CHARTERS OF
THE HONOUR OF MOWBRAY
1107-1191

a. Seal of Nigel d'Aubigny, from charter no. 3. Durham, D. & C. Archives, 1. 12. Spec. 23

b. Seal no. 1 of Roger de Mowbray, from charter no. 89. Durham, D. & C. Archives, 4. 3. Ebor. 1a

c. Seal no. 3 of Roger de Mowbray, from charter no. 145. Vyner deeds deposited at Leeds Archives, V.R. 4820

d. Seal no. 1 of Nigel de Mowbray, from charter no. 146. Vyner deeds deposited at Leeds Archives, V.R. 4832

RECORDS OF SOCIAL AND ECONOMIC HISTORY
NEW SERIES · I

CHARTERS OF
THE HONOUR OF
MOWBRAY

1107–1191

EDITED BY

D. E. GREENWAY

LONDON · *Published for* THE BRITISH ACADEMY
by THE OXFORD UNIVERSITY PRESS

*This book has been printed digitally and produced in a standard specification
in order to ensure its continuing availability*

OXFORD
UNIVERSITY PRESS

Great Clarendon Street, Oxford OX2 6DP

Oxford University Press is a department of the University of Oxford.
It furthers the University's objective of excellence in research, scholarship,
and education by publishing worldwide in

Oxford New York

Auckland Cape Town Dar es Salaam Hong Kong Karachi
Kuala Lumpur Madrid Melbourne Mexico City Nairobi
New Delhi Shanghai Taipei Toronto
With offices in
Argentina Austria Brazil Chile Czech Republic France Greece
Guatemala Hungary Italy Japan South Korea Poland Portugal
Singapore Switzerland Thailand Turkey Ukraine Vietnam

Oxford is a registered trade mark of Oxford University Press
in the UK and in certain other countries

Published in the United States
by Oxford University Press Inc., New York

ISBN 978-0-19-725926-9

TO

MY PARENTS

INTRODUCTORY NOTE TO THE
NEW SERIES

ONE of the earliest publishing ventures of the British Academy was the launching, in 1914, of the series entitled 'Records of the Social and Economic History of England and Wales' which reflected the pioneer work then being done in this field of study. The series was continued until the appearance, in 1935, of Volume IX, after which it lapsed. Since then, however, interest in social and economic history, far from abating, has greatly increased; more and more scholars have been drawn to research in the subject, and the teaching of it has so developed that it has become an integral part of the curriculum in most universities, whether in social science faculties or in departments of history. The Academy has therefore thought it appropriate to revive, with slight modification, its original project, and the volume now issued is planned as the first of a new series of 'Records of Social and Economic History'. The title of the series has been thus abbreviated to permit the introduction of material other than that relating only to England and Wales; this first volume, for instance, covers the whole honour of Mowbray and therefore includes charters concerning lands in Normandy as well as lands in ten different counties of England. The creation in the last half-century of many new local record societies and the increasing activity of many old ones have opened up fresh opportunities for the publication of social and economic records relating to a particular locality, but it is hoped that this new series will prove particularly valuable as a means of publishing material, such as that in the present volume, which does not fall within the scope of any one local record society.

E. M. CARUS-WILSON
Chairman, Records of Social and
Economic History Committee

PREFACE

WITH the death in 1481 of the child heiress Anne de Mowbray, one of the most famous and powerful of English noble families became extinct, and the ancient barony of Mowbray fell into abeyance. For almost four hundred years the family had flourished, steadily increasing its territories and titles—lords of Segrave and Gower, earls of Nottingham, Warren, and Surrey, earls marshal, and dukes of Norfolk. This book is concerned with the family's early history, and with the estate that was to form the 'power-base' for later expansion—the honour of Mowbray, which was created by king Henry I for the ancestor of the Mowbrays, Nigel d'Aubigny. The collection of charters covers the years between 1107 and 1191 and illustrates the organization of the honour of Mowbray during the first three generations of the family.

For permission to use and print the text of documents in their possession I am grateful to Mr. O. R. Bagot, the Rt. Hon. the Viscount Downe, Mr. F. W. A. Fairfax-Cholmeley, Col. A. Gregory-Hood, Major Sir Joslan Ingilby, Miss M. L. A. Strickland, Commander C. G. Vyner, and Major J. E. E. Yorke. Permission to print documents has also been kindly given by the Governing Body of Emmanuel College, Cambridge, the Deans and Chapters of Durham and York, and the Dean and Canons of Windsor. I record my thanks also for permission to print documents in the Bodleian Library, Oxford, the Borthwick Institute of Historical Research, York, the British Museum, the Archives Départementales of Calvados, the John Rylands Library, Manchester, and the Yorkshire Archaeological Society Library, Leeds. Transcripts of Crown-copyright records in the Public Record Office appear by permission of the Controller of H.M. Stationery Office.

The task of collecting the charters was greatly eased by the skill and kindness of many librarians and archivists, among whom I am especially grateful to Mr. M. Y. Ashcroft (Northallerton), Mr. C. B. L. Barr (York Minster Library), Mr. R. Bearman (Stratford on Avon), Mr. J. M. Collinson (Leeds Archives), Mr. J. E. Fagg (Durham), Miss A. G. Foster (Yorkshire Archaeological Society), Mrs. N. K. M. Gurney (Borthwick Institute), Miss S. J. MacPherson (Kendal), Mr. D. J. H. Michelmore (Yorkshire Archaeological Society), Mr. M. Snape (Durham), Dr. F. H. Stubbings (Emmanuel College, Cambridge), and the staffs of the Bodleian Library, the British Museum, the Cambridge

University Library, and the Public Record Office. I also thank Mrs. J. E. E. Yorke for her hospitality and for her help over the identification of the seals of Nigel de Mowbray.

The preparation of this edition was not without dramatic incident, and the entire work would have foundered but for the prompt action of the Sisters of St. Elizabeth of Hungary and Reverend Mother Angela, who retrieved and returned to me a precious parcel, containing the transcripts of the charters, which had been stolen from my house and abandoned in their garden.

To the Institute of Historical Research, University of London, which allowed me two months' study leave in which to complete the writing of the Introduction, and to the British Academy, which awarded me a Research Fund Grant towards the costs of research, I offer my sincere thanks.

Throughout the work I have been fortunate to be able to draw upon the expert knowledge of many scholars. For their help on various points I record my debt of gratitude to Professor C. N. L. Brooke, Professor R. R. Darlington, the late G. R. Duncombe, Mrs. P. M. Jacobs, Mr. B. Jennings, Professor M. M. Postan, and Mr. C. A. Robson. I am especially grateful to Mrs. M. M. Chibnall, from whose inspired teaching the whole enterprise sprang and who has constantly encouraged my work; to Mr. D. J. V. Fisher, who supervised my early research on the Anglo-Norman baronage; and to Professor R. W. Southern, under whose sympathetic guidance the collection of charters was completed. In the final stages of preparing the book for publication the practical help and advice of Professor E. M. Carus-Wilson and Professor C. R. Cheney has been invaluable. To two friends I am deeply grateful: to Mrs. Audrey Cornwall, who typed the entire manuscript and whose suggestions greatly improved its clarity, and to Miss Jane Sayers, who gave generous help and unfailing encouragement at every stage. Especial thanks are due to Sir Charles Clay, who read the book in manuscript and in proof and offered many valuable suggestions, and has allowed me to benefit in innumerable ways from his own immense learning.

D. E. G.

CONTENTS

ILLUSTRATIONS

ABBREVIATED REFERENCES

Ang.-Norm. Families	L. C. Loyd, *Origins of some Anglo-Norman Families*, ed. C. T. Clay and D. C. Douglas. Harleian Society ciii, 1951.
C.Ch.R.	*Calendar of the Charter Rolls preserved in the Public Record Office.* 6 vols. London, 1903–27.
C.P.R.	*Calendar of the Patent Rolls preserved in the Public Record Office (1232–1509).* 52 vols. London, 1891–1916.
Cal. Docs. France	*Calendar of Documents preserved in France, 918–1206,* ed. J. H. Round. London, 1899.
Cal. Inq. P.M.	*Calendar of Inquisitions Post Mortem . . . preserved in the Public Record Office (Henry III to Edward III).* 14 vols. London, 1904–54.
Complete Peerage	G.E.C., *The Complete Peerage of England, Scotland, Ireland, Great Britain and the United Kingdom,* revised edn. V. Gibbs *et al.* 13 vols. in 14. London, 1910–59.
Danelaw Charters	*Documents Illustrative of the Social and Economic History of the Danelaw,* ed. F. M. Stenton. British Academy, 1920.
E.H.R.	*The English Historical Review.*
E.Y.C.	*Early Yorkshire Charters.* 13 vols. Vols. i–iii, ed. W. Farrer, Edinburgh, 1914–16. *Index* (to vols. i–iii), ed. C. T. Clay and E. M. Clay, Wakefield, 1942. Vols. iv–xii, ed. C. T. Clay, Wakefield, 1935–65.
Eyton, *Itinerary*	R. W. Eyton, *Court, Household and Itinerary of Henry II.* London, 1878.
Feudal Aids	*Inquisitions and Assessments relating to Feudal Aids, 1284–1431.* 6 vols. London, 1899–1920.
Fount. Cart.	*Abstract of the Charters and other Documents contained in the Chartulary of the Cistercian Abbey of Fountains,* ed. W. T. Lancaster. 2 vols. Leeds, 1915.
Furness Coucher	*The Coucher Book of Furness Abbey.* 2 vols. in 6 parts. Vol. I, ed. J. C. Atkinson, Chetham Society new series ix, xi, xiv, 1886–9. Vol. II, ed. J. Brownbill, Chetham Society new series lxxiv, lxxvi, lxxviii, 1915–19.
Gesta Hen. II	*Gesta Regis Henrici Secundi Benedicti Abbatis,* ed. W. Stubbs. 2 vols. Rolls series xlix, 1867.
H.M.C.	Historical Manuscripts Commission.
Hatton's Book of Seals	*Sir Christopher Hatton's Book of Seals,* ed. L. C. Loyd and D. M. Stenton. Northants. Record Society xv, 1950.
Houeden	*Chronica Magistri Rogeri de Houeden,* ed. W. Stubbs. 4 vols. Rolls series li, 1868–71.
L.R.S.	Lincoln Record Society.

Léchaudé d'Anisy, *Extrait*	A. L. Léchaudé d'Anisy, *Extrait des Chartes du Calvados.* Caen, 1834–5.
Mon. Ang.	Sir W. Dugdale, *Monasticon Anglicanum*, ed. J. Caley, H. Ellis, and B. Bandinel. 6 vols. in 8. London, 1817–30.
Nichols, *Leics.*	J. Nichols, *History and Antiquities of the County of Leicester.* 4 vols. in 8 parts. London, 1795–1815.
Ord. Vit.	*Orderici Vitalis Ecclesiasticae Historiae*, ed. A. le Prévost. 5 vols. Paris, 1838–55.
Ord. Vit. (ed. Chibnall)	*The Ecclesiastical History of Orderic Vitalis*, ed. M. M. Chibnall. Vols. ii, iii. Oxford, 1969, 1972.
P.R.	*Pipe Rolls 5 Henry II to 17 John.* Pipe Roll Society, 1884–1964.
P.R. 31 Hen. I	*Magnus Rotulus Scaccarii, 31 Henry I*, ed. J. Hunter. Record Commission, 1833.
P.R. 2–4 Hen. II	*Magnus Rotulus Pipae, 2–3–4 Henry II*, ed. J. Hunter. Record Commission, 1844.
P.R.S.	Pipe Roll Society.
P.U.E.	*Papsturkunden in England*, ed. W. Holtzmann. 3 vols. Abhandlungen der Gesellschaft der Wissenschaften zu Göttingen, Phil.-Hist. Klasse, new series xxv, 3rd series xiv–xv, xxxiii. Berlin, 1930, 1935–6. Göttingen, 1952.
Priory of Hexham i	*The Priory of Hexham*, ed. J. Raine. Vol. i, Surtees Society xliv, 1864.
R.B.	*Red Book of the Exchequer*, ed. H. Hall. 3 vols. Rolls series xcix, 1896.
R.S.	Rolls series: The Chronicles and Memorials of Great Britain and Ireland during the Middle Ages, published under the direction of the Master of the Rolls. 99 vols. London, 1858–96.
Records of Templars	*Records of the Templars in England in the Twelfth Century*, ed. B. A. Lees. British Academy, 1935.
Regesta	*Regesta Regum Anglo-Normannorum*, ed. H. W. C. Davis, C. Johnson, H. A. Cronne, and R. H. C. Davis. 4 vols. Oxford, 1913–69.
Riev. Cart.	*Cartularium Abbathiae de Rievalle*, ed. J. C. Atkinson. Surtees Society lxxxiii, 1889.
S.S.	Surtees Society.
Selby Coucher	*The Coucher Book of Selby*, ed. J. T. Fowler. 2 vols. Yorkshire Archaeological Society, Record series x, xiii, 1891–3.
Stenton, *Feudalism*	F. M. Stenton, *The First Century of English Feudalism, 1066–1166.* 2nd edn. Oxford, 1961.
Stonehouse, *Axholme*	W. B. Stonehouse, *The History and Topography of the Isle of Axholme.* London, 1839.
T.R.H.S.	*Transactions of the Royal Historical Society.*
V.C.H.	*The Victoria History of the Counties of England.*

Whitby Cart.	*Cartularium Abbathiae de Whiteby*, ed. J. C. Atkinson. 2 vols. Surtees Society lxix, lxxii, 1879–81.
Wightman, *Lacy Family*	W. E. Wightman, *The Lacy Family in England and Normandy, 1066–1194.* Oxford, 1966.
Y.A.J.	*The Yorkshire Archaeological Journal.*
Y.R.S.	Yorkshire Archaeological Society, Record series.
York Min. Fasti	*York Minster Fasti*, ed. C. T. Clay. 2 vols. Yorkshire Archaeological Society, Record series cxxiii, cxxiv, 1957–8.
Yorks. Deeds	*Yorkshire Deeds.* 10 vols., ed. W. Brown, C. T. Clay, and M. J. Stanley Price. Yorkshire Archaeological Society, Record series xxxix, l, lxiii, lxv, lxix, lxxvi, lxxxiii, cii, cxi, cxx, 1909–53.

ABBREVIATIONS

Antiq.	Antiquarian
Archaeol.	Archaeological
Aug.	Augustinian
B.M.	British Museum, London
Ben.	Benedictine
Bibl.	Bibliothèque
Bibl. Nat.	Bibliothèque Nationale, Paris
Bodl.	Bodleian Library, Oxford
Cal.	Calendar, calendared
Cart.	Cartulary
Ch.	Charter
Chart.	Chartulary
Chron.	Chronicle
Cist.	Cistercian
Clun.	Cluniac
Ed.	Edited
Edn.	Edition
Gilb.	Gilbertine
Hist.	Historical
Jnl.	Journal
Libr.	Library
N.S.	New Series
P.R.O.	Public Record Office, London
Par.	Parish
Pd.	Printed
Prem.	Premonstratensian
Proc.	Proceedings
Rec. ser.	Record series
Rev.	Review
Sav.	Savigniac
Soc.	Society
Trans.	Transactions
Transl.	Translated
Univ.	University
Wap.	Wapentake

INTRODUCTION

I. THE HONOUR OF MOWBRAY

IN the redistribution of confiscated lands which followed the battle of Tinchebray (1106), king Henry I granted to Nigel d'Aubigny, the landless younger son of a minor Norman baron, a great complex of estates in England and Normandy, and thus raised him to the highest ranks of the feudal nobility. The English lands, which had belonged to a number of different tenants-in-chief at the time of the Domesday Survey, and some of which had changed hands several times in the years between 1086 and 1106, formed a massive honour which was to remain a permanent feature of the pattern of English landownership until 1481. But although the English estates comprised one of the greatest honours of the realm, it is a sign of that pre-eminence of Normandy and of Norman affairs in the minds of the Anglo-Norman barons, as well as of their kings, that the comparatively small Norman fief was regarded more highly, and its head, the little town of Montbray, was held to be the *caput* of the entire honour. Nigel d'Aubigny's son Roger was given the name *de Molbraio*, de Mowbray, and his inheritance, consisting of territories from the borders of Scotland to the south-west corner of Normandy, was called the honour of Mowbray.

Nigel d'Aubigny was the model 'new man'. He never gained any land from the family estate in Normandy, a small fief at St. Martin d'Aubigny, near Coutances, which passed from his father Roger d'Aubigny to his elder brother William.[1] Nigel's entire fortune came to him as the result of the king's favour. He joined the royal entourage in September 1101, six months after his brother William had been made *pincerna*.[2] Thereafter to his death in 1129 he seems always to have been in the royal service. The first phase of his career, when he was probably a superior kind of household knight, ended in 1107, when he received from the king his first gifts of land. In the second phase of his career, between 1107 and *c.* 1118, he was deeply involved in northern government, acting as local justiciar in Yorkshire and Northumberland;[3] during this period

---

[1] See L. C. Loyd, 'The origin of the family of Aubigny of Cainhoe', *Beds. Hist. Rec. Soc.* xix (1937), 101–9, and *Ang.-Norm. Families*, p. 7; *Complete Peerage* ix 366–7.
[2] *Regesta* ii nos. 544, 515.
[3] For the writs reflecting this work, see *Regesta* ii nos. 890–1, 917, 923, 926–7, 977, 993, 995, 1001, 1030, 1072, 1124, 1237, 1330, 1357, 1382, 1630. Cf. H. A. Cronne, 'The

b

more territories were accumulated and the honour rounded off. In his last years, from *c.* 1118 to 1129, he was constantly at the king's side, acting as adviser and military commander, and travelling with the court throughout England and Normandy.[1] It was in Normandy in November 1129 that he died.[2]

The king established Nigel d'Aubigny in Normandy by means of a reward frequently used to establish Henrician new men—marriage. In the same year, 1107, that his brother William obtained a valuable marriage,[3] Nigel was given the hand of Maud de Laigle, sister of Gilbert de Laigle and a relative of the earl of Chester, who brought with her both social status and landed property. The marriage was made possible by a papal dispensation allowing Maud's divorce from her first husband, Robert de Mowbray, the former earl of Northumbria who had been imprisoned since his rebellion and forfeiture in 1095.[4] With his wife, Nigel gained the Norman fief of Mowbray, which lay in the gently undulating country to the north of Saint-Sever-Calvados.[5] Montbray itself, where the remains of a castle and extensive fortifications are still to be seen, stands on the river Drôme, a tributary of the Vire, and has never developed into anything more than a small village. Here the custom of the wood belonged to Bayeux cathedral from before 1037,[6] and the first known lord of Montbray was earl Robert's father, Roger 'de Molbraio', who was present at the council of Lillebonne in 1066.[7] Several neighbouring villages were included in the Mowbray fee: Beaumesnil, Beslon,[8]

office of local justiciar in England under the Norman kings', *Univ. of Birmingham Hist. Jnl.* vi (1957–8) 18–38, especially p. 33.

----

[1] *Regesta* ii *passim.* He was commander at the siege of Montfort-sur-Risle in 1123 (*Ord. Vit.* iv 443).

[2] He last occurs in 1129, before 15 July (*Regesta* ii no. 1575). He had certainly died some months before September 1130 (*P.R. 31 Hen. I* pp. 137–8). Robert of Torigny (in William of Jumièges, *Gesta Normannorum Ducum,* ed. J. Marx (Rouen, 1914) p. 277) says that he retired to Bec and died there. At Durham he was commemorated on 21 or 22 November (Durham Cathedral Libr., MS. B. IV. 24 fo. 37r, and *Liber Vitae Dunelm.* [ed. J. Stevenson] (S.S. xiii) p. 147). At Lincoln he was commemorated on 26 November (*Statutes of Lincoln Cathedral,* arranged H. Bradshaw, ed. C. Wordsworth (Cambridge, 1892–7) ii p. ccxlii).

[3] This was to Maud, daughter of Roger Bigod, and brought 10 fees to William d'Aubigny (see *Complete Peerage* ix 578 n. *c*). The marriage clearly took place in 1107, when Roger Bigod's honour was in royal custody.

[4] *Ord. Vit.* iii 410; Robert of Torigny, op. cit. pp. 276–7; *Anselmi Cantuariensis Archiepiscopi Opera Omnia,* ed. F. S. Schmitt, v (Edinburgh, 1951) ep. no. 423. Nigel's wife first appears in charter no. 1 below. Nigel appears as a kinsman of the earl of Chester in [1123] (*Regesta* ii no. 1389).

[5] For the Mowbray estates in Normandy, see Map I inset.

[6] *Antiquus Cartularius Ecclesiae Baiocensis Liber Niger,* ed. V. Bourrienne (Rouen, 1902–3) i no. 21.

[7] *Ord. Vit.* (ed. Chibnall) ii 140.

[8] Charters nos. 162, 164–5; cf. below, p. xix n. 13.

Étouvy, Coulonces,[1] Margueray,[2] and probably also Landelles,[3] Saint-Vigor,[4] and Pontfarcy.[5]

In addition to this compact fee centred on Montbray, Nigel d'Aubigny gained, either in 1107 or later, a cluster of tenements to the east, in the Orne valley north-west of Argentan, none of which can be positively identified as former Mowbray estates: Château-Gontier, on the Orne,[6] and to the north Bazoches-en-Houlme (which was held of the count of Eu)[7] were both sites of castles; and there were properties nearby at Saint-Brice, Neuvy-au-Houlme,[8] Rabodanges (held of the abbey of Saint-Évroult),[9] Villers-Canivet,[10] and Proussy,[11] and probably also at Ménil-Hermei,[12] Bellou-en-Houlme,[13] Boucé,[14] and Crèvecœur.[15] To this fee was added the castle of Écouché, probably acquired from the family of Gournay in 1118, when Nigel d'Aubigny repudiated his childless first wife, Maud de Laigle, and married Gundreda de Gournay.[16] The possession of these two groups of estates in southern Normandy continued, with a break in Stephen's reign, until 1204.[17] The *servicium debitum* was five knights, and by 1172 more than eleven fees had been created.[18] It is disappointing that only a handful of the surviving charters relate to the Norman lands,[19] so that compared with the English honour the properties are very imperfectly recorded.

The process whereby Nigel d'Aubigny's English honour was created extended over some years after the first grants of c. 1107, but was probably complete by c. 1115. Although the honour was to bear the name of Mowbray, no part of the former English territories of earl Robert de Mowbray came to d'Aubigny, except perhaps two isolated manors in

[1] *Ord. Vit.* (ed. Chibnall) iii 230.   [2] Charter no. 76.
[3] Perhaps the origin of the witness Rolland de Landelles (see index); and cf. no. 402 note (p. 258 n. 9).
[4] A gift of Roger I de Mowbray was witnessed by Drogo de Sancto Vigore, possibly of Saint-Vigor-des-Monts (*Gallia Christiana* xi (Paris, 1759) instr. col. 60).
[5] See no. 402 note (p. 258 n. 8).   [6] Arr. Argentan, cant. Écouché, *R.B.* ii 629.
[7] Charter no. 19.   [8] Inquisition of 1220, pd. below as no. 402.
[9] Ibid. 'Cueleium'; also charter no. 17.
[10] Charter no. 279.   [11] No. 280.
[12] Perhaps the origin of William de Meisnilhermer and family (see index and no. 400 note).
[13] C. T. Clay, *E.Y.C.* vi 54, suggests Bellou-en-Houlme, Orne (arr. Argentan, cant. Messei), as the origin of the Bellun family (see index), but perhaps Beslon, Manche (arr. Saint-Lô, cant. Percy) is more likely.
[14] Perhaps the origin of the Buscy family, witnesses and tenants (see index).
[15] Near Putanges. Perhaps the origin of John and Robert de Crevequer, witnesses and tenants (see index).
[16] Écouché was in Gournay's lordship in 1089 (*Ord. Vit.* iii 322), but belonged to the Mowbray fee before 1190 (charter no. 277; cf. no. 402). For the events of the marriage, see *Ord. Vit.* iv 318.
[17] See F. M. Powicke, *The Loss of Normandy* (2nd edn., Manchester, 1961) pp. 345–6.
[18] *R.B.* ii 629.   [19] Charters nos. 16, 17, 19, 76, 93, 162–5, 277, 279–80.

county Durham, which rightly belonged to Durham cathedral priory, to which they were restored before 1114.[1] Henry I formed d'Aubigny's estates from the greater part of the fee which William Rufus had created for Robert de Stuteville, forfeit in 1106,[2] with substantial additions designed to enlarge and strengthen the former Stuteville lordships. The new honour consisted of holdings in six main areas, with some outlying properties, and reached into nine counties. The six main lordships of the honour were remarkably compact and their origins illustrate some of the diverse factors which worked in favour of unified fiefs at different stages of the Norman feudal settlement.

Three lordships derived through the Stuteville honour from the Domesday tenancy of Geoffrey de La Guerche, who died soon after 1093.[3] Two of the three originated in pre-Conquest estates of a compact type. In Leicestershire and Warwickshire La Guerche had taken over the lands of a single Saxon lord, Leofwine, whose heiress, Ælfgeofu, he married.[4] The Leicestershire estates were placed in the Wreak Valley and on the Wolds around the important route-centre of Melton,[5] where roads from Leicester to Grantham and from Nottingham to Oakham and Stamford crossed. Stuteville under William Rufus, and later Nigel d'Aubigny under Henry I, took over this lordship intact. In Warwickshire La Guerche had held a group of estates, also formerly Leofwine's, round Monks Kirby, east of Coventry, close to the intersection of the Fosse Way and Watling Street.[6] Supplementing this fief La Guerche had in 1086 the custody of Smite (along with other lands), formerly belonging to Aubrey de Couci. The addition of Smite to the holdings at Monks Kirby and its neighbourhood probably continued under Stuteville,[7] although it is not clear on what terms, and it was made permanent when Nigel d'Aubigny, who took over the Monks Kirby lands as tenant-in-chief, was enfeoffed by the then overlord of Smite,

---

[1] Barmpton and Skerningham, nos. 2–6; see R. W. Southern, 'The place of Henry I in English history', *Proc. British Academy* xlviii (1962) 143, and *Regesta Regum Scottorum* i, ed. G. W. S. Barrow (Edinburgh, 1960) no. 23.

[2] See *E.Y.C.* ix 1 ff. and ibid. nos. 41–4.

[3] He last occurs, in Britanny, in that year (G. A. Lobineau, *Histoire de Bretagne* (Paris, 1707) ii col. 215); and had probably died by 1094 (see A. S. Ellis, in *Y.A.J.* iv (1877) 224).

[4] See J. H. Round, in *V.C.H. Warwicks.* i 275–6; and F. M. Stenton, 'English families and the Norman Conquest', *T.R.H.S.* 4th ser. xxvi (1944) 6. His wife 'Alveva' is mentioned in *Mon. Ang.* vi (2) 996.

[5] For a map of the groups of holdings centred on Melton, see Map IIc; and cf. *Domesday Geography of Midland England*, ed. H. C. Darby and I. B. Terrett (Cambridge, 1954) p. 312.

[6] See Map IID.

[7] This is suggested by claims made by William de Stuteville in 1200–1 (*E.Y.C.* ix nos. 41–4).

the earl of Leicester, in two knights' fees there.[1] It was in the territory of Smite that Nigel d'Aubigny had a commanding castle on the Fosse Way, at Brinklow.[2] By contrast the third lordship which derived from the Domesday fee of Geoffrey de La Guerche was not an inheritance of the pre-Conquest period, but had been created between 1066 and 1086 from the holdings of at least eight pre-Conquest tenants: this formed a solid block of territory comprising the fertile and fenny Isle of Axholme in the north-west corner of Lincolnshire.[3] Its creation as a single lordship had probably come about after the Danes had used Axholme as a retreat in 1069.[4] The fief passed to Robert de Stuteville and later to Nigel d'Aubigny. By the middle of the twelfth century, and probably a good deal earlier, there was a castle in Axholme at Kinnard (Owston), on the west bank of the River Trent.[5]

These three lordships were granted to Nigel d'Aubigny soon after 1106. In Axholme, which was to be retained in demesne by generations of Mowbrays, Nigel was lord before May 1108.[6] He probably gained the other La Guerche estates at the same time, for by 1114 he had had sufficient time to oust some tenants and install others.[7]

In the north of England there were a further three compact lordships which were granted by Henry I to Nigel d'Aubigny. Unlike the three midland lordships, they were not complete by 1086, and modifications were made to them both by William Rufus for Robert de Stuteville, and by Henry I for Nigel d'Aubigny. This process reflects the comparatively slow development of royal policy and feudal institutions in the north.[8]

In the wild country to the west of the Pennines, feudal authority was still in a primitive phase at the time of Domesday Book. The areas of modern Lancashire and Westmorland which were surveyed together with the Ewcross wapentake of Yorkshire and had belonged to earl Tostig and other Saxon lords before 1066, were recorded as being in the king's own hands in 1086, but only the bare details of numbers of carucates for geld are given, and it is difficult to believe that the estates were being farmed effectively as royal demesne. After William Rufus's conquest of Carlisle in 1092, however, lordships began to be set up in the

---

[1] See note to charters nos. 77–8; also nos. 2–3, 10.

[2] *P.R. 31 Hen. I* p. 138; cf. below, p. xxx n. 12.   [3] See Map II A.

[4] *Ord. Vit.* (ed. Chibnall) ii 229; *Anglo-Saxon Chron.*, ed. D. Whitelock (1961) p. 150; cf. F. M. Stenton, *Anglo-Saxon England* (2nd edn., Oxford, 1947) p. 595.

[5] The castle is not mentioned in the Pipe Roll account of the honour in 1130, but in 1174 it was already ancient and in need of repair (see Stenton, *Feudalism* pp. 204–5). A constable of Axholme probably occurs before 1148 (charter no. 219) and later (no. 221). For a plan of the castle, see Stonehouse, *Axholme* p. 224.

[6] Charter no. 1.   [7] Nos. 2–3.

[8] Cf. Wightman, *Lacy Family* pp. 28 ff., on the Lacy and Warenne fees. For the Mowbray lands in Yorkshire, see Map III.

rear of the new frontier with Scotland. Ivo Taillebois was established in
the upper Eden, and also in an extensive block of territory which stretched
from upper Ribblesdale across the fells to Lonsdale and thence to
Kendale. This latter lordship had as its head the town of Burton in
Lonsdale, on the route south from Scotland. After Taillebois's death, in
c. 1094, the lordship of Burton and its dependent estates was probably
granted to Robert de Stuteville;[1] and some time after 1106 it was given
to Nigel d'Aubigny.[2] The early history of this remote area is obscure,
but progress towards feudalization was slow: in 1130 the castle at
Burton had for its garrison a professional knight and sergeants, and the
established tenants were not knights but drengs.[3]

The Vale of York was much more susceptible to the social changes of
the early Norman period than was Burton in Lonsdale, but here the
establishment of a settled pattern of landholding was subject to reverses
and delays which had their origin in political instability. Facing one
another across the Vale, just north of Ripon, were two lordships
which suffered many vicissitudes in the first half century of Norman
feudalism.

On the eastern slope of the Pennines lay a lordship, which originally
derived from the pre-Conquest holding of Gospatric and had a strange
history. In 1086 some of these lands, including Kirkby Malzeard and its
neighbouring vills, were still held by Gospatric, one of the few Saxon
lords to retain property in the north. Other lands, however, had already
passed out of Gospatric's possession into that of Erneis de Burun,[4] who
held Gospatric's former properties in Nidderdale in chief and those in
and around Masham as a tenancy of count Alan, lord of Richmond. This
division of Gospatric's old estate seems to have persisted under William
Rufus, who granted to Robert de Stuteville Kirkby Malzeard and its
dependent lands, but not, apparently, Masham or Nidderdale.[5] For
Nigel d'Aubigny, however, Gospatric's entire lordship in the areá was
re-created by Henry I: to the holdings around Kirkby Malzeard were

[1] For Taillebois's tenure, see W. Farrer, *Records relating to the Barony of Kendale*, ed.
J. F. Curwen (Cumb. and Westm. Antiq. and Archaeol. Soc., Rec. ser. iv–vi) i pp.
viii–x, 1; F. M. Stenton, in Hist. Monuments Comm., *Westmorland* (1936) p. liv. For
his death, see *Complete Peerage* vii 743. The evidence that the lordship passed to Stuteville is the claim of William de Stuteville in 1200–1 (*E.Y.C.* ix nos. 41–3, and see the
note to no. 43).
[2] Farrer (*Barony of Kendale* i 1) thought the grant took place before 1115; he
associated it with the grant of the honour of Lancaster to Stephen, count of Mortain,
which he dated 1114–16 (*Lancs. Pipe Rolls and Early Charters*, ed. W. Farrer (Liverpool, 1902) p. 312).
[3] *P.R. 31 Hen. I* p. 138; cf. below, p. xxx n. 12.
[4] For the greater part of Erneis de Burun's honour, see *E.Y.C.* x 1–2, 23–30.
[5] Malzeard, but not Masham nor Nidderdale, was claimed in 1200–1 (*E.Y.C.* ix
nos. 41–3).

added the former Burun lands, both in Nidderdale and in the Masham fee held of Richmond. The only properties in the great stretch of country from Ellington south to Dacre (a distance of 14 miles) that had not belonged to Gospatric were some small estates of the Liberty of Ripon. In three of these Nigel d'Aubigny was enfeoffed as the archbishop's tenant,[1] further evidence that this large and compact lordship was the result of deliberate royal policy. The entire fief was probably in Nigel's possession before 1114, and by 1130 there was a castle at Kirkby Malzeard.[2]

Only a dozen miles to the east, at the western foot of the Hambleton Hills, was Thirsk, the head of the largest and most complex of the six lordships. From Thirsk, stretching eastward over the Hambleton Hills and south-east over the Howardian Hills and through the Gilling gap into the western half of the Vale of Pickering, there ranged a series of Mowbray estates, whose accumulation into a single tenurial unit took place by stages between 1066 and c. 1114. Much of the lowland territory of this North Riding estate had belonged in 1086 to one of the most valuable of the Yorkshire fees—that of Hugh Fitz Baldric, sheriff of York from 1069 to some time after 1080, who died in 1086.[3] Fitz Baldric's fee in this area had been created out of properties deriving from several pre-Conquest landowners, but the Conqueror's policy was not consistently in favour of unified fiefs, and at Thirsk, where Fitz Baldric held 12 carucates of Tor's former holding, the king himself retained the 8 carucates which had previously belonged to Orm, a lord whom Fitz Baldric had actually succeeded in the important manors of Bagby, Hovingham, and Kirkby Moorside. When William Rufus granted the greater part of Fitz Baldric's fee to Robert de Stuteville, he added some pieces of North Riding royal demesne and parcels of land from the Mortain fee,[4] and it is likely that the union of the two Domesday estates in Thirsk, which had taken place by the time of Nigel d'Aubigny's possession, dates from the 1090s. The creation of a strong lordship here on the Scottish route to York would have been in line with Rufus's vigorous northern policy. After the confiscation of the Stuteville honour in 1106 further tenurial engineering occurred. Henry I seems to have kept all the estates near Thirsk in his own hands until after 1109.[5] When

[1] Charter no. 359; cf. nos. 2–3.　　　　[2] Nos. 2–3; *P.R. 31 Hen. I* p. 138.
[3] Cf. T. A. M. Bishop, 'The Norman settlement of Yorks.', in *Studies in Medieval History presented to F. M. Powicke* (Oxford, 1948) p. 11, and *Domesday Geography of Northern England*, ed. H. C. Darby and I. S. Maxwell (Cambridge, 1962) pp. 452–3.
[4] From royal demesne: Ellenthorpe, Harton, and Sutton (*E.Y.C.* ix 75–6, nos. 1 and note, 4 and note); from Mortain fee: Myton on Swale (ibid. i no. 354, p. 272).
[5] Cf. ibid. ix no. 3 (calendared in *Regesta* ii no. 977, where it is assigned to [1111, Lent?]).

Nigel d'Aubigny received his grants in the area, perhaps before 1114, some of the old Stuteville lands were still retained by the Crown and never became part of the Mowbray honour,[1] while there was added a knight's fee of the former Malet honour, which had been forfeit in 1106.[2] At Thirsk there was a castle by 1130, and probably also a market and borough.[3] The strategic importance of the site was demonstrated in 1138, when the Yorkshire army halted there before marching to face the Scots at the battle of the Standard.[4]

In addition to the six main lordships there were some outlying manors in different counties. In Northamptonshire, at Crick, Welford, and elsewhere, and in Warwickshire at Hampton in Arden and elsewhere, there were estates deriving from the La Guerche fee, situated at some distance from the main holdings of Monks Kirby and Brinklow.[5] But the Northamptonshire manors were themselves on important routes, and this was true also of other outliers, such as the La Guerche manors of Gainsborough in Lincolnshire (a few miles upstream from Axholme on the River Trent), and Langford in Nottinghamshire (about 25 miles from Axholme and the same from Melton Mowbray, but placed just off the Fosse Way on the Lincoln side of Newark and near to the River Trent).[6] The use of water as well as land routes also explains the grant to Nigel d'Aubigny of South Cave, in the East Riding of Yorkshire, formerly a Malet estate: it gave an important foothold on the north bank of the Humber opposite Axholme, on the road to York.[7]

Nigel d'Aubigny was raised up as lord of this great honour in order to serve the king's purposes. In Yorkshire and Northumberland he exercised authority as local justiciar between c. 1107 and c. 1118. In York itself, which continued in the Norman period its Northumbrian tradition of provincial capital, he possessed considerable property both in the city and in its suburbs.[8] The administration of finance and justice centred

[1] See *E.Y.C.* ix 73–4. The only positive evidence for Nigel d'Aubigny's possession of a former Fitz Baldric estate before 1114 relates to Middlethorpe, near York, and not in the Thirsk area; but for the likelihood that the lordship of Thirsk was in his hands by 1114, see charter no. 3 note.

[2] The Malebisse fee; see *E.Y.C.* iii 457 and below, charter no. 371.

[3] *P.R. 31 Hen. I* p. 138; cf. *V.C.H. Yorks. N.R.* ii 61, for the suggestion that the borough dated from Henry I's period of possession, and ibid. p. 59 for the siting of the market-place, abutting the east side of the castle. The borough is mentioned in two forged or interpolated charters, below nos. 203, 211, and also in a charter of Henry II (*E.Y.C.* i no. 349). Stallage and toll in Thirsk are referred to in [c. 1181] (charter no. 140).

[4] Richard of Hexham and John of Hexham, in *Priory of Hexham* i 88, 119.

[5] See Map IID.   [6] See Map IIB.   [7] See Map IIA.

[8] For unspecified parts of York, see charters nos. 3, 170, 288, 379–80. For Fishergate, see nos. 195, 304; for Skeldergate, see nos. 290–1; for Coney Street, see *E.Y.C.* i nos. 236–8. For Middlethorpe, see charters nos. 8, 55, 255, 263, 290–1, 379–80. For Heworth, cf. *Domesday Book* i fo. 328b and *Feudal Aids* vi 60.

on York castle, of which Nigel seems to have had the custody.[1] To Hugh,
the precentor of York, writing in about 1127, Nigel d'Aubigny was a
powerful figure, by virtue of both his high local standing and his close
connection with the king.[2] By taking advantage of the wide discretion
allowed by the king to his servants in the exercise of office, Nigel was
able to accumulate a large number of small properties in the north and
the midlands by ousting various ecclesiastical and lay owners; but during
a grave illness which overtook him at Durham some time between 1109
and 1114 he made peace with his conscience and penitently restored the
lands.[3]

The uncertainty of the feudal law which made possible disseisin and
disinheritance also allowed the king to make re-arrangements in the
feudal framework. Nigel d'Aubigny was granted the overlordship of two
former tenants-in-chief and their fees: before 1118 he had been given
the service of Gilbert Tison, the Domesday tenant-in-chief in Yorkshire
(chiefly East Riding), Nottinghamshire (some estates near Langford),
and Lincolnshire (a manor near Axholme),[4] and by 1124 he was overlord
also of William de Arches, who had succeeded to his father Osbern's
Domesday fief, which lay chiefly in the fertile area west of York.[5] With
little cost to himself, the king had strengthened Nigel d'Aubigny's
position in the north and had also tightened the feudal network.

The fief thus created for Nigel d'Aubigny was one of the greatest of
English honours, and owed a *servicium debitum* of sixty knights, a quota
which scarcely a dozen other honours equalled or exceeded.[6] Nigel's
establishment in these extensive territories had come about through the
beneficent operation of royal power. The history of the honour after his
death offers a striking contrast. His son Roger de Mowbray stood outside

[1] On York and its castle, see F. M. Stenton, 'York in the eleventh century', *York
Minster Hist. Tracts* (1927), and E. Miller, in *V.C.H. Yorks. City of York* pp. 25, 29.
Nigel was in possession of the castle mills (charter no. 292, cf. no. 273) and possibly
of other mills beyond Monkbridge (nos. 2–3; cf. *V.C.H. City of York* pp. 315, 506).
Custody of the mill-pool and fish-pond was closely connected with custody of the
castle gaol and gate (ibid. p. 29). Roger de Mowbray and his grandson William both
claimed custody of York castle as an hereditary right (charter no. 255; *Rotuli Litterarum
Clausarum* (Record Comm. 1833–44) i 215a; *Rotuli Litterarum Patentium* (Record
Comm. 1835) p. 143b).
[2] *Hugh the Chantor: History of the Church of York 1066–1127*, ed. C. Johnson
(1961) pp. 37, 41, 106.
[3] See the remarkable series of charters, nos. 2–10.
[4] *Lincs. Domesday and Lindsey Survey*, ed. C. W. Foster and T. Longley (L.R.S.
xix) p. 252. For the Tison fee, see *E.Y.C.* xii, especially pp. 19–23, and for a discussion
of whether Gilbert Tison's lands were forfeit in 1095, see ibid. p. 4.
[5] Charter no. 11. For the Arches fee, see *E.Y.C.* i 408–36.
[6] See J. H. Round, *Feudal England* (1895) pp. 253 ff. S. Painter, *Studies in the History
of the English Feudal Barony* (Baltimore, 1943) pp. 25 nn., makes some corrections to
Round, but in rejecting the evidence for the Mowbray quota, fails to state how it is
unsatisfactory.

the circle of royal administrators and was thus deprived of the favour which had nourished and protected Nigel's feudal authority. In the troubled conditions of the mid twelfth century, Mowbray suffered losses of land, status, and security.

Military weakness resulted in some temporary losses of territory in Stephen's reign. After a minority of nine years, Roger de Mowbray succeeded to his estates in 1138, at the age of eighteen or nineteen,[1] and fought with the victorious Yorkshire army at the battle of the Standard in August of the same year.[2] Some lands of his inheritance had already been lost: these were his estates in the Houlme district of Normandy which had been taken by count Geoffrey of Anjou in 1138.[3] Four years later his remaining Norman lands—the lordship of Montbray and its estates—were lost as the Angevin conquest of Normandy proceeded.[4] In England the territories at and near Burton in Lonsdale, which had almost certainly been ravaged by the Scots in the early summer of 1138, before Roger's coming of age, were annexed by king David in 1141 or 1142.[5]

Both the Norman lands and the lordship of Burton in Lonsdale were recovered before the end of the reign of Stephen. Soon after Roger's return from the second Crusade,[6] an opportunity arose, in May 1149, for him to regain the lost territories, by coming to terms with Henry of Anjou and David of Scotland, who were forming an alliance with earl Ranulf of Chester, in a campaign to take the city of York.[7] Roger seems to have recovered the Burton estates as a result of participating in the alliance,[8] in the terms of which king David made over to earl Ranulf the

[1] He was probably born in 1119 or 1120, his father having married Gundreda de Gournay in June 1118. According to the Byland chronicle, he was knighted in 1137 or 1138 (*Mon. Ang.* v 349*b*). His earliest charter, below, no. 32, was given in 1138 or 1139; cf. charters nos. 170, 288, 294.

[2] Ailred of Rievaulx calls him 'adhuc puerulus' in August 1138, in *Chrons. of Stephen, Hen. II and Ric. I*, ed. R. Howlett (R.S. lxxxii) iii 183. See also Richard of Hexham and John of Hexham, in *Priory of Hexham* i 86, 119; and *Ord. Vit.* v 114.

[3] *Ord. Vit.* v 108–9; cf. ibid. pp. 68, 82, for attacks in 1136 and 1137.

[4] For the process of Angevin conquest in Normandy, see J. Chartrou, *L'Anjou de 1109 à 1151* (Paris, n.d.) pp. 36–68, and C. H. Haskins, *Norman Institutions* (Cambridge, Mass., 1918) pp. 123–55.

[5] See G. W. S. Barrow, 'King David I and the honour of Lancaster', *E.H.R.* lxx (1955), 85–9.

[6] For his presence on the Crusade, see John of Hexham, in *Priory of Hexham* i 154; and charters nos. 155, 160–1, 174.

[7] See *Gesta Stephani*, ed. K. R. Potter (1955) pp. 142–3; John of Hexham pp. 159–60; *Henrici Huntendunensis Historia Anglorum*, ed. T. Arnold (R.S. lxxiv) 282.

[8] For Roger's participation, see *E.Y.C.* iii no. 1826, which refers to his 'waging war in the time of hostility on behalf of king [Henry]', and *E.Y.C.* iii nos. 1823–4, cal. as charters nos. 322–3, which date this activity before April 1153. The only campaign to which this can refer is that of 1149. For the recovery of the Lonsdale estates, see the enfeoffment charter to William son of Gilbert, no. 370; William witnesses a charter of

honour of Lancaster. Although the plan to take York came to nothing and the alliance disintegrated, there is a strong impression from the charters that Roger de Mowbray was involved in hostilities at this time— near York (he speaks of his hope of recovering custody of York castle),[1] near the Humber crossings in the East Riding,[2] and in the neighbourhood of Ripon.[3] He probably came to terms with the royal party in 1153,[4] taking no part in the Angevin campaign of that year. In the circumstances, he did not recover his Norman lands until after the treaty of West-minster, in November 1153. He was formally confirmed in his fee of Bazoches-en-Houlme in August 1154.[5]

Lands which had been lost as the result of military conquest might be —and were—regained. This was not true, however, of lands which had been granted away to military enemies. As a result of his capture by earl Ranulf of Chester at the battle of Lincoln, in January 1141,[6] Roger de Mowbray was forced to make concessions which permanently weakened his feudal authority. He was obliged to make a 'beneficial' enfeoffment to earl Ranulf's constable, Eustace Fitz John, of lands in Yorkshire, Lincolnshire, and Leicestershire, amounting to fourteen fees, for the service of eleven knights. This enfeoffment included land in Gains-borough on the Trent, where the castle and bridge were confirmed by king Stephen to earl Ranulf's brother, William de Roumare.[7] The sub-sequent history of Eustace Fitz John's estates, which descended in 1157 to his son William de Vescy, was to be exceedingly complex, perhaps as Mowbray attempted to restore his authority.[8] At any rate, in the 1140s the concessions represented a serious loss of status for Roger de Mowbray. Another sign of this, and of the power which earl Ranulf had achieved at Lincoln, was Roger's marriage, in 1142 or 1143, almost

---

earl Ranulf in [1149] (*Lancs. Pipe Rolls and Early Charters*, ed. W. Farrer (Liverpool, 1902) p. 296).

[1] Charters nos. 255, 263.

[2] Nos. 318, 322–4; cf. *E.Y.C.* i no. 183 and ii no. 1125. Also perhaps charters nos. 89–90 below, relating to Blyborough, Lincs.

[3] Nos. 102–3, 318; cf. for abnormal conditions *E.Y.C.* i no. 534.

[4] *E.Y.C.* iii no. 1823, cal. as charter no. 322, suggests that he had made peace with the royal party.

[5] Charter no. 19.

[6] John of Hexham, in *Priory of Hexham* i 134–5; *Ord. Vit.* v 128; *Henrici Hunten-dunensis Historia Anglorum*, ed. T. Arnold (R.S. lxxiv) p. 274.

[7] Reference to the enfeoffment is in charter no. 397. Cf. king Stephen's confirmation of Gainsborough to William de Roumare, probably of 1146 (*Regesta* iii no. 494). Gainsborough had been in Nigel d'Aubigny's demesne in [*c.* 1115 × 1118] (*Lincs. Domesday and Lindsey Survey*, ed. C. W. Foster and T. Longley (L.R.S. xix) p. 242); cf. charter no. 231.

[8] In 1166 William de Vescy appeared in the *carta* holding only 2 fees of the new enfeoffment (charter no. 401); for some of the complexities of the Vescy fee, see no. 397 note.

certainly at the earl's direction, to Alice de Gant, sister of Gilbert de
Gant, another of the earl's satellites.[1]

The military vicissitudes of Stephen's reign revealed grave weak-
nesses in Roger de Mowbray's feudal position. But military vulnerability
was common to all classes of society when royal authority was weak.
More serious for Mowbray was the demonstration of the legal insecurity
of his possession of his honour. This came about, also in the 1140s, as
the result of royal favour shown to Robert III de Stuteville, the grandson
of Robert I de Stuteville, most of whose forfeited lands had been granted
by Henry I to Nigel d'Aubigny. Having regained possession of some
parts of his grandfather's honour which had not passed into the Mowbray fee, supplemented by gifts out of the royal demesne,[2] Robert de
Stuteville laid claim to certain Mowbray properties in Yorkshire. Although the claims were not successful when they were first made in 1147,[3]
Roger de Mowbray was obliged to make a settlement at the beginning of
Henry II's reign, whereby Robert de Stuteville was enfeoffed in nine or
ten fees of the Mowbray honour.[4] The arrangement did not have royal
confirmation, however, and the way was left open for further Stuteville
claims. Indeed, tension between the families continued until 1201, when
another ten Mowbray fees had to be conceded to satisfy the Stuteville
appetite.[5] Throughout the period between the two settlements there
was considerable tenurial uncertainty in the Mowbray honour, which
is betrayed in many of the charters in the collection.[6]

It was perhaps in an attempt to give extra force to the judgements of
his court and to his property transactions in the face of this tenurial
uncertainty, that Roger de Mowbray brought his sons into a kind of
partnership. From an early age, even before the death of their grand-

[1] The earliest evidence of the marriage is charter no. 195, of [Feb. 1142 × June 1143].
Alice's first husband, Ilbert de Lacy, was still alive in Feb. 1141 (*Ord. Vit.* v 128), but
must have died soon after. Alice's brother, Gilbert de Gant, was himself compelled to
marry at earl Ranulf's dictation (John of Hexham, in *Priory of Hexham* i 135; and see
Complete Peerage vii 672–3). Alice was niece of earl Alan of Richmond, who was made
to do homage to earl Ranulf and surrender his castles (*Gesta Stephani*, ed. K. R. Potter
(1955) p. 77).

[2] See *E.Y.C.* ix 5–9, 65–7, 74–5 and ibid. nos. 4, 5.

[3] Byland chron., *Mon. Ang.* v 351b–352a. Although this source states that Roger de
Mowbray was in Normandy at the time, when in fact he was on the Crusade, there is
no reason to doubt the other details of the story, as Byland abbey property was involved.

[4] Charter no. 386.

[5] *E.Y.C.* ix no. 44, and cf. ibid. nos. 41–3; for a comment on the political significance
of the suit, see J. C. Holt, *The Northerners* (Oxford, 1961) p. 22.

[6] The monks of Rievaulx had difficulty in retaining their lands of the Mowbray fee
(see *E.Y.C.* ix nos. 10; 157–8 (cal. as charters nos. 247–8); 126 (cal. as no. 249);
129, 132, 161). Fountains lost land to William de Stuteville (*Fount. Cart.* i 215 (34),
216 (36); cf. charters nos. 110, 125–6). For the possibility that Byland might lose land
held of Mowbray, see no. 56. Stuteville had claims on Moreville lands of Mowbray,
see no. 154 and note, and cf. below, p. xxxi n. 3.

mother Gundreda in c. 1154, both Nigel and Robert began to attest charters and give their consent to their father's acts.[1] Nigel, the elder son, born soon after his father's marriage of c. 1142, came of age in or about 1164,[2] and was married before 1170 to Mabel, perhaps the daughter of William Patri, who held fifteen fees in Kent and a fief in Normandy quite close to Montbray.[3] Possibly on the occasion of his marriage, and certainly before 1172, Nigel was installed as lord of the Norman honour of Mowbray.[4] He held some estates of the English demesne,[5] and is found issuing charters relating to the English honour as if he shared lordship with his father.[6] Robert de Mowbray also had some lands of the demesne[7] and appears with frequency as a witness to the charters of his father and brother.[8] Both Nigel and Robert were deeply involved with Roger in the rebellion of 1174.

Insecurity of territorial right undermined the very basis of Mowbray's feudal authority and was doubtless the major factor in his participation in the rebellion of 1173–4. Other reasons for frustration certainly existed, such as the increase in the *servicium debitum* in 1168 from sixty to one hundred knights,[9] and the pressure of the king's expansionist forest policy in Yorkshire.[10] But the threat to Mowbray's position that was offered by the rise of the Stutevilles was primary. In the political sphere Mowbray was affronted by the Stutevilles' accumulation of offices of power and profit, which gave them a wide authority in the northern

---

[1] Roger's sons (not named) are first mentioned in c. 1146 (charter no. 156; and cf. *E.Y.C.* ix no. 150, cal. as charter no. 235). Nigel attests and gives consent before c. 1154 (charters nos. 101, 200, 289, 322; cf. nos. 243, 304, 390). Robert attests 1154 (no. 323), and with Nigel gives consent (no. 236). Gundreda last occurs in 1147 (Byland chron., *Mon. Ang.* v 352a; cf. charters nos. 155–6), but was probably dead by the time of the issue of no. 236 [1154] (see note to no. 236).

[2] He was present with the king at Clarendon in Jan. 1164 (*Select Charters*, ed. W. Stubbs (9th edn., Oxford, 1921) p. 164) and apparently on no other occasion before the young king's rebellion, so this was perhaps the time of his knighthood.

[3] *P.R. 16 Hen. II* p. 164; cf. charter no. 269 and note to no. 266. For the Patri estates, see I. J. Sanders, *English Baronies* (Oxford, 1960) p. 135, and *Ang.-Norm. Families* p. 76.

[4] *R.B.* ii 629.   [5] See below, p. xlv.

[6] e.g. charters nos. 123, 158, 207, 309, 328, 334, 389. Charters issued jointly by Roger and Nigel are nos. 52–4, 115, 120, 128–30 (cf. no. 163 for Normandy).

[7] See below, p. xlv.   [8] See index.

[9] *P.R. 14 Hen. II* p. 87, recording the assessment and Roger's payment on 60 fees. In 1171 the debt was discharged on 28¼ fees of Nigel d'Aubigny's creation, *P.R. 17 Hen. II* pp. 65–6 (cf. charter no. 401). The debt on Roger's own new fees, 11⅜, was outstanding till 1176, *P.R. 22 Hen. II* p. 101.

[10] From 1165 onwards tenants in the vills of the honour north of the forest of Galtres were amerced for forest offences (*P.R. 11 Hen. II* p. 51, *12 Hen. II* pp. 40 ff., *13 Hen. II* pp. 93 ff. etc.). These amercements, which even included Roger de Mowbray himself at Hovingham, seem to represent an expansion of the royal forest at this period (cf. J. C. Holt, *The Northerners* (Oxford, 1961) map 2, and M. L. Bazeley, 'The extent of the English forests in the 13th century', *T.R.H.S.* 4th ser. iv (1921) 146 ff.).

counties reminiscent of that wielded under Henry I by Roger's father Nigel d'Aubigny. Robert de Stuteville was sheriff of York,[1] his younger brother Roger was sheriff of Northumberland,[2] and his son William was granted valuable manors close to Mowbray estates in the West Riding.[3] Robert's daughter, Burga, was married to William de Vescy, son of Eustace Fitz John, and thus an alliance was formed between Mowbray's two most influential and hostile tenants.[4]

To Jordan Fantosme, the fate of the whole York area in 1174 seemed to depend on the Stutevilles:

> 'Par devers Everwic cument funt les baruns?
> E ceus d'Estutevile, tienent-il lur meisuns?'[5]

When Roger de Mowbray allied with the Scottish king, it was doubtless his hope to regain some of his father's northern authority at the expense of the Stutevilles. As in 1149, the city and castle of York figured large in his designs:

> 'La bone cité d'Everwic si est à dan Rogier,
> Par tut Everwicsire, se fait seignur clamer.'[6]

Charter evidence illustrates Roger's connection with some powerful citizens and rebels of York—William of Tickhill,[7] Hugh son of Lewin,[8] Thomas son of Elvive,[9] and Thomas son of Thomas Ultra Usam.[10]

The collapse of the rebellion in 1175 had results deeply humiliating for Roger de Mowbray—his surrender, the temporary confiscation of some of his estates,[11] and the destruction of the castles of Kinnard, Kirkby Malzeard, and Thirsk.[12] But because the monarchy had ceased

---

[1] See *E.Y.C.* ix 6.   [2] Ibid. pp. 3–4.
[3] Knaresborough and Aldborough, ibid. pp. 9–10.
[4] Ibid. pp. 8, 178–9; cf. above p. xxvii.
[5] *Chrons. of Stephen, Hen. II and Ric. I,* ed. R. Howlett (R.S. lxxxii) iii 332.
[6] Ibid. p. 284.
[7] Fined for rebellion, *P.R. 21 Hen. II* pp. 179, 182; witness to Mowbray charters, two of which were drawn up in his house in York (nos. 126–7; cf. nos. 251–2, 308–9, 347); received manor of Askham Richard (nos. 388–9).
[8] Fined for rebellion, *P.R. 21 Hen. II* pp. 180, 182; witness to charters (nos. 308–9); tenant on demesne (no. 315).
[9] Fined for rebellion, *P.R. 21 Hen. II* p. 182; witness to charters (nos. 110–11).
[10] Fined for rebellion, *P.R. 21 Hen. II* p. 180; probably witness to charters (nos. 110–11; and cf. Ernise Ultra Usam who occurs in no. 388).
[11] *P.R. 20 Hen. II* p. 143.
[12] Kinnard is said to have been destroyed at the time of its capture, in 1174 (*Giraldi Cambrensis Opera Omnia,* ed. J. S. Brewer (R.S. xxi) iv 364; *Radulfi de Diceto Opera Historica,* ed. W. Stubbs (R.S. lxviii) i 379; *Gesta Hen. II* i 68). In 1180, however, Adam Paynel was amerced 2 marks 'de castello de Insula non bene prostrato' (*P.R. 26 Hen. II* p. 53). Malzeard was partially dismantled in 1174 (Giraldus, op. cit. iv 366, says destroyed, but archbishop Roger was put in charge of the castle (*Gesta Hen. II* i 69), so it cannot have been a ruin). Malzeard and Thirsk were razed early in 1176 (ibid. p. 126; *Houeden* ii 101; cf. the reference in charter no. 131, and *E.Y.C.* ii no. 1114). There seems to be no positive evidence to support the statement of J. C. Holt

to use forfeiture as a political weapon, Mowbray suffered no permanent loss of territory. Such clemency was a sign of the strength of a king who was deliberately elevating his office above the arena of feudal conflict in order to become an arbiter and no longer a party in baronial disputes. By the standards of his grandfather, Henry II's enemies were not harshly treated. Neither were his friends greatly rewarded. The Stutevilles were not given more lands and powers; indeed, Robert de Stuteville ceased to be sheriff of York in 1175. A compromise was reached over the Mowbray quota: although in 1176 Roger was forced to pay his outstanding debt from the feudal aid of 1168, the *servicium debitum* was never again set so high, but was accepted as eighty-eight or eighty-nine knights, representing the number of fees reckoned to have existed on the honour at the death of Nigel d'Aubigny in 1129.[1] It may have been as a result of royal pressure at a time of pacification that various settlements over disputed lands in Yorkshire were made soon after the rebellion.[2] There were further disputes and settlements in the 1180s, however, and on at least one occasion the king took action which undermined Mowbray's lordship.[3]

During the last years of his life, Roger de Mowbray turned again to the crusades. As after his humiliation in the 1140s he had taken part in the second Crusade, so after the failure of rebellion in 1174–5 he undertook another pilgrimage. Whether he actually went with the count of Flanders' expedition in 1177, it is impossible to say, but in the months immediately preceding this crusade he raised substantial sums of money from Fountains abbey in aid of his journey,[4] and paid one of his rare visits to London in March 1177, just six weeks before the crusaders set

(*The Northerners* (Oxford, 1961) p. 22) that the castle of Burton in Lonsdale was destroyed at this time, but there is nothing in the documents or in the archaeological remains to suggest that it survived the 12th century (cf. *V.C.H. Yorks.* ii 27–8). T. D. Whitaker's reference to the appointment of a governor under Edward II (*A History of Richmondshire* (1823) ii 354) is based on a misunderstanding of the Patent Roll (*C.P.R. 1321–4* p. 161). The castle at Brinklow was abandoned at an early date: no masonry has been found (see P. B. Chatwin, 'Castles in Warwicks.', *Trans. Birmingham Archaeol. Soc.* lxvi (1951) 4–6). It may have suffered in Stephen's reign, or been dismantled as a result of the treaty between the earls of Chester and Leicester, some time between 1149 and 1153 (Stenton, *Feudalism* pp. 250–3, 286–8), for it stood within the area covered by the treaty and on a fee held by Mowbray of the earl of Leicester. For the Mowbray castles, see Map I.

[1] See above, p. xxix n. 9, and I. J. Sanders, *English Baronies* (Oxford, 1960) p. 146 n. 7.
[2] Charters nos. 56–7, 110–13, 119–27, 131, 327–8.
[3] In 1183–4 the king, 'for hatred of Roger de Mowbray', disseised the monks of Kirkstall of land of the Moreville fee ('The Foundation of Kirkstall Abbey', ed. E. K. Clark, Thoresby Soc. *Miscellanea* iv (1895) 182–3; cf. *P.R. 29 Hen. II* p. 48 and *30 Hen. II* p. 30). For other disputes, see, e.g., *E.Y.C.* i nos. 610, 617, and *Fount. Cart.* i 215 (33).
[4] Charter no. 111 and *Fount. Cart.* i 205 (7) (and cf. charters nos. 112–13, 120–2, 126). The journey is also mentioned in no. 388, and perhaps in no. 174.

off.[1] If he did indeed accompany the expedition, he presumably returned in the autumn of 1178. It was at about this time, after 1176 and probably before 1181, that his wife Alice de Gant died.[2] Roger again took the cross in 1185, although by this time he was about sixty-five years of age. The crusaders arrived at Jerusalem in the spring of 1186. At the disastrous battle of Hittin, on 4 July 1187, Roger was captured by the Saracens, and in the following year, not long after his ransom by the knights of the Hospital and the Temple, he died and was buried in the Holy Land.[3] There can be small doubt that love of military adventure played an important part in his career. Jordan Fantosme says of him, that he 'tuz jorz fud guerreer', and that he and Adam de Port were 'les meillurs guerriers que l'um saveit en vie'.[4]

At the time of his father's death in 1188 Nigel de Mowbray was already about forty-five years old. His possession of the honour was short. He was present at king Richard's coronation at Westminster on 3 September 1189, and on 12 December he left England on crusade with the king. He died at Acre in 1191 and was buried at sea.[5] He was survived by Robert his brother, Mabel his wife, three or four sons, and a daughter.

[1] *Gesta Hen. II* i 154; *Houeden* ii 131.

[2] She occurs last in April 1176 (charter no. 131). Although she was closely interested in benefactions to Fountains abbey, she does not appear in the series of charters of *c.* 1181 (nos. 132–41).

[3] *Gesta Hen. II* i 359, ii 10, 22; *Houeden* ii 316, 325.

[4] *Chrons. of Stephen, Hen. II and Ric. I*, ed. R. Howlett (R.S. lxxii) iii 284, 314. Cf. *Regesta Regum Scottorum* ii, ed. G. W. S. Barrow (Edinburgh, 1971) p. 22.

[5] *Gesta Hen. II* ii 80, 101, 149.

II. FEUDAL STRUCTURE

THE basic distinction between demesne and tenanted land may be observed throughout the collection of charters. Demesne is distinguished by phrases which carry the full weight of proprietary right: it is retained 'in manu', as 'proprium dominium'.[1] When demesne is alienated, it is given in enfeoffment, alms, or other forms of tenancy. Ecclesiastical interest in tenancies of the Mowbray honour has been responsible for preserving the great majority of the charters, even many for lay beneficiaries.[2] The collection therefore gives a one-sided view of the tenurial structure, and it seems appropriate here to attempt to redress the balance.

A hundred knights' fees were established on the honour before 1166. The *carta* of that year states that sixty fees had been in existence when Nigel d'Aubigny received his lands, which should probably be interpreted as meaning that he had immediately passed on to the tenants already enfeoffed the *servicium debitum* of sixty knights imposed by the king when his honour was complete, perhaps *c.* 1114. The *carta* also states that Nigel created another twenty-eight fees and that Roger de Mowbray added eleven and three-quarter fees out of demesne.[3] Eight of the fees entered under the old enfeoffment, however, those of Robert de Stuteville, were not created until after 1154, and rightly belong to Roger de Mowbray's enfeoffment.[4] After 1166 only four enfeoffments for knight service are known to have been made, and these were for fractions of fees—two halves and two quarters.[5]

Although lack of early documentation obscures the first stages of the enfeoffment process, certain facts emerge with reasonable clarity. The earliest fees were chiefly situated in the midlands, where subinfeudation had been well advanced by 1086. Nine and a half twelfth-century fees actually correspond with Domesday tenancies on the lands of Geoffrey de La Guerche, although it is not possible to prove continuity.[6] About thirty more fees were established in the midland territories during

---

[1] Charters nos. 88, 201.
[2] Nos. 340, 343–4, 348, 350–4, 359, 363, 366–9, 375, 377, 379–83, 387–8, 396.
[3] No. 401. [4] No. 386.
[5] Nos. 343, 349, 360, 364–5.
[6] Sancto Martino 2 fees in Blyborough (Lincs.) (held by Robert in 1086); Gainsborough 2 fees in Gainsborough (Lincs.) (held by Rainald in 1086); Queniborough 2 fees in Queniborough and Burton on the Wolds (Leics.) (held by William in 1086); Rames 1 fee and d'Aubigny 1 fee in Stathern (Leics.) (held by Roger and William in 1086); Wyville 1½ fees in Cold Ashby, Elkington, Sulby, Welford (Northants.) (held by Alfrid in 1086).

C

Robert de Stuteville's period of lordship and during the early years of
Nigel d'Aubigny's possession of the honour.[1] All the largest fiefs—
Camville (accounting in 1166 for 9 fees), Wappenbury (5 fees), Wyville
(5 fees), Moreville (5 fees), Daiville (4 fees), and Montfort (3¾ fees)—
were thus created between 1086 and *c.* 1114, and they were mainly
placed in the well-tenanted midland areas of Leicestershire, Warwickshire, and Northamptonshire. In these counties the pattern of military
enfeoffment was largely complete by *c.* 1114, answering for more than
forty knights.

By contrast, in the northern territories, where very few tenants had
been recorded in 1086, the fees mostly date from the period after overlordship passed to Nigel d'Aubigny. Indeed, the Pennine lordships of
Burton in Lonsdale and Kirkby Malzeard had scarcely any knights' fees
established until *c.* 1150.[2] Hired knights, such as the one who commanded
the garrison of ten hired sergeants at the castle of Burton in 1130, and
household knights, such as those who appear in Roger de Mowbray's
household in the 1140s and later, doubtless provided the honour's main
force in the north in the first half of the twelfth century.[3] Enfeoffment
in Yorkshire, particularly under Roger de Mowbray, largely took the
form of settling household knights on the land. Consequently, few
military tenants in the northern estates owed more than one knight's

[1] It is not possible to show which fees derive from Stuteville's overlordship and
which from d'Aubigny's. But the family of Camville (9 fees in Leics., Northants., and
Warwicks.) came from Canville-les-Deux-Églises, not far from the Stuteville place of
origin, Étoutteville (*Ang.-Norm. Families* p. 24), and in a genealogy of Mowbray the
vavassoria of Camville is said to have been given to Nigel d'Aubigny (*Mon. Ang.* vi
(1) 320). The same source states that the *vavassoria* of Wyville (5 fees in Northants. cf.
above, p. xxxiii n. 6) and Yorks.) was given to Nigel d'Aubigny; Hugh de 'Guidvilla'
occurs in 1077 and 1086 (*Mon. Ang.* vi (2) 996 and *Domesday Book* i fos. 219a, 230a);
Robert de 'Wituile' was a tenant of the honour before 1114 (charter no. 3). Hugh de
Rampan (1 fee in Leics.) was probably established before Nigel became lord and certainly before 1114 (no. 3; cf. witnesses to nos. 4, 5, 7); he had no known connection
with Rampan, Manche (arr. and cant. Saint-Lô). Richard de Daiville (4 old fees and
1 new fee in Leics., Notts., and Yorks.) was a tenant before 1114 (no. 3; cf. witnesses
to nos. 5, 13) and the family came from Déville, Seine-Maritime, and like Nigel
d'Aubigny were tenants of the count of Eu (*Ang.-Norm. Families* p. 37). Henry de
Montfort (3¾ fees in Warwicks.) occurs as a witness before 1114 (charters nos. 4, 5, 7);
his brother Robert was established in fees of the earl of Warwick before 1097 (*Complete
Peerage* ix 120). Geoffrey de Moreville (5 fees in Leics., Warwicks., and Yorks.) occurs
as a witness before 1129, together with a tenant of his own, Roger de Neuham (charter
no. 13). He was almost certainly related to the family from Morville, Manche, no great
distance from Morsalines, a d'Aubigny estate (*Ang.-Norm. Families* pp. 49, 70, and
note to charter no. 384; cf. for Morsalines *Regesta* ii nos. 1682, 1684). Wielard of
Wappenbury (5 fees in Leics. and Warwicks.) also occurs as witness before 1129 (charter no. 13), but his origin is unknown.
[2] Enfeoffments of Walter Buher in Masham, 1149–50 (see charter no. 174), of
William son of Gilbert in Lonsdale, Kendale and Horton in Ribblesdale, [1149] (no.
370), of William Graindorge in Winterburn and Flasby, [*c.* 1149 x?1154] (no. 150 note).
[3] See below, pp. lxi–ii.

service, and most of the fractional fees in the entire honour belonged to Yorkshire.

The three northern tenancies which did not conform to this pattern came about in exceptional circumstances. Two were the former tenancies-in-chief of Arches (probably 7 fees in 1166) and Tison (15 fees). There had been considerable subinfeudation in the Arches lands at the time of Domesday Book, and it is not improbable that the addition of these tenancies to Nigel d'Aubigny's honour was designed to counteract the effect of under-enfeoffment in his other northern estates.[1] The third exceptional northern tenancy, that of Stuteville, owed its origin to a settlement made between 1154 and 1166, by which Roger de Mowbray gave to Robert de Stuteville lands in the North Riding, for the service of nine or ten knights.[2]

The tenants thus established in the knights' fees were of widely vary-ing social groups. The origins of many of the smaller knightly tenants are obscure, but most of the tenants on the larger fees were Normans. There were, however, two notable tenants of English descent.[3] Some of the knights had extensive landed interests outside the honour. Stute-ville, Vescy, Bulmer, and Vere held lands in chief of the Crown, and the last three, with nine others, also held fees of other lords.[4] About half the military tenancies on the Mowbray honour were confined to a single county, and of those with scattered estates a third combined their chief holding with only a small tenement in second or third counties. Most fees, therefore, were based essentially in one district, many being re-stricted to a very small area and five being confined to a single manor. The holdings which were not compact, but were scattered throughout two or more counties, were chiefly the larger fiefs, of five or more fees.

---

[1] Cf. above, p. xxv.   [2] Above, p. xxviii, and charter no. 386.

[3] Henry of Arden, who held one fee in Warwicks. in 1166, was the grandson of Turkill of Warwick (see V.C.H. Warwicks. i 276–8). William son of Gilbert, enfeoffed in Lonsdale etc., was descended through his mother from a prominent English family (charter no. 370 note).

[4] In 1166 Stuteville (9 or 10 fees of Mowbray) held 8 fees in chief. Vescy (2 fees; but cf. no. 397 which gives 14 fees for the service of 11 knights) held 26 in chief, 7 of Fossard, 3 of the bishop of Durham, 1½ of Gant, and ½ of earl Simon. Bulmer (1 fee) held 3 in chief and 5 of the bishop of Durham. Vere (1 fee) held 30 in chief and 16 of 9 other lords.

Others who had larger interests outside than inside the Mowbray honour were: Montfort (3¾ fees of Mowbray) held 10¼ of the earl of Warwick; Arden (1 fee) held 5 (and his brother held another 5⅓) of the earl of Warwick; Sancto Martino (2 fees) held 2 of Roumare, ½ of Chester, and an interest of Caux; Dapifer (½ fee) held 3½ of Percy; Grammaticus (¼ fee) held 1 of Lacy and ½ of Curcy.

Others with small external estates were: Wyville (5 fees) held ½ of Warter and ½ of Foliot; Daiville (5 fees) held 1 of Caux and estates of the count of Eu. Haget (2 fees of Mowbray) held 1 of Arches and ¼ of Bulmer; d'Aubigny (1 fee) held 1 of d'Aubigny Brito.

Estates on these larger fees often included complete manors, so that scattering had the effect of creating not an uneconomic unit, but a series of economic units.

The Mowbray charters demonstrate several ways in which feudal custom was progressively defined during the twelfth century, as the personal relationship of lord and man was transmuted into a tenurial relationship of landlord and tenant. A remarkable restoration charter of Nigel d'Aubigny, given some time between 1109 and 1114, makes clear that although the idea of the heritability of knights' fees was accepted, in practice a powerful lord could actually disinherit his men, even if he felt bound to make restitution later.[1] It is noticeable that four of the twelve families whose members appear as witnesses to Nigel d'Aubigny's charters failed to survive as tenants of the honour.[2] By the time of Roger de Mowbray, fees were subject to hereditary right, and it was unusual in the middle years of the century for a knightly tenant to be dispossessed of part of his father's fee.[3] Roger's enfeoffments were made 'in fee and heredity' to men 'and their heirs'. Normally the phraseology of the charters distinguishes restorations to heirs from new enfeoffments, although there is at least one case, of c. 1150, where an heir received his father's fee in terms of a new grant.[4] By the 1180s the sophisticated form of the restoration charter, with its 'reddidisse' clause,[5] completely conceals from our view the procedure's origin, illuminated by a phrase in Nigel d'Aubigny's charter of 1109 × 1114, that the heirs of a certain man could have the land 'si eam requisierint'.

The ease with which the lord could exchange a man's land, so clearly seen in Nigel d'Aubigny's charter of restoration, is a key to the understanding of feudal ties in the early twelfth century. The lord retained in his own hand a wide power to rearrange tenancies: this satisfied a need for flexibility in a period of settlement and adaptation to local circumstances. In Nigel's charter Robert de Wyville held lands in four places which did not belong to the later Wyville fee and were therefore presumably exchanged subsequently. If tenurial conditions might be adjusted without much difficulty, this was because the relationship of lord and

---

[1] Charter no. 3.

[2] Insula family: Walter, tenant in Althorpe (Lincs.) [1109 × 1114] (no. 3); William, witness (no. 13); Geoffrey, witness (nos. 4, 5, 232; and cf. no. 170); W., witness (nos. 4, 5). Walvile: Robert, tenant [1109 × 1114] (no. 3), and witness (nos. 4, 5). Puntfreit: Ralph, witness (no. 4). Giuardvile: Richard, witness (no. 5).

[3] Ralph son of Aldelin remitted to Furness abbey all his claim to 2 carucates in Winterburn, which his father held by hereditary right on the day of king Henry I's death; this land had been granted in fee to William Graindorge (see charter no. 150 note).

[4] No. 371; *dedisse* is used with *reddidisse* in no. 383.

[5] Cf. *E.Y.C.* ix no. 137 (cal. as charter no. 361).

man was the basic nexus, and this is reflected in Nigel d'Aubigny's charter, where the emphasis is placed on the tenant and not on the terms of the tenancy. Moreover, Nigel dealt directly with all the dispossessed tenants, whether they were his immediate tenants or his sub-tenants: all were his men. A measure of his father's discretionary power remained to Roger de Mowbray. Under his lordship the practice of exchanging estates in fee persisted but became less common,[1] as did the related practice of granting augmentations of existing fees.[2] There are signs that even as late as the middle of the century, although probably not later, the lord might enter into direct contact with the tenants of his knights, issuing charters to them and confirming their gifts to religious houses, sometimes without mentioning that they did not hold their estates immediately of him.[3]

The distinctive characteristic of the knight's fee was the knight's service, but here there is much obscurity. Nowhere in all the charters is there any note of what the service of a knight entailed. The only reference to knight service on the honour before the 1140s occurs in Nigel d'Aubigny's restoration charter of 1109 × 1114 and suggests that although the amount of service was fixed and known, there might be improper demands for excessive service.[4] Roger de Mowbray's enfeoffment charters normally specify how many knights' service was due, but give no details of what was demanded. For the larger, older fiefs, which owed more than one knight's service, there are no surviving charters of enfeoffment, but none of the evidence relating to these estates suggests that there was any conception of a standard size of fee. The fact that grants were sometimes made to augment existing fees, without imposing additional service, seems to confirm this impression,[5] and three charters which concern fees owing the service of single knights show no correlation between the amounts of land involved.[6]

There was of course a world of difference between a tenant who owed the service of one or more knights and a tenant whose service was a fraction of a knight's service. The service for fractions of fees was very often a money payment. It is clear that the smallest fractional fee on the

[1] Charters nos. 139, 245, 364, 371; also 375 and cf. 116; cf. also an exchange made by Richard de Moreville (no. 384 note).
[2] Nos. 58, 338, 363, and perhaps also 342, 400.
[3] See nos. 393–4 (cf. no. 392), 347, 384; confirmations of gifts, nos. 20, 233, 240, 289, 295, 321.
[4] No. 3, final sentence concerning Robert de Walvile.
[5] See above, n. 2.
[6] Nos. 341 (Beler—10½ carucates and a mill); 356 (Coleville—evidently 12 carucates); a third charter which is rather less clear is no. 371 (Malebisse—a very large fee, perhaps 24 carucates). Nos. 381–2 relate to the reduction of Queniborough's service from two knights to one, after land from a 14-carucate holding had been granted to Selby.

Mowbray honour—for the fifteenth part of the service of one knight—
must have been held for cash.[1] Charters which give the formula—'for the
service pertaining to x carucates where y carucates makes a knight's fee'
—are concerned with the amount of scutage due from a fraction of a
fee.[2] The only clear reference to scutage relates to a quarter-fee, held for
half the service of a knight. This was a sub-tenure held by Mowbray of
the archbishop of York. Roger de Mowbray's charter for his own tenant
contains the condition that he would exact nothing except 'quando
archiepiscopus Ebor' exiget a me servicium quarte partis unius militis,
et tunc non exigam amplius nisi quantum ad servicium dimidii militis
pertinebit, secundum quod pro quarta parte unius militis a me exigetur'.[3]

The financial benefits which came to the feudal lord out of the creation
of military fees, the 'feudal incidents', took the form of irregular and
variable payments and profits. Roger de Mowbray himself paid large
sums in reliefs for two fees he held of other lords: he paid £60 of Angers
(about £15 sterling) and gave a *destrier* for his fee of the count of Eu at
Bazoches[4] and made a pledge of 100 marks for his fee of the count of
Britanny at Masham.[5] The reliefs paid by Mowbray's own tenants are
not normally revealed in the documents. The only clear case exhibits
some exceptional features which reflect the uncertain, if not arbitrary,
nature of the procedure. Robert de Arden paid 100 shillings to Nigel de
Mowbray for his half-fee in Hampton in Arden (Warwicks.).[6] This
represents twice the rate mentioned by Glanville for a knight's relief.[7] A
more surprising aspect of this case is that the occasion of Robert de
Arden's payment was not his initial establishment in the estate. Some
years earlier, Robert had bought his half-fee from Ralph de la Haia, for
50 marks, and had given a palfrey for Roger de Mowbray's confirmation,
presumably in addition to a relief.[8] The unusual nature of the fee's
origin probably explains why Nigel de Mowbray was able to exact a
second relief. But custom was obviously flexible, and allowed the taking
of additional gifts and payments when the lord could exert pressure.
During Roger de Mowbray's lifetime, Nigel had accepted a gold ring
from Robert de Arden for his consent to his father's grant of another
holding of a tenth of a fee.[9]

On the incidents of wardship and marriage, the charters are silent.

---

[1] No. 375.
[2] No. 374, of 1138 × 1148 concerning a holding of 2 carucates, where 10 carucates
made one knight's fee; cf. no. 366, referring to a holding of 60 acres, where 12 carucates
made one knight's fee, and no. 367 note.   [3] No. 359.   [4] No. 19.
[5] E.Y.C. iv no. 19 (cal. as charter no. 18 below).
[6] Charter no. 334.
[7] On this topic, see Stenton, *Feudalism* pp. 163 ff.
[8] Charter no. 333.   [9] No. 331.

We hear from the York eyre of 1218–19 that the wardship of William Malebisse was granted by Nigel de Mowbray, probably *c.* 1189, to the royal chancellor William de Longchamp, presumably for a cash payment,[1] but we have no means of knowing how the custody of minors and their estates normally operated. Similarly there are no direct statements on the marriages of wards and of widows. The marriages of heiresses to two important fees, however, bear the clear mark of Roger de Mowbray's interest. Juetta de Arches, daughter and heiress of William de Arches, and widow of Adam de Brus, was given in marriage to Roger de Flamville, one of Mowbray's frequent companions. Flamville thus gained another seven fees to hold together with his own one and a half fees.[2] After Flamville's death in *c.* 1169, Roger de Mowbray may have exerted some pressure on Juetta de Arches, possibly on the matter of her marriage, for between 1175 and 1177 she is said to have sold him the manor of Askham Richard for 220 marks.[3] Two of the four daughters and co-heirs of William Tison were married to Mowbray's household companions, Ralph de Belvoir, the steward, and his brother Robert, who were thus established in fees without cost to Mowbray himself.[4]

Much of the tenanted land of the honour was held by free tenants for rent in money or in kind. This had probably been true also at the time of Domesday Book. By the middle of the twelfth century the charters creating rented tenancies normally use the term 'in fee and heredity'. Sometimes we have glimpses of tenures going back into Nigel d'Aubigny's time,[5] and many of those in the hands of men of native ancestry must have originated in the pre-Conquest period. In Yorkshire and Lincolnshire there was a substantial class of free tenants, many of whom bore Scandinavian names. They were particularly numerous in the area round Kirkby Malzeard and Masham, where even some of the estates held as fractional fees were in the hands of men of native descent, one of them the grandson of the pre-Conquest lord of the entire area.[6] A feudal veneer had been laid in patches on the existing pattern of tenancies, so that in social and economic terms there was little to distinguish the tenants on fractions of fees from rent-paying socage tenants. Both are

---

[1] *Rolls of the Justices in Eyre for Yorks. 1218–19*, ed. D. M. Stenton (Selden Soc. lvi) no. 102.
[2] *E.Y.C.* iii 415 and charter no. 401 below; cf. *Mon. Ang.* vi (2) 971 (VII).
[3] Charters nos. 388–9 and notes.
[4] *E.Y.C.* xii 8–11; cf. below, p. lxii.
[5] e.g. charter no. 390.
[6] Uctred son of Dolfin son of Gospatric, see nos. 392–5. Other military tenants of native descent were: Roger son of Haldan de Berlay, no. 347; probably also Roger son of Geoffrey (? son of Unwin, nos. 101, 107, 109); and Ralph son of Aldelin (? son of Uctred, no. 106) nos. 383, 401 (cf. above, p. xxxvi n. 3). Cf. the large number of tenants of native origin on the Richmond and Lacy fees (see Wightman, *Lacy Family* pp. 40 ff.).

found witnessing the lord's charters and attending his honorial court, alienating or buying land, and issuing their own sealed charters.[1] That there was little tenurial distinction between some military and socage tenures is evident from the history of two post-1166 enfeoffments. One of these, for half the service of a knight, seems to have disguised the conversion of an earlier socage tenure into military fee.[2] The other, for the service of sixty acres, where twelve carucates made one knight's fee, seems later to have been converted into a socage.[3]

Rented tenancies of varying sizes were created in the twelfth century for various feoffees. A merchant of York, William of Tickhill, held the largest rented holding known on the honour: this was the vill of Askham Richard, which in Domesday Book was assessed as six carucates.[4] Some tenants of the knightly class, whose major holdings were in military fees of Mowbray or other lords, held lands in socage—usually more than one carucate—for rent,[5] or for renders such as spurs[6] or red hose.[7] Lower in the social scale were feoffees such as a reeve,[8] a miller,[9] an archer,[10] a chamberlain,[11] a cook[12] and a minstrel.[13] A fiddler received a life interest in a small estate in return for an annual render of one pound of pepper.[14] A tenant near Malzeard had one carucate of land in return for twenty lengths of cord to be rendered yearly.[15] An important class of rent-paying tenants was the religious houses, especially the Cistercian monasteries of Byland[16] and Rievaulx.[17] Some gifts said to have been made 'in pure and perpetual alms' were in reality for rent, and occasionally included

---

[1] For witness-lists, see, e.g. charters nos. 97, 101, 106, 108–9. For charters, see, e.g. nos. 59 and note, 133 and note, 270. Cf. also no. 396.

[2] Nos. 343–4.   [3] Nos. 366–8.

[4] Nos. 388–9; cf. E.Y.C. i 428.

[5] Uctred son of Dolfin in Hebden, charter no. 395; he held ¼ fee in Ilton (no. 392). Adam Fossard in Bagwith and Balk, Yorks. Deeds ii no. 30; he held 1 fee of Stuteville (E.Y.C. ix 152–60). Philip of Billinghay, in Kirkby Malzeard, B.M., Egerton MS. 2823 (cartulary of Byland) fo. 51r; he succeeded to his brother Peter's ¼ fee in Hovingham (cf. charter no. 349).

[6] Thomas de Coleville in Melton Mowbray, no. 357; he held 1 fee in Coxwold etc. (no. 356).

[7] Ralph and Robert de Belvoir in Mickley, no. 345; they held ½ fee each of Tison (E.Y.C. xii 8–11). Maud of Stonegrave in Thorpefield, B.M., Egerton MS. 2823 (cartulary of Byland) fo. 93v (cf. charter no. 65); Stonegrave held ¼ fee of Everard de Ros (R.B. i 433).

[8] Charter no. 369.   [9] No. 348.

[10] Reference in a charter of William de Mowbray, 1209 (Bodl., MS. Dodsworth 8 fo. 298r–v).

[11] Charter no. 340.   [12] No. 46.   [13] No. 200.

[14] No. 308.   [15] No. 377.

[16] Charters of Hugh Malebisse: E.Y.C. iii nos. 1836, 1845; Yorks. Deeds ii no. 36; Maud of Stonegrave: B.M., Egerton MS. 2823 (cartulary of Byland) fo. 93v; Engelram de Torp: Bodl., MS. Dodsworth 7 fo. 166r; Robert de Buscy: Bodl., MS. Dodsworth 63 fo. 62v.

[17] Charters nos. 233, 243, 287.

forensic service.[1] Various as these rented tenancies were, they had one factor in common: the extreme favourableness of their terms. Some of the free tenants paid derisory rents, and all paid at a rate considerably lower than that at which villeins paid. Many free rents in Yorkshire were at the rate of one mark per carucate, which is equivalent to 1s. 8d. per bovate,[2] while rent-paying villeins might pay rents in the region of 5s. per bovate.[3]

The great majority of the Mowbray charters relate to property of the honour which was given into the possession of various ecclesiastical corporations, chiefly monastic communities. Nigel d'Aubigny was not, it appears, a lavish benefactor: many of his gifts were in reality restorations of alienated property or confirmations of grants made by predecessors.[4] Roger de Mowbray, on the other hand, was a notable patron, 'quasi signifer liberalitatis inter omnes proceres terre'.[5] The collected charters of Roger and his son Nigel are in favour of no fewer than forty-eight religious communities, among which the Cistercians and Augustinians are the chief beneficiaries. Roger founded two important houses in Yorkshire—the Cistercian abbey of Byland and the Augustinian priory of Newburgh—and these were largely endowed by himself and his tenants.

Theoretically, the service due from frankalmoin tenancies was spiritual. The patron received a place in the prayers and a share in the spiritual benefits of the community's good works, for the health and salvation of himself and his family.[6] He might also gain a burial-place[7] and permanent remembrance after death.[8] But the foundation of a monastery

[1] Nos. 233, 241; cf. E.Y.C. iii nos. 1842, 1845. Forensic service mentioned in charters of Maud of Stonegrave (see p. xl n. 16) and Richard de Wyville: B.M., Stowe MS. 937 (cartulary of Pipewell) fo. 29v. For specific exemptions from forensic service, see charters nos. 289, 319.
[2] e.g. nos. 117, 133–4, 241, 243.   [3] Cf. no. 349, and below, p. xlviii.
[4] His gifts were to Selby (nos. 2, 9), to St. Albans (nos. 2, 3), to Bec (nos. 2, 10; exchanged in no. 11), to Monks Kirby (nos. 3, 13), to Holy Trinity, York (no. 3), to Pontigny (no. 14), to Nostell (no. 15), and to Saint-Évroult (nos. 16–17).
[5] Byland chron., Mon. Ang. v 349b.
[6] Cf. charters nos. 307 and 310, and the statement about Roger de Mowbray in Mon. Ang. v 569 (III). Special prayers for his crusade were offered by the monks of Garendon (no. 155).
[7] Nigel d'Aubigny gave his body for burial at St. Albans (nos. 2, 3), but actually died and was buried at Bec (see above, p. xviii n. 2). Cf. W. Dugdale, Baronage of England (1675–6) i 123, 125, for unsubstantiated stories about the burials of Roger de Mowbray, Gundreda de Gournay, and William de Mowbray.
[8] Nigel d'Aubigny sought commemoration at Monks Kirby (charter no. 13); for his obit at Durham and Lincoln, see above, p. xviii n. 2. Roger de Mowbray was also commemorated at Durham (Liber Vitae Dunelm., facsimile ed. A. H. Thompson (S.S. cxxxvi) fos. 16r, 42v), at Arden (Mon. Ang. iv 286 (V)) and by the Templars (ibid. vi (2) 838a–b). Alice de Gant sought remembrance at Fountains (charter no. 131) and York Minster (no. 323).

brought other compensations. As founder of the Augustinian priory of
Newburgh, Roger de Mowbray enjoyed the rights of custody during
vacancies, and licence and assent in elections: he was the convent's
'advocatus'[1] and the canons were 'his' canons.[2] During the early years
of Byland, Roger seems to have had a similar proprietary control over
the abbey's affairs, presenting the abbot-elect to the archbishop in 1142
and claiming the right to determine the abbey's religious subjection to
Savigny in 1147.[3] Such lay power, normally repudiated by the white
monks, doubtless originated and was tolerated in the unusual circumstances of Byland's foundation and early history, when a strong protector
was a necessity.[4] The close connections between Mowbray and the communities of Newburgh and Byland are illustrated by the frequency with
which Augustine and Richard, successive priors of Newburgh, and
Roger, abbot of Byland, are found attesting the charters.[5] Hospitality
seem to have been reciprocal, and the prior and the abbot seem occasionally to have travelled with the Mowbray household.[6]

These spiritual and social benefits were achieved without great cost.
The property granted to ecclesiastical tenants very rarely comprised
whole manors.[7] Often it consisted of small arable estates within manors,
so that there came to be scarcely a village in the honour without a
monastic tenant.[8] Where the estates of religious and laity were inter-
mingled, it may have happened that secular demands were made from
time to time on frankalmoin tenements.[9] As we have seen, some property
said to have been in alms was actually held for rent, and this may have
been true of many other estates ostensibly held in frankalmoin. In times
of emergency, such as Stephen's reign, ecclesiastical estates, tenants, and
goods in the Mowbray honour were subjected to harsh treatment.[10] The
lords certainly tried to wring all possible benefit out of their endowments. In several areas colonization was encouraged by grants—especially to the Cistercians—of moorland, woodland, or marsh.[11] Such gifts
greatly reduced the expense of patronage. When they were made in

---

[1] Charters of the prior of Newburgh refer to 'dominus Rogerus advocatus noster':
B.M., Cotton MS. Claud. D xi (cartulary of Malton) fo. 99r; Bodl., MS. Dodsworth 91
fo. 148r.
[2] Charters nos. 200, 208, 213.   [3] Byland chron., *Mon. Ang.* v 350b, 353a.
[4] Ibid. pp. 349 ff.
[5] See index. Augustine served in a semi-judicial capacity in charter no. 318.
[6] Augustine attested nos. 196 at Bridlington, 236 at York, and 177 at Thirsk. Roger
attested nos. 327 at Northampton, 236 at York, and nos. 110, 119, probably at York.
[7] Some of the older Benedictine houses held manors which had been granted to them
before the end of the 11th century, e.g. Selby in Crowle (Lincs.) (no. 1 note); Monks
Kirby in Monks Kirby (no. 191 note).
[8] Cf. F. M. Stenton's comment on the Danelaw, *Danelaw Charters* p. liii.
[9] Cf. *E.Y.C.* v no. 160 (cal. as charter no. 303).
[10] See charters nos. 89–90, 102–3, 255, 318, 322–4.   [11] See below, pp. xlviii–li.

return for large sums of cash—as were some of Mowbray's endowments
—they served both God and Mammon.[1]

One favoured method of ecclesiastical endowment was to grant
parish churches, which the Augustinians especially were willing to accept. All the churches of the Mowbray demesne and many of those in
the knights' fees were given to religious houses in a series of gifts which
began in the late eleventh century and culminated in the middle of the
twelfth. This process was not altogether straightforward. Problems and
disputes arose from the fact that portions of tithe in many places had
been alienated earlier.[2] In some cases lay patronage may have been
maintained even after churches had ostensibly been given away,[3] and
Mowbray's grant of many of the demesne churches to his convent of
Newburgh ensured that during vacancies, at least, he kept an interest.[4]
But although the language of the charters reveals that proprietary atti-
tudes were slow to change,[5] the transfer of ownership represented a
genuine break with the past. Roger de Mowbray had relinquished the
patronage with which he had previously rewarded his personal chaplain
and in consequence had to provide for the chaplain from other resources.[6]
The value of the churches was by no means negligible: three of the
demesne churches were given to York Minster, to form the prebend of
Masham, which was to be the most valuable of all the York prebends.[7]

---

[1] See below, pp. liv–v.

[2] e.g. Hampton in Arden, where tithes had been granted by Geoffrey de La Guerche
to Monks Kirby (*Mon. Ang.* vi (2) 996), and by Geoffrey de Stuteville to Lewes (*Cal.
Docs. France* no. 1391); settlements with these houses were made by the convent of
Kenilworth, to which the church was given by Mowbray (charters nos. 176, 178–80),
see B.M., Harley MS. 3650 fos. 36v–37r; Add. MS. 47677 fos. 34r, 34v, 35v.

[3] e.g. Askham Richard, see charter no. 388 note; Langford, no. 196 note; Hampton
in Arden, see nos. 176, 178–80, 271, 333–4, 336–7, and *V.C.H. Warwicks.* iv 85–6.

[4] For the story that Mowbray first tried to give the churches to Byland, but they
were refused by the abbot, see Byland chron., *Mon. Ang.* v 351a.

[5] Cf. the reference to Samson d'Aubigny's son being able to 'tenere and regere' a
church in charter no. 196 and the reference to 'seisin' of a church in no. 176.

[6] See below, pp. lxv–vii.   [7] Charter no. 326 note.

III. ECONOMY

THE primary function of the demesne was to feed the lord and his household. The Byland chronicle describes how the Mowbray household travelled through the demesnes, 'de manerio in manerium per varias provincias',[1] doubtless consuming certain food-rents[2] and collecting cash payments and profits. There were castles or manor-houses in all the demesne manors, and when place-dates are given in the charters they confirm the picture of the peripatetic lord and household.[3] A sign of this dependence on the demesne was the chaplain's possession, until c. 1154, of the livings of the demesne churches.[4]

Beyond a certain point, therefore, new tenancies could not be created, as there had to be a residual estate for the lord's use. At the time of Nigel d'Aubigny's death in 1129, the demesne consisted of thirteen of the largest and most valuable manors in the honour—nine in Yorkshire, two in Warwickshire, and one each in Lincolnshire and Leicestershire. By the 1170s enfeoffments had cut this down to seven manors, five of which had castles until 1174–6. One of these demesne estates, Brinklow, was to be granted out as part of the settlement with Stuteville in 1201,[5] but the others—the six manors of Burton in Lonsdale, Kirkby Malzeard, Thirsk, Hovingham, Epworth and the Isle of Axholme, and Melton Mowbray—were to be retained until the fourteenth century. Essentially, therefore, the residual level of the demesne had been reached by the 1170s. Thereafter, when pressed to create new tenancies, the lords increasingly used methods designed to preserve as much of the demesne as possible: granting to new tenants older tenancies which had been resumed,[6] buying property to grant out again,[7] inserting tenants above existing tenants,[8] and probably leasing portions of demesne.[9]

---

[1] *Mon. Ang.* v 349b–350a.   [2] See below, pp. xlvi–vii.
[3] Charters no. 294 at Welburn, no. 177 at Thirsk, no. 369 in Axholme, no. 142 (see note) at Kirkby Malzeard. Some charters are dated at York: nos. 111, 125–7, 322–3.
[4] Below, p. lxvi.   [5] *E.Y.C.* ix no. 44.
[6] Of course, this was not a new method: see, e.g., charters nos. 43, 67, 308, 346, 400.
[7] No. 249; also nos. 388–9.
[8] e.g. *York Min. Fasti* ii no. 55 (cal. as charter no. 329).
[9] This is an obscure topic in the Mowbray honour. In charter no. 306, Roger de Mowbray clearly refers to the possibility of leasing 'sive ad tempus sive imperpetuum'. In no. 315 he addresses Hamo Beler, Roger de Daiville, and Hugh son of Lewin of York 'et universis aliis hominibus suis tenentibus dominia sua in Anglia'. Beler seems to have held portions of Hovingham and Axholme, probably on leases, for his family's interest did not survive (for Hovingham, see no. 61, and *P.R. 8 Ric. I* p. 177; for Axholme, see charter no. 342 and note). Roger de Daiville received part of South Cave, in fee and heredity (no. 360), and this was not a lease, for Daiville's interest passed

There were, however, some demands on the demesne which had to be met directly. These were the tenancies held by members of the Mowbray family. Roger's mother, Gundreda de Gournay, during her widowhood from 1129, held property in the North Riding of Yorkshire and in Leicestershire, and installed several socage tenants.[1] On her death, which probably occurred between 1147 and 1154, these estates returned to demesne; some in Yorkshire were then enfeoffed to Robert de Stuteville,[2] and some in Melton Mowbray went to Roger's elder son, Nigel,[3] who also received estates in Brinklow[4] and Axholme.[5] Robert de Mowbray, the younger son, had land in Melton Mowbray,[6] and in 1195 had a dispute with Nigel's widow, Mabel, whose dowry was there.[7] Alice de Gant had as dowry some estates near Kirkby Malzeard[8] and in South Cave (which was held in demesne until the 1170s).[9] Marriage-portions operated in the other direction, and brought land into the honour. Alice de Gant brought Empingham (Rutland),[10] which was granted out in fee before 1157.[11] Nigel de Mowbray's wife, Mabel, brought Banstead (Surrey),[12] which was kept in demesne until it had to be alienated to secure William de Mowbray's release from captivity in 1217.[13]

The charters cast only a fitful light on the organization of the demesne in the twelfth century. It is clear, however, that all the manors which comprised the 'residual demesne' not only had reasonably large home farms but also formed important centres in their respective districts, many of them with markets and all of them central to an area of Mowbray lordship. Therefore they served as pivotal points of honorial administration, where courts were held and rents and services from the surrounding estates were received. Bailiffs or reeves operated in every demesne

to his descendants. Hugh son of Lewin received Askham Richard, as heir of William of Tickhill, and this was also a permanent tenancy (see *E.Y.C.* i 427–8 and charters nos. 388–9).

[1] Her estates were in Hovingham (charter no. 47; cf. no. 201); some berewicks of Kirkby Moorside–Hoveton (no. 287; cf. nos. 237, 243, 249), Welburn (nos. 232, 235; cf. nos. 236–7), and Skiplam (no. 235); Bagby (no. 300; cf. no. 302); Old Byland (Byland chron., *Mon. Ang.* v 350b; cf. charter no. 38); Thorpe Arnold, near Melton Mowbray (no. 156; cf. nos. 31, 155, 160).

[2] See no. 386.

[3] Nos. 29–30; cf. nos. 357, 387. Also Kirby Bellars (nos. 25–6).

[4] No. 329; also Withybrook (no. 83).   [5] Nos. 258–61.   [6] No. 161.

[7] *Three Rolls of the King's Court*, ed. F. W. Maitland (P.R.S. xiv) pp. 7–8; cf. *Curia Regis Rolls* i 17, 368.

[8] Charters nos. 100–1, 104–7, 131, 377.

[9] Nos. 299, 322–3. For South Cave's division between three feoffees, see nos. 343, 360.   [10] No. 182.

[11] See no. 378. For Alice's dowry of the Lacy honour, see no. 229.

[12] Nos. 266–9. Mabel was still in possession in 1198 (*Curia Regis Rolls* i 37).

[13] *Furness Coucher* II ii 291; cf. *C.Ch.R.* i 83.

estate, subject to the overriding authority of the steward.[1] Some of the reeves' activities emerge from the charters: they were concerned with the working of the demesne ploughs,[2] they oversaw woodcutting in the demesne woodlands,[3] and they supervised haymaking in the demesne meadows.[4]

The Isle of Axholme was by far the largest and the most important of the Mowbray demesnes.[5] These estates had been in 1086 the most valuable of all the lands which were to form the Mowbray honour, and they yielded in 1298 more than three times the income of the next most valuable manor, Thirsk.[6] Some of the Axholme estates, chiefly those external to the central island, were granted to ecclesiastical and lay tenants in the later eleventh and twelfth centuries,[7] but the main island, comprising Epworth, Belton, Haxey, and Owston, was mostly kept in demesne, with a complex economic organization and social structure. There were many free tenants, and in 1298 the proportion was higher than elsewhere in the honour. Some of these free tenants were doubtless the descendants of Domesday sokemen, but others, such as those who had tenancies where there had been no sokemen in 1086, had perhaps gained from marshland reclamation.[8] The growth of free tenures was not accompanied by any lessening of manorial pressures, for at the end of the thirteenth century the customary rents and services were much more onerous in Axholme than anywhere else in the honour.

One element in the demesne economy, which is visible in Axholme but nowhere else in the honour, is the system of food-rents. Some time before c. 1150, Roger de Mowbray gave to St. Mary's, York, for the monks at their cell at Sandtoft, six baskets of barley annually, to be rendered at All Saints by his men of Epworth, and also half the tithes of his foods—'omnium ciborum meorum ubicunque fuero in Haxolm'.[9] A series of charters for Nostell also shows the existence of food-rents in

---

[1] See below, p. lxiv.   [2] Charter no. 306.   [3] Nos. 185–6.
[4] Nos. 118, 124.
[5] For a map, see Map II A. For an analysis of Axholme's conservative but flourishing economy in the 16th and early 17th centuries, see J. Thirsk, 'The Isle of Axholme before Vermuyden', *Agricultural History Rev.* i (1953) 16–28. Dr. Thirsk prints a map of the Isle. See also Stonehouse, *Axholme*.
[6] The source for 1298 is the inquisition post mortem, P.R.O., C. 133/84 (8), cal. in *Cal. Inq. P.M.* iii 356 ff.
[7] Crowle had been granted to Selby before 1086 (charter no. 1 note); Sandtoft and Wroot to St. Mary's, York, before 1106 (nos. 317, 319, and notes); Hirst to Nostell between 1121 and 1129 (no. 15); land in Keadby and Althorpe to the Templars before 1185 (nos. 273, 276). Adlingfleet (Yorks., W.R.) was enfeoffed to Daiville; land in Kinnard's Ferry (Lincs.) to Sancto Martino.
[8] See F. M. Stenton's comment on Thorald son of Oviet of Owston's charter, *Danelaw Charters* no. 402, and ibid. pp. xciv–v. *Liberi homines* appear in Westwood in charter no. 264.   [9] Charter no. 317.

Axholme. Between 1121 and 1129 Nigel d'Aubigny gave to Ralph, canon of Nostell then living at Hirst, an annual payment of 15s. rent, together with 4 sesters each of malt, wheat, and rye, and 500 eels.[1] These renders, from the farm of Belton, were doubled by Roger de Mowbray, to provide for two canons at Hirst.[2] Before 1148 the wheat and rye were exchanged for 6 bovates of land,[3] and before 1166 the eels were exchanged for two fisheries.[4] By the middle of the thirteenth century, when we next have a glimpse of this property, the malt had been commuted and all the rents were in cash.[5] Nevertheless, the system of food-rents in Axholme, although archaic, was slow to disappear. The Mowbray lords were often resident in the Isle during the later twelfth and thirteenth centuries, and this factor operated against commutation. In 1298 substantial renders of malt were still being made at Haxey and Owston.[6]

The composition of the demesne labour force in Axholme in the twelfth century is not shown in the charters with any clarity. The reeve, William de Immingham, who held two bovates and a toft for a rent of 4s. and his service,[7] was in charge of the food-renders and rents paid by the villein tenants,[8] and presumably also supervised the performance of services. In 1298 the labour services in Axholme were much heavier than on any other of the Mowbray demesnes, and although there is no direct evidence, it is unlikely that the twelfth-century demesne was cultivated without a considerable villein labour force. But the presence in Axholme of quite a large number of *bordarii*, as well as *villani*, in 1086, and of some peasant tenants with holdings of less than one bovate in 1185,[9] suggests that paid labour may have played a part in demesne cultivation. In three charters where Roger de Mowbray grants away the services of Axholme men without reference to their tenements, we may well have landless estate labourers.[10]

In the Mowbray demesnes outside Axholme there must also have been some full-time labour. Only one *famulus* occurs, witnessing a charter of 1142 × 1154 relating to a North Riding demesne estate,[11] but perhaps the fourteen *prebendarii* mentioned in 1130 were in fact manorial *famuli*.[12] On the performance of labour services the documents shed little light.

---

[1] No. 15.   [2] No. 215.   [3] Nos. 215–17.   [4] Nos. 218–20.

[5] B.M., Cotton MS. Vesp. E xix (cartulary of Nostell) fo. 132r–v.

[6] At Haxey at Christmas the *bondi* rendered 3 quarters 1 bushel, and at Owston in August the *bondi* rendered 19 quarters. Also at Owston they rendered 5s. 6d. at Christmas 'pro quadam consuetudine que vocatur Yolbreweng'. Hens were rendered from Owston, Epworth, and Belton (*P.R.O.*, C. 133/94 (8) m. 7).

[7] Charter no. 369.   [8] Nos. 215–20, especially no. 219.

[9] *Records of Templars* pp. 111–12 (noted as charter no. 273), relating to Keadby and Althorpe.   [10] Charters nos. 221, 275, 339.

[11] No. 300.   [12] *P.R. 31 Hen. I* p. 137.

In Yorkshire the Templars' Inquest reveals some ploughing services and boon works at South Cave in 1185,[1] but charters deal with villein tenements,[2] and speak of *villani*[3] and *rustici*,[4] without mentioning services. We are told the names of villeins in Hovingham,[5] South Cave,[6] and Grewelthorpe,[7] and the sizes of their holdings, but not whether they owed labour dues. The inquisition of 1298 does not mention any labour services at Kirkby Malzeard: in this area in 1086 there had been some *bordarii* and in the twelfth century tenants occur with such small holdings that it is possible that they sold their labour in order to survive.[8] Tenants with minute tenements also appear in twelfth-century Thirsk,[9] where in 1298 only 100 sickle-works were owed on a demesne of over 300 acres. At South Cave we hear of *terre bubulcorum* in the 1170s.[10] In the Leicestershire and Warwickshire estates in 1086 there had been *servi* to work the demesne ploughs, as well as a number of *villani* and *bordarii*. There are few charters relating to these manors, but at Hampton in Arden we hear of 'omnes bovarii cum terris eorum'.[11]

Closely related to the demesne was the forest. The Mowbray lords claimed warren in the meres and vert of Axholme[12] and hunting rights in Farndale,[13] which passed by enfeoffment to Stuteville, and probably in Ingleborough, near Burton in Lonsdale.[14] But the area known in the thirteenth century as the 'chase of Nidderdale', attached to the manor of Kirkby Malzeard, was the chief forest of the honour, stretching from Masham to Dacre.[15] The administration was in the hands of foresters, whose first responsibility was the preservation of the game.[16] The economic resources of Nidderdale were granted away by Roger de Mowbray with a casual contempt—the abbeys of Byland and Fountains were given between them all Nidderdale, with pasture and mineral rights—but the hunting of 'stag and hind, roe-deer and wild boar and birds of prey' was jealously retained.[17] Consequently, while the Mowbray

[1] *Records of Templars* pp. 125–6.   [2] e.g. charters nos. 308–9, 311–12.
[3] At Wombleton, *E.Y.C.* ix no. 163 (cal. as charter no. 202).
[4] At Welburn, charter no. 242.   [5] No. 349.   [6] No. 343.
[7] Near Kirkby Malzeard, nos. 364–5.
[8] Nos. 66–7, 142, 147, 368; cf. in Langthorpe, *Records of Templars* p. 122.
[9] *Records of Templars* pp. 128–9.   [10] Charter no. 360.
[11] No. 333; cf. Long Lawford, *E.Y.C.* ix no. 62.
[12] See *Cal. Inq. P.M.* iii 357; and Stonehouse, *Axholme* pp. 62 ff. Cf. charter no. 1.
[13] *E.Y.C.* ix no. 114 (cal. as charter no. 238); cf. J. C. Holt, *The Northerners* (Oxford, 1961) p. 163 and n.
[14] Cf. T. D. Whitaker, *An History of Richmondshire* (1823) ii 354.
[15] *Cal. Inq. P.M.* iii 358; see also T. S. Gowland, 'The honour of Kirkby Malzeard and the chase of Nidderdale', *Y.A.J.* xxxiii (1938) 349–96.
[16] For their duties see, e.g., charters nos. 60, 120, 122. Names of foresters occur in nos. 97, 109, 112.
[17] Grants to Byland, see nos. 48–9, 52–4, 56–7, 60, 71; to Fountains, nos. 102–4, 107, 110–16, 119–27, 129, 131–2, 135; and to Temple, no. 272.

lords disported themselves in the chase, the monks of Byland and
Fountains developed sheep-farming and lead-mining in Nidderdale.[1]
In the rough and wooded areas on the fringes of Nidderdale, in
contrast to the protected area of the chase itself,[2] felling and assarting
had encouragement from the Mowbray lords. Timber rights in the
forests of Masham, Malzeard, and Brimham were granted to both
religious and lay beneficiaries—for charcoal for the Fountains forge at
Aldburgh,[3] for ordinary fuel and for making fences,[4] and for building
purposes.[5] On these eastern slopes of the Pennines we find both monastic
and lay tenants engaged in making assarts,[6] creating new settlements,
several of which appear for the first time in the Mowbray charters,[7] and
also extending the arable of older settlements, such as Kirkby Malzeard
(*mal assart*) itself.[8]

A similar pattern of colonization is discernible in Warwickshire,
where the Mowbray estates lay in the forested Arden region. For Hampton in Arden the documents are scanty, but they show clearly the steady
advance of piecemeal settlement, and before 1182 chapels had been
founded to serve the population in outlying clearings of this large parish.[9]
More information emerges concerning assarting in the vicinity of
Brinklow, itself a settlement which is first mentioned in 1130.[10] Here
the monks of Combe, who had themselves depopulated the Domesday

---

[1] See *A History of Nidderdale*, ed. B. Jennings (Huddersfield, 1967) pp. 23–85; and
A. Raistrick and B. Jennings, *A History of Lead Mining in the Pennines* (1965) pp. 31 ff.
[2] For regulations concerning cattle-folds, dogs etc., within the chase, see charters
nos. 49, 53, 56, 111, 114.   [3] Nos. 115, 135.
[4] No. 137.   [5] Nos. 272, 343, 364; cf. no. 174.
[6] For example at Brimham, see nos. 119–21, 396; at Aldburgh, no. 97; at Nutwith
and 'Flatwith', see charter of John de Wauton, *Fount. Cart.* i 20 (27); at Swetton,
charter no. 376 note; and generally no. 131.
[7] See generally *Domesday Geography of Northern England*, ed. H. C. Darby and I. S.
Maxwell (Cambridge, 1962) p. 98. Nutwith, charter no. 366 [*c.* 1170 × *c.* 1181] (*Place-
Names N.R. Yorks.* (English Place-Name Soc. v) p. 230 gives 1198 as first appearance);
Penhill, no. 272 [*c.* 1170 × 1184] (ibid. gives 1202); Galphay, no. 148 [1183 × 1186]
(*Place-Names W.R. Yorks.* v (English Place-Name Soc. xxxiv) p. 199 gives 12th
century); Littley, no. 101 [*c.* 1147 x 1155] (ibid. p. 200 gives *c.* 1180); Mickley, no. 345
[1175 × 1176] (ibid. gives *c.* 1180); Redley, no. 107 [*c.* 1147 × 1156] (ibid. p. 163 gives
1155–95).
[8] See charters nos. 67, 364; and for small holdings probably of assart origin see nos.
66–7 (cf. no. 147 for Laverton). Field-names suggesting assart are Naurethorp and
Tinchehoucroft (no. 364), Bywrtreflath (no. 66); also Flatscoh in Azerley (nos. 145,
343; *Place-Names W.R. Yorks.* v 202 gives 1481 as first appearance). On this topic see
T. A. M. Bishop, 'Assarting and the growth of the open fields', *Economic History Rev.*
vi (1935–6) 13–29.
[9] The chapels of Hampton are mentioned in charter no. (cf. no. 180 178 note). One
was Alspath (see *P.U.E.* iii no. 288). By 1221 Nuthurst and Baddesley Clinton had chapels
(B.M., Harley MS. 3650 (cartulary of Kenilworth) fo. 34*r*). Settlements at Chadwick
and Balsall first appear in charter no. 180. For Hampton in Arden and its area see also
nos. 330–8. For some comments on settlement in Arden, see B. K. Roberts, 'A study
of medieval colonization in the Forest of Arden', *Agricultural History Rev.* xvi (1968)
101–13.   [10] *P.R. 31 Hen. I* p. 138.

village of Smite,[1] made steady inroads into the woods, first grazing their animals and gathering dead wood, and then felling and assarting; meanwhile the men of Brinklow had made assarts up to the edge of what was later called 'Monks Riding'.[2] Another example from this area of the changes in village geography which occurred in the twelfth century is Withybrook, which first appears before 1182, apparently superseding in importance the Domesday settlement of Hopsford.[3]

The expansion of settlement at the expense of waste land is evident in every part of the Mowbray honour, and there are numerous references to assarts in the charters of lords and tenants.[4] A sign of this colonizing pressure is that in the vills near the royal forests of Knaresborough and Galtres in Yorkshire, many Mowbray tenants were amerced for forest offences in the 1160s and later.[5] In the neighbourhood of Coxwold, Kilburn, Yearsley, and Hovingham, there was much assarting, carried on by both monastic and lay enterprise, with new place-names appearing and old arable being extended.[6] Assarting could not continue indefinitely, and even in the woodlands of the honour which were not reserved for hunting, some trees and rough vegetation had to be retained for grazing and as a source of timber. Many charters speak of the common rights to the use of the woodland resources.[7] In thickly wooded areas, the problem of diminishing resources had not yet arisen, but by the 1170s assarting had to be limited near Kilburn and Yearsley to protect the common pastures.[8] At Hovingham Mowbray had a forester to protect the woodland.[9]

[1] See M. Beresford, 'The deserted villages of Warwicks.', *Trans. Birmingham Archaeol. Soc.* lxvi (1950) 95–6.

[2] See charters nos. 77–81, 84–8; cf. *Place-Names, Warwicks.* (English Place-Name Soc. xiii) p. 99.

[3] Charters nos. 82–3; cf. *Place-Names Warwicks.* pp. 121–2. But cf. also charter no. 13, where the chapel of Withybrook probably occurs before 1129.

[4] For some examples see nos. 15 (Axholme); nos. 168–9 (Eltisley, Cambs.); P.R.O., E. 326/849, and cf. charters nos. 192–3 (the Spinney, Melton Mowbray); no. 262 (Kirk Ella, E.R.); Bodl., MS. Dodsworth 120 B fo. 50v, and *P.R. 15 Hen. II* p. 39 (Beningbrough, N.R.); charter no. 181 (Micklethwaite, W.R.); no. 235 (Skiplam, N.R.); *E.Y.C.* ix no. 6 (Farndale, N.R.); charter no. 198 (? Thirsk, N.R.).

[5] Cf. above, p. xxix n. 10.

[6] For Kilburn, see Byland chron., *Mon. Ang.* v 351b–352a; charter no. 200; and charter of Robert de Daiville, B.M., Egerton MS. 2823 (cartulary of Byland) fo. 52v. New names appear: Stocking, Byland chron., *Mon. Ang.* v 353b (*Place-Names N.R. Yorks.* (English Place-Name Soc. v) p. 50 gives 1333 as first appearance); Airyholme (in Hovingham), nos. 34–5 [1140] (ibid. p. 49 gives 1138); Cam (in Kilburn), no. 40 [1142 × c. 1143] (ibid. p. 196 gives 1138); Oxendale (in Coxwold), no. 51 [1147 × 1164] (ibid. p. 197 gives c. 1300).

[7] Cf. the particularly interesting charters nos. 206 and 207 relating to Brandsby (N.R.).

[8] Charters of Robert de Daiville (Kilburn: B.M., Egerton MS. 2823 (cartulary of Byland) fo. 52v) and Thomas de Coleville (Yearsley: ibid. fo. 36v).

[9] See charter no. 186; cf. the forester's claim in 1298 (*Cal. Inq. P.M.* iii 492–3). Warren in Hovingham was granted in 1296, *C.Ch.R.* ii 465.

Reclamation of the waste also took place in the low-lying areas of the honour, in Yorkshire and Lincolnshire. In the fens along the Humber, south of Cave, land was taken in to form new meadows, and new place-names appear in the charters.[1] Similarly in the ill-drained western portion of the Vale of Pickering there seems to have been extension of meadow land in the twelfth century. This is suggested in charters relating to Hovingham,[2] and a case concerning Welburn (near Kirkby Moorside) illustrates how reclamation was achieved by digging drainage channels.[3] In the Isle of Axholme we hear of dykes, channels, and embankments.[4] But undrained marshland, like uncleared woodland, contained valuable resources.[5] Alan de Ryedale had to be restrained from digging up the common near Welburn, and from taking too much turf.[6] The Axholme charters speak of fisheries[7] and of turf,[8] and we can have small doubt that fowling and reeding were also carried on.[9] The winter flooding of the commons around the central isle in Axholme enriched the ground and made possible a flourishing pastoral economy.[10]

It is ironic that there should be so much evidence in the charters of the pressure to turn waste into arable, but so little word of how the arable was actually cultivated. The Axholme food-rents show that barley, wheat, and rye were grown, with barley perhaps the biggest crop.[11] Elsewhere the charters, when they do refer to crops, do so only in general terms—chiefly to *bladum*,[12] once to *seges*.[13] The number of mills grinding the grain certainly increased during the twelfth century, and yields from their rents probably rose considerably.[14]

[1] See generally *Domesday Geography of Northern England*, ed. H. C. Darby and I. S. Maxwell (Cambridge, 1962) pp. 175–6. New meadow in Cave, charters nos. 343, 360. New place-names as follows: Ousefleet, no. 318 [1142 × c. 1154] (cf. *E.Y.C.* i nos. 470, 487; *Place-Names W.R. Yorks.* ii (English Place-Name Soc. xxxi) p. 7); Broomfleet, no. 324 [1154 × 1157] (*Place-Names E.R. Yorks.* (English Place-Name Soc. xiv) pp. 222–3); probably Weedley, no. 273 [before 1185] (ibid. p. 223).
[2] In 1086 there were 32 acres of meadow in Hovingham, but more seems to be mentioned in charters nos. 47, 61, 349.
[3] *E.Y.C.* ix no. 157 (cal. as charter no. 247) of [1160 × 1169]; cf. ibid. no. 159, of 1175. Cf. also the Byland chron.'s account of drainage near Coxwold (*Mon. Ang.* v 353b).
[4] Charter no. 276; also nos. 218, 224, 264, and *P.R. 26 Hen. II* p. 52.
[5] Cf. no. 317, which refers to 'quicquid poterit lucrari de communi palude'.
[6] See above, n. 3.
[7] Nos. 2, 3, 257, 273, 276, 281, 317, 324, 373; cf., for eels, nos. 15, 215–20.
[8] No. 223; cf. also no. 148 for turbary near Kirkby Malzeard.
[9] See Stonehouse, *Axholme* pp. 63 ff.
[10] Cf. J. Thirsk, 'The Isle of Axholme before Vermuyden', *Agricultural History Rev.* i (1953) 16–28.
[11] Charters nos. 15, 215–20, 317; cf. J. Thirsk, art. cit.
[12] Charters nos. 13, 102–3, 115, 129, 135, 306.
[13] *Danelaw Charters* no. 395 (cal. as charter no. 285).
[14] For references in the charters to new mills, see nos. 2, 23, 95, 396. Rents from mills, all of them quite high, are mentioned in nos. 24, 27–8, 39, 194, 198, 273.

In three tenants' charters there are clear references to the operation
of two-field systems—in Marton (Cleveland, N.R.),[1] Hovingham,
(N.R.),[2] and Withybrook (Warwicks.);[3] there is some indication that
there were two fields also in Aldfield[4] and Kirkby Malzeard (W.R.).[5]
But references to fields, *campi*, are few and far between,[6] and several
of the arable holdings that are the subject of the gifts and exchanges
recorded in the charters lay in single blocks and were not divided between fields. Some of these were small parcels in a particular field.[7]
Others consisted of quite large compact holdings, like the *culturae* of the
demesne, as in Thorpe Arnold, next to Melton Mowbray (a *cultura* of
32 acres),[8] in Welburn (N.R.),[9] and possibly in Kirkby Malzeard.[10]
There were some compact holdings in the hands of tenants—as William
de Martona's two bovates in Kelfield (Axholme)[11] and William son of
Ucce's 18 acres in Bagby (N.R.).[12] Extension of the arable by assarts
complicated the arrangements of fields and cultures. Some holdings had
attached to them small tenements of newly asserted land,[13] and in the
area of Kirkby Malzeard and Masham a certain amount of reclamation
was undertaken by individual rather than communal enterprise.[14]

Where there was arable land there had also to be pasture. Indeed, the
larger the area under the plough, the more common pasture was needed
for the plough-oxen. There was, however, much variation from area to
area and from village to village in the balance between arable and stock,
according to the amount and quality of the pasture and meadow. The
cattle-farms which appear in the charters are found in the type of
country favoured by contemporary agricultural practice, chiefly upland
or forest.[15] It is possible that the concentration of cattle in Nidderdale,[16]

[1] *E.Y.C.* iii no. 1853.
[2] B.M., Cotton MS. Claud. D xi (cartulary of Malton) fo. 99r.
[3] B.M., Cotton MS. Vit. D xviii (cartulary of Combe) fo. 34v.
[4] *Fount. Cart.* ii 850 (3) and (4).   [5] Charter no. 67.
[6] *Campi* of Kilburn (N.R.), no. 36; of Owston (Lincs.), no. 285. *Campus* in Malzeard
(W.R.), no. 66; Laverton (W.R.), no. 147; Eltisley (Cambs.), no. 168 (but cf. no. 169).
[7] Malzeard (W.R.), 3 acres, no. 66; Bagby (N.R.), 5 acres, no. 208; Laverton (W.R.),
4 acres, no. 147; Owston (Lincs.), 4 acres, no. 282.
[8] Nos. 160–1; cf. no. 31.
[9] No. 237; cf. nos. 232, 235; *E.Y.C.* ix no. 145.   [10] Charter no. 364.
[11] Nos. 284, 373; cf. F. M. Stenton's comment, *Danelaw Charters* p. xxxiii.
[12] Charter no. 59; cf. holdings near Malzeard of 48 acres (nos. 137, 139), 35 acres
(*Fount. Cart.* i 215 (33)), and 24 acres (no. 141).
[13] Eltisley (Cambs.) nos. 168–9; North Cave (E.R.) no. 41; ? Hovingham (N.R.) no.
74; Malzeard (W.R.) no. 364; ? Axholme (Lincs.) no. 258.
[14] Cf. the pattern of ownership in Nutwith in nos. 137, 139, 141; individual assarting
at Brimham, no. 396, and at Malzeard, no. 67.
[15] See R. Trow-Smith, *A History of British Livestock Husbandry to 1700* (1957)
pp. 93–4.
[16] Cattle belonging to Fountains, at Sutton Grange, see charters nos. 115, 129, 135,
and at Birstwith, no. 114.

on the Hambleton[1] and Howardian Hills,[2] in the wooded parts of Ax-holme,[3] and perhaps in Arden[4] had its origin in the need for animals in the work of felling and carting timber. In this connection the quite large number of horses in Nidderdale may also have some relevance.[5] But the characteristic livestock of the woodlands was the pig, and although it is impossible to form any idea of the numbers of herds, references to pannage abound in charters from every part of the honour.[6] Sheep are much less frequently mentioned, but there can be small doubt that everywhere their numbers exceeded those of other stock. This was true not only in the obviously pastoral areas—the uplands of Nidderdale and the North Yorkshire Moors, where the flocks of Fountains, Byland, and Rievaulx increased and multiplied, and the marshland and meadow areas of the western Vale of Pickering, the Humber estuary, Axholme, and Leicestershire. It was also true in villages on the edge of dense wood-land. At Withybrook in Warwickshire two virgates of arable carried with them common pasture for 400 sheep;[7] at Brandsby in the North Riding two bovates of arable are connected with pasture for 200 sheep, 40 cows, and 10 sows and their litters.[8]

The charters tell us little of the commercial arrangements of the honour. It is clear, however, that the demesne manors, being the pre-dominant settlements in each area of lordship, were natural centres for exchange. There was a market at Melton Mowbray by 1077,[9] at Thirsk probably before 1130,[10] and at South Cave before 1157.[11] Evidence for markets at other demesne manors does not come until later—Brinklow by 1218,[12] Hovingham in 1252,[13] Kinnard by 1298,[14] Kirkby Malzeard and Burton in Lonsdale in 1307[15]—but there is no reason to suppose that

[1] Grant to Byland of *vaccaria* of Cam, no. 37.
[2] Newburgh had 40 cows at Brandsby, nos. 206–7.
[3] Grant to Templars of *vaccaria* of Belwood, no. 276; cf. no. 369. St. Mary's, York, was granted pasture for 10 cows in the wood of Ross, no. 317.
[4] Reference to 'Calfremedew' in no. 180; place-name of Chadwick, no. 180 etc. (see *Place-Names of Warwicks.* (English Place-Name Soc. xiii) p. 54).
[5] Pasture for 80 mares and foals, Byland, charter no. 52; cf. *Fount. Cart.* i 215 (33); *sumagii* in charter no. 56. 'Horse-croft' occurs in Axholme, no. 218, and 'Stodfald' near Muscoates (N.R.), no. 236.
[6] The largest numbers relate to herds belonging to Byland—40 near Hovingham (H.M.C., *Various Collections* ii (1903) 4) and 30 sows and 5 boars in Nidderdale (charter no. 53).
[7] Charter of Richard de Moreville, B.M., Cotton MS. Vit. D xviii (cartulary of Combe) fo. 34v; cf. ibid. fo. 33v for one virgate carrying pasture for 100 sheep in Withybrook.
[8] Charters nos. 206–7; cf. at Bagby, no. 274.
[9] *Mon. Ang.* vi (2) 996; cf. *Domesday Book* i fo. 235b.
[10] See above, p. xxiv n. 3.   [11] Charter no. 324, cf. no. 360.
[12] *Rotuli Litterarum Clausarum* (Record Comm. 1833–44) i 366b.
[13] *C.Ch.R.* i 379.   [14] *Cal. Inq. P.M.* iii 358.
[15] *C.Ch.R.* iii 78, 84.

they were not trading centres in the twelfth century. Indeed, trade was doubtless encouraged in these manors, as by levying tolls the Mowbray lords were able to share in the prosperity of neighbours and tenants. At Thirsk, where the market met in the shade of the castle, there is every sign that trade flourished under seignorial patronage. Recorded as largely waste in 1086, the town had recovered and expanded by the middle of the twelfth century, so that there was a settlement and a church on each side of Cod Beck,[1] and the arable fields stretched as far as the parish boundary towards Bagby.[2] Both lay and ecclesiastical tenants in the surrounding district were eager to have houses in this centre.[3] Doubtless the most important commodity in Thirsk's trade was wool, and by 1163, when Henry II issued his charter to the weavers of York, Thirsk was one of the Yorkshire boroughs privileged to make dyed and rayed cloth.[4]

Despite the signs of an expanding economy in the Mowbray honour in the twelfth century, it does not seem that seignorial income increased fast enough to meet the demands made on it. Certainly the yields rose from individual manors, as profits went up from direct cultivation and from rents, mills, tolls, and so on. Substantial increases on Domesday valuations are shown in the Pipe Roll accounts for the confiscated estates of Melton Mowbray and Brinklow in 1174 and Masham in 1175.[5] But the effect of these increases in yields must have been largely offset by the subinfeudation of six important demesne manors in the middle years of the twelfth century, for the income from knights' fees could never be sufficient to make up for the loss of demesne. In particular the alienation of Kirkby Moorside and its dependencies in the settlement with Robert de Stuteville may well have tipped the financial balance against Roger de Mowbray.

Certainly the evidence of some charters suggests that Mowbray's normal income was insufficient to meet the demands of an emergency: in order to raise extra cash, he accepted gifts and loans from at least three Cistercian houses. The earliest charter which refers to this use of patronage dates from the end of Stephen's reign, and suggests that force may have played a part in persuading the monks of Fountains to yield up 83 marks 'in mea magna necessitate'; shortly afterwards the abbey was compensated with mineral rights in Nidderdale.[6] Later charters illustrate refinements of this expedient. In 1172, not long before the

---

[1] See *V.C.H. Yorks. N.R.* ii 59; cf. charters nos. 203, 214.   [2] No. 208.
[3] Nos. 92, 140, 208, 273, 296 note, 348, 353, 391.
[4] See H. Heaton, *Yorks. Woollen and Worsted Industries* (Oxford, 1920) p. 28.
[5] *P.R. 20 Hen. II* p. 143; *21 Hen. II* p. 6.   [6] Charters nos. 102–3.

young king's rebellion, Roger and his sons mortgaged part of Nidderdale
to the abbey of Byland in return for 300 marks.[1] It may have been at
this time, or perhaps a little later, that Mowbray gave part of Brinklow
wood to the monks of Combe in return for their settling his debt of 80
marks to the Jews.[2] The rebellion of 1174 must have strained Mowbray's
resources to the limit, and his project to go on the crusade of 1177
necessitated the raising of further sums. Between 1174 and 1176 he
gained from the abbey of Fountains £100 and 480 marks for charters
relating to Nidderdale, and his son Nigel gained 65 marks.[3]

[1] No. 54.   [2] Nos. 84–5; cf. also no. 87.
[3] Nos. 111–13, 120–2, 124, 126; cf. a memorandum in B.M., Add. MS. 18276
(cartulary of Fountains) fo. 112r. See also no. 145 for the payment of another 30 marks.

IV. ADMINISTRATION

THE machinery evolved for making seignorial authority effective over a great estate and its tenants consisted basically in the twin institutions of the honorial court and the lord's household. Court and household had a common origin in the meetings of the lord, his family, and his followers. The Mowbray charters show that the officials of the household formed the nucleus of the court, and the intimate connection between court and household is attested by a phrase in the Byland chronicle, in which certain knights are said to be 'de curia et familia' of Roger de Mowbray.[1] Another smaller group within the same company of family, officials, and friends comes to light in the Byland chronicle and not elsewhere: this is the lord's secret council, in which the steward played an important part, as he did also in both court and household.[2]

The starting-point of a study of the honorial court must be the statement in the *Leges Henrici Primi*, that every lord may summon his man to stand to right in his court and may compel him to come, even from the remotest manor of the honour.[3] The evidence of the Mowbray charters suggests that the term 'honour' was used to apply to an area less than the entire Mowbray fief. 'Honor de Molbraio' occurs only once in the collection, and on this occasion clearly refers to the Norman honour of Montbray.[4] We hear of the 'honor de Masham'[5] and the 'honor de Malessart',[6] and perhaps also of the 'honor' of Crowle.[7] There are specific references to the lord's court meeting at Malzeard[8] and at Thirsk,[9] on both occasions dealing with local cases, and the composition of the witness-clauses of other charters suggests that Warwickshire business was transacted locally, perhaps at Brinklow.[10] Thirteenth-century evidence reveals courts also in Axholme, at Hovingham[11] and at Burton in Lonsdale.[12] It seems that the Mowbray estates were conceived as a series of honours, each with its own court, held at the appropriate demesne centre.[13]

---

[1] *Mon. Ang.* v 350b.   [2] Ibid. p. 350a; cf. Stenton, *Feudalism* pp. 74–5.
[3] 'Leges Henrici' § 55, in *Die Gesetze der Angelsachsen*, ed. F. Liebermann (Halle, 1903–16) i 575. See also the discussion in Stenton, *Feudalism* pp. 42 ff.
[4] Charter no. 165.   [5] No. 129.   [6] Nos. 131, 135.   [7] No. 1.
[8] Charter of Richard de Hedona, Vyner deeds deposited at Leeds Archives, V.R. 26.
[9] *E.Y.C.* ix nos. 166, 167.   [10] Charters nos. 332–3.
[11] See below, p. lix n. 4.
[12] In 1246, see *Yorks. Fines 1232–46*, ed. J. Parker (Y.R.S. lxvii) p. 162.
[13] Cf. F. W. Maitland, *Select Pleas in Manorial and other Seignorial Courts* (Selden Soc. ii) p. xlvii.

The address-clauses of charters—to 'all my men and friends'—reveal the general nature of the company present at the sessions of the honour court. The witness-clauses give a more precise picture. The lord's family and the members of his household were joined by a heterogeneous group of men who came from the middle and lower ranks of the free tenantry. This group included knights holding as many as five fees, as well as lesser tenants holding fractions of fees, sub-tenures or estates in socage.[1] Notably absent from the witness-clauses are tenants in the largest fees and those who had extensive interests outside the Mowbray honour. Missing too are several lesser tenants, some holding single fees and others portions of fees, chiefly in Lincolnshire and Leicestershire.

Primarily the court was a gathering called to bear witness to the actual ceremony of homage and investiture which took place at the enfeoffment of a tenant. In the later twelfth century the grant of a charter of enfeoffment became usual,[2] but in the early period, when the handing over of rod and staff was a more important part of the ceremony, the memory of the witnesses must often have been the sole record of the transaction.[3] In this connection it may be significant that the *carta* of 1166 was returned by the 'homines Rogeri de Moubrai', probably calling on their memory of enfeoffments.[4] When rearrangements of tenures were made —such as exchanges[5] or sales[6]—the court was the obvious forum. Similarly, disputes between tenants were naturally brought to the lord's court for settlement, the suitors standing as counsellors and witnesses.[7] Perambulations of boundaries were made and recognized,[8] and oaths, *affidationes*, and quitclaims were made,[9] the lord and his court attesting the resulting documents.[10] If necessary, the lord issued a mandate for reseisin.[11]

Clearly property transactions and disputes concerning mesne tenants of the honour provided most of the business of the court. A somewhat wider competence is suggested by a clause in a charter dating from the middle of the twelfth century: Roger de Mowbray orders that a sub-tenant 'pro nullo calumpniatore in placito ponatur nisi in presencia mea'.[12] This was an area where feudal jurisdiction became increasingly

[1] See, e.g., charter no. 109.
[2] Cf. the references to the return of a charter when land was restored, *E.Y.C.* ix no. 126 (cal. as charter no. 249), charter no. 116 (cf. no. 375).
[3] Cf. charters nos. 149 and 290.
[4] Charter no. 401.   [5] No. 245.   [6] Nos. 249, 333.   [7] Nos. 109, 248.
[8] Nos. 133, 236, 243.   [9] Nos. 245, 249; *E.Y.C.* ix nos. 161, 166, 167.
[10] On almost every occasion when Roger de Mowbray attests a tenant's charter this seems to have concluded a settlement; see, e.g., *E.Y.C.* i no. 238, iii no. 1836; *Fount. Cart.* i 307–8, ii 705 (6); *Yorks. Deeds* ii no. 30; B.M., Egerton MS. 2823 (cartulary of Byland) fo. 52*v*.
[11] e.g. charters nos. 90, 315, and cf. no. 254.   [12] No. 392.

vulnerable as the century proceeded.¹ In the 1160s 'ministers of the king
sent by the sheriff' were present at the settlement of a case in Mowbray's
court between a sub-tenant, Alan de Ryedale, and the convent of
Rievaulx.² The sheriff himself received the *affidatio* of Samson of
Cornwall, a Mowbray sub-tenant, concerning a quitclaim to Rievaulx,
after *affidatio* had already been made in the feudal court in the hand of
Mowbray's steward.³ Where ecclesiastics were involved, however, not
even the sheriff's court could always satisfy: Samson of Cornwall later
acknowledged his *affidatio* in the chapter of York Minster,⁴ and Rievaulx brought a counter-claim against Alan de Ryedale before papal
judges.⁵ Several Mowbray charters for the Cistercians of Fountains and
Rievaulx have clauses providing for arbitration by the chapter of York
in the event of dispute over property.⁶ This machinery was put into
operation on at least one occasion, when Fountains lost some estates
given by Mowbray and had to be given an exchange.⁷ Lay tenants who
had claims against Mowbray also tended to take their suits elsewhere:
from 1169 onwards the Pipe Rolls reveal an increasing number of land
suits against Mowbray.⁸

Beyond certain proprietary actions the jurisdiction of the Mowbray
lords did not extend very far. From the Quo Warranto proceedings of the
next century it seems that the lords were nowhere quit of suits to the
shire court. Of the rights of sake and soke, toll and team, and infangenetheof, which were enjoyed in all the Mowbray estates, only the last
involved a capital offence, and even this did not represent a high franchise. Indeed, enfeoffments very often included concessions of all these
rights, even to quite humble tenants.⁹ There is no evidence for the exercise of higher jurisdiction in the twelfth century, although the Isle of
Axholme may have formed a small franchise. Nigel d'Aubigny held the
entire 'wapentake' of Axholme in demesne, and this 'wapentake', which
did not survive as a separate unit, is mentioned also in a charter of Roger

¹ See N. D. Hurnard, 'Magna Carta, Clause 34', in *Studies in Medieval History
presented to F. M. Powicke* (Oxford, 1948) pp. 160–3.
² Charters nos. 247–8.   ³ No. 249.   ⁴ Ibid.
⁵ *E.Y.C.* ix no. 159.
⁶ Fountains: charters nos. 111–13; cf. *Fount. Cart.* i 205 (7), 208 (13), 208 (15).
Rievaulx: *E.Y.C.* ix nos. 125 (cal. as charter no. 243), 151 (cal. as charter no. 236); cf.
ibid. nos. 127–31, 153.   ⁷ Charter no. 127; cf. *Fount. Cart.* i 206 (10b).
⁸ *P.R. 15 Hen. II* p. 36; *22 Hen. II* p. 5; *23 Hen. II* p. 78; *25 Hen. II* p. 21 (cf. charter
no. 364); *26 Hen. II* p. 74 (cf. no. 372); *2 Ric. I* p. 43; *7 Ric. I* p. 91. Cf. the account
of the Stuteville claim against Mowbray 'in curia Regis', in Byland chron., *Mon Ang.*
v 352a.
⁹ The smallest estate to carry these rights was one carucate granted to Noel (charter
no. 377); cf. Stenton, *Feudalism* pp. 104–6. A place-name near Malzeard—Galphay
(W.R.)—had its origin in 'gallows enclosure' (*Place-Names W.R. Yorks.* v (English
Place-Name Soc. xxxiv) p. 199).

de Mowbray.[1] In 1327 it was stated that in Axholme from the Conquest the lords had enjoyed the right of utfangenetheof as well as infangenetheof, wreck, waif, and the assize of bread and ale.[2] In the borough of Thirsk, too, utfangenetheof was held in 1327, as well as the other rights and also hue and cry and blodewite.[3] The courts of Axholme and Thirsk were more profitable in 1298 than any of the other courts in the Mowbray lands.[4]

The routine administration was carried out by officials of the four departments of the household—those of the constable, the steward, the chaplain, and the chamberlain. Illumination of their identity and work comes only in patches, in the address- and witness-clauses of charters and other stray references, and in the narrative of the foundation of Byland abbey, written in 1197. All four chief officers are found by the 1140s, and although only the chaplain and chamberlain can be shown to occur in Nigel d'Aubigny's household, it is unlikely that his honour can have been administered without a constable and a steward. The constable habitually has precedence in the Mowbray charters over the steward, a situation paralleled in the households of the earls of Chester and of the kings of Scotland before 1162,[5] although unusual in Yorkshire, where on the honours of Richmond, Holderness, and Pontefract the steward was the main officer.[6] The only hereditary office in the Mowbray household was the chamberlainship, which unlike its equivalent at Richmond was an obscure post of low social status.[7] Presumably appointments to the other main offices were made by the personal choice of the lord. During the second half of the twelfth century the number of household officials increased, particularly in the departments of the steward and the chaplain, and there seems to have been considerable sophistication of administrative techniques.

The military organization of the Mowbray honour must have involved the constable in a variety of work of which there is scarcely a trace in the surviving documents. He was both a military commander in the field

---

[1] *Lincs. Domesday and Lindsey Survey*, ed. C. W. Foster and T. Longley (L.R.S. xix) p. 243; charter no. 369 below.

[2] *Cal. Inq. P.M.* vii 52.   [3] Ibid.

[4] Each worth 40s., while the Hallemote of Hovingham was worth 6s. 8d., and the court of Malzeard 26s. 8d. (P.R.O., C. 133/84 (8)).

[5] For Chester see *Chart. of St. Werburgh Chester*, ed. J. Tait (Chetham Soc., N.S. lxxix) pp. xlvi–vii; cf. G. Barraclough, 'Some charters of the earl of Chester', in *A Medieval Miscellany for D. M. Stenton*, ed. P. M. Barnes and C. F. Slade (P.R.S., N.S. xxxvi) p. 28. For Scotland see *Regesta Regum Scottorum* i, ed. G. W. S. Barrow (Edinburgh, 1960) pp. 31–3, 34–5.

[6] For Richmond see *E.Y.C.* iv 101–7. For Holderness see ibid. vii 292. For Pontefract see Wightman, *Lacy Family* pp. 103–5.

[7] See below, p. lxv.

and a security officer within the household, and thus was responsible for
the services of all the honorial troops, whether enfeoffed, hired, or
retained in the household. The unique feature of the constable's activities was that they often involved the lord himself: on the battlefield, as
at Northallerton in 1138 and Lincoln in 1141, and in the rebellion of
1174, Roger de Mowbray led his own forces; and in 1174 the castle of
Axholme was defended by Roger's second son, Robert.[1] The constable
was therefore drawn into a close relationship with the lord. Robert de
Daiville, who was probably constable from c. 1154 to c. 1186, and held
five knights' fees in 1166, was a constant companion, appearing as first
lay witness in no fewer than fifty charters.[2]

The castles and the services associated with them form an important
part of the constable's responsibilities. He was concerned with enfeoffments and even with the movement of villeins, for they might be required to perform castle-works.[3] The Pipe Roll of 1130 reveals something
of the manning arrangements of the castles at that time. At Burton in
Lonsdale there was a hired garrison, consisting of a knight, paid 8d. a
day, and ten sergeants, a porter, and a watchman, each paid ½d. a day.
At each of the other three castles—Kirkby Malzeard, Thirsk, and Brinklow—there was a permanent paid staff of only two—a porter and a
watchman, who each received ½d. a day.[4] These porters and watchmen
were presumably supplemented by enfeoffed tenants, although it is
difficult to believe that either of the two local constables whose names
are known can have taken command of knights, for both were of a lower
social grade. Peter of Thirsk, constable of Thirsk in the 1140s, was a
sub-tenant of Malebisse, and was not in the first rank of the honorial
baronage.[5] The constable of Axholme, Ralph de Bellun, held small
tenements probably in socage, and was also of relatively low social
status. He appears as *consistor* of Axholme, in a context which suggests
that the local constable was involved in the receipt of rents and renders,
which like scutages were doubtless paid at the castle.[6]

In time of war, a fully garrisoned castle made heavy demands on the

---

[1] *Gesta Hen. II* i 68.

[2] His only positive appearance, as 'constabularius de Insula' is in charter no. 221,
of 1138 × 1174. He heads the laymen of Mowbray's *curia* in no. 247, and leads the
witnesses in the greater number of the charters he attests.

[3] Cf. nos. 221, 242.

[4] *P.R. 31 Hen. I* pp. 137–8; and see J. O. Prestwich, 'Anglo-Norman feudalism and
the problem of continuity', *Past and Present* xxvi (1963) 46.

[5] He occurs as constable in charter no. 94; cf. nos. 20, 240.

[6] No. 219. *Consistor* is a term found on the Gant honour, whence through the
marriage of Alice de Gant to Roger de Mowbray, it may have passed into the Mowbray
administration. It seems to be synonymous with *constabularius*, see *E.Y.C.* ii nos.
1208, 1223; cf. ibid. no. 1135; and *Mon. Ang.* i 630 (IV), v 287 (IX).

resources of the neighbourhood. During the troubles towards the end
of Stephen's reign, Roger de Mowbray's men, probably from Kirkby
Malzeard, stole grain belonging to the abbey of Fountains at Ripon, and
the monks were forced to give Roger 83 marks 'in his necessity'.[1] At
about the same time, his *castrenses*—whether from Malzeard or from
Thirsk is not clear—exacted castle-works and protection money (*ten-sarie*)—from tenants of St. Mary's, York, at Myton on Swale.[2] In 1174
the *castrenses* of Axholme caused much devastation in the Lincoln
countryside, before they were taken by surprise and forced to surrender
because they had insufficient food. The castle was destroyed: 'deleta
penitus praedorum spelunca', says Giraldus.[3] When Kirkby Malzeard
was taken shortly afterwards, thirty knights and sixty archers were captured.[4] It is clear that in order to garrison these two castles and also the
castle of Thirsk, and to take a force with him to Scotland, Roger de
Mowbray must have used mercenaries, in addition to those few of his
military tenants who joined the rebellion.[5] The expense of paying and
providing for these forces was a heavy drain on Mowbray's finances.

Finally the constable had charge of the household troop. A well-
known passage in the Byland chronicle tells of three knights, 'veterani
et emeriti milites de curia et de familia domini Rogeri', who became
conversi at Byland in 1142.[6] The presence within the household of two
of these (but not the third) is verified by the witness-clauses of the
charters of the 1140s.[7] Some household companions, who were probably
household knights, were enfeoffed by Roger de Mowbray in the middle
years of the century, and some as late as the 1170s.[8] There are also some
men who occur with such frequency in the witness-lists that it seems
likely that they were resident in the household, but although most of
them had small tenements they were never given knights' fees.[9] It may
be that these men, under the constable's leadership, formed a mobile
troop of knights and sergeants who acted as the lord's bodyguard and

[1] Charters nos. 102–3.   [2] No. 318.
[3] *Giraldi Cambrensis Opera Omnia*, ed. J. S. Brewer (R.S. xxi) iv 364.
[4] Ibid. p. 366.
[5] Tenants certainly involved in the rebellion were: Roger de Arden, Hugh Malebisse, and Richard de Moreville (*P.R. 20 Hen. II* p. 143).
[6] *Mon. Ang.* v 350b, discussed by Stenton, *Feudalism* pp. 140–1.
[7] Henry de Wasprey occurs in charter no. 230, and probably came from Guêprei,
near the Mowbray lands in the Houlme area (*Ang.-Norm. Families* p. 112). Landric de
Ages occurs in charters nos. 38, 156, 177, 374, and ?403. Henry Bugge does not occur.
[8] Walter Buher (cf. no. 174); Hamo Beler (no. 341); Thomas de Coleville (no. 356);
Walter of Carlton (no. 352); Oliver de Buscy (cf. no. 401); Warin son of Simon (no.
398). Those in the 1170s were Nicholas de Bellun (no. 343), Peter of Billinghay (no.
349), Roger de Daiville (no. 360).
[9] Robert de Beauchamp, Ralph and Robert Beler, Ralph and Robert de Belvoir,
Robert and John de Crevequer, and Philip de Montpincon.

could be used for any special military task. They were probably also concerned with the hunt, which in the absence of a marshal in the Mowbray household, is likely to have come under the constable. The name of one huntsman, Alan *venator*, has survived, and it is possible that he is the same man as Alan the archer, *sagittarius*.[1] A number of grooms, falconers, and berners must also have been retained in the household, probably in the constable's charge.

Although precedence in the Mowbray household was given to the constable, the greater part of the day-to-day administrative work fell to the steward and his subordinates. The steward had great influence, as is seen from the Byland chronicle's account of the leading part he played in the secret council and of how he initially invited the monks into the Mowbray household.[2] In his office the central and the local met, for the steward's responsibility included both the domestic arrangements of the household and the administration of the demesne. It is perhaps natural that there should be more information on the names and duties of the men in the steward's department than in any other department of the Mowbray household.

The stewardship was not hereditary, as it was under the English and Scottish kings and on some twelfth-century honours, and therefore did not carry a steward's fee. This allowed the lord to appoint whomsoever he chose, and it is noticeable that there were important social differences between the four men who were stewards of Roger de Mowbray.[3] Hugh Malebisse, who appears as *dapifer* from c. 1147 to c. 1154, held one fee of the old enfeoffment in the North Riding of Yorkshire.[4] But William de Wyville, *dapifer* from c. 1154 to c. 1157, was a man of far greater property, holding five old fees of Mowbray in Northamptonshire and in the North and East Ridings, as well as half-fees of Warter and Foliot. He was the founder of the Premonstratensian house of Welford (Northants.).[5] The two *dapiferi* of the later part of Roger de Mowbray's life were of lesser social status and were closer in type to the career administrators of thirteenth-century baronial households. Ralph de Belvoir had only small rented estates in Yorkshire until he gained a half-fee in marriage with a daughter of William Tison. Roger de Cundy had a half-fee of Mowbray in scattered tenements in Leicestershire, Lincolnshire, and the West Riding of Yorkshire. As Ralph de Belvoir occurs as

---

[1] Charters nos. 97, 106.

[2] *Mon. Ang.* v 350a, discussed by Stenton, *Feudalism* pp. 73–5.

[3] For another possible Mowbray *dapifer*, see note to charter no. 403, and for two *dapiferi* who occur in spurious charters, see notes to nos. 37, 203.

[4] As *dapifer* he occurs in Byland chron., *Mon. Ang.* v 351b, and nos. 49–50, 290.

[5] As *dapifer* in no. 237; cf. no. 323. For Welford see H. M. Colvin, *White Canons in England* (Oxford, 1951) pp. 77–81; and charters nos. 281–6.

dapifer before 1169, in 1175–6, and after 1182,[1] it is clear that he either had two periods of office, or shared the steward's duties with Roger de Cundy, who is called *dapifer* in 1174 or 1175.[2] If there was a subdivision within the steward's office, the line of demarcation was not between the household and the estates, as became usual in the next century, nor was it geographical, for as we shall see both Ralph de Belvoir and Roger de Cundy performed duties in connection with the administration of the Yorkshire estates.

The steward's duties began with the provisioning of the household, as it journeyed from manor to manor. The Byland chronicle's picture of a peripatetic household, in some measure supplied directly from the demesne, is confirmed by the evidence of food-rents in Axholme and by the place-dates of some charters.[3] Providing food for the regular household and guests was a matter of some complexity, and the steward delegated part of the organization to an assistant who is called by the Byland writer the *provisor hospicii*.[4] The official meant by this phrase may be the *dispensator*,[5] although it is not until more than thirty years after the events of the chronicle that there is charter evidence for a *dispensator* in the Mowbray household, one Arnald, who attests six charters between *c.* 1170 and 1186 and each time occupies a humble position in the list of witnesses.[6] At table the lord had his butler: four butlers appear by name among the witnesses to charters—Richard,[7] Geoffrey,[8] Herbert,[9] and William.[10] Other household officials appear. An usher, Asketil *hostiarius*, occurs six times between *c.* 1142 and *c.* 1155,[11] but there is no sign of a successor in this post. We have the names of eight cooks[12] and two bakers.[13] Some entertainers come to notice—a minstrel,[14]

---

[1] Nos. 249, 315, 347; also no. 339.   [2] Nos. 110–11; also nos. 314 and 381.
[3] Above, p. xliv.   [4] Byland chron., *Mon. Ang.* v 350*a*.
[5] Ailred of Rievaulx, formerly *dispensator* of the king of Scotland, asked in a prayer to be made 'a faithful dispenser, a discreet distributor, a prudent provider' (see *Life of Ailred of Rievaulx by Walter Daniel*, ed. F. M. Powicke (1950) p. xli; cf. *Regesta Regum Scottorum* i, ed. G. W. S. Barrow (Edinburgh, 1960) pp. 32–3).
[6] Cf. the comparatively late appearance of a *dispensator* in the Chester household, *Chart. of St. Werburgh Chester*, ed. J. Tait (Chetham Soc., N.S. lxxix) p. xlvii. For Arnald see charters nos. 81, 84–5, 160, 276, 315. Baldwin *le despenser* occurs in no. 389, 1175 × 1179.
[7] No. 195.   [8] Nos. 332, 356.   [9] No. 322; he had land in York, no. 380.
[10] Nos. 147, 223, 366, 388.
[11] Nos. 40, 99, 238, 297, 304; cf. no. 38; he had land in York, *E.Y.C.* i no. 185.
[12] Serlo, charter no. 95, and for his land, no. 46. Roger, nos. 282, 332, 353–4, 373. Geoffrey, nos. 86, 277. Brisebarre, nos. 208, 275. Ralph Brisebarre, no. 81. Maurice, nos. 275, 284. Herbert, no. 388. William, no. 60.
[13] Richard, no. 235. Hugh, nos. 208, 290; in *E.Y.C.* iii no. 1572 he is called 'pistor Rogeri de Molbrai'.
[14] Bartholomew *gigator*, charter no. 202; for his land see no. 200 and *E.Y.C.* ix no. 166.

a fiddler,[1] a singer, and a *jongleur*.[2] There were doubtless also many other domestic servants.

The provisioning of the household was closely connected with the management of the demesne lands: the steward's responsibility for the one led naturally to his oversight of the other. In 1142 or 1143 the steward was directly involved in demesne management in Coxwold, where Roger de Mowbray granted to the monks of Byland 'materiem ad domos suas faciendas per providenciam dapiferi mei'.[3] It is just possible that in the early twelfth century there were local stewards administering portions of the Mowbray demesne, as there were later on the honour of Warenne,[4] and that the 'Goisbertus dapifer Rogeri de Molbrai' who appears in Warwickshire in 1130 was a local steward.[5] By the middle of the century, however, it is clear that the steward was not concerned with the details of estate organization, but supervised the work of the local officials, the reeves. This over-all supervision is seen in operation in a remarkable mandate of Roger de Cundy, *dapifer* of Roger de Mowbray, addressed to all the ministers of his lord, and relating to the render of the ninth garb from all the Mowbray demesnes in England.[6] It is impossible to say whether this document is the sole survivor of numerous writs issued by twelfth-century private stewards, or whether it was issued in the exceptional circumstance of Roger de Mowbray's absence from England in 1177 or 1186, but in either case its diplomatic form is a testimony to the advanced techniques of the Mowbray household.

The executive power of the steward had a wider aspect: he was the guardian of tenants' rights. He is addressed in many of the enfeoffment charters. Roger de Mowbray directs his *dapifer* and bailiffs and men, in a charter attested by Ralph de Belvoir *dapifer*, that no one is to cause a certain tenant injury nor place him in plea.[7] The hospital of St. Leonard's, York, had its possessions especially protected by Mowbray's steward: 'if any of my men disturb any of these [possessions] contrary to the tenor of my charter or contrary to the tenor of my men's charters, my *senescaldus* shall make and compel observance, as he loves me and the health of my soul'.[8] From acting as the lord's representative in the

---

[1] Warin *vielator* had a life tenancy, no. 308.

[2] Luke *cantor* and Warin *joculator* (? same as Warin *vielator*, above, n. 1), in *Yorks. Deeds* ii no. 32.

[3] Charter no. 40; cf. interpolated nos. 44 and 69; also Byland chron., *Mon. Ang.* v 351*b*.

[4] See *E.Y.C.* viii 242 ff.

[5] *P.R. 31 Hen. I* p. 106; he does not appear in the witness-clauses of any charters, and cannot be identified with any tenant family.

[6] Charter no. 314.   [7] No. 339.   [8] No. 313.

protection of property rights, it was but a short step for the steward to receive *affidationes* in the lord's court. We have a glimpse of this ceremony when some time between 1163 and 1169 Samson of Cornwall and his wife made a quitclaim to Roger de Mowbray and 'swore this by their own hand in the hand of Ralph de Belvoir my *dapifer* in the presence of all my court, that they would observe it for ever without ill will'.[1] It was perhaps the performance of this kind of act, having its origin in executive rather than judicial action, that was to lead in course of time to the steward's presidency of courts held in his lord's name.[2]

The financial administration of the honour is obscure. There is no shortage of chamberlains, but no evidence as to what they did. Alfred, the chamberlain under Nigel d'Aubigny from before 1124, continued in office until the 1140s,[3] and was succeeded by his son William, who held office from before 1154 and was perhaps himself succeeded by his son William before 1190.[4] Two other chamberlains appear towards the end of Roger de Mowbray's lifetime, Robert[5] and Chinon.[6] Nigel de Mowbray's personal chamberlain, both before and after his succession to the honour, was probably Augustine.[7] Unlike their counterparts on the honour of Richmond, the Mowbray chamberlains had no knights' fees attached to their office, had no high place in the witness-lists, and are never addressed in charters.[8] William and Augustine had small tenements of land for rent.[9] Whether the Mowbray chamberlains before the end of the twelfth century had any duties outside the *camera* itself, it is impossible to say—that is, beyond the care of cash, jewels, and other valuables, and the lord's bedding, clothing, and laundry arrangements. Certainly there was a great deal of work to be done in connection with the accounts of the honour, but it is not at all clear whether before the thirteenth century the *camera* was a financial office.[10] It may be that the chaplain, as in 1194, had some concern with the accounts.[11]

The office of chaplain was established early. The two chaplains who held office in the first half of the century—Guy, who occurs from before 1114 to after 1121,[12] and Samson d'Aubigny, who appears from before 1129 to c. 1154[13]—both enjoyed the livings of parish churches. Guy had

---

[1] No. 249; cf. the steward's duty in the interpolated or forged no. 53, and *C.P.R. 1388–92* pp. 160–2 (cal. as charter no. 203).
[2] Cf. Stenton, *Feudalism* pp. 77–8; N. Denholm-Young, *Seignorial Administration in England* (Oxford, 1937) pp. 66 ff.   [3] Charters nos. 11, 89, 95, 369, 383.
[4] Nos. 235, 300, etc.; for his son cf. nos. 88, 275–6, 368.   [5] Nos. 142, 252.
[6] No. 81.   [7] Nos. 329, 340.   [8] Cf. *E.Y.C.* iv 105, v 167–79.
[9] *Records of Templars* p. 125; charter no. 340.
[10] For its 13th-century character, cf. B.M., Cotton MS. Vesp. E xix (cartulary of Nostell) fo. 132r–v.
[11] Below, p. lxvii.   [12] Charters nos. 5, 7, 8, 10, 11, 15.
[13] First, (2) cf. no. 197; last nos. 109, 322.

the fat benefice of Dunton (Essex),[1] and Samson d'Aubigny had possession of no fewer than nine churches of demesne manors in Yorkshire,
Nottinghamshire, Lincolnshire, and Warwickshire.[2] During their respective periods of office, both Guy and Samson witnessed more charters
than any other members of the household. Like the personal chaplains
of the two Mowbray ladies—Gundreda's chaplain Nicholas,[3] and Alice's
chaplain Hugh[4]—they were constant companions. How far their activities extended beyond sacramental, pastoral, and advisory functions,
it is not easy to say. Like some contemporary private chaplains,[5] Guy
may have had some executive authority, for he is addressed by Nigel
d'Aubigny in a notification of a grant of land and food-renders in
Axholme.[6] He may, too, have had custody of Nigel's seal.[7] Samson
d'Aubigny was Nigel's nephew and Roger de Mowbray's cousin,[8] a man
whose social status was independent of his membership of the clergy:
he usually attests high in the witness-order and without his clerical
title. When some of the churches of the demesne were granted to the
priory of Newburgh, it was at his instance and request, but they were
granted with the condition that Samson's son, Roger, should succeed
to them,[9] and in fact when Masham was made a prebend of York,
Roger became prebendary.[10] Samson himself entered the convent of
Newburgh at the end of his life.[11] It is difficult to imagine this man per-
forming the lowly tasks of cutting parchment and writing charters,
although custody of the seal and supervision of documents written by
others might well have fallen within his province.

The clerical staff of the Mowbray household advanced during the
second half of the twelfth century to become a genuine chancery.
With the career of Robert the chaplain, who held office from before
1153[12] until after 1175,[13] an element of professionalism is introduced.
Unlike his predecessors, whose churches had been granted on their

---

[1] No. 11.
[2] Nos. 97, 175, 178, 196–7; for a similar example, see Stenton, *Feudalism* p. 85 n.
[3] Charters nos. 156, 232, 235, 300; cf. also nos. 244, 304.
[4] Nos. 101, 104, 107; cf. no. 300 and nos. 50, 108, 244.
[5] For archbishop Anselm's clerk, Baldwin, who was head of his household, see
R. W. Southern, *St. Anselm and his Biographer* (Cambridge, 1963) pp. 194–8. For earl
Roger de Montgomery's clerk, Richard de Belmeis, who was probably steward, see
J. F. A. Mason, 'The officers and clerks of the Norman earls of Shropshire', *Trans.
of Shropshire Archaeol. Soc.* lvi (1957–60) 253–4.   [6] Charter no. 15.
[7] He occurs in nos. 5 and 7, and the seal survives on nos. 2(?), 3, 5.
[8] Nos. 11, 199; cf. Byland chron., *Mon. Ang.* v 351b. Perhaps the son of a brother
of William and Nigel d'Aubigny, and therefore the brother of Humphrey d'Aubigny
(cf. *Mon. Ang.* i 164 (XVII); *Regesta* ii nos. 828 etc.).
[9] Byland chron., *Mon. Ang.* v 351b; charter no. 196.
[10] For Roger d'Aubigny as prebendary of Masham see *York Min. Fasti* ii 52.
[11] Charter no. 178; cf. the reference to his possible change of habit in no. 196.
[12] Nos. 89, 199. For another chaplain, see spurious no. 203.   [13] Nos. 128–9, 388.

deaths to various religious houses, Robert was not endowed with any ecclesiastical benefice, and must therefore have gained his living entirely within the household itself. He is a most frequent witness to charters, very often heading the list, and once having precedence in a list of men whom Roger de Mowbray describes as 'de curia mea'.[1] He accompanied Roger on at least one visit to Normandy.[2] During Robert's chaplaincy two clerks also appear, often very low in the order of witnesses, as if they were of much inferior status to Robert: these are Baldwin[3] and Peter.[4] Robert the chaplain was succeeded in office by John, who first appears in c. 1181, and continued as chaplain under Nigel de Mowbray.[5] During the 1170s and 1180s, a clerk called Robert appears with much greater frequency than John himself.[6] The impression that by this time the clerk had taken up a closer relationship with the lord than the chaplain seems to be confirmed by the fact that under Nigel de Mowbray the most prominent clerical figure was the clerk Ralph de Insula, who had been in Nigel's service for some years before the death of Roger de Mowbray.[7] Ralph had for his lifetime the tithes of the fulling-mill at Beslon, near Montbray,[8] and he accompanied Nigel to Normandy at least once.[9] In Nigel de Mowbray's period of lordship, John the chaplain witnesses no charters,[10] as if he had become detached from the intimate circle of the household, where he was replaced by the clerk.[11] But the chaplain had important administrative responsibilities, for John had charge of certain of the honour's finances at the time of Nigel de Mowbray's crusade.[12]

This small clerical department certainly produced some of the administrative documents. Although those records most likely to have been written within the household—feodaries, rentals, household accounts, and routine memoranda—have failed to leave any trace, it is evident that certain of the charters issued by the Mowbray lords were written by members of the secretariat. First, there are explicit statements in charters which survive only in copies: Baldwin the clerk wrote a charter in favour

---

[1] No. 247. He witnesses more than 50 charters.   [2] No. 163.

[3] He witnesses 15 charters between c. 1154 (nos. 240, 396) and c. 1175 (nos. 145, 388).

[4] He witnesses 21 charters from before 1166 (no. 246) to after 1182 (no. 315).

[5] He witnesses 8 charters between c. 1170 and 1186; cf. no. 87 and below, n. 12.

[6] He witnesses 20 charters from before 1172 (no. 53) to after 1188 (no. 76).

[7] Cf. nos. 123–4 of 1175 × 1176. He witnesses 21 charters of Nigel de Mowbray, six of Roger, and one of Robert.

[8] No. 165.   [9] Nos. 76, 164–5.   [10] Except perhaps no. 87.

[11] Cf. the situation in the household of the earls of Chester, where the clerk was preferred to the chaplain in the later 12th century, having custody of the gem-seal, *Chart. of St. Werburgh Chester*, ed. J. Tait (Chetham Soc., N.S. lxxix) pp. xlvii–viii.

[12] *P.R. 5 Ric. I* p. 70, recording a quittance to John the chaplain of Nigel de Mowbray of 100s. for £20 Anjou which John 'commodaverat' to Nigel in his crusade.

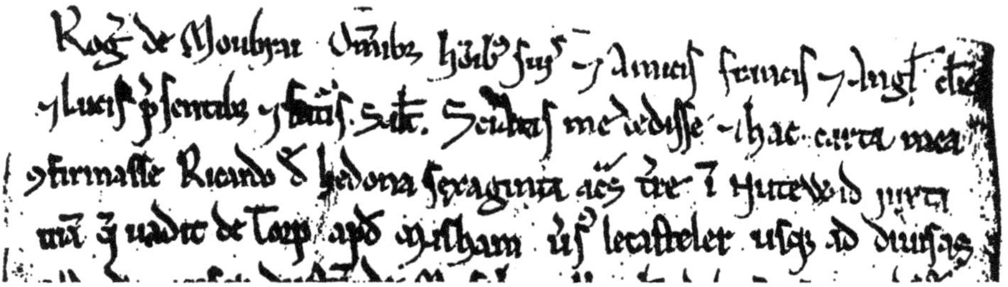

FIG. 1. Vyner deeds deposited at Leeds City Library, Archives Department, V.R. 25. Charter no. 366 in the text. Scribe i.

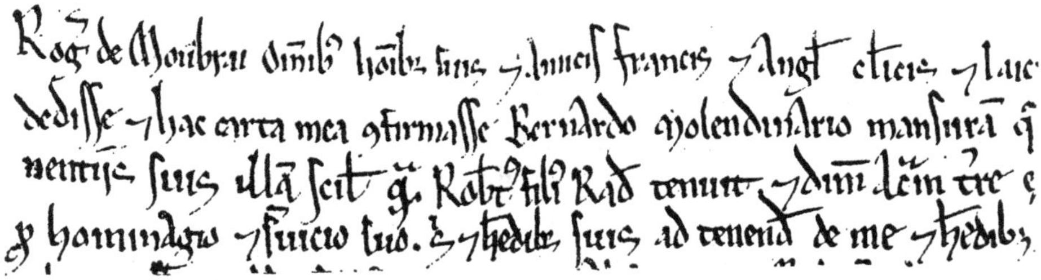

FIG. 2. Durham Dean and Chapter Muniments, 3. 1. Ebor. 4. Charter no. 348 in the text. Scribe i.

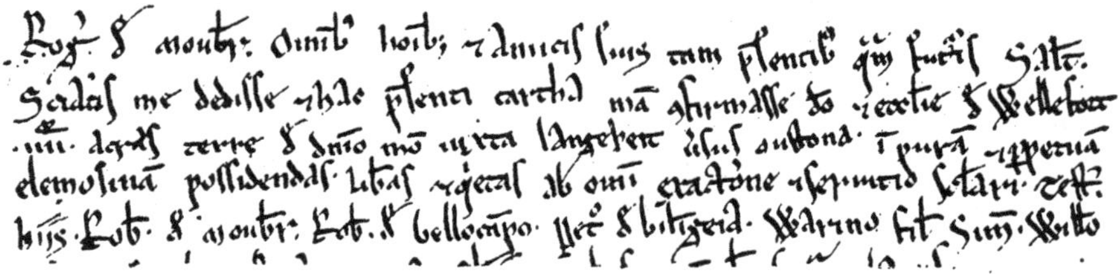

FIG. 3. Gregory-Hood deeds deposited at Shakespeare Birthplace Trust Library, Gregory-Hood charter 1364. Charter no. 282 in the text. Scribe ii.

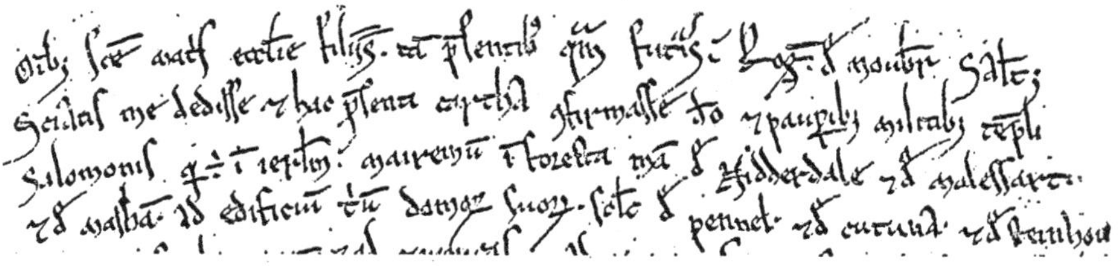

FIG. 4. Leeds, Yorks. Archaeological Society Library, Ribston Hall deeds, DD 59/xvi. Charter no. 272 in the text. Scribe ii.

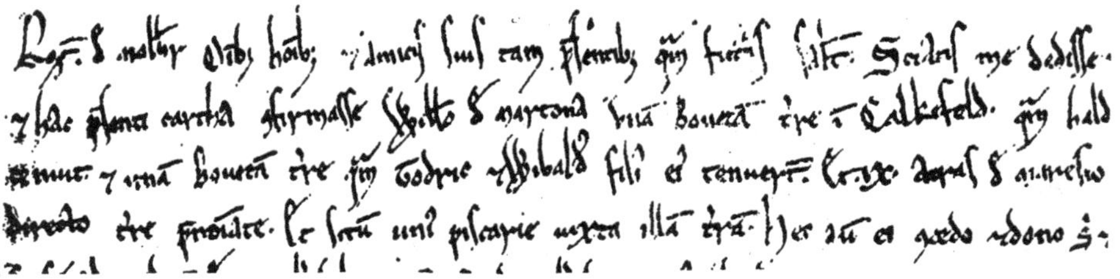

FIG. 5. B.M., Add Ch. 20847. Charter no. 373 in the text Scribe ii.

of Uctred son of Gamel[1] and another in favour of Roger de Arden,[2] and
John the chaplain wrote a charter in favour of Ralph of Queniborough.[3]
Secondly, two scribes of original charters of Roger de Mowbray can be
identified, both at work after *c.* 1170: one scribe wrote a charter for
Richard de Hedona[4] and another for Bernard the miller;[5] and a second
scribe wrote a charter for Welford,[6] another for the Templars,[7] and a
third for William de Martona.[8] Further, there is a certain regularity and
consistent economy of form in many of the charters, especially those in
favour of lay tenants, which suggests the work of a professional writing-
office. The two charters written by our first scribe have identical address-
clauses: 'Rog' de Moubrai omnibus hominibus suis et amicis Francis et
Anglis clericis et laicis presentibus et futuris salutem'. This exact phras-
ing is found in three other charters of the same period in which Roger
de Mowbray makes gifts to laymen, and in one by Nigel de Mowbray
for a layman, but as they do not survive in the original, it is impossible
to say whether these were also the work of the same scribe.[9]

It does not follow that all or even most of the Mowbray charters were
written within the household. In the case of charters for laymen, scribes
may have been casually employed,[10] or even provided by a religious house
with an interest in the property.[11] In the case of charters for religious
houses, there are strong indications that the beneficiaries often presented
for authentication charters already written by their own scribes. This
explains the variety of hands and styles to be found in the charters, and
also the marked palaeographical and diplomatic similarities between
charters for a single ecclesiastical beneficiary.[12] The surviving original
charters for Fountains, Byland, and Newburgh exhibit family like-
nesses to charters of other lords issued in their favour.[13] The form of

[1] Charter no. 396.   [2] No. 332.   [3] No. 381.
[4] No. 366; see Fig. 1.   [5] No. 348; see Fig. 2.
[6] No. 282; see Fig. 3. Cf. below, n. 9.
[7] *Records of Templars* pp. 269–70 (cal. as charter no. 272; see Fig. 4).
[8] *Danelaw Charters* no. 393 (cal. as charter no. 373; see Fig. 5). Cf. below, n. 9.
[9] Charters nos. 345–6, 360; Nigel's charter is no. 343. Two of the three charters
written by our second scribe have the address-clause: 'Rog(erus) de Moubr' [Molbr']
omnibus hominibus et amicis suis tam presentibus quam futuris salutem' (nos. 282, 373).
[10] The three original charters for laymen attested by Robert the chaplain, two of
which are attested also by Baldwin the clerk, are in different hands (nos. 339, 353, 373).
[11] Nos. 364–5, for Geoffrey de la Haia, who was a benefactor of the Templars, are
in a hand very similar to that of a Templar charter which has no connection with
Mowbray (*E. Y.C.* v no. 389, plate xxx). Charters nos. 353–4, for Roger son of Walter
of Carlton, are in a hand similar to Newburgh hands (e.g. B.M., Egerton Ch. 585).
[12] Some charters for a single house are written by the same scribe, e.g. for Newburgh,
charters nos. 205 (2) and 208; also nos. 201 and 206; and nos. 207 and 212; for Combe,
nos. 85–7; for Durham, nos. 89–90.
[13] Fountains: nos. 95, 134, 143, 145–6; cf. Vyner deeds deposited at Leeds Archives,
V.R. 19, 134, and *E. Y.C.* v nos. 367–8 and plates xxviii–ix, and ibid. vii no. 83. For

address common in twelfth-century Byland charters is found in most of the Mowbray charters for Byland: 'Eboracensi archiepiscopo totique capitulo Sancti Petri etc.'. The somewhat florid language of the Mowbray charters for Malton priory, with emphasis on the limitations of secular right, has parallels in documents of other lords for Malton.[1] The canons of Nostell apparently drew up two charters in an exceptional form, which required autograph *signa*.[2]

Once drawn up, a charter was presented for authentication. First the witnesses' names were added: in some of the documents drawn up by beneficiaries, it is evident that the witness-clauses were actually written a little later than the main text of the charters.[3] After the witnessing, the charter received authentication by sealing, for which a fee was probably charged.[4] There are surviving impressions of the seals of Nigel d'Aubigny, Samson d'Aubigny, Roger de Mowbray, Alice de Gant, and Nigel de Mowbray. Both Roger and Nigel de Mowbray had more than one seal during their careers. Roger's three seals were probably used in chronological sequence: the first before *c.* 1150–4, the second between *c.* 1150 and *c.* 1157, and the third from before 1157 to the end of his life. It is possible that Nigel de Mowbray changed his seal at the time of his father's departure on his last crusade. As in the royal chancery, the normal method of sealing until the 1150s was on a tongue cut at the lower edge of the document—*sur simple queue*;[5] from the 1150s the method increasingly favoured was to seal on a tag passed through a slit in the centre of the foot—*sur double queue*. Exceptionally the seal was appended on silk strings.[6] Most of the surviving original charters bear endorsements, but none of these endorsements can be identified as having been written within the Mowbray household. Mostly they are readily identifiable as archival endorsements made in the various religious houses. None of the surviving original charters which were in favour of laymen and remained in lay hands during the middle ages bears any endorsement.[7]

---

a charter similar to charter no. 109 below, see *E.Y.C.* xi no. 25 and plate ii. Byland: charters nos. 58, 59; cf. B.M., Add. Ch. 70693. Newburgh: charters nos. 207, 212; cf. *E.Y.C.* ix no. 23 and plate i. Combe: charter no. 81 and note.

[1] No. 183 and note.   [2] Nos. 215, 217.
[3] e.g. nos. 85–7. The witnesses to no. 212 (Newburgh) seem to be in a different hand.
[4] Cf. no. 64.
[5] Sealed in this fashion are nos. 2, 3, 5, 89, 90, 108, 109, 170, 339, 352. Cf. T. A. M. Bishop, *Scriptores Regis* (Oxford, 1961) pp. 16–18.
[6] Charters nos. 101, 134, 162, 342; cf. no. 87 on linen strings.
[7] *Danelaw Charters* no. 472 (cal. as charter no. 339); charters nos. 342, 352–4, 374. *Danelaw Charters* no. 393 (cal. as charter no. 373) has a late Welford endorsement.

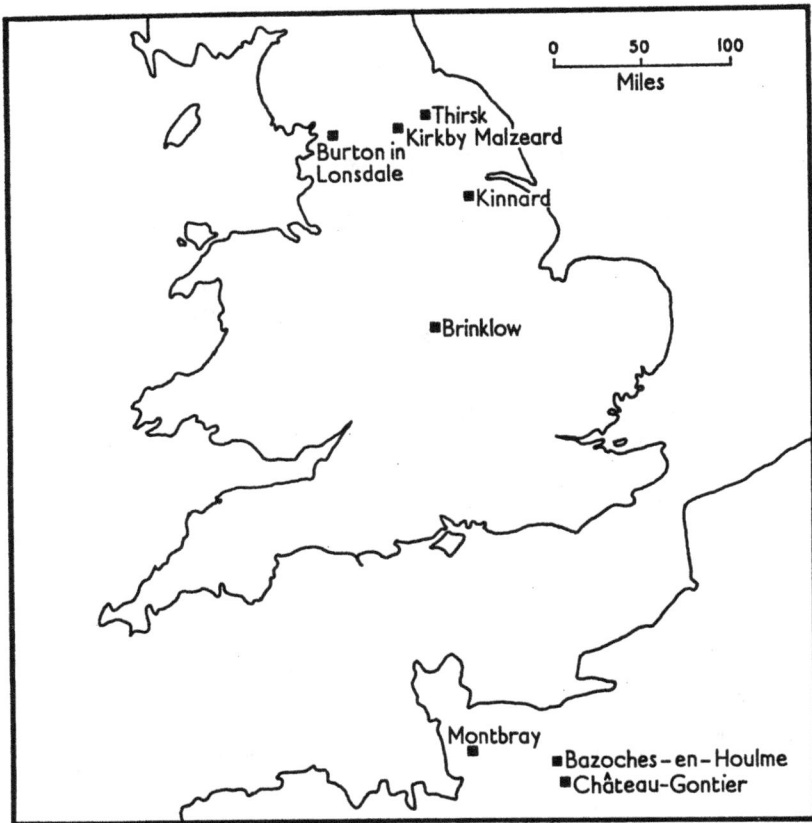

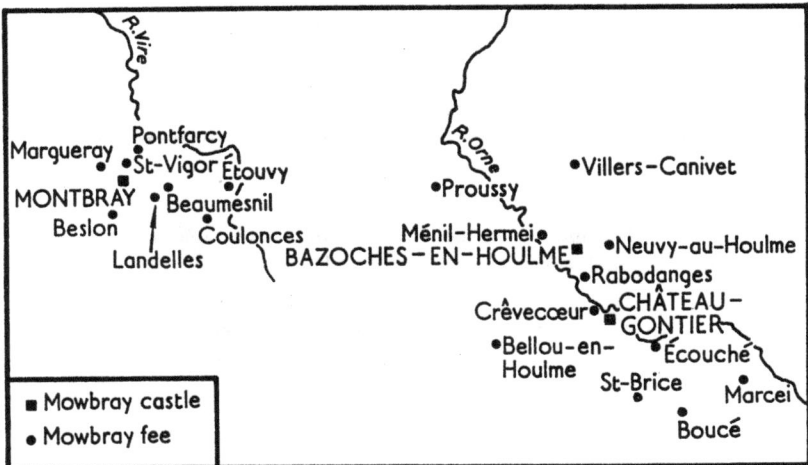

MAP I. The castles of the Honour of Mowbray, *c.* 1130
The Honour of Mowbray in Normandy

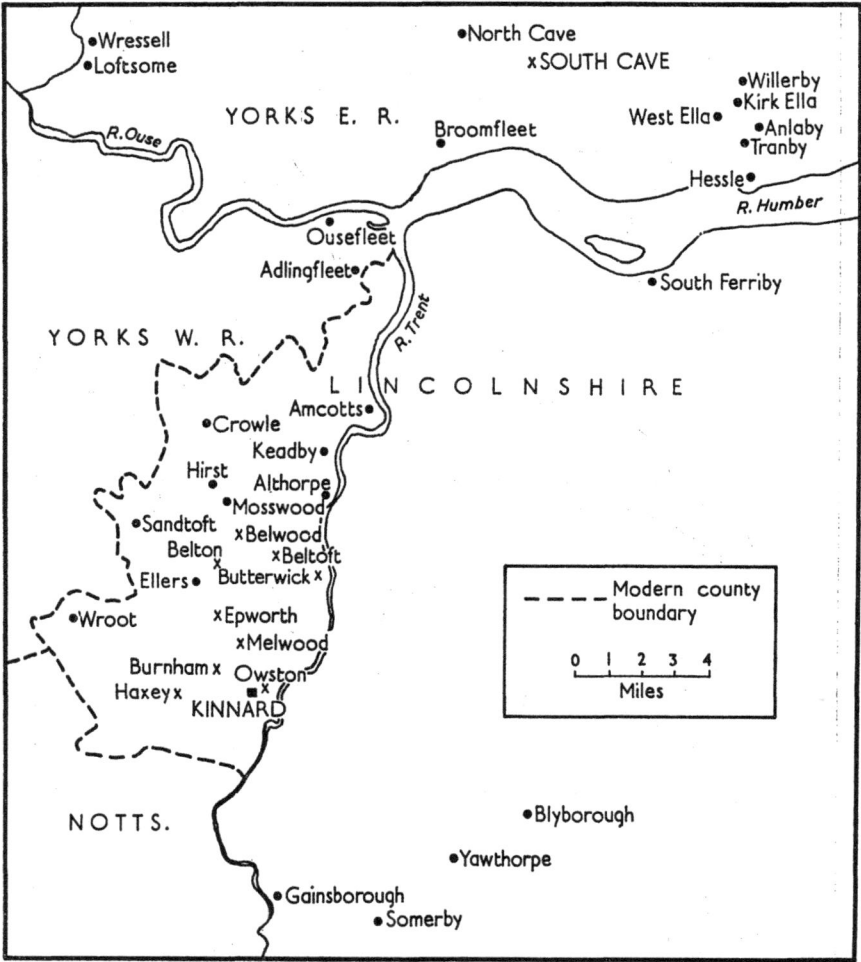

Wressell
Loftsome
North Cave
x SOUTH CAVE
Willerby
Kirk Ella
YORKS E. R.
West Ella
Anlaby
Tranby
Broomfleet
Hessle
R. Ouse
R. Humber
Ousefleet
Adlingfleet
South Ferriby
YORKS W. R.
R. Trent
L I N C O L N S H I R E
Amcotts
Crowle
Keadby
Hirst
Althorpe
Mosswood
Sandtoft
x Belwood
Belton
x Beltoft
Ellers
Butterwick x
Wroot
x Epworth
x Melwood
Burnham x
Owston
Haxey x
KINNARD

Blyborough

Yawthorpe

Gainsborough
Somerby

NOTTS.

	Modern county boundary

0 1 2 3 4
Miles

A

Map II

A. The Isle of Axholme and its neighbourhood
B. Estates in Nottinghamshire
C. Melton Mowbray and its neighbourhood
D. Brinklow and its neighbourhood

x Mowbray demesne c. 1170
● Mowbray fee c. 1170
■ Mowbray castle
□ Castle not in Mowbray honour

B

Finningley

R. Trent

Gainsborough

Serlby
Torworth

Tuxford
Egmanton
Weston

Winkburn
Kelham
Langford
Averham
Staythorpe
NEWARK ON TRENT

0   5   10
Miles

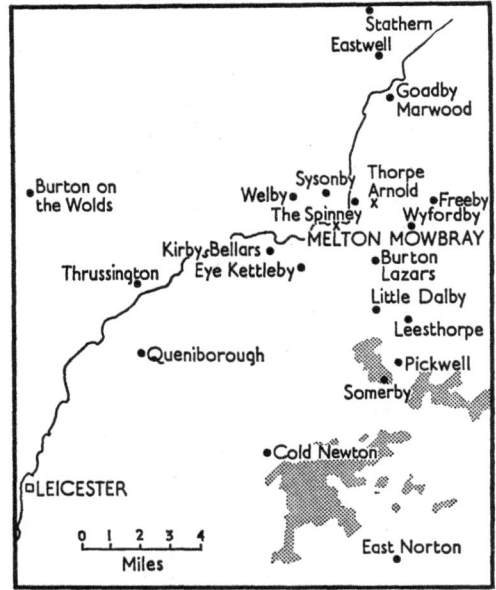

C

Stathern
Eastwell

Goadby
Marwood

Burton on
the Wolds

Welby
Sysonby
Thorpe
Arnold
The Spinney
Freeby
Wyfordby
MELTON MOWBRAY

Kirby Bellars
Eye Kettleby
Burton
Lazars
Thrussington
Little Dalby

Leesthorpe
Queniborough
Pickwell
Somerby

Cold Newton

LEICESTER

0 1 2 3 4
Miles

East Norton

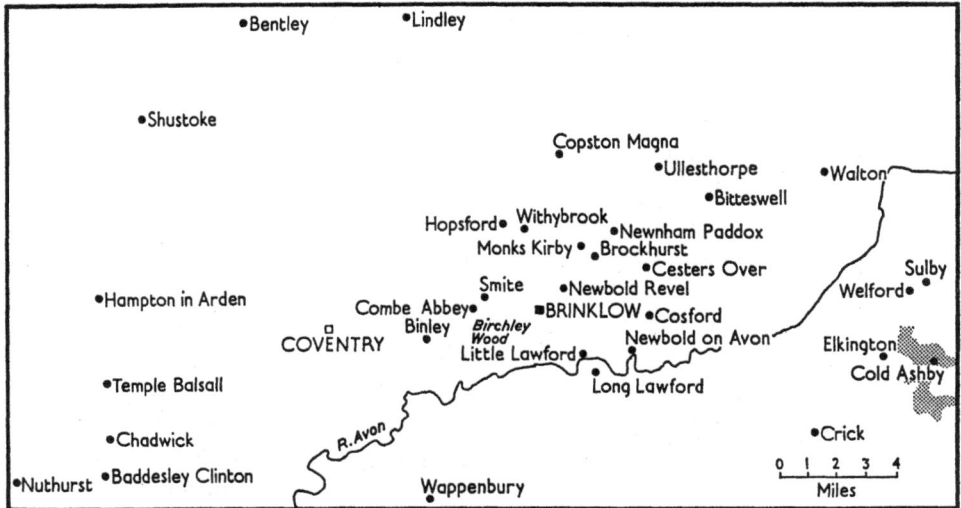

D

Bentley   Lindley

Shustoke

Copston Magna

Ullesthorpe
Walton

Bitteswell

Hopsford
Withybrook
Monks Kirby
Newnham Paddox
Brockhurst

Cesters Over
Sulby
Welford

Smite
Newbold Revel
Hampton in Arden

Combe Abbey
BRINKLOW
Cosford
Binley
Birchley
Wood
Newbold on Avon
Elkington
COVENTRY
Little Lawford
Cold Ashby

Temple Balsall
Long Lawford

R. Avon

Chadwick
Crick

Nuthurst
Baddesley Clinton

Wappenbury

0 1 2 3 4
Miles

Land over 600 ft.

NOTE ON THE EDITION

THE arrangement of the charters will be seen from the schedule below (pp. 1–3). The charters of Nigel d'Aubigny (nos. 1–17) are of considerable interest as a collection of early baronial charters and are therefore printed in full and arranged as a single group, in chronological order. The greater part of the collection consists of charters issued by other members of the Mowbray family (nos. 20–400). Roger de Mowbray is by far the most important figure, but there are charters also of Gundreda de Gournay, Samson d'Aubigny, Alice de Gant, Nigel de Mowbray, Mabel, and Robert de Mowbray. These charters are arranged in two main sections—those in favour of religious beneficiaries (nos. 20–329)[1] and those in favour of laymen (nos. 330–400)—and within either section the order of beneficiaries is alphabetical. The charters for a single beneficiary are arranged chronologically. In addition there are printed the returns of the English knights' fees in 1166 (no. 401) and the Norman fees in 1220 (no. 402), with some brief notes on the location of the fees.

With the exception of Nigel d'Aubigny's charters, which are given in full, texts are given only of charters that have not been printed before, or have appeared in editions that are either unsatisfactory or difficult to obtain. Charters already satisfactorily edited are calendared and their witnesses noted. References to lost charters are included in the collection and are numbered and arranged in the normal sequence.

Where the text of a charter is given in full, the first manuscript cited under the English heading normally gives the preferred version. Variant readings are not usually given where the text of a later copy differs from that of an original charter. In the case of original charters, the punctuation and spelling are preserved exactly. The medieval endorsements of originals are given, with the measurements of the top and left edges of the documents.[2] Brief notes on the seals are placed under the text of charters bearing seals, and full descriptions of the various seal designs will be found below, pp. lxxxii–iv. In charters surviving only in later copies, the principle has been to reconstruct the best text from the variant versions: the punctuation has been modernized and the spelling of words containing 'c', 'j', and 'v' has been regularized.

Some of the charters in the collection are of doubtful authenticity.

---

[1] See also addendum, no. 403.

[2] Endorsements and size are not given when they have already appeared in a printed edition.

Often, however, they seem to preserve genuine witness-lists, and they have been included because they can be shown to be based on genuine grants by members of the twelfth-century family of Mowbray. Forgeries not related to genuine grants are excluded. Most of the doubtful charters come from Byland abbey: a full study of the Byland forgeries must await a critical edition of the Byland chronicle and cartulary.

THE SOURCES

A FULL list of the sources of the Mowbray charters is given below. In all there survive 74 original charters, of which 63 are printed here in full. Of these, five are certainly fabricated originals,[1] but the remainder appear to be authentic and most are in a good state of preservation. The bulk of the texts in the collection comes from medieval copies of various types: cartularies are the most important, but chancery enrolments, episcopal inspeximuses, and other memoranda have yielded some texts. Of the post-medieval transcripts, those made by the seventeenth-century antiquaries, Roger Dodsworth and William Dugdale, are fruitful sources. Dodsworth's accurate texts from original charters now lost are often to be preferred to cartulary versions. In the nineteenth and twentieth centuries documents have been transcribed and then lost to view: thus the notes made by A. L. Léchaudé d'Anisy, W. Farrer, and W. T. Lancaster have been useful in adding some more texts to the collection.

Original charters of members of the Mowbray family

	Number in present edition
Caen, Archives of Calvados	
H. 6574 nos. 16, 17, 291, 292	162–5
H. 7809	277
Villers-Canivet nos. 159, 160	279, 280
Cambridge, Emmanuel College Muniments	
Box 12. A (Eltisley) no. 3	169
Durham, Dean and Chapter Archives	
3.1 Ebor. 3, 4	92, 348
4.3 Ebor. 1a, 1b, 1c, 14	89–91 (cal.)
1.12 Spec. 23, 24, 26	2, 3, 5
Halton Place, Hellifield, Yorks.	
Deeds in the possession of Major J. E. E. Yorke, nos. 55–9	49, 53, 56, 57, 60
Leeds, City Library, Archives Department	94, 95, 98, 100, 101, 105,
Deeds deposited by Commander C. Vyner,	108, 109, 134, 143, 145, 146,
V.R. 18, 20–3, 25, 27, 444, 4818–22, 4832	366, 367
Leeds, Yorkshire Archaeological Society Library	
Ribston Hall deeds, DD 59/xv–xvii	272 (cal.), 364, 365
Bradfer-Lawrence deeds, MD 335	201, 265

---

[1] Nos. 49, 53, 78, 228, 263.

Number in present edition

London, British Museum
    Additional Charters 5870, 19816, 20607, 20847   170, 284 (cal.), 286 (cal.),
        21088   342, 373 (cal.)
    Cotton Charter xvii. 123   339 (cal.)
    Egerton Charters 2141, 2144, 2168–71   58, 59, 205, 208, 212
    Harley Charters 83 C 38, 53 G 54–6   111, 192, 263, 285 (cal.)
    Portland Loan, Loans 29/242 no. 20   99

London, Public Record Office
    E. 326/8438, 11358   228, 281

Northallerton, County Record Office
    Deeds deposited by Viscount Downe   374
    Deeds deposited by Mr. F. W. A. Fairfax-   206, 207
        Cholmeley

Oxford, Bodleian Library
    Douce Charter a. 1 no. 5   97
    MS. Eng. Hist. a. 2 no. 38   268

Stratford on Avon, Shakespeare Birthplace Trust
    Library
    Deeds deposited by Colonel A. Gregory-Hood,
        nos. 37–41, 190, 191, 1364   77, 78, 81, 84–7, 282

York, Dean and Chapter Muniments
    Vicars Choral Deeds Vv 21, 22   352–4

Cartulary copies, transcripts, and confirmations of Mowbray charters

Caen, Archives of Calvados
    H. 4034   93 (cal.)
    H. 6510 (cart. of Saint-André-en-Gouffern)   163

Cambridge, Emmanuel College Muniments
    Box 12. A (Eltisley) no. 2   168 (cal.)

Durham, Dean and Chapter Archives
    Cartuarium Vetus   2–6, 91 (cal.)
    Cartuarium I–III   2–6, 91 (cal.)
    Large Register V   294

Halton Place, Hellifield, Yorks.
    Deeds in the possession of Major J. E. E. Yorke,
        no. 68   52, 54

Leeds, City Library, Archives Department
    Deeds deposited by Commander C. Vyner,
        V.R. 453, 454 (transcripts)   119, 132
    Deeds deposited by Sir J. Ingilby, no. 12   392

Leeds, Yorkshire Archaeological Society Library
    MS. 282 (R. Dodsworth's transcripts)   371, 372, 389
    MS. 405 (W. T. Lancaster's transcripts)   298
    MS. 869 (W. Farrer's MSS.) E.Y.C.   125, 142, 173, 347, 361 (cal.)

Levens Hall, Westmorland
    Register of deeds (written about 1639) in the
        possession of Mr. O. R. Bagot   370

Number in present edition

Oxford Bodleian Library (*cont.*),
  MSS. Dodsworth (*cont.*)

55 (transcripts)	106
63 (transcripts)	32 (cal.), 34–7, 38 (cal.), 44, 46, 55, 69, 172, 174, 191, 227, 281
76 (fragment of cart. of St. Mary's, York)	317, 319
91 (transcripts)	33, 72, 196, 197, 199, 201, 204, 209, 213, 349, 390
94 (transcripts)	37, 39 (cal.), 43, 50, 55, 69, 194 (cal.), 196, 197, 202 (cal.), 210, 214, 357, 399
95 (transcripts)	265, 293
110 (transcripts)	350
120 B (transcripts)	295, 296, 300–2, 311, 312
121 (transcripts)	359
144 (transcripts)	167
145 (transcripts)	55

MSS. Dugdale:

12 (transcripts)	78, 80, 82, 84–6, 88, 350
13 (transcripts)	330–8, 384

MSS. Rawlinson:

B 449 (cart. of Fountains)	94–7, 99, 102, 104, 107–9, 111, 114–16, 119–22, 124, 125, 127, 129–32, 134, 136, 142–4, 270, 363, 366–8, 375
B 455 (cart. of St. Leonard's, York)	303 (cal.), 308, 309
MS. Topography Yorks. d. 11 (transcripts)	75
Yorks. Rolls 21 (cart. of Hebden family)	392–5
University College MS. 170 (cart. of Fountains)	117, 128

Paris, Bibliothèque Nationale
  MSS. Latin 11055, 11056 (cart. of Saint-
  Évroult)   16, 17

Rouen, Bibliothèque Municipale
  MS. Y. 201 (Cartulaire de Normandie)   93 (cal.)

Stratford on Avon, Shakespeare Birthplace Trust
  Library
  Deeds deposited by Colonel A. Gregory-Hood,
  no. 519   13, 192, 193

Whitwell, Yorks.
  Cartulary of Whitby in the possession of Miss   8, 288, 289 (cal.), 290, 291,
  M. L. A. Strickland[1]   379, 380

Windsor Castle, St. George's Chapel, Dean and
  and Chapter Muniments
  XI. G. 11   10, 11

[1] Miss Strickland kindly allowed me to consult this MS. at the County Record
Office, Northallerton.

Number in present edition

York, Borthwick Institute of Historical Research
  Register of archbishop Melton   359
York, Dean and Chapter Muniments
  Magnum Registrum Album   3, 7, 321–4 (cal.)
  MS. xvi A.1 (cart. of St. Mary's, York) 316 (cal.), 318

Untraced charters   267, 269, 274, 355, 361

THE SEALS

FOR ease of reference, detailed descriptions are given here of the seals used by members of the Mowbray family.

NIGEL D'AUBIGNY

Surviving examples: nos. 2, 3, 5, all of [June 1109 × Feb. 1114]; also a detached seal perhaps belonging to no. 4, of [June 1109 × Feb. 1114].

Appearance: round, 6·1 cm. diameter; equestrian, knight facing right; wearing hauberk of mail and ?helmet; bearing sword and shield showing the inside.

Legend: + SIGILLVM : NIGELLI · DE ALBINNEIO

Described: W. Greenwell and C. H. Blair, 'Durham seals', *Archaeologia Aeliana* 3rd ser. vii (1911) 274 no. 40 (from all surviving examples).

Illustrated: ibid. plate XVI (from charter no. 3).

See Frontispiece (*a*) (from no. 3).

SAMSON D'AUBIGNY

Surviving example: no. 97, of [1138 × Oct. 1153].

Appearance: vesica, 5·4 × 3·5 cm.; ecclesiastical figure facing front; wearing ?mass vestments; holding book in right hand (left hand broken off).

Legend: SIGILLVM SAMSOИ[.] DE A[.]BAИEIO[. . .]OS

ROGER DE MOWBRAY

Seal no. 1

Surviving examples: nos. 89 [*c.* 1150], 98 [1142 × *c.* 1154], 99 [1142 × *c.* 1154].

Appearance: round, 7 cm. diameter; equestrian, knight facing right; wearing hauberk of mail and conical pointed helmet with nasal; bearing sword and shield showing the inside; horse has breast-band.

Legend: + SIGILLVM : ROG[.]R[.] DE MVLBRAI

Described: W. Greenwell and C. H. Blair, 'Durham seals', *Archaeologia Aeliana* 3rd ser. ix (1913) 315 no. 1838 (from charter no. 89); 'Blyborough Charters', ed. K. Major, in *A Medieval Miscellany for D. M. Stenton* (P.R.S., N.S. xxxvi), no. 2 (from no. 89).

Illustrated: Greenwell and Blair, plate VII (from no. 89).

See Frontispiece (*b*) (from no. 89).

Seal no. 2

Surviving examples: nos. 77 [*c.* 1150], 90 [*c.* 1150], 109 [Oct. 1154 × *c.* 1157].

Appearance: round, 7·6 cm. diameter; equestrian, knight facing right; wearing hauberk of mail and helmet with nasal; bearing sword and shield; horse galloping.

Legend: + SIGILLVM : ROGERI [. . .]OLBRAIO

Described: W. Greenwell and C. H. Blair, 'Durham seals', *Archaeologia Aeliana* 3rd ser. ix (1913) 315 no. 1839 (from charter no. 90); 'Blyborough Charters' no. 3 (from no. 90).

Illustrated: 'Blyborough Charters' plate XVI (from no. 90).

Seal no. 3

Surviving examples: nos. 49 [1147 × *c.* 1154] (fabricated), 56 [*c.* 1173 × 1180], 58 [*c.* 1181], 84 [*c.* 1170 × 1186], 91 [*c.* 1160 × 1170], 92 [*c.* 1170 × 1186], 95 [1138 × 1145] (renovation), 111 [Aug. 1174 × June 1175], 125, March 1176, 134 [*c.* 2 Feb. 1181], 145 [*c.* 1175 × 1186], 162 [Aug. 1154 × 1157], 201 [1147 × 1155], 205(1) [*c.* 1145 × 1186], 272 [*c.* 1170 × 1184], 348 [*c.* 1170 × 1186], 353 [1154 × 1166], 364 [*c.* 1170 × 1184], 366 [*c.* 1170 × *c.* 1181], 373 [*c.* 1170 × 1184]; also B.M., Egerton Ch. 585 [*c.* 1177 × 1181] (see no. 68 note), and Add. Ch. 70692 (forgery) (see no. 38 note).
Drawings or descriptions of lost examples: nos. 160 [1175 × 1186], 336 [*c.*1170 × 1184], 347 [*c.* 1176].
Appearance: round, 8·3 cm. diameter; equestrian, knight facing right; wearing hauberk of mail, long surcoat with tasselled fringe, and rounded helmet with nasal; bearing sword with maunch and shield with large pointed boss; surcoat, helmet, and shield decorated with *fleur-de-lys*; horse galloping, with breast-band.
Legend: + SIGILLVM ROGERI DE MOLBRAI:
Described: W. Greenwell and C. H. Blair, 'Durham seals', *Archaeologia Aeliana* 3rd ser. ix (1913) 314 no. 1837 (from charters nos. 91, 92, 348); ibid. no. 1840 (from charters nos. 125, 142); 'Blyborough Charters' no. 4 (from no. 91); W. de G. Birch, *Catalogue of Seals in the B.M.* ii (1892) nos. 6219–24 (from nos. 111, 373, and Egerton Ch. 585).
Illustrated: Greenwell and Blair plate VII (from no. 91); *Cat. Seals B.M.* ii plate X (from no. 111); A. L. Léchaudé d'Anisy, *Recueil de Sceaux Normands et Anglo-Normands* (Caen, 1834) plate VI no. 6 (very inaccurate drawing of seal from charter no. 162).
See Frontispiece (*c*) (from no. 145).

ALICE DE GANT

Surviving examples: nos. 100 [*c.* 1144 × May 1155], 101 [*c.* 1147 × May 1155].
Drawing of lost example: no. 106 [*c.* 1144 × Nov. 1156].
Appearance: vesica, 6 × 4·1 cm.; female figure facing front; wearing long robe and cloak; holding bird in right hand and ?*fleur-de-lys* in left.
Legend: worn and broken off in surviving examples; given by Dodsworth (no. 106) as: SIGILLVM : ALICIE GAVNT

NIGEL DE MOWBRAY

Two seals of very similar design:
General appearance: round, equestrian, knight facing right; wearing hauberk of mail, surcoat, and rounded helmet with nasal; bearing sword and shield; horse trotting, with breast-band and diapered saddle.
Legend: + SIGILLVM NIGELLI : DE : MOLBRAI
Distinguishing features of the two designs:

Seal no. 1

7 cm. diameter; shield has prominent rounded boss; in legend second 'I' in SIGILLVM is placed above horse's ears, and horse's right foot is placed just before 'N' of NIGELLI.
Surviving examples: nos. 53 [*c.* 1160 × 1172], 57 [*c.* 1173 × 1180], 146 [*c.* 1175 × 1186], 286 [*c.* 1170 × 1190], 365 [*c.* 1170 × 1184], 367 [*c.* 1170 × *c.* 1181].

Described: W. de G. Birch, *Catalogue of Seals in the B.M.* ii (1892) nos. 6217–18 (from charter no. 286 and an untraced charter).
See Frontispiece (*d*) (from no. 146).

Seal no. 2

6·9 cm. diameter; boss on shield scarcely visible; horse has square bit; in legend second 'I' in SIGILLVM is placed below horse's ears, and horse's right foot is placed inside 'N' of NIGELLI.
Surviving examples: nos. 165 [*c.* 1170 × 1190], 280 [*c.* 1170 × 1190], 342 [1186 × 1190].
Untraced example: no. 361 [1186 × 1190].
Drawing of lost example: no. 337 [*c.* 1170 × 1190].
Described: W. de G. Birch, *Catalogue of Seals in the B.M.* ii (1892) nos. 6215–16 (from charters nos. 342, 361).
Illustrated: A. L. Léchaudé d'Anisy, *Recueil de Sceaux Normands et Anglo-Normands* (Caen, 1834) plate VI no. 8 (from charter no. 280).

THE CHARTERS

SCHEDULE

TEXTS

1 *Notification by Nigel d'Aubigny of his demise to Selby (Ben., Yorks., W.R.) of his claim on Crowle (Axholme, Lincs.), which Geoffrey de La Guerche had sold to abbot Benedict; and of his concession of wapentake and warren, sake and soke, etc.*

[1107 × 1115, probably before May 1108]

Cartulary copy: B.M., Add. MS. 37771 fo. 206*r* (old fo. 203*r*).
Pd., *Selby Coucher* ii no. 1197.

Notum sit omnibus hominibus tam Francis quam Anglis quod ego Nigellus de Albineio dimisi ecclesie Sancti Germani de Seleby et monachis ibidem Deoque Sancto Germano de Seleby servientibus calumpnias quas habebam super terram Sancti Germani, scilicet super Crullam et silvam ejusdem ville quam villam vendiderat Gaufridus de la Wyrca quartus antecessor meus in eodem honore Benedicto primo abbati ecclesie Sancti Germani Selebye. Et sciatis quod ego concessi eisdem monachis ut habeant suum wapentack' et suam warrennam et omnia que eidem ville adjacent cum soca et saca et thol et theam et infangthef, et si mei homines clamorem super homines abbatis habuerunt ut intraturi sunt s[cilicet]*ᵃ* recepturi veniant. Et ob hoc effectus sum ego N. plenarie frater ecclesie Sancti Germani et abbas missurus est semper in eadem ecclesia unum monachum et pascere debet unum pauperem in elemosinam pro me et pro uxore mea et pro Gaufrido et pro omnibus antecessoribus nostris et pro omnibus benefactoribus ejusdem ecclesie. Hujus rei testes sunt R.[1] abbas ecclesie Sancti Albani etc.

NOTE. The reference to Nigel's wife indicates that this settlement cannot have been made before 1107. It was confirmed by Henry I before 1115, and probably before May 1108.[2] Geoffrey de La Guerche (for whose gift see *Selby Coucher* ii no. 1196) is referred to as Nigel's fourth predecessor, the intervening two predecessors being—in all probability—Robert and Geoffrey de Stuteville.[3]

ᵃ *suamet*, or *seisinam*, suggested by J. T. Fowler, *Selby Coucher*, but *scilicet* seems more likely.

[1] Richard d'Aubigny, abbot of St. Albans (1097–1119), who was probably Nigel's paternal uncle (see L. C. Loyd, 'The origin of the family of Aubigny of Cainhoe', *Beds. Hist. Rec. Soc.* xix (1937) 105–6).
[2] *Regesta* ii no. 889.
[3] Cf. *E.Y.C.* ix 2, 119 and n. 1 (and below, no. 319 note).

2 *Notification by Nigel d'Aubigny to king H(enry I) of his restorations of lands to St. Peter's, York (secular cathedral), and its hospital, to Durham (Ben. cathedral), to Serlo the monk, and to St. Mary's, York (Ben.), and his gifts to St. Albans (Ben., Herts.), to Bec (Ben., Calvados, France), to Lewes (Clun., Sussex), and to Selby; and request for royal confirmation.*

[June 1109 × Feb. 1114]

> Original charter: Durham, D. & C. Archives, 1. 12. Specialium 24. Cartulary copies: Durham, Cartuarium Vetus fo. 64*r*, Cartuarium II fo. 208*v*; Bodl., MS. Carte 177 fo. 41*r*. Also copied: B.M., Cotton MS. Claud. D iv fo. 62*r–v*. Pd. (incompletely), *Feodarium Prioratus Dunelmensis*, ed. W. Greenwell (S.S. lviii) p. 151 n., from the original charter.

Karissimo domino suo Regi Anglorum .H. Nig(ellus) de Albini fidele seruitium. Precor uos karissime domine in quo post Deum tota mea est fiducia ut quia ego uester dum potui et uos ueraciter dilexi et uobis fidelissime seruiui in necessitate mea pro Dei dilectione et uestra dulcissima nobilitate mei misereamini. Cum enim ego et in seruitio uestro et in aliis operibus meis peccata maxima et bona uel nulla uel modica fecerim :' de uestra confisus bonitate dulcissima terrulas quasdam quas de ęcclesiis habebam . ipsis ęcclesiis reddidi et dedi. Precor igitur uos karissime domine et quia corporaliter non possum . pedibus Maiestatis uestrę spiritualiter obuolutus cum lacrimis et singultibus exoro . ut quod ipsis ecclesiis reddidi . et aliis ęcclesiis de dominio meo pro redemptione anime mee dedi . Maiestatis uestre pietas ita concedat et confirmet . ne ab aliquo uiolari queat ullo tempore. Terrę autem quas ego reddidi ęcclesiis :' hę sunt. Eboracensi ecclesię Helprebi[1] . et Sclenigforde[2] . et Granteleie[3] . et in Cnardeforde[4] carrucatam . et dimidiam. Hospitio pauperum fratrum eiusdem ecclesię .ii. carrucatas terrę in Hameseie.[5] Ecclesię Dunelmensi et Sancto Cuthberto .ii. maneria que Walthef filius Alsi de me tenebat ultra Teisa . scilicet Bermentun[6] et Schirningeham[7] . et quicquid ad eas pertinet. Et Sarloni monacho dimidiam carrucatam terrę.[8] Et abbatie Sanctę Marię de Eboraco . molendinos illos quos abbas fecerat super stagnum . et si ipsi molendini deteriorantur propter nouos molendinos meos . uolo ut frater meus restauret illud damnum abbatię de redditibus molendinorum meorum. Hę sunt terrę quas ego dedi ęcclesiis. Eswalle in Chent[9] et quicquid ad eam pertinet dedi Deo et abbatię Sancti Albani quia ad

---

[1] Helperby, Yorks., N.R.   [2] Sleningford, Yorks., W.R.
[3] Grantley, Yorks., W.R.   [4] In Skelden, Yorks., W.R.
[5] Upper Helmsley, Yorks., N.R.
[6] Barmpton, co. Durham.   [7] Skerningham, co. Durham.
[8] Middlethorpe, Yorks., W.R.; cf. no. 8.
[9] Easole Street in Nonington, Kent.

eandem ecclesiam me sepeliendum disposui. Esmid[1] dedi Deo et Sanctę Marię Beccensis abbatię. Monasterio Sancti Pancratii de Lewes et monachis concessi et dedi terram de Meltun[2] . sicut eos indissaisitos inueni . et molendinum quendam quem ipse in uadimonium habebam . ita eisdem concessi et dedi . sicut eum in manu mea habebam. Deo et abbatie Sancti Germani de Salebi concessi et dedi Hamescote[3] . et piscinam quę illi adiacet quę uocatur Grasgard. Non de seruitio meo sed de bonitate uestra piissime domine confido.

Endorsements: *de Bermetun et Scirnigaham* (12th cent.); *Carta Nic'li de Albini'* / *Prima .xii. specialium C. 2* (later medieval hands).

Size: 18·6 × 6·2 cm.

Seal: almost certainly one of the two detached seals in a packet, 1. 12 Spec. 26✣. (see above, p. lxxxii); was appended on tongue, with tie.

NOTE. For the date, see note to no. 5 below.

3 *Notification by Nigel d'Aubigny to his brother W(illiam) of his appointment of William as his heir; and request to William to superintend the restorations Nigel made to St. Peter's, York, and its hospital, to Durham, to Serlo the monk, and to St. Mary's, York, and his gifts to St. Albans, to Bec, to Lewes, to Selby, to Monks Kirby (Ben. alien, Warwicks.),[4] and to Holy Trinity, York (Ben. alien);[5] and notification of his restitutions or exchanges to certain laymen, and request to William to make restitutions or exchanges to certain other laymen.*   [June 1109 × Feb. 1114]

Original charter: Durham, D. & C. Archives, 1. 12. Specialium 23. Cartulary copies: Durham, Cartuarium Vetus fo. 65r, Cartuarium I fos. 237v–238r, Cartuarium II fos. 207v–208r; York, D. & C. Muniments, Registrum Magnum Album III fos. 29r–30r.

Pd., *Historians of the Church of York*, ed. J. Raine (R.S. lxxi) iii no. xxxix, from the original charter and the York Register; R. Surtees, *History and Antiquities of Durham* (1816–40) iii 395, and (incompletely) *Feod. Prior. Dunelm.* p. 151 n., from the original charter.

Karissimo domino et fratri suo .W. Nig(ellus) de Albini salutem et fraternam dilectionem. Ex quo nati fuimus uterque uos de mea necessitate et auxilio . et me de uestris satis exoratos existimo. Precor igitur uos frater karissime ut cum per Dei misericordiam naturali et carnali uinculo coniuncti simus . hoc alter ad alterum cum necessitas euenerit . in operibus ostendamus. Ecce frater karissime peccata mea maxima et iniquitates Dei misericordia diutius tolerare non ualens ⸱⁊ flagella iusticię suę carni meę miserrime misericorditer admouit ne per peccatricem insolentiam anima mea ęternam mereretur gehennam. Ego si

[1] Smite, Warwicks.   [2] Melton Mowbray, Leics.
[3] Amcotts, in Axholme, Lincs.   [4] Dependency of St. Nicholas, Angers, France.
[5] Dependency of Marmoutier, Tours.

quidem quod in prosperitate mea melius facere potuissem uos quem
super omnes diligo . honoris mei et rerum mearum constitui heredem .
eo uidelicet tenore . ut redditiones terrarum quas ego Eboracensi et
Dunelmensi feci ęcclesiis . pro salute animę meę et redemptione peccatorum meorum . et quia ipse terrę ęcclesiis illis iure adiacent reddidi
et concessi . et donationes terrarum quas ego sancte Beccensi ęcclesię .
et abbatię Sancti Albani et monasterio Sancti Pancratii et abbatię Sanctę
Marię de Eboraco . et abbatię Sancti Germani de Salebi . et redditiones
terrarum quas hominibus meis quos exhereditaueram feci . et escambia
quę pro terris illis hominibus meis quibus eas dederam reddidi . nullo-
modo uiolare presumatis . sed ut donatio mea firma sit et stabilis .
uestris uiribus et omnium amicorum nostrorum faciatis. Terrę autem
quas ego reddidi ęcclesiis ꞏ́ hę sunt. Eboracensi ęcclesię . Helprebi . cum
feudo Bonefacii et Scleningeforde . et Granteleie . et in Cnardeforde .i.
carrucatam et dimidiam. Hospicio pauperum fratrum eiusdem ęcclesię
.ii. carrucatas terrę in Hameseie. Ęcclesię Dunelmensi et Sancto CUTH-
BERTO .ii. maneria quę Waltef filius Alsi de me tenebat ultra Teisa .
scilicet Bermentun et Scirmingeham . et quicquid ad eas pertinet.
Sarloni monacho dimidiam carrucatam terrę. Abbatię Sancte MARIĘ
de Eboraco . molendina illa quę*a* abbas fecerat super stagnum . et si
ipsa molendina*b* deteriorantur propter noua molendina mea*c* . uolo frater
mi ut restauretis illud dampnum abbatię de redditibus molendinorum
meorum. Hę sunt terrę quas ego dedi ęcclesiis Eswalle in Chent et quicquid ad eam pertinet et totam decimam de Cundale in Eboraciscira[1] .
uidelicet in messe . et in molendinis et in piscinis . et in omnibus rebus
de quibus decimę dantur dedi Deo et abbatię Sancti Albani . quia ad
eandem ęcclesiam me sepeliendum disposui. Esmid dedi Deo et Sanctę
Marię Beccensis abbatię. Monasterio Sancti Pancratii de Lewes et
monachis concessi et dedi terram de Meltun . sicut eos indissaisitos
inueni . et molendinum quoddam quod*d* ipse in uadimonium habebam
ita eisdem concessi et dedi . sicut eum in manu mea habebam. Deo et
abbatię Sancti Germani de Salebi concessi et dedi Hamescote . et
piscinam quę illi adiacet quę uocatur Grasgard. Deo et ęcclesię Sancti
Nicholai quę est in Circebi concessi et dedi ęcclesiam de Neweboldē[2] .
cum terris et decimis suis. Ęcclesię Sancti Trinitati dedit*e* .iii. mansiones
domorum in Eboraco et decimam molendinorum. Hę sunt terrę quas
ego reddidi hominibus exheredatis. Videlicet Rodb(erto) de Cambos

---

a Word endings written by the same scribe, over erasures. Previously *molendinos
illos quos.*   *b* Previously *ipsos molendinos.*   *c* Previously *nouos molendinos
meos.*   *d* Previously *quendam quem.*   *e* *Sic.*

---

[1] Cundall, Yorks., N.R.   [2] Newbold on Avon, Warwicks.

totam terram suam et heredibus suis . eo tenore . ut R. de Cambos uel heredes sui teneant illam de Rodb(erto) de Wituile . et ipsi .R. de Wituile dedi Langliuetorp[1] . et Circebi[2] . et Mildebi[3] . et seruitium Liulfi de terra de Graftun.[4] Willelmo fili[a] Warini dedi Torntun[5] cum .iiii. carrucatis terrę et cum hominibus qui in eis sunt . propter illas duas carrucatas terrę et dimidiam . quas ipse reddidi elemosinę Sancti PETRI . et Sarloni monacho. Raulfo de Paueli reddidi totam terram suam et pecuniam sicuti eam melius habuerat. Raulfo de Buce reddidi suam terram. Wence suam terram reddidi . sicut eum saisitum inueni. Filiis Anseis reddidi terram patris sui . ut teneant illam sub Hugone de Rampan et ipsi Hugoni dedi .ii. carrucatas terrę in Circebi[6] in escambio . ubi ipse aliam suam terram habebat. Butin reddidi terram suam de Smid[7] et pecuniam suam quam ipse monstrare potuerit quod perdidit. Et tu Willelme frater meus redde Giraldo escambium suum . et Burnulfo nemus suum de Hantona[8] . et Vnfrido Hastingo terram suam de Note-herst[9] quam ipse Nig(ellus) seruabat . et Russello de Landeforde .i. carrucatam. Terram de Landeleie[10] quę fuit Rannulfi de Landeforde uolo ut reddas eam heredibus Rannulfi . si eam requisierint. Hoc est escambium quod ego dedi Ric(ardo) de Dauiduile . Frethebi[11] totam . preter .vii. bouetas quas Aluredus tenet . et in Alebi[12] .iii. carrucatas et dimidiam . et dimidiam bouetam. Et Waltero de Insula Aletorp[13] de Insula in escambio terrę suę. Et tu Willelme frater meus . redde Rod-berto de Waluile escambium suum ad ualens ad terminum suum . et non faciat seruitium quousque hoc habeat nisi pro .i. milite.

Endorsements: *Nig' de Albeinni de Berm'tun et Skirningham* (12th or 13th cent.); *Prima .xii. specialium B. 2* (later medieval hand).

Size: 21 × 30·5 cm.

Seal: seal of Nigel d'Aubigny (above, p. lxxxii), white wax varnished; appended on tongue projecting from centre of foot of document. See Frontispiece (*a*).

NOTE. For the date see note to no. 5 below.

This charter shows that Nigel d'Aubigny was in possession of the lordships of Melton Mowbray, Monks Kirby, and Axholme before February 1114. The evidence is less clear on his possession of the lordships of Kirkby Malzeard and Thirsk. Certainly he already held, illegally, the lands which were later to be held as a quarter-fee of the archbishop of York (Sleningford, Grantley,

---

[a] *Sic.*

[1] Langthorpe (par. Kirby Hill), Yorks., N.R.
[2] Kirby Hill, Yorks., N.R.
[3] Milby (par. Kirby Hill), Yorks., N.R.
[5] ? Thornton Bridge, Yorks., N.R.
[7] Smite, Warwicks.
[9] Nuthurst, Warwicks.
[10] ? Lindley, Leics.
[12] Welby, Leics.

[4] Grafton, Yorks., W.R.
[6] Probably Kirby Bellars, Leics.
[8] Hampton in Arden, Warwicks.
[11] Freeby, Leics.
[13] Althorpe, in Axholme, Lincs.

and Skelden), and the proximity of these estates to Kirkby Malzeard renders it likely that Malzeard was also in his possession by 1114, as were some other estates deriving from the pre-Conquest holding of Gospatric (Kirby Hill and ? Thornton Bridge). The only property in the charter from Hugh Fitz Baldric's fee is Serlo's land in Middlethorpe (cf. p. 6 n. 8), but Cundall, a former Mortain holding, is close to many of the former Fitz Baldric estates at and near Thirsk. It is unlikely that Thirsk and its related properties were granted to Nigel d'Aubigny much later than c. 1114, and certainly not later than c. 1118, when his period of northern administration came to an end.

Of the lay tenants mentioned in the charter, three—Robert de Wyville, Hugh de Rampan, and Richard de Daiville—were certainly ancestors of military tenants of 1166,[1] but the four places in which Wyville was granted land by this charter did not remain parts of the Wyville fee. William son of Warin's exchange was the subject of another charter, no. 7. Humphrey Hastings was the ancestor of the Hastings family, sub-tenants of Moreville.[2]

4 *Request by Nigel d'Aubigny to Ranulf (Flambard), bishop of Durham, and the congregation of St. Cuthbert, for intercession and pardon, at a time of grave illness, and notification of his restoration to Durham of the two manors of Barmpton and Skerningham (co. Durham).* [June 1109 × Feb. 1114]

Cartulary copies: Durham, D. & C. Archives, Cartuarium Vetus fo. 64v, Cartuarium II fo. 208v. (Original charter lost, formerly Durham D. & C., I. 12 Specialium 25,[3] mentioned in Repertorium Magnum.) Also copied: B.M., Cotton MS. Claud. D iv fo. 62v.
Pd., *Feod. Prior. Dunelm.* pp. 151–2 n., from Cartuarium II.

Ranulfo Dunelmensi episcopo et omni congregationi Sancti Cuthberti Nig(ellus) de Albini salutem. Dei misericordiam et Sancte Marie Sanctique confessoris Cuthberti vestramque intercessionem piissimam[a] requiro ut mei misereamini, quia Deus omnipotens sua justicia gravi me infirmitate corporis percussit et hic jaceo graviter vexatus nesciens quid michi amodo evenire debeat. Et propterea rogo ut pro me sitis sicut pro fratre vestro et amico esse debetis. Et volo ut sciatis quod ego pro redemptione anime mee reddo et dono Sancto Cuthberto et ecclesie Dunelmensi illa duo maneria que Waldef[b] filius Alsi de me tenebat ultra Teisam scilicet Bermetun et Scirningeham.[c] Et inde Sanctum Cuthbertum nunc facio resaisiri. T(estibus),[d] Th. archiepiscopo, et W.

---

[a] *piissimam intercessionem*, Cart. II.   [b] *Walthef*, Cart. II.   [c] *Scirnyngham*, Cart. II.   [d] Cart. Vet. version ends, and witnesses written in margin in 15th-cent. hand. Text from this point is from Cart. II.

---

[1] See no. 401, and Fees [21], [16], [24].   [2] See Fees [22].
[3] Perhaps one of the two detached seals in a packet, I. 12 Spec. 26·⁙· (see above, p. 7) belonged to this lost charter.

de Lile,*a* et R.¹ de Walvile,*b* et Ra(dulfo) de Puntfreit,*c* et Henrico de Monteforti, et Hugone de Rampan,*d* et Gosfrido de Lile.*e* Valete.

NOTE. For the date, see note to no. 5 below.

5 *Notification by Nigel d'Aubigny to Th(omas), archbishop of York, the sheriffs of York and Northumberland, and his brother William, of his restoration to Durham of the two manors which Waltheof son of Alsi held of him, namely Barmpton and Skerningham; and request to William to maintain the restoration.* [June 1109 × Feb. 1114]

> Original charter: Durham, D. & C. Archives, 1. 12 Specialium 26. Cartulary copies: Durham, Cartuarium Vetus fo. 64*v*, Cartuarium II fo. 209*r*; Bodl., Carte 177 fo. 41*r*. Also copied: B.M., Cotton MS. Claud. D iv fo. 62*v*. Pd., *Feod. Prior. Dunelm.* p. 152 n., from the original charter.

Th.'*f* Eboracensi archiepiscopo . et vicecomitibus Eboraci et de Nor-humbrelande . et omnibus baronibus . et Willelmo karissimo fratri suo . et omnibus amicis et hominibus suis Francis et Anglis . Nig(ellus) de Albini salutem et amicitiam. Sciat dilectio uestra amici karissimi quod ego pro dilectione Dei et redemptione animę meę reddidi et dedi Deo et Sancto CUTHBERTO et [ecclesi]ę*g* Dunelmensi illa duo maneria que Walthef filius Alsi de me teneb[at ultr]a*g* Teisa . uidelicet . Bermentune . et Schirlingeham . et quicquid a[d eas per]tinet.*g* Ideo autem ęcclesiam Dunelmensem et beatum Cuthbertum et nullum alium heredem de predictis terris facio . quia ecclesię illi iure ad[iac]ent*g* . nec eas amplius ad dampnationem animę meę retinere audeo [sed]*g* ecclesię illi et beato Cuthberto spontanea uoluntate reddo et don[o. Ma]ndo*g* igitur tibi et precor Willelme frater meus . ut sicut Deum et animam meam [diligis]*g* nullo modo hanc meam donationem uiolare presumas . sed fir[miter]*g* tenere studeas. T(estibus) Th.' archiepiscopo . et Mah-(ilde) coniuge mea . et Gwidone capell(ano) . et Hugone cap(ellano)*h*. et Rodb(erto) de Maisnil et W. de Lile . et Hug(one) de Rampan . et Rodb(erto) de Waluile . et Ric(ardo) de Dauiduile . et Henr(ico) de Monteforti . et Gosfrido de Lile . et Ric(ardo) de Giuarduile.

Endorsements: *De Bermet' et Scirn'* (12th cent.); *C. Nig' de Albein[. .] de vill'/ Prima .xii. [S]pecialium .E.2.* (later medieval hands).

Size: 15·8 × 12·1 cm.

a *Lyle,* Cart. Vet. margin.   *b* *Walevile,* Cart. Vet. margin.   *c* *Ponifrett,* Cart. Vet. margin.   *d* *Rampay',* Cart. Vet. margin.   *e* *Lyle,* Cart. Vet. margin.   *f* *Thome,* carts.   *g* Charter damaged; text supplied from Cart. Vet.   *h* Carts. and Cotton version end.

---

¹ Presumably Robert, cf. no. 5.

Seal: seal of Nigel d'Aubigny above (p. lxxxii), white wax varnished; on reverse, cross of St. Cuthbert rudely scratched in the wax, with the letters CU. Now detached, but formerly appended on tongue, with tie.

NOTE. The identification made in the cartulary copies, of archbishop 'Th' of the original charter with archbishop Thomas [II (June 1109–Feb. 1114)],[1] is rendered virtually certain by the appearance in the witness-list of Maud de Laigle, the first wife of Nigel d'Aubigny, whom he repudiated in 1118. Thurstan, although elected and enthroned in 1114, was not consecrated until Oct. 1119 and was out of the country for much of the intervening period, and is therefore most unlikely to be identified as 'Th'. 'Thomas' is written in full in the texts of nos. 6 and 10, and Maud appears also in nos. 7 and 10. The witness-list of the present charter is so similar to those of nos. 7, 9, and 10, that it must be regarded as certain that all four charters were given on the same occasion. The phraseology and content of these charters strongly suggest that they are of an even date with nos. 2–4, 6, and 8. The entire series nos. 2–10, therefore, has been assigned to the period of Thomas's archiepiscopate, June 1109–Feb. 1114.

6 *Notification by Nigel d'Aubigny to Thomas, archbishop of York, of his concession to Durham of the land of Barmpton.*

[June 1109 × Feb. 1114]

Cartulary copies: Durham, D. & C. Archives, Cartuarium Vetus fo. 64*r*, and Cartuarium II fo. 209*r*; Bodl., MS. Carte 177 fo. 41*r*. (Original charter lost, formerly Durham D. & C., 1.12 Specialium 27, in Repertorium Magnum.) Pd., *Feod. Prior. Dunelm.* p. 152 n., from Cartuarium II.

Thome archiepiscopo Eboracensi et omnibus baronibus et fidelibus regis et suis Nigellus de Albinico*a* salutem. Sciatis me concessisse pro anima patris et matris mee et redemptione peccatorum meorum ecclesie Sancti Cuthberti terram de Bermetun*b* quietam et solutam de omni servicio. Testibus,*c* Rodberto de Sigillo etc.

NOTE. Probably of even date with nos. 2–5 and 7–10, see note to no. 5 above.

7 *Notification by Nigel d'Aubigny to Th(omas), archbishop of York, the sheriff and barons of Yorkshire, and his brother William, of his restoration to St. Peter's hospital, York, of 2 carucates in Upper Helmsley (Yorks., N.R.) which he had taken from them, and of his gift of Thornton (? Bridge, Yorks., N.R.) to William son of Warin, in exchange for those 2 carucates.*

[June 1109 × Feb. 1114]

a *Albini*, Cart. II.   *b* *Bermeton'*, Carte II; *Bermetona*, Bodl. Carte   *c* Cart. Vet. and Bodl. Carte versions end here.

---

[1] Sir Charles Clay's analysis of the charters of Thomas and Thurstan, archbishops of York, suggests that 'Th.' was the usual abbreviation for Thomas, and that Thurstan was usually abbreviated as 'T.' (see *Y.A.J.* xxxvi (1945) 134–5).

Cartulary copy: York, D. & C. Muniments, Registrum Magnum Album III
fo. *29r.*
Pd., *Historians of the Church of York,* ed. J. Raine (R.S. lxxi) iii no. xxxviii.

Th(ome) Ebor(acensi) archiepiscopo et vicecomiti et omnibus baronibus comitatus Ebor(acensis) et Willelmo fratri suo et omnibus amicis et omnibus suis Francis et Anglis Nigellus de Albeni salutem et amicitiam. Sciat dilectio vestra amici karissimi quod ego pro dilectione Dei et redemptione anime mee reddidi et dedi Deo et Sancto Petro et ecclesie Ebor(acensi) et victui pauperum fratrum qui ecclesie illi adjacent ij carucatas terre in Hameseie quas ego eis abstuleram et Willelmo filio Warini cui eas dederam dono Thornetun in excambio videlicet quatuor carucatas terre cum omnibus hominibus qui in eis sunt. Mando igitur tibi et precor Willelme frater meus ut sicut Deum et animam diligis nullo modo hanc meam donationem violare presumas sed firmiter tenere studeas. T(estibus), Th(ome) archiepiscopo, et R. Dunelm(ensi) episcopo,[1] et Math(ilde) conjuge mea, et Guidone cap(ellano), et Roberto de Mainil, et Hugone de Rampan, et Henrico de Monte forti.

NOTE. For the date see note to no. 5 above.
Thornton Bridge later formed part of the Daiville fee,[2] and the sub-tenant at the end of the 12th century was Ranulf de Sules.[3]

8 *Notification by Nigel d'Aubigny to [Thomas,] archbishop of York, of his restoration to the church of All Saints, Fishergate, York (cell of Whitby, Ben., Yorks. N.R.), and prior Serlo, of ½ carucate in (Middle)thorpe with the tenants therein.*   [June 1109 × Feb. 1114]

Cartulary copy: cartulary of Whitby, in the possession of Miss M. L. A. Strickland of Whitwell, York, fo. *65v.*
Pd., *Whitby Cart.* i no. 261.

Thome[a] venerabili archiepiscopo Ebor(acensi) ecclesie et karissimo[b] domino suo et amico et omnibus Sancti Dei ecclesie cultoribus et amicis suis Nigellus de Albinni salutabiles[c] famulatus. Notum sit tam futuris quam presentibus quod ego reddidi Deo et ecclesie Omnium Sanctorum dimidiam carucatam terre in Thorp, cum ospitibus qui in ea sunt, scilicet ecclesie que est in Fisergate apud Eboracum, quam volo ut Serlo prior habeat, et alii monachi ejusdem loci. [Testibus][d] vobis Thom(a), et Rann(ulfo) Dunelmensi episcopo, et Ricardo Sancti Albani abbate, et Guidone capellano meo, et aliis.

a Johanne, MS.   *b kõmo,* MS.   *c salutibiles,* MS.   *d* Omitted in MS.

---

[1] Ranulf Flambard.   [2] See Fees [24].   [3] *V.C.H. Yorks. N.R.* ii 101.

NOTE. For the date, see note to no. 5 above.

The church of All Saints had been given to Whitby by king William Rufus, probably in 1091 or 1092.[1] Serlo the prior is probably Serlo the monk of nos. 2 and 3.

9 *Notification by Nigel d'Aubigny to R(obert Bloet), bishop of Lincoln, the sheriff and barons of Lincolnshire, and William his brother, of his gift to Selby for lighting their church, of one carucate in Amcotts (Axholme, Lincs.).*   [June 1109 × Feb. 1114]

> Cartulary copy: B.M., Add. MS. 37771 fo. 208r (old fo. 205r).
> Pd., *Selby Coucher* ii no. 1215, and (incompletely) *Mon. Ang.* iii 500 (X).

R. Lincoln(iensi) episcopo [et]ᵃ vic(ecomiti) et baron(ibus) comitatus Linc(olnie) et Willelmo fratri suo et omnibus amicis et hominibus suis Francis et Anglis Nigellus de Albini salutem. Notum sit omnibus vobis quod ego pro redemptione anime mee dedi Sancto Germano et monachis de Seleby ad luminare ejusdem ecclesie unam carucatam in Amecotes cum omnibus que ei adjacent, in puram elemosinam liberam et quietam ab omni seculari servicio. Test(ibus), Th(oma) archiepiscopo, et R. Dunelm(ensi) episcopo[2] etc.

NOTE. For the date, see note to no. 5 above.

10 *Notification by Nigel d'Aubigny to R(obert de Limesey), bishop of Chester, and W(illiam de Montfort), abbot, and the congregation of Bec, of his gift to Bec of Smite (Warwicks.), for the monks' kitchen, with the consent of R(obert) count of Meulan.*   [June 1109 × Feb. 1114]

> Pd., *Select Documents of the English Lands of the Abbey of Bec*, ed. M. M. Chibnall (Camden 3rd ser. lxxiii) no. xxxv, from Windsor, St. George's Chapel, D. & C. Muniments, XI. G. 11, charter roll.

R. Cestrensi episcopo et W. Beccensis ecclesie abbati omnique congregationi sibi commisse et omnibus fidelibus suis tam Francis quam Anglis, Nigellus de Albin' salutem. Sciat dilectio vestra amici mei et domini quod ego pro Dei dilectione et anime mee redemptione dedi Deo et Sancte Marie Becci Esmitam cum omnibus adjacentibus tam in pratis quam in planis et nemoribus, et nominatim ad coquinam monachorum. Hanc vero donationem sciatis me fecisse concessione domini R. comitis

---

ᵃ Omitted in MS.

---

[1] *E.Y.C.* ii no. 863; also pd. *Whitby Cart.* ii no. 527; cal. *Regesta* i no. 421.
[2] Ranulf Flambard.

Mellenti. Testibus, Thoma Eboracen(si) episcopo, et Rannulfo Dunelmensi episcopo, et M.[1] uxore mea, et Guidone capellano et aliis.

NOTE. This charter clearly belongs to the same series as nos. 2–9 above; cf. note to no. 5.

11 *Notification by Nigel d'Aubigny to A(ubrey) de Vere, of his concession to Bec of £20 worth of land in Dunton (Essex), with the same stock as William de Arches held there of him, and the church of Dunton after the death of Guy his chaplain, in exchange for Smite, which he had previously given; and precept to Aubrey to give the monks seisin of the land at Martinmas.*

[1109 × 1124]

Pd., *Select Documents of Bec* no. xxv, from charter roll (see above, no. 10).

Nigellus de Alb' A. de Ver salutem. Scias me concessisse et reddidisse ecclesie Sancte Marie Beccen' xx libratas terre in Dontona in Essessa, scilicet domos et nemus et totum dominium et ecclesiam post mortem Guidonis capellani mei, cum illa instauratione cum qua Willelmus de Arch' eam de me habuit, pro escambio terre de Smit(a) quam ante dederam Sancte Marie, et superplus siquid fuerit habeat Willelmus de instauratione, si vero minus perficiatur de suo. Et volo et precipio ut monachos de predicta terra saisias et a festo Sancti Martini in antea habeant inde omnes redditus ad illam terram pertinentes, et teneant bene et quiete et honorabiliter sicut unquam melius et quietius eam habui. Et scias tu et homines mei et amici me hoc fecisse de terra supradicta benigno concessu uxoris mee, existentibus hujus rei Sansone nepote meo, Alveredo camerario et pluribus aliis.

NOTE. This charter provides the earliest evidence that Nigel d'Aubigny had been granted the overlordship of William de Arches.

12 *Gift by Nigel d'Aubigny to St. Mary's, York, of lands and tithes, unspecified.*   [c. 1107 × 1129]

Confirmation by Roger de Mowbray: pd., *E.Y.C.* ix no. 136, cal. no. 316 below.

13 *Confirmation by Nigel d'Aubigny to St. Nicholas, Angers (i.e. dependency at Monks Kirby, Warwicks.), of gifts made by Geoffrey de La Guerche, of the church of Kirby and the chapel of 'Hildebrok',[2] the manor of Copston (Magna), and the tithes of Kirby, Brockhurst, Wappenbury, Newbold (on*

---

[1] Maud de Laigle.
[2] This is probably Withybrook, the advowson of which belonged to Monks Kirby priory (cf. W. Dugdale, *Antiquities of Warwicks.* 2nd edn. W. Thomas (1730) i 75).

Avon), (*Long*) *Lawford, Hampton in Arden* (*all Warwicks.*), *Crick*
(*Northants.*), *Melton* (*Mowbray*) (*Leics.*), *and Axholme* (*Lincs.*); *and
additional gift of the church of Newbold* (*on Avon*).   [1109 × 1129]

Inspeximus of 1285: Gregory-Hood deeds deposited at Stratford on Avon,
Shakespeare Birthplace Trust Libr., Gregory-Hood Ch. 519 (5).

Sciant omnes tam presentes quam futuri quod ego Nigellus Dei gratia
de Albiniaco pro salute domini mei Regis Henrici et pro remedio anime
mee omniumque parentum affinium et amicorum cunctorumque predecessorum et successorum meorum imperpetuum tam vivorum quam
defunctorum, concedo Deo et ecclesie beati Nicholai Andegavis et
monachis inibi Deo servientibus in manu domni Lamberti predicte
ecclesie abbatis omnes possessiones quas Gausfridus de Wirchia eis in
elemosinam dedit, et elemosinas omnes quas homines ejusdem Gausfridi
servientibus Sancti Nicholai per maneria sua contulerunt. Concedo
dico*a* scilicet ecclesiam de Chircheberia et capellam de Hildebrok, que
adjacet predicte ecclesie, cum omnibus decimis et molendino et terris
que ipsi et homines sui habent in Chircheberia et in Brocaherst. Et
totum manerium de Copestuna cum omnibus appendiciis suis. Et
preterea decimas de dominio maneriorum istorum: Wappenberie,
Newebold, Leleford, Crece, Meltune, Hamptuna, Axiholm, in bladio
et pecunia, in caseo et lana, in pisce et pasnagio, in theloniis et molendinis et hominibus quos in eisdem maneriis ad colligendas et conservandas
decimas suas possident. Et volo ut ita firme et libere et quiete et honorifice
usque in eternum habeant et teneant, sicuti tempore Gausfridi de Wirchia
firmius, liberius, quietius et honorificentius habuerunt et tenuerunt,
qui primus predicta beneficia contulit Deo et Sancto Nicholao. Superque
hec omnia adicio eis ex mea parte et do ecclesiam de Newebold in elemosinam cum decimis et terris et possessionibus ad eandem ecclesiam
pertinentibus et quicquid Baldricus presbyter tenet, post mortem ejus
habeant et teneant. Et de omnibus incrementis et instaurationibus que
faciam in dominio omnium maneriorum que fuerunt Gausfridi de
Wirchia, scilicet in carucis et molendinis et restaurationibus pecuniarum
et omnium rerum de quibus decima reddi debet in quibus maneriis
monachi decimas tenent, do eis decimam. Et in Chircheberia dono et
concedo pecunie eorum pasturam cum mea propria pecunia in omnibus
locis, et hominibus eorum ubicunque sint pasturam cum hominibus
meis ubique communem. Et ita firme et stabiliter hec omnia Deo et
Sancto Nicholao concedo et dono sicuti aliquis umquam alicui ecclesie
elemosinam firmius et stabilius concessit et dedit, cum soka et saca et

a Sic in MS., perhaps for *concedo et dico* (instead of the more usual *do*).

toll et team et infanghenefetheof. Hanc vero concessionem et donationem posui ego Nigellus super altare Sancti Nicholai in Chircheberia cum textu Ewangelii, presente Lamberto abbate, cum quo abbatum beneficia et fraternitatem Andegavensis ecclesie beati Nicholai susceperam. Ipse vero abbas et fratres qui cum eo erant concesserunt michi ex parte sua et ex parte tocius conventus tantum post obitum meum fieri pro me quantum pro uno eorum abbate. Hujus rei testes sunt: Rogerius de Camvilla, Wielardus de Wapenberia, Willelmus de Insula, Gausfridus de Morvilla, Ricardus de David villa, Rogerus de Niweham, et alii multi ex parte Nigelli; ex parte vero abbatis: Theobaldus magnus, Theobaldus minor, Johannes de Sancto Georgio, Ranulphus, Rotholandus monachi; de laicis: Petrus Haldene, Michael camerarius, David Lancea acuta, Sawardus cocus, Salidus diaconus et multi alii quos longum est enumerare.

NOTE. The charter should presumably be dated after nos. 2 and 3, i.e. after 1109.

14 *Gift by Nigel d'Aubigny to Pontigny (Cist., Yonne, France) of land in Aldburgh (Yorks., N.R.) on the east bank of the River Ure.* [1114 × 1129]

Reference in a charter of Roger de Mowbray for Fountains: no. 95 below.

NOTE. Pontigny was founded in 1114. It is possible that Pontigny intended to have a daughter-house in Yorkshire, but nothing came of it, and by 1145 the land at Aldburgh had been given to Fountains.

15 *Notification by Nigel d'Aubigny to Guy the chaplain and Jeralmus and all his bailiffs and men of the Isle of Axholme (Lincs.), of his gift to the 'monastery' of Hirst and Ralph, the canon of Nostell (Aug., Yorks., W.R.) staying there, and all canons staying there subsequently, of the dwelling-place of Hirst (Axholme), the wood for assarting, and the marsh, and various foodrents, etc.* [1121 × 1129, perhaps 1121 or 1122]

Cartulary copy: B.M., Cotton MS. Vesp. E xix fo. 131r (old p. 323).
Pd., *Mon. Ang.* vi (1) 101 (I).

Nigellus de Albun' Widoni cap(ellano) et Jeralmo et omnibus ballivis et omnibus hominibus suis de Insula salutem. Sciatis me dedisse et concessisse monasterio de Hyrst et Radulfo canonico ibidem inhabitanti et post ipsum Radulfum canonicis ibi Deo servientibus in manu semper prioris Sancti Osuualdi, pro Dei amore et pro salute anime mee, in puram et perpetuam elemosinam, habitationem in Hyrst et totum illud nemus ad sartandum et ad usus suos et marais quod est circa Hirst et de Hirst usque in Don, et xv solidos et quatuor sesteras de brais et quatuor sesteras frumenti et quatuor sesteras siliginis et dimidium .M. anguillarum in uno quoque anno. Et concedo eis commune ubique in bosco et in plano, in pascuis et in aquis. Et precipio quod annona ipsorum sit molendinata in molendino meo super Trentam in Insula sine multura et post illam annonam quam invenient in tremeia. Test' etc.

NOTE. There had probably been a settlement of clerks at Nostell since 1114, perhaps ruled by the Ralph of the present charter. In 1121 or 1122, when the Augustinian priory was established with Adelulf (later bishop of Carlisle) as prior, Ralph may have gone to live at the cell of Hirst. He is perhaps to be identified with 'Ralph Aldlaue', who is said to have died on 12 May 1128.[1]
An abstract of this charter is inserted before the table of contents of the cartulary of Selby.[2]

16 *Gift by Nigel d'Aubigny to Saint-Évroult (Ben., Orne, arr. Argentan, cant. La Ferté-Fresnel, France) of 2 parts of the tithes of Villers (?-en-Ouche, arr. Argentan, cant. La Ferté-Fresnel).*   [probably 1124 × 1129]

Confirmation by Henry I [1124 × 1129]: cartulary copy, Paris, Bibl. Nat. MS. Lat. 11056 fo. 25v.
Pd., *Ord. Vit.* v 202; cal. *Regesta* ii no. 1595.

... duas partes decime de Vilers, quas Nigellus de Albineio eis dedit, scilicet duas garbas de dominio et de tota villa, et duas partes decime similiter de vitulis et agnis et porcellis, et de ortis tocius ville, et de illis rebus de quibus consuetudo est, et de caseis et de lana et de omnibus rebus de quibus decima juste debet dari, et duas partes etiam decime de molendino ejusdem ville ...

17 *Gift by Nigel d'Aubigny to Saint-Évroult of 2 parts of the tithes of Villers; and agreement concerning 'Cullei' (Rabodanges, Orne, arr. Argentan, cant. Putanges), which the monks conceded to Nigel (excepting the church and 2 parts of the tithes), for which Nigel was to render to the king the service of one knight.*   [probably 1124 × 1129]

Confirmation by Henry I [1124 × 1129]: Paris, Bibl. Nat., MS. Lat. 11055 fo. 21r–v.
Pd., *Ord. Vit.* v 200–1; cal. *Regesta* ii no. 1595.

... duas partes tocius decime de Villaris, garbarum videlicet lini, canabi et leguminum et ortorum et fructuum omnium virgultorum ejusdem ville et omnium de quibus decima juste dari debet, habendas

---

[1] See A. H. Thompson, *Priory of St. Mary, Bolton* (Thoresby Soc. xxx) 24–30, whose account is more convincing than that of W. E. Wightman, 'Henry I and the foundation of Nostell priory', *Y.A.J.* xli (1963) 57–60.
[2] *Selby Coucher* i 2.

et possidendas de dono et largitione predicti Nigelli meaque concessione et confirmatione in perpetuam, liberam et quietam elemosinam, ita quod de ea nemini preter Deum servicium aliquod facere tenebuntur. Concedo preterea et presenti carta mea confirmo prefatis abbati et monachis subscriptam conventionem inter eos et sepe dictum Nigellum in presencia mea factam super villa que Culleium dicitur super Olnam. Concesserunt namque idem abbas et monachi memorato Nigello quicquid habebant in supradicta villa, quam de dono dominorum Gretesmenil*a* in elemosina possidebant, tenendum de ipsis abbate et monachis in feodum et hereditatem, excepta ecclesia cum duabus omnium decimarum suarum et molendinorum ejusdem ville partibus, ita quod per eorum manum et submonitionem servicium unius militis quod inde michi debetur faciet prefatus Nigellus in meis negociis et exercitibus, et pro relevamento terre et regalibus serviciis et taliis abbatie Sancti Ebrulfi a me vel heredibus meis concessis, licebit prefatis abbati et monachis in eadem villa justiciam suam facere quociens sibi viderint expedire, nec poterit idem Nigellus vel heredes ejus milites vel alios homines ejusdem ville ad alias consuetudines trahere quam ad eas quas de jure debebant abbati et monachis Sancti Ebrulfi facere, quin abbas et monachi, si clamorem inde fecerint, justiciam super eum faciant in illa villa donec congrue emendetur. Similiter et pro omnibus forifactis aliis et emendis ipsius Nigelli versus abbatem et predictos monachos . . .

NOTE. Although the royal charter cannot be accepted as it stands, for there is obviously much interpolation, it may well have been based on a genuine agreement concerning Cullei made at the same time as the grant of the tithe of Villers.[1]

18 *Confirmation by Alan 'comes Anglie et Britannie' to Roger de Mowbray of Masham (Yorks., N.R.) with its appurtenances, by specified bounds, to hold as Nigel d'Aubigny his father held it of count Stephen, Alan's father, for the service of one knight; and quitclaim of any other right after the acquittance of the pledge of Masham, which had been made by Roger to Alan for 100 marks silver.* [1138 × 1145]

Pd., *E.Y.C.* iv no. 19, from P.R.O., Pat. Roll 20 Hen. VI pt. ii (C. 66/452) m. 6. Also pd., *C.P.R. 1441–6* p. 72, and *Registrum Honoris de Richmond* [ed. R. Gale] (1722) app. no. clxvii.

Testibus, Scolland' seneschaldo, Radulfo filio Rib(aldi), Hugone filio Gernag(ani), Herveio filio Acharii, Rogero filio Gieumer, Alano

a Sic in MS.

[1] For a discussion of the Cullei agreement, see C. H. Haskins, *Norman Institutions* (Cambridge, Mass., 1918) pp. 11–14.

pincerna, Roberto le chamberleng, Copsi filio Arkilli, Theobaldo clerico, Sansone de Albeni, Bertram Haget, Aldelino de Aldefeld'.

> NOTE. The charter clearly records a genuine grant and a genuine witness-list, although its boundaries are obviously interpolated. See *E.Y.C.* iv 21–2.

19 *Confirmation by John, count of Eu, to Roger de Mowbray of the whole fief which Roger's father held of the count's father at Bazoches-en-Houlme (Orne, arr. Argentan, cant. Putanges), and release of the £20 which the count was entitled to receive.*   26 August 1154

> Transcript, from an original charter formerly in the Archives of Manche:[1]
> P.R.O., Transcripts (Léchaudé d'Anisy's Cartulaire de la Basse-Normandie)
> P.R.O. 31/8/140B pt. ii pp. 33–4.
> Pd. (abstract), *Cal. Docs. France* no. 595, from the transcript.

In nomine Sancte et Individue Trinitatis. Notum sit etc. quod ego Johannes Dei gratia comes Augensis concessi et reddidi domino Rogero de Molbraio totum feodum quod pater suus a patre meo tenuit apud Basecas et preter hoc donavi ei et concessi de jure meo illas xx libras quas pater suus patri meo pro eodem feodo reddere consueverat. Pro hac autem donatione et concessione idem Rogerus de Molbraio dedit michi unum dextrarium et lx libras Andegavensium. Teste Roberto de Sancto Petro, Henrico Hose, Guidone de Boveincurt, Fretello de Sancto Hylario, Roberto de Gillemercurt, Hugone de Gurnaio, Galeranno vicecomite Lexoviens', Roberto de Buzi, Olivero de Auge et Savarino fratre ejus, Roberto de Crevecort, Henrico de Rumera, Radulfo de Meholdini et Willelmo fratre ejus. Anno ab incarnatione Domini MCLIIII, vij kalendas Septembris, Rege Francorum Ludovico, duce Normannorum Henrico.

20 *Confirmation by Roger de Mowbray to Arden (Ben. nuns, Yorks., N.R.) of the conventual site and 3 carucates in Arden, given by Peter de Hotona.*
[*c.* 1147×1169]

> Memorandum of 2 Feb. 1405: B.M., Add. Ch. 20544.
> Pd., *Mon. Ang.* iv 285 (I), from a document formerly in the Hatton library (? now the Add. Ch.).

Universis sancte ecclesie filiis Rogerus de Mowbray salutem. Notum sit vobis me concessisse et presenti carta confirmasse pro salute mea et meorum Deo et Sancto Andree et sanctimonialibus de Ardena, in liberam et perpetuam elemosinam et ab omni terreno servicio imperpetuum quietam et liberam et nulli alii abbathie subjectam, donationem

---

[1] Destroyed at Saint-Lô in 1944.

Petri de Hotona quam fecit et carta sua confirmavit predictis sanctimonialibus in liberam et perpetuam elemosinam, scilicet ipsum locum
ubi abbathia sedet cum tribus carucatis terre in prefata Herdena, cum
omnibus pertinenciis suis et libertatibus in bosco, in plano et in mora
et in pascuis et in stagnis et in molendinis. Hiis testibus, Rogero de
Flammavilla, Bertram Haget, Hamund Beler, Willelmo filio Eng[e]l-
(rami), Radulfo de Belvaer, Radulfo canonico et aliis.

> NOTE. William son of Engelram's first occurrence belongs to *c.* 1147 × *c.* 1154,
> possibly *c.* 1147 (no. 200). Roger de Flamville had probably died by 1169 (no.
> 377 note). If the Bertram Haget in the witness-list is the elder Bertram, the
> date could be put back to before 1165, for he had been succeeded by William
> Haget by that date (no. 363 note).
>
> Peter de Hotona (? Sand Hutton) was probably the same man as Peter
> of Thirsk, a sub-tenant of Malebisse (see no. 240 note).

21 *Gift by R(oger) de Mowbray to Bridlington (Aug., Yorks., E.R.) of one
carucate in Fraisthorpe (E.R.) and ½ carucate in Marton (par. Bridlington).*
[1142 × *c.* 1150]

Cartulary copy: B.M., Add. MS. 40008 fo. 157r (old fo. 153r).
Pd., *Abstract of the Chart. of Bridlington*, ed. W. T. Lancaster (Leeds, 1912)
p. 206.

Omnibus ecclesie fidelibus R. de Moubray salutem. Sciatis me concessisse et dedisse in perpetuam elemosinam Deo et Sancte Marie et
canonicis de Brid(elintona) unam carrucatam terre de feudo meo in
Fraistingthorp' et dimidiam carrucatam in Martona liberam et quietam
et solutam ab omnibus rebus et serviciis sicut justam et legitimam elemosinam meam. Hiis testibus, Gund(reda) matre ejus, Mathia de Ropeyn
et Gilberto fratre ejus, abbate de Begdland,[1] priore de Novoburgo,[2]
Olivero de Bosceio, Radulfo de Widvilla, Waltero de Riva.

> NOTE. The appearance of the prior of Newburgh indicates that this gift was
> made after 1142, perhaps even after *c.* 1145. Matthew de Rampan does not
> occur after *c.* 1150 (see note to no. 35). The land here given was confirmed to
> Bridlington by pope Eugenius III before 1153.[3]

22 *Gift by R(oger) de Mowbray to Bridlington of one carucate in Fraisthorpe
and ½ carucate in Marton; and confirmation of one carucate in Sherburn
(Yorks., E.R.), given by Robert de Wyville.*   [*c.* 1154 × 1169]

Cartulary copy: B.M., Add. MS. 40008 fo. 166r (old fo. 162r).
Pd. (transl.), *Abstract of the Chart. of Bridlington* p. 216.

R. de Molbray universis sancte ecclesie filiis salutem. Sciatis me dedisse ecclesie Sancte Marie de Bridel(intona) et canonicis ibidem Deo

---

[1] Roger.   [2] Augustine.   [3] *P.U.E.* iii no. 87.

servientibus in elemosinam liberam et ab omni re preter Danageldum quietam unam carucatam terre in Freistingthorp et dimidiam carucatam terre in Martona. Preterea ecclesie Sancte Marie de Brid(elintona) concessi et hac mea carta confirmavi unam carucatam terre in Schirburn' quam Robertus de Withvilla ecclesie Sancte Marie predicte dedit in elemosinam liberam et quietam ab omni re preter Danegeld'. Hiis testibus, Rogero de Condeio, Rogero de Flamevilla, Waltero de Lariver, Hugone Malebissa, Thoma de Colevilla, Roberto de Buscy, Hamone Belier, Waltero de Carletona, Roberto de Crevequer, Rogero de Daltona, Waltero Buer'.

NOTE. Thomas de Coleville first occurs after 1154 (see no. 356 note). Roger de Flamville probably died by 1169 (no. 377 note). If Walter of Carlton was the man of that name who was father of Roger of Carlton, he was probably dead by 1166 (nos. 352–3 notes).

Robert de Wyville occurs in a charter of 1109 × 1114 (no. 3), and last occurs 1130 × 1136.[1] It seems likely that his gift in Sherburn had been made some time before Mowbray's confirmation in the present charter, and certainly before 1153, for it was confirmed by pope Eugenius III.[2] For the Wyville fee, see Fees [21].

23 *Gift by Roger de Mowbray to the lepers of St. Lazarus, Jerusalem (Burton Lazars, Leics.) of 2 carucates, a messuage, and the site of a mill in Burton Lazars.* [*c.* 1154 × Sept. 1162]

Cartulary copy: B.M., Cotton MS. Nero C xii fo. 3*r* (old p. 1).
Pd., *Mon. Ang.* vi (2) 632 (I), and Nichols, *Leics.* ii (1) app. p. 128.

In nomine patris et filii et spiritus sancti amen. Rogerus de Moubrei omnibus hominibus suis et amicis Francis et Anglis tam futuris quam presentibus salutem. Sciatis me dedisse et hac presenti carta mea confirmasse Deo et Sancte Marie et leprosis Sancti Lazari Jerusalem duas carugatas terre in Burtona et super aquam ejusdem ville masagium unum et sedem cujusdam molendini, pro salute anime mee et pro anima patris mei et matris mee et pro animabus antecessorum meorum, tenendum de me et de heredibus meis in perpetuam elemosinam libere et quiete ab omni seculari actione. Preterea sciatis me concessisse et hac carta mea bono animo et bona voluntate confirmasse Deo et Sancte Marie et leprosis Sancti Lazari de Jerusalem quicquid homines mei eis dederunt vel daturi sunt in terris in aquis in pratis in pascuis in nemoribus in planis in pecuniis tenendum de eis in perpetuam elemosinam libere et quiete ab omni seculari servicio. T(estibus), Nigello filio meo, Rodberto

[1] *E.Y.C.* ii no. 783; cf. *P.R. 31 Hen. I* p. 137.
[2] *P.U.E.* iii no. 87.

filio meo, Rodberto de Aivilla, Hugone Mal'bissa, Radulfo de Belverico, Thoma de Colevilla, Oliver de Busci, Roberto fratre suo, Roberto capellano meo.

NOTE. Thomas de Coleville first occurs after 1154 (no. 356 note). This charter is probably the foundation charter of the hospital of Burton Lazars, which was certainly in existence by Sept. 1162.[1] Oliver de Buscy had been succeeded by Robert de Buscy by 1166 (no. 401).

24 *Gift by Roger de Mowbray to the hospital of Burton Lazars of 3 marks from the rents of his mills in the castle of Thirsk (Yorks., N.R.); also gifts by Herbert and Ralph of Queniborough.*   [*c.* 1154×1165]

Cartulary copy: B.M., Cotton MS. Nero C xii fo. 3*v* (old p. 2).

In nomine patris et filii et spiritus sancti amen. Notum sit omnibus tam futuris quam presentibus quod ego Rogerus de Molbray dono [et]*a* concedo leprosis Sancti Lazari de Hierl'm pro salute anime mee et pro animabus omnium parentum meorum patris matris mee filiorum et omnium amicorum meorum in castello de Tresch tres marcas de propriis reditibus scilicet molendinorum meorum. Et hoc confirmo literis meis et signo sigillo meo ut donum meum ratum sit usque imperpetuum. Teste Herberto de Cunniburgo qui dat ac etiam predictis leprosis de reditibus molendini sui in Cocowaldo[2] uno quoque anno dimidiam marcam argenti pro remedio anime sue; Redulfo*b* quoque teste de Conniburgo qui eisdem leprosis dat pro anima sua uno quoque anno dimidiam marcam. Valete.

NOTE. If no. 23 is the foundation charter of the hospital, this gift must belong to the period after *c.* 1154. Herbert of Queniborough had been succeeded by his brother Ralph by 1166 (no. 401).[3]

25 *Gift by Nigel de Mowbray to the hospital of Burton Lazars of Peter son of Geoffrey and his tenement in Kirby (Bellars) (Leics.).*

[*c.* 1170×1184]

Cartulary copy: B.M., Cotton MS. Nero C xii fo. 45*r* (old p. 93).

Nigellus de Moubrai omnibus sancte matris ecclesie filiis presentibus et futuris salutem. Sciatis me dedisse et concessisse et hac carta mea confirmasse Deo et fratribus leprosis de Sancto Lazaro de Jerusalem Petrum filium Galfridi et ten(ementum) suum totum, scilicet dimidiam carucatam terre et quartam partem molendini de Kirkebi, in puram et

---

a Omitted in MS.   *b* *Sic.*

---

[1] *P.R. 8 Hen. II* p. 2.   [2] Coxwold, Yorks., N.R.   [3] And see Fees [15].

perpetuam elemosinam libere et quiete tenendum ab omnibus secularibus serviciis et exactionibus pro salute anime mee et animarum antecessorum meorum. Hiis testibus, comite Simone, Roberto de Moubr',
Hugone Maleb', Hamone Beler, Roberto de Borci, Philippo de Munpincun, Roberto de Bellocampo, Roberto Beler, Willelmo cam(erario)
et aliis multis.

NOTE. Philip de Montpincon does not occur before *c.* 1170 (no. 376 note).
Simon, earl of Huntingdon, died in 1184.[1] Five of these witnesses occur in
no. 59, and four in no. 141, both of *c.* 1181.

26 *Confirmation by Roger de Mowbray to the hospital of Burton Lazars of*
Peter son of Geoffrey of Kirby (Bellars) with his tenement, given by Gilbert
de Rampan and Nigel de Mowbray. [*c.* 1170 × 1184]

Cartulary copy: B.M., Cotton MS. Nero C xii fo. 45*r* (old p. 93).

Rogerus de Moubr' omnibus sancte matris ecclesie filiis presentibus et
futuris salutem. Sciatis me concessisse et presenti carta mea confirmasse
Deo et fratribus leprosis Sancti Lazari de Jerusalem donationem quam
Gilbertus de Rampayn et Nigellus filius meus eisdem fecerunt Petrum
scilicet filium Gaufridi de Kirkebi cum toto ten(emento) suo, scilicet
dimidiam carucatam terre et quartam partem unius molendini, in puram
et perpetuam elemosinam possidenda libera et quieta ab omni exactione
et servicio seculari pro salute anime mee et animarum omnium antecessorum meorum. Hiis testibus, comite Simone, Roberto de Moubr', Hugone
Maleb', Hamone Beler, Roberto de Boci, Roberto de Bellocampo, Willelmo camerario, Roberto Beler, Philippo de Munpincun et aliis multis.

NOTE. For the date, see note to no. 25. In 1166 Hugh de Rampan held
one fee.[2]

27 *Gift by Roger de Mowbray to the hospital of Burton Lazars of 2s. p.a. from*
the rent of the mill of Masham (Yorks., N.R.). [*c.* 1166 × 1186]

Cartulary copy: B.M., Cotton MS. Nero C xii fo. 4*v* (old p. 4).

Universis sancte ecclesie filiis Rogerus de Moulbrai salutem. Notum sit
omnibus tam presentibus quam futuris me dedisse et presenti carta
confirmasse in liberam et perpetuam elemosinam Deo et Sancto Lazaro
de Jerusalem duos solidos in molendino de Massam pro anima Walteri
de Buri. Quicunque predictum molendinum tenuerit reddet fratribus de
Sancto Lazaro de Jerusalem annuatim predictum censum ad festivitatem
Sancti Michaelis. Hiis testibus, Ricardo priore de Novoburgo, Roberto

---

[1] See *Complete Peerage* vi 645.   [2] No. 401, Fees [16].

de Daivilla, Radulfo de Baver, Thoma de Colevilla, Turgisio filio
Ma[l]g(eri), Roberto Beler, Wilardo de Sancto Agn', Roberto capellano.

NOTE. Walter Buher last occurs *c.* 1166 × 1173 (nos. 305–6) and was dead by
1177.[1] Richard, prior of Newburgh, last occurs in Nov. 1181, and had been
succeeded by Sept. 1186.[2] If the gift was made shortly after the death of Walter
Buher, as seems likely, a date between *c.* 1170 and *c.* 1176 is probable. 'Wilard
de Sancto Agn'', who occurs as 'Wielard de Seint Annhel' in no. 109, is
perhaps to be identified with 'Eulard de Sancto Aniano', who witnesses a charter of Walter Buher.[3]

28 *Gift by Roger de Mowbray to the hospital of Burton Lazars of 2s. p.a. from
the rent of the mill of Masham.* [*c.* 1166 × 1186]

Cartulary copy: B.M., Cotton MS. Nero C xii fo. 4*v* (old p. 4).

Notum sit omnibus sancte matris ecclesie filiis presentibus et futuris
quod ego Rogerus de Molbraio dedi et hac mea carta confirmavi Deo
et Sancte Marie et leprosis de Sancta Civitate de Jerusalem duos solidos
sterlingorum de redditu molendini de Massam a quocunque predictum
tenente molendinum recipiendos annuatim ad festum Sancti Michaelis,
in liberam et quietam et puram et perpetuam elemosinam pro anima
Walteri Buhere et pro salute anime mee et omnium antecessorum
meorum. T(estibus) his, Nigello de Molbraio, Roberto de Daievilla,
Hugone Malebisse, Radulfo de Belveer, Willelmo de Daievilla, Roberto
de Belveer, Roberto capellano ad capell(am), Roberto de Bello campo,
Roberto filio Rogeri, Waltero de Maisnil et aliis multis tam clericis quam
laicis.

NOTE. For the date, see note to no. 27.

29 *Gift by Nigel de Mowbray to the hospital of Burton Lazars of the tenement
of Richard de Thorp [? in Thorpe Arnold, Leics.].* [*c.* 1166 × 1186]

Cartulary copy: B.M., Cotton MS. Nero C xii fo. 3*r–v* (old pp. 1–2).

Universis sancte matris ecclesie filiis Nigellus de Moubrai salutem.
Sciatis me dedisse et hac carta mea confirmasse Deo et infirmis hospitalis
Sancti Lazari de Jerusalem in puram et perpetuam elemosinam pro
anima mea et antecessorum meorum tenementum Ricardi de Torp quod
tenuit de me in terra et prato de meo dominio. Et volo et firmiter precipio ut prefatus Ricardus et heredes sui illud teneant a fratribus
prefate domus. Hiis testibus, David fratre Regis[a] Scotie, Herberto filio

---

[a] *Ric'*, MS.

---

[1] *P.R. 23 Hen. II*, p. 78; and note to no. 143 below.   [2] See *E.Y.C.* ix 248–9.
[3] *York Min. Fasti* i no. 35.

Ricardi, Hamone Beler, Roberto capellano, Warino filio Simonis, Ricardo Davverys, Ridecot.

> NOTE. Warin son of Simon first occurs in 1166 (see no. 398 note). The gift was made during Roger de Mowbray's lifetime (see no. 30). If David of Scotland was really called earl (of Huntingdon), as he appears in no. 31, the date would need to be either 1173 × 1174 or 1185 × 1186.[1] The tenement was presumably in Thorpe Arnold (cf. nos. 31, 387).

30 *Confirmation by Roger de Mowbray to the hospital of Burton Lazars of the tenement of Richard de Thorp, given by his son Nigel de Mowbray.*

[*c.* 1166 × 1186]

> Cartulary copy: B.M., Cotton MS. Nero C xii fos. 3*v*–4*r* (old pp. 2–3).

Universis sancte matris ecclesie filiis tam presentibus quam futuris Rogerus de Molbrai salutem. Sciatis me concessisse et carta mea confirmasse donationem quam Nigellus filius meus fecit Deo et infirmis hospitalis Sancti Lazari de Jerusalem, scilicet tenementum Ricardi de Thorp' quod tenuit in terra et prato dominei[a] mei in liberam et puram et perpetuam elemosinam possidendum. Quare volo et firmiter precipio ut prefatus Ricardus et heredes ejus illud teneant a fratribus predicte domus pro salute anime mee et animarum predecessorum meorum. T(estibus) his, David fratre Regis Scotie, Roberto capell(ano), Herberto filio Ricardi, Hamone Beler, Warino filio Simonis, Ridecot et aliis multis.

> NOTE. For the date, see note to no. 29.

31 *Gift by Roger de Mowbray to the hospital of Burton Lazars of a meadow and 12 acres of arable between Melton Mowbray and Thorpe Arnold (Leics.), which Richard de Thorp held.*   [*c.* 1166 × 1186]

> Cartulary copy: B.M., Cotton MS. Nero C xii fo. 4*r* (old p. 3).

Universis sancte matris ecclesie filiis ad quos presens scriptum pervenerit Rogerus de Moubrai salutem in Domino. Noverit universitas vestra me dedisse et concessisse et hac presenti carta mea confirmasse Deo et Sancte Marie et fratribus leprosis de Jerusalem et eorum fratribus sanis in Anglia commorantibus quoddam pratum vocatum Alnetescroft et duodecim acras terre arabilis in quadam cultura de dominio meo inter Meltonam et Thorp' scilicet contra Ailmeresbrigge quas Ricardus de

---

[a] *Sic.*

---

[1] See *Complete Peerage* vi 646.

Thorp' in tempore Gundredis matris mee tenuit, in puram et perpetuam elemosinam liberam solutam et quietam ab omni servicio seculari et exactione, pro salute anime mee et pro animabus patris mei et matris mee[a] et antecessorum meorum et sucessorum meorum. Et sciendum est quod ego Rogerus de Moubrai et heredes mei prenominatum pratum scilicet Alnetescroft et duodecim acras terre prenominatas predictis fratribus contra omnes homines et omnes feminas imperpetuum waranti-zabimus. Ut autem hec carta stabilis et inviolata permaneat hoc presens scriptum sigilli mei appositione corroboravi. His testibus, comite David fratre Regis Scotie, Roberto capellano, Herberto filio Ricardi, Hamone Beler, Warino filio Simonis, Ridecot.

NOTE. For the date, see note to no. 29. The warranty- and sealing-clauses of this charter, however, suggest that it was compiled in the next century, per-haps to make up for the lack of definition in nos. 29 and 30.

32 *Gift by Roger de Mowbray, with the consent of Robert d'Aunay and the monks of Whitby, to abbot Gerold and his convent (Sav., later Byland) of the place of Hood (par. Kilburn, Yorks., N.R.), with the wood and plain around it.* [1138 or 1139]

Pd., *E.Y.C.* ix no. 115, from B.M., Egerton MS. 2823 fo. 42*v* (old fo. 147*v*), and Bodl., MS. Dodsworth 63 fos. 11*v*, 18*r*.

Hiis testibus, Sampsone de Albeneyo, Rogero de Cundy, Gundrea matre Rogeri de Molbray, Helya de Sancto Martino, et ceteris.

NOTE. The Byland chronicle gives 1138 as the date of this gift, which is Byland's first endowment.[1] The date of the abbey's foundation is given as 23 December 1138 in the Cistercian annals,[2] and also in a 13th-century list of the daughters of Savigny.[3] A marginal note in John of Hexham's chronicle places the foundation before Christmas 1138.[4] The charter may have been issued a little later than the actual settlement, as was often the case with monastic foundation charters.[5]

Gerold and his monks had originally gone out from Furness to found a daughter-house at Calder in 1135, but were driven from the site by the Scottish invasions of 1137. They remained at Hood from 1138 to 1142 or 1143 (see

[a] *mei*, MS.

---

[1] *Mon. Ang.* v 349*b*.
[2] *Cisterciensium . . . Annalium*, ed. A. Manrique (Lyons, 1642–59) i 360; also *Jnl. British Archaeol. Assoc.* xxvi (1870) 285.
[3] Desroches, in *Mémoires de la Société des Antiquaires de Normandie*, 2nd ser. x (1853) 270; cf. P.R.O., Transcripts (Léchaudé d'Anisy's Cartulaire de la Basse-Normandie) P.R.O. 31/8/140B pt. iii p. 115.
[4] *Priory of Hexham* i 115 n. *v*; *Symeonis Dunelmensis Opera Omnia*, ed. T. Arnold (R.S. lxxv) ii 289 n. *a*.
[5] See V. H. Galbraith, in *Cambridge Hist. Jnl.* iv (1934) 205–22.

no. 194), when they moved to Old Byland (no. 38). From Old Byland the convent moved again in 1147 to Stocking in Coxwold (no. 44). The final migration was made in 1177, to New Byland (cf. no. 68).[1]

33 *Gift by [Roger] de Mowbray and Gundreda to Byland of the land of Scackleton (Yorks., N.R.), i.e. 3 carucates.* [c. 1138×c. 1140]

Transcript, from an original charter formerly in St. Mary's Tower, York: Bodl., MS. Dodsworth 91 fo. 93v.

Robertus[a] de Molb' et Gundreda mater ejus omnibus hominibus suis et omnibus fidelibus sancte ecclesie salutem. Sciatis nos dedisse et concessisse Deo et Sancte Marie et monachis de Bealland terram de Scachelden, videlicet tres carucatas, liberam et quietam ab omni negotio seculari, cum omnibus pertinenciis suis in boscis et in planis et in aquis[b] et in omnibus, pro salute nostra et pro animabus anthiscessorum[c] nostrorum et in perpetuam elemosinam. His testibus, Willelmo de Menuham, Matthia de Romppein, Olivero de Bosceio, Waltero de Rivera, Willelmo de Stutevilla, Olivero de Olgrs.

NOTE. It seems likely that this joint charter of Roger and his mother belongs to the earliest period of his majority. According to the Byland chronicle, Scackleton was given in 1140.[2] The reference to the monks of 'Bealland', however, suggests later tampering, for the convent was at Hood until 1142 or 1143 (see no. 35 below).
The names of some of the witnesses present problems. The first may be William de Meisnilhermer (for whom see no. 400 note), and the second is clearly Matthew de Rampan, but Oliver de Olgrs is otherwise unknown. The appearance of William I de Stuteville is unexpected at this early date, as his first certain occurrence is 1147.[3] A rather similar witness-list appears in no. 35 (another suspicious text), and it may be that *Stutevilla* in the present charter should be emended to *Widevilla* (Wyville).

34 *Gift by Roger de Mowbray to Byland of the land of Airyholme and a cultura between the fields of Coxwold and Kilburn (all Yorks., N.R.).*

[c. 1140]

Transcript, from a lost portion of the Byland cartulary (Byland chron.): Bodl., MS. Dodsworth 63 fos. 13v–14r. Cartulary copy: B.M., Egerton MS. 2823 fo. 30v (old fo. 133v).

Ebor(acensi) archiepiscopo et omnibus sancte ecclesie filiis Rogerus de Molbray salutem. Sciatis me dedisse et confirmasse Deo et monachis

---

[a] Read *Rogerus.*   [b] *adquis*, MS.   [c] *Sic.*

[1] For the narrative of these events see Byland chron., *Mon. Ang.* v 349 ff.; cf. C. T. Clay, in *Y.A.J.* xxxviii (1955) 9–11; and D. Nicholl, *Thurstan Archbishop of York* (York, 1964) pp. 201–4.
[2] *Mon. Ang.* v 350a, and cf. note to no. 38 below.
[3] See *E.Y.C.* ix 3, 100, and no. 19 (cal. no. 239 below).

Sancte Marie de Bellalanda terram de Erghun que jacet juxta[a] Holthorp'
per has divisas, scilicet de Braydestamkelde usque ad Thrispol. Do
etiam eis et confirmo in perpetuam similiter elemosinam liberam et
quietam ab omni calumpnia, pro salute anime mee et omnium fidelium,
culturam de Deneshous que jacet inter campos Cukewale et Killeburne.
Test(ibus) Willelmo de Wydevilla,[b] Rogero de Cundy, Willelmo de
Muntpincun, Willelmo de Curcy, Radulpho Beler etc.

> NOTE. In the transcript of the Byland chronicle, this charter is placed under
> 1140.[1] Airyholme was confirmed to Byland in 1154/5 by Adrian IV.[2] As in
> the previous charter (no. 33), the reference to Byland suggests later tampering.
> The description of 'Erghun' as lying next to Howthorpe identifies this as
> Airyholme rather than Angram. 'Deneshous' is also called 'Edeneshous'
> (no. 72).

35

*Gift by Roger de Mowbray to Byland of his land of Scackleton, i.e. 3
carucates, with rights of pasture at Hovingham, and the land of Airyholme
(all Yorks., N.R.).* [1140]

> Transcript, from a lost portion of the Byland cartulary (Byland chron.):
> Bodl., MS. Dodsworth 63 fo. 13v. Cartulary copy: B.M., Egerton MS.
> 2823 fo. 111v (old fo. 217v).

Ebor(acensi) archiepiscopo totique capitulo Sancti Petri et omnibus
sancte ecclesie filiis Rogerus de Moubray[c] salutem. Sciatis me dedisse
et confirmasse Deo et monachis Sancte Marie de Begthlanda et successoribus eorundem in puram et perpetuam elemosinam terram meam de
Skakiltena,[d] scilicet tres carucatas cum omnibus pertinenciis suis cum
boscis et planis, moreis[e] et pasturis cum omnibus aisiamentis que ego et
mater mea habuimus sine retentamento, et communam pasture per
totam terruram et forestam meam de Hovingham[f] omni[g] tempore ubicunque averia mea et hominum meorum pascent. Ad hec do eis totum
Erghun in bosco, terra et prato cum omnibus pertinenciis ad faciendum
de omnibus prescriptis suam voluntatem sicut de suo proprio imperpetuum. Et ego et heredes mei totam hanc donationem eisdem monachis
et successoribus suis semper debemus[h] manutenere et warantizare contra
omnes homines et feminas. Hiis testibus, Willelmo de Meynill',[i] Mathia
de Ramporn', Olivero de Busceyo, Willelmo de Widevilla, etc.

> NOTE. In the transcript of the Byland chronicle, this charter is placed under
> 1140.[3] If this is correct, there must have been some subsequent tampering

---

[a] *inter,* Dodsw. 63.   [b] *Widdevilla,* Dodsw.   [c] *Munbray,* cart.   [d] *Scakildena,*
cart.   [e] *moris,* cart.   [f] *Hovyunham,* cart.   [g] *cum,* cart.   [h] Omitted
in Dodsw. MS., supplied from cart.   [i] *Morvill',* Dodsw.

---

[1] Omitted in *Mon. Ang.* v 350a.   [2] *P.U.E.* iii no. 96.
[3] Omitted in *Mon. Ang.* v 350a.

with this and with nos. 33-4 and 36-7 (possibly also no. 38), for until 1142 or 1143 the convent was not at Byland, but at Hood. The properties conveyed were confirmed by Adrian IV in 1154/5.[1] The appearance of Matthew de Rampan in the witness-list of this charter suggests a date before c. 1150.[2] But the warranty-clause is suspicious, being in the style of the next century. Possibly the charter is a conflation of nos. 33 and 34 and a third charter concerning Hovingham (perhaps that mentioned in Egerton MS. 2823 fo. 43v).

36 *Gift by Roger de Mowbray to Byland of all Rose Hill, to the west of Rye Dale (Yorks., N.R.) and wood as far as the fields of Kilburn.*   [c. 1140]

> Transcript, from a lost portion of the Byland cartulary, fo. 234v: Bodl., MS. Dodsworth 63 fo. 73r.

Rogerus de Molbray archiepiscopo Ebor(acensi) et capitulo Sancti Petri et fratribus sancte matris ecclesie salutem et Dei benedictionem. Notum sit vobis me dedisse et concessisse Deo et Sancte Marie et fratribus de Belande totam Rosebergam per Reddel west et per caput de Trenemore de west et omnem boscum usque ad campos de Kilburne et ad terras. Testibus, Sampsone de Albeneio, Roberto de Daivilla, Roberto Bosco, Mathia de Rampan', Willelmo de Ripar(ia) etc.

> NOTE. According to the Byland chronicle, 'Roseberg' was given in 1140 (see no. 37 below). The appearance of Matthew de Rampan[2] and of Robert Boscer[3] suggests a date before c. 1150.

37 *Gift by Roger de Mowbray to Byland of Great and Little Wildon, Rose Hill, his vaccary of Cam (par. Kilburn) and his wood, 3 carucates in Scackleton, all Airyholme, and common pasture at Hovingham.*   [1140]

> Transcript, from an original charter formerly in St. Mary's Tower, York: Bodl., MS. Dodsworth 94 fo. 8r–v. Transcript, from a lost portion of the Byland cartulary (Byland chron.): MS. Dodsworth 63 fo. 13v (lacks last 4 witnesses).

Ebor(acensi) archiepiscopo et omnibus sancte ecclesie filiis Rogerus de Molbrai salutem. Sciatis me dedisse concessisse et per hanc cartam confirmasse Deo et Sancte Mariei et abbati Geroldo de Beghland ac monachis ejus et successoribus eorum ad supervivendum imperpetuum magnam Wildonam et parvam Wildonam cum omnibus pertinenciis, Roseberg' et vaccariam meam de Camb cum omnibus pertinenciis et totum boscum meum per latera more, et tres carucatas terre cum pertinenciis in Scakilden, et totum Erghum in bosco terra et pratis cum

---

[1] *P.U.E.* iii no. 96.

[2] He appears in eight other early charters of Roger de Mowbray, nos. 21, 33, 36, 94-5, 177, 321, 370. Cf. also no. 403 note.

[3] He appears in three other charters of the 1140s, in two of which Matthew de Rampan also occurs, nos. 95, 370, 374.

pertinenciis, et communam pasture omni tempore in terrura boscis et pasturis de Hovingham. Hec omnia do tibi abbati Geroldo tuisque successoribus ad petitionem domini archiepiscopi Thurstani et Gundree matris mee pro anima patris mei et omnium mortuorum in liberam puram et perpetuam elemosinam. Istam donationem meam ego et heredes mei debemus defendere guarantizare et acquietare Sancte Marie et monachis ad sustentationem et vitam imperpetuum. His testibus, Gundrea matre mea, Roberto fratre meo, Sampsone de Albeney, Elia de Sancto Martino, Georgio dapifero, Ingelero capellano, Hugone de Mala Bissa, P.[1] de Tresc et aliis.

NOTE. In the transcript of the Byland chronicle this charter is placed under 1140.[2] But many of its features invite suspicion. In addition to the anachronism 'abbot Gerold of Byland', which has parallels in nos. 33–6 (and possibly no. 38), the sophisticated language and the warranty-clause suggests later interpolation. The witness-list is difficult to accept, for there is no other occurrence of Robert, the brother of Roger de Mowbray. George the *dapifer* occurs only in this charter and in the narrative of the Byland chronicle.[3] The only other George to appear in Mowbray documents is George de Sancto Martino, who attests a charter for Byland 1147 × c. 1154 (below, no. 49), where his name follows that of Hugh Malebisse, the *dapifer*. It is not improbable that the forger or interpolator of the present charter understood George de Sancto Martino to have been *dapifer*, and this erroneous information passed into the Byland chronicle.

38 *Gift by Roger de Mowbray to the monks of Byland of the vill of Byland on the Moor (Old Byland, Yorks., N.R.) by specified bounds, with the church of the vill.* [1142 × June 1143]

Pd., *E.Y.C.* iii no. 1833, from transcript of a lost portion of the cartulary of Byland (Byland chron.), Bodl., MS. Dodsworth 63 fo. 15v.

Hiis testibus, Sampsone de Albeneio, Rogero de Cundi, Helia de Sancto Martino, Hugone de Mainilhermer, Petro de Tresk, Landrico de Ages, Asketino, Hugone Malebis, Hamone Beler.

NOTE. The transcript of the Byland chronicle gives the date of this charter as c. 8 Sept. 1143.[4] But its true date is established by comparison with *E.Y.C.* ix no. 119 (cal. no. 39 below). The detailed boundaries and warranty-clause, however, invite suspicion, and although the witness-clause is consistent with the date assigned above, the text of the charter was obviously subject to interpolation at a later date. Old Byland was part of Gundreda's dowry, and the convent moved from Hood and remained there until 1147.[5]

A forged charter of Roger de Mowbray, with a witness-clause very similar to that of the present charter, is not included in the series of texts, as there is

---

[1] Presuambly Peter.   [2] Omitted in *Mon. Ang.* v 350a.
[3] *Mon. Ang.* v 350a.   [4] Charter omitted in *Mon. Ang.* v 350b.
[5] See Byland chron., *Mon. Ang.* v 350b–351a, and below. no. 44.

no evidence in the Byland cartulary or the chronicle, or in any other source, that the estate purporting to have been given, 'Eskeberg', was actually granted to Byland in the twelfth century. The witnesses to the charter, which is written in a hand of the fourteenth century, are as follows: Samson d'Aubigny, Roger de Cundy, Elias de Sancto Martino, [Peter] of Thirsk, Landric de Ages, Asketil, Hugh Malebisse, and Hamo Beler.[1]

39 *Gift by Roger de Mowbray to Byland of 20s. in his mill of Coxwold in exchange for Hood, which at his petition the monks had demised to the canons who had come from Bridlington to build their cell.* [1142×c. 1143]

Pd., *E.Y.C.* ix no. 119, from Bodl., MS. Dodsworth 94 fo. 77v (no witnesses).

NOTE. This gift is clearly associated with the previous charter, and with *E.Y.C.* ix nos. 118, 120 (cal. nos. 194–5 below), relating to the foundation of Newburgh priory at Hood.

40 *Gift by Roger de Mowbray to Byland of land at Cam and common pasture of the forest of Coxwold and material for building the monks' dwellings.* [1142×c. 1143]

Cartulary copy: B.M., Egerton MS. 2823 fo. 17r (old fo. 105r).

Ebor(acensi) archiepiscopo et omnibus suis hominibus Francis et Anglis et omnibus sancte ecclesie filiis Rogerus de Molbray salutem. Sciatis me dedisse Deo et monachis Sancte Marie de Bellalanda in perpetuam elemosinam liberam solutam et quietam pro salute anime mee et meorum terram de Cambe et communem pasturam foreste de Cukwald' et materiem ad domos suas faciendas per providenciam dapiferi mei. Hiis testibus, Gundrea matre mea, Sampsone de Albeneio, Rogero de Cundi, Petro de Tresc, Asketino ostiario, etc.

NOTE. The last four witnesses occur in no. 38, and therefore the present charter probably belongs to the same occasion, when the monks were about to move from Hood to their new site at Old Byland. On the other hand, the content of the grant seems to connect it with the move from Old Byland to the site near Coxwold, in 1147 (see no. 44 below).

41 *Gift by Roger de Mowbray to Byland of ½ carucate and 5 acres in (North) Cave (Yorks., E.R.) with toft and croft and liberties and easements; and an undertaking that neither he nor his heirs would receive the men of another order within that vill and territory to the injury of the monks.* [1138×1147]

Pd., *E.Y.C.* iii no. 1827, from B.M., Egerton MS. 2823 fo. 22r (old fo. 124r).

---

[1] B.M., Add. Ch. 70692; seal no. 3 of Roger de Mowbray (see above, p. lxxxiii), red wax, appended on tag.

Testibus, Sampsone de Albeneio, Herberto de Cunibergh,[1] Roberto de Dayvilla, Rogero de Flammavilla etc.

NOTE. Farrer assigned this charter to the period between 1145 and 1160. But the land in North Cave was confirmed to Byland in 1154/5 by Adrian IV,[2] and according to the Byland chronicle it was given in or before 1147 (see no. 44 below). All four witnesses appear in a charter of 1138 × 1148 (no. 374 below). It is even possible that the land was given while the monks were still at Hood. For a charter concerning the liberties of this land, see *E.Y.C.* iii no. 1828 (cal. below, no. 62).

42 *Grant by Roger de Mowbray to Byland of easements in his forests of Nidderdale (Yorks., W.R.), Coxwold, Bagby, Balk, Hovingham, and Scackleton (all N.R.).* [1142 × 1147]

Cartulary copy: B.M., Egerton MS. 2823 fo. 70*v* (old fo. 177*v*).

Ebor(acensi) archiepiscopo totique capitulo Sancti Petri et omnibus sancte ecclesie filiis presentibus et futuris Rogerus de Molbray salutem. Sciatis me dedisse et concessisse et hac presenti carta confirmasse Deo et monachis Sancte Marie de Beghlanda omnia communa aysiamenta in pastura in materia in viis et semitis et aquis per omnes forestas meas de Niderdala et Cukwald' et Bagby et Balk' et Hovingham et Scakeldena. Et ut habeant liberos et congruos introitus et exitus sibi et hominibus et averiis suis et sint quieti de pannagio de hiis propriis porcis per omnes predictas forestas meas. Hanc autem donationem feci Deo et predictis monachis in perpetuam elemosinam liberam solutam et quietam ab omni terreno servicio et exactione seculari pro salute anime mee et omnium antecessorum et heredum meorum. Et ego et heredes mei manutenebimus et warantizabimus predictis monachis istam donationem contra omnes homines imperpetuum. Hiis testibus, Sampsone de Albaneyo, Willelmo de Arches, Radulfo de [. . . . . .]ll'[a] etc.

NOTE. This gift was obviously made after that in no. 40, of 1142 × c. 1143. Easements in all Mowbray's forests were confirmed by Adrian IV in 1154/5.[3] The Byland chronicle states that the gift was made in or before 1147 (see no. 44 below), and the witness-list is consistent with a date between 1142 and 1147. The phraseology of the charter, however, is suspicious, and suggests later interpolation.

43 *Confirmation by Roger de Mowbray to Byland of 2 carucates in Fawdington (Yorks., N.R.), given by Humphrey de Mandeville.* [c. 1147]

Transcripts from an original charter formerly in St. Mary's Tower, York: Bodl., MSS. Dodsworth 7 fo. 135*v*, 94 fos. 12*v*–13*r* (lacks last 9 witnesses).

[a] Possibly [*Wydevi*]*ll'*.

[1] Presumably Queniborough (Leics.).   [2] *P.U.E.* iii no. 96.   [3] Ibid.

Eboracensi archiepiscopo totique capitulo Sancti Petri et omnibus sancte ecclesie filiis Rogerus de Molbrai[a] salutem. Sciatis me dedisse et hac[b] carta mea confirmasse Deo et monachis Sancte Marie de Beghlanda duas carucatas terre in Faldington, illas scilicet quas Humfridus de Mande-villa[c] tenuit de feudo meo et servicium earum, cum omnibus pertinenciis earum in terris et in aquis in bosco et in plano in pratis et pasturis et omnibus aliis aisiamentis ad easdem carucatas pertinentibus, per omnia ita libere et plenarie sicut pater meus ante me et ego post eum easdem carucatas liberius unquam et plenius tenuimus una nocte et die. Hanc autem donationem feci eis in puram et perpetuam elemosinam liberam propriam solutam et quietam a me et ab heredibus meis et ab omni terreno servicio et exactione seculari imperpetuum pro salute anime mee et omnium antecessorum et heredum meorum. Et hanc donationem tam ego quam heredes mei eis monachis manutenebimus et warantizabimus contra omnes homines imperpetuum. His testibus, Samsone de Al-beneio,[d] Hereberto de Moravilla, et Ricardo filio ejus, Willelmo de Arches, Roberto de Daivilla, [e]Bertramo Haget, et Willelmo filio ejus, Rogero de Flam'villa, Willelmo de Widevilla, Waltero de Riparia, Petro de Tresc,[e] et Waltero de Karlatuna.

NOTE. Fawdington was confirmed to Byland by Adrian IV in 1154/5,[1] and according to the Byland chronicle was given in or before 1147 (see no. 44 below). The witness-list is identical to that of no. 44, with the addition of the last name.

44 *Gift by Roger de Mowbray to Byland of the forest of Cam by specified bounds and land at Coxwold; and confirmation of Murton, Wildon, Rose Hill, Scackleton, Cam, Fawdington, Snilesworth, and Airyholme (all Yorks., N.R.), and of land in Axholme (Lincs.), North Cave (Yorks., E.R.), and Ampleforth (Yorks., N.R.), and easements in all his forests.*

[1147]

Transcripts, from a lost portion of the cartulary of Byland (Byland chron.):
Bodl., MS. Dodsworth 63 fos. 18v–19r, 32v–33r.

Ebor(acensi) archiepiscopo et toti capitulo Sancti Petri et omnibus hominibus suis Francis et Anglis et omnibus sancte matris ecclesie fidelibus Rogerus de Moubray salutem. Sciatis me dedisse concessisse et presenti carta confirmasse Deo et monachis Sancte Marie de Bella-landa totam forestam scilicet Cambe et circa abbathiam ipsorum per

---

a *Mowbray*, Dodsw. 94.   *b* *presenti*, inserted Dodsw. 94.   *c* *Maundevill*, Dodsw. 94.   *d* *Sampsone de Albeneyo*, Dodsw. 94.   *e-e* These names given in nominative case in MS.

---

1 *P.U.E.* iii no. 96.

has divisas scilicet sicut via de Heth vadit per moram et descendit ad
fundum vallis que est inter Killeburna et Middlebergam et per fundum
vallis usque Gillesbrigge et exinde sicut Fulsic vadit juxta Cambisheved
ab occidente usque Brine et exinde sicut vallis vadit a septentrionali plaga
Brine ubi Grundelousekelda cadit in ipsam vallem et inde vadit ad
Whiteker et cadit in Mykelbek sub molendino monachorum, super hoc
tantum incrementi quantum Willelmus de Mainilhermer cui dederam
terram de Cukwald ipsis monachis concessione mea superaddidit scilicet
stagnum molendini et sub stagno usque ad latam viam et ultra stagnum
ab oriente latitudine xl perticarum et inde sicut lata via que vadit Ampil-
fordiam venit ad Holbek et inde sursum per medium Burtoft usque ad
moram. Do etiam eis et confirmo Beghland' Mortonam Wildonam Rosebergam Skakeldonam Cambe Faldingtonam Snyelesworth Erghum et
terram in Thirneholme de Insula Haxiholm' et terram quam dedi eis
in Cava et Ampilford et omnia terris istis adjacentia in terra et aqua in
bosco et plano in viis et semitis et in omnibus aliis aisiamentis et libertatibus suis et per omnes forestas meas plenarie que illis necessaria
fuerunt per providenciam dapiferi mei. Hanc donationem solutam et
ab omni calumpnia quietam et ab omni terreno servicio et exactione
seculari liberam dono et confirmo Deo et predictis monachis in perpetuam elemosinam pro salute anime mee et patris et matris mee et
omnium antecessorum et heredum meorum. Volo igitur et precipio
omnibus hominibus meis ut predicti monachi hec omnia bene et in pace
honorifice et quiete teneant in boscis et in planis et in terris et in aquis
in pratis et pasturis et in omnibus aliis locis et rebus et pertinenciis suis.
Hujus donationis et confirmationis testes sunt hii Sampson de Albeneyo,
Herbertus de Morvilla, et Ricardus filius ejus, Willelmus de Arches,
Robertus de Daivill, Bertramus Hagat, Willelmus filius ejus, Rogerus de
Flammavill, Willelmus de Widevill, Walterus de Ryvaria, Petrus de
Thresc.

NOTE. The transcript of the Byland chronicle states that by this charter, given
in 1147, Roger de Mowbray gave to the monks their third conventual site,
'duas carucatas de terra vasta in territorio de Cukwald' 'per estimationem
dapiferi sui'.[1] Much of the property actually conveyed in the charter was confirmed to Byland by Adrian IV in 1154/5.[2] Peter of Thirsk's last occurrence
is 1154 (no. 236 and probably no. 241),[3] and William de Arches died in
c. 1154 (no. 359 note). But the specification of the boundaries of the forest of
Cam is suspicious, and there may well have been interpolation or tampering
with a genuine charter of 1147 which granted the forest of Cam and the land
near Coxwold. For a gift of land by William de Meisnilhermer, see H.M.C.,
Various Collections ii (1903) 4 (and cf. below, nos. 50–1, 400).

[1] This charter is omitted in the edition of the chronicle in *Mon. Ang.* v 351*b*.
[2] *P.U.E.* iii no. 96.   [3] Cf. nos. 37–8, 40, 43, 238, 400.

45 *Notification by Roger de Mowbray to Eustace Fitz J(ohn) and his ministers and men of his grant to Byland that they may make any exchanges of land.*
[*c.* 1147]

Cartulary copy: B.M., Egerton MS. 2823 fo. 70*v* (old fo. 177*v*).

Rogerus de Moubray Eustachio filio J. et omnibus ministris suis et hominibus Francis et Anglis de Ebor(aci)siria salutem. Sciatis me dedisse et concessisse Deo et Sancte Marie et abbati et monachis de Beylanda pro salute mee anime quod si possint monachi de Beylanda invenire aliquem qui velit escambiare cum monachis aliquam terram pro suis terris hospitatis vel inhospitatis que terra propinquior et utilior ipsis monachis fuerit, illud escambium concedo ex mea parte ad voluntatem monachorum tenere tam libere tam quiete quam liberius quam quietius aliquam elemosinam tenent. Test(ibus), Sampsone, Willelmo de Arch', Roberto de Dayvilla etc.

NOTE. All three witnesses attest nos. 43 and 44, apparently of 1147. Eustace Fitz John did not return from Scotland until after November 1143.[1] It is possible that this charter is connected with no. 198 and therefore relates to Brignall (Yorks., N.R.), where both Roger de Mowbray and Eustace Fitz John had interests (see no. 297 note).

46 *Confirmation by Roger de Mowbray to Byland of 10 bovates in Ellington (Yorks., N.R.), given by Serlo the cook.* [1138 × *c.* 1150]

Reference in a charter of Roger, abbot of Byland, for Jervaulx [*c.* 1150]: transcript from lost portion of the cartulary of Byland (Byland chron.) fos. 15 ff., Bodl., MS. Dodsworth 63 fo. 51*r*.
Pd., *Mon. Ang.* v 572 (VII).

... decem bovatas terre in Ellington, quas Serlo cocus prius dedit nobis, per concessionem Rogeri Moubray, fundatoris nostre abbatie de Bellalanda ...

NOTE. Ellington was part of the Masham fee held by Mowbray of the Richmond honour. Serlo the cook attests no. 95, of 1138 × 1145. He gave the land, together with ten oxen and ten cows, and six mares and their foals, when he entered Byland as a *conversus*.[2]

47 *Gift by Gundreda (de Gournay) to Byland of a meadow in Hovingham (Yorks., N.R.).* [1147 × *c.* 1154]

Cartulary copy: B.M., Egerton MS. 2823 fo. 43*v* (old fo. 148*v*).

Ebor(acensi) archiepiscopo et omnibus sancte ecclesie filiis Gundrea mater Rogeri de Molbray salutem. Sciatis me dedisse et concessisse Deo et monachis Sancte Marie de Bellalanda pratum meum de Hovyngham,

---

[1] He was at Durham in November 1143 (*Symeonis Dunelmensis Opera Omnia*, ed. T. Arnold (R.S. lxxv) i 154) and at Huntingdon in *c.* 1145 (*Early Scottish Charters prior to A.D. 1153*, ed. A. C. Lawrie (Glasgow, 1905) no. 177).
[2] Byland chron., *Mon. Ang.* v 571*b*.

scilicet salcetum ab australi parte de Tuf' sicut Hardingcroe vadit, totum pratum a septentrionali plaga de Tuf' usque ad pratum ecclesie, in perpetuam elemosinam liberam solutam et quietam ab omni servicio et calumpnia, pro salute anime mee patris et matris mee et omnium fidelium. Hiis testibus, Willelmo de Widavylla, Adam Lovell', Ernaldo de Vilers etc.

NOTE. This gift presumably belongs to the period after the removal to the site near Coxwold. Gundreda probably died *c.* 1154 (see no. 236 note). The appearance of Adam Luvel suggests that the charter was given later, rather than earlier, in the period assigned.[1]

48 *Gift by Roger de Mowbray to Byland of 2 bovates in Kirkby Malzeard (Yorks., W.R.) and grant of easements in Nidderdale.* [1147 × *c.* 1154]

Cartulary copy: B.M., Egerton MS. 2823 fo. 51*r* (old fo. 157*r*).

Ebor(acensi) archiepiscopo et omnibus filiis sancte matris ecclesie Rogerus de Molbray salutem. Notum sit vobis me dedisse et presenti carta confirmasse Deo et monachis Sancte Marie de Beghlanda in perpetuam elemosinam solutam quietam liberam ab omni terreno servicio duas bovatas terre in Malasart, cum omnibus pertinenciis suis in bosco et plano, in pratis et pasturis et omnibus aysiamentis. Concessi etiam predictis monachis per omnem forestam meam de Niderdala communia aysiamenta, scilicet materiam et mineriam ferri et decimam plumbarie mee et fontem salis et pasturam et cetera domui sue necessaria scilicet in perpetuam elemosinam. Hiis testibus, Sampsone de Albaneio, Hereberto de Moravilla, Ricardo Burdet etc.

NOTE. Presumably this gift was made after the general gift of easements in the Mowbray forests, no. 42 of 1142 × 1147 and no. 44 of 1147. It probably preceded the next charter.

49 *Notification by Roger de Mowbray to his bailiffs, reeves, foresters, and ministers, of his gift to Byland of 2 stags and 3 hinds p.a. from his forest of Nidderdale for the use of the monks' infirmary; and regulations concerning the monks' pasture rights in Nidderdale.* [1147 × *c.* 1154]

Fabricated original charter: Yorke deeds at Halton Place, no. 56. Cartulary copy: B.M., Egerton MS. 2823 fos. 76*v*–77*r* (old fos. 183*v*–184*r*).

Rog(erus) de Molbrai omnibus balliuis . propositis . forestariis . et ministris suis . ac omnibus hominibus Cristianis salutem. Significo

[1] His attestations chiefly belong to the 1160s and 1170s, but he does occur as early as *c.* 1147 × *c.* 1157 (no. 371) and 1154 × 1157 (no. 243).

vobis vniuersis quod ego dedi concessi et hac carta mea confirmaui Deo
et monachis Sancte Marie de Begthland(a) in puram et perpetuam
elemosinam duos ceruos et tres bissas ad opus infirmorum monachorum
capiendos annuatim in foresta mea de Nidderdale. Et quod fratres
ipsorum monachorum ac pastores et custodes pasture sue in Nidderdale
libere ac licite inperpetuum ferant cum eis et habeant infra pasturam
monachorum feroces canes mastivos in vinculis . cornua et alia arma
sua. Ita quod homines qui arma portant nec canes eorum malum non
faciant feris meis . quas michi et heredibus meis volo quod saluent et
custodiant. Quod si malum eis fecerint ꞉ tunc abbas illum vel illos statim
repellet de valle et de suo seruicio. Nec fratres monachorum commo-
rantes in Nidderdale quicquam facient . nec dabunt forestariis meis vel
heredum meorum quasi de iure vel consuetudine inperpetuum ꞉ nisi
tantum quod sua sponte sibi dare voluerint . et hoc debito tempore
semper et competenti . ut fratres eorum importunitate numquam
graventur. Hec omnia ego Rog(erus) et heredes mei predictis monachis
et successoribus suis guarantizabimus et manutenebimus contra omnes
homines imperpetuum. Testes sunt Gundrea mater mea . Nigellus et
Robertus filii mei . Hug(o) Malabestia dapifer meus . Georgius de
Sancto Martino . Willelmus de Widuilla . Thom(as) de Coleuilla .
Walwannus de Insula et alii.

Endorsement: .*Carta. Rogeri de Molbrai de canibus habendis et cornubus in valle
et aliis contentis .Nidderdale. B' .j.iiij. .pur'.* (contemporary, perhaps same hand
as face).

Size: 19·3 × 10·9 cm.; 2 cm. turn-up.

Seal: right-hand half of seal no. 3 of Roger de Mowbray (above, p. lxxxiii), green
wax; poor impression, legend not visible on surviving half; appended on tag.

Script: charter hand of ? early 13th cent.

NOTE. Comparison with no. 60 suggests that the present charter was fabricated to supply details lacking from the genuine grant. The witness-clause
may be taken from an authentic charter. Gundreda probably died in c. 1154
(see no. 236 note), and by that time Hugh Malebisse had been superseded as
dapifer by William de Wyville (cf. no. 237).

50 *Confirmation by Roger de Mowbray to Byland of the vill of Thorpe le
Willows (par. Coxwold, Yorks., N.R.), given by William de Wyville.*

[1147 × c. 1154]

Transcript, from an original charter formerly in St. Mary's Tower, York:
Bodl., MS. Dodsworth 94 fo. 29v.

Eboracensi archiepiscopo et omnibus suis hominibus Francis et Anglis
et omnibus sancte matris ecclesie filiis Rogerus de Mowbray salutem.

Sciatis me dedisse concessisse et presenti carta mea confirmasse Deo et monachis Sancte Marie de Bellanda donationem quam Willelmus de Wydevilla dedit Deo et monachis predictis, totam scilicet villam de Thorp in perpetuam elemosinam liberam solutam et quietam ab omni terreno servicio, pro salute anime mee et omnium meorum, per easdem metas per quas dedi eam Radulfo de Wydevilla et Willelmo fratre ejus in terra et aqua et bosco. Hiis testibus, Hugone Malabisse dapifero meo, Rogero de Flamvilla, Roberto de Dayvilla, Waltero de Rivaria, Willelmo de Stayngriva, Rogero de Cundy, Hugone capellano, Rogero filio Petri de Tresc.

NOTE. This charter was issued after no. 44, which refers to a gift made by William de Meisnilhermer, who was Ralph de Wyville's predecessor in his fee (cf. no. 400). Hugh Malebisse ceased to be *dapifer* by 1154 (see note to no. 49). For William de Wyville's gifts, see H.M.C., *Various Collections* ii (1903) 4, and Bodl., MS. Dodsworth 91 fo. 122*r–v*; for his fee, see below, Fees [21].

51 *Confirmation by Roger de Mowbray to Byland of Thorpe le Willows, by specified bounds, given by William de Wyville.* [1147 × 1164]

Cartulary copy: B.M., Egerton MS. 2823 fo. 36*r* (old fo. 141*r*), partially illegible through damp, the lacunae being supplied from William de Wyville's charter, ibid.

Ebor(acensi) archiepiscopo et toti capitulo Sancti Petri et omnibus sancte ecclesie filiis Rogerus de Molbray salutem. Sciatis me concessisse et hac carta mea confirmasse Deo et monachis Sancte Marie de Bellal(anda) in perpetuam elemosinam liberam solutam et quietam ab omni terreno servicio pro salute anime mee et omnium meorum donationem illam quam Willelmus de Wydevilla dedit Deo et predictis monachis, totam scilicet terram de Thorp' per easdem divisas et metas per quas dedi eam Radulfo de Wydevilla et Willelmo fratri ejus in terra et aqua et bosco [scilicet] communionem silve que est inter Thorp' et Everleyam, id est medium contra medium in [bosco et] pastura per viam que vadit per mediam Thursedenam ad Hovyngham et erga Cuke[wald], silvam que est inter Oxedalam et veterem viam que descendit de Hesthou et vadit per [Uffisthwe]it usque ad ductum et inde del nord' sicut ductus ipse venit ad Sighe[desbriggam] inde del north' de Whiteker sicut Mychelbec cadit in Whiteker et inde usque ad divisam Ampilforde. Hiis testibus, Roberto de Dayvilla, Rogero de Flammavilla, Hugone Malebisse etc.

NOTE. This specification of the bounds of the land given in no. 50 must have been made subsequently, but before 1164, when it was confirmed by Henry II.[1]

[1] Bodl., MS. Dodsworth 7 fo. 105*r*.

52 *Gift by Roger de Mowbray, and his sons Nigel and Robert, to Byland of pasture in Nidderdale for 80 mares and their foals.*   [before 1172]

> Memorandum of late 13th century (after 1278): Yorke deeds at Halton Place, no. 68.

Memorandum quod dominus Rogerus de Molbray et Nigellus ac Robertus filii ejus dederunt nobis, per quandam cartam suam nunc dampnatam, pasturam in Nidderdale ad equas lxxx et pullos earum etc. in puram et perpetuam elemosinam.

> NOTE. The memorandum clearly states that this gift preceded that made in no. 53, and also the loan of 1172, recorded below as no. 54. The association in the present gift of Roger's two sons, if indeed the memorandum correctly reflects the lost charter, suggests a date after *c.* 1160.

53 *Gift by Roger de Mowbray and his son Nigel to Byland of part of western Nidderdale by specified bounds, as pasture for 30 sows and 5 boars, with regulations for the preservation of the game.*   [*c.* 1160 × 1172]

> Fabricated original charter: Yorke deeds at Halton Place, no. 57 (not completely legible).

+ Eboracensi archiepiscopo . totique capitulo Sancti Petri et omnibus fidelibus Christi presentibus et futuris Roger[us de] Molbraio et Nigellus filius [meus salutem. Sciatis] quod nos dedimus et concessimus et presenti carta confirmauimus monachis Sancte Marie de Beglanda quandam partem foreste nostre in Niderdale . que infra subscriptas diuisas continetur . uidelicet a parte meridiana sicut aqua que de [. . . . .] diuidit uallem a plano lande de [. . . . .] parte occidentali de Brunehou usque ad Quernesidam et inde usque ad [. . . . .] et inde usque ad Niderhou et [a parte] aquilonali a Niderhou per caput de Niderdala usque ad Aldolureslund et a parte orientali ab Aldoluerslund usque ad Bakeste[inebec et] sicut Bakesteinebec descendit in Nid. Ita quod nullius aueria habebunt communia [cum averiis] predictorum monachorum infra prenominatas diuisas. Concessimus quoque eis totum boscum ad occidentem Bakesteinebec ad ea que sibi et pecoribus suis fuerint neccessaria. Et habebunt sui [tenentes] in predicta pastura triginta sues cum tota sequela sua duorum annorum . et quinque uerres . ita tamen quod omnes porci remouebuntur ab illa pastura quindecim diebus ante natiuitatem Sancti Johannis Baptiste . et quindecim diebus post idem festum propter fetus ceruarum. Fratres uero et pastores monachorum facient sibi logias et faldas pecoribus suis in predicta pastura ubi uoluerint . et habebunt canes in uinculis et cornua . et paruos canes ad custodiendas curtes suas . et facient fenum ubi et quantum uoluerint in predicta pastura. Set ibi non arabunt neque seminabunt . et facient sibi et pecoribus suis in uno uel in duobus ad plus locis herbergiamentum et ortum. Forestarii uero nostri uel heredum nostrorum non inquietabunt nec ullam molestiam ingerent fratribus uel pastoribus siue pecoribus monachorum infra suprascriptas diuisas prenominate pasture. Quando autem inuenerint pecora monachorum extra predictas diuisas ? non capient ex eis plura quam duo neque imparcabunt. Concessimus etiam eis ducere pecora sua ad predictam pasturam et inde reducere per terras nostras libere et sine disturbatione extra blada et prata. Seculares uero pastores monachorum qui mittendi sunt in prefatam pasturam affidabunt coram senescallo nostro quod non capient aliquem de feris nostris . neque de auibus que alias capiunt in tota foresta nostra de Niderdala. Quod si quis eorum conuictus fuerit aliquem feram uel auem interdictam cepisse ? mercedem suam amittet . et de domo Beglandia eicietur. Quicquid uero infra memoratas diuisas continetur [tam nemus quam pasturam] exceptis solum modo feris et auibus que alias capiunt . dedimus et confirmauimus predictis monachis ad tenendum de nobis et heredibus nostris cum omnibus aisiamentis et pertinentiis suis in perpetuam elemosinam liberam solutam et quietam ab omni terreno seruicio et exactione seculari pro salute animarum nostrarum . et omnium antecessorum et heredum nostrorum. Monachi autem reddent annuatim nobis et heredibus nostris in recognitionem unam marcam argenti . scilicet dimidiam marcam ad Pentecostn' . et dimidiam marcam ad festum Sancti Martini. Et nos et heredes nostri manutenebimus et warantizabimus fideliter predictis monachis prenominatam pasturam cum pertinentiis suis contra omnes homines in perpetuum. His testibus . Rob(erto) de Daiuilla . Hug(one) Malebis . Thoma de Coleuilla . Ham(one) Beler . Rad(ulfo) de Beuuair . Rogero filio Gaufr(idi) . Nicholao de Bellun . Rob(erto) filio Rogeri . Rog(ero) filio Hug(onis) . Rob(erto) clerico.

Endorsements: *Rogerus de Moubray de quadam parte foreste de Niderdale . redd'*
.i. marcam annuatim. Nidd'. B'.j.j. (13th cent.).

Size: 15 × 27 cm.; 1·6 cm. turn-up.

Seals: two slits in turn-up for seals on tags, the one on the left missing; on the right, seal no. 1 of Nigel de Mowbray (above, p. lxxxiii), brown wax varnished; appended on tag.

NOTE. The 13th-century memorandum places this gift after that recorded above as no. 52, and before the transaction given below as no. 54. The witness-list of the present charter accords well with such a date, i.e. between *c.* 1160 and 1172. Five of the witnesses appear in *c.* 1160 × 1169 (no. 247) and six in

1163 × 1169 (no. 249). One of these, Nicholas de Bellun, does not appear earlier. Robert son of Roger occurs first after 1164 (no. 268) and Roger son of Geoffrey in 1166 (no. 401).

The memorandum describes the gift as follows: 'Postea [i.e. after no. 52] idem Rogerus et Nigellus filius ejus dederunt nobis quandam partem foreste sue de Nidderdale infra certas metas et divisas ad .xxx. sues et .v. verres, reddendo sibi et heredibus suis in recognitionem unam marcam argenti.'

Although there is no reason to doubt that the charter records a genuine gift and preserves a genuine witness-clause, the document itself is written in a hand which belongs to the end of the twelfth century, or the beginning of the thirteenth, and the clauses containing the regulations clearly reflect conditions of this later period, long after the original grant of pasture.

The occasion of such forgery or interpolation may have arisen in the 1190s or 1200s. Byland had an agreement over Nidderdale with Fountains in 1198.[1] The Byland chronicle, although it does not provide any information about Nidderdale, was written in c. 1197 and involved much elaboration of charters. In August 1204 a settlement was made by papal judges delegate between Byland and William de Mowbray over Middlesmoor,[2] which was the subject of the transaction of 1172, no. 54.

54 *Gift by Roger de Mowbray, and his sons Nigel and Robert, to Byland of part of Nidderdale, as pasture for 80 mares in mortgage in return for 300 marks, with conditions for its redemption after 10 years.*   1172

Memorandum of late 13th century (after 1278): Yorke deeds at Halton Place, no. 68 (not completely legible).

Contigit postea[a] quod predictus Rogerus et duo filii ejus[b] ad sua magna et ardua negotia faciendum CCC marcas argenti a nobis mutuaverunt, scilicet a festo Sancti Andree Apostoli[3] anno gracie MCLXX secundo per quoddam scriptum cyrographatum nunc dampnatum [com]posuerunt et dimiserunt nobis in vadimonium quandam partem foreste sue de Nidderdale per certas metas et divisas in cyrographo nominatas, scilicet tali conditione: quod quolibet anno decem annorum decideret una dimidia marca de predictis CCC marcis pro firma scilicet ejusdem pasture; et finitis decem annis prenominatis Rogerus et filii ejus persolverent nobis prenominatas CCC marcas, exceptis tantum quinque marcis allocatis pro firma ejusdem pasture, et recipient libere et quiete suam pasturam[c] preter illam pasturam ad lxxx equas quam Rogerus et filii ejus prius dederant que nobis deberet remanere.[c] Et si Rogerus et

---

[a] *per processum temporis* inserted.   [b] *Nigellus et Robertus* inserted.
[c-c] Deleted; *post x annos* inserted.

---

[1] *Fount. Cart.* i 215-16; Yorke deeds at Halton Place, no. 60.
[2] Yorke deeds, no. 61; cal. from cartulary copy, *Letters of Pope Innocent III*, ed. C. R. and M. G. Cheney (Oxford, 1967) no. 554.
[3] 30 November.

filii ejus non persolvissent nobis predictas CCC marcas, quinque tantum marcas [. . . . .] post decem annos, tota predicta pastura remaneret nobis [? in perpetuum. . . . .] de anno in annum donec totam [. . . . .] Rogero vel filiis ejus recuper[. . . . .] marca quolibet [. . . . .]cidente de dictis CCC marcis pro firma ejusdem pasture. Et sciendum quod cum decem anni prenominati integre et plenarie fuissent completi, nulla omnino solutio pecunie memorate per predictos Rogerum vel filios ejus nobis facta fuit, preter firmam annualem. Et sic predicta pastura remansit nobis per spacium circiter viginti duorum annorum, post decem annos completos, scilicet usque ad tempus domini Willelmi filii Nigelli de Molbray.

NOTE. The memorandum continues the history of the property (which the endorsement identifies as Middlesmoor and Heathfield) until after the succession to the Mowbray honour of Roger son of Roger in 1278.

55 *Gift by Roger de Mowbray to Byland of Middlethorpe (Yorks., W.R.).*

[*c.* 1154×1175]

Transcripts, from an original charter formerly in St. Mary's Tower, York: Bodl., MSS. Dodsworth 94 fo. 42*r*, 145 fo. 45*r*. Also transcript from a lost portion of the cartulary of Byland fo. 232: MS. Dodsworth 63 fo. 71*v* (lacks last 4 witnesses).

Ebor(acensi) archiepiscopo totique capitulo Sancti Petri et omnibus sancte ecclesie filiis Rogerus de Mowbray salutem. Sciatis et notum sit omnibus vobis me dedisse et concessisse et ista presenti carta mea confirmasse Deo et ecclesie Sancte Marie de Bellalanda et monachis ibidem Deo servientibus et imperpetuum servaturis quoddam manerium meum juxta Ebor(acum) nomine Thorp', cum omnibus suis pertinenciis ac libertatibus et cum serviciis libere tenentium simul cum wardis releviis eschaetis ac cum omnibus nativis ejusdem ville et eorum sequelis cum terris et ten(ementis) pratis pascuis pasturis turbariis moris vastis et ceteris rebus omnibus predicte ville et manerio de Thorp' pertinentibus, prout evidenter patent per antiquas metas videlicet fossata ac veteres perambulationes, tenendum et ªhabendum imperpetuum. Hec omnia et singula cum omnibus suis pertinenciis liberis introitibus et exitibus infra villam et extra et in omnibus aliis locis rebus et communis prope et procul dicto manerio et dominio spectantibus, de me et heredibus meis in liberam puram et perpetuam elemosinam solutam et quietam ab omni seculari servicio et demanda. Et ego prefatus Rogerus et heredes mei et assignati nostri manutenebimus warantizabimus et defendemus omnia suprascripta, cum omnibus suis pertinenciis predicte ecclesie et

ª⁻ª Omitted in Dodsw. 145.

monachis et eorum posteris, sicut puram liberam et perpetuam elemosinam nostram contra omnes gentes imperpetuum.[a] Test(ibus), Waltero de Bruer,[1] Rogero de Cundy, Walter de Riparia, Hugone de Malabissa, Thoma de Colvill, Roberto de Bever, Ricardo de Avers, Germano capellano et aliis.

> NOTE. Thomas de Coleville first occurs after 1154 (see no. 356 note). Walter de Riparia was dead by 1175 (no. 204 note). The charter, however, gives every appearance of being a later forgery, and was probably fabricated in connection with disputes over the property in the later thirteenth century. In 1251 Henry abbot of Byland was in dispute with William de Malteby over 13 bovates in Middlethorpe.[2] In 1272 Adam abbot of Byland and the dean and chapter of York fined an agreement over the manor of Middlethorpe, the abbot of Selby also putting in his claim.[3] For Selby's interest and another forged charter, see nos. 255, 263.

56 *Gift by Roger de Mowbray to Byland of part of western Nidderdale, within specified bounds.* [*c.* 1173 × 1180]

> Original charter: Yorke deeds at Halton Place, no. 58. Cartulary copy: B.M., Egerton MS. 2823 fo. 76*v* (old fo.183*v*) (lacks last 11 witnesses).

Eboracensi archiepiscopo totique capitulo Sancti Petri . et uniuersis sanctę ęcclesię filiis Rog(erus) de Molbr' . salutem. Sciatis me dedisse . et hac carta mea confirmasse Deo et monachis Sanctę Marię de Beghlanda . totam illam partem forestę meę de Niderdala . quę intra has diuisas continetur . scilicet sicut Higherfeldebec uenit de diuisis de Crauena et cadit in Nid . et ita sursum per filum aquę de Nid . usque aquam magnę Stenes . et sic per aquam de Stenes usque ad diuisas de Crauena . et inde per diuisas de Crauena usque ad diuisas contra Higherfeldebec. Intra has diuisas monachi predicti ędificabunt . sartabunt . et arabunt ubicunque uoluerint. Nec ego nec heredes mei quicquam intra prescriptas diuisas retinemus . nisi feras tantum et aues que alias capiunt. Reliqua uero omnia in terra et aqua . in bosco et plano . in pratis et pasturis . in uiis et semitis . subtus terram et super terram . cum omnibus aisiamentis et libertatibus quas ego unquam melius habui in terra illa . habebunt monachi ad faciendum inde quicquid uoluerint in perpetuum. Habebunt etiam conuenientes et sufficientes introitus et exitus sibi et hominibus suis . aueriis et sumagiis suis et carectis suis . per terram et forestam meam usque ad loca sua . sine aliqua contradictione et impedimento. Nec forestarii nostri de aliqua re se intromittent intra predictas diuisas nisi de feris et auibus tantum que alias capiunt ;

---

[1] Presumably Walter Buher.
[2] *Yorks. Fines 1246–72*, ed. J. Parker (Y.R.S. lxxxii) p. 50.
[3] Ibid. p. 183.

nec ueniunt nec redibunt ad loca monachorum que ibi habuerint nisi ad unum tantummodo quem monachi assignauerint . et tunc nichil aliud exigent a fratribus quam quod illis uoluerint fratres loci illius donare. Hanc donationem eis concedo et confirmo in perpetuam elemosinam . puram . propriam . solutam et quietam . liberam a me et ab heredibus meis . et ab omni terreno seruitio et exactione seculari in perpetuum. Et hanc donationem eis tenebimus et warantizabimus et ego et heredes mei contra omnes homines in perpetuum. Et si aliquando euenerit quod non possimus eam illis warantizare . uel ego uel heredes mei :' dabimus eis escambium ad ualentiam et aisiam eorum. Hanc donationem feci eis pro salute animę meę . et patris et matris meę . et omnium antecessorum . et heredum meorum. His testibus . Roberto abbate de Fontibus . Ricardo priore et capitulo de Neuburgh . Nigello et Rob(erto) filiis . Hug(one) Malebissa . Radulfo de Beuuer . Willelmo de Daiuilla . Philippo de Muntpinzun . Hamone Beler . Adam Luuel . Nicholao de Belum . Radulfo clerico de Insula . et Petro clerico . Rob(erto) Beler . et Rogero de Daiuilla . Rob(erto) de Daiuilla . Thom(a) de Coleuilla.

Endorsement: *Rogeri de foresta irg' Higerfeldebec et Stenes . Nidderdale | B'. j. jj.* (late 12th or early 13th cent.).

Size: 14·2 × 39·5 cm.; 3·3 cm. turn-up.

Seal: seal no. 3 of Roger de Mowbray (above, p. lxxxiii), brown wax; appended on tag.

NOTE. The gift was probably made after the mortgage arrangement of 1172, no. 54 above. Robert, abbot of Fountains, died in 1180.[1]

57 *Confirmation by Nigel de Mowbray to Byland of part of western Nidderdale given by his father Roger.* [*c.* 1173 × 1180]

> Original charter: Yorke deeds at Halton Place, no. 59. Cartulary copy: B.M., Egerton MS. 2823 fo. 76v (old fo. 183v) (lacks last 6 witnesses).

Eboracensi archiepiscopo totique capitulo Sancti Petri . et omnibus sanctę ęcclesię filiis . Nigellus de Molbr' salutem. Sciatis me concessisse et hac carta mea confirmasse Deo et monachis Sancte MARIE de Beghlanda . in puram et perpetuam elemosinam . propriam . liberam . solutam . et quietam . ab omni terreno seruitio et exactione seculari in perpetuum donationem illam quam pater meus Rog(erus) de Molbr.' fecit eis de illa parte foreste de Niderdala que intra has diuisas continetur . scilicet intra Higherfeldbec et Stenes a Nid . usque ad diuisas de Crauena . per omnia ita libere solute et quiete sicut carta donationis patris mei eis testatur. Hanc donationem concessi predictis monachis et

---

[1] See C. T. Clay in *Y.A.J.* xxxviii (1955) 18.

confirmaui pro salute animę meę et patris et matris me*a* et uxoris meę Mabilię et omnium antecessorum et heredum nostrorum. Et ego et heredes mei hanc donationem tenebimus et warantizabimus eis contra omnes homines in perpetuum. Hiis testibus Rog(ero) de Molbr' patre meo . et Rob(erto) fratre meo . Ricardo priore et capitulo de Neuburgh . Rob(erto) abbate Font' . Hog' Malab'sa*b* . Rad(ulfo) de Beuuer . Willelmo de Daiuilla . Philippo de Muntpinzun . Ham(one) Beler . Adam Luuel . Nicholao de Bellun . Rad(ulfo) clerico . Petro clerico . Rob(erto) Beler . Rog(ero) de Daiuilla.

Endorsements: *Carta Nigelli de Molbr' . de confirmatione Highefeld . et Stenes. | .Nidderdale. B' .j' .iij.* (late 12th or early 13th cent.).

Size: 12·8 × 19 cm.; 2·3 cm. turn-up.

Seal: seal no. 1 of Nigel de Mowbray (above, p. lxxxiii), red wax; appended on tag.

NOTE. It is clear from the witness-list that this charter belongs to the same occasion as no. 56.

58 *Confirmation by Roger de Mowbray of Hugh Malebisse's gift to and agreements with the monks of Byland concerning Bagby (Yorks., N.R.).*

[*c.* 1181]

Original charter: B.M., Egerton Ch. 2144.
Pd. (transl.), *Yorks. Deeds* ii no. 37, from the original charter then in the possession of Sir Ralph Payne-Gallwey.

Eborac(ensi) archiepiscopo totique capitulo Sancti Petri et omnibus sanctę ęcclesię filiis . Rog(erus) de Moubrai salutem. Sciatis me concessisse et hac carta mea confirmasse Hugoni Malabisse et heredibus eius donationem et conuentiones quas fecit monachis Sancte Marię de Beghlanda . de uilla de Baggebi cum omnibus pertinenciis suis et libertatibus sicut carta ipsius purportat quam habet de me de predicta terra quam terram dedi in creisiamentum illi . sui feudi militis. His test(ibus) Rob(erto) de Molbrai . Herberto filio Ric(ardi) . Philippo de Muntpinzun . Henrico de Lubham . Henrico de Moald . Rob(erto) de Beucamp . Rogero filio Gaufridi . Roberto clerico . Philippo de Karlet' . Gocelino filio Gocelini.

Endorsement: *confirmacio Rogeri de Mo[.]bray* (13th–14th cent.).

Size: 8·5 × 10 cm.; 1·3 cm. turn-up.

Seal: fragment of seal no. 3 of Roger de Mowbray (above, p. lxxxiii), red wax; legend broken off; appended on tag.

NOTE. Five of these witnesses appear in no. 141 and four in no. 142 of *c.* 1181. Hugh Malebisse's quitclaims concerning Bagby survive in original charters

---

a *Sic* in charter; *mee* in cart.   *b* *Sic* in charter; *Hugone Malabissa* in cart.

B.M., Egerton Chs. 2139, 2143 (transl. in *Yorks. Deeds* ii nos. 35, 26). Hugh held one fee in 1166.[1]

59 *Confirmation by Roger de Mowbray to Byland of 18 acres in Bagby, given by him to William son of Ucce.* [*c.* 1181]

Original charter: B.M., Egerton Ch. 2141.
Pd. (transl.), *Yorks. Deeds* ii no. 31, from the original charter then in the possession of Sir Ralph Payne-Gallwey.

Eborac(ensi) archiepiscopo totique capitulo Sancti Petri et omnibus sancte ecclesie filiis . Rog(erus) de Molbrai salutem. Sciatis me concessisse et hac carta mea confirmasse Deo et monachis Sancte Marie de Beghlanda in puram et perpetuam elemosinam propriam . liberam . solutam . et quietam ab omni terreno seruitio et exactione seculari imperpetuum illam partem terre meę et bosci in terrura de Baggebi quam dedi Willelmo filio Huke quam scilicet terram dedi ei in escambium illius terre quam antea dedi ei . uidelicet decem et octo acras. Dedi etiam eis totam terram et boscum recta linea a predicta terra Willelmi antedicti usque ad boscum Hospitalarium. Concessi etiam predictis monachis facere fossatum suum in meo quantum terra eorum durat usque a[d bo]*a*scum Hospitalarium. Hec autem omnia dedi eis in puram et perpetuam elemosinam pro salute anime mee et antecessorum et heredum meorum. Et ego et heredes mei predicta omnia antedictis monachis manutenebimus et warantizabimus contra omnes homines in perpetuum. His testibus . Rob(erto) filio meo . Philippo de Muntpincun . Rob(erto) de Belchamp Henrico de Lubbeham . Rob(erto) Beler . Johanne cappellano*b* Rob(erto) scriptore . Willelmo le Blund . Hug(one) Malebissa.

Endorsement: *Carta confirmationis Rogeri de Molbrai . de donatione Willelmi filii Hucke de Baggebi* (12th cent.); *BAGG'. B' .I.xx* (late 12th or early 13th cent.).

Size: 13·6 × 20·4 cm.

Seal: missing; no tongue, no turn-up.

NOTE. Four of these witnesses appear in no. 58, and five in no. 143, of *c.* 1181 (cf. nos. 134, 136, 140-2). William son of Ucce's charter for Byland is B.M., Egerton Ch. 2140 (transl. in *Yorks. Deeds* ii no. 32). For a charter of Roger de Mowbray granting an exchange to William son of Ucce, see below, no. 399.

60 *Confirmation by Roger de Mowbray to Byland of 2 stags and 3 hinds p.a. from his forest of Nidderdale for the use of the monks' infirmary.* [*c.* 1147 × 1186]

Original charter: Yorke deeds at Halton Place, no. 55.

---

a Charter damaged.   *b* *Sic.*

---

[1] See nos. 371, 401, and Fees [23].

Eboracensi archiepiscopo . et toti capitulo Sancti Petri . et omnibus suis hominibus Rog(erus) de Molbrai . salutem. Sciatis me concessisse . et hac presenti carta confirmasse in perpetuam elemosinam liberam solutam . et quietam ab terreno seruitio et exactione seculari . a me et ab heredibus meis . quod monachi de Beghlanda ad opus infirmorum suorum annuatim habeant in foresta mea de Niderdala duos ceruos et tres bissas. Et has feras eis concedo ut capiant quocunque anni tempore uoluerint et eo modo quo [. . . . .]^a uoluerint per notitiam forestariorum meorum. Et hanc donationem eis confirmo tenendam de me . et de heredibus meis in perpetuum pro salute anime mee et meorum. His testibus . Nigello de Molbr' . Roberto capellano . Rad(ulfo) de Belu[. .]^{b}r . Roberto de [. . . . .: . . .]^b Willelmo coco.

Endorsements: *Carta ROGERI DE* (remainder clipped) (12th cent.); *.Nidderdale. B' .j'. iij.* (13th cent.).

Size: 13·5 × 9·7 cm.; turn-up clipped off.

Seal: missing; was presumably appended on tag through turn-up now clipped off.

NOTE. The first three witnesses suggest a date after *c.* 1147.[1] This charter is probably the genuine basis of the fabricated no. 49.

61 *Confirmation by Roger de Mowbray to Byland of 10 acres of meadow in Hovingham (Yorks., N.R.), given by Hamo Beler.*   [1154 × 1186]

Cartulary copy: B.M., Egerton MS. 2823 fo. 43v (old fo. 148v), partially illegible through damp, some of the lacunae being supplied from Hamo Beler's charter, ibid.

Ebor(acensi) archiepiscopo totique capitulo Sancti Petri et omnibus [sancte ecclesie filiis Rogerus de Molbray salutem.] Sciatis me concessisse et hac carta mea confirmasse [Deo et Sancte Marie et monachis] de Beghlanda in puram et perpetuam elemosinam liberam et propriam solutam et q[uietam ab omni terreno servicio et exactione seculari] donationem illam quam Hamo Beler fecit eisdem monachis [de decem acris prati in Hovyngham, scilicet] pratum juxta ductum aque que currit de Hovyngham versus [Fritonam juxta culturam que vocatur Holover] sicut fossatum quod monachi fecerunt complectitur, sicut [carta Hamonis Beler testatur. Et] hanc donationem predictis monachis concedo et confirmo [. . . . .] et pro salute anime mee liberam omnimodis a me et heredibus meis [imperpetuum, presente Nigello] filio meo

---

^{a} Illegible; ? *ipsi* (cf. no. 71). ^{b} Illegible.

---

[1] For Ralph de Belvoir, see no. 345 note. For Robert the chaplain, see above, p. lxvi.

qui testis et concessor est hujus rei et Roberto fratre [ejus, et Ricardo priore de Neuburgo etc.].

Heading: Confirmatio Rogeri de Molbray de dictis decem acris prati.

NOTE. Richard, prior of Newburgh, held office between 1154/7 and 1181/6.[1] It is possible that this charter and nos. 62 and 64 were given on the same occasion: if so, the *terminus a quo* of this and no. 62 would be *c.* 1170 (see note to no. 64). Hamo Beler held one new fee in 1166,[2] but the land at Hovingham was probably not held for knight service.

62 *Notification by Roger de Mowbray that when he gave to Byland the land which they have in (North) Cave (Yorks., E.R.), he also gave and confirmed all the liberties belonging to the land.* [1154 × 1186]

Pd., *E.Y.C.* iii no. 1828, from B.M., Egerton MS. 2823 fo. 22r (old fo. 124r).

Testibus, Ricardo priore de Novoburgo, Roberto de Molbray etc.

NOTE. For the date, see note to no. 61. Farrer assigned this charter to the period between 1160 and 1175, which he thought was the term of office of Richard, prior of Newburgh. For the original gift, see *E.Y.C.* iii no. 1827 (cal. above, no. 41).

63 *Confirmation by Roger de Mowbray to Byland of 4 acres of meadow in Islebeck (Yorks., N.R.), given by Roger of Carlton.* [1154 × 1186]

Reference in a charter of Roger of Carlton for Byland [1154 × 1186]: B.M., Egerton Ch. 2161.
Pd. (transl.), *Yorks. Deeds* ii no. 242, from the original charter, then in the possession of Sir Ralph Payne-Gallwey.

. . . quatuor acras prati iuxta Yserbec . sicut Rogerus de Molbrai illis concessit . . .

NOTE. The confirmation is also mentioned in the Byland cartulary, Egerton MS. 2823 fo. 46v. Roger of Carlton inherited his father's fee after 1154.[3]

64 *Grant by Roger de Mowbray to Byland of freedom from fees for his seal or the seals of his heirs.* [c. 1170 × 1186]

Cartulary copy: B.M., Egerton MS. 2823 fo. 70v (old fo. 177v).

Ebor(acensi) archiepiscopo totique capitulo Sancti Petri et omnibus sancte ecclesie filiis tam presentibus quam futuris Rogerus Molbray salutem. Sciatis me concessisse et hac carta mea confirmasse Deo et monachis Sancte Marie de Beghlanda in puram et perpetuam elemosinam

[1] See *E.Y.C.* ix 248.   [2] See nos. 341–2, 401, and Fees [43].
[3] See nos. 352–4, 401, and Fees [44].

quod nichil dabunt pro sigillo meo vel heredum meorum habendo, quotiens ego sive heredes mei nec aliqui hominum nostrorum aliquam eis donationem seu elemosinam contulerimus, set libere habebunt tam sigillum meum quam heredum meorum absque alicujus exactione temporalis seu secularis impensionis tam in donationibus quam in confirmationibus sibi factis et faciendis. Hanc libertatem dedi eis pro salute anime mee et omnium antecessorum et heredum meorum imperpetuum. Hiis testibus, Ricardo priore et capitulo de Neuburgh, Roberto de Molbray filio meo, Philippo de Muntpinzun etc.

NOTE. Philip de Montpincon does not occur before c. 1170 (see no. 376 note).

65 *Confirmation by Roger de Mowbray to Byland of 12 bovates in Thorpefield (par. Thirsk, Yorks., N.R.), given by Maud of Stonegrave and Simon her son; and quitclaim of service.* [c. 1170 × 1186]

Transcript, from an original charter formerly in St. Mary's Tower, York: Bodl., MS. Dodsworth 7 fos. 165v–166r. Cartulary copy: B.M., Egerton MS. 2823 fo. 93v (old fo. 199v) (lacks last 2 witnesses).

Eboracensi[a] archiepiscopo totique capitulo Sancti Petri et omnibus sancte ecclesie filiis Rog(erus) de Molbrai[b] salutem. Notum sit vobis me concessisse et hac carta mea confirmasse Deo et monachis Sancte Marie de Beghlanda[c] imperpetuum donationem illam quam Mathilda de Steyngriva et Symon filius ejus fecerunt eis de duodecim bovatis terre in Torp juxta Tresc[d] cum omnibus pertinenciis earum per omnia ita libere solute et quiete sicut carta eorum illis proportant.[e] Sed et quietas eisdem monachis clamo imperpetuum caligas illas de scarlat quas michi et heredibus meis annuatim dare debuerant pro servicio predicte terre. Hec omnia eis concedo et confirmo in puram et perpetuam elemosinam liberam propriam solutam et quietam a me et ab heredibus meis et ab omni terreno servicio et exactione seculari imperpetuum pro salute anime mee et omnium antecessorum et heredum meorum. Et hanc elemosinam tam ego quam heredes mei manutenebimus et warantizabimus contra omnes homines imperpetuum. His testibus, Roberto de Daivilla,[f] [Hugone][g] Malabissa, Thoma de Colevilla, Hamundo [Beler],[g] Radulfo de Bevveir,[h] [Roberto][g] de Bucei,[i] Philippo de Muntpinzun, Roberto clerico filio Willelmi camerarii de Insula.

NOTE. The gift by Maud and Simon of Stonegrave must have been made after the death of Maud's husband, William of Stonegrave, which occurred

---

[a] *Ebor'*, cart.   [b] *Molbray*, cart.   [c] *Bell'*, cart.   [d] *Thorpe juxta Thresk'*, cart.   [e] *perportant*, cart.   [f] *Daivill*, cart.   [g] Omitted in MS. Dodsw., supplied from cart.   [h] *Bevveyr'*, cart.   [i] *Buscy*, cart.

after 1170.¹ For the charter given by Maud and Simon of Stonegrave, see B.M., Egerton MS. 2823 fo. 93*v* (old fo. 199*v*) and cf. also Bodl., MS. Dodsworth 7 fo. 165*r*.

66 *Gift by Roger de Mowbray to Byland of Alfnaf his man of Kirkby Mal-zeard (Yorks., W.R.) with 2 tofts and 3 acres of land.* [*c.* 1170×1186]

Cartulary copy: B.M., Egerton MS. 2823 fo. 51*r* (old fo. 157*r*).

Ebor(acensi) archiepiscopo et omnibus sancte ecclesie filiis Rogerus de Molbray salutem. Sciatis me dedisse et hac carta mea confirmasse Deo et monachis Sancte Marie de Beghlanda Alfnaf hominem*ᵃ* meum de Malasart et toftum ipsius, cum tofto ei propinquiore versus orientem, culturam etiam quandam terre nominatim trium acrarum in campo de Malasart, que cultura vocatur Bywrtreflath. Hec omnia concedo eis dono et confirmo in perpetuam elemosinam puram propriam liberam solutam et quietam ab omni terreno servicio et exactione seculari a me et heredi-bus meis imperpetuum. Hiis testibus, Herberto filio Ricardi, Alano de Limesia, Rogero filio Aye, Johanne de Crevequer etc.

NOTE. The occurrence of Alan de Limesey and Roger son of Aye suggests a date not earlier than *c.* 1170.²

67 *Gift by Roger de Mowbray to Byland of a toft and 7 acres in Kirkby Malzeard.* [*c.* 1170×1186]

Cartulary copy: B.M., Egerton MS. 2823 fo. 51*r* (old fo. 157*r*).

Ebor(acensi) archiepiscopo totique capitulo Sancti Petri et omnibus sancte ecclesie filiis Rogerus de Molbray salutem. Sciatis me dedisse et hac carta mea confirmasse Deo et monachis Sancte Marie de Beghlanda unum toftum in Malasart, totum illum scilicet toftum quod fuit Gamelli de Niderdala del North' ejusdem ville per omnia ita plenarie sicut pre-dictus Gamellus eundem toftum unquam plenius habuit, et tres acras terre inter Epedeceos³ et Kyrkeby que feriunt super viam que vadit inter Kyrkeby et Laverton', quatuor et acras terre inter Morthwayt et Kesebek circa sartam Rogeri presbiteri, communia etiam aysiamenta per totum territorium ejusdem ville et liberos et convenientes introitus et

---

ᵃ hominem repeated in MS.

---

¹ He occurs 1170×1175, *E.Y.C.* iii no. 1878 and v no. 137. For some notes on the Stonegrave family, see *E.Y.C.* vi 122.
² Alan de Limesey occurs also in nos. 145, 262, 272, 276, 307, 336. Roger son of Aye occurs in no. 119 (cf. *E.Y.C.* v no. 122).
³ Perhaps 'Eppecros' which occurs in no. 147 below.

exitus sibi et hominibus suis et averiis suis que ibi habuerint. Hec omnia dedi eisdem monachis in puram et perpetuam elemosinam propriam liberam solutam et quietam ab omni terreno servicio et exactione seculari imperpetuum. Et ego et heredes mei hanc donationem eis manutenebimus et warantizabimus contra omnes homines imperpetuum pro salute anime mee et omnium antecessorum et heredum meorum. Hiis testibus, Nigello de Molbray filio meo, Philippo de Muntpinzun, Roberto de Bello Campo etc.

NOTE. Philip de Montpincon does not occur before c. 1170 (see no. 376 note).

68 *Confirmation by Roger de Mowbray to Byland of land and rights near Yearsley (Yorks., N.R.), given by Thomas de Coleville.*   [1177 × 1186]

Cartulary copy: B.M., Egerton MS. 2823 fo. 36v (old fo. 141v), only partially legible through damp, some of the lacunae being supplied from Thomas de Coleville's charters, ibid. fos. 36v and 37r.

Ebor(acensi) archiepiscopo et toti capitulo Sancti Petri Ebor(aci) [et omnibus hominibus] Francis et [Anglis] et omnibus sancte ecclesie filiis Rogerus de Molbr' salutem. [Sciatis] me [concessi]sse et confirmasse Deo et monachis Sancte Marie de Bellalanda in perpetuam elem[osinam] liberam solutam et quietam de terreno servicio donationem illam quam Thomas de Colevilla [eis dedit in Ber]sclyva et Bur[toft] et de omni terra que est inter Thorp' et stagnum molendini ipsorum [monachorum et de] terra que [est ab] aquilonali parte Whiteker et de viginti acris terre [in bosco inter Thorp et Eversleyam] et de mortuo bosco accipiendo ad necessaria illius loci de Thorp' [et] de communi pastura habenda p[er boscum] ejusdem loci et de quadraginta porcis in tempore pa[stionis] habendis in predicto bosco Eversle si[ne pannagio]. Hec omnia eis concedo et confirmo tenenda in perpetuam elemosinam sicut carta Thome de Colavilla quam monachi habent testatur pro salute anime mee et patris et matris [mee et] omnium [? antecessorum] meorum. Concedo etiam eis et confirmo scilicet in perpetuam elemosinam viam unam inter [abbatiam] suam et Wildonam sicut testatur cyrographum inter eos et Thomam de [Colavilla] et [? divisas] que in eodem cyrographo continetur. Hiis testibus, Roberto de Bucy, War[ino ? filio Simonis] etc.

NOTE. A reference to the 'new abbey' in Thomas de Coleville's agreement concerning the road from Wildon[1] gives the earliest date of this confirmation as 1177. Thomas held one new fee in 1166.[2]

[1] Bodl., MS. Dodsworth 91 fos. 76r and 121v.
[2] See nos. 356-7, 401, and Fees [40].

There survive the two matching halves of a chirograph agreement between Byland and Newburgh, probably of *c.* 1177 × 1181, concerning land between Oxendale and Gilling (cf. above, no. 51), which mentions Thomas de Coleville's rights to pannage at Thorpe le Willows. One of the surviving halves bears the seals of both Roger de Mowbray (seal no. 3, above, p. lxxxiii) and Thomas de Coleville.[1]

69 *Confirmation by Roger de Mowbray to Byland of the site of the abbey and various neighbouring lands, and gifts by Hugh Malebisse, William de Wyville, Maud of Stonegrave, William de Mandeville, Thomas de Coleville, Robert de Daiville, and others.* [1177 × 1186]

> Pd., *Mon. Ang.* v 348 (VI), from an *inspeximus* by Thomas de Mowbray and Segrave, earl marshal, dated 21 July 1385 (transcribed in Bodl., MSS. Dodsworth 10 fos. 187r–188r, 94 fos. 3r–5r) (version A). Also transcripts from a lost portion of the cartulary of Byland (Byland chronicle): Bodl., MS. Dodsworth 63 fos. 34r–35r (version B); and from an original charter formerly in St. Mary's Tower, York: Bodl., MS. Dodsworth 94 fos. 1r–2v (version C).

Hiis testibus, Nigello et Roberto filiis meis,[a] [b]Swano magistro hospitalis Sancti Petri,[b] et Pagano fratre ejusdem domus, [c]Olyvero de Buscy, Johanne Crevequer, Roberto capellano et alio Roberto de Mowbray capellano, Roberto Beler, Waltero de Meynill, Rogero de Erdena, Walkelino, Willelmo filio Ucce, Thoma capellano et aliis.

> NOTE. This confirmation must have been granted after the monks had been established at their final site in 1177. Comparison of the three versions suggests that successive interpolations were made to what may have been a genuine charter.

70 *Confirmation by Nigel de Mowbray to Byland of the new abbey and all lands of his fee given by his father Roger and by others.* [1177 × 1190]

> Cartulary copy: B.M., Egerton MS. 2823 fo. 70v (old fo. 177v).

Omnibus sancte ecclesie fidelibus Nigellus de Molbray salutem in Domino. Sciatis me pro salute anime mee et Rogeri patris mei et

---

[a] *meis* omitted in B, which inserts *Rogeri de Molbray.* [b-b] B reads: 'magistro Swano hospicii Sancti Petri Ebor ''. [c] From this point to end, B reads: 'Roberto capellano et alio capellano, Olivero de Bucy, Roberto Crevequer et Johanne fratre ejus, Roberto Beler, Waltero de Mainill, Rogero de Erdena, Walkelino, Willelmo filio Ucce'. C reads: 'Roberto capellano de Mowbrai, Thoma capella, Olivero de Bucy, Roberto Crevequer, Johanne fratre ejus, Roberto Beler, Waltero de Maynill, Rogero de Erdena, Willelmo filio Ucce et aliis multis'.

---

[1] B.M., Egerton Ch. 585; also Newburgh Priory deeds deposited at Northallerton, County Record Office; cartulary copy in B.M., Egerton MS. 2823 fo. 81r–v; pd. (abstract), H.M.C., *Various Collections* ii (1903) 4.

omnium antecessorum et heredum meorum concessisse et confirmasse Deo et Sancte Marie matri ejus et abbati et monachis Beghlande et successoribus suis novam abbatiam suam et omnes terras cum pertinenciis quas habent de feudo meo quocunque loco, sive per Rogerum patrem meum sive per alios, in liberam puram et perpetuam elemosinam quietam de omnibus serviciis imperpetuum. Et ego et heredes mei istam confirmationem contra omnes gentes predictis monachis et eorum successoribus warantizabimus et defendemus imperpetuum. Testes sunt, Robert Dayvilla, Willelmus frater ejus, Hugo de Malabestia, Robertus Bellcampo, Hamo Beler.

NOTE. The confirmation was clearly issued after the establishment at Byland, 1177. Possibly it was made after Roger de Mowbray's departure on crusade, 1186, or his death, 1188.

71 *Confirmation by Nigel de Mowbray to Byland of 2 stags and 3 hinds p.a. from the forest of Nidderdale for the use of the monks' infirmary, and of freedom from fees for his seal or the seals of his heirs.* [1186 × 1190]

Cartulary copy: B.M., Egerton MS. 2823 fo. 77r (old fo. 184r).

Ebor(acensi) archiepiscopo totique capitulo Sancti Petri et omnibus sancte ecclesie filiis Nigellus de Molbray salutem. Sciatis me dedisse et concessisse et hac mea carta confirmasse monachis Sancte Marie de Bellal(anda) ad opus infirmorum suorum annuatim in foresta mea de Niderdala duos cervos et tres bissas in perpetuam elemosinam liberam et quietam ab omni terreno servicio et exactione seculari pro salute anime mee et omnium antecessorum et heredum meorum. Et concessi eis ut capiant has feras quocunque amodo tempore voluerint et eo modo quo ipsi voluerint per noticiam forestariorum meorum. Concessi etiam eis quod nichil dabunt pro sigillo meo vel heredum meorum. Sed habebunt libere sigillum meum et heredum meorum absque omni exactione seculari sicut carta patris mei testatur quotiens ego vel heredes mei vel homines mei eis aliquid contulerimus quolibet modo. Et ego et heredes mei warantizabimus predictis monachis hec omnia contra omnes homines imperpetuum. Hiis testibus, Roberto de Moubray fratre meo, Willelmo et Roberto filiis meis, Rogero de Sancto Martino, Rogero de Dayvilla, Radulpho clerico etc.

NOTE. This confirmation by Nigel of his father's gifts in nos. 49, 60, and 64 must have been made after Roger's departure on crusade.

72 *Confirmation by Nigel de Mowbray to Byland of Great and Little Wildon, Rose Hill, 'Edeneshous', a road from Wildon to the abbey, and pasture in Coxwold.* [1186 × 1190]

Transcript, from an original charter formerly in St. Mary's Tower, York: Bodl., MS. Dodsworth 91 fos. 121v–122r.

Ebor(acensi) archiepiscopo totique capitulo Sancti Petri et omnibus sancte ecclesie filiis Nigellus de Molbray salutem. Sciatis me concessisse et hac charta mea confirmasse Deo et monachis Sancte Marie de Belelanda donationem illam quam pater meus Rogerus de Mubray fecit eis de Magna Wildona et Parva Wildona et de Roseberch cum omnibus pertinenciis suis in bosco et plano in pratis et pasturis et omnibus aisiamentis ad illas terras pertinentibus sicut carte patris mei testantur. Concedo etiam eis et confirmo culturam de Edeneshous et viam que vadit a Wildonia usque ad novam abbatiam que debet habere tres perticatas in latitudine et pasturam in Cucuwalt que dedit eis Thomas de Colevilla. Hec omnia concedo et confirmo propria libera soluta et quieta ab omni terreno servicio et exactione seculari in puram et perpetuam elemosinam pro salute anime mee et patris mei et matris mee et omnium antecessorum et heredum meorum imperpetuum. Et ego Nigellus et heredes mei hanc concessionem et confirmationem manutenebimus et warantizabimus eis contra omnes homines imperpetuum. Hiis testibus, Roberto fratre meo, Willelmo filio et herede meo, Gaufrido Hagate, Richardo de Widevilla, Hamone Beler, Radulfo de Bevver, Rogero de Dayvilla, Rogero de Sancto Martino, Henrico de Riparia, Roberto Buscy, ...ᵃ Luvel, Waltero de Grimeston.

NOTE. The confirmation of nos. 34, 36, 37, and 68 clearly belongs to Nigel's period as lord of the honour, and was given on the same occasion as nos. 73–5.

73 *Confirmation by Nigel de Mowbray to Byland of various lands in (North) Cave, Fawdington, Thorpefield, Thirsk, and Bagby, given by various tenants.* [1186 × 1190]

Cartulary copy: B.M., Egerton MS. 2823 fos. 71v–72r (old fos. 178v–179r).

Omnibus sancte ecclesie filiis has literas visuris vel audituris Nigellus de Molbray salutem. Sciatis me concessisse et presenti carta mea confirmasse Deo et monachis de Beghlanda dimidiam carucatam terre in Cava et Faldyngtonam secundum conventiones que facte sunt inter eos et Humfridum de Mandevilla et Walterum de Riparia et heredes eorum; duodecim etiam bovatas terre in Thorpe juxta Thresk quas habent ex donatione Mathild(is) de Staingrive et Symonis filii ejus cum omnibus pertinenciis earum, per omnia ita proprie libere solute et quiete sicut in cartis eorum continetur. Set et quietas eisdem monachis clamo caligas illas de scarlat quas michi et heredibus meis annuatim dare debuerant

ᵃ *Sic*; presumably *Adam* omitted.

pro servicio predicte terre. Concedo etiam eis et confirmo conventiones que facte sunt inter eos et Willelmum nepotem et heredem Engeleri de Thresk, scilicet de terra de Thorp' juxta Thresk', de una bovata terre in Bagby et de tribus bovatis in Thresk' quas Engelerus avunculus ejus dedit et carta sua confirmavit Deo et predictis monachis. Concedo etiam eis et confirmo servicium Willelmi filii Ucce et heredum suorum et donationem illam quam fecit eis de terra sua in Bagby sicut carta ejus testatur et unum etiam toftum in Thresk' quod fuit Galfrido Harpin et alterum quod tenent Rogerus filius Walteri Harkesinall' et Jordanus socius ejus cum omnibus pertinenciis suis et libertatibus et liberis consuetudinibus. Hec omnia concedo predictis monachis et confirmo propria libera soluta et quieta ab omni terreno servicio et exactione seculari cum omnibus pertinenciis suis in bosco et plano in pratis et pasturis cum omnibus aliis aysiamentis sicut carte datorum testant in puram et perpetuam elemosinam pro salute anime mee et patris et matris mee et omnium antecessorum et heredum meorum. Et ego et heredes mei hanc concessionem et confirmationem manutenebimus et warantizabimus eis contra omnes homines imperpetuum. Hiis testibus, Roberto fratre meo, Willelmo filio meo et herede, Galfrido Hagat, Ricardo de Widevilla, Hamone Beler etc.

NOTE. For the date, see note to no. 72. For some of the earlier charters relating to these properties, see above, nos. 41, 43, 59, 65.

74 *Confirmation by Nigel de Mowbray to Byland of land in Scackleton, Hovingham, and Airyholme, given by Gundreda de Gournay, Roger de Mowbray, and Hamo Beler.* [1186×1190]

Cartulary copy: B.M., Egerton MS. 2823 fo. 111*v* (old fo. 217*v*).

Ebor(acensi) archiepiscopo totique capitulo Sancti Petri et omnibus sancte ecclesie filiis Nigellus de Moubray salutem. Sciatis me concessisse et presenti carta mea confirmasse Deo et monachis de Beghlanda terram de Scakilden, tres scilicet carucatas quas pater meus Rogerus de Moubray et mater ejus Gundrea eis dederunt cum bosco et communem pasturam per totam forestam de Hovyngham ubicunque averia hominum ejusdem ville pascunt. Concedo etiam eis et confirmo pratum de Hovyngham quod habent ex donatione domine Gundree avie mee per divisas et metas que continentur in carta ejus, et ex donatione Hamonis Beler decem acras prati in Hovyngham et quinque acras terre in terrura ejusdem ville in loco qui vocatur Speules et dimidiam marcam argenti annuatim de molendinis ejus de Hovyngham sicut carte ejus testantur. Concedo etiam eis et confirmo terram de Erghom que [jacet]*ᵃ* juxta Holthorp per divisas que continentur in carta patris mei Rogeri de Moubray. Has omnes divisas concedo eis et [confir]*ᵃ*mo puras liberas solutas et quietas ab omni terreno servicio et exactione seculari cum omnibus pertinenciis suis [in boscis]*ᵃ* et planis in aquis et viis et semitis in pratis et pasturis et omnibus aliis aisiamentis in puram et perpetuam elemosinam pro salute [anime mee]*ᵃ* et patris et matris mee et omnium antecessorum et heredum meorum. Et ego et heredes mei hec omnia manutenebimus et warant[izabimus contra]*ᵃ* omnes homines imperpetuum. Hiis testibus, Roberto fratre meo, Willelmo filio meo et herede, Galfrido Hagat, Ricardo de Widevilla etc.

NOTE. For the date, see note to no. 72. For the earlier charters relating to these properties, see nos. 33–5, 37, 47, and 61.

75 *Confirmation by Nigel de Mowbray to Byland of agreements concerning Scawton, Murton, and Snilesworth (Yorks., N.R.), made between the monks and Hugh Malebisse.*   [1186 × 1190]

Transcript, from a lost portion of the cartulary of Byland fo. 60: Bodl., MS. Top. Yorks. d. 11 fo. 258r.

Confirmatio Nigelli de Molbray totius Beghelandie et ecclesie et ex dono Hugonis Malebysse totum planum fundi vallis que est inter Beghelandiam et Scaltonam et Mortonam secundum conventiones quas fecerunt inter se, et Snigleswath etc. Testibus, Roberto fratre, Willelmo filio et herede etc.

NOTE. For the date, see note to no. 72. For Hugh Malebisse's charter, given during Roger de Mowbray's lifetime, see *E.Y.C.* iii nos. 1836, 1846, Bodl., MSS. Dodsworth 94 fo. 18r–v, Top. Yorks. d. 11 fo. 258r.

76 *Gift by Nigel de Mowbray, with the consent of Mabel his wife, to the hermitage of La Colombe (Ben., Manche, arr. Saint-Lô, cant. Percy), of 4 acres next to the church of Margueray (Manche, arr. Saint-Lô, cant. Percy).*   [1188 × 1190]

Transcript, from an original charter formerly in the Archives of Orne, Alençon (now missing): P.R.O., Transcripts (Léchaudé d'Anisy's Cartulaire de la Basse-Normandie) P.R.O. 31/8/140B pt. i p. 212.
Pd. (abstract), *Cal. Docs. France* no. 649, from the transcript.

Notum sit vobis omnibus ad quos presens scriptum pervenerit quod ego Nigellus dominus de Monbrai assensu et concessione Mabire*ᵇ* uxoris mee et filiorum meorum pro salute anime mee et decessorum meorum

ᵃ Illegible through damp.   *ᵇ Sic.*

dedi et concessi ecclesie Sancte Marie de heremitagio de Columba in perpetuam elemosinam iiij acras juxta ecclesiam Sancte Marie de Margerei, libere et quiete possidendas ex omnibus actionibus secularibus. His testibus, Roberto capellano, Willelmo Malaherba, Nicholao de Beslii, Radulfo clerico, Roberto clerico, Willelmo de Maisnileio et aliis.

Seal: broken.

NOTE. The hermitage was a dependency of Saint-Sauveur-le-Vicomte, and was founded in 1188.[1]

77 *Confirmation by Roger de Mowbray to Combe (Cist., Warwicks.) of the land of Smite, given by Richard de Camville for the foundation of the abbey, and quitclaim of knight service; and gift of dead wood in Birchley (in Brinklow, Warwicks.) and pasture and quittance of pannage.* [*c.* 1150]

Original charter: Gregory-Hood deeds deposited at Stratford on Avon, Shakespeare Birthplace Trust Libr., Gregory-Hood Ch. 191.

Episcopo Couentruwię . et vniuersis sancte ecclesię fidelibus . et omnibus hominibus suis Francis et Anglis . tam presentibus quam futuris . Rogerius de Moulbraio . salutem. Quoniam ad nos pertinet . in hiis que de iure nostro sunt . seruos Dei fouere . et beneficiis temporalibus ampliare ꝰ notum uobis facio me dedisse et concessisse . et presentis cartule testimonio confirmasse in perpetuam elemosinam totam terram de Smite in terra et aqua . in bosco et plano . in pratis et pascuis . quam Richardus de Camuilla tenuit de me et dedit Deo et monachis Sancte Marie de Cumba . ad fundandam abbatiam ordinis Cistercii . sicut ipse Richardus dedit . et per cartam suam confirmauit ꝰ liberam et quietam a seruicio unius militis quod ipse Richardus annuatim michi debebat . et ab omni seculari seruicio. Concedo etiam predictis monachis in bosco meo de Burchtleio mortuum boscum . et pasturam pecoribus suis . et ut porci sui quieti sint de pannagio. His testibus . Rogero abbate Bellelande . Roberto de Daiuilla monacho . Herberto de Moreuilla et Richardo filio eius . Willelmo de Arches . Roberto de Daiuilla . Bertranno Haget . et Willelmo filio eius . Rogero de Flammauilla . Willelmo de Camuilla . Radulfo de Beluer . et Roberto fratre suo . et Radulfo de Bethlum.

Endorsement: *ROG' de Moulbraio de terra de Smita* (12th cent.).

Size: 28·8 × 10·7 cm.; 1·2 cm. turn-up.

Seal: seal no. 2 of Roger de Mowbray (above, p. lxxxii), brown wax varnished; appended on tag and enclosed in green silk seal-bag.

---

[1] *Gallia Christiana* xi (Paris, 1759) instr. col. 252.

NOTE. The foundation of Combe by Richard de Camville took place on 10 July 1150. This confirmation was probably made very shortly after Camville's original gift.[1] One of the witnesses, William de Arches, died in c. 1154 (below, no. 359 note). The gift by Roger de Mowbray and Richard de Camville was confirmed by Henry II, probably in January 1155.[2]

Roger held Smite of the earl of Leicester; for his enfeoffment of Richard de Camville, see below, no. 350. The present charter formed the basis of the interpolated version below, no. 78.

78 *Interpolated version of no. 77.*

> Fabricated original charter: Gregory-Hood deeds deposited at Stratford on Avon, Shakespeare Birthplace Trust Libr., Gregory-Hood Ch. 190. Cartulary copies: B.M., Cotton MSS. Vit. A i fo. 37*v* (lacks 6 witnesses); Vit. D xviii fo. 1*v* (fragment). Transcript, from cartulary of Combe fo. 50*v* (Vit. D xviii before Cotton fire); Bodl., MS. Dugdale 12 p. 113.
> Pd., *Mon. Ang.* v 584 (III), from Vit. A i.

Waltero Dei gratia episcopo Couintrensi . et vniuersis sancte ecclesie fidelibus . tam presentibus quam futuris . Rog(erus) de Molbraio salutem. Quoniam ad nos pertinet in hiis que de iure nostro sunt . seruos Dei fouere et beneficiis temporalibus ampliare ; notum uobis facio me concessisse . et presentis carte testimonio confirmasse Deo et Sancte Marie et monachis de Cumba in puram et perpetuam elemosinam pro salute anime mee et omnium parentum meorum totam terram de Smita quam Ricardus de Camuilla de me tenuit per seruitium unius militis . et eisdem monachis dedit ad fundandam abbatiam Cisterciensis ordinis. Totam autem predictam terram de Smita . tam in terris asisis quam in hominibus . cum toto dominico . in bosco et plano . in pratis et pascuis . in uiis et aquis . in sichis et moris . concessi predictis monachis de Cumba liberam . solam[a] et quietam ab omni seculari seruitio . sicut ipse Ricardus illam dedit eis . et per cartam suam confirmauit. Et ut quieti sint ab illius militis seruitio quod idem Ricardus michi debebat . et ego comiti de Legrecest(ria) . seruitium autem alterius militis quem eidem comiti debeo . fiet de Brinkelawe . ita quod ego nec heredes mei aliquod seruitium seculare a predictis monachis exigemus. Concedo etiam predictis monachis in bosco meo de Burtleia mortuum boscum . et pasturam pecoribus ipsorum . et ut eorum porci quieti sint de pasnagio. T(estibus) . Rogero de Flamuilla . Herberto de Moreuilla et Ricardo filio ipsius . Will(elmo) de Arches . Rob(erto) de Daiuilla . Bertranno Haget et Will(elmo) filio ipsius . Willelmo de Camuilla . Radulfo de Belueir . et Rob(erto) fratre ipsius . Radulfo de Betlum . et multis aliis.

---

[a] *Sic* in all versions for *solutam*).

---

[1] *Mon. Ang.* v 584 (I).   [2] *C.Ch.R.* i 351; cf. Eyton, *Itinerary* pp. 3–4.

Endorsement: *Carta Rogerii de Molbraio de Smita* (12th cent.).

Size: 14·1 × 15·2 cm.; 2·4 cm. turn-up.

Seal: missing; was appended on tag.

> NOTE. This charter is an interpolated version of the genuine no. 77, but the script is perhaps not later than the 1170s or 1180s. The occasion of the fabrication was probably the demand for knight service by Mowbray or Leicester, perhaps 1174. A charter of Robert, earl of Leicester, confirms the gift, and quitclaims the service of one knight due from Smite, recording that the service of another knight is due from Mowbray for Brinklow.[1]

79 *Gift by Roger de Mowbray to Combe of part of his wood called Birchley (in Brinklow, Warwicks.).*   [*c.* 1150 × Jan. 1182]

> Cartulary copy: B.M., Cotton MS. Vit. A i fo. 40v.

Episcopo Cestrie et universis sancte ecclesie fidelibus et omnibus hominibus suis Francis et Anglis tam presentibus quam futuris Rogerus de Moubrai salutem. Notum vobis facio me dedisse et concessisse et presentis cartule testimonio confirmasse in perpetuam elemosinam Deo et monachis de Cumba quandam partem nemoris mei que dicitur Borchleia a via que dicitur Heshcetelweie usque ad viam que dicitur Morweie et inde usque ad divisas de Billn'[a] et pratum quod est de dominio meo quod est a stagno ipsorum monachorum usque ad divisas de Billn'. Teste Nigello filio meo et herede concessu et prece hanc donationem feci.

> NOTE. This gift was made before no. 80 and was perhaps made not long after no. 77.

80 *Notification by Nigel de Mowbray to Richard (Pecche), bishop of Coventry (1161–82), of his confirmation to Combe of the land of Smite, given by Roger de Mowbray for the foundation of the abbey, and of dead wood in Birchley and pasture and quittance of pannage; and also of a part of the wood of Birchley given separately by Roger de Mowbray.*

[Apr. 1161 × Jan. 1182]

> Cartulary copies: B.M., Cotton MSS. Vit. A i fo 38v (lacks last 3 witnesses); Vit. D xviii fo. 14r–v (fragment). Transcript from cartulary of Combe fo. 53r (Vit. D xviii before Cotton fire): Bodl., MS. Dugdale 12 p. 115.

Ricardo Dei gratia episcopo Cestrie et omnibus sancte ecclesie filiis Nigellus de Moubray salutem. Sciatis me concessisse et per hanc cartam meam confirmasse donationem illam quam Rogerus de Moubrai

---

[a] *Brandon'* erased in MS.

[1] B.M., Cotton MS. Vit. A i fos. 37v–38r.

pater meus fecit Deo et Sancte Marie de Cumba et monachis ordinis Cisterciensis ibidem Deo servientibus in perpetuam elemosinam, scilicet totam terram de Smita in terra et aqua in bosco et plano in pratis et pasturis ad fundandam abbatiam ordinis Cist(erciensis). Concedo etiam predictis monachis in bosco meo quod dicitur Burchleia mortuum boscum et pasturam pecoribus suis et ut porci sui quieti sint de pannagio et quandam partem nemoris mei de Borchleia separatim quam pater meus dedit eis et per cartam suam confirmavit, que incipit a via que dicitur Hethwittelweie usque ad viam que dicitur Moreweia usque ad divisas de Billneia. Et hanc donationem patris mei quam ego concessi et per cartam meam confirmavi volo ut habeant monachi de Cumba in pace et honorifice liberam et quietam ab omni terreno servicio et exactione seculari. Hiis testibus, Hugone Malebisse, Radulfo de Belveir, Hamone Belier, Roberto de Buci, Willelmo de Daivilla, Roberto Belier et multis aliis.

81 *Notification by Roger de Mowbray to Richard (Pecche), bishop of Coventry, of his gift to Combe of part of his wood of Brinklow, called Birchley.*

[*c.* 1170 × Jan. 1182]

Original charter: Gregory-Hood deeds deposited at Stratford on Avon, Shakespeare Birthplace Trust Libr., Gregory-Hood Ch. 39. Cartulary copies: B.M., Cotton MSS. Vit. A i fo. 40v (lacks last 16 witnesses); Vit. D xviii fo. 10v (fragment) (lacks last 10 witnesses).

Ricardo Dei gratia episcopo Cestrie et . omnibus hominibus et amicis suis Francis . et Anglis . et omnibus fidelibus sancte ecclesie tam presentibus quam futuris Rogerus de Molbraio salutem. Quoniam ad nos pertinet seruos Dei semper et ubique pro posse nostro confouere . et ex possessionibus que iuris nostri sunt ampliare ꝉ [ic]ᵃcirco notum sit omnibus filiis sancte ecclesie . quod ego Rogerus de Molbraio concessi et in perpetuam elemosinam [don]ᵃaui Deo et ecclesie Sancte Marie de Cumba . et monachis ibidem Deo seruientibus . de nemore meo de Brincalawa quod dicitur Burhtleia . totam illam partem nemoris que est a uia que uocatur Walewei . scilicet ab illa Waleweia que propinquior est Brincalawie . et que totum boscum penetrat per transuersum ꝉ usque ad diuisas Brandonie et Bileneie. Sciant igitur omnes hanc cartam legentes et legi audientes . quod ego Rogerus de Molbraio hanc donationem feci Deo et monachis de Cumba . et hac presenti carta mea confirmaui . pro salute mea et omnium heredum meorum . et pro animabus patris et matris mee et omnium antecessorum meorum ꝉ ut iidem

ᵃ Charter damaged; text supplied from carts.

monachi de Cumba per concessionem meam . et per warantizationem meam et heredum meorum contra omnes homines . teneant et habeant in perpetuam elemosinam . totam predictam partem nemoris . et quicquid intra prenominatos terminos habetur . bene et in pace . et omnino tam libere et quiete quam ego unquam liberius et quietius eandem posses-sionem tenui. His t(estibus) . Rog(ero) sacerdote de Brincalawa . Hug(one) Malebisse . Philippo de Muntpincun . Rob(erto) de Cotes . Petro clerico meo . Herberto Putot . Durando de Brincalawa . Simone filio Rogeri . Will(elmo) filio Herberti . Willelmo Gramario . Rad(ulfo) filio Ricardi . Will(elmo) de Wauera . Osberto de Brettuna Alano Fossard . Ernaldo dispensatore . Chinone camerario . Rad(ulfo) Bisebar[.]ᵃ coco . et aliis multis.

Endorsement: *Rog' de Molbraio de boscho de Brinchelawa* (12th-cent. hand, very similar to that of face).

Size: 20·6 × 13·7 cm.; 3 cm. turn-up.

Seal: missing; was appended on tag.

Script: same hand as that of Gregory-Hood Ch. 194, a charter of Gerard de Camville, addressed to Richard (Pecche), bishop of Coventry.

NOTE. Philip de Montpincon does not occur before *c.* 1170 (no. 376 note). Richard Pecche, bishop of Coventry, died in January 1182.
   A charter of Geoffrey de la Haia reveals that this land was held by him of Mowbray and he received 41 marks from the monks for his gift.[1] Haia lost his estate in Brinklow and was given an exchange before 1184, possibly 1179 (below, nos. 364-5).

82 *Confirmation by Roger de Mowbray to Combe of 2 virgates in Withybrook (Warwicks.), given by Richard de Moreville.* [c. 1170 × Jan. 1182]

Cartulary copies: B.M., Cotton MSS. Vit. A i fo. 39r (lacks last 3 witnesses); Vit. D xviii fo. 8r (fragment). Transcript, from cartulary of Combe fo. 54r (Vit. D xviii before Cotton fire): Bodl., MS. Dugdale 12 p. 115.

Rogerus de Moubray omnibus hominibus et amicis suis Francis et Anglis salutem. Sciatis quod ego Rogerus concessi et hac presenti carta mea confirmavi pro salute anime mee et omnium meorum Deo et abbatie mee de Cumba hanc libertatem perpetuo habendam scilicet ut monachi ejusdem loci liceat habere et tenere libere et quiete et per-petualiter illas duas virgatas terre in Withibrocᵇ quas Ricardus de More-villa homo meus in perpetuam elemosinam illis dedit. Et preterea ut liceat eisdem monachis de Cumba perquirere et habere libere et quiete de feodo meo ubicunque et de quocunque et quantumcunque potuerint

---
ᵃ Charter damaged. ᵇ *Widebroc*, Vit. D xviii.

[1] B.M., Cotton MS. Vit. A i fos. 38r, 41v.

sive in elemosinam illis donatum fuerit sive etiam ipsi proprio catallo suo aliquid emere vel conquirere potuerint salvo servicio regis. His testibus, Hugone Malebisse, Gaufrido de la Haia, Roberto de Bealcamp, Petro de Belingeia et Philippo de Belingeia fratre ejus, Philippo de Mumpincun.

NOTE. Philip de Montpincon does not occur before *c.* 1170 (no. 376 note). This confirmation must have preceded no. 83. The charter of Richard de Moreville (who held 5 fees of Mowbray in 1166)[1] is summarized in MS. Dugdale 12 p. 115. Withybrook was presumably a post-Domesday settlement in the Domesday territory of Hopsford.[2]

83 *Confirmation by Nigel de Mowbray to Combe of 6 virgates of his demesne in Withybrook, given by Richard de Moreville.*   [*c.* 1170 × Jan. 1182]

Cartulary copies: B.M., Cotton MSS. Vit. A i fo. 75*r*; Vit. D xviii fo. 36*v* (fragment).

Omnibus amicis suis Nigellus de Moubray salutem. Sciatis quod ego Nigellus de Moubrai concessi et hac presenti carta mea confirmavi Deo et ecclesie beate Marie de Cumba de feodo meo scilicet de dominio meo de Withybroch sex virgatas terre cum gardino et cum curte et cum pratis et cum omnibus pertinenciis ejusdem terre ut teneant et habeant perpetualiter totam predictam possessionem tam libere et quiete sicut Ricardus de Morevilla illam eis donavit et carta sua confirmavit. Hiis testibus.

NOTE. This confirmation was clearly made after no. 82. Richard de Moreville's charter is addressed to Richard Pecche, bishop of Coventry (1161–82).[3]

84 *Gift by Roger de Mowbray to Combe of part of the wood of Brinklow, by specified bounds, for which the monks gave him 80 marks.*   [*c.* 1170 × 1186]

Original charter: Gregory-Hood deeds deposited at Stratford on Avon, Shakespeare Birthplace Trust Libr., Gregory-Hood Ch. 37 (damaged). Cartulary copies: B.M., Cotton MSS. Vit. A i fo. 40*r* (lacks last 10 witnesses); Vit. D xviii fo. 9*v* (fragment). Transcript, from cartulary of Combe fo. 55*r* (Vit. D xviii before Cotton fire): Bodl., MS. Dugdale 12 p. 116 (lacks last 4 witnesses).

Omnibus sancte matris ecclesie filiis presentibus et futuris Rogerus [de Moubray salutem. Sciatis me]*a* dedisse et concessisse et hac carta mea presenti confirmasse [monachis Sancte Marie de Cumba]*a* quandam

a Charter damaged; text supplied from carts.

---

[1] No. 401, Fees [22].
[2] See *Place-Names Warwicks.* (English Place-Name Soc. xiii) p. 121.
[3] B.M., Cotton MS. Vit. A i fo. 74*v*.

partem de bosco . meo . de Brinkalaue . illam scilicet [partem nemoris cum terra que]ᵃ infra est a Morweia . usque ad uiam . que est inter predictum ne[mus et inter terram arabilem de Brin]ᵃkelaue . et a Walweia . que est inter illam partem nemoris . [quam iidem monachi prius de me habuerunt]ᵃ usque ad diuissas de Brandune . et item a diuis[is de Brandona usque Morweiam. Hanc a]ᵃutem donationem feci illis . pro Dei amore et pro sa[lute anime mee et filiorum meorum et pro ani]ᵃmabus patris et matris mee et omnium antecessorum meorum et [successorum meorum ut habeant et teneant o]ᵃmnem predictam donationem liberam et solutam et quietam . ab [omnibus seruiciis et omni seculari exactio]ᵃne in perpetuam elemosinam . ad velle suum . inde faciendum [ad sartandum vel custodiendum.]ᵃ Monachi uero prefati . michi quater uiginti marcas . in caritate dederunt . [Hiis testibus, Roberto de Davilla,]ᵃ Waltero Briton(e) . Ham(one) Bel(er) . Ham(one) Lestrange . Philippo de Munpincun . He[nrico de Rokeby, Roberto de Billn',ᵇ]ᵃ Rob(erto) de Wauera . Will(elmo) cam(erario) . Petro filio Ham(onis) Lestrange Rad(ulfo) filio Ric(ardi) [Roberto Beler, Ernaldo]ᵃ dispens(atore)ᶜ . Rad(ulfo) filio Galfr(idi) . Rob(erto) clerico . Rannuldoᵈ de Mandeuilla . Rob(erto) filio [Girardi, et multis aliis.]ᵉ

Endorsement: *Rog' de Molbrai de parte nemoris de Brinkelaue ad custodiend' et sartand' et ad velle suum faciend'* (? 12th cent.).

Size: 10·8 × 13·8 cm.; 1·2 cm. turn-up.

Seal: seal no. 3 of Roger de Mowbray (above, p. lxxxiii), white wax varnished; appended on tag, and enclosed in seal-bag of white linen.

NOTE. Philip de Montpincon does not occur before *c.* 1170 (see no. 376 note).

85 *Similar gift by Roger de Mowbray to Combe of part of his wood of Brinklow, by specified bounds, for which the monks acquitted his debt to the Jews of 80 marks.* [*c.* 1170 × 1186]

> Original charter: Gregory-Hood deeds deposited at Stratford on Avon, Shakespeare Birthplace Trust Libr., Gregory-Hood Ch. 38. Cartulary copies: B.M., Cotton MSS. Vit. A i fo. 40r (lacks witnesses); Vit. D xviii fos. 9v–10r (fragment). Transcript, from cartulary of Combe fo. 55v (Vit. D xviii before Cotton fire): Bodl., MS. Dugdale 12 p. 116 (lacks witnesses).

Omnibus sancte ecclesie fidelibus tam presentibus quam futuris ? Rogerius de Mulbraio salutem. Sciatis me dedisse et concessisse et hac presenti carta mea confirmasse monachis Sancte Marie de Cumba quandam partem de bosco meo de Brinchelawa . illam partem .

ᵃ Charter damaged; text supplied from carts. and ends.   ᶜ MS. Dugdale version ends.
ᵇ Vit. A i version adds *et aliis*
ᵈ *Sic* (? for *Rannulfo*).
ᵉ Charter damaged; text supplied from Vit. D xviii.

scilicet . nemoris cum terra que infra est a Moreweia usque ad uiam
que est inter predictum nemus et inter terram arabilem de Brinkelawa
et a Waleweia usque ad uiam que uenit de Brinchelawa ad Brandonam .
et a diuisis de Brandon(a) . usque ad sartum . quod homines de
Brinchelawa tenent . et de angulo sarti illorum per Morweiam . usque
ad uiam predictam que tendit ad Brandonam. Hanc autem donationem
feci illis monachis pro Dei amore et Sancte Marie . pro salute anime
mee et filiorum meorum . et pro animabus patris et matris mee . et
omnium antecessorum meorum et successorum . ut habeant et teneant
omnem predictam donationem liberam et solutam . et quietam ab omnibus seruitiis . et omni seculari exactione . in perpetuam elemosinam ad
velle suum inde faciendum . scilicet ad sartandum . uel ad custodiendum. Preterea omnes qui hanc cartam legerint uel legi audierint ? scire
uolo ? quod ego Rog(erius) de Molbraio . et omnes heredes mei . hanc
donationem prescriptam . predictis monachis de Cumba contra omnes
homines et calumpnias warantizabimus.[a] Et simul ad uniuersitatis
uestre notitiam peruenire uolo ? quod prefati monachi de Cumba .
caritatiue de quater .xx. marcas . erga Iudeos me acquietauerunt. His
testibus . Rob(erto) de Daiuill(a) . Waltero Briton(e) . Ham(one)
Bel(er) . Ham(one) Lestrange . Philippo de Muntpincun . Henr(ico)
de Rokebi . Rob(erto) Bel(er) . Rob(erto) de Waura . Will(elmo)
cam(erario) . Petro filio Ham(onis) Lestrange . Rad(ulfo) filio Ric(ardi) .
Rob(erto) de Bileneia . Ernald(o) dispensat(ore) . Rad(ulfo) filio
Gaufrid(i) . Rob(erto) clerico . Rannulfo de Mendeuill(a) . Rob(erto)
filio Gerardi.

Endorsement: *Rogeri de Molbrai de bosco de Brinkelauue* (12th cent.).

Size: 18·3 × 15·3 cm.; 4 cm. turn-up.

Seal: missing; was appended on tag.

Script: same hand as that of nos. 86 and 87.

NOTE. The witness-clause is identical to that of no. 84.

86 *Confirmation by Nigel de Mowbray to Combe of part of the wood of Brinklow, called Birchley, given by Roger de Mowbray.* [*c.* 1166 × 1190]

> Original charter: Gregory-Hood deeds deposited at Stratford on Avon,
> Shakespeare Birthplace Trust Libr., Gregory-Hood Ch. 40. Cartulary
> copies: B.M., Cotton MSS. Vit. A i fos. 40v–41r (lacks witnesses); Vit. D
> xviii fo. 11r (fragment). Transcript, from cartulary of Combe fo. 55 (Vit. D
> xviii before Cotton fire): Bodl., MS. Dugdale 12 p. 116.

Omnibus sancte matris ecclesie filiis tam presentibus quam futuris .
Nigellus de Molbraio salutem. Notum sit omnibus filiis sancte ecclesie

[a] From here in lighter ink, perhaps written a little later.

quod ego Nigellus de Molbraio concessi et hac presenti carta mea confirmaui Deo et ecclesie Sancte Marie de Cumba et monachis ibidem Deo seruientibus donationem illam quam pater meus Rogerius de Mulbraio predictis monachis de Cumba in puram et perpetuam elemosinam sicut carta ipsius testatur donauit de nemore suo de Brincalawa quod dicitur Burthleia . totam illam . scilicet partem nemoris . que est a uia que uocatur Walewei . scilicet ab illa Waleweia . que propinquior est Brincalawie . et que totum boschum penetrat per transuersum ./ usque ad diuisas Brandonie et Bileneie. Sciant igitur omnes hanc cartam legentes et legi audientes . quod ego Nigellus . de Molbraio hanc concessionem feci Deo et monachis de Cumba . et hac presenti carta mea confirmaui pro salute mea . et omnium heredum meorum . et pro animabus patris et matris mee . et omnium antecessorum meorum ./ ut iidem monachi de Cumba per concessionem meam . et per warantizationem meam et heredum meorum contra omnes homines et calumpnias . teneant et habeant in perpetuam elemosinam . totam predictam partem nemoris . et quicquid inter prenominatos terminos habetur . bene et in pace . et omnino tam libere et quiete . quam pater meus unquam liberius et quietius eandem possessionem tenuit.[a] His testibus . Fulchon(e) de Castellione . Nichol(ao) de Bellon' . Gaufrido de Haia . Petro fratre ejus . Gaufrido coco.

Endorsement: *Nigellus de Molbrai de bosco de Brinkelaua* (12th cent.).

Size: 20·8 × 12·7 cm.; 2 cm. turn-up.

Seal: missing; was appended on tag.

Script: same hand as that of nos. 85 and 87.

NOTE. The occurrence of Geoffrey de la Haia suggests a date after *c*. 1166 (see no. 364 note).

87 *Confirmation by Nigel de Mowbray to Combe of a wood, given by Roger de Mowbray, for which Nigel received from the monks 12 marks and the remittance of a debt of 3 marks and 9s.*   [1177 × 1190]

Original charter: Gregory-Hood deeds deposited at Stratford on Avon, Shakespeare Birthplace Trust Libr., Gregory-Hood Ch. 41. Cartulary copies: B.M., Cotton MSS. Vit. A i fo. 41*r–v* (lacks last 12 witnesses); Vit. D xviii fo. 11*r–v* (fragment).

Omnibus sancte matris ecclesie filiis tam presentibus quam futuris ./ Nigellus de Molbraio salutem. Sciatis me concessisse et hac presenti carta mea confirmasse Deo et Sancte Marie et monachis de Cumba illam donationem nemoris quam pater meus Rogerius de Molbraio dedit

[a] From here in lighter ink, perhaps written a little later.

predictis monachis de Cumba . sicut carta ipsius testatur ? et uolo ut habeant hanc donationem liberam et quietam ab omni seruitio et exactione seculari in puram et perpetuam elemosinam . per diuisas que in carta patris mei quam monachi de eadem donatione nemoris ab eo habent exprimuntur . scilicet a Waleweia usque ad uiam que uenit de Brinchelawe ad Brandonam . et a diuisis de Brandona usque ad sartum quod homines de Brinchelawe tenent . et de angulo sarti illorum per Morweiam usque ad uiam predictam que tendit ad Brandonam. Hanc autem prescriptam confirmationem ego Nigellus de Molbraio feci prenominatis monachis de Cumba pro amore Dei et pro salute anime mee et pro animabus patris et matris mee . et omnium meorum . et insuper eandem donationem ego et heredes mei contra omnes homines et calumpnias ipsis monachis warantizabimus.[a] Preterea omnes qui hanc cartam legerint uel legi audierint scire uolo ? quod prenominati monachi de Cumba caritatis respectu .xij. marcas argenti . michi dederunt . et iij. marcas . et ix. solidos de debito quod domui illi per fidem interpositam et per pignus debueram ? michi remiserunt. His testibus . Baldewin(o) priore de Kerkebi . Rob(erto) de Molbraio . Rog(ero) de Arden(a) . Rog(ero) de Sancto Martin(o) . Rob(erto) de Castellione . Rad(ulfo) de Bisegge . Johanne capellano meo . Rob(erto) capellano de Brinkelaue . Alardo de Widebroc . Hug(one) de Lutherwrd' . et Rogero filio ejus . Rad(ulfo) de Turstenestun(a) . Will(elmo) filio Durandi . et Adam et Rogero fratribus ejus.

Endorsement: *Confirm' Nigelli de Molbrai* (12th cent.).

Size: 21·4 × 14·3 cm.; 2·9 cm. turn-up.

Seal: missing; was appended on linen strings.

Script: same hand as that of nos. 85 and 86.

NOTE. Baldwin, prior of Monks Kirby, presumably held office after Richard of Cornwall, who became abbot of Whitby in 1177 (no. 192 note).

88 *Gift by Nigel de Mowbray to Combe of land near Brinklow.*

[1186 × 1190]

Cartulary copies: B.M., Cotton MSS. Vit. A i fo. 38*v* (lacks last 2 witnesses); Vit. D xviii fo. 14*r* (fragment). Transcript, from cartulary of Combe fo. 53*r* (Vit. D xviii before Cotton fire): Bodl., MS. Dugdale 12 p. 114.

Omnibus hominibus suis Francis et Anglis Nigellus de Moubray salutem. Sciatis me dedisse et concessisse Deo et Sancte Marie et monachis de Cumba illam terram que remansit in manu mea a Moreweia usque ad sartum hominum de Brinkelawe et ex alia parte a nemore filiorum

---

[a] From here in lighter ink, perhaps written a little later.

Duranti usque ad sartum de Brinkelawe, pro salute mea et uxoris mee et
filiorum meorum et amicorum meorum in puram et perpetuam elemosinam liberam et quietam ab omni seculari servicio et exactione ad
faciendum totum velle suum sicut de alia terra sua quam habent de me
et de patre meo. His testibus, Roberto de Cuneburc, Rogero de Sancto
Martino, Hugone de Ranb', Roberto de Moubray, Willelmo le chamb-
(erer) et Roberto fratre suo et multis aliis.

NOTE. It is likely that this gift was made during Nigel de Mowbray's lordship
of the honour.

89 *Confirmation by Roger de Mowbray to Durham (Ben. cathedral) of 6
bovates and part of the church of Blyborough (Lincs.), given by Robert de
Sancto Martino, saving his service.*   [*c.* 1150]

Pd., 'Blyborough Charters', ed. K. Major, in *A Medieval Miscellany for D. M.
Stenton*, ed. P. M. Barnes and C. F. Slade (P.R.S., N.S. xxxvi) pp. 206–7,
from original charter, Durham, D. & C. Archives, 4. 3. Ebor. 1a.

His presentibus testibus Roberto de Daivilla et Willelmo de Romara et
Radulfo de Bellon et Willelmo de Crochelai et Avveredo camerario et
Roberto capellano et multis aliis.

Seal: seal no. 1 of Roger de Mowbray (above, p. lxxxii), white wax varnished;
appended on tongue. See Frontispiece (*b*).

Script: same hand as that of no. 90.

NOTE. Robert de Sancto Martino's gift is recorded in a chirograph of 1148/9.[1]
He had probably succeeded Elias de Sancto Martino in his fee, and when he
entered the convent of Durham in 1148/9 his heir was his son, Robert, presumably brother or father of Roger the tenant of 2 fees in 1166 (no. 401).[2]
For Nigel d'Aubigny's gifts to Durham, see nos. 2–6.

90 *Mandate by Roger de Mowbray to Oliver de Bocleville and his wife, ordering them to allow the prior and convent of Durham to hold their land (in
Blyborough) in peace.*   [*c.* 1150]

Pd., 'Blyborough Charters' p. 207, from original charter, Durham, D. & C.
Archives, 4. 3. Ebor. 1c; plate, ibid. no. XVI (no witnesses).

Seal: seal no. 2 of Roger de Mowbray (above, p. lxxxii), white wax varnished;
appended on tongue.

Script: same hand as that of no. 89.

NOTE. The final clause of this mandate—'et volo et precipio quod in pace
teneant ne clamorem amodo audiam'—recalls the usages of the royal chancery.[3]

[1] 'Blyborough Charters' p. 206.   [2] See Fees [8].
[3] Cf. *Regesta* iii no. 257, for Durham, discussed ibid. iv 17. Cf. also a mandate of
Ranulf Flambard, bishop of Durham, pd. in *Durham Episcopal Charters 1071–1152*, ed.
H. S. Offler (S.S. clxxix) no. 20.

91 *Confirmation by Roger de Mowbray to Durham of 6 bovates in Blyborough, given by Robert de Sancto Martino.* [*c.* 1160 × 1170]

Pd., 'Blyborough Charters' p. 208, from original charter, Durham, D. & C. Archives, 4. 3. Ebor. 1b (and later copy, 4. 3. Ebor. 14) and cartulary copies, Cartuarium Vetus fo. 59*v*, Cartuarium III fo. 118*v*.

Teste Nigello filio meo et herede . Rodberto de Deivevila . Thomas de Colevila . Rodberto de Busci . et multis aliis.

Seal: seal no. 3 of Roger de Mowbray (above, p. lxxxiii), white wax varnished; appended on tag.

92 *Gift by Roger de Mowbray to Durham of a toft in Thirsk (Yorks., N.R.), which was Walter the clerk's,[1] and Walter himself.* [*c.* 1170 × 1186]

Original charter: Durham, D. & C. Archives, 3. 1. Ebor. 3.

Rogerus de Mulbrai omnibus uidentibus et audientibus has literas tam futuris quam presentibus salutes. Sciatis me dedisse et hac carta presenti confirmasse Deo et Sancto Cuthberto de Dunelmo et monachis ibidem Deo seruientibus in puram et perpetuam elemosinam toftum unum in Tresch quod fuit Walteri clerici cum omnibus pertinentiis suis et ipsum Walterum. Volo etiam ut predicti monachi predictum toftum teneant libere et quiete ab omni seculari seruicio et sine omni uexatione sicut alias terras suas liberius tenent. Precipio itaque ne quis heredum uel successorum uel hominum meorum de hac elemosina eos uexare uel inquietare presumat. His testibus . Roberto de Mubrai . Philippo de Munpinchun . Rob(erto) Beler . Rob(erto) de Belchamp . Willelmo filio Ingel(rami) . Rob(erto) filio Matildis . Radulfo filio Ricardi . Alano Fossard . Ricardo Baccun . Bernardo molendinario . Willelmo camerario . Willelmo filio Roberti de Kneiuetu' . Helia de Walesend' . Bertramo de Nesham . Philippo de Lindeseie Johanne capellano . Roberto clerico . et ceteris multis.

Endorsements: *C. R. de Mubrei* (? late 12th cent.); *in villa de Trek* (13th cent.); *de tofto Walteri | 3ª. 1ᵉ. Ebor'. C. 1.* (later medieval hands).

Size: 17·1 × 9·5 cm.; 1·9 cm. turn-up.

Seal: seal no. 3 of Roger de Mowbray (above, p. lxxxiii), white wax varnished; legend broken off; appended on tag.

NOTE. The appearance of Philip de Montpincon (cf. no. 376 note) and Alan Fossard suggests a date after *c.* 1170 (cf. nos. 81, 127, 142, 147, 368).

1 It is possible that Walter, who was apparently a villein, was not a clerk, and that *Clericus* should be understood as a surname.

93 *Confirmation by Roger de Mowbray to St. John's hospital, Falaise (Calvados) of land, 'terram plantationis' [? in Villers], given by Philip of Bazoches and Fulk his brother.* [Aug. 1154×March 1157]

> Confirmation by Henry II, [Jan. × March] 1157; pd., *Recueil des Actes de Henri II*, ed. L. V. Delisle and E. Berger (Paris, 1909–27) i no. XXXV, from an original charter in Caen, Archives of Calvados, H. 4034, and cartulary copy in Cartulaire de Normandie, Rouen, Bibl. Municipale, Y. 201 fos. 32, 64. Also pd. (transl.), *Cal. Docs. France* no. 613; noted and dated Eyton, *Itinerary* p. 21.

> NOTE. It is unlikely that this gift belongs to the earliest period of Roger's Norman lordship, for Bazoches was lost from 1138, and Falaise itself fell to Geoffrey of Anjou in 1141.[1] Roger did not recover Bazoches until August 1154, and the gift may well belong to his Norman visit on that occasion (above, no. 19).

94 *Confirmation by Roger de Mowbray to Fountains (Cist., Yorks., W.R.) of wood on both sides of the River Ure near Masham (Yorks., N.R.), given by earl Alan.* [1138×1145]

> Original charter: Vyner deeds deposited at Leeds Archives, V.R. 21. Cartulary copies: B.M., Cotton MS. Tib. C xii fo. 26r; Bodl., MS. Rawlinson B 449 fo. 24r (lacks last 3 witnesses); B.M., Egerton MS. 3053 fo. 3r (lacks all witnesses); Add. MS. 18276 fo. 4v (abstract).
> Pd. (transl.), *Fount. Cart.* i 15 (4), from Cotton MS.

Rog(erus) de Mubrai . omnibus hominibus suis Francis et Anglis . videntibus et audientibus has litteras . salutem. Sciatis me concessisse et hac mea carta confirmasse Deo et monachis ecclesie Sancte Marie de Font' totum boscum quod comes Alanus eis dedit . quod pertinet ad Masham . ex illa par*ᵃ* Jor qua Burt' consistit . et ex alia parte predicte aque . Rumoram et Bramleiam concedo et confirmo eisdem . sicut carta predicti comitis testatur et purportat. Teste Samsone de Avbeni . Petro constabulario de Tresc . Gvillelmo del Mainilhermer et Hug(one) fratre eius . Mathia de Ramp' . et Gilleberto fratre eius.

Endorsements: *Confirm' Rogeri de Mubrai de bosco de Masham. XXV | Aldeburg.* (probably late 12th cent.); *iiii* (? 13th cent.); *Aldeburgh carta 4* (? 15th cent.). Size: 14·5 × 8·2 cm.; 2·4 cm. turn-up. Seal: missing; was appended on tag.

> NOTE. The confirmation probably followed shortly after earl Alan's gift, of before 1145.[2] The witnesses are consistent with such a date. For earl Alan's enfeoffment of Roger de Mowbray in Masham, see no. 18.

ᵃ *Sic* in charter; *parte*, carts.

[1] See C. H. Haskins, *Norman Institutions* (Cambridge, Mass., 1918) p. 129.
[2] *E.Y.C.* iv no. 18.

95 *Gift by Roger de Mowbray to Fountains of Aldburgh (Yorks., N.R.), for a grange.* [1138×1145]

Original charter: Vyner deeds deposited at Leeds Archives, V.R. 18. Cartulary copies: B.M., Cotton MS. Tib. C xii fo. 24v; Bodl., MS. Rawlinson B 449 fo. 20r (lacks last 9 witnesses); B.M., Egerton MS. 3053 fo. 3r (lacks all witnesses); Add. MS. 18276 fo. 4v (abstract).
Pd., *Mon. Ang.* v 306 (LII) (lacks last 9 witnesses), from the original charter; (transl.) *Fount. Cart.* i 14 (1a), from Cotton MS.

Omnibus sancte ecclesie filiis presentibus et futuris Rog(erus) de Mubrai . salutem. Sciatis me pro salute anime mee et uxoris mee ac liberorum meorum . et patris mei et matris mee omniumque parentum meorum dedisse in elemosinam monachis Sancte Marie de Fontanis Aldeburgam in grangiam . solutam et quietam ab omnibus seruiciis . et quicquid ad eam pertinet . ex illa parte Jori fluminis . in bosco et plano . et campis et pratis et aquis . sicut pater meus Nigellus de Albinio dedit eam antiquitus monachis Pontiniacensibus et communem pasturam ex altera parte aque in Svintun et in Rumor et in Nutewith . et ex eadem parte firmamentum stagni sui ad molendinum faciendum. Hii sunt testes . Samson de Albinio . Mathias de Rampainne . Rad(ulfus) de Bellu' Gvalt(erus) de Lariuera . Odo de Neusu' . Rob(ertus) Boscher . Ricardus nepos Samsonis . Alfredus camerarius . Gvalt(erus) de Carletona . Serlo cocus . Vctredus frater Ricardi de Kirkebi . Rad(ulfus) carbo . Ketel filius Vctredi de Ilketvn;

Endorsements: *ALDEBVRG* (contemporary); *.iii. duplicatur* (in red ink, 13th cent.); *Aldeburgha carta prima duplicatur* (? 14th cent.).

Size: 17·5 × 11 cm.; 2·2 cm. turn-up.

Seal: seal no. 3 of Roger de Mowbray (above, p. lxxxiii), white wax varnished; legend broken off; appended on tag.

NOTE. The grange of Aldburgh was confirmed to Fountains by Eugenius III, 29 Jan. 1146.[1] Although the terms and witnesses of the charter are perfectly consistent with the date assigned, it seems that the charter itself is a 'renovation'.[2] It bears the third seal of Roger de Mowbray, which is not otherwise found until after 1154 (above, p. lxxxii). The script is similar in style to the hands of other Fountains charters belonging to 1181 and later (nos. 134, 143, 145–6).

96 *Confirmation by Roger de Mowbray to Fountains of Dacre (Yorks., W.R.), given by Bertram Haget.* [1138×1145]

Cartulary copies: B.M., Add. MS. 40009 fo. 9v (old p. 18); Bodl., MS. Rawlinson B 449 fo. 143r; B.M., Add. MS. 18276 fo. 46r (abstract).
Pd. (transl.), *Fount. Cart.* i 204 (4), from Add. MS. 40009.

1 *P.U.E.* iii no. 54.
2 On this subject, see T. A. M. Bishop, *Scriptores Regis* (Oxford, 1961) p. 35.

Notum sit omnibus presentibus et futuris quod ego Rogerus de Mul-braiᵃ concedo et confirmo donationem de Dacra quam Bertrannus Haget dedit in elemosinam monachis Sancte Marie de Fontibus et in bosco et in plano etᵇ pratis et in aquis et in omnibus aliis rebus ad eundem locum juste pertinentibus. Teste ipso Bertranno, Samsone clerico, Hugone filio Jernagoti.ᶜ

> NOTE. The confirmation was almost certainly made at the same time as, or very shortly after, Bertram Haget's gift.[1] The grange of Dacre was confirmed to Fountains by Eugenius III, 29 Jan. 1146.[2] For Roger de Mowbray's original gift of Dacre to Bertram Haget, see below, no. 363, and Fees [4].

97 *Agreement made by Samson d'Aubigny, between Fountains and the church of Masham, concerning the tithes of Aldburgh.*   [1138 × Oct. 1153]

> Original charter: Bodl., Douce Ch. a. 1, no. 5. Cartulary copy: Bodl., MS. Rawlinson B 449 fo. 21r–v.

CIROGRAPHUM

Notum sit omnibus istas litteras uidentibus uel audientibus hanc esse compositionem inter ecclesiam de Fontibus et ecclesiam de Messaham . quod ecclesia de Fontibus annis singulis dabit ecclesie de Messaham ad cereum Paschalem de cera quod ualeat .vi. denarios . pro decima cuius-dam terre que uocabatur Aldeburch. Precium quidem paruum est . quia non fuit ibi multum terre arabilis quando primum data est eis . sed fere totum monachi postea sartauerunt. Teste domno Samsone de Albin' per cuius manum hec compositio facta est . Waltero capellano de Watlos . Waltero filio Landrici capellano de Insula . Svano capellano de Massaham . Adam filio Chetel . Walterio filio Rogerii forestarii . Tom(a) clerico de Massam . Iohanne forestario . Alano uenatore . Fulcone filio Ricardi . Ricardo Bruseuilan . Keteman filio Chetel . Gos-patric de Massam . Symo(ne) filio Uctredi.

> Endorsements: *De decimis.* / *de Masham* / [.]*caldel'.* / *Aldeburc.* (12th cent.).
> Size: 12·6 × 14·6 cm.; 3·2 cm. turn-up.
> Seal: seal of Samson d'Aubigny (above, p. lxxxii), red wax; formerly appended on tag, but now detached.

> NOTE. Aldburgh was given to Fountains after 1138 (no. 95). This settlement was confirmed by Henry Murdac, archbishop of York, who died in Oct. 1153.[3] Samson d'Aubigny had the livings of Masham and of several other churches of the Mowbray demesne (see no. 196 and note).

ᵃ *Mubrai*, MS. Rawl.   ᵇ MS. Rawl. inserts *in*   ᶜ *Jarn'*, MS. Rawl.

[1] *Fount. Cart.* i 203 (2).   [2] *P.U.E.* iii no. 54.
[3] See papal bull of 27 May 1163, *P.U.E.* iii no. 144.

98 *Gift by Roger de Mowbray to Fountains of land near Sutton (Grange)* *(Yorks., W.R.), by specified bounds.* [1142 × c. 1154]

> Original charter: Vyner deeds deposited at Leeds Archives, V.R. 4821. Cartulary copies: Manchester, John Rylands Libr., Lat. MS. 224 fos. 286v–287r; B.M., Add. MS. 18276 fo. 234r (abstract).
> Pd. (transl.), *Fount. Cart.* ii 704 (5), from Rylands MS.

ROG(erus) DE MVLBR'. omnibus hominibus suis . et ceteris legentibus uel audientibus litteras has ⫶ salutem. Sciatis me concessisse monachis Sanctę MARIE de Fontibus in puram et perpetuam elemosinam pro animabus patris et matris męę . et mea . et uxoris męę . omniumque parentum meorum ⫶ quicquid meum est inter terram Suttunę . et quendam riuulum meantem infra Redlaiam iuxta fontem quem adaquandis pecoribus suis illis dedi . et ab eodem riuulo recta linea prescidente inflexionem eiusdem riuuli uersus aquilonem usque ad tres spinas sitas in quodam monte petroso . et inde usque ad quendam magnum salicem sub margine siluę quę uocatur Litlahaga . et inde usque ad quandam uiam quę iacet in fundo uicinę uallis . et per eandem uiam ⫶ quantum terra illorum durat. Testibus his ⫶ quorum hic nomina subscribuntur . domina Gundreda matre mea . Hugone del Mainil Heremer . et fratre ejus Willelmo . et Ric(ardo) Burdet . et Walt(ero) de Lariuera . et Rad(ulfo) de Bellun . et Alano de Ridala.

> Endorsement: *Carta Rog' de quadam terra iuxta Sutt'. | Sutt'. | Rog' de Mub'* (12th cent.); *A* (? 12th cent.); *iii* (? 13th cent.); *Sutton 4. 4* (? 15th cent.).
>
> Size: 15·2 × 10·7 cm.; 2 cm. turn-up.
>
> Seal: seal no. 1 of Roger de Mowbray (above, p. lxxxii), white wax varnished brown; appended on tag.

> NOTE. The reference to Roger's wife gives the earliest possible date as 1142, and the appearance of Gundreda de Gournay among the witnesses shows that the charter cannot have been given later than c. 1154 (no. 236 note).

99 *Confirmation by Roger de Mowbray to Fountains of land from Swanley (Grange) to Wainforth (in Markington, Yorks., W.R.) and 5 feet of arable to make a fosse, given by Aldelin of Aldfield and his son Ralph.*

[1142 × c. 1154]

> Original charter: B.M., MSS. Loans 29/242 no. 20 (Portland loan). Cartulary copies: Bodl., MS. Rawlinson B 449 fo. 129r (lacks last 10 witnesses); B.M., Add. MS. 18276 fo. 77v (abstract).
> Pd. (transl.), *Fount. Cart.* ii 851 (7), from detached leaves of cartulary of Fountains vol. ii (i.e. now B.M., Add. MS. 40009, which no longer contains this text) (gives all witnesses). Also pd. (abstract), H.M.C., *13th Report*, app. ii, *MSS. of Duke of Portland*, ii (1893) 4, from the original charter then at Welbeck.

Sciant omnes homines mei et amici uniuersique matris ęcclesię filii ?
quod ego ROGERVS de Mulbrai concedo . et per hanc meam cartam
stabiliter confirmo . donationem terre illius quam Aldelin de Aldefeld
et RADVLFVS filius eius donauerunt . et cęteri filii eius concesserunt ?
Sancte MARIE de Fontibus et monachis ibidem Deo seruientibus . in
liberam et perpetuam elemosinam . scilicet de Suaneslæie usque ad
uadum de Wainesford . et quinque pedes de terra arabili ad fossam
faciendam. Hii sunt testes . domina Gund(reda) . Radulfus filius
Aldelin . Will(elmus) frater eius . Will(elmus) de Mainilhermer .
Rad(ulfus) de Bell' . Rog(erus) de Daltun . Walt(erus) filius Aluredi .
Alanus de Ridale . Rog(erus) de Condeio . Anfretillus*a* hostiarius .
Walt(erus) Wincebag . Ricardus clericus de Stodleia . Amelin filius
Aldeli(ni).

Endorsements: *Rogerii de Molb'. | De don'. Aldel'.* (12th cent.); *vii | Fontes
carta .7. | .7.* (later medieval hands).

Size: 19·6 × 9·4 cm.; 1·2 cm. turn-up.

Seal: fragment of seal no. 1 of Roger de Mowbray (above, p. lxxxii), brown wax
varnished; appended on tag.

NOTE. Four of the witnesses, including Gundreda de Gournay, appear in
no. 98 above. Land given by Aldelin of Aldfield was confirmed to Fountains
by pope Adrian IV, 23 November 1156.[1] For Aldelin's charter, see *Fount.
Cart.* ii 850. Ralph son of Aldelin held ¼ fee in 1166.[2]

100 *Gift by Alice de Gant to Fountains of part of her wood of 'Esseslach' [nr.
Sutton Grange][3] (? Azerley, Yorks., W.R.), by specified bounds.*

[c. 1144 × May 1155]

Original charter: Vyner deeds deposited at Leeds Archives, V.R. 4819. Cartu-
lary copies: Manchester, John Rylands Libr., Lat. MS. 224 fo. 287v;
B.M., Add. MS. 18276 fo. 234r (abstract).
Pd. (transl.), *Fount. Cart.* ii 705 (8), from Rylands MS.

Notum sit omnibus sancte matris ecclesie quod ego Aaliz de Gant' dedi
monachis Sancte Marie de Fontibus partem de bosco meo de Esseslach .
a uia petrosa usque ad Wallescroft et de Wallescroft ultra Cumbedene
usque ad siccum salicem . iuxta Peruuinetres et sic recte usque fontem
in feudo et in pura elemosina pro anima mea et domini mei et filiorum
meorum. Teste Noel Rad(ulfo) de Rubeo Monte et Rad(ulfo) [uice]*b*-
comite Herberto fabro de Esseslach et Stephano homine uicecomitis
et Blacheman.

a Sic, for *Asketillus.*   *b* Illegible in charter.

---

[1] *E.Y.C.* i no. 80.
[2] Charters nos. 383, 401, and Fees [29]; cf. nos. 129–30.
[3] See *Place-Names W.R. Yorks.* v (English Place-Name Soc. xxxiv) p. 199.

Endorsements: *Carta Aaliz de Gant . de parte boschi de Esselac. Sutth'.* (12th cent.); *xii* (? 13th cent.); *Sutton'. 7.* (? 15th cent.).

Size: 10·6 × 5·9 cm.; 0·9 cm. turn-up.

Seal: seal of Alice de Gant (above, p. lxxxiii), white wax; legend broken off; appended sideways on tag.

NOTE. The gift was almost certainly made before Henry II's confirmation, May 1155,[1] and anyway before no. 105, of before 1156. The reference to Alice's sons shows that it cannot have been made before *c.* 1144.

101 *Gift by Alice de Gant to Fountains of the wood of Littley (Yorks., W.R.),[2] by specified bounds.* [*c.* 1147 × May 1155]

> Original charter: Vyner deeds deposited at Leeds Archives, V.R. 4818. Cartulary copies: Manchester, John Rylands Libr., Lat. MS. 224 fo. 287*v*; B.M., Add. MS. 18276 fo. 234*r* (abstract).
> Pd. (transl.), *Fount. Cart.* ii 705 (7), from Rylands MS.

Notum sit omnibus sancte matris ecclesie filiis quod ego Aliz de Gant pro anima mea et domini mei et natorum meorum dedi monachis Sancte Marie de Fontibus in feudo et in elemosina boscum de Litleahe a via petrosa usque ad finem xx percarum et inde recto tramite usque ad Piruinetres et hinc usque ad barram. Test(e) filio meo Nigello et mecum eam dante et Roberto fratre eius et Rad(ulfo) de Bellu' et Rad(ulfo) de Rubeo Monte et Hug(one) capell(ano) . et Wlrico et Hereberto de eadem uilla et Leurico et Siwardo et Gaufrido filio Vnwine

Endorsement: *Aeliz de Gant de Litleahe.* (12th cent.); *v* (? 13th cent.); *Sutton. 6.* (? 15th cent.).

Size: 11·6 × 7·1 cm.

Seal: seal of Alice de Gant (above, p. lxxxiii), white wax; legend broken off; appended sideways on silk strings passed through broad slit (? intended for parchment tag) at centre of foot of document; no turn-up.

NOTE. The charter was probably given before Henry II's confirmation.[1] The active participation of Alice's sons may well suggest that this gift was made towards the end of the suggested period. The parchment of the document is ruled for four more lines after the end of the text.

102 *Grant by Roger de Mowbray to Fountains of necessaries in his forest of Nidderdale, in recompense for grain taken by his men in Ripon; and permission to remove the grange of Dacre within one league.* [1151 × May 1155]

> Cartulary copies: Bodl., MS. Rawlinson B 449 fo. 144*r*; B.M., Add. MS. 18276 fo. 47*r* (abstract).

---

[1] *E.Y.C.* i no. 76.   [2] Lost, see *Place-Names W.R. Yorks.* v 200.

Eboracensi archiepiscopo et omnibus sancte ecclesie filiis et omnibus suis hominibus tam presentibus quam futuris Rogerus de Mubrai salutem. Sciatis me dedisse et concessisse Deo et monachis Sancte Marie de Fontibus plenarie necessaria sua in foresta mea de Niderdala in pastura et pastione in ferro et plumbo et materia et in omnibus necessariis suis. Hanc donationem facio eis primum in recompensatione bladi quod dominus Henricus Ebor(acensis) archiepiscopus dedit eis quod homines mei ceperunt in Ripun, deinde in perpetuam elemosinam solutam quietam et ab omni calumpnia liberam pro salute anime mee et patris et matris et uxoris mee et filiorum meorum. Promitto eis etiam ut si aliquando voluerint grangiam suam de Dacra removere ab eo loco in quo nunc sita est usque ad unam leugam, habeant facultatem transferendi in meo dominio quacunque parte voluerint. His testibus, Rogero abbate de Beheland, Gervasio et Landrico monachis, Willelmo et Hugone conversis, Radulfo Belero.

NOTE. The gift of necessaries in Nidderdale was confirmed by Henry II in May 1155.[1] The earliest date is 1151, when Henry Murdac received the temporalities of the archbishopric. If Henry Murdac was still alive when this charter was issued, the latest possible date would be Oct. 1153. Another version of this charter, no. 103, gives the names of four additional witnesses.

103 *Grant by Roger de Mowbray to Fountains of mineral rights in his forest of Nidderdale, in recompense for grain taken by his men in Ripon and for 83 marks which the monks gave him in his necessity.*

[1151 × May 1155]

Cartulary copy: B.M., Add. MS. 40009 fos. 14v–15r (old pp. 28–9).
Pd. (transl.), *Fount. Cart.* i 207 (11).

Eboracensi archiepiscopo et omnibus sancte ecclesie filiis et omnibus hominibus tam presentibus quam futuris Rogerus de Molbr' salutem. Sciatis me pro salute anime mee dedisse concessisse et hac presenti carta mea confirmasse Deo et Sancte Marie et monachis de Fontibus plenarie omnem materiam eris ferri et plumbi et cujuscunque metalli et lapidum in foresta mea de Niderdale in quocunque loco subtus terram vel supra inventam seu inveniendam imperpetuum, habendam eis et eorum successoribus in liberam puram et perpetuam elemosinam quietam ab omni servicio et exactione seculari ineternum, in grodis minis et mineris et omnibus aliis pertinenciis et libertatibus suis sine aliquo retenemento mei vel heredum meorum. Hanc donationem feci eis in recompensationem bladi sui quod homines mei ceperunt ab eis apud Ripon(am) et

---

[1] *E.Y.C.* i no. 76.

octoginta trium marcarum quas michi in mea magna necessitate dederunt et etiam pro salute anime mee et patris et matris, uxoris et filiorum
meorum, in liberam elemosinam sine aliqua calumpnia imperpetuum
possidendam. Hiis testibus, Rogero abbate de Beheland, Gervasio et
Landrano monachis, Willelmo et Hugone conversis, Radulfo Beler,
Nigello filio meo, Hugone Malebisse, Rodeberto de Buscy, Thoma
hostrifer[a] et aliis.

NOTE. This is clearly another version of no. 102.

104 *Confirmation by Alice de Gant to Fountains of necessaries in the forest of
Nidderdale, given by Roger de Mowbray, for which confirmation Alice
received 3 marks from the monks.* [1151 × May 1155]

> Cartulary copies: B.M., Add. MS. 40009 fos. 16v and 1r (old pp. 32 and 1);
> Bodl., MS. Rawlinson B 449 fo. 150v (lacks all witnesses).
> Pd. (transl.), *Fount. Cart.* i 208 (17a), from Add. MS.

Sciant omnes qui has litteras legerint vel audierint tam presentes quam
futuri quod ego Aaliz de Gant[b] uxor Rogeri de Mulbrai[c] presenti carta
concessi ex parte mea illam donationem quam fecit predictus dominus
meus Rogerus monachis Sancte Marie de Fontibus, scilicet ut habeant
plenarie necessaria sua in foresta de Niderdala in pastura et pastione, in
ferro et plumbo, in materia et in omnibus necessariis suis, sicut in ejus
carta continetur in perpetuam elemosinam solutam quietam et ab omni
calumpnia liberam, pro salute nostra et filiorum nostrorum, patrum ac
matrum nostrarum. In hac concessione accepi ab eis tres marcas, ut
posteri sciant quia hec confirmatio rata erit imperpetuum. Test(ibus),
Roberto filio domini Rogeri de Mulbrai, Hugone capellano, Ricardo
clerico de Malesart, Noel.

> NOTE. The confirmation probably belongs to the same time as the gift by
> Roger de Mowbray, nos. 102 and 103 above. Cf. also no. 107 below.

105 *Confirmation by Roger de Mowbray to Fountains of a gift in Littley made
by Alice de Gant, and of land in Redley with common pasture in Winksley
(Yorks., W.R.), given by Ralph de Bellun.* [c. 1144 × Nov. 1156]

> Original charter: Vyner deeds deposited at Leeds Archives, V.R. 4822. Cartu-
> lary copies: Manchester, John Rylands Libr., Lat. MS. 224 fos. 287v–288r;
> B.M., Add. MS. 18276 fo. 234r (abstract).
> Pd. (transl.), *Fount. Cart.* ii 705 (9), from Rylands MS.

Notum sit omnibus tam presentibus quam futuris . quod ego ROG(erus)
de Mubraio concessi et confirmo monachis Sancte Marie de Fonteines

---

[a] *Sic* (for *hostricer*).   [b] *Gaunt*, MS. Rawl.   [c] *Mubray*, MS. Rawl.

donationem quam Aaliz de Gant vxor mea illis dedit per medium
Litlehage . a barra usque ad viam petrosam . sicut diuisio facta est . et
post ultra uiam petrosam usque ad Wallescroft ¿ ultra Cumbedene .
usque ad siccum salicem iuxta Pirwinetres . et sic recte usque ad fontem.
Et super hoc concedo et confirmo eis terram de Redleia . quam Rad-
(ulfus) de Bellun eis in elemosinam dedit cum communi pastura de
Winkesleia . scilicet a barra ipsa de Redleie . inferius sicut fossatum
uadit usque ad capud calcede versus Aserlagh in bosco et plano. Huius
rei sunt testes . Rob(ertus) de Aievilla . Hug(o) Malebisse . Ol[i]u(erus)
de Buzci . Rad(ulfus) Beler . Rog(erus) de Cundi Rad(ulfus) de
Rubeomonte . Rad(ulfus) vicecom(es) . Herb(ertus) faber de Aser-
la[g]ᵃh . Steph(anus) homo vicecom(itis) . Blacheman.

Endorsements: *Confirmatio Rog' de Mubrai de donacione . Aliz de Gant . et de
donacione Rad' de Bellun | Sutt'.* (12th cent.); *.A.* (late 12th or early 13th cent.);
xiii (? 13th cent.); *Sutton' 8* (? 15th cent.).

Size: 16·5 × 8·3 cm.; 2 cm. turn-up.

Seal: missing; was appended on tag, which survives, and bears part of an ink
drawing (? a decorated initial).

NOTE. The gift by Ralph de Bellun[1] was confirmed to Fountains by Adrian
IV, 23 Nov. 1156.[2] The last five witnesses occur in Alice de Gant's charter,
no. 100, of *c.* 1144 × May 1155. Ralph de Bellun probably held a socage tenure
(cf. no. 343 note).

106 *Gift by Alice de Gant to Fountains of land near Redley.*

[*c.* 1144 × Nov. 1156]

Transcript, from an original charter formerly in the possession of Samuel
Roper of Monks Kirby: Bodl., MS. Dodsworth 55 fo. 125r. Cartulary
copy: Manchester, John Rylands Libr., Lat. MS. 224 fo. 287r-v.
Pd., *Mon. Ang.* v 310 (LXXII), from an original charter formerly in St.
Mary's Tower, York. Also pd. (transl.), *Fount. Cart.* ii 705 (6), from
Rylands MS.

Universis sancte matris ecclesie filiis notum sit quod ego Aaliz de Gant
dedi et concessi ecclesie Sancte Marie de Fontibus terram sicut divisa
incipit apud calcedum de Redlaia usque ad barram et a barra usque ad
viam petrosam et inde usque ad Walescroft ᵇet de Walescroftᵇ usque ad
rogum³ ᶜet deindeᶜ usque adᵈ quercum et sic recte usque ad Stainlai
quantum terra mea durat. Hanc terram dedi primum ad ipsam ecclesiam
construendam deinde in puram et perpetuam elemosinam pro salute
anime mee et domini mei et patris et matris mee et filiorum meorum.

ᵃ Illegible in charter.   ᵇ⁻ᵇ Omitted in Rylands MS.   ᶜ⁻ᶜ Omitted in MS.
Dodsw.   ᵈ Omitted in MS. Dodsw.

¹ *Fount. Cart.* ii 705 (6).   ² *E.Y.C.* i no. 80.   ³ Probably a lime-kiln.

Teste Roberto filio meo qui hanc donationem concessit et super altare optulit, et Ricardo clerico, Uctredo filio Wallef, Radulfo filio Aldelini et Hamelino fratre suo, Noel, Ricardo nepote[a] Samsonis de Albinio, Ketello filio Siwardi, Galfrido filio Siwin, Pagano homine Noel, Gamel de Stodlay, Radulfo parmentario[b] Ebor', Willelmo cursore meo, Uctredo homine[c] Noel, Alano sagittario, Aldelino filio Uctredi de Stodley.

Dodsworth notes: 'In dorso: Carta AAliz de Gant de Welescroft. Sutton'. Drawing of seal of Alice de Gant (above, p. lxxxiii); appended sideways on tag.

NOTE. Presumably this gift belongs to the same period as nos. 100–1, 105.

107 *Confirmation by Alice de Gant to Fountains of necessaries in the forest of Nidderdale and permission to remove the grange of Dacre within one league; of land and wood in Littley; and of land of Redley given by Ralph de Bellun.*
[*c.* 1147 × Nov. 1156]

> Cartulary copies: B.M., Add. MS. 40009 fo. 1*r–v* (old pp. 1–2); Bodl., MS. Rawlinson B 449 fo. 150*v* (lacks witnesses); B.M., Add. MS. 18276 fo. 47*r–v* (abstract).
> Pd. (transl.), *Fount. Cart.* i 208 (17b), from Add. MS. 40009.

Sciant qui has litteras legerint vel audierint [d]presentes et futuri[d] quod ego Aaliz de Gant[e] uxor Rogeri de Mulbr'[f] presenti[g] carta mea concessi ex parte mea illam donationem quam fecit predictus dominus meus Rogerus monachis Sancte Marie de Fontibus, scilicet ut habeant plenarie necessaria sua in foresta de Niderdala in pastura et pastione, in ferro et plumbo, in materia et in omnibus necessariis suis, sicut in ejus carta continetur in perpetuam elemosinam solutam quietam et ab omni calumpnia liberam, pro salute nostra et filiorum nostrorum, patrum et matrum nostrarum. Concedo etiam ut si aliquando voluerint grangiam suam de Dacher[h] removere ab eo loco in quo nunc sita est usque ad unam leugam habeant facultatem transferendi quacunque parte voluerint sicut in carta domini mei Rogeri continetur. In hac benigna mea concessione accepi ab eis x marcas argenti ut posteri sciant quia hec confirmatio rata erit imperpetuum. His testibus, [i]Hugone capellano, Ricardo clerico de Malesart, Waltero de Buheri, Radulfo Beler, Rodberto de Busci, Radulfo de Rubeo monte, Gilberto de Rampagne, Radulfo filio Aldelin, Hamundo Beler, Uctredo filio Walthefi, Goscelino Veilleken, Noel.[i] Super hoc etiam concedo et in perpetuam elemosinam

---

[a] *nepos*, MSS.   [b] *parmentarius*, MSS.   [c] *filio*, MS. Dodsw.   [d-d] *etc.*, MS. Rawl.   [e] *Gaunt*, MS. Rawl.   [f] *Mubray*, MS. Rawl.   [g] *per*, MS. Rawl.   [h] *Dacra*, MS. Rawl.   [i-i] Omitted in MS. Rawl.

eis presenti*a* carta confirmo boscum videlicet*b* et terram per medium Litlehae a barra usque ad viam petrosam sicut divisio facta est et post ultra viam petrosam usque ad Walescroft et de Walescroft ultra Cumbedene usque ad siccum salicem juxta Piruuinetries*c* et sic recte usque ad fontem. In hac concessione et confirmatione testes hii fuerunt*d* Nigellus filius meus qui hoc mecum dedit et Robertus frater ejus, *e*Radulfus de Bellu', Radulfus de Rubeo monte, Hugo capellanus, Vlricus, Herbertus de eadem villa, et Leuricus, Siwardus, Gaufridus filius Unwine.*e* Ratam etiam habeo et hac carta confirmo donationem Radulfi de Bellun terre de Redlay, scilicet a barra ipsius Redlay inferius sicut fossatum vadit usque ad caput calcede versus Aserlagh*f* in bosco et plano. His testibus qui presentes affuerunt quando Radulfus hanc terram obtulit super altare de Fontibus, Rogero videlicet et domino meo,*g* Waltero de Buheri, Radulfo de Beler, Austello forte,*h* Rodberto de Busci, Hamundo Beler. Hii etiam hujus mee concessionis et confirmationis testes sunt et Walterus de Crocheslei.

NOTE. This confirmation was probably made at the time Ralph de Bellun made his gift, i.e. before November 1156 (see note to no. 105). The Nidderdale charters are nos. 102–4; for Littley, see nos. 100–1, 105; and for Redley cf. no. 105.

108 *Confirmation by Roger de Mowbray to Fountains of land from 'Smithehusawat' to 'Gretgata' (? nr. Masham, Yorks., N.R.), given by Turgis son of Malger.* [c. 1150 × 1156]

Original charter: Vyner deeds deposited at Leeds Archives, V.R. 20. Cartulary copies: B.M., Cotton MS. Tib. C xii fo. 27*v*; Bodl. MS. Rawlinson B 449 fo. 21*r* (lacks last 10 witnesses); B.M., Egerton MS. 3053 fo. 4*r* (lacks all witnesses); Add. MS. 18276 fo. 5*r* (abstract).
Pd. (transl.), *Fount. Cart.* i 16 (9), from Cotton MS.

Rog(erus) de Molb' . omnibus sanctę ęcclesię filiis . salutem. Sciatis me presenti carta confirmasse illam donationem quam Turgisius filius Malgeri fecit ęcclesię Sancte Marię de Fontibus in puram et perpetuam elemosinam . et confirmationem quam Galt(erus) de Buher de eadem terra monachis fecit . scilicet de Smithehusawat usque ad Gretgata . et sicut Gretgata tenditur usque in Elrebec . et exinde inferius sicut Elrebec . cadit in Jor. T(estes) Rob(ertus) cap(ellanus) . Rog(erus) de Cundi . Hug(o) cap(ellanus) . Nigellus filius meus . Hug(o) Maleb' . Rob(ertus) de Daiu' . Rog(erus) de Flammeu' . Galt(erus) de la Riu' .

a per, MS. Rawl.   *b scilicet*, MS. Rawl.   *c Pirewinetres*, MS. Rawl.
d sunt, MS. Rawl.   *e-e* Omitted in MS. Rawl.   *f Asserlagh*, MS. Rawl.
g MS. Rawl. ends.   *h Austellus fortis*, MS.

Rad(ulfus) de Bell' . Willelmus Hag' . Galt(erus) de Karlet' . Suanus de Tornet' . Runci.

Endorsement: *Aldeburc | Confirmatio donationis Turgisii* (12th cent.); *carta.9* (? 14th cent.); *ix. a good* (late 15th cent.).

Size: 13·4 × 9·8 cm.

Seal: missing; was appended on tongue from left of document; probably stub of tie-tag below.

NOTE. The witnesses to this confirmation are the same as those to Walter Buher's confirmation of Turgis son of Malger's gift,[1] and Walter Buher did not have land in this area until *c.* 1150 (below, no. 174). Turgis son of Malger's gift was confirmed by Adrian IV, 23 Nov. 1156.[2] For Turgis son of Malger's gift, see *Fount. Cart.* i 16 (7).[3]

109 *Notification by Roger de Mowbray to Roger (of Pont l'Évêque), archbishop of York (1154–82), of the settlement in his court of the dispute between the monks of Fountains and the sons of Drogo the forester concerning the land of Aldburgh (Yorks., N.R.).* [Oct. 1154 × c. 1157]

Original charter: Vyner deeds deposited at Leeds Archives, V.R. 23. Cartulary copies: B.M., Cotton MS. Tib. C xii fo. 34*r*; Bodl., MS. Rawlinson B 449 fo. 21*v* (lacks last 17 witnesses); B.M., Egerton MS. 3053 fo. 4*v* (lacks all but first two witnesses); Add. MS. 18276 fo. 5*v* (abstract). Pd. (transl.), *Fount. Cart.* i 20 (29), from Cotton MS.

Rog(ero) Dei gratia Ebor(acensi) archiepiscopo . et capitulo ecclesie Sancti Petri Ebor' . omnibusque sancte matris ęcclesię filiis . tam presentibus quam futuris ꞁ Rog(erus) de Molb' . salutem. Super calumpnia et controuersia illa quę agitabatur inter monachos de Fontibus et filios Drog(onis) forestarii . scilicet . de terra Aldeburch ꞁ sciatis quod in presentia mea et coram filiis et hominibus meis in unum conuenientes pacificati sunt et concordati . et omnem querimoniam dimiserunt . et ex utraque parte omnem calumpniam quietam clamauerunt . Test(es) . Nigellus et Rob(ertus) filii mei . Hug(o) filius Jernag(ani) . et Jernag(anus) filius eius . Samson de Alb' . Ric(ardus) de Malesart . et Huctr(edus) frater eius . Rad(ulfus) de Bellun . Hamund Beler . Turg(isius) filius Malg(eri) . Galt(erus) de Carlet' . Rollandus de Landel' . Rad(ulfus) filius Aldel(ini) . Wielard de Seint Annhel . Goscel(inus) Uelleken . Rob(ertus) filius Arnald(i) . Pharaman filius Vnuuin(i) . et Gaufr(idus) frater eius . Jernag(anus) de Tanef' . et Dolf(inus) frater eius . Willelmus filius Rog(eri) forest(arii) . Ketellus prepositus de Masham.

[1] *Fount. Cart.* i 16 (8).   [2] *E.Y.C.* i no. 80.
[3] Also original charter, Vyner deeds deposited at Leeds Archives, V.R. 19.

Endorsements: *Rog' de Molb' super terra que erat in calumnia | inter monachos de Font' et fil' Drogonis | Aldeburc | .C.1* (12th cent.); *.xiii.* (in red ink, 13th cent.); *Aldeburgh' carta 29 | xxix* (later medieval hands).

Size: 16·8 × 11·1 cm.

Seal: seal no. 2 of Roger de Mowbray (above, p. lxxxii), white wax varnished; appended on tongue.

NOTE. Samson d'Aubigny does not occur after *c.* 1157 (see no. 178 note).

110 *Gift by Roger de Mowbray to Fountains of part of his forest of Nidderdale from Dacre south to Killinghall and from Dacre north to Bewerley.*

[At York. Aug. 1174 × June 1175]

Cartulary copies: B.M., Add. MS. 40009 fos. 9v–10r (old pp. 18–19); Add. MS. 18276 fo. 46r–v (abstract).

Pd. (transl.), *Fount. Cart.* i 204 (5), from Add. MS. 40009.

Eboracensi archiepiscopo et capitulo Sancti Petri Eborac(i) et omnibus filiis sancte matris ecclesie Rogerus de Molb' salutem. Sciatis me dedisse et presentis carte testimonio confirmasse Deo et ecclesie Sancte Marie de Font(ibus) quandam partem foreste mee de Niderdala, scilicet totum quod continetur ex occidentali parte fluminis Nid a grangia eorum de Dacra deorsum usque Killinghala et ab eadem grangia sursum duas leugas usque ad rivulum qui descendit in Nid juxta saltum de Beuerli et inde sursum usque ad caput de Gisleclif inter duas rupas que supereminent Beuerli; de Gisleclif usque Forsegillebec ubi via que venit de Dacra transit Forsegillebec et sic per semitam usque ad Rudelez; deinde usque ad rivum de Walkesbrunne et per Walkesb' deorsum usque ad viam que protenditur versus Thorescros et postea per altum kiminum usque ad Salterkelda et inde usque ad calcedum de Roudunscaha et postea donec iterum descendat in Nid, excepta culta terra de Gillinghala. Concessi etiam eis vias suas consuetudinarias cum ponte suo et preter eas unam novam viam xxx pedum latitudinis ubi eis commodius fuerit. Hanc*ᵃ* donationem per predictas divisas feci eis in puram et perpetuam elemosinam et ita in liberam et propriam possessionem ut nichil ibi michi retineam preter cervum et cervam, aprum et capriolam et aves que alias capiunt. Sed et forestarii mei nullam potestatem ibi habebunt nec de re aliqua se intromittent nisi de predictis feris et avibus custodiendis. Et si calumpnia aliqua super predicta donatione aliquando emerserit ego vel heredes mei acquietabimus et guarentabimus eis. Si autem guarentizare non poterimus excambium illis dabimus ad valitudinem juxta considerationem abbatum et fratrum trium ecclesiarum scilicet Rievallensis, Fontanensis et Beeland. Hec omnia concessimus et confirmavimus in presencia capituli Eborac(i) ego et filii mei Nigellus et

ᵃ Han, MS.

Robertus et ipsum capitulum Eborac(i) horum omnium testem et fide-jussorem posuimus. Test(es), capitulum Eborac(i), abbas Clemens Sancte Marie Ebor', et Rogerus abbas Beel', Gaufridus prior ecclesie Sancte Marie Ebor', Philippus prior Sancte Trinitatis Ebor', magister Suanus de hospitali, Willelmus Tillemer, Gaufridus filius Rom', Rogerus de C(un)di dapifero, Hugo Maleb', Radulfus de Bellun, Galterus de Carlet', Robertus de Busci, Warinus filius Symonis, Johannes de Crevequer, Radulfus de Beeluer, Robertus filius Codric[a] Ebor', Thomas filius Elvive, Thomas filius Thome Ebor' et Adam frater ejus, Galterus de Mainil, Helte de Boidele.

NOTE. This gift must have been made after Roger de Mowbray's reconciliation with the king in August 1174, and before the royal confirmation to Fountains, probably in June 1175.[1] The king's enfeoffment of William de Stuteville in Knaresborough, in July 1175,[2] probably included the land south of Dacre, which Fountains had lost by March 1176 (nos. 126-7).

111 *Agreement between Fountains and Roger de Mowbray concerning the monks' rights in Nidderdale, for which Roger received 120 marks, Nigel 10 marks, and Robert one mark.* At York [Aug. 1174 × June 1175]

Original charter: B.M., Harley Ch. 83 C 38. Cartulary copies: B.M., Add. MS. 40009 fos. 11v–12r (old pp. 22–3); Bodl., MS. Rawlinson B 449 fo. 149v (lacks all but first witness); B.M., Add. MS. 18276 fo. 46v (abstract). Pd. (transl.), *Fount. Cart.* i 205 (8), from Add. MS. 40009.

CIROGRAPHVM

Notum sit omnibus legentibus et audientibus litteras istas . hanc . esse . conuentionem inter ęcclesiam de Font' . et dominum Rogerium de Molb' . quod si aliquando contigerit ut quoquomodo aliquam partem perdant de eo quod in foresta dedit eis in proprium . pro communi . quo uti solebant . et pro aliqua calumpnia seu molestia . seua[b] donatione . sicut in carta sua continetur libere uti non poterint . si guarentizare non poterit . capitulum de Beel' . sine offensione ipsius Rogerii et heredum suorum reddet fratribus Fontanensibus cartam priorem . quam sub hac conditione conseruandam acceperunt . et ipsi fratres de Font' . utentur aisiamentis foreste de Niderd' . sicut in eadem carta continetur . donec suam excambionem habeant . et recepta excambione . iterum cartam reponent in Beel'. Edificia ibi non facient . nisi . per ipsum Rog(erium) preter logias et faldas . ad custodienda animalia. Et hoc sciendum . quod pro predicta donatione . ęcclesia de Font' . dedit Rogerio in adiutorium itineris sui Ierosol' .c.xx. marcas . et filio suo Nigello .x. marcas . pro assensu . et Rob(erto) filio suo .i. marcam. Hoc

[a] *Sic* (for *Godric*).   [b] *Sic* in all versions; *sua* intended.

[1] *Fount. Cart.* i 205 (6).   [2] *E.Y.C.* i no. 508.

etiam statutum est inter eos . quod seruientes de Dacra securitatem facient fide uel iuramento fratribus eiusdem loci . quod de feris non capient eiusdem foreste . uel de auibus quas in carta sua dominus Rog(erius) sibi retinuit . et si quis deprehensus fuerit . monachi de eo rectum facient . prout capitulum Eborac(i) decreuerit. T(estes) . capitulum Ebor' . Gauf(ridus) prior Ebor' Phil(ippus) prior . Sancte Trinitatis Ebor' . magister Suanus de hospit(ali) . Will(elmus) Tillemer. Nig(ellus) filius Rog(erii) . Rog(erius) de C'di dapifer . Hugo Maleb' . Rad(ulfus) de Bellun . Galt(erus) de Karlet' . Rob(ertus) de Busci . War(inus) filius Symonis . Johannes de Creuequer . Rad(ulfus) de Beeluer . Rob(ertus) filius Godric Ebor' . Thom(as) filius Eluiue . Tom(as) filius Tom(e) Ebor' et Adam frater eius. Apud Eboracvm.

Endorsements: *Cirographum de Niderdala. | Dacra.* (12th cent.); *Hec est eadem penitus cum . . precedente istam. Duplicata enim* (13th cent.); *.viij.* (13th or 14th cent.).

Size: 12·5 × 20·5 cm.; 1·8 cm. turn-up.

Seal: seal no. 3 of Roger de Mowbray (above, p. lxxxiii), red wax varnished; appended on tag (a second slit in turn-up for tag for a second seal, ? never appended).

    NOTE. For the date, see note to no. 110. This agreement was confirmed by the chapter of York.[1]

112 *Similar agreement between Fountains and Roger de Mowbray.*
                    [At York. Aug. 1174 × June 1175]

    Cartulary copy: B.M., Add. MS. 40009 fo. 12r–v (old pp. 23–4).
    Pd. (transl.), *Fount. Cart.* i 206 (9a).

Notum sit omnibus legentibus et audientibus litteras ipsas hanc esse conventionem inter ecclesiam de Font(ibus) et Rogerum de Molb', quod si aliquando contigerit ut quoquomodo aliquam partem perdant de eo quod in foresta dedit eis in proprium pro communi quo uti solebant et pro aliqua calumpnia seu molestia sua donatione sicut in carta sua continetur libere uti non poterint, si guarentizare non poterit, capitulum de Beeland sine offensione ipsius Rogeri et heredum suorum cartam priorem quam sub hac conditione conservandam accepit, reponet super altare beati Petri Eborac(i) per manum canonicorum domno abbati de Font(ibus) iterum reddendam. Et ipsi fratres de Font(ibus) utentur aisiamentis foreste de Niderdala sicut in eadem carta continetur donec suam excambionem habeant, et recepta excambione iterum cartam reponent in Beel(anda). Edificia ibi non facient nisi per ipsum Rogerum

    [1] *Fount. Cart.* i 205 (7).

preter logias et faldas ad custodienda animalia. Et hoc sciendum quod pro predicta donatione ecclesia de Font(ibus) dedit Rogero in adjutorium itineris sui Jerosol' cxx marcas et filio suo Nigello x marcas pro assensu et Roberto filio suo unam marcam. Hoc etiam statutum est inter eos quod servientes de Dacra securitatem facient fide vel juramento fratribus ejusdem loci, quod de feris non capient ejusdem foreste nec de^a avibus quas in carta Rogeri sibi retinuit. Et si quis deprehensus fuerit monachi de eo rectum facient prout capitulum Ebor(aci) decrevit. T(estes), capitulum Ebor(aci), Gaufridus prior Ebor', Philippus prior Sancti Trinitatis Ebor', magister Suanus de hospit(ali) Ebor', Guillelmus Tillemir, Nigellus filius^b Rogeri, Rogerus de C(un)di dapif(er), Hugo Malebisse, Radulfus de Bellun, Galterus de Carlet', Robertus de Busci, Garin filius Symonis, Johannes de Crevequer, Radulfus de Beluer, Robertus filius Codrici Ebor', Thomas filius Eluuie^c Ebor', Tomas et Adam filii Thome Ebor', Uctredus forestarius Rogeri de Molb'.

NOTE. For the date, see note to no. 110.

113 *Similar agreement between Fountains and Nigel de Mowbray.*

[At York. Aug. 1174 × June 1175]

Cartulary copies: B.M., Add. MS. 40009 fo. 2*r–v* (old. pp. 3–4); Add. MS. 18276 fo. 47*v* (abstract).
Pd. (transl.), *Fount. Cart.* i 209 (19), from Add. MS. 40009.

Notum sit omnibus legentibus et audientibus litteras istas hanc esse conventionem inter ecclesiam de Fontibus et Nigellum de Mubray, quod si aliquando contigerit ut quoquomodo aliquam partem perdant de eo quod in foresta dedit eis in proprium pro communi quo uti solebant et pro aliqua calumpnia seu molestia sua donatione sicut in carta sua continetur libere uti non poterint, si guarentizare non poterit, capitulum de Beelland sine offensione ipsius Nigelli vel heredum suorum cartam priorem quam sub hac conditione conservandam accepit, reponet super altare beati Petri Eboraci per manum canonicorum domno abbati de Fontibus iterum reddendam. Et ipsi fratres de Fontibus utentur aisiamentis foreste de Niderdale sicut in eadem carta continetur donec suam excambionem habeant, et recepta excambione iterum cartam reponent in Beelland. Edificia ibi non facient nisi per ipsum Nigellum preter logias et faldas ad custodienda animalia. Et hoc sciendum quod pro predicta donatione ecclesia de Fontibus dedit Rogero patri meo in adjutorium itineris sui^d Jerosolimis centum xx marcas argenti et michi Nigello filio suo decem marcas argenti pro assensu et Roberto fratre meo

---

^{a} Altered from *ne*, MS. ^{b} *Phil'*, MS. ^{c} ? Read *Elvive*. ^{d} *suis*, MS.

unam marcam. Hoc etiam statutum est inter nos quod servientes de Dacra securitatem facient fide vel juramento fratribus ejusdem loci, quod de feris non capient ejusdem foreste nec de avibus quas Rogerus pater meus et ego Nigellus in cartis nostris nobis retinemus. Et si quis deprehensus fuerit monachi de eo rectum facient prout capitulum Eboraci decreverit.

NOTE. For the date, see note to no. 110.

114 *Grant by Roger de Mowbray to Fountains of licence to make buildings and an enclosure for their cows and calves at Birstwith (Yorks., W.R.) and for the cattle-men there.*   [1151 × March 1176]

Cartulary copy: Bodl., MS. Rawlinson B 449 fo. 150v.

Notum sit omnibus audientibus hanc cartam quod ego Rogerus de Mubray petitione fratris Roberti licenciam dedi et hac carta confirmavi monachis de Font(ibus) ut habeant et faciant sibi eddifficia et ortum ad vaccas et vitulos suos ad Birstad et ad pastores averiorum suorum que ibi sunt. Et ego Nigellus filius suus hoc idem eis in perpetuam elemosinam confirmavi. Teste Thoma etc.

NOTE. The grant must have been made after the monks gained rights of pasture in Nidderdale, after 1151 (nos. 102–3), and before they lost the land south of Dacre belonging to the Knaresborough forest, in 1175 (cf. nos. 126–7).

115 *Gift by Roger de Mowbray and Nigel his son to Fountains of dead wood for the monks' forge at Aldburgh; and confirmation of common pasture in Azerley and Winksley and of ½ carucate in Brimham (Yorks., W.R.).*
[c. 1160 × March 1176]

Transcript, from an original charter formerly in St. Mary's Tower, York: Bodl., MS. Dodsworth 7 fo. 31v (lacks last witness). Cartulary copies: B.M., Cotton MS. Tib. C xii fo. 25r–v; Bodl., MS. Rawlinson B 449 fo. 20r (lacks last witness); B.M., Egerton MS. 3053 fo. 3r–v (lacks all witnesses); Add. MS. 18276 fo. 4v (abstract).
Pd. (transl.), *Fount. Cart.* i 15 (2), from Cotton MS.

Rogerus de Mubrai[a] et Nigellus filius ejus omnibus literas has legentibus et audientibus salutem. Sciatis nos dedisse et presenti carta confirmasse monachis de Fontibus[b] mortuum boscum in foresta nostra de stante et de jacente quicquid folium non portat ubicunque capere voluerint, ad carbonem faciendum ad forgiam suam de Aldeburga.[c] Item confirmavimus eis ad grangiam suam de Suttun communem pasturam de Aserlagh

---

[a] *Molb'*, Cotton MS.   [b] *Font'*, Cotton MS.   [c] *Aldeb'*, Cotton MS.

et Winchesle^a per totum preter de blado et de prato omnibus bobus illius grangie et xxv vaccis, et quando non sunt in labore in foresta nostra ibunt ad pascendum diebus et noctibus. Et ad utendas has pasturas villarum scilicet et foreste habebunt vias ubi oportunum eis fuerit in cujuscunque manus predicte ville devenerint. Preterea confirmavimus predictis monachis dimidiam carucatam^b terre in Birnebem in bosco et plano, pratis et pasturis et aquis et in omnibus aliis aisiamentis ad tenendum tam libere sicut ego Rogerus de Mubrai^c eam fratribus de Templo carta mea confirmavi. Hec omnia confirmavimus eis in perpetuam elemosinam solutam liberam et quietam ab omni servicio^d pro animabus nostris et omnium parentum nostrorum. Test(es) Landricus monachus de Beeland(a),^e Robertus de Mubrai^c filius Rogeri de Mubrai,^c Hugo Malebiss,^f Robertus de Busci qui affidaverunt hec omnia tenenda Hamund Beler.

NOTE. Nigel de Mowbray cannot have been associated in a joint charter with his father before c. 1160. The gift must have preceded no. 119, of Sept. 1175 × March 1176. For the gift of ½ carucate in Brimham to the Templars, see no. 270.

116 *Notification by Roger de Mowbray that Rainald de Mildeby restored and quitclaimed to him one carucate in Brimham, which Roger then gave to Fountains.* [c. 1160 × March 1176]

Cartulary copies: Bodl., MS. Rawlinson B 449 fo. 91r; B.M., Add. MS. 18276 fo. 31r–v (abstract).

Rogerus de Mubray omnibus videntibus et audientibus has litteras salutem. Sciatis quod Reynaldus^g de Mildeby reddidit michi et quietam clamavit illam carucatam terre quam dedi ei in Birnebem in expectatione servicii sui et cartam meam quam inde habuit michi cum illa terra reddidit. Et ego ipsam terram et eandem cartam domui de Font(ibus) in perpetuam elemosinam dedi et carta mea confirmavi.

NOTE. The gift must have been made after no. 115, but before no. 119. For Roger's original gift to Rainald de Mildeby, see no. 375.

117 *Confirmation by Roger de Mowbray to Fountains of Caldwell (Yorks., N.R.), i.e. 5 carucates, given by William Haget.* [c. 1160 × March 1176]

Cartulary copies: B.M., Add. MS. 37770 fo. 209v (old p. 420); Bodl., Univ. Coll. MS. 170 fo. 75r (old fo. 107r) (lacks last witness); B.M., Add. MS. 18276 fo. 132r (abstract).
Pd. (transl.), *Fount. Cart.* ii 486 (4), from Add. MS. 37770.

^a *Winchesl'*, Cotton MS.   ^b *carrucatam*, Cotton MS   ^c *Molb'*, Cotton MS.
^d *omnibus serviciis*, Cotton MS.   ^e *Beel'*, Cotton MS.   ^f *Malebisse*, Cotton MS.
^g *Arnaldus*, Add. MS.

Eboracensi archiepiscopo et omnibus sancte matris ecclesie filiis Rogerus
de Mulbrai*a* salutem. Notum vobis sit me concessisse et hac mea carta
confirmasse Deo et Sancte Marie et ecclesie de Fontibus et fratribus
ibidem Deo servientibus Caldewellam cum omnibus pertinenciis suis
scilicet quinque carrucatas terre, duas carrucatas et dimidiam in puram
et perpetuam elemosinam, reliquas vero duas et dimidiam in perpetuam
elemosinam reddendo Willelmo Haget et heredibus suis pro illis duabus
carrucatis et dimidia singulis annis duas marcas et dimidiam pro omnibus serviciis que ad terram pertinent. Et ipse Willelmus et heredes sui
guarentizabunt eis terram predictam et adquietabunt de omnibus serviciis que ad terram pertinent. Istam donationem ego et Nigellus filius
meus concedimus et confirmavimus sicut carta Willelmi testificat et
confirmat. Testes, Nigellus de Mulbrai,*a* Robertus de Mulbrai,*a*
Robertus de Busci, Johannes Crevequer, Robertus de Beluer.

NOTE. John de Crevequer first occurs after *c.* 1160 (no. 319). The charter
was certainly given before 1176 (see no. 128). For William Haget's gift, see
Fount. Cart. ii 486 (3). William held 2 fees in 1166.[1]

118 *Gift by Roger de Mowbray to Fountains of 20 cart-loads of hay from the
meadow of 'Wacaldaseing' (in Kirkby Malzeard, Yorks., W.R.).*
[*c.* 1166×March 1176]

Cartulary copies: B.M., Add. MS. 37770 fo. 77*v* (old p. 154); Add. MS.
18276 fo. 109*v* (abstract).
Pd. (transl.), *Fount. Cart.* i 413 (22), from Add. MS. 37770.

Rogerus de Mubray omnibus filiis sancte ecclesie presentibus et futuris
salutem. Sciatis me dedisse et presenti carta confirmasse Deo et ecclesie
Sancte Marie de Fontibus et monachis ibidem Deo servientibus in
puram et perpetuam elemosinam viginti carratas feni in prato de
Wacaldaseing solute et quiete de omnibus serviciis. Et quando monachi
de Fontibus predictum fenum falcare voluerint, monstrabunt baillio de
Malessart et baillius de Malessart monstrabit eis ubi falcare debeant.
Teste, Roberto capellano, Baldewino clerico, Radulfo clerico, Petro de
Belinghe, Herberto filio Ricardi, Rogero de Erdene, Radulfo de Novilla,
Roberto de Belscam.

NOTE. Peter of Billinghay does not appear until after *c.* 1166 (no. 349 note).
The gift was confirmed by Nigel de Mowbray between Sept. 1175 and March
1176, and his charter includes a clause which explains the reason for the
present grant (no. 124, p. 94 and n.).

a Mubrai, Univ. Coll. MS.

[1] No. 401, Fees [4].

119 *Gift by Roger de Mowbray to Fountains of Brimham, by specified bounds.*
[Sept. 1175 × March 1176]

Transcripts, from an original charter formerly in St. Mary's Tower, York:
Bodl., MS. Dodsworth 7 fo. 170r–v; Vyner deeds deposited at Leeds
Archives, V.R. 454. Cartulary copies: Bodl., MS. Rawlinson B 449 fo. 88r;
B.M., Cotton MS. Tib. C xii fo. 229v (lacks last 8 witnesses); Add. MS.
18276 fo. 30v (abstract).
Pd., *Mon. Ang.* v 307 (LVIII), from MS. Rawlinson; (transl.), *Fount. Cart.*
i 145 (2), from Cotton MS.

Eboracensi archiepiscopo et capitulo Sancti Petri Ebor(aci) et omnibus
sancte matris ecclesie filiis *ᵃpresentibus et futurisᵃ* Rogerus de Mubraiᵇ
salutem. Sciatis me dedisse et presenti carta confirmasse Deo et ecclesie
Sancte Marie de Fontibus totam terram de Birnebem cum omnibus
pertinenciis suis in bosco et plano pratis et aquis et pasturis in viis et
semitis per rectas divisas plenarias scilicet de Felebriggebec usque ad
metas de Rippelei sicut unquam melius et liberiusᶜ tenui. Hanc donationem per directasᵈ divisas feci predicte ecclesie in perpetuam
elemosinam et ita in liberam et propriam possessionem et ad sartandum
et donandum et vendendum, ita quod terra ubi nemus est cum tota alia
terra de Birnebem imperpetuum ecclesie predicte de Fontibus remanebit et quod nichil ibi michi retineam preter cervum et cervam, aprum et
capreolam et aves que alias capiunt. Sed et forestarii mei non habebunt
ibi potestatem nec de aliqua re se intromittent nisi de predictis feris et
avibus custodiendis. Et si aliqua calumpnia super predicta terra aliquando evenerit, ego et heredes mei predictam terram cum omnibus
pertinenciis suis monachis garentizabimus et acquietabimus ab omnibus
serviciis et consuetudinibus que ad terram pertinent et defendemus
contra omnes homines ita ut libere et in pace omnia teneant. Hec omnia
concessimus et confirmavimus *ᵉin presencia capituli Sancte Marie
Eborac'ᵉ* ego et Nigellus filius meus et Robertus filius meus in presencia
Clementis abbatis et in presencia Roberti decani et capituli Sancti Petri
Ebor(aci). Hiis testibus, Rogeroᶠ abbate de Beal(anda), Landrico monacho ejus, Philippo priore Sancte Trinitatis, magistro Suano de hospitali,
Roberto capellano Rogeri, Rogero de Kaove, Willelmo de Munzpinzun,ᵍ
Thoma filio Vivet,¹ Roberto de Daivilla, Hugone deʰ Malebissa, Turgis

---

ᵃ–ᵃ Omitted in Cotton MS.   ᵇ *Molb'*, Cotton MS.   ᶜ Cotton MS. inserts
illam terram.   ᵈ *predictas*, Cotton MS.   ᵉ–ᵉ Omitted in MS. Dodsw.
ᶠ Cotton MS. version has all witnesses' names in nominative case.   ᵍ *Mun-
pinceun*, Cotton MS.   ʰ Omitted in Vyner transcript.

---

¹ Perhaps Thomas son of Ulf, the moneyer, who is identified by Professor Cronne
with Thomas de Everwic' filius Ulvieti who occurs in 1130 (H. A. Cronne, *The Reign
of Stephen* (1970) p. 237).

filio Maugeri, Radulfo de Bavveir, Hamund Beler, Helia de Ferlint', Rogero de Bavent, Willelmo de Daivilla, Roberto de Busci, Thoma de Colevilla, Henrico de Lubbaham, Roberto de Bavveir, Rogero filio Aie, Ricardo de Insula, Willelmo de Rainevilla, Rannulfo de Glanvilla tunc vicecomite Ebor', Radulfo de Mundaivilla, Thoma Darel, Gaufrido de Neovilla, Ada filio Normanni, Bertrammo Haget, Adam Luvel, Radulfo de Ebor(aco), Stephano de Killum et de comitatu aliis multis.[a]

NOTE. Ranulf de Glanville was sheriff from Michaelmas 1175, and Brimham was confirmed by Nigel de Mowbray before March 1176 (no. 124). Henry II issued a confirmation, probably in January 1177.[1]

120 *Agreement between Fountains and Roger de Mowbray and his sons Nigel and Robert concerning the monks' rights in Brimham, for which Roger received 350 marks.*   [Sept 1175 × March 1176]

Cartulary copies: Bodl., MS. Rawlinson B 449 fo. 88r–v; B.M., Add. MS. 18276 fos. 30v–31r (abstract).
Pd., *Mon. Ang.* v 307 (LIX), from MS. Rawlinson.

Notum sit omnibus sancte matris ecclesie filiis hanc esse conventionem inter monachos de Font(ibus) et dominum Rogerum de Molb' et filios suos Nigellum et Robertum quod Rogerus et filii sui concesserunt et dederunt et carta sua confirmaverunt Deo et ecclesie Sancte Marie de Font(ibus) in perpetuam elemosinam totam terram de Birnebem, cum omnibus pertinenciis suis in bosco et plano, pratis et aquis et pasturis, in viis et semitis, per rectas divisas suas plenarias scilicet de Felebrigge-bec usque ad metas de Rippeleia, sicut unquam melius et liberius illam terram tenuerunt. Et hanc terram cum pertinenciis suis imperpetuum habebunt monachi solutam quietam ab omni servicio et consuetudine et ita in liberam et propriam possessionem et ad sartandum et donandum et vendendum, ita quod terra ubi nemus est cum tota alia terra de Birne-bem imperpetuum predicte ecclesie de Font(ibus) remanebit et quod nichil Rogerus et filii sui ibi retinuerunt preter cervum et cervam, aprum et capreolam et aves que alias capiunt. Sed et forestarii mei non habebunt ibi potestatem nec de aliqua re se intromittent nisi de predictis feris et avibus custodiendis. Hoc etiam statutum est inter nos quod servientes de Birnebem securitatem facient fide vel juramento fratribus ejusdem loci quod de feris non capient ejusdem foreste, neque de avibus quas in carta sua Rogerus et filii sui sibi retinuerunt. Et si aliquis de servien-tibus monachorum deprehensus fuerit monachi de eo rectum facient

[a] MSS. give *alii multi.*

[1] *Fount. Cart.* i 297 (6); cf. witnesses at Northampton in Jan. 1177, in Eyton *Itinerary* p. 210.

prout capitulum Eboraci decreverit. Et propter hanc conventionem Rogerus de Mub' accepit a monachis cccl marcas argenti. Ad hoc tenendum et garentizandum et defendendum monachis imperpetuum contra omnes homines et contra omnes feminas Rogerus de Mub' et filii ejus Nigellus et Robertus fidem affidaverunt et Robertus de Daivilla, Radulfus de Bavveir, Hugo Maleb', Turgis filius Malgeri, Robertus Busci. Et pro concessione et confirmatione hujus conventionis Nigellus filius Rogeri de Mub' v marcas a monachis recepit. Testes, capitulum ecclesie Sancte Marie Ebor', Philippus prior Sancte Trinitatis, magister Suanus.

NOTE. Almost certainly this agreement belongs to the same time as no. 119.

121 *Similar agreement between Fountains and Nigel and Robert de Mowbray, for which Nigel received 5 marks.* [Sept. 1175 × March 1176]

Cartulary copies: Bodl., MS. Rawlinson B 449 fos. 88v–89r; B.M., Add. MS. 18276 fo. 31r (abstract).

Notum sit omnibus sancte ecclesie filiis hanc esse conventionem inter monachos de Font(ibus) et Nigellum de Mub' et Robertum fratrem ejus quod Nigellus et Robertus frater ejus concesserunt et dederunt et carta sua confirmaverunt Deo et ecclesie Sancte Marie de Fontibus in perpetuam elemosinam totam terram de Birnebem, cum omnibus pertinenciis suis in bosco et plano, pratis et aquis et pasturis, in viis et semitis, per rectas divisas suas plenarias scilicet de Felebriggebec usque ad metas de Rippeleia, sicut unquam melius et liberius Rogerus de Mub' pater eorum illam terram tenuit. Et hanc terram cum pertinenciis suis imperpetuum habebunt solutam quietam ab omni servicio et consuetudine et ita in liberam et propriam possessionem et ad sartandum et donandum et vendendum, ita quod terra ubi nemus est cum tota alia terra de Birnebem imperpetuum predicte ecclesie de Font(ibus) remanebit et quod nichil Nigellus et filii sui sibi retinuerunt preter cervum et cervam, aprum et capreolam et aves que alias capiunt. Sed et forestarii Nigelli non habebunt ibi potestatem nec de aliqua re se intromittent nisi de predictis feris et avibus custodiendis. Hoc etiam statutum est inter eos quod servientes de Birnebem securitatem facient fide vel juramento fratribus ejusdem loci quod de feris non capient ejusdem foreste neque de avibus quas Nigellus et filii sui in carta sua sibi retinuerunt. Et si aliquis de servientibus monachorum deprehensus fuerit monachi de eo rectum facient prout capitulum Ebor(aci) decreverit. Et propter hanc concessionem Rogerus de Mub' pater eorum accepit a monachis cccl marcas. Et pro hac concessione et confirmatione hujus conventionis

Nigello de Mubrai v marcas dederunt. Ad hoc tenendum et warentandum et defendendum monachis imperpetuum contra omnes homines et contra omnes feminas Rogerus de Mubrai et filii ejus Nigellus et Robertus fidem affidaverunt, et Robertus de Daivilla, Radulfus de Bavveir, Hugo Maleb', Turgisius filius Malgeri, Robertus de Busci. Testes, capitulum Ebor', Philippus*a* prior Sancte Trinitatis.

NOTE. Almost certainly this agreement belongs to the same time as nos. 119–20.

122 *Confirmation by Roger de Mowbray to Fountains of their grange of Dacre; and gift of an increment to its lands between Dacre and Bewerley, for which Roger received £100.*   [Sept. 1175 × March 1176]

Cartulary copies: B.M., Add. MS. 40009 fo. 15*r–v* (old pp. 29–30); Bodl., MS. Rawlinson B 449 fo. 143*r–v* (lacks last 14 witnesses); B.M., Add. MS. 18276 fo. 47*r* (abstract).
Pd. (transl.), *Fount. Cart.* i 207 (12), from Add. MS. 40009.

Eboracensi archiepiscopo et capitulo Sancti Petri Ebor(aci) et omnibus sancte ecclesie filiis presentibus et futuris Rogerus de Molbr' salutem. Sciatis me dedisse et presenti carta confirmasse Deo et ecclesie Sancte Marie de Fontibus et monachis ibidem Deo servientibus grangiam de Dacra cum omnibus pertinenciis suis in bosco et plano et omnibus aliis rebus et locis et libertatibus sicut in cartis meis continetur. Preterea dedi eis et confirmavi ad incrementum sicut rivus de Beuerlai cadit in Nid ubi vetus capella fuit et inde sicut Nid venit usque Hiherfeldebec et inde sicut Hiherfeldebec pertingit usque ad divisas de Cravene. Hanc donationem per plenarias predictas divisas feci monachis de Fontibus solutam et quietam in puram et perpetuam elemosinam et ita in liberam et propriam possessionem quod nichil ibi michi vel heredibus meis retineam preter cervum et cervam, aprum et capriolam et aves que alias capiunt. Set et forestarii mei nullam potestatem ibi habebunt nec de re aliqua se intromittent nisi de predictis feris et avibus custodiendis. Et ego et heredes mei hec omnia guarentabimus eis in bosco et plano et acquietabimus de omnibus serviciis et consuetudinibus imperpetuum. Et sciendum quod pro donatione predicti incrementi monachi de Fontibus dederunt michi de caritate sua centum libras argenti. Testes, capitulum Sancti Petri Ebor', Philippus prior Sancte Trinitatis Ebor', Gualterus de Templo, Symon et Hamun et Willemus de Buum, Radulfus de Langetoft vicarii Sancti Petri, Paulinus de Ledes, Gamel de Dunesford, Robertus filius Symonis de Seel, Robertus capellanus

a Philpus, MS.

Rogeri de Molb', Robertus de Daivilla et Willelmus frater ejus, Torphinus filius Roberti filii Copsi, Gillebertus de Briddeshala, Radulfus Magnus, Galterus de Ros, Osbertus de Schipwic, Willelmus Nobilis.

NOTE. This confirmation is clearly of even date with nos. 123–4. Roger, archbishop of York, issued a confirmation.[1]

123 *Confirmation by Nigel de Mowbray to Fountains of part of the forest of Nidderdale from Dacre south to Killinghall and from Dacre north to Bewerley, given by Roger de Mowbray.* [Sept. 1175 × March 1176]

Cartulary copies: B.M., Add. MS. 40009 fos. 1*v–2r* (old pp. 2–3); Add. MS. 18276 fo. 47*v* (abstract).
Pd. (transl.), *Fount. Cart.* i 209 (18), from Add. MS. 40009.

Eboracensi archiepiscopo et capitulo Sancti Petri Eboraci et omnibus filiis sancte matris ecclesie Nigellus de Mubrai salutem. *Continues as Roger de Mowbray's charter, no. 110, to:* ... Hanc confirmationem... scilicet Rievallensis, Fontanensis et Beeland. Hec omnia concessi et confirmavi in presencia capituli Eboraci. Testes capitulum Ebor(aci), Philippus prior Sancte Trinitatis, Galterus de Templo, Symon, Hamo, Guillelmus de Buhu', Radulfus de Langetoft vicarii Sancti Petri Eboraci, Gamel de Dunesfort, Paulinus de Ledes, Robertus capellanus Rogeri de Moubray, Robertus de Daivile et Guillelmus frater ejus, Torphinus filius Roberti filii Copsi, Gilebertus de Brideshale, Radulfus Magnus, Gauterus de Ros, Osbertus de Scipwic, Guillelmus Nobilis, Radulfus clericus de Insula.

NOTE. The land concerned in this confirmation was lost by March 1176 (nos. 126–7). The confirmation was made at the same time as no. 124, after Sept. 1175.

124 *Confirmation by Nigel de Mowbray to Fountains of various gifts (specified) made by his father Roger and his mother Alice de Gant, for which Nigel received 50 marks.* [Sept. 1175 × March 1176]

Cartulary copies: B.M., Add. MS. 40009 fos. 3*r–5r* (old pp. 5–9); Bodl., MS. Rawlinson B 449 fo. 144*r* (lacks last 18 witnesses).
Pd., *Mon. Ang.* v 309 (LXXI), from MS. Rawlinson; (transl.) *Fount. Cart.* i 210 (21), from Add. MS.

Eboracensi archiepiscopo et capitulo Sancti Petri Eboraci et omnibus sancte matris ecclesie filiis presentibus et futuris Nigellus de Molb' salutem. Sciatis me dedisse et presenti carta confirmasse in perpetuam elemosinam Deo et ecclesie Sancte Marie de Fontibus et monachis

[1] *Fount. Cart.* i 208 (13).

ibidem Deo servientibus donationes quas pater meus Rogerus de Molbr' fecit eis et cartis suis confirmavit in perpetuam elemosinam scilicet Aldeburgam in grangiam, solutam*a* et quietam ab omnibus serviciis et quicquid ad eandem pertinet, ex illa parte Jori fluminis in bosco et plano in campis et pratis et aquis sicut avus meus Nigellus de Albinio dedit eam antiquitus monachis Pontiniacensibus et communem pasturam ex altera parte aque et ex ipsa eadem parte firmamentum stagni sui ad molendinum faciendum. Confirmavi etiam illis illam donationem quam Turgisius filius Malgeri fecit eis in puram et perpetuam elemosinam. Et confirmationem quam Galterus de Bueri de eadem terra monachis fecit scilicet de Smithuswat usque ad Gretgata et sicut Gretgata tenditur usque in Elrebec' et exinde inferius sicut Elrebec cadit in Jor. Confirmavi etiam monachis mortuum boscum in foresta mea de stante et jacente quicquid folium non portat ubicunque capere voluerint ad carbonem faciendum ad forgiam suam de Aldburg. Item confirmavi eis quicquid patris mei fuit inter terram de Suttuna et quendam rivulum meantem infra Redlaiam juxta fontem quam adaquandis pecoribus suis illis dedit et ab eodem rivulo recta linea precidente inflexionem ejusdem rivuli versus aquilonem usque ad tres spinas sitas in quodam monte petroso, et inde usque ad quendam magnum salicem sub margine silve que vocatur Litlehage et inde usque ad quandam viam que jacet in fundo vicine vallis et per eandem viam quantum terra illorum durat. Et preterea confirmo donationem quam Aaliz de Gant mater mea illis dedit per medium Litlehaga a barra usque ad viam petrosam sicut divisio facta est et post ultra viam petrosam usque ad Walescroft et de Walescroft ultra Cumbedena usque ad siccum salicem juxta Pirwinetres et sic recte usque ad fontem. Item confirmavi eis ad grangiam suam de Suttuna communem*b* pasturam de Aserlagh et de Wincheslai per totum preter de blado et prato omnibus bobus illius grangie et xxv vaccis et quando non sunt in labore in foresta mea ibunt ad pascendum diebus et noctibus. Et ad utendum his pasturis villarum scilicet et foreste habebunt vias ubi eis oportunum fuerit in cujuscunque manus predicte ville devenerint. Et ut difficiant et estupent unam viam que vadit per mediam culturam de Suttuna quia eis nocebat,[1] dedi etiam eis et confirmavi in perpetuam elemosinam xx carratas feni in prato de Wacaldesheng solute et quiete de omnibus serviciis et quando predictum fenum falcare voluerint, monstrabunt ballivo*c* de Malesart et ipse ballivus de Malesart monstrabit eis ubi falcare debeant. Item confirmavi eis donationem terre illius

---

a solam, Add. MS.   *b* commuonem, MSS.   *c* balivo in Add. MS.

[1] This interesting clause is not found in the charter making the gift of 20 cart-loads of hay (no. 118).

quam Aldelin de Aldefeld et Radulfus filius ejus donaverunt et ceteri filii ejus concesserunt predictis monachis in perpetuam elemosinam scilicet de Suanlei usque ad vadum de Wainesford et quinque pedes de terra arabili ad fossatum faciendum. Item confirmavi eis totam terram de Birnebem cum omnibus pertinenciis suis in bosco et plano pratis et aquis et pasturis in viis et semitis per rectas divisas plenarias scilicet de Felebriggebec usque ad metas de Rippelei sicut umquam melius et liberius illam terram pater meus tenuit. Hanc donationem et confirmationem per predictas divisas feci monachis in perpetuam elemosinam et ita in liberam et propriam possessionem et ad sartandum et donandum et vendendum. Ita quod ubi nemus est cum tota alia terra de Birnebem inperpetuum ecclesie de Fontibus remanebit et quod nichil ibi michi retineam preter cervum et cervam, aprum et capreolam et aves que alias capiunt. Set et forestarii mei non habebunt ibi potestatem nec de aliqua re se intromittent nisi de predictis feris et avibus custodiendis. Et si aliqua calumpnia super predictam terram aliquando evenerit, ego et heredes mei predictam terram cum omnibus pertinenciis suis monachis warentabimus et acquietabimus ab omnibus serviciis et consuetudinibus que ad terram pertinent et defendemus contra omnes homines ita ut libere et in pace omnia teneant. Super hec omnia dedi et confirmavi ecclesie de Fontibus grangiam de Dacra cum omnibus pertinenciis in bosco et plano et omnibus aliis rebus et locis et libertatibus sicut in cartis patris mei continetur. Preterea dedi eis et confirmavi in incrementum sicut rivus de Beuerlay cadit in Nid ubi vetus capella fuit et inde sicut Nid venit usque Higherfeldebec et inde sicut Higherfeldebec pertingit usque ad divisas de Cravena. Hanc donationem per plenarias predictas divisas feci monachis de Fontibus solutam et quietam in puram et perpetuam elemosinam et ita in liberam et propriam possessionem quod nichil ibi michi vel heredibus meis retineam preter cervum et cervam, aprum et capreolam et aves que alias capiunt. Set et forestarii mei nullam potestatem ibi habebunt nec de re aliqua se intromittent nisi de predictis feris et avibus custodiendis. Et ego et heredes mei hec omnia guarentabimus eis in bosco et plano et acquietabimus de omnibus serviciis et consuetudinibus imperpetuum. Confirmavi etiam eis terram de Redlay quam Radulfus de Beellun eis in elemosinam dedit scilicet a barra ipsius Redlai inferius sicut fossatum vadit usque ad caput calcede versus Azerlagh in bosco et plano. Hec omnia supradicta dedit et confirmavit pater meus Rogerus de Molb' per cartas. Et ego Nigellus filius et heres ejus dedi et confirmavi per hanc cartam meam. Et sciendum quod pro donatione et confirmatione mea monachi de Fontibus dederunt michi l marcas. Testes, capitulum Sancti Petri Eboraci, Philippus prior

Sancte Trinitatis Ebor(aci), Galterus de Templo, Simon et Hamun et Willelmus de Buum et Radulfus de Langetoft et Willelmus vicarii Sancti Petri, Paulin de Ledes, Gamel de Dunesford, Robertus filius Simonis del Seel, Robertus capellanus Rogeri de Molb', Radulfus clericus Nigelli, Robertus de Daivill' et Willelmus frater ejus, Torphinus filius Roberti filii Copsi, Gillebertus de Briddeshala, Radulfus Magnus, Galterus de Ros, Osbertus de Schipwic, Willelmus Nobilis.

NOTE. The gift of Brimham, which is included in this confirmation, was not made until after Sept. 1175 (no. 119). The list of witnesses indicates that the confirmation was made at the same time as no. 123, before March 1176. For the gifts confirmed, see above, nos. 95, 99–101, 105, 107–8, 115, 118–22.

125 *Gift by Roger de Mowbray to Fountains of land between Pateley Bridge and Yeadon (Yorks., W.R.).* At York, 8 March 1176

Transcript, from an original charter formerly in the possession of the Revd. William Greenwell, B. 3: Leeds, Yorks. Archaeol. Soc. Libr., MS. 869 (Farrer MS.) E.Y.C. box 8 (with a note: *not to be printed*). Cartulary copies: B.M., Add. MS. 40009 fos. 12v–13r (old pp. 24–5); Bodl., MS. Rawlinson B 449 fo. 143v (lacks last 6 witnesses); B.M., Add. MS. 18276 fo. 46v (abstract).
Pd., *Mon. Ang.* v 309 (LXX), from MS. Rawlinson; (transl.) *Yorks. Deeds* i no. 157, from the original charter in the possession of Greenwell; (transl.), *Archaeologia Aeliana* 4th ser. vii (1930) 85, from the original charter then in the possession of Dr. C. H. Hunter Blair; (transl.) *Fount. Cart.* i 206 (9b), from Add. MS. 40009.

Rogerus de Mubrai omnibus hominibus suis et omnibus audientibus has literas salutem. Sciatis me dedisse et hac mea carta confirmasse Deo et monachis Sancte Marie de Fontibus quicquid continetur inter Patleiagate et Jwdene. Hoc dedi eis in puram et perpetuam elemosinam liberum et quietum ab omni servicio et ab omni re que ad terram pertinet et quietum de me et omnibus heredibus meis imperpetuum sine excambio illis dando si forte aliqua occasione quicquam de eo perdiderint, et tamen pro omni posse nostro illud eis guarantabimus sicut proprium jus nostrum quod eis in perpetuum dedimus sine omni retenemento nostri vel heredum nostrorum. Teste, Roberto de Mubrai, Roberto de Aievilla, Hugone Malebisse, Radulfo de Belvaco, Roberto de Belscamp, Adam Luvel, Philippo de Munpinctun, Roberto le Norreis, Radulfo filio Aldelini, Roberto de Trehanton. Facta fuit hec carta apud Eboracum viij idus Martii anno incarnationis Domini MCLXXV.

Endorsement: *Dakre Cart. 9.*
Seal: fragment of seal no. 3 of Roger de Mowbray (above, p. lxxxiii).

126 *Gift by Roger de Mowbray to Fountains of land on eastern Nidderdale (Dallow Moor), by specified bounds, in recompense for land to the south of Dacre which the monks had lost; for which gift Roger received 10 marks.*
At York, 9 March 1176

Cartulary copy: B.M., Add. MS. 40009 fo. 13r–v (old pp. 25–6).
Pd. (transl.), *Fount. Cart.* i 206 (10a).

Eboracensi archiepiscopo et decano et capitulo Sancti Petri Ebor(aci) Rogerus de Mubrai salutem. Sciatis me dedisse et hac mea carta confirmasse Deo et monachis de Fontibus quicquid infra has divisas continetur scilicet totam Niderdala ex illa parte aque deversus le est Jwdene sursum in longum Nid usque ad Beckermote et totum saltum de Loftushum et illum saltum de Popeltun et de Beckermote sursum usque ad moram et sic usque ad Frostildehau et inde usque ad Hameldun et inde usque ad Dalhagha et totum Dalhagha deorsum ex utraque parte quantum durat et inde transversus moram deversus Scheldene usque ad divisas archiepiscopi et inde deversus le west usque ad Jwdene. Hec omnia dedi eis primum in recompensationem illius terre et bosci quod perdiderunt el suth de Dacra, postea partim in perpetuam elemosinam quia quando ego vel heredes mei fecerimus eos recuperare libere et quiete hec quod perdiderunt el suth de Dacra dabunt nobis lx marcas et tam illud quod perdiderunt quam hoc quod in recompensationem a me receperunt eis imperpetuum remanebunt. Et quando hanc cartam de hoc habuerunt de me Rogero dederunt michi de predicta pecunia in testimonium et in memoriam decem marcas. Et ego et heredes mei hec omnia predicta eis guarentabimus et defendemus adversus omnes calumpniatores ita quod ipsi facient de hiis omnibus quicquid voluerint sicut de sua libera et propria et perpetua possessione soluta quieta et libera ab omni servicio et consuetudine et ab omni re ad terram pertinente. Test(ibus), Roberto de Mubray filio meo, Roberto de Belscamp, Philippo de Muntpinzun, Roberto de Trehamtun, Guillelmo[a] Gramarie, Guillelmo filio[b] Herberti de Saue, Guillelmo[a] de Tikehill'. Teste etiam Philippo priore et capitulo Sancte Trinitatis. Facta fuit hec carta apud Ebor(acum) in domo Guillelmi de Tikehil anno incarnationis Domini MCLXXV, vij idus Martii.

NOTE. This charter was confirmed by Robert the dean and the chapter of York,[1] and by Henry II, probably in January 1177 (see no. 119 note). Fountains had lost the land south of Dacre to William de Stuteville.[2]

---

[a] *Guillelmus*, MS.   [b] *Guillelmus filius*, MS.

---

[1] *Fount. Cart.* i 206 (10b).   [2] Ibid. pp. 215–16; cf. above, no. 110 note.

127 *Gift by Roger de Mowbray to Fountains of land on eastern Nidderdale (Dallow Moor), by specified bounds, and all Lofthouse, in recompense for land to the south of Dacre which the monks had lost.*

At York, 18 March 1176

Cartulary copies: B.M., Add. MS. 40009 fo. 14*r–v* (old pp. 27–8); Bodl., MS. Rawlinson B 449 fo. 143*v* (lacks last 11 witnesses); B.M., Add. MS. 18276 fos. 46*v*–47*r* (abstract).
Pd., *Mon. Ang.* v 309 (LXIX), from MS. Rawlinson; (transl.) *Fount. Cart.* i 207 (10c), from Add. MS. 40009.

Eboracensi archiepiscopo et decano et capitulo Sancti Petri Eboraci et omnibus sancte ecclesie filiis presentibus et futuris Rogerus de Mubrai salutem. Sciatis me dedisse et hac mea carta confirmasse Deo et monachis Sancte Marie de Fontibus quicquid continetur infra has divisas scilicet totum Niderdala ex illa parte aque deversus le est de Jwdenebec sursum in longum Nid usque ad Beckermote et inde sursum usque ad moram et sic usque ad Frostildehau et de Frostildehau usque ad Hameldun et inde usque ad Dalhagha et totum Dalhaga deorsum ex utraque parte quantum durat et inde transversus moram deversus Sceldene usque ad divisas archiepiscopi et inde deversus le west usque ad Jwdenebec; et preterea totum Loftushum cum pertinenciis suis. Hec omnia dedi in puram et perpetuam elemosinam et in recompensationem illius terre et illius bosci quod dedi eis el suth de Dacra quod perdiderunt. Et ego et heredes mei omnia predicta eis guarentabimus imperpetuum et defendemus adversus omnes calumpniatores, ita quod ipsi facient de hiis omnibus predictis quicquid voluerint sicut de sua libera et propria et perpetua possessione soluta quieta et libera ab omni servicio et consuetudine et ab omni re que ad terram pertinet. Sciendum est etiam quod quandocunque ego Rogerus de Mubray vel heredes mei libere et quiete deliberavimus eis hoc quod perdiderunt el suth de Dacra quod tenuerunt de me hoc quod dedi eis in recompensationem propter hoc quietum ab eis michi vel heredibus meis remanebit. Teste, Roberto decano et capitulo Eboraci, Philippo priore Sancte Trinitatis, Roberto de Mubrai, Willelmo de Tikehil, Roberto Daievilla, Hugone Malebisse, Radulfo de Belvaco, Adam Luvel, Philippo*ᵃ* de Muntpinzun, Roberto de Belscamp, Petro clerico, Roberto de Trehamt', Radulfo filio Aldelini, Roberto de Cotes, Guillelmo le Gramarie, Alano*ᵇ* Fossard. Facta fuit hec carta apud Ebor(acum) in domo Guillelmi de Tikehil xv kalendas Aprilis anno incarnationis Domini MCLXXV.

ᵃ Philippus, MS.   *ᵇ Alanus*, MS.

128 *Confirmation by Roger de Mowbray and Nigel his son to Fountains of Caldwell (Yorks., N.R.), i.e. 5 carucates, given and quitclaimed by Geoffrey Haget; Roger and Nigel received 3 marks.* [At York, March 1176]

> Cartulary copies: B.M., Add. MS. 37770 fo. 211r (old p. 423); Bodl., Univ. Coll. MS. 170 fo. 75v (old fo. 107v) (lacks 7 witnesses); B.M., Add. MS. 18276 fo. 132r (abstract).
> Pd. (transl.), *Fount. Cart.* ii 487 (8), from Add. MS. 37770.

Rogerus de Mubrai et Nigellus filius ejus omnibus videntibus et audientibus has litteras salutem. Sciatis nos concessisse et hac carta nostra confirmasse in perpetuam elemosinam Deo et ecclesie Sancte Marie de Font(ibus) et monachis et fratribus ibidem Deo servientibus totam Caldewellam scilicet quinque carrucatas terre cum omnibus pertinenciis suis et aisiamentis in prato et pastura et in omnibus locis ita libere et quiete sicut in carta Galfridi Haget quam inde habent continetur. Et ipse Galfridus et heredes sui eandem terram eis guarentizabit cum omnibus pertinenciis suis et aisiamentis et adquietabit ab omnimodo servicio et consuetudine et exactione que ad terram pertinent sicut liberam et perpetuam elemosinam suam et fratrum suorum Guillelmi et Bertrammi. Et sciendum quod pro hac confirmatione nostra monachi dederunt nobis tres marcas argenti. Teste, Roberto capellano, Roberto de Aivilla, Hugone Malebisse, *a*Radulfo de Bevveir, Hamone Beler, Roberto de Buzci,*a* Ada Luvel,*b* Herberto filio Ricardi, Roberto le Norreis, Petro clerico, Roberto de Novilla.

> NOTE. Five of the witnesses to this confirmation occur in the charters dated at York on 8 March 1176 (no. 125) and 18 March 1176 (no. 127). For an earlier confirmation concerning Caldwell, see above, no. 117. The gift by Geoffrey Haget was confirmed by Henry II, probably in Jan. 1177 (see no. 119 note).

129 *Gift by Roger de Mowbray and Nigel his son and heir to Fountains of a road for their cattle to go from Aldburgh to the moor between Swinton and Nidderdale; and confirmation of land in Swinton (Yorks., N.R.), given by Turgis son of Malger, and land in Aldfield (W.R.), given by Ralph son of Aldelin.* [At York, March 1176]

> Cartulary copies: B.M., Cotton MS. Tib. C xii fo. 26r–v; Bodl., MS. Rawlinson B 449 fo. 20v (lacks last 6 witnesses); B.M., Egerton MS. 3053 fo. 3v (lacks all witnesses); Add. MS. 18276 fo. 5r (abstract).
> Pd. (transl.), *Fount. Cart.* i 16 (6), from Cotton MS.

Notum sit omnibus sancte ecclesie filiis presentibus et futuris quod ego Rogerus de Mubrai et ego Nigellus filius et heres ejus dedimus et hac

---

a-a Omitted in Univ. Coll. MS.   *b* Univ. Coll. MS. version ends.

nostra carta confirmavimus Deo et ecclesie Sancte Marie de Font(ibus) et monachis et fratribus ibidem Deo servientibus unam viam tante latitudinis quantum necesse fuerit per quam averia sua de Audeburg'[a] exire possint ad pascendum ad pasturam suam in mora inter Suintun et Niderdala que mora pertinet ad honorem de Masham. Hanc viam habebunt per terram et feudum nostrum ubi eis utilius fuerit extra bladum et pratum sine omni impedimento nostri vel hominum nostrorum. Et nos et heredes nostri eandem viam cum predicta pastura eis guarentizabimus imperpetuum sicut puram et perpetuam elemosinam nostram et ab omni terreno servicio liberam. Et preterea confirmavimus eis totam terram illam quam Turgisus[b] filius Malgeri et Albrea uxor ejus eis dederunt in territorio de Suint'[c] scilicet inter Rumore et Gredgate[d] sicut in carta Turgisi[e] continetur quam monachi inde habent. Confirmavimus etiam eis totam terram illam quam Radulfus filius Aldelin et filii ejus Guillelmus et Ricardus eis dederunt in territorio de Aldefeld'[f] ita libere et quiete et plenarie sicut in cartis eorum continetur. Et sciendum quod predicta via trium percarum latitudinis erit et postquam in predicta pastura pernoctaverint, non longius ibunt in predicta pastura quam ut sequenti die redire possint ad carrucam. Teste, Roberto capellano, Roberto de Aievilla, Hugone Malebise,[g] Radulfo de Belveir, Hamone Beler, Roberto de Busci, Adam Luvel, Herberto filio Ricardi, Roberto le Norreis, Petro clerico, Roberto de Novilla.

NOTE. This gift and confirmation is clearly of an even date with no. 128. For an earlier confirmation of Turgis son of Malger's gift, see no. 108. Ralph son of Aldelin's charters are *Fount. Cart.* ii 850 (3) and (4). Ralph was himself present at York in March 1176 (nos. 125, 127).[1]

130 *Confirmation by Roger de Mowbray and Nigel his son to Fountains of 44 acres [in Aldfield], given by Ralph son of Aldelin.* [At York, March 1176]

Cartulary copies: Bodl., MS. Rawlinson B 449 fo. 129*v*; B.M., Add. MS. 18276 fo. 77*v* (abstract).
Pd. (transl.), *Fount. Cart.* ii 851 (5), from detached leaves of cartulary of Fountains vol. ii (i.e. now B.M., Add. MS. 40009, which no longer contains this text).

Omnibus sancte matris ecclesie filiis tam presentibus quam futuris Rogerus de Mubrai et Nigellus filius ejus salutem. Sciatis nos et heredes

---

[a] *Aldeburga*, MS. Rawl. [b] *Turgisius*, MS. Rawl. [c] *Suintun*, MS. Rawl.
[d] *Gretegate*, MS. Rawl. [e] *Turgisii*, MS. Rawl. [f] *Aldefelda*, MS. Rawl.
[g] *Malebisse*, MS. Rawl.

---

[1] For his fee, see nos. 383, 401, Fees [29]; cf. above, no. 99.

nostros concessisse et cartis nostris confirmasse donationem quam Radulfus filius Aldelini de Aldefeld fecit monachis de Font(ibus), scilicet xl et iiij acras terre sicut in carta jamdicti R. continetur, in puram et perpetuam elemosinam possidendam liberam et quietam ab omni servicio et exactione seculari. Testibus his, Roberto capellano, Roberto de Daivilla, Hugone Malebise et aliis multis.

Fount. Cart. adds to these the following witnesses:

Thomas de Coleville, Ralph de Belveeir, Peter clericus, 'and many others'.

NOTE. Five of these witnesses occur in no. 129, and four in no. 127.

131 *Confirmation by Alice de Gant to Fountains of whatever they have of her dowry in the honour of Kirkby Malzeard, in Nidderdale, and in Azerley, and all Brimham (Yorks., W.R.), as given by Roger de Mowbray and her sons Nigel and Robert; for which confirmation Alice received a gold ring.*

10 April 1176

> Transcript, from an original charter formerly in St. Mary's Tower, York: Bodl., MS. Dodsworth 7 fo. 171r. Cartulary copies: Bodl., MS. Rawlinson B 449 fo. 91r; B.M., Add. MS. 18276 fo. 31r.
> Pd., *Mon. Ang.* v 310 (LXXIII), from MS. Rawlinson.

Eboracensi archiepiscopo et omnibus sancte matris ecclesie filiis Alicia de Gaunt uxor Rogeri de Mubrai salutem. Sciatis me de mea bona et libera voluntate et sine omni exactione alicujus hominis concessisse et hac mea carta confirmasse in perpetuam elemosinam Deo et monachis Sancte Marie de Fontibus quicquid habent de dote mea in bosco et plano, pratis et aquis, pasturis, essartis et terris cultis que pertinent ad honorem de Mallesart et ad Nidderdale et ad villam de Asserlac, et preterea totam Birnebem cum omnibus pertinenciis suis et aisiamentis in bosco et plano et in omnibus aliis locis et rebus ad eam pertinentibus, ita quiete libere et integre et plenarie sicut inde continetur in cartis prenominati domini mei Rogeri de Mubray, et in cartis filiorum meorum Nigelli et Roberti. Et sciendum quod ecclesia de Fontibus recepit me in omnibus orationibus et beneficiis suis et faciet post decessum meum pro me plenarium servicium in missis et psalteriis sicut pro monacho ejusdem domus fieri solet. Hanc concessionem et confirmationem feci predicte ecclesie post Pascha scilicet iiij idus Aprilis anno incarnationis M°. C°. LXX° VI°, eo anno quo oppida de Tresc et de Malessart prosternabantur. Et in testimonium et in rememorationem dederunt michi predicti monachi unum annulum aureum.

132 *Gift by Roger de Mowbray to Fountains of all the beasts and birds of the forest of Brimham, for the monks' infirmary.* At Fountains, 2 Feb. 1181

> Transcripts, from an original charter formerly in St. Mary's Tower, York: Bodl., MS. Dodsworth 7 fo. 171*r*; Vyner deeds deposited at Leeds Archives, V.R. 453. Cartulary copies: Bodl., MS. Rawlinson B 449 fo. 90*r*; B.M., Add. MS. 18276 fo. 31*r* (abstract).

Omnibus sancte ecclesie filiis presentibus et futuris Rogerus de Mubrai[a] salutem. Sciatis me dedisse et hac mea carta confirmasse Deo et monachis Sancte Marie de Fontibus in puram et perpetuam elemosinam omnes feras et aves totius foreste de Birnebem ad infirmatoria sua. Hanc donationem feci eis solutam quietam et liberam ab omni servicio et consuetudine de me et omnibus heredibus meis imperpetuum et ita in propriam possessionem quod nec nos nec aliquis alius per nos de re aliqua infra predictam forestam se intromittet. Sed predicti monachi habebunt custodiam foreste et ferarum et avium que in ea fuerint per suos proprios forestarios sine omni retinemento mei vel heredum meorum. Facta autem fuit hec carta ad Fontes in hospicio die purificationis Sancte Marie anno incarnationis Domini MCLXXX. Hii sunt testes, Willelmus de Vesci, Galterus de Boelebec,[b] Radulfus de Bavveir.

133 *Confirmation by Roger de Mowbray to Fountains of all Bramley (Grange) (Yorks., W.R.), given by Swain de Thornton, for a rent to Roger of 2 marks p.a.* [At Fountains, *c.* 2 Feb. 1181]

> Cartulary copies: B.M., Cotton MS. Tib. C xii fo. 222*r–v*; Egerton MS. 3053 fo. 6*v* (lacks all witnesses); Add. MS. 18276 fo. 29*r* (abstract). Pd. (transl.), *Fount. Cart.* i 141 (3), from Cotton MS.

Omnibus audientibus et videntibus has litteras presentibus et futuris Rogerus de Mubrai[c] salutem. Sciatis me concessisse et hac mea carta confirmasse Deo et monachis ecclesie Sancte Marie de Fontibus totam Bramleiam cum omnibus pertinenciis suis et aisiamentis in bosco et plano in pratis et pasturis et aquis et in omnibus locis et rebus ad terram illam pertinentibus, quam Bramleiam Suanus de Tornetun a me emit, tenendam et habendam in feudo et hereditate de me et heredibus meis tantummodo pro duabus marcis per annum. Hanc Bramleiam cum omnibus pertinenciis et aisiamentis, per divisas quibus ego et probi homines mei perambulavimus et predictam ecclesiam saisiavimus, ita libere et quiete ecclesie de Fontibus confirmavi sicut predictus Suanus eam ecclesie de Fontibus dedit et carta sua confirmavit, reddendo annuatim michi et heredibus meis pro omni servicio et consuetudine et

---

[a] *Mub'* MS. Rawl.   [b] *Boolebec*, MS. Rawl.   [c] *Moubray*, Egerton MS.

omni re ad terram pertinente duas marcas argenti, dimidium ad Pent-
(ecosten) et dimidium infra octavas Sancti Martini. Hii sunt testes,
Guillelmus de Vescy, Gualterus de Bolebec, Radulfus de Belvair,
Radulfus filius Aldelini, Rogerus filius Galfridi, Robertus Beler,
Robertus de Beuscamp, Philippus de Muntpinzon, Johannes de Creve-
quer, Johannes de Burt', Robertus clericus.

NOTE. The first two witnesses occur in only two other Mowbray charters
(nos. 132 and 134). Their conjunction in the present charter and in no. 134
with Ralph de Belvoir strongly suggests that these two charters were issued at
the same time as no. 132, 2 Feb. 1181 at Fountains. Bramley was confirmed
to Fountains by pope Lucius III, 23 March 1183.[1] For Swain de Thornton's
charter, see *Fount. Cart.* i 140 (1).[2] The boundaries of Bramley are given in no.
134. At the time of Domesday Book Gospatric held 2 carucates in Bramley.

134 *Gift by Roger de Mowbray to Fountains of all Bramley, by specified bounds,*
for a rent of 2 marks p.a. [At Fountains, *c.* 2 Feb. 1181]

Original charter: Vyner deeds deposited at Leeds Archives, V.R. 444. Cartulary copies: B.M., Cotton MS. Tib. C xii fo. 222v; Bodl., MS. Rawlinson
B 449 fo. 22r (lacks last 7 witnesses); B.M., Egerton MS. 3053 fos. 6v–7r
(lacks all witnesses); Add. MS. 18276 fo. 29v (abstract).
Pd., *Mon. Ang.* v 306 (LIV), from MS. Rawlinson; (transl.) *Fount. Cart.* i
141 (4), from Cotton MS.

Omnibus sancte ecclesie filiis presentibus et futuris Rog(erus) de
Mubrai salutem. Sciatis me dedisse et hac mea carta confirmasse Deo et
monachis ecclesie Sancte Marie de Fontibus totam Bramleiam . in
bosco et plano . in prato et pastura et mora . et aquis . et in omnibus
locis et rebus que infra has diuisas continentur . scilicet a fossato eorum
quod incipit ad Musebec et uadit usque ad grossam quercum que est
sub cilio collis qui est sub sepi de Bramleia . et inde transuersus boscum
sub cilio predicti collis usque ad sursam cuiusdam sichet iuxta uiam
que uadit de Bramleia ad Malessart . et per illud sichet deorsum
usque ad Kesebec . et per Kesebec sursum usque ad moram . et transuersus moram usque ad diuisas Johannis de Watt' . et inde sicut diuise
Johannis uadunt usque ad Sienderhav . et inde deorsum usque ad
Musekelda . et inde usque ad prenominatum fossatum monachorum .
quod est diuisa inter eos . et Torp et Malesart. Totam hanc terram cum
omnibus rebus et aisiamentis que infra predictas diuisas continentur .
habebunt monachi imperpetuum . solutam quietam et liberam ab omni
seruicio et consuetudine et ab omni re ad terram pertinente . tantummodo pro duabus marcis per annum . dimidium infra octavas Pent' .

[1] *P.U.E.* iii no. 346.
[2] Also *Mon. Ang.* v 306 (LIII). Original charter, Vyner deeds deposited at Leeds
Archives, V.R. 445.

et dimidium infra^a Sancti Martini. Et ego Rog(erus) et heredes mei .
omnia predicta eis guarentabimus et acquietabimus ab omni re et seruicio quod ad terram pertinet pro predicta firma . sine omni retenemento mei et heredum meorum imperpetuum. Hii sunt testes . Gvillelmus
de Vesci . Gvalt(erus) de Bolebec . Rad(ulfus) de Belvair . Rad-
(ulfus) filius Aldel(ini) . Rog(erus) filius Galf(ridi) . Rob(ertus) Beler .
Rob(ertus) de Belscamp . Philippus de Muntpinzun . Johannes de
Burt' . Rob(ertus) clericus;

Endorsements: *Confirmatio Rogeri de Mubrai Bramlei* (12th cent.); *iiii | Brame-
lay carta .x.* (later medieval hands).
Size: 21 × 17·6 cm.; 2·2 cm. turn-up.
Seal: seal no. 3 of Roger de Mowbray (above, p. lxxxiii), green wax varnished;
appended on red and green silk strings.

NOTE. For the date, see note to no. 133.

135 *Gift by Roger de Mowbray to Fountains of dead wood in his forest pertaining
to the honour of Kirkby Malzeard, and various specified pasture rights.*

1181/2

Cartulary copies: Manchester, John Rylands Libr., Lat. MS. 224 fo. 288*r–v*;
B.M., Add. MS. 18276 fo. 234*v* (abstract).
Pd. (transl.), *Fount. Cart.* ii 706 (10), from Rylands MS.

Eboracensi archiepiscopo et omnibus sancte ecclesie filiis presentibus et
futuris Rogerus de Mubray salutem. Sciatis me dedisse et hac mea
carta confirmasse Deo et monachis ecclesie Sancte Marie de Fontibus
mortuum boscum in foresta mea que pertinet ad honorem de Malessart
de stante et jacente quicquid folium non portat ubicunque capere
voluerint ad carbonem faciendum ad forgias suas de Aldburg et pasturam in eadem foresta xxv vaccis et uno tauro ad grangiam suam de
Sutht' et aliis xx vaccis in communi pastura predicte foreste ad Laverton'
logiam suam et communem pasturam de Aserlach et de Wynkesleya per
totum extra bladum et pratum in cujuscunque manus predicte ville
devenerint. Et quando boves de Sutht' non fuerint in labore ibunt ad
pascendum in predicta foresta diebus et noctibus. Et ad utendum hiis
pasturis scilicet villarum et predicte foreste habebunt vias ubi eis oportunum fuerit. Concessi etiam predicte ecclesie et hujus carte testimonio
donavi quod nec ego nec heredes mei unquam recolligemus aliquem
hominem de relligione in terra vel bosco vel pastura que pertinent ad
honorem de Malessart exceptis monachis de Fontibus plus vel aliter
quam recolligebantur eo anno quo hanc donationem predicte ecclesie
feci, hoc est anno incarnationis Domini MCLXXX primo. Et ego et

^a octavas seems required.

heredes mei omnia predicta eidem ecclesie guarentabimus imperpetuum et acquietabimus et defendemus ab omni servicio et consuetudine et ab omni re que ad terram pertinet sicut puram et perpetuam elemosinam meam. Hiis testibus, Henrico de Aubeni, Philippo*a* de Muntpinzun, Guarino filio*b* Symonis, Herberto filio*b* Ricardi, Roberto de Belscamp, Roberto Tancart, Roberto Beler, Hugone filio Guillelmi de Leleia, Ricardo de Belscamp, Radulfo et Roberto clericis.*c*

NOTE. This is a confirmation of no. 115, with additional pasture.

136 *Gift by Roger de Mowbray to the infirm brethren of Fountains of 6 stags p.a. in his forest of Nidderdale, to be taken by his huntsmen.*   [*c.* 1181]

> Cartulary copies: B.M., Add. MS. 40009 fo. 16*r* (old p. 31); Bodl., MS. Rawlinson B 449 fo. 144*r* (lacks last 2 witnesses).
> Pd. (transl.), *Fount. Cart.* i 208 (14), from Add. MS.

Omnibus sancte ecclesie filiis presentibus et futuris Rogerus de Moubr'*d* salutem. Sciatis me pietatis intuitu dedisse et hac carta mea confirmasse fratribus infirmis de Fontibus sex cervos imperpetuum annuatim capiendos per venatores meos in foresta mea de Niderdala quacunque sacione ipsi fratres voluerint. Ita quidem ut integre habeant et coreos*e* et carnes predictorum cervorum preterea que canum usibus congruunt*f* si cum*g* canibus capti fuerint. Si vero sagittariis occisi fuerint totaliter habeant quicquid ex eis habere voluerint. Hiis testibus, Hereberto filio Ricardi, Warino filio Symonis, Philippo de Muntpinc', Roberto Beler, Rogero filio Gaufridi, Roberto de Bellocampo.

> NOTE. All these witnesses, except Roger son of Geoffrey, appear in no. 135, of 1181/2.

137 *Gift by Roger de Mowbray to Fountains of a thicket (? orchard) in Laverton (Yorks., W.R.), by specified bounds, 48 acres of cultivated land, common pasture for 100 sheep, and wood for burning and making fences.* [*c.* 1181]

> Cartulary copies: B.M., Add. MS. 40009 fos. 172*v*–173*r* (old pp. 344–5); Add. MS. 18276 fo. 80*v* (abstract).
> Pd. (transl.), *Fount. Cart.* i 307 (18), from Add. MS. 40009.

Omnibus sancte ecclesie filiis presentibus et futuris Rogerus de Moubr' salutem. Sciatis me dedisse et presenti carta confirmasse Deo et ecclesie Sancte Marie de Fontibus et monachis ibidem Deo servientibus quoddam frutectum in territorio de Lavertona, videlicet quicquid infra has divisas

---

a *Philippus*, MS.   *b* *filius*, MS.   *c* *clerici*, MS.   *d* *Mubrai*, MS. Rawl.   *e* *corios*, MS. Rawl.   *f* *conveniunt*. MS. Rawl., with marginal note *vel congruunt*.   *g* *tam*, Add. MS.

continetur: scilicet de Leyrwad deorsum in longum aque usque ad divisas terre Johannis de Crevequer et inde sursum aque ad terram cultam de Lavertona et inde usque ad Steinbrigge et inde usque ad Doddekeld et sic iterum usque ad Leyrwad. Et preterea dedi eis et confirmavi in eodem territorio de Lavertona xl et viij acras terre culte versus orientem de Steynbrigge. Et habebunt in communi pastura centum oves. Et accipient de meo foresto per visum forestariorum meorum ad ardendum ibidem et ad sepes faciendas. Hec omnia dedi eis et confirmavi concessu Nigelli filii mei in puram et perpetuam elemosinam solutam quietam et liberam ab omni servicio et consuetudine et exactione et ab omni re ad terram pertinente. Ita ut ego et heredes mei hec omnia eis guarentabimus et acquietabimus imperpetuum et defendemus adversus omnes homines. Teste, Nigello de Moubr', Radulfo de Belu(er), Herberto filio Ricardi, Thoma de Colevilla, Rogero filio Gaufridi, Roberto monoculo serviente meo, Uvieth.

NOTE. This gift was probably made at the same time as nos. 138–9. Land and pasture in Laverton was confirmed by Lucius III, 23 March 1183.[1]

138 *Confirmation by Nigel de Mowbray to Fountains of the previous gift by Roger de Mowbray.*　　　　　　　　　　　　　　　　　　　　　[*c.* 1181]

Cartulary copies: B.M., Add. MS. 40009 fo. 173*r–v* (old pp. 345–6); Add. MS. 18276 fo. 80*v* (abstract).
Pd. (transl.), *Fount. Cart.* i 307 (19), from Add. MS. 40009.

Omnibus sancte ecclesie filiis presentibus et futuris Nigellus de Moubr' salutem. Sciatis me concessisse et hac mea carta confirmasse Deo et ecclesie Sancte Marie de Font(ibus) et monachis ibidem Deo servièntibus donationem quam pater meus fecit eis in territorio de Lavertona, scilicet frutectum quoddam per has divisas videlicet de Leirwad deorsum in longum aque usque ad divisas terre Johannis de Crevequer et inde sursum usque ad terram cultam de Lavertona et inde usque ad Steinbrigge et inde usque ad Doddekeld et sic iterum usque ad Leirwad; et preterea xl et viij acras terre culte in eodem territorio versus orientem de Steinbrigge. Et in communi pastura habebunt centum oves. Et accipient de foresto meo per visum forestariorum meorum ad ardendum ibidem et ad sepes faciendas. Hec omnia concessi eis et confirmavi in puram et perpetuam elemosinam solutam quietam et liberam ab omni servicio et consuetudine et exactione et ab omni re ad terram pertinente. Et ego et heredes mei hec omnia eis guarentabimus et acquietabimus imperpetuum et defendemus adversus omnes homines sicut in carta

[1] *P.U.E.* iii no. 346.

patris continetur. Teste, Thoma de Colevilla, Hamone Beler, Rogero filio Gaufridi, Nicolao de Behlun, Johanne de Crevequer, Roberto Beler, Radulfo clerico Nigelli[a] de Moubr', Roberto de Belcamp, Sansone sellario Ebor'.

NOTE. This confirmation was probably made at the same time as no. 139.

139 *Similar gift by Roger de Mowbray to Fountains, adding also 12 acres between Kirkby Malzeard and Azerley.* [*c.* 1181]

Cartulary copy: B.M., Add. MS. 40009 fo. 172r–v (old pp. 343–4).
Pd. (transl.), *Fount. Cart.* i 307 (18a).

Omnibus sancte ecclesie filiis presentibus et futuris Rogerus de Mobr' salutem. Sciatis me dedisse et hac carta confirmasse Deo et ecclesie Sancte Marie de Fontibus et monachis ibidem Deo servientibus quoddam frutectum in territorio de Lavertona scilicet quicquid continetur infra has divisas videlicet de Lairwad deorsum in longum aque usque ad divisas terre Johannis de Crevequer et inde sursum usque ad terram cultam de Lavertona et inde usque ad Steinbrigge et inde usque ad Doddekelde et sic iterum usque ad Leirwad; et preterea xl et viij acras terre culte in eodem territorio versus orientem de Steinbrigge et xij acras quas Warinus filius Symonis tenuit quas excambiavi inter Malessart et Aserle. Et preterea habebunt in communi centum oves et accipient de meo foresto per visum forestariorum meorum ad ardendum ibi et ad sepes faciendas. Hec omnia dedi eis et confirmavi in puram et perpetuam elemosinam solutam quietam et liberam ab omni servicio et consuetudine et exactione et ab omni re ad terram pertinente. Et ego et heredes mei hec omnia eis guarentizabimus et acquietabimus et defendemus adversus omnes homines imperpetuum. Teste, Thoma de Colevilla, Hamone Beler, Rogero filio Gaufridi, Nicolao, Johanne de Crevequer, Roberto Beler, Radulfo clerico Nigelli de Mobr', Roberto de Bellocampo, Herberto filio Ricardi, Warino filio Symonis, Philippo de Montepinc'.

NOTE. Six of these witnesses occur also in no. 135, of 1181/2. Warin son of Simon held ⅔ new fee in 1166[1] and his descendants held land in Malzeard and Azerley.[2]

[a] *Nigello*, MS.

---

[1] Nos. 398, 401, Fees [46].
[2] *Book of Fees*, ed. H. C. Maxwell Lyte (1920–31) ii 1461.

140 *Gift by Roger de Mowbray to Fountains of a* mansura *in Thirsk (Yorks., N.R.).* [*c.* 1181]

> Cartulary copies: Manchester, John Rylands Libr., Lat. MS. 224 fo. 357*r*;
> B.M., Add. MS. 18276 fo. 243*v* (abstract).
> Pd. (transl.), *Fount. Cart.* ii 737 (1), from Rylands MS.

Omnibus sancte ecclesie filiis presentibus et futuris Rogerus de Moubr' salutem. Sciatis me dedisse et concessisse et hac mea carta confirmasse Deo et monachis ecclesie Sancte Marie de Fontibus unam mansuram in Tresc, illam scilicet quam Robertus filius Basilye tenuit prope portam de Kilvingtona in puram et perpetuam elemosinam solutam quietam et liberam ab omni servicio et consuetudine et exactione seculari cum omnibus libertatibus et liberis consuetudinibus quietam de stallagio et tolneto et omnibus reliquis consuetudinibus. Et poterint monachi ibi edificare et quicquid voluerint de eadem terra facere sicut de sua propria et libera ac perpetua possessione. Hiis testibus, Philippo de Mumpinc', Roberto de Bello campo, Roberto Beler, Roberto clerico, Roberto filio Matildis, Radulfo filio Ricardi, Willelmo Gramatico et aliis multis clericis et laicis.

> NOTE. The first four witnesses appear in nos. 133 and 134, of *c.* 2 Feb. 1181, and also in no. 135, of 1181/2.

141 *Confirmation by Roger de Mowbray to Fountains of 24 acres between Laverton and Braithwaite (Yorks., W.R.), given by Jocelin Veillekin.*
[*c.* 1181]

> Cartulary copies: B.M., Add. MS. 40009 fos. 180*v*–181*r* (old pp. 360–1);
> Add. MS. 18276 fo. 82*r* (abstract).
> Pd. (transl.), *Fount. Cart.* i 312 (32), from Add. MS. 40009.

Omnibus sancte ecclesie filiis presentibus et futuris Rogerus de Mubrai salutem. Sciatis me concessisse et hac mea carta confirmasse Deo et monachis ecclesie Sancte Marie de Fontibus in puram et perpetuam elemosinam xxiiij acras terre inter terram de Lavertun et Brathwait, illas scilicet quas Gozelinus Vellieken obtulit secum super altare de Fontibus quando se ibi reddidit. Hanc*a* terram concessi et confirmavi monachis per requisitionem predicti Gozelini in liberam puram et perpetuam elemosinam solutam quietam et liberam ab omni servicio et consuetudine et exactione imperpetuum et omni re que ad terram pertinet et per concessionem et requisitionem Gozelini filii predicti Gozelini. T(estibus), Roberto de Mubrei, Hamone Beler, Rogero filio Ge[o]f(ridi), Philippo de Muntp', Roberto de Belcham, Radulfo filio Aldelini, Huctred

a Han, MS.

de Stodl', Roberto clerico,[a] Radulfo filio Ricardi, Johanne capellano[b] et multis aliis.

NOTE. Five of these witnesses appear in no. 133, of *c*. 2 Feb. 1181, and four in nos. 139 and 140, of *c*. 1181. The gift by Jocelin Veillekin[1] and this confirmation may have been made at the same time as nos. 137–9, of *c*. 1181, which also concern Laverton.

142 *Confirmation by Roger de Mowbray to Fountains of land in Nutwith (Yorks., N.R.), which Richard de Hedona gave; and quitclaim of rent of a pound of pepper p.a.*

[At Kirkby Malzeard, *c*. 1176×March 1183, probably *c*. 1181]

Transcript, from an original charter formerly in the possession of the Revd. William Greenwell, B. 2: Leeds, Yorks. Archaeol. Soc. Libr., MS. 869 (Farrer MS.) E.Y.C. box 8. Cartulary copies: B.M., Cotton MS. Tib. C xii fo. 29*v*; Bodl., MS. Rawlinson B 449 fo. 23*r* (lacks last 6 witnesses); B.M., Egerton MS. 3053 fos. 5*v*–6*r* (lacks all witnesses); Add. MS. 18276 fo. 5*v* (abstract).
Pd. (transl.), *Yorks. Deeds* i no. 346, from the original charter in the possession of Greenwell; (transl.) *Archaeologia Aeliana* 4th ser. vii (1930) 84, from the original charter then in the possession of Dr. C. H. Hunter Blair; (transl.) *Fount. Cart.* i 18 (17), from Cotton MS.

Rogerus de Moub' omnibus sancte ecclesie filiis presentibus et futuris salutem. Sciatis me concessisse et presenti carta mea confirmasse Deo et monachis ecclesie Sancte Marie de Fontibus donationem quam Ricardus de Hedune eis fecit de terra quam ei dedi pro servicio et homagio suo in Nutewith et circa, videlicet per has divisas sicut Musebec descendit in Museschod usque in Jor et sic sursum Jor usque ad divisas Johannis de Waut' et sic per Rig usque in Musescoh excepta carrucata terre que fuit Aldredi et duabus bovatis Ackemanni[c] et vj acris Liulfi. Servicium etiam ejusdem terre scilicet unam libram piperis annuatim dedi et quietum clamavi Deo et prefate ecclesie pro salute anime mee et omnium antecessorum et heredum meorum. Et ego et heredes mei hec omnia eis guerentabimus et acquietabimus et defendemus contra omnes homines sicut puram et perpetuam elemosinam nostram solutam quietam et liberam ab omni terreno servicio de me et heredibus meis imperpetuum. Hiis testibus, Rogero de Albeni, Rogero filio Gaufridi, Roberto Beler, Philippo de Munpincun, Roberto clerico, Roberto camerario, Henrico dispen(satore), Henrico de Lubeham, Alano Fossard.

[a] *Robertus clericus*, MS. Cotton MS.   [b] *Johannes capellanus*, MS.   [c] *Acke manerii*,

---

[1] *Fount. Cart.* i 312 (31).

Endorsement (given in *Yorks. Deeds*): *Aldeburgh Carta 17 .xvij.*
Seal: seal no. 3 of Roger de Mowbray (above, p. lxxxii), white wax.

> NOTE. Roger de Mowbray made his gift to Richard de Hedona after *c.* 1176 (no. 368). Nutwith was confirmed by Lucius III, 23 March 1183.[1] Richard de Hedona's gift was made in the court of Roger de Mowbray at Kirkby Malzeard, in the presence of at least six of these witnesses.[2] The second, third, fourth, and fifth witnesses occur in charters of *c.* 1181 (nos. 133–4, cf. nos. 136, 139–40).

143 *Confirmation by Roger de Mowbray to Fountains of land in 'Flatwith'*[3] *and Nutwith, given by John de Wauton.*   [*c.* 1176 × March 1183]

> Original charter: Vyner deeds deposited at Leeds Archives, V.R. 22. Cartulary copies: B.M., Cotton MS. Tib. C xii fos. 33*v*–34*r*; Bodl., MS. Rawlinson B 449 fos. 21*v*–22*r* (lacks last 3 witnesses); B.M., Egerton MS. 3053 fo. 5*r* (lacks all witnesses); Add. MS. 18276 fo. 5*v* (abstract).
> Pd. (transl.), *Fount. Cart.* i 20 (28), from Cotton MS.

Omnibus audientibus et videntibus has litteras . Rog(erus) de Mubrai ." salutem. Sciatis me concessisse et hac mea carta confirmasse Deo et monachis ecclesie Sancte Marie de Fontibus . quicquid Johannes de Watt' dedit eis in Fladwith et in Nutewith . in bosco et in plano . et in omnibus locis et rebus que continentur infra illas diuisas que nominantur in carta predicti Johannis quam ipsi de eo habent. Hanc confirmationem feci eis in puram et perpetuam elemosinam . pro salute anime mee . patris et matris et omnium antecessorum meorum . ita quod facient de predicta terra quicquid uoluerint . sicut de sua libera et propria et perpetua possessione . sine omni retenemento mei uel heredum meorum; Hii sunt testes . Johannes capellanus . Rob(ertus) de Mubrai . Philippus de Muntpinzun . Rob(ertus) de Bevscamp . Rob(ertus) Beler . Ricardus de Bevscamp . Rob(ertus) de RICVS.;

> Endorsements: *Nutewyd. Flattewid* (early 13th cent.); *xxviii* (late 13th or 14th cent.); *Aldeburgh'. | carta . 28.* (15th cent.).
> Size: 12·7 × 11·2 cm.; 2·8 cm. turn-up.
> Seal: missing; was appended on tag.

> NOTE. This confirmation falls within the same broad chronological limits as no. 142. John de Wauton's charter is *Fount. Cart.* i 20 (27). Wauton had succeeded Walter Buher in the fee of Masham (cf. nos. 27, 174). Buher was certainly dead by September 1177,[4] and perhaps by April 1176, which is the date assigned by Eyton to a royal charter referring to John de Wauton's custody of Buher's heirs.[5]

[1] *P.U.E.* iii no. 346.
[2] Original charter, Vyner deeds deposited at Leeds Archives, V.R. 26; cf. *Mon. Ang.* v 307 (LVII).
[3] Presumably not Flawith in Alne (Bulmer wapentake), but a place near Nutwith.
[4] *P.R. 23 Hen. II* p. 78.   [5] Eyton, *Itinerary* p. 201; P.R.O., D.L. 10/38.

144 *Confirmation by Robert de Mowbray to Fountains of gifts made by his father Roger and his brother Nigel.* [*c.* 1175 × 1186]

Cartulary copies: B.M., Add. MS. 40009 fo. 5*r* (old p. 9); Bodl., MS. Rawlinson B 449 fo. 151*r* (lacks last 6 witnesses).
Pd. (transl.), *Fount. Cart.* i 211 (22), from Add. MS.

Eboracensi archiepiscopo et decano et capitulo Sancti Petri Eboraci et omnibus legentibus et audientibus litteras istas Robertus de Mubrai salutem. Sciatis me dedisse et presenti carta confirmasse Deo et ecclesie Sancte Marie de Fontibus et monachis ibidem Deo servientibus in perpetuam elemosinam omnes donationes et confirmationes quas pater meus Rogerus de Mubray et Nigellus filius ejus fecerunt predicte ecclesie de Fontibus et cartis suis confirmaverunt. Hanc donationem et confirmationem feci monachis de Fontibus ut omnia solute quiete et libere imperpetuum possideant sicut in cartis patris mei et domini Nigelli filii sui continetur. Et ego et heredes mei hec omnia predictis monachis guarentizabimus et acquietabimus imperpetuum. Teste, Rogero de Mubrai patre meo, et domino Nigello fratre meo, Roberto de Daivile et Guillelmo fratre ejus, Guillelmo Bacun, Roberto capellano Rogeri de Mubrai, Radulfo de Insula clerico Nigelli de Mubrai, Roberto de Belscamp'.

NOTE. Presumably this confirmation belongs to the period after the large gifts made by Roger and Nigel de Mowbray in 1174–5 (nos. 110–13). Possibly it was made at the same time as Nigel's confirmation of Sept. 1175 × March 1176, no. 124.

145 *Gift by Roger de Mowbray to Fountains of 43 acres in the wood of Littley (Yorks., W.R.), for which the monks gave him 30 marks.* [*c.* 1175 × 1186]

Original charter: Vyner deeds deposited at Leeds Archives, V.R. 4820.
Cartulary copies: Manchester, John Rylands Libr., Lat. MS. 224 fo. 286*r–v*; B.M., Add. MS. 18276 fo. 234*r* (abstract).
Pd. (transl.), *Fount. Cart.* ii 704 (3), from Rylands MS.

Rog(erus) de Mubrai . omnibus sancte ecclesie filiis presentibus et futuris .' salutem Sciatis me dedisse et hac mea carta confirmasse Deo et monachis ecclesie Sancte Marie de Font' . in liberam et perpetuam elemosinam . quadraginta et tres acras terre in bosco de Litelhage . scilicet inter Flatscoh et Gredgate que uadit versus Holwat . latere ad latus juxta illam rodam que fuit diuisa . inter boscum eorum et boscum meum. Hanc terram dedi eis solutam quietam et liberam ab omni seruicio et consuetudine et ab omni re ad terram pertinente. Et ego et heredes mei eandem terram monachis guarentabimus inperpetuum et defendemus aduersus omnes homines . sicut liberam et perpetuam elemosinam . ita quod monachi de Fontibus facient de hac predicta

terra quicquid uoluerint sicut de sua propria et perpetua possessione .
sine omni retinemento nostri uel heredum meorum Et sciendum quod
quando hanc terram eis dedi . et super altare Sancte Marie de Font' per
hanc cartam meam optuli .*monachi dederunt michi Rogero de Mubrai .
in recompensationem et in testimonium xxx.^{ta} marcas argenti. Testes .
Nigellus et Rob(ertus) filii mei . Rad' de Bevuair . Rad' filius Audel' .
Nichol' de Bellun . Gilleb' de Arches . Rog' de Bellun . Rob' de
Bevscamp . Baldewino clerico^a . Petro clerico^a Ric' de Bevscamp .
Alano^a de Limeseia.

Endorsements: *Littelhage | Carta Rog. de Mubray de xliii acris* (12th cent.); *.A.*
(? 13th cent.); *Quere primam cartam de Sutton in thecis de Fontibus videlicet carta
prima* (14th cent.); *Sutton. 2* (15th cent.).

Size: 16·1 × 13·6 cm.; 2·5 cm. turn-up.

Seal: seal no. 3 of Roger de Mowbray (above, p. lxxxiii), green wax varnished;
appended on tag. See Frontispiece (*c*).

NOTE. This gift clearly belongs to the period after no. 124.

146 *Confirmation by Nigel de Mowbray to Fountains of his father's gift in the
wood of Littley, for which the monks gave Nigel a palfrey worth 2 marks.*
[*c.* 1175 × 1186]

Original charter: Vyner deeds deposited at Leeds Archives, V.R. 4832.
Cartulary copies: Manchester, John Rylands Libr., Lat. MS. 224 fo. 286*v*;
B.M., Add. MS. 18276 fo. 234*r* (abstract).
Pd. (transl.), *Fount. Cart.* ii 704 (4), from Rylands MS.

Nigellus de Mubrai . omnibus sancte ecclesie filiis presentibus et futuris
salutem. Sciatis me concessisse et presenti carta confirmasse Deo et
ecclesie Sancte Marie de Fontibus et monachis ibidem Deo seruientibus
totam illam terram quam pater meus Rog(erus) de Mubrai eis dedit in
bosco de Littelhage . scilicet . inter Flatscoh et Gredgate que uadit
deuersus Holwat . latere ad latus iuxta illam rodam que fuit diuisa inter
boscum suum et boscum meum. Hanc terram concessi et confirmaui eis
in liberam et perpetuam elemosinam solutam quietam et liberam ab
omni seruicio et consuetudine et ab omni re ad terram pertinente. Et ego
et heredes mei eandem terram eis guarentabimus imperpetuum . et
defendemus aduersus omnes homines . ita quod monachi de Font'
facient de terra illa quicquid uoluerint . sicut de sua propria et libera
et perpetua possessione sine omni retenemento mei uel heredum meorum.
Et sciendum . quod quando hanc terram monachis confirmaui .* ipsi
dederunt michi in recompensationem unum palefridum de precio duarum marcarum. Teste Rad(ulfo) de Bevuair Nicholao de Bellun .

^a *Sic* in charter and Rylands cart.

Gilleb(erto) de Arches . Rog(ero) de Beellun . Baldewino clerico . Petro clerico Rad(ulfo) clerico de Insula . Rob(erto) de Bevcamp . Ric(ardo) de Beucamp . Alano de Milesei.*a*

Endorsements: *Conf. Nig. de Mubrai de bosco in Litelhae.* (12th cent.); *Sut'. | .A.* (late 12th or early 13th cent.); *Sutton. 3* (15th cent.); *ii* (?).

Size: 13·8 × 13 cm.; 2 cm. turn-up.

Seal: seal no. 1 of Nigel de Mowbray (above, p. lxxxiii), green wax varnished; appended on tag. See Frontispiece (*d*).

NOTE. For the date, see note to no. 145.

147 *Confirmation by Roger de Mowbray to Fountains of 6 acres in Nutwith (Yorks., N.R.) and 4 acres in Laverton (W.R.), given by Roger son of Roger.* [*c.* 1176 × 1186]

> Cartulary copies: B.M., Cotton MS. Tib. C xii fo. 34*r–v*; Egerton MS. 3053 fo. 6*r* (lacks all witnesses); Add. MS. 18276 fo. 6*r* (abstract).
> Pd. (transl.), *Fount. Cart.* i 20 (30), from Cotton MS.

Rogerus de Mubrai*b* omnibus audientibus et videntibus has litteras salutem. Sciatis me concessisse et hac mea carta confirmasse Deo et monachis ecclesie Sancte Marie de Font(ibus) in puram et perpetuam elemosinam illas sex acras terre quas Rogerus filius Rogeri eis dedit in Nutewith et carta sua confirmavit, scilicet illas quas Liolf filius Suani de Torp tenuit de predicto Rogero fratre suo et alias quatuor acras quas isdem*c* Rogerus filius Rogeri eis dedit in campo de Lavert', scilicet inter pratum Roberti de Vado et Eppecros[1] el west vie que vadit ad Kirkeby. Hanc terram confirmavi eis ut teneant et habeant eam ita libere et quiete et plenarie sicut carta predicti Rogeri*d* purportat et testatur. Hii sunt testes, Alanus Fossart, Radulfus filius Ricardi, Robertus clericus, Guillelmus pincerna, Radulfus Chinun, Rannulfus clericus, Rogerus de Bellun, Ricardus filius Rogeri, Rogerus Kide, Alexander de Mideltun.

> NOTE. This confirmation is clearly later than no. 142. It may, therefore, belong to the period after *c.* 1181. If Roger son of Roger was the son of Roger son of Geoffrey (a tenant of 1166),[2] a date after *c.* 1181 would be certain (cf. nos. 136–7, 139, 141).

148 *Confirmation by Roger de Mowbray to Fountains of Galphay (Yorks., W.R.), sold to the monks by John de Crevequer.* [1183 × 1186]

> Cartulary copy: B.M., Add. MS. 18276 fo. 8*or* (abstract).

Rogerus de Moubrai omnibus etc. salutem. Sciatis Johannem de Crevequer vendidisse monachis de Font' totam terram suam de Galghagh et

---

a *Sic* in charter and Rylands cart.; *Limesei* presumably intended (cf. no. 145).
b *Moubr'*, Egerton MS. *c* *idem*, Egerton MS. *d* *Roberti*, MSS.

[1] Perhaps the place which is called 'Epedeceos' in no. 67.
[2] See no. 401, Fees [29].

omne jus quod in ea unquam habuit eis quietum clamasse coram me de
se et cunctis ejus heredibus imperpetuum, me etiam concessisse et hac
mea carta confirmasse eandem venditionem scilicet totum Galghagh Deo
et prefatis monachis, per divisas plenarias cum omnibus pertinenciis et
aisiamentis suis in bosco et plano in viis et semitis in moris et mariscis in
pratis et pasturis in aquis stagnis et turbariis et in omnibus omnino locis
et rebus ad eandem terram pertinentibus, ita plene et integre sicut ego
et Nigellus filius meus ea prefato Johanni pro homagio et servicio suo
dedimus et confirmavimus, extra partem terre et turbarii quam Nicholas
de Bellun acquisivit de Johanne et extra xx acras terre quas idem
Johannes dederat hospitalariis. Concessi et etiam et confirmavi eisdem
monachis xvj acras terre quas prefatus Nicholas predicto Johanni accre-
vit et unum toftum quod idem Johannes dedit eisdem monachis in
Malasart cum una acra terre in alneto juxta domum Gocelini Veilleken'.
Preterea dedi et quietum clamavi Deo et prefatis monachis totum servicium prefatarum terrarum quietum et liberum de me et heredibus
meis in finalem elemosinam pro salute anime mee et heredum meorum.
Et ego et heredes mei omnia supradicta eis warantizabimus et acquietabimus sicut propriam elemosinam solutam quietam et liberam ab omni
servicio.

Another record of the confirmation: B.M., Add. MS. 18276 fo. 8or.
Rogerus de Mowbray confirmavit nobis venditionem quam Johannes
Crevequer nobis fecit in puram elemosinam quietam ab omnibus sicut
in carta septima plenius continetur.

NOTE. Galphay is not mentioned in Lucius III's confirmation of 23 March
1183.[1]

149 *Notification by Roger de Mowbray of John de Crevequer's restoration to
him of the land of Galphay, and of his gift of that land to Fountains.*

[1183 × 1186]

Cartulary copy: B.M., Add. MS. 18276 fo. 8or (abstract).

Rogerus de Moubray omnibus etc. salutem. Sciatis quod Johannes de
Crevequer reddidit michi et quietum clamasse totum feodum suum quod
de me tenuit scilicet terram de Galghagh et homagium quod michi fecit
reddit et ego eum inde quietum clamavi et hoc fecit cum fusto et baculo
coram paribus suis de se et heredibus suis et ego eandem terram ejus
consilio et consensu ecclesie de Font(ibus) dedi in puram elemosinam
etc.

NOTE. For the date, see note to no. 148.

[1] *P.U.E.* iii no. 346.

150 *Gift by Roger de Mowbray to Furness (Sav., Lancs.) of half the service of a knight in Winterburn (Yorks., W.R.), in scutage, Danegeld, and ten-mentale, quit of all service, which the monks are to retain in alms if William Graindorge forfeits anything.* [c. 1149 × 1166]

> Pd., *Furness Coucher* II ii 373 (24), from B.M., Add. MS. 33244 fo. 140v (no witnesses).
>
> NOTE. The gift was confirmed by Roger of Pont l'Évêque, archbishop of York (1154–81), between 1155 and 1166.[1] It is unlikely that William Graindorge gained his fee in Winterburn and Flasby before c. 1149,[2] but he may have been in possession before 1154. By that time Ralph son of Aldelin had been confirmed in his father's fee in Aldfield and Studley (W.R.), but not in Winterburn (no. 383). The possibility, mentioned in the present charter, that William Graindorge might forfeit some of his land may have arisen from the fact that Winterburn had belonged by hereditary right in 1135 to Aldelin of Aldfield: Ralph son of Aldelin issued a quitclaim to Furness after 1154.[3]

151 *Similar gift by Nigel de Mowbray to Furness.* [? c. 1149 × 1166]

> Pd., *Furness Coucher* II ii 373 (25), from B.M., Add. MS. 33244 fos. 140v–141r (no witnesses).

152 *Notification by Roger de Mowbray of his confirmation to Furness of all Winterburn, given by William Graindorge.* [c. 1149 × 1186]

> Pd., *Furness Coucher* II ii 372 (22), from B.M., Add. MS. 33244 fo. 140r (no witnesses).

153 *Confirmation by Roger de Mowbray to Furness of Winterburn with its appurtenances, and wood and pasture of Flasby (Yorks., W.R.), given by William Graindorge.* [c. 1149 × 1186]

> Pd., *Furness Coucher* II ii 372 (23), from B.M., Add. MS. 33244 fo. 140v (no witnesses).

154 *Confirmation by Nigel de Mowbray to Furness of Selside and Birkwith (Yorks., W.R.), given by Richard de Moreville and Avice his wife and their heir William de Moreville.* [Sept. 1189 × 1190]

> Pd., *Furness Coucher* II ii 338 (5), from B.M., Add. MS. 33244 fo. 124v.

Hiis testibus, Henrico decano Eboracensi, Hamone cantore, Nicholao, Jernaga, Adam de Thornouer canonicis de Eboraco etc.

> NOTE. Henry Marshal became dean of York on 16 Sept. 1189.[4] The gift by Richard and Avice de Moreville was made in return for 300 marks to acquit their lands from the hands of William de Stuteville.[5]

---

[1] *Furness Coucher* II ii 373–4 (26).   [2] See above, p. xxvi; cf. no. 401, Fees [45
[3] *Furness Coucher* II ii 375 (27 and 28).
[4] See C. T. Clay, in *Y.A.J.* xxxiv (1939) 372–3.
[5] *Furness Coucher* II ii 334 (1).

155 *Notification by Roger de Mowbray to G(odfrey), abbot of Garendon (Cist., Leics.), of his concession of whatever Gundreda (de Gournay) will give of her lands; and request for the monks' prayers during Roger's forthcoming pilgrimage.* [c. 1146]

> Cartulary copy: B.M., Lansdowne MS. 415 fo. 21r.
> Pd., Nichols, *Leics.* ii (1) app. p. 135.

G. abbati de Gerold' venerabili patri et domino Rogerus de Mubrai humilitatis et obediencie obsequium. Exaudivi preces Gundr(edis) matris mee de negotio et commodo abbatie vestre et finaliter concedo vestre ecclesie quantumcunque G. mater mea dabit vestre ecclesie de terris suis. Sed humiliter pro Dei amore et meo servicio vos ut patrem spiritalem et conventum vestrum requiro, quatinus vestris orationibus et precibus dum in hac peregrinatione fuero interesse possim, cum rediero quicquid a me rationabiliter postulabitis libentissime concedam. Et ego Rogerus abbas de Beilande his verbis et petitionibus interfui et hujus concessionis testis sum et ero.

> NOTE. The second Crusade, to which Roger refers (see no. 160), was preached at Easter 1146, and Roger must have left England by May 1147.

156 *Gift by Gundreda (de Gournay) to Garendon of 32 acres and a meadow (in Thorpe Arnold, Leics.).* [c. 1146]

> Cartulary copy: B.M., Lansdowne MS. 415 fo. 21r.
> Pd., Nichols, *Leics.* ii (1) app. p. 135.

Gundredis mater Rogerii de Mubrai omnibus fidelibus sancte ecclesie salutem. Sciatis me dedisse et concessisse Deo et monachis Sancte Marie de Gerold' pro anima Nigelli domini mei et pro salute Rogeri filii mei et filiorum suorum et mea triginta et duas acras terre et pratum quod eidem terre adjacet in perpetuam elemosinam concessu Rog(erii) filii mei. Teste, Rogero abbate de Beallanda, Landrico de Age, Nicholao capellano, Gilleberto de Rampainne.

> NOTE. Doubtless this charter was issued at the same time as no. 155 (see no. 160).

157 *Confirmation by Roger de Mowbray to Garendon of 4 carucates in Welby (Leics.), given by Geoffrey Haget.* [1166 × Aug. 1181]

> Cartulary copy: B.M., Lansdowne MS. 415 fo. 11v.
> Pd., Nichols, *Leics.* ii (1) app. p. 137.

Universis sancte matris ecclesie filiis Rogerus de Mobrai salutem. Sciatis me concessisse et hac carta mea confirmasse Deo et ecclesie Sancte Marie

Geroud' et monachis ibidem Deo servientibus pro salute anime mee et patris mei et omnium antecessorum meorum donationem Gaufridi Haget, scilicet iiij carrucatas terre in Alebi cum omnibus pertinenciis suis quas idem G. tenet de feodo meo in eadem villa. Concedo igitur quatinus prefati monachi donationem illam in perpetuam elemosinam teneant liberam et quietam ab omni terreno servicio, ita tamen ut predictus G. regi et michi et heredibus meis servicium faciat quantum pertinet ad feodum illud sicut carta illius testatur. T(estibus), Nigello filio meo, Roberto de Buci.

NOTE. Geoffrey Haget did not succeed his brother William in the Haget fee until after 1166 (no. 401).[1] The grange of 'Halebi' was confirmed to Garendon by pope Alexander III, before Aug. 1181.[2]

158 *Confirmation by Nigel de Mowbray to Garendon of 4 carucates in Welby, given by Geoffrey Haget.* [1166 × Aug. 1181]

Cartulary copy: B.M., Lansdowne MS. 415 fo. 21r.
Pd., Nichols, *Leics.* ii (1) app. p. 135.

Universis sancte matris ecclesie filiis Nigellus filius Rogerii de Mubrai salutem. Sciatis me concessisse et hac carta mea confirmasse Deo et ecclesie Sancte Marie de Gerold' et monachis ibidem Deo servientibus pro salute anime mee et omnium antecessorum meorum donationem Galfridi Haget, scilicet quatuor carrucatas terre in Alebi cum omnibus pertinenciis suis quas idem Galfridus tenet de feodo meo in eadem villa. Concedo igitur quatinus prefati monachi donationem illam in perpetuam elemosinam teneant liberam et quietam ab omni terreno servicio, ita tamen ut predictus Gaufridus regi et michi et heredibus meis servicium faciat quantum pertinet ad feudum illud sicut carta illius testatur. His t(estibus), Rogero de Mubrai patre meo, Roberto de Buci, Gilleberto de Sukearmunt, Rogero de Canvilla, Willelmo filio Roberti de Notinh'.

NOTE. For the date, see note to no. 157.

159 *Confirmation by Roger de Mowbray to Garendon of land (4 carucates etc. in Burton on the Wolds, Leics.), given by Hugh and Asketil de Berges and Ralph of Queniborough and his brothers.* [c. 1160 × 1183]

Cartulary copies: B.M., Lansdowne MS. 415 fos. 8v (lacks 5 witnesses), and 19r.
Pd., Nichols, *Leics.* iii (2) 810.

Rogerus de Mubrai omnibus sancte ecclesie filiis presentibus et futuris salutem. Sciatis me concessisse et hac carta mea confirmasse donationem

---

[1] For the Haget fee, see Fees [4].　　　　　　[2] *P.U.E.* i no. 182.

elemosine quam Hugo de Berges et Asketillus filius ejus et Radulfus de
Queniburc et fratres ejus dederunt Deo et monachis Sancte Marie de
Gerold'.[a] T(estibus), Waltero de Camvilla, Toma de Wappenb', Ricardo
de Morvilla, Willelmo de Rudevill, Rogero de Condi, Willelmo Malebisse, Ricardo filius Hernis.

> NOTE. The date is likely to have been after *c.* 1160, as Ralph of Queniborough
> and four of the witnesses occur in the *carta* of 1166 (no. 401).[1] Richard de
> Moreville was probably dead by 1183 (no. 384 note).

160 *Confirmation by Roger de Mowbray to Garendon of a* cultura *of land before
Thorpe Arnold (Leics.), i.e. 32 acres, given by Gundreda his mother before
he set out for Jerusalem for the first time with king Louis of France; they
may have an exchange of land if they wish.* [1175 × 1186]

> Pd., *Hatton's Book of Seals* no. 8, from facsimile in the custody of Northants
> Record Society.

Testibus his . Philippo de Munpinzun . Roberto Beler . Willelmo
camerario . Ricardo de Queniburc' . Johanne elemosinario . Waltero
de Malton' . Ragenaldo . Rogero Banastre . Ærnaldo dispensatore .
Roberto clerico . et multis aliis.

> Drawing of seal no. 3 of Roger de Mowbray (above, p. lxxxiii), yellow; appended
> on tag.

> NOTE. The reference to Roger's first journey to Jerusalem shows that the
> charter was issued after 1175 (no. 174 note).

161 *Confirmation by Robert de Mowbray to Garendon of a* cultura *before
Thorpe Arnold, as in no. 160, and of an exchange between the monks and
Arnald de Bois.* [1175 × 1189]

> Cartulary copy: B.M., Lansdowne MS. 415 fo. 11*r*.
> Pd., Nichols, *Leics.* ii (1) app. p. 135.

Universis sancte matris ecclesie filiis Robertus de Mulbrai salutem.
Sciatis me concessisse et hac carta mea confirmasse in liberam et puram
et perpetuam elemosinam Deo et ecclesie Sancte Marie Geroud' et
monachis ibidem Deo servientibus pro salute anime mee et omnium antecessorum et heredum meorum quandam culturam terre ante Torp quam
Gund(reda) mater mea[2] concessione patris mei monachis dedit in elemo-

---

[a] Two or three words erased in both copies.

---

[1] For the Queniborough fee, see nos. 381–2 and Fees [15].
[2] Gundreda was not the mother but the grandmother of Robert de Mowbray, as
correctly stated a little later in this charter (*avia*).

sinam pro xxxij acris cum chevesciis et prato ad eam pertinente libera et quieta ab omni seculari servicio, sicut inde saisiti fuerunt per aviam meam antequam Rogerus de Mulbrai pater meus primo arriperet iter eundi Jerosolimam cum rege Francorum Lodovico, videlicet totam illam culturam que est de feodo Meltone inter viam que ducit a Spineto versus Meltonam et divisam ipsius culture et feodo de Torp cum chevesciis et quodam prato eidem culture adjacenti quod dicitur Rubr' pratum et quicquid amplius est in predicta cultura quam xxxij acre totum integre predictis monachis confirmavi. Concessi etiam ut escambium quod inde factum est inter monachos et Ernaldum de Bosco et heredes ejus firmiter teneatur et stabile sit quamdiu monachi voluerint vel si monachi in futurum alibi escambium acceperint. Hanc confirmationem feci monachis postquam pater meus confirmaverat eis eandem terram et postquam terra de Maltona*a* data fuit michi in feodum et hereditatem pro homagio et servicio meo. Et ego et heredes mei hanc elemosinam eis warantizabimus. T(estibus), Radulfo de Queniburc, Gilleberto de Setgrave.

NOTE. If genuine, this confirmation belongs to the period after no. 160, i.e. after 1175. Arnald de Bois's exchange was made before 1189.[1]

162 *Gift by Roger de Mowbray to Saint-André-en-Gouffern (Sav., Calvados) of the tithe of his mills at Montbray, Beslon, and Beaumesnil, and the tithe of pannage in his park of Beslon (Manche).*   [Aug. 1154 × 1157]

Original charter: Caen, Archives of Calvados, H. 6574 no. 291.
Pd. (French), Léchaudé d'Anisy, *Extrait* i 442 (no. 283).

Rog(erus) de Molbraio episcopo de Sancto Laudo et omnibus sancte matris ecclesie filiis et omnibus hominibus suis clericis et laicis Franchis et Anglicis tam presentibus quam futuris *?* salutem. Sciatis me dedisse et concessisse et hac presenti carta mea confrimasse*a* Deo et Sancte Marie et abb(ati) de Sancto Andrea et omni conventui decimam totam de molendinis meis videlicet de Mobraio et de Beslon et de Bel maisnil et decimam de pasnagio videlicet de parco meo de Beslon in perpetua elemosina pro anima patris mei et matris mee et salute mea. Quare volo et firmiter precipio omnibus ministris et ballivis meis . quia, predicta ecclesia hanc elemosinam prenominatam habeat et teneat libere et quiete et honorifice. His testibus Nigello filio meo . et Oliverio de Boche . et Roberto fratre suo . et Radulfo Beler et Hamone fratre suo . Roberto

---

a *Sic.*

---

de Creuecor . et Radulfo de Bello visu . et Sanson Beler . et Sanson Loisel . et Rog(ero) de Ardena . et pluribus aliis.

Endorsements: *de redditu Moub' ii* (late 12th cent.); *It' Moubrai .b.iiii[or].* (13th cent.); *Mombray* (later medieval hand).

Size: 20·3 × 11·5 cm.; 1·2 cm. turn-up.

Seal: seal no. 3 of Roger de Mowbray (above, p. lxxxiii), red wax; appended on white and blue silk strings.

> NOTE. The gift was almost certainly made on a visit to Normandy. Nigel de Mowbray cannot have taken part in such a visit before that of 1154 (cf. no. 93). Ralph Beler was dead by 1157.[1]

163 *Grant by Roger (de Mowbray) and Nigel his son to Gouffern of freedom of selling, buying, and travelling in all their English and Norman lands.*

At Bazoches [Aug. 1154×1186]

Original charter: Caen, Archives of Calvados, H. 6574 no. 16. Cartulary copy: Archives of Calvados, H. 6510 fo. 23r.

Pd. (transl.), *Cal. Docs. France* no. 596;[2] (French) Léchaudé d'Anisy, *Extrait* i 442 (no. 284).

.R. de Mobraio . et Nigellus filius eius . cunctis baronibus iusticiis pretoribus ceterisque ministris suis . presentibus et futuris ⸴ salutem. Omnibus vobis notum sit . monachis Sancti Andreę quitanciam omnium rerum suarum in vendendo et in emendo transitumque faciendo. per totam terram nostram Anglie scilicet . atque Normannie ⸴ pro salute animarum nostrarum atque parentum . omnimodam in perpetuum nos concessisse. Unde mandamus posteris nostris atque per presentem cartam rogamus et monemus ut quod pro communi utilitate a nobis factum est . atque concessum ⸴ ipsi teneant ratum et illibatum. Statuimus autem et prohibemus ⸴ ut nullus nostrorum . predictos monachos fratres nostros . super his quę supracommemoravimus audeat unquam inquietare . vel quicquam molestie inferre. Quod si presumpserit ⸴ sciat se periculum irę nostrę nimis incurrere. Testibus Roberto capellano . Ric(ardo) . Boteri . Rad(ulfo) de Balueer . Rad(ulfo) de Meisheldin . et Gullelmo fratre suo. Apud Basochas fuit factum br(eve)

Endorsements: *Rog' de Moubraio . de quitantia* (late 12th or early 13th cent.); *a.vi.* (13th cent.).

Size: 22·9 × 12 cm.; 1·2 cm. turn-up.

Seal: missing; was appended on tag.

> NOTE: Bazoches was not recovered until Aug. 1154 (no. 19). If the grant was made before Nigel de Mowbray was given lordship of the Norman estates, the latest date would be *c.* 1170.

---

[1] See *E.Y.C.* ix 212.

[2] Round wrongly gives the place of deposit of this and of no. 164 as the Archives of Manche [at Saint-Lô, destroyed 1944].

164 *Confirmation by Nigel de Mowbray to Gouffern of the tithe of his mills at Montbray, Beslon, and Beaumesnil, and the tithe of pannage of his park of Beslon.*   [*c.* 1170 × 1190]

Original charter: Caen, Archives of Calvados, H. 6574 no. 17.
Pd. (transl.), *Cal. Docs. France* no. 599;[1] (French) Léchaudé d'Anisy, *Extrait* i 443 (no. 287).

Venerabili domino et patri suo Dei gratia Constanc' episcopo . et omnibus matris ecclesie filiis . universis quoque hominibus suis Francis et Anglicis tam presentibus quam futuris ? Nigellus de Molbraio . salutem. Sciatis me dedisse et concessisse et hac presenti carta mea et sigillo meo confirmasse Deo et Sancte Marie . et abbati et omni conventui de Sancto Andrea . totam decimam de molendinis meis videlicet de Molbraio . et de Beslon . et de Belmaisnil . et decimam de pasnagio videlicet de parco meo de Beslon . in perpetua elemosina pro anima patris et matris mee et salute mea. Quare volo . et firmiter precipio omnibus ministris et ballivis meis . quod predicta ecclesia hanc elemosinam prenominatam habeat et teneat libere et quiete et honorifice. Mando etiam et precipio omnibus successoribus meis ut hanc donationem et elemosinam liberam et quietam predicte ecclesie defendant et ipsi teneant et teneri faciant. Huius rei testes sunt hii . Radulfus clericus . Willelmus . Malerba . Radulfus de Belveer . Willelmus de Alenchum . Willelmus de Torignei . Albericus de Alenchum . Radulfus . Bufart . et alii.

Endorsements: *Carta Nigelli de Molbraio . de redditu de Molbraio* (12th cent.); *It' Moubrai b.iiii^{or}.* (13th cent.).

Size: 18·4 × 16·5 cm.; 2·6 cm. turn-up.

Seal: missing; was appended on tag.

NOTE. The confirmation probably belongs to Nigel de Mowbray's period of lordship of the Norman lands. The reference to his father's soul may indicate that it belongs to the period after 1188.

165 *Gift by Nigel de Mowbray to Gouffern of the tithe of rent from his fulling-mill of Beslon, after the death of Ralph de Insula his clerk.*
                                                  [*c.* 1170 × 1190]

Original charter: Caen, Archives of Calvados, H. 6574 no. 292.
Pd. (French), Léchaudé d'Anisy, *Extrait* i 442 (no. 285).

Omnibus sancte matris ecclesie filiis Nigellus de Moibraio^a salutem. Notum sit vobis me dedisse et concessisse monachis Sancti Andree de Gofer in perpetuam elemosinam pro salute anime mee et omnium antecessorum meorum totam decimam redditus molendini mei folerez de

---

^{a} *Sic.*

[1] See note to no. 163.

Beslon . quo omnes panni honoris de Moibraio[a] ex debito fullantur. Hanc autem decimam dedi eis et concessi post decessum Radulfi de Insula clerici mei cui illam prius dederam pro amore Dei possidendam. Et ut monachi prefati loci elemosinam illam liberam et omnino quietam post decessum prefati clerici in perpetuum possideant ꞉ presentis scripti testimonio et huius presentis sigilli mei munimine feci sigillari et confirmari. Testibus his . magistro Ranulfo canonico de Falesia . magistro Willelmo canonico . Willelmo Malerbe . Roberto de Castelon . Radulfo clerico . Gaufrido coquo . Roberto de Noui . Ricardo de Richemont . et aliis.

Endorsements: *Nigelli de Molbraio* (12th cent.); *It' Moubrai .b.iiii[or]*. (13th cent.).
Size: 13·3 × 12 cm.; 2·6 cm. turn-up.
Seal: seal no. 2 of Nigel de Mowbray (above, pp. lxxxiii–iv), red wax; appended on tag, to which tie-tag loosely attached.

NOTE. For the date, see note to no. 164. All Roger and Nigel de Mowbray's gifts were confirmed by William, bishop of Coutances (1179–99).[1]

166 *Confirmation by Roger de Mowbray to Guisborough (Aug., Yorks., N.R.) of land in Barningham and Newsham (N.R.), given by Walter Bardulf.*
[*c.* 1170 × 1186]

Transcript, from an original charter formerly in St. Mary's Tower, York: Bodl., MS. Dodsworth 7 fo. 45*r*.
Pd., *Cartularium Prioratus de Gyseburne*, ed. W. Brown (S.S. lxxxvi, lxxxix) ii no. 1125, from the transcript.

Rogerus de Mubrai omnibus hominibus suis et amicis clericis et laicis presentibus et futuris salutem. Sciatis me concessisse et h(ac) c(arta) m(ea) confirmasse Deo et Sancte Marie de Giseb' et canonicis ibidem Deo servientibus donationem illam quam Walterus Bardulf illis fecit, scilicet quicquid habuit in Berningham et Neus secundum quod carta prefati Walteri testatur quam inde habent. Hiis testibus, Roberto de Bussei, Roberto Beler, Nicholao de Daivill, fratre Terry de Naburc, Roberto de Upilium, Johanne capellano, Roberto clerico et multis aliis.

Drawing of seal, circular, 'very fair on horsebacke'; appended on tag.

NOTE. The appearance of John the chaplain suggests a date after *c.* 1170.[2] Walter Bardulf gave the land to Guisborough for as much service as pertains to six carucates, where twenty carucates makes one knight's fee.[3] Four carucates in Barningham and two in Newsham were held by Mowbray of the honour of Richmond.[4]

[a] *Sic.*

---

1 Léchaudé d'Anisy, *Extrait* i 443 (no. 286).
2 Cf. nos. 59, 87, 92, 143, 208, 210.
3 *Cart. de Gyseburne* ii no. 1126.   4 *E.Y.C.* iv 11–12.

167 *Confirmation by Roger de Mowbray to Haverholme (Gilb., Lincs.) of 3 carucates in Stathern (Leics.), given by Ralph de Rames and his brothers.*
[1139×1148]

Transcript, from fo. 55 of the lost cartulary of Haverholme: Bodl., MS. Dodsworth 144 fo. 93r.

Cunctis Christi fidelibus Rogerus de Mubrai salutem. Notum sit vobis me dedisse etc. monialibus de Haverholm concessionem quam Radulfus de Rames et fratres sui eis concesserunt, scilicet illas tres carucatas terre in Stakethirne quas predictus Radulfus de Rames de me tenuit.

NOTE. The charter must have been given after the foundation of Haverholme, 1139, and while the house was still a nunnery, before 1148.[1] Ralph de Rames's charter is MS. Dodsworth 144 fo. 93r. In 1166 William de Rames held one fee of Mowbray.[2]

168 *Confirmation by Roger de Mowbray and Nigel de Mowbray to St. Mary and Leticia the nun and her sisters (later Hinchingbrooke, Ben. nuns, Hunts.) of a wood, 15 acres, and the chapel of Papley (in Eltisley, Cambs.), given by Roger de Cundy.*
[c. 1160×May 1169]

Confirmation by Nigel, bishop of Ely, [c. 1160×May 1169]: Cambridge, Emmanuel Coll. Muniments, Box 12. A (Eltisley) no. 2 (original charter).

. . . donationem quam Rogerus de Cundeio et Rogerus de Mobraio et Nigellus filius eius eis fecerunt . et chartis suis confirmauerunt in liberam et perpetuam elemosinam videlicet totum boscum Rogeri de Cundeio in Pappele et quinque acras de sarto et decem alias lucrabiles in campo . et locum capelle de Pappelle . . .

NOTE. If the confirmation by Nigel de Mowbray was a separate charter, it is unlikely to have been given before c. 1160. In any case, bishop Nigel's charter must have been given after c. 1158 (for it is attested by Richard Fitz Neal as archdeacon of Ely) and before the bishop's death in May 1169.
Although the origin of the Mowbray interest in Eltisley is obscure,[3] this charter sheds some light on the early history of the nunnery. The reference to the 'locum capelle de Pappelle' suggests that the nuns had not yet moved to St. James, Huntingdon (Hinchingbrooke). In a private charter of the same period they are called the nuns of Papley.[4] Leland's account of an earlier settlement at Eltisley before the removal to Hinchingbrooke is therefore confirmed.[5] The removal took place before the issue of no. 169, that is before 1190.

[1] R. Graham, *S. Gilbert of Sempringham and the Gilbertines* (1901) pp. 31–3.
[2] No. 401, Fees [19].
[3] Cf. no. 305 note; and for the Cundy fee, see Fees [27].
[4] Cambridge, Emmanuel Coll. Muniments, Box 12. A (Eltisley) no. 1.
[5] Cf. *V.C.H. Hunts.* i 390; D. Knowles and R. N. Hadcock, *Medieval Religious Houses* (1953) pp. 212, 213.

169 *Confirmation by Nigel de Mowbray to Hinchingbrooke of Roger de Mowbray's concession of Roger de Cundy's gift in Eltisley.*   [1186×1190]

> Original charter: Cambridge, Emmanuel Coll. Muniments, Box 12. A
> (Eltisley) no. 3.

Omnibus sancte matris ecclesie filiis tam presentibus quam futuris
Nigellus de Mubrai salutem. Sciatis me concessisse et hac carta confirmasse Deo et Sancte Marie et sanctimonialibus Sancti Iacobi de
Huntend(onia) concessum quem pater meus Rog(erus) de Munbrai eis
fecit scilicet super donacionem quam eis fecerat Rog(erus) de Cundui
in territorio de Auteresle in campis et in omnibus locis in perpetuum
habendis sicut in carta prefati patris mei continetur. His testibus
Rog(ero) de Seint Martin Rob(erto) de Castll' Ricard(o) Bacun Radulfo
clerico et multis aliis

Endorsement: *Nigell' de Mobary* (12th cent.).

Size: 13·5 × 7 cm.; 1·9 cm. turn-up.

Seal: missing; was appended on tag.

N O T E. All the witnesses appear in no. 342, of 1186 × 1190.

170 *Gift by Roger de Mowbray and G(undreda de Gournay) to the Hospitallers
of one mark p.a. [in York].*   [c. 1138]

> Original charter: B.M., Add. Ch. 19816.

. Rog(erus) . de Molb' et .G. mater eius omnibus suis hominibus
Francis et Anglicis . salutem. Sciatis nos concessisse et confirmasse Deo
et hospitali Ierlm' ·⁄ per unum quemque annum .i. m(arcam). argenti
pro anima patris mei . et in remissionem omnium peccatorum nostrorum ·⁄ statuto termino ad festiuitatem Sancti Michaelis. Iterum
precipio ut .G. de Insula tradat*a* hanc .m(arcam). illis qui ei hanc
cartam attulerint; Valete;

Endorsement: *Rog. de Mobar^i. | de Eboraco | s' j. marc' argenti.* (12th-cent.
hands).

Size: 19·6 × 5·4 cm.

Seal: missing; was appended on tongue from left foot of document, probably
with tie-tongue.

> N O T E. This joint charter of Roger and his mother presumably dates from the
> beginning of Roger's majority. G. de Insula was perhaps Geoffrey de Insula,
> who occurs in nos. 4, 5, 232.

a Altered from *tradet* in charter.

171 *Confirmation by Roger de Mowbray to the Hospitallers of the churches of Winkburn and Averham (Notts.), given by Henry Hose II.*

[1154 × c. 1174]

Confirmation by king John, 30 Aug. 1199: pd., *E.Y.C.* xii no. 114, from P.R.O., Charter Roll 1 Jo. (C. 53/1) m. 17. Also pd. *Rotuli Chartarum* (Record Comm., 1837) I i 16a; *Mon. Ang.* vi (2) 808 (XVIII).

NOTE. Henry Hose could not have gained an interest in the Tison lands, through his wife Avice or Amice, until after the death of Adam Tison, who was still living in 1154.[1] If the confirmation was made before Henry Hose's death, it must have been before c. 1174.[2]

172 *Gift by Roger de Mowbray to the abbey of Charity (later Jervaulx, Sav., Yorks., N.R.) and Peter the monk of land and wood from 'Brigwath' to 'Witeberecuade' (? near Masham, Yorks., N.R.).*

[c. 1146]

Transcript, from a missing portion of the cartulary of Byland (Byland chron.) fos. 15 ff.: Bodl., MS. Dodsworth 63 fo. 43v.
Pd., *Mon. Ang.* v 569 (IV).

Rogerus de Molbray omnibus ministris suis et hominibus suis de Eborasciria Francis et Anglis salutem. Sciatis me dedisse et concessisse Deo et Sancte Marie de Caritate et Petro monacho et fratribus suis de abbatia super Jor flumen totam terram et boscum totum sicut semita vadit de Brigwath usque Witeberecuade et preter hoc ad piscandum in Higlamare et warrennam et pasturam totius nemoris mei. Et volo quod habeant hanc terram usque in Jor liberam et quietam sicut terra potest esse libere et in elemosinam. Teste, Rogero abbate de Bellalanda.

NOTE. Peter and his three brethren from Savigny settled at Fors in 1145.[3] No. 174 states that this gift was made before Roger de Mowbray's departure on crusade in 1147. 'Witebech' is mentioned in earl Alan's enfeoffment of Roger de Mowbray in Masham.[4]

173 *Notification by Roger de Mowbray to Roger (of Pont l'Évêque), archbishop of York, of his confirmation to Jervaulx of Colsterdale (Yorks., N.R.), given by [earl] Conan.*

[1156 × 1171]

Transcript, from an unknown source: Leeds, Yorks. Archaeol. Soc. Libr., MS. 869 (Farrer MS.) E.Y.C. box 8 (in the hand of William Brown).

Rogero archiepiscopo Ebor(acensi) et ejus capitulo et omnibus hominibus suis Anglis et Normannis Rogerus de Mowbray salutem. Cum dominus meus Conanus [comes]*a* Richm(undie) dederit monachis de

---

a Blank in MS. Cf. *E.Y.C.* iv no. 29.

[1] See *E.Y.C.* xii 7.   [2] Ibid. p. 135.
[3] See *Mon. Ang.* v 568 (I) and *E.Y.C.* iv nos. 23, 24, 27.
[4] *E.Y.C.* iv no. 19 (cal. above as no. 18).

Jorevalle totam Colsterdale que se extendit versus Masham usque
Spromgile volo et bene concedo pro me et heredibus meis quod ipsi
monachi illam habeant et teneant in puram et perpetuam elemosinam
imperpetuum salva tantum michi et hominibus meis communa pasture
propriis animalibus nostris. Volo similiter quod ipsi monachi habeant
semper communem in omnibus ubicunque et in quibuscunque liberi
homines mei de Mashamshir solent communicare in terra aqua et bosco
per omne tempus anni. Et istius concessionis mee conscribantur ut
testes etc.

NOTE. The confirmation was probably made soon after the monks moved to
the site near East Witton, to be called Jervaulx, in 1156.[1] Earl Conan died in
1171.[2]

174 *Testification by Roger de Mowbray that before he first went to Jerusalem
and four years before Walter Buher had land in Mashamshire, Roger gave
to Jervaulx land at 'Brigwath' and pasture and timber in all his wood of
Mashamshire.* [1175 × 1186]

Transcript, from a missing portion of the cartulary of Byland (Byland chron.)
fos. 15 ff.: Bodl., MS. Dodsworth 63 fo. 43v.
Pd., *Mon. Ang.* v 569 (V).

Omnibus qui has litteras sunt visuri Roger de Molbray salutem. In
veritate testificor quod antequam prima vice irem ad Jerusalem in
peregrinatione et quatuor annis antequam Walterus Bury haberet
terram in Mashamshir' dedi abbathie que tunc vocabatur de Caritate
nunc vocatur de Jorevalle terram quam monachi tenent apud Brigwath
et pasturam et maremium de toto bosco meo de Mashamshire in perpetuam et liberam elemosinam sicut cartule mee quas monachi inde
habent testantur. Et si quis voluerit ipsas cartulas contradicere vel
falsificare ego et heredes mei parati erimus defendere et warantizare
ubique.

NOTE. The reference to Mowbray's first visit to Jerusalem (1146–7) suggests
a date after 1175, when his second journey was contemplated (cf. no. 111).
Walter Buher, who was evidently enfeoffed in Masham in 1149–50, was dead
by 1177 (no. 143 note), but this testification may have been made after his
death.

175 *Notification by Samson d'Aubigny to Roger (de Clinton), bishop of Coventry (1129–48), of his gift to Bernard, prior of Kenilworth (Aug., Warwicks.), of the church of Smite with the chapel of Brinklow (Warwicks.);
and request for episcopal confirmation.* [c. 1145]

Cartulary copies: B.M., Harley MS. 3650 fo. 31r; Add. MS. 47677 fo. 34r.

[1] Cf. *E.Y.C.* iv. no. 29.   [2] Ibid. p. 93.

Venerabili patri et domino suo Rogero Dei gratia Cest(rensi)[a] episcopo Sanson[b] de Albineio clericus suus[c] salutem. Noverit paternitas vestra dedisse me et concessisse in elemosinam ecclesiam de Smita domno Bernardo[d] priori Kennell'[e] voluntate et assensu domni Rogeri de Mulbraio patroni mei, cum capella de Brinchelau et omnibus aliis ejusdem ecclesie pertinenciis. Quare precor vestram dignationem quatinus ipsum priorem inde saisiatis et hanc nostram donationem vestra auctoritate confirmetis et manuteneatis. Valete.

NOTE. For the date, see note to no. 177 below.

176 *Notification by Roger de Mowbray to R(oger de Clinton), bishop of Coventry (1129–48), of his gift to Bernard, prior of Kenilworth, of the churches of Smite and Hampton in Arden (Warwicks.); and request for episcopal confirmation.* [c. 1145]

Cartulary copies: B.M., Harley MS. 3650 fo. 28r; Add. MS. 47677 fo. 34r.

Venerabili domino suo et patri R. Dei gratia Cestrensi[a] episcopo Rogerus de Multbrai[f] salutem et obsequium. Noverit vestra paternitas me ecclesiam de Smita et ecclesiam de Hamtona[g] in Ardena cum omnibus pertinenciis suis in elemosinam[h] concessisse et in usum religionis dedisse [i]pro salute anime mee et patris mei et matris et parentum meorum[i] et hoc consilio et industria domini[j] Bernardi prioris de Kining'[k] Deo opitulante peragere institui. Unde paternitatem vestram rogo quatinus hanc meam donationem episcopali auctoritate confirmetis et inde domnum Bernardum priorem saisietis.[l] Valete.

NOTE. For the date, see note to no. 177 below.

177 *Confirmation by Roger de Mowbray, at the petition of Samson d'Aubigny, to Kenilworth of the church of Smite.* At Thirsk [c. 1145]

Cartulary copies: B.M., Harley MS. 3650 fo. 29r–v; Add. MS. 47677 fo. 33v (abstract).

Rogerus de Mulbr' omnibus hominibus et amicis suis Francis et Anglis salutem. Sciant omnes tam posteri quam presentes quod ego Rogerus de Mulbr' pro animabus patris mei et matris mee et aliorum predecessorum meorum et pro salute mea temporali et eterna et petitione Samson de Albeneio concessi et in perpetuam elemosinam[m] donavi ecclesie Sancte

[a] *Cestrensis*, Harl. MS. [b] *Sapson*, Harl. MS. [c] Omitted in Add. MS.
[d] *Bernardi*, Harl. MS. [e] *Kining'*, Harl. MS. [f] *Mulbray*, Add. MS.
[g] *Hamptona*, Add. MS. [h] *ecclesiam*, Harl. MS. [i-i] Omitted in Add. MS.
[j] *donavi*, Harl. MS. [k] *Kenell'*, Add. MS. [l] *sansietis*, Harl. MS.
[m] *elemosina*, Harl. MS.

Marie de Kining' et canonicis ibi Deo servientibus ecclesiam de Smita manerio meo cum omnibus pertinenciis suis liberam et quietam ab omni servitio et exactione seculari. Quare volo et firmiter statuo ut prefati canonici eandem ecclesiam de Smita habeant et teneant bene et in pace libere et honorifice cum terris et decimis, pratis et pascuis et omnibus aliis rebus ad ipsam pertinentibus nec quisquam heredum vel hominum meorum eos deinceps super hac elemosina mea inquietare vel aliquo modo perturbare presumat. Hujus mee donationis sunt testes, predictus Samson de Alben', Augustinus prior de Cucuwald', Reinerius cellararius, Thomas canonicus, Willelmus de Merlou, Hugo de Mais-nilhermer et Willelmus frater ejus et Landricus de Age et Matheus de Rampanna. Apud Tresc.

NOTE. The appearance of Augustine, 'prior of Coxwold', strongly suggests that this charter was issued at the time of the Augustinians' removal in c. 1145 from Hood to a site near Coxwold, to be called Newburgh. Roger de Clinton issued a confirmation before his departure on crusade in 1147.[1] For some further notes on the date of nos. 175-7, see note to no. 196.

178 *Notification by Samson d'Aubigny to R(ichard Pecche), bishop of Coventry (1161-82), of his gift to Kenilworth of the livings of the churches of Smite and Hampton in Arden, which had been confirmed by Roger (de Clinton), bishop of Coventry, and by Roger de Mowbray.*   [Apr. 1161 × 1179]

Cartulary copy: B.M., Add. MS. 47677 fo. 35r-v.

Reverendo et domino R. Dei gratia Coventr(ensi) episcopo et universo capitulo Coventr(ie) ecclesie frater Samson de Albineio canonicus de Novob(urgo) salutem. Veritati tenentur amici veritatis perhibere testimonium. Inde est quod ego precibus fratrum nostrorum canonicorum de Kenell' humiliter annuens litteris presentibus vobis significandum duxi quod personatum ecclesiarum de Smita et de Hamptona in Ardena que canonice fueram adeptus intuitu pietate et amore religionis concessi canonicis de Kenell'. Et quicquid juris in eisdem ecclesiis habueram prenominate ecclesie in perpetuam possessionem donavi quantum ad me spectabat. Has vero ecclesias bone memorie Rogerus tunc Coventr(ensis) episcopus post hanc a me factam cessionem ecclesie de Kenell' episcopali qua fungebatur auctoritate perpetuo possidendas concessit assensu et petitione Rogeri de Mowbray fundi illius domini in quo predicte ecclesie de Smita et de Hamptona site sunt et carta sua confirmavit quam habent in ecclesia sua supradicti canonici etc.

[1] B.M., Harley MS. 3650 fos. 34v-35r.

NOTE. Richard Pecche confirmed to Kenilworth the church of Smite, with the chapel of Brinklow, and the church of Hampton, with its chapels, before 1179.[1] Samson d'Aubigny's last positively dated occurrence belongs to Apr. 1153 (no. 322), and no charter in which he appears has a terminal date later than 1157 (cf. nos. 240, 399). His retirement into Newburgh probably took place, therefore, c. 1154.

179 *Promise by Roger de Mowbray to Kenilworth to warrant the church of Hampton in Arden.*   [c. 1170 × 1184]

> Cartulary copy: B.M., Harley MS. 3650 fo. 23r (probably also Add. MS. 47677 fo. 33v, abstract).

Rogerus de Molbraio hominibus et amicis suis et omnibus sancte ecclesie fidelibus salutem. Sciant omnes ad quos litere iste pervenerint quod ego warantizo ecclesie beate Marie de Kining' et canonicis ibidem Deo servientibus ecclesiam de Hamt(ona) in Ardena cum omnibus pertinenciis et libertatibus suis quam donavi eis in perpetuam elemosinam pro animabus patris et matris mee et pro salute mea et meorum temporali et eterna in tempore Rogeri quondam Cestrensis episcopi et carta mea quam habent super hoc confirmavi. His testibus, Roberto de Daivilla, Hugone Malebr'a,[2] Radulfo de Bevv', Adam de Siltun, Petro de Biligheia, Philippo fratre ejus, Petro clerico, Adam Luvel, Roberto de Buci, Hamone Beler, Adam capellano et multis aliis tam clericis quam laicis.

> NOTE. This and the following charter were issued at the same time, when both Robert de Arden and his successor Peter de Arden (instituted before 1179)[3] were dead, and when Roger de Arden made a detailed confirmation to Kenilworth.[4] Peter of Billinghay was dead by 1184 (no. 349 note).

180 *Confirmation by Roger de Mowbray to Kenilworth of the church of Hampton in Arden, with chapels, lands, tithes, etc., with 3 virgates and other property specified.*   [c. 1170 × 1184]

> Cartulary copies: B.M., Harley MS. 3650 fo. 23r–v; Add. MS. 47677 fo. 33r–v (incomplete and lacks witnesses).

Rogerus de Molbraio hominibus et amicis suis et omnibus sancte ecclesie fidelibus salutem. Sciant omnes ad quos litere iste pervenerint quod ego pro animabus patris et matris mee et aliorum predecessorum et amicorum meorum et pro salute mea et heredum meorum in perpetuam elemosinam concessi et donavi ecclesie beate Marie de Kining' et canonicis ibidem Deo servientibus ecclesiam de Hamtona in Ardena, cum capellis terris et decimis et omnibus pertinenciis et libertatibus

---

[1] B.M., Harley MS. 3650 fos. 35r, 40r–v   [2] Presumably Malebisse.
[3] B.M., Harley MS. 3650 fos. 39v–40r.
[4] Ibid. fos. 22v–23r. For the Arden family see below, nos. 330–9.

suis, et nominatim cum duabus virgatis terre, una que antiquitus fuit in dominio ecclesie et alia que dicitur virgata Godrici, sine tofta et cum crofta que dicitur Chirchecroft, et cum terra et prato de Hingstesfea et terra et prato de Snelles medwe *a*et terra apud Blacalremedew et terra apud Siwrchesle et prato quod dicitur Tuelfacremedew, et uno homine apud Blacalremedew*a* et uno homine inter Calfremedew et [terram]*b* Gaufridi, et in Hamtona cum omnibus mansuris a mansura que fuit*c* Elfston usque domum Uhtredi et cum mansura Osberti Ruffi et mansura que fuit Roberti et alia mansura que proxima est juxta illam et cum mansura que fuit Alicie vidue, et apud Beleshale dimidia virgata terre que reddit iij solidos, apud Chedelesvvich uno bordagio*d* quod reddit xij*e* denarios. Quare volo*f* et firmiter statuo ut canonici predicte ecclesie de Kining' habeant imperpetuum hanc meam elemosinam cum prescriptis terris et cum omnibus pertinenciis et libertatibus suis in bosco et plano in pratis et pasturis et omnibus locis ad ipsam pertinentibus liberam et quietam ab omni servicio et exactione seculari et ut nullus heredum vel hominum meorum hanc meam donationem aliquo modo perturbare presumat eam presentis carte mee et sigilli mei testimonio confirmavi. Hiis testibus, Roberto de Daivilla, Hugone Maleb', Radulfo de Bevv', Adam de Siltun, Petro de Bilingheia et Philippo fratre ejus, Adam Luvel, Roberto de Buci, Hamone Beler, Adam capellano et multis aliis tam clericis quam laicis.

NOTE. This and no. 179 show that the gift to the Templars of the church of Hampton, 1161 × 1163 (no. 271), was ineffective.

181 *Confirmation by Roger de Mowbray to Kirkstall (Cist., Yorks., W.R.) of Micklethwaite (W.R.), given by Herbert de Moreville and Richard his son.*
[May 1147 × 1162]

Confirmation by Henry II, [1155 × 1162]: pd., *E.Y.C.* iii no. 1452, from *Mon. Ang.* v 535–6 and from a transcript of a Dodsworth MS. (untraced). Also confirmation by Henry II, [1170 × 1173]: pd., *E.Y.C.* iii no. 1461 and *C.Ch.R.* iv 46–7, from P.R.O., Charter Roll, 1 Edw. III (C. 53/114) m. 20; and *Coucher Book of Kirkstall*, ed. W. T. Lancaster and W. P. Baildon (Thoresby Soc. viii) no. 307, from P.R.O., D.L. 42/7 fo. 62v.

NOTE. The convent which had been founded at Barnoldswick in May 1147 was moved to Kirkstall in 1152 or 1153.[1] It is impossible to say whether Moreville's gift and Mowbray's confirmation were made before or after the move. For the Moreville fee, see Fees [22].

a-a Omitted in Harl. MS.   *b* *hominam* in both MSS.   *c* *fecit*, Harl. MS.
d *bordario*, Harl. MS.   *e* *iix*, Harl. MS.   *f* Add. MS. version adds *etc.* and ends.

---

[1] See C.T. Clay, in *Y.A.J.* xxxviii (1955) 23–4.

182 *Confirmation by Roger de Mowbray to Lincoln (secular cathedral) of the church of Empingham (Rutland), as held of any of Roger's predecessors, namely Gilbert de Gant and Walter his son and Gilbert de Gant son of Walter; provided that if anyone shall attempt to prove that the said church never was nor ought to be a prebend of Lincoln, the present charter shall not prevent Roger from acting in accordance with his right.* [1142 × 1186]

> Pd., *Registrum Antiquissimum of Lincoln*, ed. C. W. Foster (L.R.S. xxviii) ii no. 318, from Lincoln D. & C., A/1/5 (Registrum Antiquissimum) fo. 36 (no witnesses).

> NOTE. Mowbray's right in Empingham presumably originated in his marriage to Alice, sister of Gilbert de Gant the younger. If the charter was issued after the death of Gilbert the younger, the earliest date would be 1156.[1]

183 *Confirmation by Roger de Mowbray to Malton (Gilb., Yorks., N.R.) of the church of Norton (E.R.), given by Roger de Flamville and his wife Juetta de Arches.* [c. 1150 × July 1169]

> Cartulary copy: B.M., Cotton MS. Claud. D xi fo. 55r.

Cunctis Christi fidelibus Rogerus de Mumbray salutem. Vobis omnibus innotescat quod donationem ecclesie de Nortona quam Rogerus de Flamevilla in cujus fundo sita est et domina Jueta de Arches uxor predicti Rogeri contulerunt monasterio beate Marie et canonicis de Malt(ona), hanc utique donationem ego quantum ad me pertinet ratam habeo et hac carta mea eis confirmo. Et jus universum predicte ecclesie de Nortun pertinens, quantum persone laice licet concedere, ego predictis canonicis concedo et hac mea carta confirmo in puram et perpetuam elemosinam, quatinus plenissima securitate possideant et quiete et libere nullo eis nomine meo inquietudinem ullam inde importante. Hiis t(estibus) etc.

> NOTE. Malton was founded c. 1150. The gift was confirmed by pope Alexander III, 30 July 1169.[2] This charter contains pious phrases—'quantum persone laice licet concedere,' etc.—reminiscent of those found in other lords' charters for Malton.[3] Roger de Flamville held 8½ fees in 1166, of which 7 were in right of his wife Juetta de Arches.[4] The 1½ fees in his own right included Norton and the lands in no. 184.

---

[1] See *Complete Peerage* vii 673.   [2] *P.U.E.* i no. 112.
[3] Cf. *Mon. Ang.* vi (2) 970 (II), 972 (X); and B.M., Cotton MS. Claud. D xi fo. 55r.
[4] No. 401, Fees [1].

184 *Confirmation by Roger de Mowbray to the hospital of Norton (dependency of Malton) of the church of Marton (Yorks., W.R., Claro wapentake) and 12 bovates in Welham (E.R.) and 8 bovates in Norton, given by Roger de Flamville and his son Hugh.* [c. 1150 × July 1169]

Cartulary copy: B.M., Cotton MS. Claud. D xi fo. 58r.

Omnibus sancte ecclesie filiis Rogerus de Moubray salutem. Sciatis quod concessi et hac carta mea confirmavi donationem quam fecerunt Rogerus de Flamvilla et Hugo filius suus hospitali pauperum de platea apud Northon', scilicet ecclesiam de Martona cum suis pertinenciis, et xij bovatas in Wellom cum suis pertinenciis, et viij bovatas terre in Northona cum suis pertinenciis, et omnino quicquid[a] unus eorum vel alter seu ambo eidem loco concesserunt vel in futurum concessuri sunt. Ego confirmo eidem elemosinarie habendum et tenendum bene et in pace liberum et quietum ab omni servicio et omni exactione de me et heredibus meis imperpetuum. T(estibus), Roberto etc.

NOTE. This charter should be assigned to the same limits as no. 183.

185 *Gift by Roger de Mowbray to Malton of 40 cart-loads of wood p.a. from his wood of Hovingham (Yorks., N.R.), for the canons' kitchen.* ? [c. 1150 × 1186]

Cartulary copy: B.M., Cotton MS. Claud. D xi fo. 99r.

Rogerus de Molb' omnibus fidelibus suis[b] salutem. Notum sit omnibus hominibus meis tam presentibus quam futuris me Rogerus de Molb' concessisse et dedisse et hac mea carta confirmasse in perpetuam elemosinam tam libere quam liberius aliqua elemosina religiosis donari potest xl kareas de meo bosco in Hovingham per unum quemque annum semper de anno in annum canonicis de Maltona ad coquinam suam pro salute anime mee et omnium antecessorum meorum. Hujus mee donationis et concessionis testes sunt etc.

NOTE. This gift is said to have been alienated without licence in 35 Edward III (1361),[1] but the charter seems to belong to the twelfth century.

186 *Precept of Roger de Mowbray to his reeve, forester, and men of Hovingham, concerning his gift to Malton of 40 cart-loads of wood p.a.* ? [c. 1150 × 1186]

Cartulary copy: B.M., Cotton MS. Claud. D xi fo. 99r.

[a] *quicquic*, MS.   [b] *dedi*, MS

---

[1] B.M., Add. MS. 24688 (late 15th-cent. register of Mowbray) fo. 15v.

Rogerus de Munbray preposito suo et forestario et hominibus suis de Hovingham salutem. Precipio vobis quod sicut me diligitis, faciatis canonicos meos de Maltuna habere plenarie et integre xl carateas de meo bosco in Hovingham de anno in annum sicut carta mea quam eis inde dedi in puram et perpetuam elemosinam testatur.

NOTE. See note to no. 185.

187 *Gift by Roger de Mowbray to Malton of all his land in Dalby (Yorks., N.R.) and pasture pertaining.* [*c.* 1150×1186]

Cartulary copy: B.M., Cotton MS. Claud. D xi fo. 99r.

Cunctis Christi fidelibus Rogerus de Mumbray salutem. Notum sit vobis me concessisse et dedisse et hac mea carta confirmasse in perpetuam elemosinam, tam libere quam liberius aliqua elemosina potest religiosis donari, totam partem meam de terra de Dalbi et pasturam que pertinet ad hanc terram, plenarie sicut ego plenarius et liberius vel pater meus habuit hanc terram in Dalbi et pasturam ad eam pertinentem canonicis de Malt(ona) Deo imperpetuum ibidem servientibus sine omni exactione et sine omni seculari servicio, quantum ad me et ad meos heredes pertinet, pro salute anime mee et patris mei et matris mee et filiorum meorum et omnium consanguineorum meorum tam vivorum quam mortuorum. Hujus etiam mee elemosine testes sunt etc.

188 *Confirmation by Roger de Mowbray to Malton of 3 acres of arable and 2 acres of meadow in Hovingham, given by Philip of Billinghay.* [*c.* 1170×1186]

Cartulary copy: B.M., Cotton MS. Claud. D xi fo. 98v.

Omnibus hoc scriptum visuris vel audituris Rogerus Moubray salutem in Domino sempiternam. Noveritis me concessisse et hac presenti carta mea confirmasse Deo et beate Marie, priori et conventui de Malt(ona), tres acras terre arabilis et duas acras prati in territorio et pratis de Hovingham, illas videlicet quas habent de dono Philippi de Bilinghay quemadmodum continetur in carta ejusdem, tenendas et habendas dictis priori et conventui libere quiete et pacifice, quietas et solutas ab omni servicio et exactione ad me et heredes meos pertinentibus sicut aliqua elemosina liberius melius et quietius viris religiosis potest dari et confirmari, ita quod nec ego nec heredes mei aliquid exigere in posterum de predictis poterimus in futuris. Et ego vero et heredes mei omnia predicta predictis priori et conventui de omnibus serviciis secularibus exactionibus et demandis acquietabimus et defendemus in perpetuum. In cujus rei test(imonium) etc. Hiis testibus etc.

NOTE. Peter of Billinghay received land in Hovingham after *c.* 1170 (no. 349). The gift by Philip, his brother, may have been made after Peter's death, in 1184 (see no. 349 note).

189 *Confirmation by Nigel (? Roger) de Mowbray to the hospital of Norton of 12 bovates in Welham and the church of Marton, given by Roger de Flamville.* [? 1186×1190, or *c.* 1150×1154]

Cartulary copy: B.M., Cotton MS. Claud. D xi fo. 58*r*.

N. de Moubray dap' et omnibus hominibus et fidelibus suis salutem. Notum sit omnibus vobis quod donationem quam fecit Rogerus de Flamevilla elemosinarie domui de platea ad caput pontis Northon', scilicet de xij bovatis terre in Wellom et de ecclesia de Marthona cum suis pertinenciis quas predictus Rogerus concessit jamdicte domui in perpetuam elemosinam et liberam ab omni servicio quod ad eum vel heredes suos pertinet. Ego concedo et hac presenti carta mea confirmo et precipio quod stabilis sit et firma ad omnes dies imperpetuum. Teste, domina matre mea et cet(eris).

NOTE. The address to his *dapifer* and men seems to suggest that this charter was given during Nigel de Mowbray's period of lordship 1186–1190, but the attestation of his mother shows that this is impossible, as Alice de Gant almost certainly predeceased her husband. If 'N.' has been incorrectly supplied for 'R.', however, the difficulty would disappear: the charter would then belong to the period *c.* 1150×*c.* 1154.

190 *Confirmation by Roger de Mowbray to Meaux (Cist., Yorks., E.R.) of pasture for 200 sheep in the common of (Kirk or West) Ella (E.R.), given by Robert de Belvoir.* [1182×1186]

Record of gifts, in B.M., Cotton MS. Vit. C vi fo. 26*r*.

NOTE. The gift was confirmed also by John de Belvoir, son of Robert, and by Ralph de Belvoir and Constance his wife. The Belvoir interests in the Tison fee originated from the marriages of Robert and Ralph de Belvoir to two of the daughters and coheirs of William Tison, who died between *c.* 1170 and 1180.[1] The chronicle of Meaux puts Robert de Belvoir's gift after 1182.[2]

[1] See *E.Y.C.* xii 8–11; for the Belvoir lands of Mowbray, see below, nos. 345–6.
[2] *Chronica de Melsa*, ed. E. A. Bond (R.S. xliii) i 227.

191 *Confirmation by Roger de Mowbray to Monks Kirby (Ben. alien, War-wicks.)[1] of the churches of Monks Kirby and Langford (Notts.), given by Geoffrey de La Guerche, and the church of Newbold on Avon (Warwicks.), given by Nigel d'Aubigny.* [c. 1154 × 1165]

Transcript, from an original charter formerly in the Court of Augmentations: Bodl., MS. Dodsworth 63 fo. 104r.
Pd., *Mon. Ang.* vi (2) 996 (II), from the original charter 'in bibl. Deuvesiana'.[2]

Omnibus sancte matris[a] filiis tam presentibus quam futuris Rogerus de Mulbraio salutem. Sciatis me concessisse et hac presenti carta mea confirmasse Deo et ecclesie Sancti Nicholai de Kirkebi et monachis ibidem Deo servientibus pro salute anime mee et antecessorum et successorum meorum omnia tenementa sua et beneficia a predecessoribus meis sibi collata, scilicet ecclesiam de Kirkeby et ecclesiam de Landeford cum omnibus pertinenciis suis quas Galfridus de Wirchia eis in perpetuum dedit, et ecclesiam de Neubold quam Nigellus de Albineio eis similiter dedit et concessit. Preterea volo atque firmiter precipio ut omnes quibus dedi dominia mea cujuscunque sint conditionis sive sunt clerici sive laici omnes decimas ad predictas ecclesias expectantes absque omni impedimento et vexatione reddant. Nulli enim dedi vel donasse prohibeo aut warantizare nisi quod meum erat. Hiis testibus, Roberto de Deivilla, Hugone Malebisse, Hereberto de Morevill, Thoma de Wappenbire, Hamone Beler, Richardo de Morevill, Rogero de Ardena, Roberto de Buci, Roberto de Bellocampo, Radulfo Brusebarre.

NOTE. Robert de Beauchamp first occurs after 1154 (nos. 246, 353–4). Herbert de Moreville had been succeeded by his son Richard by 1166 (no. 401). The church of Langford, which is not mentioned in the charters of Geoffrey de La Guerche[3] and Nigel d'Aubigny (nos. 3, 13), became part of the prebend of Masham in York Minster (nos. 325–6), having also been given by an ineffective grant to Newburgh (no. 196 and note).

192 *Confirmation by Nigel de Mowbray to Monks Kirby of gifts in lands and tithes etc. in Axholme (Lincs.), Melton Mowbray and the Spinney (Leics.), and Hampton in Arden.* [c. 1160 × May 1177]

Original charter: B.M., Harley Ch. 53 G 55. Also *inspeximus* of 1285: Gregory-Hood deeds deposited at Stratford on Avon, Shakespeare Birthplace Trust Libr., Gregory-Hood Ch. 519 (3).

---

[a] ? Add *ecclesie*.

---

[1] Dependency of St. Nicholas, Angers.
[2] But not among the MSS. listed by A. G. Watson, *The Library of Sir Simonds D'Ewes* (1966), and not among Harley Charters.
[3] *Mon. Ang.* vi (2) 996.

Pd., *Mon. Ang.* vi (2) 996 (III), from the original charter then 'in bibl. Deuvesiana' (but Bodl., MS. Dodsworth 110 fo. 17v says 'penes Hen. St. Georg.').[1]

Nigellus de Mulbrai omnibus clericis et baronibus et ceteris hominibus suis tam presentibus quam futuris salutem. Sciatis me concessisse et hac carta confirmasse Deo et Sancte MARIE et ecclesie Sancti Nicholai de Kirkebi et priori et monachis ibidem Deo seruientibus omnes donationes terras decimas et elemosinas et omnia cetera beneficia que data sunt eis ab antecessoribus meis per maneneria[a] mea scilicet Axiholm . Meltune . et de Spineto quod est de dominio meo et de Hantuna in Ardena et ceteris maneriis sicut carte Gosfridi de Wirchia et Nigelli aui mei et Rogeri patris mei testantur. Quapropter uolo et firmiter precipio ut predicti monachi omnia tenementa prefata et pasnagias et decimas et cetera beneficia sua in bosco et plano libere et quiete et honorifice teneant sicut melius et liberius tenuerunt in tempore regis Henrici predecessoris nostri et tempore Nigelli aui mei et Rogeri patris mei. Volo etiam ut quemcunque teneant tenorem ·' quod ipsi prefati monachi habeant omnia iura sua. Et iterum uolo et precipio quod homines Sancti Nicholai qui in prefatis uillis manent habeant communem in bosco et plano et in pastura sicut ipsi qui melius habent ex uicinis suis qui tenent talem tenuram et omnes libertates et consuetudines quas tempore regis Henrici et Nigelli aui mei habuerunt. Insuper prohibeo ut nullus exigat ab eis auxilia uel operationes aut aliquas seculares exactiones. His testibus . Ric(ardo) Cornub(iensi) priore de Kirkebi . Renaldo monacho . [b]Waltero monacho . Siwardo monacho . Baldwino monacho .[b] Waltero de Camuilla . Hug(one) Malebisse . Hamone Beler . Nichol(ao) de Bellun .[c] Rob(erto) Beler . Rob(erto) de Waura . Anketil de Creft . Will(elmo) de Waura Adam Cornewaille . Rog(ero) de Neuham . Jordano capellano de Kirkebi . Rob(erto) diacono . Dreo subdiacono.

Endorsement: *Confirmatio Nigelli de Moubray.* (13th cent.).

Size: 20·7 × 9·9 cm.; 1·4 cm. turn-up.

Seal: missing; was appended on tag.

NOTE. Nicholas de Bellun does not occur before *c.* 1160 (no. 343 note) and Nigel de Mowbray did not issue his own charters until after that date. Richard, prior of Monks Kirby, was elected abbot of Whitby in May 1177.[2]

---

[a] *Sic* in Harley Ch.; *inspeximus* gives *maneria.*   [b–b] Omitted in *inspeximus.*
[c] *Inspeximus* version ends.

---

[1] For MSS. that D'Ewes derived from St. George, see A. G. Watson, *The Library of Sir Simonds D'Ewes* (1966) pp. 35–6.
[2] *Gesta Hen. II* i 166.

193 *Confirmation by Roger de Mowbray to Monks Kirby of lands and benefices given by his predecessors, their tithes to be rendered without impediment, especially from the Spinney and Hampton in Arden; and confirmation of tithe of pannage in Hampton in Arden and in Axholme.* [*c.* 1170×1186]

Inspeximus of 1285: Gregory-Hood deeds deposited at Stratford on Avon, Shakespeare Birthplace Trust Libr., Gregory-Hood Ch. 519 (2).

Omnibus sancte matris ecclesie filiis tam presentibus quam futuris Rogerus de Moubr' salutem. Sciatis me concessisse et hac presenti carta mea confirmasse Deo et ecclesie Sancti Nicholai de Kirkeby et monachis ibidem Deo servientibus omnia tenementa sua et beneficia a predecessoribus meis sibi collatis, in bosco et plano, in viis et semitis, in pratis et pascuis, in aquis et stagnis et molendinis, in decimis et aliis elemosinis, que scilicet Gaufridus de le Wyrche et ceteri antecessores mei eis dederunt et cartis suis confirmaverunt. Et que ego eis concessi, dedi et confirmavi tenenda atque possidenda absque omni contradictione et impedimento, adeo libere, quiete et honorifice, in puram et perpetuam elemosinam, sicut ea in aliquo tempore liberius vel quietius tenuisse perhibentur. Preterea volo atque firmiter precipio ut omnes quibus dedi dominia mea cujuscunque sint conditionis, sive sint clerici sive laici, omnes decimas ad predictam spectantes ecclesiam absque omni impedimento et vexatione reddant. Maxime autem de Spineto quod est juxta Meltoniam, scilicet de dominio meo quod monachi de Lewes tenent, et de dominio meo de Hamptuna in Ardena, quod donavi Rogero de Ardena,[1] que ad jamdictam ecclesiam spectare dinoscuntur, sine impedimento et absque diminutione, persolvantur. Nulli enim eorum dedi vel donasse perhibeo aut warantizo nisi quod meum erat. Concessi etiam eis et confirmavi decimam pasnagii de Hamptona in Ardena et de Haxiholm in puram et perpetuam elemosinam possidendam. Prohibeo ergo ne quis prenominatas detineat nec injuriam aliquem sive molestiam predicte facere presumat ecclesie. Test(ibus) his, Roberto de Daievilla, Hugone Maleb', Roberto de Bocy, Philippo de Munpincon, Roberto Beler.

NOTE. Philip de Montpincon does not occur before *c.* 1170 (no. 376 note).
A settlement over the tithes of the Spinney was made between Richard prior of Monks Kirby and the monks of Lewes before 1177.[2] The tithes of Hampton in Arden were in dispute between Monks Kirby and Kenilworth: an agreement was made before papal judges delegate some time between 1167 and 1182.[3]

---

[1] Perhaps referring to no. 331 below.   [2] P.R.O., E. 326/8649.
[3] B.M., Harley MS. 3650 (cartulary of Kenilworth) fos. 36v–37r.

194 *Confirmation by Roger de Mowbray of the agreements made between Roger abbot of Byland and the canons of Hood (later Newburgh, Aug., N.R.), namely that for the peace of Robert d'Aunay the abbot demised to the canons the place of Hood, on condition that there should be founded there for Roger de Mowbray an abbey of canons with a full convent observing the order of canons according to the rule of St. Augustine; and notification that Samson d'Aubigny gave in exchange to the abbot 20s. p.a. from the mill of Coxwold.*

[1142 × c. 1143]

Pd., *E.Y.C.* ix no. 120, from Bodl., MS. Dodsworth 94 fo. 77v (no witnesses). Also pd., *Mon. Ang.* vi (1) 322 (III), supposedly from Cotton MS. Cleop. C iii fo. 301.[1]

NOTE. For Roger de Mowbray's charter for Byland, see *E.Y.C.* ix no. 119 (cal. above, no. 39). Roger, abbot of Byland, issued a charter in favour of the canons, describing himself as 'servus servorum Dei'.[2]

195 *Gift by Roger de Mowbray, for the souls of Nigel d'Aubigny his father and Gundreda his mother and for the health of himself and Alice his wife, to Hood and Augustine the prior and canons, of the church of St. Andrew, York, beyond the Foss in Fishergate, with a* mansura *formerly belonging to Thurstan de Montfort, and also the man named Thorbrand dwelling there.*

[Feb. 1142 × June 1143]

Pd., *E.Y.C.* ix no. 118, from Bodl., MS. Dodsworth 7 fo. 168r. Also pd. *Mon. Ang.* vi (1) 320 (V), from the original charter formerly in St. Mary's Tower, York.

Hiis testibus, Willelmo decano et capitulo Sancti Petri Eboraci, Samsone de Albaneio, Helia de Sancto Martino, Roberto Maltalent, Radulfo de Withvilla et Willelmo fratre suo, Ricardo pincerna.

NOTE. Thurstan de Montfort held 3¾ fees of Mowbray in 1166.[3]

196 *Gift by Samson d'Aubigny to Newburgh of the churches of Haxey, Owston, Epworth, Belton, (Axholme, Lincs.), Langford (Notts.), Masham (Yorks., N.R.), and Kirkby Malzeard (Yorks., W.R.).*

[c. 1145]

Transcripts from an original charter formerly in St. Mary's Tower, York: Bodl., MSS. Dodsworth 91 fo. 65r–v, 94 fo. 75r (incomplete).
Pd., *Mon. Ang.* vi (1) 319 (IV) from the original charter; (abstract) J. Fisher, *History of Masham* (1895) p. 530.

Omnibus ecclesie filiis Sampson*a* de Albinneio salutem. Notum sit vobis me concessisse et dedisse in elemosinam Augustino priori ecclesie Sancte Marie de Neuburgo et successoribus ejus et fratribus in eadem ecclesia

a *S. in Dodsw. 91.*

---

[1] This is a transcript of a genealogy of Mowbray which does not contain any charters. [2] B.M., Egerton MS. 2823 fo. 42v.
[3] No. 401, Fees [25]; cf. also *E.Y.C.* ix 65–7.

imperpetuum substituendis ecclesiam de Haxeia et ecclesiam de Oustuna et ecclesiam de Apewrda et ecclesiam de Beltona et ecclesiam de Lande-ford et ecclesiam de Massam et ecclesiam de Malesart, cum terris et decimis et omnibus eisdem adjacentibus pro anima Nigelli de Albinneio et antecessorum meorum.[a] Hanc donationem feci in hunc modum quod ego ipsas ecclesias tenebo libere et quiete dum in laicali habitu vivere voluero, et postquam ego habitum mutavero aut ex hac vita decessero Rogerus filius meus tenebit quatuor ecclesias de Insula et quintam de Landeford pro quinque marcis annuatim reddendis priori de Neuburgo. Ecclesiam vero de Massam tenebit de ecclesia de Neuburgo liberam et quietam ex omni exactione. Ecclesiam quoque de Malesart tenebit ipse de priore et Richardus de ipso sicut de me tenuit libera[m], soluta[m], et quieta[m]. Et post decessum Richardi vel post mutationem vite ejus, frater ejus Uchtredus eodem modo tenebit eam. Predictus autem Richardus habebit in custodia eundem Rogerum puerum cum ecclesia de Massam. Et de ipsa ecclesia providebit puero necessaria per consilium et considerationem prioris. Alias vero quinque ecclesias habebit prior sub tutela sua et inde providebit puero necessaria per consilium Ricardi donec ad talem etatem venerit, ut ipse sibi et suis providere noverit et predictas ecclesias tenere et regere. Si ante obitum meum puer obierit, post decessum meum ipse ecclesie libere et quiete remanebunt ecclesie de Neuburgo. Hec donatio facta est in presencia prioris Berlentone et capituli ejusdem ecclesie, per consilium ejusdem Bernardi prioris Ber-lentone, presente Augustino priore Neuburgi et hanc actionem con-cedente.

NOTE. The latest possible date is Oct. 1153 (cf. no. 199 below). It seems probable that the churches were granted when the canons moved from Hood to a site in Coxwold, called Newburgh, c. 1145,[1] and the Byland chronicle suggests that negotiations for Samson's gift may have begun before the removal from Hood.[2] For Samson's gifts of churches to another Augustinian house, Kenilworth, made also c. 1145, see nos. 175–7. The churches of Masham, Malzeard, and Langford were later granted to become a prebend of York Minster, with Roger d'Aubigny as first prebendary (below, nos. 325–6), although Langford had apparently been given to Monks Kirby by Geoffrey de La Guerche (see no. 191).

197 *Gift by Roger de Mowbray to Newburgh of the churches of Masham, Kirkby Malzeard, Langford, Haxey, Owston, Epworth, and Belton, as given by Samson d'Aubigny.* [c. 1145]

Transcripts, from an original charter formerly in St. Mary's Tower, York: Bodl., MSS. Dodsworth 91 fos. 22v–23r, 94 fo. 75r.

[a] Version in Dodsw. 94 ends.

---

[1] See *E.Y.C.* ix 206.   [2] *Mon. Ang.* v 351b.

Pd., *Mon. Ang.* vi (1) 319 (III).

Universis ecclesie filiis Rogerus de Moubrai[a] salutem. Notum vobis facio me concessisse et dedisse et presentis carte testimonio confirmasse Deo et ecclesie Sancte Marie et canonicis de Novoburgo in perpetuam elemosinam pro animabus patris mei et matris mee ecclesiam de Massaham[b] et ecclesiam de Malesart et ecclesiam de Landeford et ecclesiam de Haxey[c] et ecclesiam de Oustona et ecclesiam de Apewrda[d] et ecclesiam de Beltona cum terris et decimis et omnibus ad ipsas pertinentibus. Assentiente pariter et donante Sampsone de Albeneio[e] cui Nigellus pater meus eas antea[f] donaverat. Hiis testibus, Rogero abbate de Bellalandia,[g] Samsone de Albeneio, Rogero de Condeio, Hugone sacerdote, Ricardo clerico de Malesart, Rogero de Flamevilla,[h] Olivero de Buci,[i] Roberto de Daivilla,[j] Willielmo de Withvilla,[k] Willielmo de Cracehelaio.[l]

NOTE. This confirmation probably belongs to the same time as no. 196, *c.* 1145. The latest possible date, 1153, is given by no. 199.

198 *Gift by Roger de Mowbray to Newburgh of 5s. p.a. in his mill of Thirsk* (*Yorks., N.R.*) *for acquittance to Byland, until he shall give them ½ carucate in Brignall* (*N.R.*). [*c.* 1147]

Cartulary copy: B.M., Egerton MS. 2823 (cart. of Byland) fo. 83*v* (old fo. 190*v*).

Rogerus de Mowbray universis sancte ecclesie filiis salutem. Sciatis me concessisse Deo et beate Marie et canonicis meis de Novoburgo in liberam elemosinam quatuor solidos annuatim in prefato[m] molendino meo de Thresk' pro adquietand(is) monach(is) de Bellalanda donec eis in perpetuam elemosinam dedero dimidiam carucatam terre in Brigeshalam vel alibi. Dedi eis quintum solidum in prefato[n] molendino pro adquietand(is) prefatis monachis de decimis sartorum Acce et Willelmi. Hii quinque solidi reddendi sunt ab illo qui molendinum tenuerit de firma ejusdem molendini, et hiisdem temporibus et terminis quibus firma redditur. Hiis testibus, Rogero abbate de Bellal(anda) cum monachis suis, Nigello filio meo, Waltero de Ryparia etc. Set sciendum quod

---

[a] *Mowbray*, Dodsw. 94. [b] *Massam*, Dodsw. 94. [c] *Haxei*, Dodsw. 94.
[d] *Appewrda*, Dodsw. 94. [e] *Albeneis*, Dodsw. 94. [f] *ante*, Dodsw. 94.
[g] *Bellalanda*, Dodsw. 94. [h] *Flamavill*, Dodsw. 94. [i] *Buscy*, Dodsw. 94.
[j] *Daivill*, Dodsw. 94. [k] *Withvill*, Dodsw. 94. [l] *Crockelaio*, Dodsw. 94.
[m] *Sic.* The charter immediately preceding this charter in Egerton MS. 2823 fo. 83*v* is cal. below, no. 200. The two charters are stated in the cartulary to be: 'Copie duarum cartarum de Registro de Novoburgo extracte, quas canonici ejusdem loci habuerunt de domino Rogero de Mowbray pro decima Magne Wyldone et decimis sartorum Acci et Willelmi.' [n] *profato*, MS.

monasterium de Gyseburne habet istam carucatam terre in Thresk' et tenet illam de monasterio N[ovoburgo]^a mansum illius e[...]^a ad[.....]^a-torem partem ville de Thresk'.

NOTE. This charter is probably to be connected with no. 45, which has been dated *c.* 1147. Brignall belonged to the honour of Richmond.[1] Neither Roger de Mowbray nor Eustace Fitz John, who made claims to the vill (no. 297 and note), had any apparent right there. Perhaps their claims were made during the interval between earl Alan's return to Britanny in 1145[2] and Roger de Mowbray's departure on the second Crusade in 1147.

199 *Notification by Roger de Mowbray to H(enry Murdac), archbishop of York, of his gift to Newburgh of his right in the churches of Masham, Kirkby Malzeard, and Langford; and request for archiepiscopal confirmation.*
[Dec. 1147 × Oct. 1153]

Transcripts, from an original charter formerly in St. Mary's Tower, York: Bodl., MSS. Dodsworth 7 fo. 131*v*, 91 fo. 22*r*.

Venerabili patri et domino H. Dei gratia Eboracensi archiepiscopo Rogerus de Moubrai salutem. Noverit discretio vestra me pro salute anime mee et omnium antecessorum et heredum meorum donasse et hac carta mea confirmasse Deo et ecclesie Sancte Marie de Novoburgo ex novo in feudo meo fundate^b et^c canonicis ibidem imperpetuum regulariter viventibus in liberam et puram et perpetuam elemosinam quicquid juris habui in ecclesiis de Massam et Malesard et Landeford et quicquid laicus potest in ecclesiis conferre alicui collegio religioso me illis in eisdem ecclesiis imperpetuum contulisse. Et quantum ingens sollicitudo vestra, qua sacram religionem plantare et plantatam fovere sat agitis cunctis nota est iccirco vestram suppliciter exhoro clemenciam quatinus divini amoris intuitu huic donationi mee accomodetis assensum et scripti vestri auctoritate sepedictas ecclesias predictis canonicis imperpetuum confirmetis. Nolo latere benignitatem vestram me hanc illis fecisse donationem voluntate et supplicatione Samsonis de Albeneia cognati mei qui prefatas ecclesias tenet. Hiis testibus, Roberto capellano, Rogero de Flammavilla, Willelmo de Widevilla, Radulfo Beler, Turgisio filio Malgeri.

NOTE. Henry Murdac was consecrated in Dec. 1147, and died in Oct. 1153. Archiepiscopal confirmation was presumably withheld (see note to no. 325 below).

^{a} Illegible through damp. ^{b} *fundata*, Dodsw. 7. ^{c} Omitted in Dodsw. 7.

[1] See *E.Y.C.* v 332-3. [2] Ibid. iv 90.

200 *Notification by Roger de Mowbray that with the consent of Nigel his son he had given to Augustine the prior and his canons[1] of Newburgh the land of Little Wildon, which Bartholomew gigator had surrendered to him; and had given them a carucate in Thirsk, which they had given to Bartholomew and his heirs for a pound of incense or 12d. p.a., for acquittance of the tithe of Great Wildon to Byland; and had also given them all the assarts made by their men in Kilburn (all Yorks., N.R.).* [c. 1147×c. 1154]

Pd., *E.Y.C.* ix no. 165, from B.M., Egerton MS. 2823 (cart. of Byland) fo. 83v (old fo. 190v).

Hiis testibus, Gundrea matre mea, Aleliz uxore mea, Sampsone de Albaneyo, Rogero abbate et capitulo de Bellalanda, Radulpho de Wynclyva,[a] Hugone Camino, Willelmo de Stutevylla, Olyvero de Buscy, Roberto de Dayvyll, Odone de Newsom, Willelmo filio Hengeleri, Wartero[b] de Carletona, Petro de Hotona.

NOTE. Sir Charles Clay assigns the charter to 1145×1157, but Nigel de Mowbray did not attest charters until c. 1147, and it seems that Gundreda died by c. 1154 (see no. 236 note). It is possible that this gift belongs to the same time as no. 198, perhaps c. 1147.

201 *Confirmation by Roger de Mowbray to Newburgh of one carucate in Hovingham (Yorks., N.R.), given by Gundreda.* [1147×1155]

Original charter: Leeds, Yorks. Archaeol. Soc. Libr., MD 335, Bradfer-Lawrence collection. Transcripts, from an original charter formerly in St. Mary's Tower, York: Bodl., MSS. Dodsworth 7 fo. 148r, 91 fo. 32r–v. Pd. (abstract), *Yorks. Deeds* vii no. 374, from the original charter then in the possession of Sir Thomas Pilkington.

Uniuersis sancte ecclesie fidelibus Rog(erus) de Moubrai salutem. Sciatis me concessisse et dedisse et presenti cartula confirmasse in elemosinam Deo et ecclesie Sancte Marie de Nouoburgo . unam carrucatam terre in Hovingham . quam prius mater mea .G. dederat prefate ecclesie . et per cartam suam confirmauerat plenarie in bosco et plano in pratis et pascuis Quod si contigerit me prefatum manerium in manu mea tenere et in proprio dominio meo ? et ipsam carucatam terre escambire uoluero ? aliam pro ipsa dabo ad ualentiam ipsius . et ad libitum supradicte ecclesie infra tenuram meam Eboracisire. Quod si non fecero ? in perpetuam elemosinam remanebit Nouoburgensi ecclesie. His testibus . Hugone de Gurnai auunculo meo . A. abbate Rieuall(is) . Rogero abbate Bellalandie . Rog(ero) de Flameuilla .

[a] Probably *Wythvilla* is intended.   [b] *Sic*, probably in error for *Waltero*.

[1] *canonicis meis.*

Roberto de Daiuilla . Hug(one) Maleb' . Waltero de Riparia . Roberto de Busci . Nigello capellano.

Endorsement: *De vna carrucata terre in Houingham* (late 12th or early 13th cent.).

Size: 17 × 17·5 cm.; 3 cm. turn-up.

Seal: seal no. 3 of Roger de Mowbray (above, p. lxxxiii), red wax; appended on tag.

Script: same hand as that of no. 206.

NOTE. Ailred became abbot of Rievaulx in 1147,[1] and Hugh de Gournay was dead by 1155.[2] Hovingham belonged to Gundreda's dowry: if, as seems probable from this charter, she was still in possession, the date could be put back a little, as she died by c. 1154 (see note to no. 236).

202 *Gift by Roger de Mowbray, for the health of his soul and that of Alice his wife, to Richard the prior and the canons of Newburgh of all his land in Wombleton (Yorks., N.R.); and confirmation of his earlier gift to Augustine the prior and the canons of the church of Welburn (N.R.) with 6 bovates and the chapel of Wombleton with 2 bovates.* [1154 × 1157]

Pd., *E.Y.C.* ix no. 163, from Bodl., MS. Dodsworth 94 fo. 78v.

Hiis testibus, Roberto de Molbraio filio meo, Rogero de Flammavilla, Thoma de Colvilla, Willelmo de Whitevilla, Olivero de Buscy, Gilberto de Gaunte, Rogero [de] Cundi, Radulpho Beler, Silvestro presbitero, Johanne Grosso, Bartholomeo gigatore, et aliis.

203 *Gift by Roger de Mowbray to Newburgh and prior Richard, of the church of Newburgh and various neighbouring lands, and the churches of Hood, Coxwold, Thirsk, Kirby Hill, Cundall, Hovingham, Welburn, Kirkby Moorside (all Yorks., N.R.), St. Andrew's in York, Masham (N.R.), Kirkby Malzeard (W.R.), Langford (Notts.), Haxey, Owston, Epworth, and Belton (Axholme, Lincs.), with chapels and lands, and the chapelry of the household after the death of Roger de Cundy.* ? [1154 × 1157]

Pd., *C.P.R. 1388-92* pp. 160-2, from P.R.O., Patent Roll 13 Ric. II pt. ii (C. 66/329) m. 26.

Hiis testibus, Roberto capellano, Rogero de Flamvilla, Willelmo de Widevilla, Radulpho Beler, Turgiso filio Malgeri.

NOTE. The appearance of prior Richard indicates a date after 1154,[3] and Ralph Beler apparently died by 1157.[4] But this witness-clause is identical with that of no. 199, of 1147 × 1153, and the charter contains much obviously

[1] *Life of Ailred of Rievaulx by Walter Daniel*, ed. F. M. Powicke (1950) p. xci.
[2] *P.R. 2-4 Hen. II* p. 24.   [3] See *E.Y.C.* ix 248.   [4] Ibid. p. 212.

interpolated matter.[1] It is therefore impossible to know how much credence should be given to information contained in the charter and not found elsewhere, for example its references to Walter de Riparia as *dapifer* in *c.* 1145 and to Roger de Cundy as chaplain *c.* 1154. For Cundy cf. no. 322.

204 *Confirmation by Roger de Mowbray to Newburgh of a gift made by Walter de Riparia* [? *in Brandsby, Yorks., N.R.*]. [*c.* 1154 × 1175]

> Transcript, from an original charter formerly in St. Mary's Tower, York: Bodl., MS. Dodsworth 91 fo. 11*v*.

Omnibus sancte ecclesie filiis Rogerus de Molbrai salutem. Notum sit vobis me concessisse et presenti carta mea confirmasse in liberam et perpetuam elemosinam Deo et Sancte Marie de Novoburgo donationem quam fecit Walterus de Riparia in terra et pastura et in omnibus sicut carta predicti Walteri continetur. Hiis testibus, Toma de Colevilla, Radulpho vic[ec]om(ite), Radulpho de Rugem', Willelmo de Davilla, Roberto Beler, Roberto capellano.

> NOTE. Thomas de Coleville first occurs after 1154 (see no. 356 note) and Robert Beler first occurs in 1154 (no. 240; cf. no. 243). Walter de Riparia, who was presumably still alive when the confirmation was issued, was dead by 1175.[2]
>
> The text of Walter de Riparia's charter is not known to survive, but the land given was possibly in Brandsby (Yorks., N.R.), which was part of the knight's fee held in 1166.[3]

205 *Confirmation by Roger de Mowbray to Newburgh of ½ carucate in Bagby (Yorks., N.R.), given by Roger de Cundy.* [*c.* 1145 × 1186]

(1)

> Original charter: B.M., Egerton Ch. 2168.
> Pd. (transl.), *Yorks. Deeds* ii no. 43, from the original charter then in the possession of Sir Ralph Payne-Gallwey.

Rogerus de Molbraio . vniuersis sancte ecclesie filiis salutem. Notum sit uobis me concessisse et presenti carta confirmasse Deo et Sancte Marie et canonicis meis de Nouoburgo in liberam et quietam et perpetuam elemosinam donationem quam fecit eis Rog(erus) de Cund' . uidelicet de dimidia carucata terre in territorio de Baggabi iuxta Tresch. His testibus . Rog(ero) de Cund' . Rob(erto) capellano de Land' . Gaufrido sacerdote . Ham(one) Beler . Willelmo camerario . Roberto de Cund'.

---

[1] *E.Y.C.* ix 202.   [2] *P.R. 21 Hen. II* p. 181.   [3] Nos. 206–7, 401, and Fees [5].

Endorsement: *De dimidia carrucata terre in Bagebi* (12th cent.).

Size: 15·6 × 8·6 cm.; 2·2 cm. turn-up.

Seal: seal no. 3 of Roger de Mowbray (above, p. lxxxiii), red wax; legend broken off; appended on tag.

(2)

Original charter: B.M., Egerton Ch. 2169.

Rogerus de Moubr' vniuersis sanctę ecclesię filiis . salutem. Notum sit uobis me concessisse et presenti carta confirmasse Deo et Sanctę Marię et canonicis meis de Nouoburgo in liberam et quietam et perpetuam elemosinam donationem quam fe[cit]*ᵃ* eis Rogerus de Cund' . uidelicet de dimidia carrucata terrę in te[rri]*ᵃ*torio de Baggebi iuxta Tresch. His testibus Rogero de Cund' . R[o]*ᵃ*berto capellano de Land' . Gaufrido sacerdote . Hamundo Beler . Willelmo camerario . Roberto de Cund'.

Endorsements: *Carta Rogeri de Mubrai de dim' caruc' terre in Baggebi. | de dim' caruc' in Baggebi.* (12th cent., both endorsements in same hand: same hand as endorsement on Egerton Ch. 2170 (no. 212 below)).

Size: 13 × 8·2 cm.; 2·5 cm. turn-up.

Seal: fragment of green wax; appended on tag.

Script: same hand as Egerton Ch. 2171 (no. 208 below).

NOTE. Roger de Cundy held ½ fee of Mowbray in 1166.[1]

206 *Confirmation by Roger de Mowbray to Newburgh of 2 bovates in Brandsby, with certain tofts, rights, and pasture, given by Henry de Riparia.*

[1166 × 1186]

Original charter: Fairfax-Cholmeley deeds, deposited at Northallerton, North Riding R.O., ZQG.

Omnibus sancte matris ecclesie filiis Rog(erus) de Molbrai salutem. Sciatis me concessisse et presenti carta confirmasse Deo et Sancte Marie de Nouoburgo et canonicis ibidem seruientibus in liberam et perpetuam elemosinam donationem illam quam eis fecit Henricus de Riparia uidelicet duas bouatas terre in Brandesbi que fuerunt Geroldi in Brachanehou et ubicunque alibi iacuerint cum tofto illo quod fuit Fredegest . totam etiam terram illam que iacet inter Stubsiche et exitum de Steresbi sub Suertecole cum tofto ill[o]*ᵇ* et crofto que fuerunt Rob(erti) presbiteri uiginti etiam scheppas carbonum a[nnuatim inperpetuum de m]*ᶜ*ortuo boscho suo. Homines etiam canonicorum qui prefatam terram in[habitabunt habebunt plen]*ᶜ*ariam communam in boscho et plano et pastura ad [edificandum et ardendum. Predict]*ᶜ*i etiam

ᵃ Charter damaged.   *ᵇ* Illegible.   *ᶜ* Charter damaged; text supplied from no. 207.

---

[1] No. 401, Fees [27].

cano[nici ha]*ᵃ*bebunt in prefata villa toftum illud quod f[uit Gamel et pasturam ad ducentas]*ᵃ* oues et ad quadraginta uaccas et ad decem [sues cum nutrim]*ᵃ*entis suis. His testibus Ricardo de Wiuile . Willelmo de Laceles . Adam Luuel . Herberto filio Ricardi . Rob(erto) Beler . Rolando de Landeles . Willelmo de Fribi . Rad(ulfo) clerico . Roberto filio Rogeri . Petro nepote Ric(ardi) prioris.

Endorsement: *Cart'*[........]*ᵇ* *terra de* [.......]*ᵇ* (contemporary).

Size: 14·4 × 17 cm.; 3 cm. turn-up.

Seal: missing; traces of red wax; was appended on tag.

Script: same hand as no. 201.

NOTE. Henry de Riparia succeeded to his father Walter's fee between 1166 and 1175.¹ Walter had probably made a gift to Newburgh in Brandsby (no. 204).

207 *Confirmation by Nigel de Mowbray to Newburgh of the gift of Henry de Riparia, as in no. 206.*   [1166 × 1186]

Original charter: Fairfax-Cholmeley deeds, deposited at Northallerton, North Riding R.O., ZQG.

Omnibus sancte matris ecclesie filiis . Nig(ellus) de Molbraio . salutem. Sciatis me concessisse et presenti carta confirmasse Deo et Sancte Marie de Nouob(urgo) et canonicis ibidem Deo seruientibus in liberam et perpetuam elemosinam donationem illam quam eis fecit Henr(icus) de Riparia sicut carta ipsius testatur . uidelicet duas bouatas terre in Brandesbi que fuerunt Geroldi in Bracnehou . et ubicunque alibi iacuerint . cum tofto illo quod fuit Fredegest . totam etiam terram illam que iacet inter Stubesich et exitum de Steresbi sub Suertecole cum tofto et crofto . que fuerunt Rob(erti) presbiteri . viginti etiam scheppas carbonum annuatim inperpetuum de mortuo boscho suo.*ᶜ* Homines etiam canonicorum qui prefatam terram inhabitabunt . habebunt plenariam communam in boscho et plano et pastura ad edificandum et ardendum. Predicti etiam canonici habebunt in predicta uilla toftum illud quod fuit Gamel . et pasturam ad ducentas oues . et ad quadraginta uaccas . et ad decem sues cum nutrimentis suis. Hiis testibus . Ricardo de Wiuile . Willelmo de Laceles . Adam Luuel . Hereberto filio Ric(ardi) . Rob(erto) Beler . Rollando de Landeles . Willelmo de Fribi . Rad(ulfo) clerico . Roberto filio Rogeri . Petro nepote .R. prioris.

ᵃ Charter damaged; text supplied from no. 207.   *ᵇ* Charter damaged.
ᶜ *sueo*, MS., with *e* underdotted for deletion.

¹ See no. 401; cf. *P.R. 21 Hen. II* p. 181.

Endorsement: *Confirmatio Nigelli de Mubrai de terra de Brandesbi* (early 13th cent.).

Size: 16 × 8 cm.; 1·2 cm. turn-up.

Seal: missing; was appended on tag.

Script: hand probably the same as that of text of no. 212.

NOTE. This charter was clearly given on the same occasion as no. 206.

208 *Gift by Roger de Mowbray to Newburgh of 5 acres in Bagby and 2 tofts in Thirsk.* [*c.* 1170 × 1186]

Original charter: B.M., Egerton Ch. 2171.

Vniuersis sanctę matris ecclesię filiis . Rog(erus) de Moubrai . salutem. Notum sit uobis me concessisse et dedisse et hac carta confirmasse Deo et Sanctę Marię et canonicis meis de Nouob(urgo) quinque acras terrę de territorio de Baggebi proximas fossato de Tresch*a* iuxta uiam quę uadit uersus Sanctum Felicem . et unum toftum in Tresch iuxta barram uersus Kiluingtonam ab australi parte uię inter domum Roberti coluse et domum Vmfridi . et aliud toftum in Tresch inter toftum Helie filii Elwini . et Willelmi filii Roberti telarii . in puram et liberam et perpetuam elemosinam cum omnibus pertinenciis et liberis consuetudinibus suis. His testibus . Roberto de Moubrai . Adam capellano . Phil(ippo) de Muntpincun . Willelmo filio Engel(rami) . Roberto de Beuchamp . Johanne capellano . Roberto clerico . Brisebarre et Chinun . Willelmo Gramatico . Willelmo de Wafre . Hug(one) pistore . et Roberto fratre eius . Waltero et Rogero diaconis.

Endorsements: *De toftis Ernaldi* (12th cent.); *Bagby* (13th or 14th cent.).

Size: 16·4 × 9·3 cm.; 1·8 cm. turn-up.

Seal: missing; was appended on tag.

Script: same hand as Egerton Ch. 2169 (no. 205 (2) above).

NOTE. Philip de Montpincon does not occur before *c.* 1170 (see no. 376 note). Brisebarre and Chinon also occur only after *c.* 1170 (nos. 81, 274–5). Five of the witnesses appear in *c.* 1181 (no. 141).

209 *Confirmation by Roger de Mowbray to Newburgh of the advowson of Brafferton (Yorks., N.R.), given by Henry de Riparia.* [*c.* 1170 × 1186]

Transcript, from an original charter formerly in St. Mary's Tower, York: Bodl., MS. Dodsworth 91 fos. 11v–12r.

Rogerus de Moubrai universis sancte matris ecclesie filiis salutem. Sciatis me concessisse et dedisse et presenti carta confirmasse donationem illam quam Henricus de Riparia fecit ecclesie et canonicis de

―――――

a Altered in MS. from *Tresc*.

Novoburgo me presente et assentiente, astante etiam Jeremia archidiacono de Clivelandia et assentiente[a] et prebente, scilicet jus patronatus in ecclesia de Braffertona quod eis dedit in liberam et perpetuam elemosinam, cartam suam etiam prefatus Henricus super hac donatione vobis presentibus et astantibus super altare ecclesie de Novoburgo optulit. Hiis testibus, Jeremia archid(iacono), Arnisio priore de Martona, Nigello de Moubra,[b] Henrico de Riparia, Magistro Adam Arrab', Johanne clerico et Ricardo clerico archid(iaconi).

NOTE. The period of office of Jeremy, archdeacon of Cleveland, began c. 1170.[1] Henry de Riparia's charter and archdeacon Jeremy's confirmation are found in MS. Dodsworth 91 fos. 12v–13r.[2]

210 *Gift by Roger de Mowbray to Newburgh of moorland near Kirkby Malzeard (Yorks., W.R.).* [c. 1175 × 1186]

Transcript, from an original charter formerly in St. Mary's Tower, York: Bodl., MS. Dodsworth 94 fo. 78r.

Universis sancte matris ecclesie filiis Rogerus de Mowbray salutem. Notum sit vobis me concessisse et dedisse Deo et Sancte Marie et canonicis meis de Novo Burgo in puram et liberam et perpetuam elemosinam totam terram cum nemore sicut Keldebec vadit in Kesebec contra obviando Ketelsmor usque Rauthmire cum toto Rauthmire et inde ascendendo usque Ketelsmor et inde per transversum usque Ruchau qui super moram est et de Reuchau descendendo[c] iterum in Kesebec, salvo uno exitu viginti perticarum de latitudine quem homines de Malesar et de Torp habebunt ad averia sua usque ad moram. Hec dedi et presenti carta confirmavi predictis canonicis meis imperpetuum pro salute anime mee et antecessorum meorum et heredum meorum cum plenaria pastura animalibus suis ibidem commorantibus per totam forestam meam tam in bosco quam in mora et cum quietatione pasnagii sui. His testibus, Roberto de Mowbray filio meo, et Willelmo nepote meo, Philippo de Muntpincun, Roberto Beler, Roberto de Belcamp, Johanne et Waltero capellanis, Toma de Colevilla, Hamundo Beler, Sampsone Beler, Roberto de Beler.[3]

Seal: 'on horsback with a faire seale'.

NOTE. Roger de Mowbray's grandson William was not born until 1171 or later,[4] and so this charter cannot have been given before c. 1175 and may well have been given several years later.

[a] *assensum*, MS.   [b] *Sic.*   [c] *descendo*, MS.

[1] See C. T. Clay, in *Y.A.J.* xxxvi (1947) 412–13.
[2] For the Riparia fee, see Fees [5].   [3] ? Robert de Belvoir.
[4] He was said to be 14 years old in 1185 (*Rotuli de Dominabus*, ed. J. H. Round (P.R.S. xxxv) pp. 9–10) but he did not succeed to his father's honour until 1194 (*P.R. 6 Ric. I* p. 160).

211 *Gift by Roger de Mowbray to Newburgh of the site of the priory and neigh-*
bouring lands, and the churches of Hood, Coxwold, Thirsk, Hovingham,
Welburn, Kirkby Moorside, Kirby Hill, and Cundall.

Pd., *Mon. Ang.* vi (1) 318 (I), from an original charter formerly in the possession of Thomas, Lord Fauconberg (transcribed in Bodl., MS. Dodsworth
45 fo. 69r–v).

NOTE. The witnesses are the same as those to a charter of William de Mowbray, to which they clearly belong.[1] Although the phraseology of the present
charter suggests interpolation or forgery, the property mentioned may well
have been given by 1154.[2]

212 *Confirmation by Nigel de Mowbray to Newburgh of ½ carucate in Bagby,*
given by Roger de Cundy. [*c.* 1160 × 1190]

Original charter: B.M., Egerton Ch. 2170.
Pd. (transl.), *Yorks. Deeds* ii no. 44, from the original charter then in the
possession of Sir Ralph Payne-Gallwey.

Vniuersis sancte ecclesie filiis . Nigellus de Molbraio salutem. Notum
sit uobis me concessisse et presenti carta confirmasse Deo et Sancte
Marie de Nouoburgo dimidiam carrucatam terre in territorio*a* de
Bagebi . quam Rogerus de Condeio prefate ecclesie donauit. Hanc
igitur eandem terram eidem ecclesie confirmo in liberam et perpetuam
elemosinam. His testibus*b* Rob(erto) capell(ano) . Will(elmo) filio
Ingel(rami) . Ric(ardo) canonico . Adam capell(ano) . Rad(ulfo) de
Torp . jun(iore).

Endorsement: *Carta Nigelli de Mubrai de dim' caruc' terre in Baggebi.* (12th
cent.: same hand as endorsement on Egerton Ch. 2169 (no. 205 (2) above)).

Size: 12·2 × 9·4 cm.; 2·3 cm. turn-up.

Seal: missing; was appended on tag.

Script: hand of main portion probably the same as that of no. 207.

NOTE. Nigel de Mowbray probably did not begin to issue his own charters
before *c.* 1160. This confirmation was evidently made on an occasion after the
confirmation by Roger de Mowbray (no. 205).

213 *Confirmation by Nigel de Mowbray to Newburgh of gifts made by his*
father and by various tenants. [1186 × 1190]

Transcripts, from an original charter formerly in St. Mary's Tower, York:
Bodl., MSS. Dodsworth 7 fo. 131r–v, 91 fos. 2r–3r.

Nigellus de Molbraio omnibus sancte matris ecclesie filiis salutem.*c*
Sciatis me concessisse et presenti carta confirmasse Deo et Sancte Marie

a Altered in MS. from *territoria.*   *b* From here in lighter ink, almost certainly
a different hand.   *c* *salutem* repeated in Dodsw. 7.

[1] *Mon. Ang.* vi (1) 318 (II).   [2] Cf. *E.Y.C.* ix nos. 58, 112.

et canonicis meis de Novoburgo in liberam et perpetuam elemosinam unam carucatam terre in Hovingham cum omnibus pertinenciis suis; duas etiam bovatas terre apud sartum quas habent de donatione Radulfi de Belvero; quatuor etiam bovatas terre in Brandesbi cum pastura et ceteris aisiamentis in eadem villa sicut carta Henrici de Riparia testatur; unam etiam bovatam terre in Tresc que fuit Willelmi filii Ketelli quam habent in escambium pro bovata terre de Coltona; item quinque acras terre de territorio de Baggabi juxta viam que vadit versus Sanctum Felicem; et unum toftum in Tresc juxta barram versus Kilvington inter domum Roberti colus et domum Umfridi; aliud etiam toftum inter toftum Helie filii Elfwini et toftum Willelmi filii Roberti; insulam etiam de Tresc que fuit Ricardi sacerdotis et bovatam terre cum tofto quam idem Ricardus tenuit et toftum illud quod fuit Basilie cum libertate vie que de ipsa insula vadit ad villam. Hec omnia eisdem canonicis concedo et presenti carta confirmo sicut pater meus eisdem donaverat et cartis suis confirmaverat. Ratam etiam habeo et presenti carta confirmo donationem illam quam eisdem canonicis fecit pater meus et carta sua confirmavit, totam scilicet terram cum nemore sicut Keldebec cadit in Kesebec contra obviando Ketelsmor usque Rauthmire, cum tota Rauthmire et inde ascendendo usque ad Ketelsmore et inde transversim usque Ruthhau qui est super moram et Ruthhau iterum in Kesebec, salvo uno exitu xx perticarum de latitudine quem homines de Malesart et de Thorp habent ad averia sua usque moram. Adjeci autem ex proprio dono eisdem canonicis pratum illud quod fuit Augustini Althete et liberum exitum hominibus et averiis suis de mansione illorum ad villam de Malesart. Hec omnia concessi et presenti carta confirmavi predictis canonicis meis in liberam et perpetuam elemosinam cum plenaria pastura animalibus suis in territorio de Malesart commorantibus per totam forestam meam tam in bosco quam in mora et ut quieti sint de pannagio reddendo. Quecunque etiam predictis canonicis meis a liberis hominibus feudi mei collata sunt rationabiliter et conferenda presentis scripti testimonio confirmo. Hiis testibus, Roberto de Molbrai, Rogero de Sancto Martino, Rogero de Daivilla, Nicholao de Bellun, Radulfo de Belvero, Roberto de Busci, Radulfo clerico, Radulfo filio Radulfi, Henrico nepote Radulfi de Belvero, Willelmo filio Geradi,[a] Hugone Barilth, Ricardo Golle.[b]

NOTE. The confirmation clearly belongs to Nigel de Mowbray's period as lord of the Mowbray honour. For some of the gifts confirmed in this charter, see above, nos. 201, 208, 210 (cf. also nos. 206–7), and below, no. 264, for Coulton (Yorks., N.R.).

[a] *Gerrardi*, Dodsw. 91.   [b] *Gelle*, Dodsw. 91.

214 *Confirmation by Nigel de Mowbray to Newburgh of all the gifts made by his father.* [1186 × 1190]

Transcript (? incomplete), from an original charter formerly in St. Mary's Tower, York: Bodl., MS. Dodsworth 94 fo. 75*v*.

Universis sancte ecclesie filiis Nigellus de Mowbray salutem. Notum sit vobis me concessisse et presentis carte testimonio confirmasse Deo et Sancte Marie de Novo Burgo canonicisque ibidem Deo servientibus omnes donationes patris mei sicut carte ejus testantur, videlicet in ecclesiis in terris et ceteris possessionibus: ipsum locum in quo abbatia eorum fundata et ecclesiam Sancte Marie de Hod cum terra et bosco de*a* sub proximis montibus, ecclesiam de Cukewald cum novem bovatis terre in eadem villa et cum capellis ad ipsam ecclesiam pertinentibus, ecclesiam de Tresc cum una carucata terre, capellam Sancti Jacobi cum duabus bovatis terre in ipsa villa, ecclesiam de Kyrkeby juxta pontem de Burgo, ecclesiam de Condalia, ecclesiam de Hovingham, ecclesiam de Welleburna, ecclesiam de Massam, ecclesiam de Malesart, ecclesiam de Landeford, ecclesiam de Haxeia, ecclesiam de Owstona, ecclesiam de Appewrd, ecclesiam de Beltona, cum terris et decimis et omnibus aliis rebus ad ipsas ecclesias pertinentibus.

NOTE. This confirmation, if genuine, probably dates from Nigel de Mowbray's period of lordship.

215 *Notification by Roger de Mowbray to Alexander, bishop of Lincoln (1123–48), and to his own men, of his gift to Hirst (Axholme, Lincs.) and Nostell (Aug., Yorks., W.R.) of 30s., 8 sesters of malt, and 1,000 eels to be rendered by his men from the farm of Belton (Axholme), and also of 6 bovates in 'Lithesm' in exchange for grain, for the sustenance of two canons (at Hirst) and their servants.* [1138 × Feb. 1148]

Cartulary copy: B.M., Cotton MS. Vesp. E xix fo. 131*r* (old p. 323).

Rogerus de Mubrai Alexandro Dei gratia Lincoln(iensi) episcopo et omnibus successuris episcopis Lincoln(iensibus) et omnibus heredibus suis atque baronibus et omnibus ministris suis et hominibus Francis et Anglis salutem. Sciatis me dedisse et concessisse monasterio de Hirst' et ecclesie Sancti Osuualdi de Nostlat et canonicis ejusdem ecclesie in predicto monasterio Deo et Sancte Marie servientibus pro salute anime mee et pro animabus patris et matris mee et omnium parentum meorum in elemosinam imperpetuum, unoquoque anno scilicet solidos xxx et viij sextarios de brasio et unum milliarium anguillarum quos dabunt eis homines mei de firma mea de Beeltona, illi videlicet ad quos

a ? a word omitted.

illos misi et constitui ita ut nulli prepositorum meorum accipiant censum neque brasium nec anguillas ab illis hominibus quos elemosinam meam predictis canonicis dare constitui neque eos aliquo modo disturbent vel contristent. Insuper dedi eis et concessi vj bovatas terre in Lithesm cum terra Gladwini ad victum duorum canonicorum et servientium suorum in loco bladi quod eis ante donaveram. Concessi quoque eis communitatem pascuorum in bosco et in plano sicut meo dominico et pasnagium suum et hominum suorum pro amore Dei clamo eis quietum imperpetuum. Volo igitur et precipio ut hec elemosina mea cum omnibus tenuris suis sit libera et quieta ab omni exactione servicii secularis et consuetudine, sicut ulla elemosina quietior est et liberior. Et ut hec donatio mea firma imposterum et illibata consistat presentis cartule mee auctoritate et attestatione atque proprie manus mee subscriptione confirmo. +++.

NOTE. This gift doubles that made by Nigel d'Aubigny, above, no. 15.

216 *Similar notification by Roger de Mowbray to bishop Alexander and to his own men, of his gift to Hirst and to Robert, canon of Nostell.*

[1138 × Feb. 1148]

Cartulary copy: B.M., Cotton MS. Vesp. E xix fo. 131r–v (old pp. 323–4).

Rogerus de Mulbr' Alexandro Dei gratia Lincoln(iensi) episcopo et omnibus post eum successuris episcopis Linc(olniensibus) et omnibus heredibus suis atque baronibus et omnibus hominibus suis Francis et Anglis salutem. Sciatis me dedisse et concessisse imperpetuum in elemosinam monasterio de Hirst et Roberto canonico regulari ecclesie Sancti Osuualdi et cunctis fratribus canonicis post eum futuris in eodem loco Deo et Sancte Marie servientibus pro animabus patris et matris mee et pro salute anime mee et heredum meorum, scilicet unoquoque anno xxx solidos denariorum de firma mea de Beltona et viij sextarios de brasio et unum milliarium anguillarum quos dabunt eis homines mei de firma mea de Beltona, illi videlicet ad quos illos misi et constitui ita ut nulli prepositorum meorum accipiant censum neque brasium nec anguillas ab illis hominibus quos elemosinam meam predictis canonicis dare constitui neque eos aliquo modo inde disturbent. Insuper dedi eis et concessi imperpetuum vj bovatas terre in Littlehesim cum terra Gladewini. Concessi quoque eis communitatem pascuorum in bosco et in plano sicut meo dominio et pasnagium suum et hominum suorum pro Dei amore clamo eis quietum imperpetuum. Volo igitur et precipio ut hec elemosina mea cum omnibus tenuris et hominibus ad predictum locum de Hirst pertinentibus sit libera et quieta ab omni exactione et consuetudine servicii secularis, sicut ulla elemosina quietior est et liberior imperpetuum. Et ut hec donatio mea firma imposterum et illibata consistat presentis cartule mee auctoritate confirmo. Teste etc.

217 *Similar notification by Roger de Mowbray to bishop Alexander, and to his own men, of his gift to Hirst and to Warin, canon of Nostell.*

[1138×Feb. 1148]

Cartulary copy: B.M., Cotton MS. Vesp. E xix fo. 132r (old p. 325).

Rogerus de Mubrai Alexandro Dei gratia Linc(olniensi) episcopo et omnibus successuris episcopis Linc(olniensibus) et omnibus heredibus suis atque baronibus et omnibus ministris suis et hominibus Francis et Anglis salutem. Sciatis me dedisse et concessisse monasterio de Hirst et Garino canonico ecclesie Sancti Osuualdi et cunctis fratribus canonicis post eum futuris in eodem loco Deo et Sancte Marie servientibus pro salute anime mee et pro animabus patris et matris mee et omnium parentum meorum in elemosina imperpetuum, unoquoque anno scilicet solidos xxx et viij sextarios de brasio et unum milliarium anguillarum quos dabunt eis homines mei de firma mea de Beltona, illi videlicet ad quos illos misi et constitui ita ut nulli prepositorum meorum accipiant censum nec brasium nec anguillas ab illis hominibus quos elemosinam meam predictis canonicis dare constitui nec eos aliquo modo inde disturbent vel contristent. Insuper dedi eis et concessi vj bovatas in Litthehesin cum terra Gladewini ad victum duorum canonicorum et servientium suorum in loco bladi quod eis ante donaveram. Concessi quoque eis communitatem pascuorum in bosco et in plano sicut meo dominico et pasnagium suum et hominum suorum pro amore Dei clamo eis quietum imperpetuum. Volo igitur et precipio ut hec elemosina mea cum omnibus tenuris suis sit libere et quiete ab omni exactione servicii secularis et consuetudine, sicut ulla elemosina quietior est et liberior. Et ut hec donatio mea firma imposterum et illibata consistat presentis cartule mee atque proprie manus mee subscriptione confirmo. +++. Test' etc.

218 *Gift by Roger de Mowbray to Hirst and Osbert Silvanus canon of Nostell of the wood of Hirst and the marsh, 30s. and 8 sesters of malt p.a., fisheries in the Rivers Don and Idle, and 6 bovates in 'Litteshesel'.* [1148×1166]

Cartulary copy: B.M., Cotton MS. Vesp. E xix fo. 131v (old p. 324).
Pd., *Mon. Ang.* vi (1) 101 (II).

Rogerus de Mubrai omnibus heredibus suis et hominibus et universis sancte ecclesie filiis salutem. Sciatis me dedisse et concessisse et presenti scripto confirmasse in puram elemosinam imperpetuum loco de Hirst in Insula et Osberto Silvano canonico et omnibus ei successuris in eodem loco sub obediencia capituli Sancti Osuualdi pro anima patris mei Nigelli et matris mee Gundree et pro salute mea et heredum meorum totum nemus quod vocatur Hirst et Hirstesic et marays de Hirstesic usque Risebrigam sicut jacet inter nemus de Hirst et Estsinord et Houkeswra et Horsecroft et marays inter locum de Hirst et Eppen et totum marays et fossatum usque Don; et unoquoque anno xxx solidos denariorum de firma mea de Beltona et octo sextaria brasii quos dabunt eis homines mei de Beltona, illi scilicet homines quos censum suum eis reddere constitui ita quod nullus prepositorum meorum nec censum nec brasium hoc ad opus meum accipiat ab illis hominibus sed canonicis meis dentur sine omni disturbatione. Preter hoc dedi et concessi eisdem canonicis pro uno miliario anguillarum quod eis unoquoque anno concesseram, piscarias in aquis Don et Yddel quas de me tenebant Svenus de Beltona et Reginaldus frater ejus et reddere michi solebant unum milliarium anguillarum. Insuper dedi eis et concessi vj bovatas terre in Litteshesel cum terra Gladwini et pannagium suum et hominum suorum in omnibus boscis meis in Insula clamo eis quietum imperpetuum et concessi eisdem canonicis meis et hominibus suis omnem communitatem in bosco et plano in marays et aquis et omnibus aliis in quibus homines mei habent communitatem. Volo igitur et precipio ut hec elemosina mea cum omnibus tenuris suis et hominibus sit libera et quieta ab omni exactione et consuetudine seculari de me et de omnibus hominibus. Hiis etc.

NOTE. This charter clearly belongs to the same time as no. 220, which is addressed to Robert de Chesney, bishop of Lincoln (1148-66).

219 *Notification by Roger de Mowbray to Ralph de Bellun his 'consistor' (? constable)[1] of Axholme, and William de Immingham his reeve, of his decision to have his men pay directly to the canons of Hirst his gift of 30s. and 8 sesters of malt p.a., instead of through the agency of his reeves as formerly, because the reeves frequently failed to make the payments.* [1148 × 1166]

Cartulary copy: B.M., Cotton MS. Vesp. E xix fos. 131v-132r (old pp. 324-5).

Rogerus de Mubrai Radulfo de Bellun consistori suo de Insula et Willelmo de Imingahaga preposito suo et omnibus post eos futuris consistoribus et prepositis et omnibus hominibus suis de Insula Francis et

[1] Cf. above, p. lx n. 6.

Anglis salutem. Sciatis me concessisse et statuisse et presentis cartule mee attestatione confirmasse canonicis meis de Hirst elemosinam meam quam dudum eis dederam, scilicet xxx solidos denariorum et viij sextarios brasii unoquoque anno quas solebant accipere de manibus prepositorum meorum de firma mea, sed quia sepius eveniebat eis inde fallacia propter incuriam et oblivionem prepositorum, ab eis requisitus concessi eis et statui ut ipsi canonici non accipiant amplius a prepositis, sed amodo ex meo precepto manu sua accipiant ab hominibus meis censum quem dare debuerant michi ad eosdem terminos ad quos alii homines mei dant, ita quod nullus prepositorum meorum predictis canonicis aliquo modo inde disturbet. Ketellus dabit v solidos, Macusus v solidos, Lefwinus et Wlmarus v solidos, Baredchrakin v solidos, Gamel filius Normani iiij solidos et ix denarios, Elwinus de Humelt' iiij solidos et j denarium, Ernui filius Spratlini ij solidos et ij denarios. De brasio similiter illis statui: Lefwinus Basei dabit eis ij sextarios, Eilwardus ij sextarios, Willelmus filius Sweni ij sextarios, Macus dimidium sextarium, Wlmarus Rudda dimidium sextarium, Robertus et Berewaldus unum sextarium. Pro uno milliario anguillarum quod solebant eis dare Swenus et Reinaldus frater ejus ex meo dono, concessi eisdem canonicis piscarias in aqua, videlicet in Don et in Hiddel, que solebant michi reddere unum milliarium quoque anno. Precipio itaque ut amodo imposterum illi homines qui hic nominati sunt et scripti et eorum successores et heredes reddant censum suum et brasium unoquoque anno predictis canonicis sicut michi ipsi debuissent, quia hoc est meum proprium et dominicum quod datum est in elemosinam servis Dei pro salute tam corporis quam anime mee. Volo igitur et precipio ut idem canonici omnes tenuras suas quas[a] me tenent bene et honorifice et libere et quiete teneant, sicut ulla elemosina honorificentius et liberius et quietius tenetur.[b] Test' etc.

NOTE. This charter clearly belongs to the same time as no. 220, which is addressed to Robert de Chesney, bishop of Lincoln (1148–66).

220 *Notification by Roger de Mowbray to Robert (de Chesney), bishop of Lincoln (1148–66), of his gift to Hirst and Osbert Silvanus canon of Nostell of 30s. and 8 sesters of malt p.a., fisheries in the Rivers Don and Idle, and 6 bovates in 'Litthehesim'.*   [Dec. 1148 × Dec. 1166]

Transcript, from an original charter in St. Mary's Tower, York: Bodl., MS. Dodsworth 8 fo. 196v. Cartulary copy: B.M., Cotton MS. Vesp. E xix fo. 131v (old p. 324) (lacks all witnesses).
Pd., *Mon. Ang.* vi (1) 101 (III), stated to be from the cartulary copy, but actually from the original charter.

[a] ? supply *de.*   [b] *tenet*, MS.

+ Rogerus de Molbr'*a* Rodberto*b* Dei gratia Lincolliensi episcopo et omnibus post eum futuris episcopis Lincoll(iensibus) et omnibus heredibus suis atque baronibus et omnibus hominibus suis Francis et Anglis salutem. Sciatis me dedisse et concessisse in elemosinam imperpetuum monasterio de Hirst in Insula et Osberto Silvano canonico de ecclesia Sancti Oswaldi et omnibus canonicis post eum successuris in eodem loco Hirst Deo et Sancte Marie servientibus pro salute anime mee et pro animabus patris et matris mee et heredum meorum, scilicet unoquoque anno xxx solidos denariorum de firma mea de Beltona et viij sextarios de brasio quos dabunt eis homines mei de firma mea de Beltona, illi videlicet homines quos censum suum eis reddere constitui ita ut nullus prepositorum meorum censum nec brasium ad opus meum accipiat ab illis hominibus sed canonicis meis dentur libere et sine aliqua disturbatione. Pro uno milliario anguillarum quod eisdem canonicis unoquoque anno concesseram et dederam, concessi prefato Osberto Silvano piscarias in aqua, videlicet Don et Iddel*c* quas tenebant de me Suenus de Beltona et Reinaldus*d* frater ejus et michi inde reddere solebant unum milliarium anguillarum. Insuper dedi et concessi predicto loco Hirst .vj. bovatas terre in Litthehesim*e* cum terra Gladwini.*f* Et eidem Osberto et omnibus canonicis post eum futuris in eodem loco pro amore Dei et suo concessi et dedi in elemosinam imperpetuum nemus totum quod vocatur Hirst et pasnagium*g* suum et hominum suorum clamo eis quietum imperpetuum. Volo igitur et precipio ut hec elemosina mea cum omnibus tenuris suis et hominibus sit libera et quieta et soluta ab omni exactione et consuetudine servicii secularis sicut ulla elemosina liberior et quietior et solutior est. Test(ibus), Roberto de Davidvilla, Radulfo de Bellun, Willemo filio Talborti.*h*

NOTE. An Osbert Salvain, canon of Nostell, occurs *c.* 1180 × 1200,[1] but the man mentioned in the present charter may be the same as Osbert Salvain, canon, who occurs in a charter for Welbeck, 1154 × *c.* 1160.[2]

221 *Notification by Roger de Mowbray to Robert de Daiville, his constable of Axholme, and William de Immingham, the reeve, of his gift to the canons of Hirst of Jerelmus, son of Bared his man of 'Drac'*.　　[1138 × 1174]

Cartulary copy: B.M., Cotton MS. Vesp. E xix fo. 131*r* (old p. 323).

a Mubrai, cart.	*b Roberto*, cart.	*c Yddel*, cart.	*d Reg'*, cart.
e Littehesun, cart.	*f Gladewini*, cart.	*g pannagium*, cart.	*h* Corrected

in MS. from *Turberti*, which is reading of *Mon. Ang.*

---

[1] *E.Y.C.* vi no. 109.
[2] See *E.Y.C.* xii 99 n. 3 for the suggestion that he was canon of Radford priory.

Rogerus de Mulbr' Roberto de Davidvilla constabulario suo de Insula
et Willelmo de Himinghaga preposito et omnibus hominibus suis de
Insula salutem. Sciatis me dedisse et concessisse Deo et Sancte Dei
Genetrici Marie et canonicis de Hirst', Jerelmum filium Bared hominis
mei de Drac', liberum et quietum de meo homagio ad serviendum
predictis canonicis regularibus in tota vita sua sicut homo suus proprius
ex meo dono et concessione. Hujus doni testes sunt etc.

NOTE. The castle of Axholme (at Kinnard) was destroyed in 1174. 'Drac'' has
not been identified: it is unlikely to be Drax (Yorks., W.R.), which belonged
to the Paynel fee.

222 *Confirmation by Roger de Mowbray to Nun Monkton (Ben. nuns, Yorks.,*
W.R.), of the churches of Thorp Arch, Kirk Hammerton, Askham Richard,
and Kirkby (Hall, near Great and Little Ouseburn), and 6 carucates in
Nun Monkton and ½ carucate in Kirk Hammerton (all W.R.), given by
William de Arches and Elias de Hou.   [Dec. 1147×c. 1154]

Confirmation by king John, 28 March 1200: *Rotuli Chartarum* (Record
Comm., 1837) I i 41*b*–42*a*, from P.R.O., Charter Roll 1 Jo. (C. 53/1) m. 18.

NOTE. The gift by William and his wife Juetta de Arches was made in the
presence of Henry Murdac, archbishop of York (Dec. 1147–Oct. 1153).[1]
Roger de Mowbray's confirmation, which was probably issued before William
de Arches' death in *c.* 1154 (see no. 359 note), may have been made at the
same time as the original gift. Elias de Hou had been enfeoffed by William de
Arches in lands in Kirk Hammerton, Kirkby, Hebden, and Appletreewick,
some time between 1140 and 1147.[2]

223 *Gift by Roger de Mowbray to North Ormsby (Gilb., Lincs.) of a* mansura
of one acre in Butterwick (Axholme, Lincs.) and an allowance of turf.
                                                        [*c.* 1170×1186]

Pd., *Transcripts of Charters relating to Gilbertine Houses*, ed. F. M. Stenton
(L.R.S. xviii) p. 70 (66), from P.R.O., Exch. Mem. Roll (E. 159) no. 185,
Easter, m. xii (Ormsby series).

Testibus hiis, Nigello de Moubray, Roberto de Moubray, Radulfo de
Belvario, Ada Lovell', Willelmo camerario, Baldevino clerico, Gaufrido
Brunham, Willelmo pincerna et aliis multis clericis et laicis.

NOTE. The appearance of William *pincerna* and of Geoffrey de Burnham
suggests a date after *c.* 1170.[3]

[1] *E.Y.C.* i no. 535.   [2] Ibid. no. 534.
[3] Cf. for William *pincerna* charters no. 147, 366, 388. Cf. for Geoffrey de Burnham
nos. 224, 275, 284.

224 *Gift by Roger de Mowbray to North Ormsby of a* mansura *of one acre in Kinnard's Ferry (Axholme).* [*c.* 1170 × 1186]

> Pd., *Transcripts of Charters relating to Gilbertine Houses* p. 71 (67), from P.R.O., Exch. Mem. Roll (E. 159) no. 185, Easter, m. xii.

Hiis testibus, Willelmo Basset, Philippo de Kimba et Willelmo filio suo, Nigillo*ᵃ* de Sapertune, Waltero decano, Willelmo camerario, Roberto del Belchamp, Galfrido de Brunham, Roberto clerico et aliis multis.

> NOTE. For the date, see note to no. 223.

225 *Gift by Roger de Mowbray to Pipewell (Cist., Northants) of Elkington (Northants).* [Sept. 1143 × 1159]

> Cartulary copy: B.M., Cotton MS. Calig. A xiii fo. 39*v* (old fo. 33*v*).

[E]piscopo Cestrensi omnibusque sancte ecclesie filiis et omnibus suis hominibus tam Francis quam Anglis Rogerus de Mobrai salutem. Sciatis me dedisse et concessisse Deo et abbatie Sancte Marie de Pip' Idindun et omnia illi adjacentia in plano et bosco in elemosinam puram et quietam pro salute anime mee et pro anima patris mei et matris mee et pro animabus omnium fidelium. Testes sunt, Robertus, etc.

> NOTE. Pipewell was founded 13 Sept. 1143. The grange of Elkington was confirmed by Henry II, before 1159.[1] Elkington belonged to the fee of Welford, held by the Wyville family.[2]

226 *Confirmation by Roger de Mowbray to Pipewell of Long Lawford and Thurnmill (in Little Lawford, Warwicks.), given by Robert de Stuteville.* [1159]

> Cartulary copy: B.M., Cotton MS. Calig. A xiii fo. 134*r* (old fo. 123*r*).

[R]ogerus de Molbraio [.]*ᵇ* Cestrensi episcopo et omnibus sancte matris ecclesie filiis salutem. Notum sit vobis me concessisse et hac cartula mea confirmasse donationem quam Robertus de Stutevilla fecit Deo et Sancte Marie et monachis de Pip' in perpetuam elemosinam solutam*ᶜ* liberam et ab omni terreno servicio quietam, scilicet villam de Lallef' et quicquid ei pertinet de feudo Roberti de Stutevilla et Tirnemolend'. Hiis t(estibus).

> NOTE. Robert de Stuteville's gift is said to have been made in 1159, in a confirmation charter by Robert's brother John, which is addressed to Walter Durdent, bishop of Coventry (Oct. 1149–Dec. 1159), and must be of the same

---

ᵃ Sic.   *ᵇ Space left for initial.*   *ᶜ solam, MS.*

[1] *C.Ch.R.* i 207.
[2] Cf. Northants Survey in *V.C.H. Northants.* i 379; below, Fees [21].

date.¹ Roger de Mowbray's confirmation probably belongs to the same year, and certainly precedes by some years his confirmation of Apr. 1161 × Jan. 1182 (no. 227).

227 *Notification by Roger de Mowbray to Richard (Pecche), bishop of Coventry (1161–82), of his confirmation to Pipewell of land in Long Lawford, Thurnmill, Newbold on Avon, and Cosford (Warwicks.), given by Robert de Stuteville.* [Apr. 1161 × Jan. 1182]

> Transcript, from an original charter formerly in the Court of Augmentations: Bodl., MS. Dodsworth 63 fo. 87r.

Ricardo episcopo Cestrensi Rogerus de Molbraio salutem. Notum sit vobis nos concessisse et presenti cartula nostra confirmasse Deo et monachis in Pippewell' donationem quam Robertus de Stutevilla monachis de Pipp' fecit in Longa Lallford', Thirnlend, et Neubold, Cosford vel alibi de feudo nostro, ex dono dicti Roberti vel aliorum quorumcunque donatorum suorum in elemosinam puram liberam et ab omni seculari servicio quietam et solutam. Hii sunt testes,ᵃ Siwardus et Matheus capellanus, magister Reginaldus Arundell, Walterus Bidun, Hugo de Rampania et alii.

> NOTE. The charter invites comparison with John de Stuteville's charter, *E.Y.C.* ix no. 62. Robert de Stuteville's charter is B.M., Cotton MS. Calig. A xiii fo. 130v.

228 *Confirmation by Roger de Mowbray to Pipewell of lands in Cold Ashby and Elkington (Northants).*

> Forged original charter: P.R.O., E. 326/8438.

Episcopo Linc' et omnibus sancte matris ecclesie filiis presentibus et futuris et omnibus hominibus meis tam Francis quam Anglicis . Rog-(erus) de Molbraio salutem. Notum sit vobis omnibus me concessisse et presenti carta mea confirmasse et pro me et heredibus meis quietum clamasse Deo et monachis Sancte Marie de Pipewell' omnes terras et omnia ten(ementa) et quicquid habent tam in bosco quam in plano de feodo meo in Coldesseby et in Eltindona et in territoriis earumdem villarum et quicquid ibi vel alibi de feodo meo ex dono cuiuscunque Christiani vel Judei rationabiliter habere poterunt . in elemosinam perpetuam . liberam . puram et ab omnibus terrenis seruiciis

---

ᵃ The witnesses are then given in the ablative case in MS.

---

¹ B.M., Cotton MS. Calig. A xiii fos. 130v–131r; also B.M., Stowe MS. 937 fo. 38v. Cf. *C.Ch.R.* i 207, and *E.Y.C.* ix no. 62.

consuetudinibus sectis cur(iarum) seu rebus cunctis ad me vel heredes meos qualitercunque spectantibus quietam et solutam in perpetuum pro salute anime mee patris mei matris mee et omnium fidelium vt in pace requiescant . Amen. Hiis testibus Roberto de Daiuilla . Rogero de Flameuuilla . Hascullo de Venucio . Henr(ico) de Rumissi Baldrico de Buchy Gundrea matre mea Aelizia uxore mea cum multis aliis.

Endorsement: *Rogeri Moubray.*

Size: 10·5 × 8·6 cm.

Seal: missing; was appended on tag.

Script: hand cannot be earlier than 1250, and probably nearer 1300.

> NOTE. This charter is probably based on a genuine confirmation (cf. no. 225). The third, fourth, and fifth witnesses do not occur in twelfth-century charters. The last two witnesses were probably added to lend credibility to the fabrication.

229 *Gift by Alice de Gant to Pontefract (Clun., Yorks., W.R.) of one carucate in Ingoldmells (Lincs.), for the soul of Ilbert de Lacy her first husband, which Henry de Lacy confirmed.* [1142 × 1154]

> Pd., *E.Y.C.* iii no. 1494, from B.M., Add. MS. 50754 fo. 74r (old fo. 67r) (then at Woolley Hall). Also pd., *Mon. Ang.* v 125 (XII); *Chart. of Pontefract*, ed. R. Holmes (Y.R.S. xxv, xxx) ii no. 409.

Hujus donationis testes sunt, Willelmus filius Walteri de Wella, Salomon filius ejus, Gocelinus de Aufort, Ricardus de Smydetona, Rannulfus frater ejus, Willelmus pistor monachorum, Rainaldus filius Anketilli de Dardingtona.

> NOTE. Alice de Gant married Roger de Mowbray in 1142 or 1143. The gift and Roger's confirmation were mentioned in archbishop Theobald of Canterbury's confirmation charter, of 1153 × 1154.[1] Four of the witnesses to Henry de Lacy's charter[2] appear at Thirsk in c. 1145 (above, no. 177).

230 *Confirmation by Roger de Mowbray to Pontefract of one carucate in Ingoldmells, given by Alice de Gant.* [1142 × 1154]

> Cartulary copy: B.M., Add. MS. 50754 fo. 74r (old fo. 67r).
> Pd., *Mon. Ang.* v 125 (XIII); *Chart. of Pontefract* ii no. 410.

Rogerius de Molbrai omnibus hominibus suis cunctisque sancte matris ecclesie fidelibus salutem. Sciatis quod confirmo et concedo monachis de Pontefr(acto) carrucatam terre in Ingoluesmeles quam uxor mea dedit eis pro salute corporum et animarum nostrarum et pro anima

---

[1] *E.Y.C.* iii no. 1475; also pd., A. Saltman, *Theobald, Archbishop of Canterbury* (1956) no. 202.　　　　[2] *E.Y.C.* iii no. 1495.

prioris domini sui Ilberti de Lasci liberam et quietam ab omnibus
serviciis sicut decet elemosinam in plano in aquis in pratis et in omnibus adjacentibus predicte terre. Hujus donationis testes sunt, Samson
capellanus ipsius Rogerii, Willelmus Peverel, Ricardus Burdet, Turgis
de Molbrai,[1] Henricus de Wasprez, Walterus de Daivilla.

NOTE. For the date, see note to no. 229.

231 *Confirmations by Roger de Mowbray to Revesby (Cist., Lincs.) of land in
Gainsborough (Lincs.), given by William de Roumare, earl of Lincoln, and
by William Tison, and quitclaim of the service of William Tison [of
Gainsborough].*   [1142 × 1161]

Record of charters: pd., *E.Y.C.* xii no. 105, from B.M., Egerton MS. 3058.

NOTE. Revesby was founded in 1142. The confirmations were probably made
before the death of William de Roumare, which occurred before 1161,
perhaps before 1159.[2]

232 *Gift by Gundreda de Gournay to Rievaulx (Cist., Yorks., N.R.) of her
demesne within specified bounds in Welburn (N.R.), with the meadow of
'Gildehusedale' and common pasture.*   [c. 1138 × c. 1143]

Pd., *E.Y.C.* ix no. 149, from B.M., Cotton MS. Julius D i fo. 38*v* (old
fo. 34*v*). Also pd. (incompletely), *Riev. Cart.* no. 56.

His testibus, Nicholao capellano, Johanne clerico de Hovincham,
Waltero de la Rivere, Rogero de Flammevile, Benedicto de Wimbeltun,
Henrico de Maltun, Unspac de Hovincham, Gaufrido de Insula,
Willelmo de Witvile.

233 *Confirmation by Roger de Mowbray to Rievaulx of Stainton (par. Hawnby,
Yorks., N.R.), given by Stephen de Meinil.*   [1143 × 1147]

Pd., *E.Y.C.* iii no. 1843, from B.M., Cotton MS. Julius D i fos. 47*v*–48*r* (old
fos. 43*v*–44*r*). Also pd. (incompletely), *Riev. Cart.* no. 71.

His testibus, Ælredo abbate de Sancto Laurentio, Samsone de Albini,
Willelmo converso de Fontibus, Rainaldo Puehero.

NOTE. Farrer's date, 1154 × 1164, is incorrect, because Ailred was abbot of
Revesby from 1143 to 1147.[3] Stephen de Meinil's charter, *E.Y.C.* iii no. 1842,
must also be dated accordingly. Stainton was part of the Malebisse fee.[4]

---

[1] Turgis de Mowbray does not appear elsewhere. Perhaps this is an error for 'Turgis
filius Malgeri'.
[2] See *Complete Peerage* vii 669 and n.
[3] See *Life of Ailred of Rievaulx by Walter Daniel*, ed. F. M. Powicke (1950) pp.
lxi–ii, lxix, xci.   [4] See *E.Y.C.* iii no. 1845, and Fees [23].

234 *Confirmation by Roger de Mowbray to Rievaulx of land in Wombleton (Yorks., N.R.), given by Benedict son of Gervase.* [1145 × c. 1152]

> Pd., *E.Y.C.* ix no. 146, from B.M., Cotton MS. Julius D i fo. 43r (old fo. 39r). Also pd. (incompletely), *Riev. Cart.* no. 63.

His testibus, Waltero de la Rivere, Rogero de Flammevile, Radulfo Beler, Rogero de Cundi.

> NOTE. For Benedict son of Gervase's charter, with boundaries, see *E.Y.C.* ix no. 145. Benedict was perhaps Benedict of Wombleton, who witnessed no. 232 above.

235 *Gift by Gundreda de Gournay to Rievaulx of her cultivated land in demesne in Skiplam and land which she and her son had within specified bounds between Welburn, Wombleton, and Fadmoor (all Yorks., N.R.), reserving to her and her men of Welburn common of pasture and facilities; and confirmation of any gifts, sales, or exchanges made by her men of Welburn.* [1144 × 1154]

> Pd., *E.Y.C.* ix no. 150, from B.M., Cotton MS. Julius D i fo. 38r (old fo. 34r). Also pd. (incompletely), *Riev. Cart.* no. 55.

His testibus, Nicholao capellano, Waltero presbitero, Engelram presbitero ejusdem ville,[1] Gerardo de Limesia, Henrico [de] Rumelli, Arnaldo de Vilers, Samson[e de] Cornwalia, Radulfo et Waltero fratribus Engelrami presbiteri, Willelmo camerario filio Aluredi, Ricardo filio Suani, Jacobo clerico, Ricardo pistore, Robba, Stir.

236 *Gift by Roger de Mowbray to Rievaulx, for the souls of his father Nigel and his mother Gundreda, with the consent of his heirs Nigel and Robert, of Welburn within specified bounds, as his men had perambulated them in his presence.* [1154]

> Pd., *E.Y.C.* ix no. 151, from B.M., Cotton MS. Julius D i fos. 38v (old fo. 34v), 41r (old fo. 37r) (two versions). Also pd. (incompletely), *Riev. Cart.* nos. 57, 60.

His testibus, domino Rogerio Eborac(ensi) archiepiscopo, Roberto decano, Johanne thesaurario, Radulfo archidiacono, Roberto archidiacono, Thoma de Rainevilla, Nicholao de Treili, Geroldo filio Serl(onis), Serlone fratre ejus, Symone de Sigillo, Johanne filio Letholdi, Thoma filio Paul(ini), Thoma Sottavag(ina), Arnulfo Sottavag(ina), Osberto Arundel, Gilberto filio Fulchonis, Theobaldo clerico domini episcopi Dunelm(ensis), Roberto capellano, Rogero abbate de Beilanda, Augustino priore de Noveb(urgo), Willelmo de Widevilla, Roberto de

[1] i.e. Welburn.

Daivilla, Rogero de Flammevilla, Hugone Malebestia, Waltero de la
Rivere, Radulfo Beler, Petro de Tresc, Roberto de Busci, Rolando de
Land(eles), Philippo de Logi, Hamundo Beler, Willelmo de Steinegrif,
Waltero de Karlet(on), Arnaldo de Vilers, Alano de Flamevilla.

NOTE. A royal confirmation and *inspeximus* of 1327, Patent Roll 1 Edw. III
pt. ii (P.R.O., C. 66/167) m. 8, printed *Riev. Cart.* pp. 413–14,[1] has an almost
identical text, and the following witnesses: Robert the dean, John the
treasurer, Ralph the archdeacon, John son of Letold, Nicholas de Trailli,
Osbert Arundel, Roger abbot of Byland, Augustine prior of Newburgh,
William de Wyville, Robert the chaplain, Robert de Daiville, Roger de
Flamville, Hugh Malebisse, Thomas de Coleville, Oliver de Busci, Robert
de Busci. See Sir Charles Clay's notes to *E. Y.C.* ix no. 151. For a perambulation of the neighbouring vill, 'Hoveton', see below, no. 243.

The property disposed of in this charter, Welburn, had belonged to the
dowry of Gundreda de Gournay (above, nos. 232, 235), who last occurs in
1147.[2] The fact that her rights are not mentioned may well suggest that she
had died by the time of the charter's issue, and this seems to be confirmed by
the terms of no. 237. In this connection, the reference to Gundreda under
1155 in the Byland chronicle,[3] cited by Sir Charles Clay in his note to the
present charter, cannot be used to show that Gundreda was still alive, as
the chronicler simply states that Roger de Mowbray confirmed her gifts to
Byland in that year.

237 *Gift by Roger de Mowbray to Rievaulx of Welburn, including the culture
on the other side of the river towards 'Hoveton',[4] which his father and afterwards his mother held in demesne.*　　[1154]

Notification by Robert the dean and the chapter of York of this gift made in
their presence, pd., *E. Y.C.* ix no. 153, from B.M., Cotton MS. Julius D i
fo. 158r (old fo. 141/2). Also pd. (incompletely), *Riev. Cart.* no. 229.

Hujus donationis testes sunt, Robertus decanus, Johannes thesaurarius,
Robertus archidiaconus, Radulfus archidiaconus, Sym(on) de Sigillo,
Nicholaus de Trelli, Thomas de Reinevill', Geroldus, Serlo, Nicholaus
filius Durandi, Arnulfus Sottawag(ina), Achardus filiusA lani, Gillebertus filius Fulconis, Thomas filius Paul(ini), Stephanus de Arraz
canonici, Thomas Sottawag(ina), Paul(inus), Osbertus Arundel, Alexander, Normannus, Ketel presbiteri, Willelmus de Wituill' dapifer
Rogeri, Rogerus de Cond(i), Radulfus Beler, Alanus de Flammeuill'.

NOTE. This charter was almost certainly issued at the same time as no. 236,
although the culture mentioned in this notification (and in another notification
by archbishop Roger)[5] is not mentioned in no. 236. For another gift in the
presence of the chapter of York at this period, see no. 243.

---

[1] Briefly noticed, *C.P.R. 1327–30* p. 134.　　[2] Byland chron., *Mon. Ang.* v 352a.
[3] Ibid. p. 353b.　　[4] See below, no. 287 note.
[5] *Riev. Cart.* no. 223.

238 *Gift by Roger de Mowbray to Rievaulx of two woodlands, namely Middle-head in Farndale and Dowthwaite, and common pasture of the valley of Farndale (Yorks., N.R.), saving the wild game.* [1138×c. 1155]

> Pd., *E.Y.C.* ix no. 114, from B.M., Cotton MS. Julius D i fo. 42v (old fo. 38v). Also pd. (incompletely), *Riev. Cart.* no. 62.

Teste, Samsone de Alb(ineio) et Petro de Tresc, Ricardo clerico de Mal(tun) et Gil(leberto) filio Petri, et Anschetillo ostrar(io) et Waltero Parar' et Ricardo des Escal(ers) et Johanne scriptore et Waltero de la Rivere, Reinaldo le Poer.

239 *Confirmation by Roger de Mowbray to Rievaulx of land near Murton (par. Hawnby, Yorks., N.R.), given by William I de Stuteville.* [1138×1157]

> Reference in a charter of William I de Stuteville [×1157]: pd., *E.Y.C.* ix no. 19, from B.M., Cotton MS. Julius D i fo. 57v (old fo. 53v). Also pd. (incompletely), *Riev. Cart.* no. 89.
>
> NOTE. For the date, see *E.Y.C.* ix 100. This charter may show that the Stuteville enfeoffment (below, no. 386) had already taken place.

240 *Confirmation by Roger de Mowbray to Rievaulx of common pasture near Arden (Yorks., N.R.), given by Peter of Thirsk.*

[1142×1157, probably 1154]

> Cartulary copy: B.M., Cotton MS. Julius D i fo. 40r–v (old fo. 36r–v). Pd. (incompletely), *Riev. Cart.* no. 58.

Omnibus sancte matris ecclesie filiis Rogerus de Molbrai salutem. Sciatis me concessisse et presenti carta confirmasse donationem Petri de Tresc quam ipse in presencia mea fecit Deo et ecclesie Sancte Marie Rievall(is) et monachis ibidem Deo servientibus in elemosinam perpetuam, scilicet communem pasturam more sue et bosci sui quam ipse Petrus habet inter villam suam Hardenie et grangiam monachorum de Hesteskeid, ita scilicet quod monachi singulis annis dabunt Petro et heredibus suis dimidiam marcam argenti ad Pentecosten pro omnibus rebus et consuetudinibus et interrogatis. Ego vero et heredes mei petitione ipsius Petri hanc donationem monachis contra omnes homines warantizabimus et adquietabimus. Quare volo et firmiter precipio ut monachi predictam pasturam bene et in pace libere et quiete plenarie et integre teneant et habeant in elemosinam perpetuam. His testibus, Augustino priore de Neuburc, Roberto magistro de hospitali Eboraci, Samsone de Albeni, Rogero de Cundi, Rogero de Flammevilla, Radulfo Beler, Waltero de Larivere, Waltero de Cartona, Radulfo de Belun,

Willelmo filio Egkeler, Roberto Beler, Alano de Flammevilla, Bald(wino) clerico.

NOTE. Although Peter of Thirsk's gift is said to have been made in 1158,[1] the outside limits of date are given by the occurrence of Augustine, prior of Newburgh.[2] Augustine and five others of these witnesses also appear in 1154, no. 236. Peter of Thirsk's last occurrence is 1154 (see no. 44 note). The land was presumably a subtenancy of Malebisse.[3]

241 *Agreement made by Roger de Mowbray with the monks of Rievaulx, that he will acquit Stainton to them and concede seisin of the vill to no man, except of 2 marks rent p.a. which the monks owe him.*

[1142 × 1157, probably 1154]

Pd., *E.Y.C.* iii no. 1844, from B.M., Cotton MS. Julius D i fo. 47v (old fo. 43v). Also pd. (incompletely), *Riev. Cart.* no. 70.

His testibus, Rogero abbate de Belanda, Augustino priore de Novoburgo, Roberto clerico, Radulfo Beler, Radulfo de Beelun, Roberto de Busci, Philippo de Luzi, Petro de Tresc.

NOTE. Farrer's date, 1150 × 1165, must be incorrect, because Augustine, prior of Newburgh, held office between 1142 and 1157.[4] Six of these eight witnesses also appear in 1154, no. 236. For an earlier confirmation of Stainton, see no. 233. At the time of Domesday Book, Robert Malet held 2 carucates in Stainton.

242 *Grant by Roger de Mowbray to Rievaulx of all his* rustici *of Welburn* (*Yorks., N.R.*), *giving them liberty to move and settle elsewhere.*

[1154 × 1157]

Pd., *E.Y.C.* ix no. 152, from B.M., Cotton MS. Julius D i fo. 43r (old fo. 39r). Also pd. (incompletely), *Riev. Cart.* no. 64.

Teste, Willelmo de Wivilla, Rogero de Flammevilla, Radulfo Beler, Hugone Mala bissa, Waltero Buherie, Roberto capellano, Roberto de Daiewilla, Radulfo de Bethlun.

243 *Gift (or confirmation) by Roger de Mowbray to Rievaulx of all 'Hoveton'* (*Yorks., N.R.*)[5] *within specified bounds, as his men had perambulated them in his presence; rendering 2 marks of silver p.a. at Michaelmas to Robert Beler and his heirs.*

[1154 × 1157]

Pd., *E.Y.C.* ix no. 125, from B.M., Cotton MS. Julius D i fo. 44v (old fo. 40v). Also pd. (incompletely), *Riev. Cart.* no. 66.

---

[1] *Riev. Cart.* p. 261.   [2] See *E.Y.C.* ix 248.   [3] See Fees [23].
[4] See *E.Y.C.* ix 248.   [5] See below, no. 287 note.

Hujus donationis et conventionis ego et Nigellus filius meus capitulum Eborac(ense) et ipsam ecclesiam Eborac(ensem) horum omnium testem et fidejussorem inter nos et domum Rievall(ensem) constituimus . . . His testibus, Turstino de Munford, Willelmo de Widevilla, Rogero de Flamevilla, Roberto de Daivilla, Waltero Bueri, Hugone Malab(isse), Rogero de Cundi, Olivero de Busci, Radulfo de Busci, Hamundo Beler, Roberto Beler, Waltero de Karlet(un), Waltero de la Rivere, Radulfo de Bethlum, Adam Luvel.

NOTE. At the time of Domesday Book, Hugh Fitz Baldric held 2 carucates in 'Hoveton'.

244 *Confirmation by Roger de Mowbray to Rievaulx of the meadow in the terri-tory of Scawton called Oswaldeshenge (Yorks., N.R.), given by Hugh Malebisse.* [c. 1160 × c. 1165]

Cartulary copy: B.M., Cotton MS. Julius D i fo. 108r–v (old fo. 101r–v). Pd. (incompletely), *Riev. Cart.* no. 156.

Rogerus de Molbrai omnibus sancte matris ecclesie filiis salutem. Sciatis me concessisse donationem Hugonis Malebestie de prato quod dicitur Hoswald Henge in territorio de Scaltuna et hac presenti carta mea confirmasse domui Rievall(ensi) et fratribus ibidem Deo servien-tibus prout carta prenominati Hugonis de predicta donatione testatur. T(estibus), Ricardo priore de Novo Burgo, Rainero canonico, Rogero de Cundi, Nicholao capellano, Ricardo sacerdote, Hugone capellano, Rolando Haget, Hamone de Beler, Roberto de Molbrai.

NOTE. The Rievaulx cartulary places Malebisse's gift after 1160 and before the abbacy of Silvan, which began in 1167.[1] Rolland Haget, one of the wit-nesses to this charter, probably died before 1166, being succeeded by his brother William.[2] Hugh Malebisse's charter is found in *Riev. Cart.* no. 74,[3] and from its attestation by John the treasurer of York must be dated 1154 × 1162.

245 *Acquittance by Roger de Mowbray to Rievaulx of their bounds of Welburn against Robert de Daiville, who issued a quitclaim in his presence by reason of the exchange which he (Roger) had given him.* [c. 1160 × 1165]

Pd., *E.Y.C.* ix no. 155, from B.M., Cotton MS. Julius D i fo. 108r (old fo. 100r). Also pd. (incompletely), *Riev. Cart.* no. 155.

His testibus, magistro Suano, priore de Noburc,[4] Roberto capellano, Roberto [de] Daivilla, Waltero Buhuri, Nigello filio domini, Roberto

---

[1] *Riev. Cart.* p. 261.
[3] For the Malebisse fee, see charter no. 371 and Fees [23].
[2] Charter no. 401.
[4] Richard.

fratre ejus, Radulfo de Bellun, Olivero de Buthci, Roberto de Crevequer, Waltero de Carletun, Hugone Malebisse.

NOTE. Both Oliver de Buscy and Walter of Carlton were probably dead by 1166 (nos. 23, 352–4 notes). This charter and Robert de Daiville's confirmation of the bounds are referred to by tenants of Daiville, *E.Y.C.* ix nos. 140, 141. In 1166 Robert de Daiville held 4 old fees and one new.[1] For quitclaims in Welburn by two other Mowbray tenants at the same period, see ibid. nos. 161, 162.[2]

246 *Gift by Roger de Mowbray to Rievaulx of Welburn and 'Hoveton', except the church of Welburn with 6 bovates of land which belonged to it; and undertaking not to assist anyone in the exaction of the tithes of those places.* [1154 × 1166]

Pd., *E.Y.C.* ix no. 154, from B.M., Cotton MS. Julius D i fo. 107*v* (old fo. 100*v*). Also pd. (incompletely), *Riev. Cart.* no. 154.

His testibus, Roberto capellano, Hugone Malebisse, Roberto de Bellocampo, Radulfo Chinun, Petro clerico.

247 *Notification by Roger de Mowbray of the settlement made before him in his court of the dispute between Alan de Ryedale and the convent of Rievaulx, after a wager of battle, about the moor lying between Welburn and Bowforth and extending to Cowldyke, being common to the three vills of Welburn, 'Hoveton', and Bowforth (all Yorks., N.R.).* [c. 1160 × 1169]

Pd., *E.Y.C.* ix no. 157, from B.M., Cotton MS. Julius D i fo. 106*r* (old fo. 99*r*). Also pd. (incompletely), *Riev. Cart.* no. 153.

His testibus de ministris regis a vicecomite missis, David lardener regis, Gaufrido Fossard, Odone de Neus(um), Willelmo Dod, Ivone de Bolthebi; de vicinis nostris, Richero de Walesanth et Willelmo fratre ejus, Jukelo de Alvert(un), Petro de Surdeval, Willelmo de Magnebi, Roberto de Sproxt(un), Symone de Steinegrif et Henrico fratre ejus; de curia mea, Roberto capellano, Nigello et Roberto filiis meis, Roberto de Daivilla, Hugone Malab(isse), Radulfo de Bavvair et Roberto fratre ejus, Thoma de Colev(illa), Roberto de Busci, Nicholao de Bellun, et multis aliis.

[1] No. 401 and Fees [24], [38]. [2] Cf. also *E.Y.C.* i no. 164.

248 *Notification by Roger de Mowbray of his perambulation of the moor before Bowforth and of the testimony of his neighbours and barons that the moor was common pasture for Welburn, 'Hoveton', and Bowforth, which common of pasture he had given to Rievaulx, forbidding Alan de Ryedale to disturb the monks therein, with the assent of Nigel and Robert his sons.*

[*c.* 1160 × 1169]

> Pd., *E.Y.C.* ix no. 158, from B.M., Cotton MS. Julius D i fo. 42*r* (old fo. 38*r*). Also pd. (incompletely), *Riev. Cart.* no. 61.

His testibus, Eng(elram) presbitero de Wellebr(una), Willelmo clerico de Kirkebi, Rogero de Flamvilla, Hugone Malebestie, Waltero de Karletun'.

> NOTE. If the last witness was the same man as the father of Roger of Carlton, he probably died by 1166 (nos. 352–4 notes).

249 *Confirmation by Roger de Mowbray to Rievaulx of all 'Hoveton' within specified bounds, and gift of 4 bovates which Samson of Cornwall had held there of the gift of the grantor's mother, and which the grantor had purchased for 20 marks from Samson and his wife, who made an affidation in the hand of Ralph de Belvoir, the grantor's steward, in the presence of the whole court, and then in the hand of Ranulf de Glanville the sheriff, afterwards acknowledging their affidation in the chapter of St. Peter's, York.*

[1163 × 1169]

> Pd., *E.Y.C.* ix no. 126, from B.M., Cotton MS. Julius D i fo. 45*r* (old fo. 41*r*). Also pd. (incompletely), *Riev. Cart.* no. 67.

His testibus, Roberto capellano, Rannulfo de Glanvile vicecomite, Willelmo [de] Albervilla, Roberto de Daivilla, Hugone Maleb(isse), Rogero de Flammev(illa), Ricardo de Widev(illa), Thoma de Colev(illa), David larder(er), Thoma filio ejus, Radulfo de Belveer, Roberto fratre ejus, Roberto de Busci, Adam Luvel, Ham(undo) Beler, Roberto Beler, Jordano le Envaise, Nicholao de Bethlum, Gaufrido de Stultav(illa), Gerardo de Glanvila, Rogero [de] Bavent, Baldrico clerico.

250 *Similar confirmation by Nigel de Mowbray to Rievaulx.*   [1163 × 1169]

> Cartulary copy: B.M., Cotton MS. Julius D i fos. 46*v*–47*r* (old fos. 42*v*–43*r*). Pd. (incompletely), *Riev. Cart.* no. 68.

Omnibus sancte matris ecclesie filiis Nigellus de Molbrai salutem. Sciatis quod quatuor bovatas terre cum pertinenciis suis quas Samson de Cornuwala tenuit in Hovet' pater meus propria pecunia sua id est xx marcis argenti ab ipso Samsone et uxore ejus emit. Et ipsi in curia patris mei nobis eas quietas clamaverunt pro summa predicte pecunie sine reclamatione et calumpnia in posterum de se et heredibus suis et hoc propria manu sua affidaverunt in manu Radulfi de Belveer coram multis testibus sine malo ingenio se servaturos imperpetuum ac postea eandem affidationem in capitulo Sancti Petri Ebor(aci) et coram Rannullo^a vice-comite recognoverunt quod scilicet numquam de terra predicta reclama-tionem vel calumpniam nec per se nec per alium quemlibet facient. Hanc terram cum emisset pater meus et in manu sua quietam et sine alicujus calumpnia tenuisset monachis Rievall(ensibus) cum tota reliqua terra de Hovet' in perpetuam elemosinam dedit et carta sua confirma-vit. Hec omnia sicut pater meus Rogerus de Molbrai predictis monachis dedit et carta sua confirmavit ego similiter eis concessi et presenti carta mea confirmavi libera et quieta ab omnibus consuetudinibus et auxiliis et assisis et omni terreno servicio nisi quod Roberto Beler tamen duas marcas argenti pro omni servicio terreno annuatim persolvent. Quod si de hac elemosina mea predictus Samson vel uxor ejus vel aliquis alius amodo calumpniam fecerit temporibus meis vel temporibus heredum meorum nos inter eos et omnes homines erimus et adquietabimus et warantizabimus eis hec omnia in puram et perpetuam elemosinam. His t(estibus), Rogero abbate de Bellelanda, Waltero priore ejusdem loci, Landrico cellarario, Roberto capellano, Roberto de Daivilla, Rogero de Flamavilla, Hugone Malebissa, Radulfo Belveer, Roberto fratre suo, Roberto de Busci, Balduino clerico.

NOTE. Seven of these witnesses appear also in Roger's gift, no. 249.

251 *Confirmation by Nigel de Mowbray to Rievaulx of 'Hoveton', within specified bounds, given by Roger de Mowbray.* [1163 × 1169]

> Cartulary copy: B.M., Cotton MS. Julius D i fos. 108v–109r (old fos. 101v–102r).
> Pd. (incompletely), *Riev. Cart.* no. 157.

Omnibus sancte ecclesie filiis Nigellus de Molbrai salutem. Sciatis me concessisse et presenti carta confirmasse Deo et ecclesie Sancte Marie Rievall(is) et monachis ibidem Deo servientibus sicut pater meus eis dederat et carta sua confirmaverat totam Hovetonam in bosco et plano et pratis^b et aquis et pascuis et divisis sicut via que vocatur Meregate jacet inter boscum de Kirkebi et de Hovet' et vadit usque ad Watermor et illinc sicut recte divise vadunt inter boscum de Faddemor et boscum de Hovet' usque ad Hallewad et similiter per omnes divisas quas melius et plenius habuit tempore Henrici regis liberam et quietam ab omni

---

^a *Sic.*   ^b *patris,* MS.

terreno servicio et seculari exactione in perpetuam elemosinam . . .^a predicti monachi pro omnibus consuetudinibus persolvent. Ipse etiam Robertus Beler me presente et annuente hanc predictam terram similiter ut ego liberam et quietam in perpetuam elemosinam voluntate spontanea predictis monachis dedit et concessit. Excepto quod duas marcas argenti Robertus et heredes sui a predictis monachis annuatim recipient. Ego quidem et heredes mei totum servicium quod Robertus et heredes sui pro eadem terra facere debebant Deo et ecclesie Rievall(ensi) quietum in perpetuum clamamus et istam terram et predictam conventionem monachis de Rievalle inperpetuum contra omnes homines warantizabimus et adquietabimus. His testibus, Roberto capellano, Rogero de Flamevilla, Roberto de Daivilla, Hugone Malebisse, Roberto de Belvair, Roberto de Busci, Roberto Beler, Willelmo de Tikehil, Baldewino clerico.

NOTE. Seven of these witnesses appear also in no. 249. For Roger de Mowbray's gift, see above, no. 243.

252 *Confirmation by Nigel de Mowbray to Rievaulx of Welburn, within specified bounds, as perambulated by Roger de Mowbray's men and given by him.* [1163 × 1169]

Cartulary copy: B.M., Cotton MS. Julius D i fos. 43*v*–44*v* (old fos. 39*v*–40*v*). Pd. (incompletely), *Riev. Cart.* no. 65.

Omnibus sancte matris ecclesie filiis Nigellus de Molbrai salutem. Sciatis me concessisse et presenti carta mea confirmasse Deo et ecclesie Sancte Marie Rievall(is) et monachis ibidem Deo servientibus pro anima patris mei Rogeri et matris mee et omnium antecessorum meorum in perpetuam elemosinam donationem ejusdem patris mei scilicet Welleburnam cum omnibus pertinenciis suis in bosco et plano et marescho et pratis et aquis et pasturis cum viis et semitis et divisis que subter nominantur: ab occidente scilicet de Wellebr' sicut Fragate vadit subtus Lund usque in viam de Wimbelt' et inde sicut ipsa via vadit inter boscum de Wimbelt' et Lund usque ad Tunge et inde sicut divise inter Wimbelt' et Wellebr' tendunt usque ad Mapelbusch et Loccu' et Slectes et ita sicut divise tendunt usque ad Langaran et inde usque ad Apalgard ad divisas de Cliveland et Midelhovet; ex orientali parte de Wellebr' est divisa sicut Redover descendit de Blawat unde oritur ab orientali parte de Midelhovet usque ad Hallewat et a Blawat item usque ad divisas de Cliveland; ex parte meridiana sicut via vadit inter Wimbelt' et Wellebr' usque Midelhirst et ab australi parte de Midelhirst sicut vallis dividit inter certam terram et marescum usque Stodfald' et inde recta

^a One and a half lines erased in MS.

linea versus Holm usque in Holebec et communem pasturam more que jacet ante Buleford' que est communis his tribus villis Wellebr' Hovet' Buleford usque ad Coldic. Has divisas homines patris mei ipso presente perambulaverunt et juramento recognoverunt eas esse rectas divisas inter Wellebr' et villas que circa eam sunt. Hec omnia concedo et confirmo eis libera et quieta ab omnibus consuetudinibus et auxiliis et geldis et assisis et omni terreno servicio. Quod si de hac elemosina patris mei et mea vel divisis predictis eis aliquis amodo calumpniam fecerit temporibus meis vel temporibus heredum meorum vel etiam per placitum dirationaverit ego et heredes mei inter eos et omnes homines erimus et adquietabimus et warantizabimus eis hec omnia in puram et perpetuam elemosinam . . .*a* ita ut libera semper et integra hec elemosina nostra remaneat domui Rievall(ensi) inperpetuum. Hanc donationem et conventionem ego manu mea affidavi tenendam in manu Roberti decani sub presencia domini Rogeri archiepiscopi et totius capituli Eboraci et ipsam ecclesiam Eboracensem horum omnium testem et fidejussorem inter me et monachos constitui ita ut si aliquando ego vel heredes mei ab hac conventione deviaverimus ipsa ecclesia ad hec exequenda nos ecclesiastica revocet disciplina. His testibus, Rogero abbate de Bellalanda, Waltero priore ejusdem loci, Ricardo priore de Novoburgo, Landrico cellarario, Roberto capellano, Roberto de Daivilla, Rogero de Flamv', Radulfo de Belveer, Roberto fratre suo, Roberto de Busci, Rogero Barr', Waltero de la Rivere, Roberto Belchamp, Willelmo de Tikahill, Roberto camerario, Baldewino clerico.

NOTE. Cf. witnesses to nos. 249–51. For Roger de Mowbray's gift, see above, no. 236.

253 *Confirmation by Roger de Mowbray to Rufford (Cist., Notts.) of land in Averham (Notts.), given by William Tison.* [July 1146 × Nov. 1156]

Pd., *E.Y.C.* xii no. 111, from B.M., MSS. Loans no. 41 fos. 36*v*–37*r*.

Hiis testibus, Landrico monacho, Josberto canonico de Chenilwurt, Hugone Malebisse, Alano de Flammavilla, Waltero de Larivere, Petro de Surdesvals, Willelmo fratre ejus, Rogero de Condi, Willelmo de Crocheslai, Radulfo Carbun, Symone de Sancto Clero, Willelmo monacho de Rievalle.

NOTE. The gift made by William and Adam Tison, almost certainly in Averham, was confirmed to Rufford by pope Adrian IV, 8 Nov. 1156.[1] This

---

a Almost a whole line erased in MS.

---

[1] *P.U.E.* i no. 62.

confirmation was probably made at the same time as Adam Tison's.[1] The only other Mowbray charter attested by Simon de Sancto Claro, no. 303, where Roger de Cundy and William de Crocheslai also appear, probably belongs to *c.* 1154 × 1157.

254 *Notification by Roger de Mowbray to Leising and Chetell and his men of Acaster (Selby) (Yorks., W.R.) of his gift to Selby (Ben., Yorks., W.R.) of the land of Acaster.*   [1143 × 1153]

Cartulary copy: B.M., Add. MS. 37771 fo. 104r (old fo. 103r).
Pd., *Selby Coucher* i no. 557.

Rogerus de Moubray Leising' et Chetell' et omnibus hominibus de Acastra salutem. Sciatis me dedisse et concessisse Deo et Sancte Marie et Sancto Germano et E. abbati et monachis de Seleby terram de Acastra totam de feudo meo liberam et quietam in perpetuam elemosinam sic quod pro nullo disseisiantur. Et si aliquis eos disseisiaverit ego ipse resaisio eos per hoc breve meum et latorem brevis.

> NOTE. Elias Paynel was abbot of Selby from 1143 to 1153.[2] Acaster had been given by Osbert the sheriff before 1129.[3] Mowbray's confirmation is mentioned in a charter of king Stephen, 1154.[4] For gifts by Nigel d'Aubigny to Selby, see nos. 1-3, 9.

255 *Gift by R(oger) de Mowbray to Selby of his manor of Middlethorpe (Yorks., W.R.), in satisfaction for losses he inflicted on the church; and promise to give an exchange when he shall recover custody of the castle of York.*

                                                            [? 1143 × 1153]

Cartulary copy: B.M., Add. MS. 37771 fo. 108r (old fo. 107r).
Pd., *Selby Coucher* i no. 582.

R. de Moubray omnibus sancte ecclesie filiis et omnibus hominibus suis tam Francis quam Anglis salutem. Notum sit omnibus vobis me dedisse et concessisse Deo et ecclesie Sancti Germani de Seleby et monachis ibidem Deo servientibus quoddam manerium meum juxta Ebor(acum) nomine Thorp cum omnibus pertinenciis suis in puram elemosinam liberam et quietam ab omni seculari servicio pro anima mea et animabus antecessorum meorum et pro malefactis et dampnis que intuli predicte ecclesie ita ut monachi prefati suam voluntatem de predicto manerio quodcunque maluerint faciant. Ea tamen conventione ut quando recuperabo custodiam castelli Ebor(aci) dabo eisdem monachis excambium

---

[1] *E.Y.C.* xii no. 110; William Tison's charter is ibid. no. 109.
[2] *Selby Coucher* i pp. [33]-[45].
[3] Ibid. i no. 556; cf. *Cartae Antiquae* (P.R.S., N.S. xxxiii) ii no. 455.
[4] *Regesta* iii no. 817.

ad valenciam et ad voluntatem eorum in Ebor(aci)schir'. Et postquam excambium habuerint remanebit predictum manerium in dominio meo. Monachi autem quamdiu predictum manerium in manu sua habuerint vel aliquis per illos debeo illis contra omnes homines et de rebus omnibus manerium illud warantizare. Teste, Waltero de Bueri etc.

NOTE. Perhaps this charter refers to the hostilities in the Selby area between 1143 and 1153.¹ Farrer assigned this charter to the period 1147–54 (Leeds, Yorks. Archaeol. Soc. MS. 869).² Roger de Mowbray granted the manor to Byland c. 1154 × 1175 (no. 55 above). Cf. also no. 263 below.

256 *Notification by Roger de Mowbray to William (Fitz Herbert), archbishop of York (1143–47 and 1153–54), of his restoration to Selby of the land of Acaster (Selby).* [Sept. 1143 × 1147, or Oct. 1153 × June 1154]

Cartulary copy: B.M., Add. MS. 37771 fo. 104r (old fo. 103r).
Pd., *Selby Coucher* i no. 558.

Rogerus de Moubray Willelmo gratia Dei Ebor(acensi) archiepiscopo et omnibus sancte matris ecclesie filiis salutem. Notum sit vobis omnibus me reddidisse et concessisse Deo et Sancto Germano de Seleby et monachis ibidem Deo servientibus terram de Acastra totam que de feodo meo est liberam et quietam in perpetuam elemosinam pro salute mea et pro anima patris mei et pro animabus antecessorum meorum. Test(e), Willelmo de Merlow, Willelmo de Arches etc.

257 *Gift by R(oger) de Mowbray to Selby of his part of a fishery in the River Trent, called 'Crasgarth'.* [1138 × 1177]

Cartulary copy: B.M., Add. MS. 37771 fo. 206r (old fo. 203r).
Pd., *Selby Coucher* ii no. 1198.

R. de Moubray omnibus ecclesie sancte filiis et hominibus omnibus suis tam Francis quam Anglis salutem. Notum sit omnibus vobis me dedisse et concessisse Deo et ecclesie Sancti Germani de Seleby et monachis ibidem Deo servientibus totam meam partem cujusdam piscarii in Tranta que Crasgarth vocatur pro anima mea et animabus antecessorum meorum in puram et perpetuam elemosinam liberam et quietam ab omni seculari servicio. Teste, Waltero Buere, Rogero de Cundy etc.

NOTE. Walter Buher was dead by 1177 (no. 143 note). This fishery had already been given to Selby by Nigel d'Aubigny (above, nos. 2, 3, 'Grasgard').

¹ See Wightman, *Lacy Family* pp. 76–8. ² Cf. also *Complete Peerage* ix 370 n.

258 *Gift by Roger de Mowbray to Selby of 6 bovates in 'Elvestvayth' (? nr. Ellers, Axholme, Lincs.) and 5 acres; and confirmation of Tuncroft and the crofts in Mosswood (Axholme), given by Nigel de Mowbray.*

[1160×1184]

Cartulary copy: B.M., Add. MS. 37771 fo. 204*v* (old fo. 201*v*).
Pd., *Selby Coucher* ii no. 1190.

Rogerus de Moubray omnibus sancte matris ecclesie filiis tam presentibus quam futuris salutem. Sciatis me dedisse et presenti carta mea confirmasse Deo et ecclesie Sancti Germani de Seleby et Gilberto de Ver' abbati de Seleby et monachis ibidem Deo servientibus vj bovatas terre in Elvestvayth et circa et v acras que intersunt illis bovatis quas excambiavi villanis de Beltona, scilicet totam terram quam Radulfus defendebat pro duabus bovatis et illam quam Agamundus defend(ebat) pro una bovata et unam quam Gocelinus defendebat pro una bovata et illam quam Gaufridus def(endebat) pro una bovata et illam quam Elfiat defendebat pro una bovata, et dominicos porcos suos ejusdem loci quietos a pannagio in Moswoda. Et preter hec concessi et confirmavi donationem quam Nigellus filius meus fecit eidem abbati et eidem ecclesie scilicet Tuncroft et omnes croftos qui sunt in Moswoda. Hec omnia dedi et confirmavi eis libera et quieta ab omni seculari servicio et exactione in puram et perpetuam elemosinam libere quiete et honorifice sicut liberam elemosinam cum omnibus libertatibus et liberis consuetudinibus libere elemosine pertinentibus in bosco et plano in viis et semitis in pratis et pascuis et in omnibus locis. Testibus hiis, Nigello de Moubray, Roberto de Bocy etc.

NOTE. Gilbert de Vere was abbot of Selby from 1160 to 1184.[1] Crofts of the abbot of Selby in Mosswood are mentioned in no. 276.

259 *Similar gift by Roger de Mowbray to Gilbert de Vere, abbot of Selby.*

[1160×1184]

Cartulary copy: B.M., Add. MS. 37771 fo. 204*v* (old fo. 201*v*).
Pd. (incompletely), *Selby Coucher* ii no. 1191.

Rogerus de Moubray omnibus sancte matris ecclesie filiis tam presentibus quam futuris salutem. Sciatis me dedisse et hac presenti carta confirmasse Gilberto de Ver abbati de Seleby vj bovatas terre in Elvestvait et circa et v acras que intersunt illis bovatis quas excambiavi villanis de Beltona scilicet totam terram quam Radulfus defendebat pro duabus bovatis et illam quam Agamundus defend(ebat) pro una bovata et illam quam Gocelinus defend(ebat) pro una bovata et illam quam

_____
[1] *Selby Coucher* i p. [50]; *Houeden* ii 288.

Gaufridus def(endebat) pro j bovata et illam quam Elfriad defendebat pro j bovata, et dominicos porcos suos ejusdem loci quietos a pannagio in Moswoda. Et preter hec concessi et confirmavi ei donationem quam Nigellus filius meus ei fecit scilicet Tuncroft et omnes croftos qui sunt in Moswoda. Hec omnia dedi et confirmavi ei libera et quieta ab omni seculari exactione et servicio in puram et perpetuam elemosinam libere quiete et honorifice sicut liberam elemosinam cum omnibus pertinenciis libertatibus et liberis consuetudinibus libere elemosine pertinentibus in bosco et plano in viis et semitis in pratis et pascuis et in omnibus locis. Concessi etiam predicto abbati Gilberto donare predictam terram cuicunque voluerit absque aliqua contradictione sive ecclesie sue sive alii ecclesie sive clerico sive laico et cuicunque dederit concessi et confirmavi cum supradictis libertatibus imperpetuum possidendam. Testibus hiis, Nigello de Moubray, Rogero de Bocy etc.

NOTE. For the date, see note to no. 258.

260 *Confirmation by Nigel de Mowbray to Selby of 6 bovates in 'Elvestvait' and 5 acres, given by Roger de Mowbray; and gift of Tuncroft and all crofts in Mosswood.* [1160×1184]

Cartulary copy: B.M., Add. MS. 37771 fo. 205r (old fo. 202r).
Pd. (incompletely), *Selby Coucher* ii no. 1193.

Nigellus de Moubray omnibus sancte matris ecclesie filiis tam presentibus quam futuris salutem. Sciatis me concessisse et hac presenti carta confirmasse donationem quam Rogerus de Moubray pater meus fecit Deo et ecclesie Sancti Germani de Seleby et Gilberto de Ver abbati de Seleby et monachis ibidem Deo servientibus vj bovatas terre in Elvestvait et circa et v acras que intersunt illis bovatis quas excambiavit villanis de Beltona scilicet totam terram quam Radulfus defendebat pro duabus bovatis et illam quam Agamundus defendebat pro una bovata et illam quam Gocelinus defendebat pro una bovata et illam quam Gaufridus defendebat pro j bovata et illam quam Elfuat defendebat pro j bovata et dominicos porcos suos ejusdem loci quietos a pasnagio in Moswoda. Et preter hec dedi et concessi eis de mea donatione Tuncroft et omnes croftos qui sunt in Moswoda. Hec omnia concessi et confirmavi eis libera et quieta ab omni seculari servicio et exactione in puram et perpetuam elemosinam libere quiete et honorifice sicut liberam elemosinam cum omnibus libertatibus et liberis consuetudinibus libere elemosine pertinentibus in bosco et plano in viis et semitis in pratis et pascuis et in omnibus locis. Testibus, Roberto de Boceo, Willelmo de Notingham etc.

NOTE. For the date, see note to no. 258.

261 *Similar confirmation and gift by Nigel de Mowbray to Gilbert de Vere, abbot of Selby.* [1160 × 1184]

> Cartulary copy: B.M., Add. MS. 37771 fo. 204*v* (old fo. 201*v*).
> Pd. (incompletely), *Selby Coucher* ii no. 1192.

Nigellus de Moubray omnibus sancte matris ecclesie filiis tam presentibus quam futuris salutem. Sciatis me concessisse et hac presenti carta mea confirmasse donationem quam Rogerus de Moubray pater meus fecit Gilberto de Ver' abbati de Seleby vj bovatas terre in Elvestvait et circa et quinque acras que intersunt illis bovatis quas excambiavit villanis de Beltona scilicet totam terram quam Radulfus defendebat pro ij bovatis, et illam terram quam Agamundus defend(ebat) pro una bovata et illam terram quam Gocelinus def(endebat) pro j bovata et illam terram quam Gaufridus def(endebat) pro una bovata et illam terram quam Elfuat defendebat pro una bovata, et dominicos porcos suos ejusdem loci quietos a pannagio in Moswoda. Et preter hec dedi concessi ei de mea donatione Tuncroft et omnes croftos qui sunt in Moswoda. Hec omnia concessi et quieta clamavi ab omni seculari servicio et exactione in puram et perpetuam elemosinam libere quiete et honorifice sicut liberam elemosinam cum omnibus libertatibus et liberis consuetudinibus libere elemosine pertinentibus in bosco et plano in viis et semitis in pratis et pascuis et in omnibus locis. Concessi etiam predicto abbati Gilberto donare predictam terram cuicunque voluerit absque ulla contradictione sive ecclesie sue sive alii ecclesie sive clerico sive layco. Et cuicunque dederit concessi et confirmavi cum supradictis libertatibus imperpetuum possidendam. Hiis testibus, Roberto de Bocy etc.

NOTE. For the date, see note to no. 258.

262 *Confirmation by Roger de Mowbray to Selby of the lordship and advowson of the church of Kirk Ella (Yorks., E.R.), and of a* mansura *there, and of certain assarts, which render 4s. p.a., all given by William Tison.*

[*c.* 1170 × 1186]

> Pd., *E.Y.C.* xii no. 6, from B.M., Add. MS. 37771 fo. 136*r* (old fo. 135*r*).
> Also pd., *Selby Coucher* ii no. 753.

Testibus hiis, Alano de [?] Lims', Roberto de Bello campo, Alexandro de Berk', Petro clerico, Willelmo camer(ario), etc.

NOTE. William Tison's charters are *E.Y.C.* xii nos. 5, 45.

263 *Confirmation by Nigel de Mowbray of the exchange and agreements which the monks of Selby and William de Malteby made with the monks of Byland concerning Middlethorpe (Yorks., W.R.).*

Forged original charter: B.M., Harley Ch. 53 G 54.

Ebor(acensi) archiepiscopo totique capitulo Sancti Petri et uniuersis sancte ecclesie filiis Nigellus de Molbray salutem. Notum sit vobis me concessisse et hac mea carta confirmasse excambium factum atque conuenciones illas quas monachi de Seleby et Willelmus de Malteby miles fecerunt inter se et monachos Belleland' de manerio de Thorpa iuxta Ebor(acum) quod manerium cum suis pertinenciis monachi de Seleby habuerunt per cartam ex dono et concessione domini Rogeri de Molbray patris mei. Et quia in dicta carta patris mei fuit vna clausula conuencionalis videlicet vt prefati monachi de Seleby suam voluntatem de predicto manerio quodcunque maluerint faciant. Ea tamen conuencione ut quando recuperauerit custodiam castelli Ebor(aci) daret eisdem monachis excambium ad valenciam et ad voluntatem eorum in Ebor(aci) Schira pro dominio predicti manerii. Ego uero Nigellus filius et heres antedicti Rogeri non obstante aliqua conuencione aut condicione ratifico et confirmo abbati et conuent(ui) de Bellalanda et eorum successoribus imperpetuum predictum manerium de Thorp' cum omnibus suis pertinenciis et libertatibus cum seruiciis libere tenencium cum wardis eskeatis releuiis similiter cum omnibus natiuis et eorum sequelis eiusdem ville una cum terris tenementis pratis pascuis et pasturis turbariis moris wastis et ceteris rebus omnibus predicte ville de Thorp' pertinentibus prout euidenter patet per antiqua fossata et alias ceteras metas et diuisas. tenenda et habenda hec omnia cum suis pertinenciis et libertatibus prenominatis liberis introitibus et exitibus infra villam et extra et in omnibus locis rebus et communis prope et procul dicto manerio et dominio spectantibus de me et heredibus meis in liberam puram et perpetuam elemosinam solutam et quietam ab omni seculari seruicio seu demanda. Et ego prefatus Nigellus de Molbray et heredes mei ac assignati nostri manutenebimus warantizabimus et defendemus omnia suprascripta cum omnibus suis pertinenciis predictis abbati et conuentui et eorum posteris ac ecclesie Sancte Marie de Bellalanda sicut liberam puram et perpetuam elemosinam nostram contra omnes gentes imperpetuum. Et ut hec mea confirmacio concessio ratificacio et quieta clamacio rata et stabilis perseueret imperpetuum presenti scripto sigillum meum apposui. Hiis testibus. Roberto fratre meo Waltero de Riparia. Hug(one) de Mala Bestia Roberto Dayvilla. Rob(erto) de Buscy. Herberto filio Ricardi. Thoma de Colevylla. Roberto de Beu'. Bernardo Burdun. et aliis.

No medieval endorsement.

Size: 16·9 × 24 cm.; 2·7 cm. turn-up.

Seal: missing; turn-up has no slit for tag.

Script: hand of later 13th cent.

NOTE. It is impossible to assign a date to this charter, which is suspect both in form and in script. If it were genuine, or based on a genuine charter, we should expect it to belong to Nigel de Mowbray's period of lordship of the honour, 1186–90, but the witnesses seem to belong to an earlier period, four of them attesting Roger de Mowbray's charter for Byland, granting Middle-thorpe, and also almost certainly a forgery, assigned to *c.* 1154 × 1175 (no. 55). The occasion of the forgery probably arose in the third quarter of the thirteenth century, when there were disputes over Middlethorpe (no. 55 note).

264 *Gift by Roger de Mowbray to Master Gilbert and the order of Sempringham (Lincs.) of land and rights in Westwood (Axholme, Lincs.) [later held by Newstead, Gilb., Lincs.].* [1154 × 1186]

Cartulary copy: B.M., Cotton MS. Claud. D xi (cart. of Malton) fo. 99*r*.

Omnibus sancte matris filiis ad quos presens carta pervenerit Rogerus de Munbray salutem in domino. Sciatis quod pro salute anime mee et animarum omnium antecessorum meorum et pro salute heredum meorum dedi et concessi et hac mea carta confirmavi Deo et beate Marie virgini Marie*ᵃ* et magistro Gyleberto de Sempingham et universe congregationi totius ordinis de Semplingham in liberam et perpetuam elemosinam unam carucatam terre aride et thoftum unum, scilicet octoginta et unam acras in parco de Westwde et totum mariscum juxta carucatam illam in parte aquilonari usque ad vetus fossatum, libere et quiete absque alterius communione insuper et communem pasturam circa villam de Westwode in campis et boscis, introitibus et exitibus, in mariscis, in viis et semitis et in aquis et in omnibus locis talia asiamenta et communia qualia habere debent liberi homines predicte ville, secundum quod pertinet ad unam carucatam terre. Dedi etiam predicte congregationi et concessi in liberam et perpetuam elemosinam duas bovatas terre cum tofto uno in territorio de Austun super Trente ex parte australi et occidentali de Kelefeld et totum commune illius territorii in omnibus locis et libertatibus quantum pertinere debet ad duas bovatas, et unam bovatam terre cum omnibus pertinenciis suis in Coltum quam canonici de Noburc tenuerunt unde dedi eis excambium. Hec omnia warantizabo eis et heredes mei post me imperpetuum erga omnes homines ut prosit anime mee uberius, libere et quiete ab omni seculari servicio consuetudine et exactione et de omni omnino re seculari sicut aliqua elemosina liberius dari aut warantizari potest. Hiis t(estibus) etc.

Marginal note: 'Canonici de Novo Loco tenent terram illam'.

ᵃ Sic.

NOTE. Newburgh was given an exchange in Thirsk for the bovate in Coulton (Yorks., N.R.) after 1154.[1] This charter, although it bears signs of forgery, probably represents a genuine gift. The occasion of forgery may well have been Sempringham's suit against William de Mowbray at the Lincolnshire eyre of 1202.[2]

265 *Confirmation by Roger de Mowbray to Sinningthwaite (Cist. nuns, Yorks., W.R.) of the foundation gift by Bertram Haget, and of 3½ carucates in Bilton, Thorpe Underwood, Widdington, and Elwicks (Yorks., W.R.), given by Geoffrey Haget.* [1173 × 1186]

Original charter: Leeds, Yorks. Archaeol. Soc. Libr., MD 335, Bradfer-Lawrence collection. Transcripts, from an original charter formerly in St. Mary's Tower, York: Bodl., MSS. Dodsworth 8 fo. 138*v*, 95 fo. 42*v* (then in the custody of Charles Fairfax).

Pd., *Mon. Ang.* v 464 (I), from the original charter at St. Mary's, York.

Rog(erus) de Mubrai . omnibus filiis sancte ecclesie presentibus et futuris . salutem. Sciatis me concessisse et presenti carta confirmasse . illam donationem in bosco et plano et omnibus aisiamentis . quam Bertram Hagat homo meus dedit sanctimonialibus de Sinningtuaith'. Et insuper concedo et confirmo illis illam terram cum omnibus aisiamentis et pertinentiis quam Galfridus Hagat . filius predicti Bertrami eisdem dedit . quando sororem suam receperunt . scilicet . dimidiam carrucatam in Biletun . et unam carrucatam et dimidiam . in Torp . carrucatam in Witintun . et dimidiam . in Elnewic . et si predictus Galfridus aliquid superaddere voluerit ? concedo quod inperpetuum ratum habeatur. Hanc confirmationem feci eis inperpetuam*a* elemosinam . solutam . quietam . et liberam . de omnibus seruitiis et consuetudinibus ad terram pertinentibus . de me et omnibus heredibus meis inperpetuum. Teste Roberto capellano . Roberto de Daivile . Rad(ulfo) de Beuvair . Herberto filio Ricardi . Rad(ulfo) de Novile . Rob(erto) de Beuscap*b* . Hug(one) de Flamevile .

Endorsement: *Confirmamentum Rogeri de Mubrai de Sannawaþ* (12th cent.).

Size: 13·5 × 13 cm.; 2·2 cm. turn-up.

Seal: missing; was appended on tag.

NOTE. This confirmation is presumably subsequent to pope Alexander III's confirmation, dated 18 Dec. 1172, which mentions Geoffrey Haget's gift of *two* carucates.[3] Bertram Haget's foundation of the nunnery was confirmed by Henry II in the summer of 1155.[4] These were estates held by Haget of the Arches fee.[5]

a Sic.   *b* Sic; presumably *Beuscamp* intended.

1 B.M., Cotton MS. Claud. D xi fo. 99*r*; cf. above, no. 213.
2 *Select Civil Pleas* i (1200–1203), ed. W. P. Baildon (Selden Soc. iii) no. 228.
3 *E.Y.C.* i no. 200.
4 *Mon. Ang.* v 468 (XII); cf. Eyton, *Itinerary* pp. 10–11.   5 See Fees [1].

266 *Notification by Nigel de Mowbray to H(enry of Blois), bishop of Winchester (1129–71), of his gift to Southwark (Aug., Surrey) of the advowson of the church of Banstead (Surrey).*   [1164 × Aug. 1171]

> Pd., *Hatton's Book of Seals* no. 433, from facsimile in the custody of Northants. Record Society (no witnesses).
> Drawing of seal (? no. 1 *or* 2) of Nigel de Mowbray, red wax; appended on tag.

> NOTE. A more positive reason for assigning the charter to the period after 1164 than that given by Loyd and Lady Stenton is provided by no. 267.
> Banstead was the dowry of Mabel, wife of Nigel de Mowbray, whose marriage took place before 1170.[1] Her parentage is obscure.[2] The name of her father is almost obliterated in the *Rotuli Curiae Regis* for 1194, but seems to end in -*tus* or -*cus*.[3] The heading to Dugdale's text of Mabel's charter, no. 269, calls her the daughter of William Patri, and *W. Patricus* would fit the lacuna in the king's court roll. William Patri was among the king's enemies in the rebellion of 1173–4.[4]

267 *Gift by Nigel de Mowbray to Southwark of the church of his manor of Banstead, which he received in marriage with his wife.*   [1164 × Aug. 1171]

> Pd., *Mon. Ang.* vi (1) 171 (VI), from 'Collect. Aug. Vincent gen.' (first edn. ii (1661) 85).[5]

Nigellus de Moubray omnibus amicis et hominibus suis Francis et Anglis salutem. Notum vobis facio me dedisse et presenti carta confirmasse Deo et canonicis de Suthwerke ecclesiam de manerio meo de Benestede quod cum uxore mea in matrimonium accepi etc. Testibus, Hamelino de Warenna et Rogero de Moubray.

> NOTE. Hamelin de Warenne did not take the name Warenne until his marriage to Isabel de Warenne in 1164.[6] Presumably the charter belongs to the same period as no. 266.

268 *Gift by Nigel de Mowbray to Southwark of an orchard within specified bounds, and 5 acres in Banstead.*   [1164 × 1186]

> Original charter: Bodl., MS. Eng. Hist. a. 2 no. 38.
> Pd., F. Turner, 'Addington charters of St. Mary Overie', *Surrey Archaeol. Collections* xxxi (1918), pp. 134–5, with facsimile; and H. C. M. Lambert, *History of Banstead in Surrey* (Oxford, 1912–31), ii app. 1 p. 84.

---

[1] *P.R. 16 Hen. II* p. 164.
[2] See Ethel Stokes's discussion in *Complete Peerage* ix 372 n.
[3] *Three Rolls of the King's Court*, ed. F. W. Maitland (P.R.S. xiv) p. 42.
[4] *Gesta Hen. II* i 45. See also above, p. xxix.
[5] The charter or transcript is perhaps now among the Vincent MSS. in the College of Arms, but has not been traced.   [6] See *E.Y.C.* viii 18 and n. 9.

Nigell(us) de Moubrai omnibus hominibus suis Francis et Anglis et vniuersis sancte matris ecclesie filiis tam presentibus quam futuris ? salutem. Notum sit omnibus uobis me concessisse et dedisse et hac mea carta confirmasse Deo et beate Marie et canonicis ecclesie Sancte Marie de Sudwurch' in liberam et perpetuam elemosinam . pomerium quod est apud aquilonem inter ecclesiam de Benested' et uiam que graditur apud domum Vitalis de Sutt' . et inter uiam que ducit ad curiam meam et semitam que in occidente ducit ad ecclesiam . et .v. acras in Hamma . habendum et possidendum sicut liberam et perpetuam et quietam elemosinam ex omni seclari*a* seruitio et exactione tenendum de me et de heredibus meis eternaliter. Hanc uero elemosinam optuli super altare Sancte Marie in ecclesia de Sudwerch' pro salute mea et uxoris mee et omnium pripinquorum*a* meorum. His test(ibus) . Ric(ardo) de Hasting' . Will(elmo) capell(ano) . Rog(ero) de Moubrai . Ric(ardo) de Aluers . Rob(erto) de Buci Rob(erto) filio Rog(eri) . Vital(e) de Sutt' . Will(elmo) de Coueh' . Goc(elino) uinator(e) . Rad(ulfo) uinator(e) . Rad(ulfo) Bucell' . Walt(ero) de Well' . Michael(e) filio Rad(ulfi) de Cornh' . Petro preposito . et aliis quam pluribus.

Endorsements: *Karta donationis Nigelli de Molbrai de pomerio et de terra de Benestede. | .Karta donat'.Nigelli de Molbrai de pomerio . et de terra . de Benestede* (12th cent.).

Size: 26·4 × 12·7 cm.

Seal: missing; was appended on tag.

269 *Gift by Mabel, wife of Nigel de Mowbray, to Southwark of one of the virgates in Banstead which Ralph 'Vineton' held of Nigel and her.*

[1164 × 1190]

Pd. in abbreviated form, *Mon. Ang.* vi (1) 172 (VII), from 'Collect. Aug. Vincent gen.' (first edn. ii (1661) 85).[1]

Carta Mabiliae filiae Willielmi Patrio, uxoris Nigelli de Moubray. Notum sit presentibus et futuris quod ego Mabilla uxor domini Nigelli de Moubray concessi canonicis de Suthwerke unam de virgatis terrae quas Radulfus Vineton tenuit de Nigello domino meo et marito et de me, reddendo inde ad curiam de Benstede etc.

NOTE. In 1178 Ralph *vinitor* had Nigel de Mowbray's Surrey lands 'in vadio', and rendered Nigel's forest amercements.[2] For a note on Mabel's parentage, see above, no. 266.

a Sic.

---

[1] See above, p. 180 n. 5.   [2] *P.R. 24 Hen. II* p. 133.

270 *Confirmation by Roger de Mowbray to the Templars of ¼ carucate in Brimham (Yorks., W.R.), given by Richard son of Archil.*

[*c.* 1150 × 1169]

Cartulary copies (Fountains): B.M., Cotton MS. Tib. C xii fo. 229r; Bodl., MS. Rawlinson B 449 fo. 91r (lacks last 6 witnesses); B.M., Add. MS. 18276 fo. 30v (abstract).
Pd. (transl.), *Fount. Cart.* i 145 (1), from Cotton MS.

[O]mnibus sancte ecclesie filiis *ᵃtam presentibus quam futurisᵃ* Rogerus de Mulbrei*ᵇ* salutem. Sciatis quod ego dedi et litteris meis et carta confirmavi dimidiam carucatam terre in Birnebem militibus Templi Salomonis quam eis Ricardus filius Archilli*ᶜ* dedit, liberam et quietam et omni servicio immunem sicut aliquam aliam terram in aliquo loco melius et liberius tenent in prato in bosco in aqua et in communibus pascuis. Test(ibus), Roberto de Deivill, Rogero de Flameigvilla, Waltero Buhered, Willelmo de Steingreve, Hugone*ᵈ* Malebissa, Waltero de Charletona, Radulfo de Bellun.

NOTE. All but two of these witnesses occur in 1154 (no. 236), and four occur in 1147 × *c.* 1154 (no. 50). Roger de Flamville probably died by 1169 (no. 377 note). If Walter of Carlton was the same man as the father of Roger of Carlton, the date could be put back to before 1166 (nos. 352–3 notes).

The monks of Fountains held this ½ carucate of the Templars by 1176 (see no. 115 above), and in 1185 they paid 10s. on a 20-year lease.[1]

271 *Gift by Roger de Mowbray to the Templars of the church of Hampton in Arden (Warwicks.), saving the right of Robert clerk of Arden during his life.*

[probably Apr. 1161 × March 1163]

Confirmation by Richard Pecche, bishop of Coventry (1161–82): cartulary of Kenilworth, B.M., Harley MS. 3650 fo. 40r.

. . . ecclesiam de Hamptona in Ardena cum omnibus pertinenciis suis, ad preces et petitionem Rogeri de Molbreio qui eandem ecclesiam eis concessit et carta sua confirmavit, salvo jure quod in predicta ecclesia habet Robertus clericus de Ardena quamdiu vixerit . . .

NOTE. The reference to the prayers and petition of Roger de Mowbray suggest that the gift itself was made during Richard Pecche's episcopate, after 1161. The church of Hampton in Arden, which had previously been given by Samson d'Aubigny and Roger de Mowbray to Kenilworth (nos. 175–8), was not included in Henry II's confirmation of churches to Kenilworth, of 8 March 1163.[2] This gift to the Templars, therefore, may well have been made before the royal confirmation to Kenilworth, but it was ineffective (see nos. 179–80). Robert, clerk of Arden, was archdeacon of Lisieux (no. 334) and subtenant of Montfort in Hampton in Arden (no. 330).

ᵃ⁻ᵃ Omitted in MS. Rawl., which has *etc.*   *ᵇ Mubray*, MS. Rawl.   *ᶜ Arkilli*, MS. Rawl.   *ᵈ Hugo*, MS.

---

[1] *Records of Templars* p. 122.   [2] *C.Ch.R.* iii 277; cf. Eyton, *Itinerary* p. 60.

272 *Grant by Roger de Mowbray to the Templars of timber in his forests of Nidderdale, Malzeard (Yorks., W.R.) and Masham (N.R.), for building three houses—Penhill, East Cowton, and Stanghow (all N.R.).*
[*c.* 1170 × 1184]

Pd., *Records of Templars* pp. 269–70, from an original charter at Ribston Hall, now deposited at Leeds, Yorks. Archaeol. Soc. Libr., DD 59/xvi. Also pd., *Y.A.J.* viii (1884) 273 (XVI).

Testibus his . Nigello de Moubr' . Roberto capellano . Petro de Biling' . Alano de Limmesi . Roberto de Bellocampo . Philippo de Munpincun . Willelmo camerario . Petro clerico . Willelmo Gramario . Simone filio Rogeri . Roberto filio Rogeri.

Endorsements: *Rich'* (late 12th or early 13th cent.); *Rog' Munbrai de mer' in Netherddale Malsard et Massam* (later medieval hand).

Size: 15·4 × 11·2 cm.; 1·9 cm. turn-up.

Seal: fragmento f seal no. 3 of Roger de Mowbray (above, p. lxxxiii), white wax, varnished; appended on tag.

Script: same hand as that of nos. 282 and 373. See Fig. 4 (above, p. lxviii).

NOTE. The appearance of Philip de Montpincon gives the earliest possible date (no. 376 note). Peter of Billinghay had died by 1184 (no. 349 note). Perhaps this grant was made before Roger de Mowbray's promise of 1181 to the monks of Fountains not to allow any other men of religion into his forest of Nidderdale (no. 135).

273 *Record of various gifts by Roger de Mowbray to the Templars.*
[before 1185]

Pd., *Records of Templars*, from Templars' Inquest of 1185: P.R.O., Exch., King's Remembrancer, Misc. Books, Ser. I (E. 164), no. 16.

Various tenements in Balsall (Warwicks.), the rents totalling £10. 14s. 10d. (£10. 5s. 7d. in MS.) (*Records of Templars* pp. 33–5).

The church of Althorpe and chapel of Burnham (Axholme, Lincs.), the rent of each being 4s. (ibid. pp. 78, 99).

Land in the Isle of Axholme, some in demesne for 2 ploughs and some at rents in Keadby and Althorpe, and a mill and a fishery, in all totalling 7 marks less 2d. (ibid. pp. 111–12).

2 bovates in 'Torp' (? Langthorpe, par. Kirby Hill, Yorks., N.R., or Grewelthorpe, W.R.), the rents totalling 6s. 6d. (ibid. p. 122).

3 carucates in 'Wichele' (probably Weedley, nr. South Cave, Yorks., E.R.) in demesne, and one carucate in South Cave, of which the rents totalled 58s. 8d. and one mark (ibid. pp. 125–6).

Various tenements in Thirsk (Yorks., N.R.), the rents totalling 17*s*. (ibid. pp. 128–9).

The mill under the king's castle at York, held by Henry of Fishergate for a rent of 15½ marks (ibid. p. 132).

> NOTE. These are the gifts recorded in the Inquest for which no charters survive. The advowson of Althorpe was shared with St. Leonard's, York, (no. 307).[1]

274 *Gift by Roger de Mowbray to the Templars of a toft of 8 acres, and 120 acres of good land in the territory of Bagby (Yorks., N.R.), and other small pieces of land (specified); pasture for 300 sheep, 40 animals besides the oxen, and 40 pigs in the wood without pannage; and necessaries in the wood for building, fuel and making fences.* [*c.* 1170 × 1185]

> Pd. (transl.), *Yorks. Deeds* ii no. 47, from an original charter then in the possession of Sir Ralph Payne-Gallwey.[2]

Witnesses: Robert de Mubrai, Ralph de Beauveir, Herbert son of Richard, Robert de Busci, Hugh de Beauveir, Herbert (?) de Dalton, Robert de Bello campo, William son of Engelram, Henry de Lubbeham, Robert Beler, Peter the clerk, Chynna, Robert son of Richard, and many others both clerks and laymen.

> NOTE. Henry of Lubbenham (Leics.) does not occur until after *c.* 1170.[3] The gift was made before the Templars' Inquest of 1185.[4]

275 *Gift by Roger de Mowbray to the Templars of Berner of Beltoft and his service (probably in Axholme, Lincs.).* [*c.* 1170 × 1186]

> Pd., *Records of Templars* p. 258, from B.M., Cotton MS. Nero E vi fo. 273*v*.

Hiis testibus, Roberto de Daivilla, Waltero Daivilla, Roberto Beler, Philippo de Munpincun, Roberto de Bellocampo, Hada de Alathorpe, Samsone Takell', Galfrido de Brunham, Willelmo camerario et Willelmo filio suo, Mauricio coco, Brisebare coco, Roberto clerico, et multis aliis.

> NOTE. Eight of the witnesses appear in no. 284, of *c.* 1170 × 1186. Five appear in no. 276, of 1182 × 1186, and it is probably for this reason that Miss Lees assigns the present charter to '*c.* 1184' (see note to no. 276). But nos. 284 and 276 have only three witnesses in common, and it seems wiser to leave the limits of this charter fairly wide, as no. 284.

> [1] Cf. *Rot. R. Grosseteste*, ed. F. N. Davis (Canterbury and York Soc., x) pp. 148–9, 155.
> [2] This charter was not among those which became B.M., Egerton Chs. 2139–74 (*B.M. Quarterly* vii (1933) 118).
> [3] His earliest positively dated appearance is 1175 × 1176 (no. 119); cf. nos. 58–9, 142, 346, 349, 360.
> [4] *Records of Templars* p. 128.

276 *Gift by Roger de Mowbray, with the consent of his heirs Nigel and Robert, to the Templars of all his land of Keadby by specified bounds, part of his wood and marsh of Mosswood, and the vaccary, land, and wood in Belwood (Axholme).*   [1182 × 1186]

> Pd., *Records of Templars* pp. 254–8, from B.M., Cotton MS. Nero E vi fo. 273r–v. Also pd., *Mon. Ang.* vi (2) 840 (XXVII).

Hiis testibus, Alano capellano de Templo, Petro clerico, Roberto de Dayvilla, Hugone Malebissa, Radulfo de Beavver, Hamone Beler, Galfrido de la Hayl, Warino filio Simonis, Nicholao de Bellun, Alano de Lymesy, Willelmo camerario, Philippo de Munpesun, Roberto de Bellocampo, Willelmo filio camerarii, Radulfo filio Ricardi, Ernaldo dispensatore, multisque aliis.

> NOTE. Six of the witnesses to this charter appear in no. 315, of 1182 × 1186. This gift is not mentioned in the Templars' Inquest of 1185, and may belong to the year before Roger's final crusade, i.e. 1185–6. It is dated 'c. 1184' by Miss Lees, on the ground that Alan de Limesey died by 1185, but the reference she gives is to Gerard de Limesey.[1] For the details of the estate, see *Records of Templars* p. 111.

277 *Grant by Nigel de Mowbray to Troarn (Ben., Calvados) of freedom of buying and selling and other rights in Écouché (Orne, arr. Argentan).*
[c. 1170 × 1190]

> Original charter: Caen, Archives of Calvados, H. 7809.
> Extract pd., R. N. Sauvage, *L'Abbaye de Saint-Martin de Troarn* (Caen, 1911) p. 227 n. 5.

Notum sit omnibus sancte ecclesie fidelibus ad quos presentes littere peruenerint quod ego Nigellus de Molbraio dedi et concessi ecclesie Sancti Martini de Troarno et monachis ibidem Deo seruientibus pro salute anime mee et omnium amicorum meorum plenariam quitantiam in uilla mea de Escocheio de omnibus rebus suis emendis et uendendis transitumque facientibus de passagio et theloneo et omnibus aliis consuetudinibus. Et ut predicti monachi istam donationem in perpetuam elemosinam sine aliqua contradictione et molestia heredum meorum possiderent ∴ presentis scripti testimonio et presentis sigilli mei munimine feci sigillari et confirmari. Testibus his . Roberto de Boseual monacho de Sancto Andrea[2] . Roberto Banaste . Ricardo Bacon . Gaufrido coco . aliisque quam pluribus.

> Endorsement: probably medieval, but so faded as to be illegible.
> Seal: missing; was appended on tag.

> [1] *Rotuli de Dominabus*, ed. J. H. Round (P.R.S. xxxv) pp. xxviii, 51 and n.
> [2] i.e. of Gouffern (cf. nos. 162–5).

278 *Gift by Roger de Mowbray to Vaudey (Cist., Lincs.) of 10 acres in Burton Lazars (Leics.).*   [1147 × 1186]

> Confirmation by Richard I, 7 Sept. 1189: pd., *Mon. Ang.* v 490 (I), from P.R.O., Cartae Antiquae (C. 52) W no. 6.
>
> NOTE. Vaudey was founded 23 May 1147.

279 *Gift by Roger de Mowbray to Villers-Canivet (Sav. nuns, Calvados, arr. Caen, cant. Falaise) of the vill of Villers.*   [c. 1154 × 1186]

> Original charter (damaged): Caen, Archives of Calvados, Abbaye de Villers-Canivet no. 160.
> Pd. (French), Léchaudé d'Anisy, *Extrait* ii 295 (2).

[Rogerus de]*ᵃ* Molb' . salutem. Sciatis omnes quod ego Rog(erus) de Molb' dedi et concessi Deo [et Sancte Marie]*ᵃ* villam de Vilers cum omnibus aliis rebus sine aliquo retentu . et quicquid [..... ....]*ᵇ* de me . videlicet seruitium equi . et auxilium feodale . et mea [......... .....]*ᵇ* sicut suam puram et liberam et quietam et perpetuam elemosinam . [pro animabus]*ᵃ* Nigelli de Aubigneio . et matris mee Gondree . et omnium heredum [meorum. Et ut hec]*ᵃ* mea donatio et elemosina de me et de heredibus meis in [perpetuum teneatur et]*ᵃ* de nostris propriis contra omnes homines . et in omnibus rata et [stabilis et inconcussa]*ᵃ* possideatur . presenti carta . et mei sigilli testimonio con[firmavi. Teste R]*ᵃ*ic(ardo) Boteri . et pluribus aliis.

Endorsement: not now visible, as charter is mounted.

> NOTE. This is the earliest surviving charter relating to the nunnery of Villers-Canivet, which is said to have been founded by Roger de Mowbray.[1] Some authorities give the date of foundation as *c.* 1127, and others give *c.* 1140. The nunnery was evidently in existence before Savigny and her dependencies entered the Cistercian order in 1147. The present charter seems to belong to the period after the death of Gundreda de Gournay (see no. 236 note). The sole witness occurs also in no. 163, of Aug. 1154 × 1186, and in no. 280, of *c.* 1170 × 1190.

280 *Gift by [Nigel de Mowbray] to Villers-Canivet of the church of Proussy (Calvados, arr. Vire, cant. Condé-sur-Noireau).*   [c. 1170 × 1190]

> Fragment of an original charter: Caen, Archives of Calvados, Abbaye de Villers-Canivet no. 159 (Proussy).
> Pd. (French), Léchaudé d'Anisy, *Extrait* ii 295 (3).

ᵃ Charter damaged; suggested readings in brackets.   *ᵇ* Charter damaged.

---

[1] A copy, made on 29 Dec. 1634, which is listed by Léchaudé d'Anisy, is based on a grossly conflated version of this charter, *Extrait* ii 294–5; Archives of Calvados, Abbaye de Villers-Canivet no. 163.

[Nigellus de Molbraio . . . .]ᵃbus uniuersis in Domino salutem.
Nouerint uniuersi tam presentes quam futuri [quod ego Nigellus pro
salute anime mee]ᵃ et uxoris mee et omnium antecessorum meorum et
successorum dedi [Deo et Sancte Marie et]ᵃ monialibus de Uilers
ecclesiam de Proceio concedentibus filiis [meis Willelmo . . . .]ᵃ
Philipo . et quicquid iuris in predicta ecclesia habebam ipsis [monialibus
dedi in perpetuum. Et ut hec]ᵃ donatio mea firma et inconcussa permaneat scripto [presenti atque sigillo m]ᵃeo uolui communiri. Testibus
istis . Nicholaus de Bel[lun . . . . Rad]ᵃulfus chericusᵇ. Richad'ᵇ
Boteri . Robertus Lupus.

Endorsement: *Carta Nigelli de Moubraio de ecclesia de Broceio* (13th cent.).

Seal: fragment of seal no. 2 of Nigel de Mowbray (above, pp. lxxxiii–iv);
appended on tag.

281 *Gift by Roger de Mowbray to Welford (Prem., Northants.) of a fishery in
the River Trent and one acre near Wildsworth (Lincs.), for building
a house.*   [Dec. 1155 × 1165]

> Original charter: P.R.O., E. 326/11358. Transcript, from the original charter
> then in the Court of Augmentations: Bodl., MS. Dodsworth 63 fos. 96v–
> 97r.
> Pd., T. Madox, *Formulare Anglicanum* (1702) no. CCCCXXIII, from the
> original charter.

Rogerius de Molbray omnibus hominibus suis Francis et Anglis et
uniuersis sancte ecclesie fidelibus presentibus et futuris salutem. Sciatis
me dedisse et presenti cartula confirmasse Deo et Sancte Marie et
abbatie de Welleford' et canonicis ibidem Deo seruientibus pro salute
anime mee et antecessorum et successorum meorum in liberam . puram
et perpetuam elemosinam vnam piscariam in Trenta que uocatur
Doddesgard' . et vnam acram terre iuxta Trentam in Lindeseia prope
Wiueleswurth' ad unam mansionem faciendam et duas acras prati . et
communem pasturam et quicquid ad eandem terram pertinet. Et uolo
ut predicti canonici hanc terram teneant liberam quietam et solutam ab
omni seruicio et consuetudine et exactione seculari ad me et ad heredes
meos pertinente inperpetuum. Hiis testibus . Nigell(o) de Molbray . R.
de Daiuilla¹ . H. Malebisse² . R. de Beluer . Oliu(ero) de Buci.

Endorsements: *R--EE | Giddegard' | C Thurnholm dat iiij* (later medieval hands).

Size: 19·2 × 9·3 cm.

Seal: missing; was appended on tag.

ᵃ Charter damaged; suggested readings in brackets.   ᵇ *Sic.*

---

¹ Presumably Robert rather than Roger de Daiville.
² Hugh Malebisse.

NOTE. Welford (also known as Sulby) was founded in Dec. 1155, by a Mowbray tenant and *dapifer*, William de Wyville.[1] Oliver de Buscy had been succeeded by Robert de Buscy by 1166 (no. 401).

282 *Gift by Roger de Mowbray to Welford of 4 acres of his demesne next to 'Langebeit', near Owston (Axholme).*   [*c.* 1170 × 1184]

Original charter: Gregory-Hood deeds deposited at Stratford on Avon, Shakespeare Birthplace Trust Libr., Gregory-Hood Ch. 1364.

Rog(erus) de Moubr' . omnibus hominibus et amicis suis tam presentibus quam futuris salutem. Sciatis me dedisse et hac presenti cartha[a] mea confirmasse Deo et ecclesie de Wellefort .iiii.[or] acras terre de dominio meo iuxta Langebeit uersus Oustona . in puram et perpetuam elemosinam possidendas . liberas et quietas ab omni exactione et seruitio seculari. Test(ibus) hiis . Rob(erto) de Moubr' . Rob(erto) de Bellocampo . Petro de Bilingeia . Warino filio Sim(onis) . Willelmo cam(erario) . Petro clerico . Rogero coco et aliis multis . tam clericis quam laicis.

Endorsements: *De .iiii.[or] acris terre extra parci fossam / Rogeri de Molbrai* (late 12th- or early 13th-cent. hands); *Medlwode* (late 13th or early 14th cent.).

Size: 14·2 × 6·6 cm.; 2·2 cm. turn-up.

Seal: missing; was appended on tag.

Script: same hand as that of nos. 272 and 373. See Fig. 3 (above, p. lxviii).

NOTE. Five of these seven witnesses occur in no. 343, of *c.* 1170 × 1184.

283 *Confirmation by Roger de Mowbray to Welford of the church of Welford and land of Sulby (Northants.) and other gifts.*   [1155 × 1186]

Confirmation by Edward II, 14 March 1316: P.R.O., Patent Roll, 9 Edw. II pt. ii (C. 66/145) m. 2.
Pd., *Mon. Ang.* vi (2) 903 (V); briefly mentioned, *C.P.R. 1313–17* p. 491.

. . . Concessionem, donationem et confirmationem quas Rogerus de Moubray fecit quondam abbati de Wellefordia, nunc abbati de Suleby nuncupato, et fratribus cum eo Deo servientibus de ecclesia de Welleford, et tota terra de Suleby, cum pertinentiis suis; in pratis, et pascuis, turbariis, stagnis et aquis, molendinis, semitis et viis, in Axiholm, et Tirneholm; et de terra Gamelli, et Gaufridi; et mansura una de Torkes'; ac etiam de terris, quas Radulphus filius Jacobi eis dedit in Welleford; et de terra a domo Petri filii Gaufridi, usque ad locum qui vocatur Gidescard, in insula de Axiholme, iuxta Trentam, sicut Trenta continet; et

---

[a] *Sic*; cf. spelling by same scribe in charters cal. nos. 272, 373.

[1] H. M. Colvin, *White Canons in England* (Oxford, 1951) pp. 77–9. For the Wyville fee, see Fees [21].

inde usque ad Tirneholm, cum pratis, et mariscis, et piscariis; et duabus acris ultra Trentam, cum una mansura; et de uno molendino in predicta terra juxta Trentam . . .

NOTE. Mowbray's lordship of the Welford fee, held by Wyville, derived from the Domesday honour of Geoffrey de La Guerche. The land of Sulby had been part of the Domesday fee of Reinbuedcurt, which Robert Foliot gained in marriage some time between 1154 and 1163,[1] and in 1166 there seems to have been some dispute between Foliot and Mowbray, for in the *carta* of that year Mowbray is said to hold 1½ fees of Foliot for which 'detinet michi servicium'.[2]

284 *Confirmation by Roger de Mowbray to Welford of land in Kelfield (Axholme), given by William de Martona, for a rent to Roger of 8s. p.a.*
[*c.* 1170 × 1186]

Pd., *Danelaw Charters* no. 394, from B.M., Add. Ch. 5870.

Hiis testibus . Roberto de Molbrai . Philippo de Munpincun . Roberto Beler . Willelmo camerario . Willelmo filio eius . Samson Takel . Baldewino clerico . Gaufrido de Brunham . Gaufrido filio eius . Mauricio coco . Ricardo Bruning . Reinaldo preposito de Houstun . Roberto clerico . et multis aliis.

Size: 16·6 × 12 cm.

Seal: missing; was appended on tag, no turn-up.

NOTE. Philip de Montpincon does not occur before *c.* 1170. For the date, see note to no. 275. For Roger de Mowbray's gift to William de Martona, see no. 373 below.

285 *Gift by Nigel de Mowbray to Welford, and the brethren of that house dwelling in the Isle of Axholme,[3] of common pasture in the fields of Owston, pasture in Melwood, and licence to keep a mastiff.*   [*c.* 1170 × 1190]

Pd., *Danelaw Charters* no. 395, from B.M., Harley Ch. 53 G 56; noticed, *Hatton's Book of Seals* no. 176.

Hiis testibus . Rogero de Aubeni . Roberto de Mubrai . Ricardo de Withuilla . Rogero de Condeio . Radulfo clerico meo . Warino diacono . et aliis multis.

Size: 12·7 × 9 cm.; 2·2 cm. turn-up.

Seal: missing; was appended on tag.

NOTE. The charter presumably belongs to the period after nos. 282 and 284. Roger de Cundy does not otherwise occur after 1186, and it is therefore possible that this and the following charter were given before Roger de Mowbray's departure on crusade.

[1] Stenton, *Feudalism* p. 264.
[2] *R.B.* i 332; cf. A. Saltman, *Theobald, Archbishop of Canterbury* (1956) no. 277.
[3] The canons had a grange at Melwood (see H. M. Colvin, *White Canons in England* (Oxford, 1951) p. 80 n.).

286 *Similar gift by Nigel de Mowbray to Welford, and the brethren of that house dwelling in the Isle of Axholme, of common pasture in the fields of Owston, pasture in Melwood, and licence to keep a mastiff.*

[*c.* 1170 × 1190]

Pd., *Danelaw Charters* no. 396, from B.M., Add. Ch. 21088.

Hiis testibus . Rogero de Aubeni . Roberto de Mubrai . Ricardo de Wiuilla . Rogero de Cundi . Radulfo clerico meo . Warino diacono.

Size: 14·1 × 7·5 cm.; 2 cm. turn-up.

Seal: fragment of seal no. 1 of Nigel de Mowbray (above, p. lxxxiii), white wax; appended on tag.

NOTE. For the date see note to no. 285.

287 *Gift by Gundreda de Gournay to St. Michael's hospital, Whitby (Yorks., N.R.) at the request of Robert d'Aunay, master of the hospital, of 2 bovates in 'Hoveton' (N.R.) with a toft.* [1130 × 1138]

Pd., *E.Y.C.* ix no. 123, and *Whitby Cart.* ii no. 572, from a record of the gift in B.M., Add. MS. 4715 fo. 178r.

NOTE. 'Hoveton' is a lost vill which lay between Welburn and Kirkby Moorside.[1] The record in the Whitby cartulary[2] notes that by the time of abbot Ailred of Rievaulx, who began his rule in 1147, Rievaulx held the two bovates, rendering 6s. p.a. to St. Michael's hospital. The tenancy originated before Nov. 1160, when Rievaulx's interest was confirmed in a papal bull.[3]
    Robert d'Aunay was a relative of Gundreda: according to the Byland chronicle he was her 'avunculus sive nepos'.[4]

288 *Gift by Roger de Mowbray and Gundreda de Gournay to Whitby (Ben.) of a* mansura *in York, rendering 3s. p.a., to satisfy the abbey's claim to the church of St. William of Hood (Yorks., N.R.).* [1138 × 1140]

Pd., *E.Y.C.* ix no. 116, from *Whitby Cart.* i no. 259 from cartulary (now in the possession of Miss M. L. A. Strickland of Whitwell, York) fo. 65r.

Teste, Turstino archiepiscopo, et Radulfo episcopo,[5] et Willelmo decano, et Gaufrido Turcopula, et Bertramo Agat, et Rogero diacono et aliis.

NOTE. Hood was the original site of the convent of Byland, founded 1138 or 1139.[6] The *mansura* in York was perhaps the one at Foss Bridge, confirmed in the papal bull of 1145 × 1148.[7]
    For Nigel d'Aubigny's gift to a cell of Whitby in York, see above, no. 8.

---

[1] *E.Y.C.* ix 212; and cf. ibid. no. 125 (cal. above, no. 243).
[2] Cf. *Whitby Cart.* i no. 382 for another record of the same gift.
[3] *Riev. Cart.* no. 250.   [4] *Mon. Ang.* v 350a.
[5] Ralph Noel, bishop of Orkney.
[6] See *E.Y.C.* ix no. 115 (cal. above, no. 32).   [7] *E.Y.C.* i no. 872.

289 *Quitclaim by Roger de Mowbray to Whitby of the service due to him from 2 carucates in Toulston (Yorks., W.R.), given by Fulk (son of Reinfrid) the* dapifer.   [*c.* 1147 × *c.* 1154]

> Pd., *E.Y.C.* i no. 532, and *Whitby Cart.* i no. 82, from cartulary (Strickland) fo. 19*r–v.*

Testibus, Gundree[a] matre mea, Nigello filio meo, Atheliza uxore mea, Roberto de Davidvilla, Rogero de Flammavilla, Waltero de Riparia, Herberto de Quenigburc et aliis.

> NOTE. Farrer's date, 1141 × *c.* 1150, is too early, as Nigel de Mowbray did not begin to attest charters until *c.* 1147 or later, and Gundreda de Gournay probably died *c.* 1154 (see above, no. 236 note). Toulston belonged to the Arches fee.[1] Fulk, *dapifer* of William de Percy, died before *c.* 1135.[2]

290 *Confirmation by Roger de Mowbray to Whitby of the estate which Rainald Puher sold to the abbey, i.e. 6 bovates in (Middle)thorpe and 4* mansurae *in York.*   [*c.* 1147 × *c.* 1154]

> Cartulary copies: cartulary of Whitby (Strickland) fos. 64*v* (A), 72*r–v* (B). Pd., *Whitby Cart.* i nos. 256, 282.

Rogerus de Moubrai[b] omnibus hominibus suis Francis et Anglis salutem. Notum sit vobis et omnibus videntibus vel audientibus has litteras me concessisse et dedisse ecclesie de Wyteby[c] et monachis ibidem Deo servientibus in liberam et perpetuam elemosinam totam tenuram quam Reginaldus Puer[d] de me tenuit et quam reddidit et reliquid[e] in manu mea, scilicet vj bovatas terre in Thorp et iiij[or] mansuras in Eboraco, tres scilicet in Sceldergate[f] et unam super ripam fluminis Use ubi ipse manebat. Hec[g] autem dedi eis pro anima patris et matris mee et pro salute mea et filiorum meorum in exscambium[h] dimidie carucate unde habent cartam patris mei. Reginaldus[i] autem Puer[d] vendidit ecclesie prefate de Wyteby[c] totum jus quod habuit in prefata terra et reliquid[e] mihi ad opus illorum et ego reddidi eis et saisivi per idem lignum per quod et recepi illud. Hiis testibus, Nigello filio meo, Hugone Malebisse dapif(ero),[j] Roberto de Daievilla[k] et aliis.

> NOTE. Hugh Malebisse was steward from *c.* 1147 to *c.* 1154.[3] For Roger de Mowbray's enfeoffment of Rainald Puher, see below, nos. 379–80.

---

[a] *Sic* in MS.   [b] *Moubray,* B.   [c] *Whiteby,* B.   [d] *Poer,* B.   [e] *Sic.*
[f] *Skeldergata,* B.   [g] *Hoc,* A.   [h] *excambium,* B.   [i] *Rog',* A.
[j] *dapi fil',* B.   [k] B adds: 'Rogero de Cundi, Rodberto capellano, Johanne de Crevequer, Rogero de Ardenne, Radulfo de Popelitun, Rodberto de Cundi, Dren filio Nicholai canon', Radulfo de Crammavilla, Hugone pistore, Hugone de Neuponte'.

---

[1] See below, Fees [1] and [31].   [2] *E.Y.C.* xi 92–4.   [3] See above, p. lxii.

291 *Confirmation by R(oger) de Mowbray to Whitby of the estate which Rainald Puher held of him in York.* [c. 1150×1169]

Cartulary copies: cartulary of Whitby (Strickland) fos. 65r (A), 73r (B). Pd., *Whitby Cart.* i no. 257.

Archiepiscopo Ebor(acensi) et capitulo Sancti Petri et omnibus qui has viderint vel audierint litteras R. de Munbrai*ᵃ* salutem in Christo. Sciatis omnes me dedisse et per hanc cartam confirmasse Deo et Sancte Hylde de Wyteby*ᵇ* et monachis ibidem Deo servientibus terram quam Reginaldus Poer de me tenuit in Thorp, scilicet vj bovatas terre cum prato ad eas pertinente et cum communi aisiamento ejusdem ville, et iiij°ʳ mansuras in Eboraco, tres scilicet in Sceldergate*ᶜ* et unam super ripam fluminis Use *ᵈ*[. . . . . pro salute mea]*ᵈ* et anima mea et pro animabus heredum et parentum meorum in liberam et puram et perpetuam elemosinam ab omni servicio et consuetudine et exactione seculari quietam, ut ego et heredes mei in vita et in morte specialiter simus in orationibus eorum. Ego autem et heredes mei hanc elemosinam et donationem prenominatis monachis de Wytebi*ᵇ* warantizabimus contra omnes homines et si aliquo casu eam non poterimus warantizare, dabimus illis exscambium ad valenciam. Hiis testibus, Willelmo de Steinegrive, Rogero de Flamevile,*ᵉ* Waltero de Templo, Waltero de Turchelbi, Waltero de Larivere et aliis.*ᶠ*

NOTE. The charter was issued after no. 290, and the appearance of Walter of the Temple suggests a date not earlier than c. 1150.[1] Roger de Flamville probably died by 1169 (see no. 377 note).

292 *Confirmation by Roger de Mowbray to Holy Trinity, York (Ben. alien),[2] of the tithe of the mills of the castle of York, given by his father Nigel d'Aubigny and confirmed by Roger of Pont l'Évêque, archbishop of York.* [1138×Nov. 1181, probably after Oct. 1154]

Confirmation by Henry II [May 1175×July 1188]: pd., *E.Y.C.* vi no. 6, from P.R.O., Patent Roll 4 Edw. IV pt. ii (C. 66/509) m. 12. Also pd., *C.P.R. 1461–67* p. 376.

NOTE. Presumably Mowbray's confirmation was made before the death of Roger of Pont l'Évêque, archbishop of York, in November 1181. If it was made during the archbishop's pontificate, the date would be after October 1154. For Nigel d'Aubigny's gift of the tithe of the mills, see no. 3.

ᵃ *Mulbray*, B.　　ᵇ *Whiteby*, B.　　ᶜ *Skeldergate*, B.　　ᵈ⁻ᵈ Presumably some words omitted.　　ᵉ *Flamelive*, A.　　ᶠ B adds: 'Willelmo de Magneby, dominis, Willelmo de Houchesgard, Hyvone de Ugylbordby, Cliberno Biscop, Normanno coco, Hugone hospitario, Gaufrido de Bosco, Thoraldo Francigena et multis aliis'.

1 His earliest occurrence is c. 1150×1159 (*E.Y.C.* iii no. 1500) and his last 1175× 1176 (above, no. 122), and perhaps later, 1170×1185 (*E.Y.C.* iii no. 1845).
2 Dependency of Marmoutier, Tours.

293 *Confirmation by Roger de Mowbray to St. Clement's, York (Ben. nuns), of land in York by the River Ouse, given by Ralph de Belvoir and his wife Constance.* [1162 × 1175]

> Transcript, from an original charter formerly in St. Mary's Tower, York (in the custody of Charles Fairfax): Bodl., MS. Dodsworth 95 fo. 43r.

Sciant omnes fideles tam futuri quam presentes quod ego Rogerus de Molbrai concessi et hac mea carta confirmavi sanctimonialibus Sancti Clementis donationem illius terre in Eboraco juxta Usam quam videlicet Radulfus de Beavver et Constancia sponsa sua eis fecerunt et sicut in eorum carta inde continetur. Hii sunt t(estes), Robertus de Daivilla, Robertus Buci, Willelmus camerarius, Adam Luvel, Nicholaus de Betl', Willelmus Bacun, Nicholaus Daiveill, Nicholaus presbyter.

> NOTE. The appearance of Nicholas de Bellun suggests a date after *c.* 1160 (no. 343 note). Ralph de Belvoir's charter[1] is attested by Swain, master of St. Leonard's hospital, who was not in office until after 1162. Ralph's gift was confirmed by Henry II in 1175.[2] His wife Constance was a daughter and coheir of William Tison (no. 190 note).[3]

294 *Gift by Roger de Mowbray to St. Leonard's hospital, York, of a thrave of corn from each plough on his Yorkshire demesne lands; and precept to his bailiffs to render the gift annually.* At Welburn [1138 × *c.* 1143]

> Cartulary copies: B.M., Cotton MS. Nero D iii fo. 59v (old fo. 57v); Durham, D. & C. Archives, Large Register V fo. 38v.

Rogerus de Molbrai omnibus hominibus suis et amicis et maxime bailivis suis salutem. Sciatis me dedisse et concessisse in elemosinam fratribus hospitalis Sancti Petri Ebor(aci) de unaquaque caruca nostri dominii per totam Eboraci sciram unam travam garbarum; et illud precipio bailivis meis ut tradant ubicunque sim[a] una vice per annum, et hec[b] pro remissione peccatorum meorum et parentum meorum. Hujus doni testes sunt, Samson de Alb',[c] et Vitalis de Cava sacerdos,[d] et Helias de Seint Martin.[e] Apud Wellebrune.[f]

> NOTE. Elias de Sancto Martino attests four other charters which belong to the period before 1143,[4] and he was almost certainly dead before 1148.[5] Welburn (Yorks., N.R.) was in the dowry of Gundreda de Gournay.[6]

[a] *sint*, Durham Reg.   [b] *hoc*, Durham Reg.   [c] *Sampson de Albie*, Durham Reg.   [d] *sacerdos* omitted in Durham Reg.   [e] *Elias de Saint Martini*, Durham Reg.   [f] *Welleburn'*, Durham Reg.

---

[1] Bodl., MS. Dodsworth 8 fo. 141v.   [2] *E.Y.C.* i no. 359.
[3] For estates held by Ralph de Belvoir, see nos. 345–6 and notes.
[4] Nos. 32, 37–8, 195. Cf. also no. 374.   [5] See no. 89, note.
[6] See nos. 232, 235–7.

For Nigel d'Aubigny's gifts to the hospital see above, nos. 2, 3, 7.

The hospital was an ancient foundation attached to St. Peter's, York.[1] During the twelfth century it became increasingly independent of the cathedral establishment, and came to be known as the hospital of St. Leonard. In the charters of this collection it is called indifferently St. Peter's or St. Leonard's, but to achieve consistency St. Leonard is the dedication given in the headings.

295 *Confirmation by Roger de Mowbray to St. Leonard's hospital, York, of lands held of Henry of Beningbrough.*   [probably 1138 × May 1148]

Extract, from fo. 4 of a lost volume of the cartulary of St. Leonard's, York: Bodl., MS. Dodsworth 120 B fo. 49v.[2]

Rogerus de Molbrai confirm(at) hospitali Sancti Petri Ebor(aci) quicquid Henricus de Beningburg homo suus predicto hospitali dedit, tam de terris quas hospitale tenet de Henrico et heredibus suis in feodo et hereditate, quam de elemosinis ab eo in perpetuam elemosinam collatis etc.

NOTE. Land in Beningbrough (Yorks., N.R.) was confirmed to the hospital by Eugenius III, 7 May 1148,[3] and also by Adrian IV, 19 Jan. 1157.[4] Henry of Beningbrough held of the Arches fee.[5]

296 *Confirmation by Roger de Mowbray to St. Leonard's hospital, York, of land in Thirsk (Yorks., N.R.).*   [probably 1138 × May 1148]

Extract, from fo. 194 of a lost volume of the cartulary of St. Leonard's, York: Bodl., MS. Dodsworth 120 B fo. 78r.

Rogerus de Molbray omnibus amicis et hominibus etc. confirmat terram in Tresc hospitali beati Petri Ebor(aci). [Testibus,][a] Gu(i)l(lelm)o capellano Roberti decani, Rogero de Cundeio, W(illelm)o de Merlou, Rogero de Flamevilla, Olivero de Busci, Philippo de Lugi, Radulfo Beler, Radulfo de Belluuer,[b] Gualtero de Carleton.

NOTE. A *mansura* in Thirsk was confirmed to the hospital by Eugenius III, 7 May 1148.[6] William de Merlou occurs in two other charters of the mid 1140s,[7] and also in the next charter, no. 297, which has the same witnesses as the present charter, and may belong to *c.* 1147.

---

[a] Omitted in MS.   [b] ? read *Bellun.*

---

[1] See *Mon. Ang.* vi (2) 608–9.

[2] For this source, see D. E. Greenway, 'A lost cartulary of St. Leonard's hospital, York', *Y.A.J.* xlii (1968) 178–80.

[3] *P.U.E.* i no. 44.   [4] Ibid. no. 64.

[5] See Fees [1].   [6] *P.U.E.* i no. 44.   [7] Above, nos. 177, 256.

297 *Confirmation by Roger de Mowbray to St. Leonard's hospital, York, of the church of Brignall (Yorks., N.R.) and a bovate of land, with 2 bovates of land anciently given to that church; which gift had been made to the hospital by William de Logi, his man, who was holding the vill of him.*

[probably 1138×May 1148]

> Pd., *E.Y.C.* v no. 385, from B.M., Cotton MS. Nero D iii fo. 17*v* (old fo. 15*v*), and P.R.O., Charter Roll, 22 Edw. I (C. 53/80) m. 9. Also pd. (abbreviated), *Mon. Ang.* vi (2) 612 (XIV), from Charter Roll; (transl.), *C.Ch.R.* ii 441 (16).

Testibus, Guillelmo capellano Roberti decani de Manfeld, Gaufrido filio Wlstani, Rogero de Cundeio, Guillelmo de Merlen, Rogero de Flamavilla, Olivero de Buci, Philippo de Lugi, Radulfo Beler, Radulfo de Bellun, Galtero de Carlatuna, Ascatino hostiario, et multis aliis.

> NOTE. Roger de Mowbray's gift was confirmed to the hospital by Theobald, archbishop of Canterbury, 1150×1154.[1] Two other charters, one certainly and one possibly concerning Brignall, which may be connected with the present charter, have been dated *c.* 1147 (nos. 45, 198). The witnesses, with two additional names, are the same as those to the previous charter, no. 296 which was probably issued before May 1148. Some years later, William de Vescy confirmed to the hospital 'the promise of Eustace [Fitz John] his father to give the church of Brignall'.[2] Neither Mowbray nor Fitz John had any apparent right to Brignall, which belonged to the Richmond honour.[3]

298 *Confirmation by Roger de Mowbray of the settlement between Thomas 'Guacclinus' and St. Leonard's hospital, York, concerning 3 carucates in Stockton on the Forest (Yorks., N.R.).* [1138×May 1148]

> Transcript, from an original charter formerly belonging to Mr. M. F. Middelton: Leeds, Yorks. Archaeol. Soc. Libr., MS. 405 (W. T. Lancaster's collections vol. v) p. 17.

Roggerus de Molbraio archiepiscopo Ebor(acensi) et capitulo Beati Petri et dapifero suo et omnibus ministris et amicis suis Francis et Anglis salutem. Sciatis me concessisse [   ]*a* sigillo confirmasse conventionem et pactum quod est inter Thomam Guacclinum hominem meum et fratres hospitalis Sancti Petri Eborac(i) de tribus carucatis in Stocatuna quas tenet de me, pro quibus fratres hospitalis reddent supradicto Thome et heredibus suis xx solidos singulis annis imperpetuum, x solidos ad festum Sancti Martini et decem in Pentecosten, et hoc pro omnibus geldis et consuetudinibus et auxiliis et serviciis, excepta relevatione quam ipsi heredi meo de illa terra facient et Danageldo quod

---

a Space in transcript for 2 or 3 words.

---

[1] *E.Y.C.* i no. 185 (see no. 299 below).   [2] *E.Y.C.* v no. 386
[3] Ibid. pp. 332 ff., and cf. above, no. 198 note.

per totam Angliam cucurrerit. Ipse Thomas Guacelinus et heredes sui facient michi et heredibus meis omne servicium quod super illa terra venerit et ipse Thomas guarantizabit fratribus hospitalis illam terram contra omnes. Teste, Radulfo de Wivilla, et Olyvero de Buci, et Gualtero Wincebag, et Johanne capellano, et Radulfo[a] de Davilla, et Rotberto de Buci, et Guillelmo de Manel heremer, et Helya de Sancto Martino.

Lancaster notes: '12th-century seal gone'.

NOTE. Three carucates in Stockton were confirmed in the papal bull of 7 May 1148.[1] The witness-clause suggests that the charter was given in the 1140s. Thomas Guacclinus is, however, otherwise unknown, unless he is to be identified with Thomas de Walchingham, who attests no. 396.

This estate was presumably that which belonged to the honour of Richmond and was later confirmed to the hospital by Geoffrey son of Reiner.[2]

299 *Gift by Roger de Mowbray, with the consent of Alice his wife, to St. Leonard's hospital, York, of the land of Broomfleet (nr. South Cave, Yorks., E.R.), and 5 carucates in Heslington (E.R.).* [1142 × 1154]

Confirmation by Theobald, archbishop of Canterbury, including also gifts made in nos. 297, 300, 324, [1150 × 1154]: pd., *E.Y.C.* i no. 185, and A. Saltman, *Theobald, Archbishop of Canterbury* (1956) no. 285, from B.M., Cotton MS. Nero D iii fo. 39r. Also confirmation by Henry II, [1155 × 1158]: pd., *E.Y.C.* i no. 173, and *C.Ch.R.* ii 438-9, from P.R.O., Charter Roll, 22 Edw. I (C. 53/80) m. 9.

NOTE. The *terminus a quo* is given by the appearance of Alice de Gant as wife of Roger de Mowbray. A reference is made to the hospital's land in Broomfleet in a charter of 1154 × 1157.[3] For Heslington, cf. below, no. 303.

300 *Gift by Gundreda (de Gournay) to St. Leonard's hospital, York, of 4 bovates in Bagby (Yorks., N.R.).* [1142 × 1154]

Transcript, from an original charter formerly in St. Mary's Tower, York: Bodl., MS. Dodsworth 7 fo. 14r. Also transcribed from fo. 90 of a lost volume of the cartulary of St. Leonard's, York: MS. Dodsworth 120 B fo. 61v (lacking six witnesses).
Pd., *Mon. Ang.* vi (2) 609 (VII) from the original charter.

Archiepiscopo Eborac(ensi) totique capitulo Sancti Petri Ebor' et Rogero de Mulbrai filio suo cunctisque sancte matris ecclesie filiis tam futuris quam presentibus domina Gundreda uxor Nigelli de Albini salutem. Notum sit vobis me Deo et Sancto Leonardo et pauperibus hospitalis Sancti Petri Ebor(aci) dedisse quatuor bovatas terre in Baggabi

---

[a] ? read *Roberto*.

---

[1] *P.U.E.* i no. 44.
[3] *E.Y.C.* iii no. 1825 (cal. below, no. 324).

[2] *E.Y.C.* iv nos. 120, 121.

plenarie in campo et bosco et prato et pastura, liberas et quietas et immunes ab omnibus geldis et consuetudinibus et auxiliis et ab omni humano servicio sicut liberam et perpetuam elemosinam, et hoc pro anima domini mei et pro filio meo Rogero et pro salute anime mee et pro animabus omnium antecessorum meorum. Isti sunt testes, Nicolaus capellanus, Hugo capellanus, Aliz de Gant, Radulfus de Bellunt', Arnaldus de Vilers, Paulinus medicus de Eboraco, Ezeg'n prepositus, Rogerus clericus, Willelmus camerarius, Walterus famulus domine, Unspacus de Hosingham,[a] Hugo filius Aectioni et multi alii et Walterus de Larivera.

NOTE. The appearance of Alice de Gant gives the *terminus a quo*. The gift was confirmed by archbishop Theobald, 1150 × 1154,[1] and by Roger de Mowbray, *c*. 1154 × 1157 (below, no. 302).

301 *Confirmation by Roger de Mowbray to St. Leonard's hospital, York, of one carucate in Theakston (Yorks., N.R.), given by Robert de Musters.*
[*c*. 1145 × 1157]

Extract, from fo. 197 of a lost volume of the cartulary of St. Leonard's, York: Bodl., MS. Dodsworth 120 B fo. 78*v*.

Rogerus de Mulbrai archiepiscopo Ebor(acensi) et capitulo Sancti Petri omnibusque salutem. Sciatis me concessisse et carta mea confirmasse hospitali Sancti Petri Ebor(aci) unam carucatam terre in Textun quam Robertus Musters homo meus eis dedit. Test(es), Robertus de Laundeles, Rogerus de Cundeo, Willelmus de Wivilla, Radulfus Beler, Walterus de Carlaton, Oliver de Busci, Walterus de la Rivere, Willelmus de Crochesley.

NOTE. A *mansum* and one carucate in Theakston were confirmed by Adrian IV, 19 Jan. 1157,[2] and Ralph Beler died by 1157.[3] As Theakston belonged to the honour of Richmond, the confirmation probably belongs to the period after earl Alan's return to Britanny, in 1145 (cf. above, no. 198 note).

302 *Confirmation by Roger de Mowbray to St. Leonard's hospital, York, of his mother Gundreda's gift of 4 bovates in Bagby.* [*c*. 1154 × 1157]

Transcript, from an original charter formerly in St. Mary's Tower, York: Bodl., MS. Dodsworth 7 fo. 14*r*. Extract, from fo. 90 of a lost volume of the cartulary of St. Leonard's, York: Bodl., MS. Dodsworth 120 B fo. 61*v*.

Notum sit archiepiscopo Ebor(acensi) et capitulo Sancti Petri omnibusque sancte matris ecclesie filiis tam futuris quam presentibus quod

---

[a] *Sic*, presumably for *Hovingham*.

[1] *E.Y.C.* i no., 185, cf. no. 299 above.   [2] *P.U.E.* i no. 64.
[3] See *E.Y.C.* ix 212.

ego Rogerus de Mulbrai et heredes mei damus et concedimus et confirmamus Deo et pauperibus hospitalis Sancti Petri Eboraci illas quatuor bovatas terre in Baggabi, liberas et quietas ab omnibus geldis et auxiliis et consuetudinibus et ab omni humano servicio immunes, quas domina Gundreda mater mea eisdem pauperibus dedit et carta sua confirmavit pro anima patris mei et pro anima sua et pro meipso et meis heredibus. Hanc elemosinam carta mea dictis pauperibus confirmo liberam et quietam in bosco et in plano et in pastura ab omni humano servicio sicut puram et perpetuam elemosinam. Isti sunt testes,[a] Nigellus filius domini, Robertus capellanus, Walterus Buheria, Radulfus Beler, Walterus de Carlat', Thoma de Colavilla, Berner mag(ister) Nigelli, Oliverus[b] de Buci, Willelmus de Crocheslai, et Hugo presbyter, et Ricardus presbyter et multi alii.

NOTE. It is probable that Roger issued this confirmation after Gundreda's death, which had probably occurred by 1154 (no. 236 note). Ralph Beler was dead by 1157.[1] In Henry II's confirmation, of 1158 × 1166 (? 1158), Roger, not Gundreda, is named as the donor.[2]

303 *Confirmation by Roger de Mowbray to St. Leonard's hospital, York, of land of his fee in Heslington (Yorks., E.R.), given by Robert son of Copsi.*

[c. 1154 × 1157]

Pd., *E.Y.C.* v no. 160, from Bodl., MS. Rawlinson B 455 fo. 167r.

Testes, prior ecclesie Sancte Marie et Willelmus monachus et Daniel pater ejus et Reginaldus Puher, Willelmus de Wivilla, Rogerus de Condeio, Robertus capellanus, Radulfus Beler, Willelmus de Crocheslei, Simon de Sancto Claro, Robertus[c] de Ripun, Radulfus[d] de Bellun, Hamundus Beler.

NOTE. Ralph Beler died by 1157.[3] William de Wyville's high place in the witness-order suggests he may have been *dapifer* at this time, therefore after c. 1154.[4] Robert son of Copsi's charters, *E.Y.C.* v nos. 156–8, however, belong to the period before 1148. Five carucates in Heslington were confirmed to the hospital by Theobald, archbishop of Canterbury, before 1154 (see above, no. 299).

[a] The witness-list of Dodsworth 120 B fo. 61v reads: 'Walter Buher, Rad. Beler, Hamo Beler, Walter de Carlton, Thos. de Colevilla, Oliver de Buci'.   [b] *Oliveri*, MS.   [c] *Roberto*, MS.   [d] *Radulfo*, MS.

---

[1] See *E.Y.C.* ix 212.   [2] *E.Y.C.* i no. 175.   [3] See *E.Y.C.* ix 212.
[4] See above, p. lxii.

304 *Confirmation by Roger de Mowbray to St. Leonard's hospital, York, of a toft with an orchard* (virgultum) *in Fishergate* (*York*)*, given by Gynabois.*

[*c.* 1147 × 1165]

Pd., *E.Y.C.* i no. 332, from B.M., Cotton MS. Nero D iii fo. 120r (old fo. 127r).

Testes, Nigellus filius meus et heres, qui presens fuit et hoc concessit; Nicholaus capellanus, Rogerus de Cundi, Oliver de Buci, Walterus de Bueri, Rogerus de Flammavilla, Herbertus de Morvilla, Hugo Malabissa, Walterus de la Rivera, Walterus de Carlatuna, Robertus de Daivila, Radulfus de Bellun, Willelmus filius Wuer, Willelmus filius Wualonis, Hamo Beler, Willelmo de Crokaslai, Aschatillus hostiarius.

NOTE. Farrer's *terminus ad quem*, 1165, was doubtless dictated by the appearance of Herbert de Moreville, who had been succeeded in his fee by 1166 (see no. 401). But his *terminus a quo*, 1155, seems doubtful. Asketil *hostiarius* does not otherwise occur later than *c.* 1155.[1] In view of the reference to Nigel de Mowbray's consent, the earliest possible date is *c.* 1147.

Robert, master of the hospital, granted this *mansura* to St. Cuthbert, Durham, in exchange for two *mansurae* at Skelton in Howden.[2]

305 *Confirmation by Roger de Mowbray to St. Leonard's hospital, York, of the church of Eltisley* (*Cambs.*)*, given by Roger de Cundy.*

[*c.* 1166 × March 1173]

Transcript, from an original charter formerly in St. Mary's Tower, York: Bodl., MS. Dodsworth 7 fo. 329r.

Notum sit omnibus sancte matris ecclesie filiis tam futuris quam presentibus quod ego Rogerus de Molbrai et heredes mei concedimus et confirmavimus donationem illam quam fecit Rogerus Condeio de ecclesia sua de Eltesleia, quam dedit Deo et pauperibus hospitalis Sancti Petri in puram et perpetuam elemosinam in presencia nostra. Isti sunt testes, Nigellus de Molbrai, Robertus frater ejus, Rogerus de Condeio, Walterus Buheri, Hugo Malebisse, Radulfus de Bellun, Rolandus de Landeles, Warinus filius Simonis, Hamo Beler, Robertus Beler, Robertus de Crevequer, Radulfus de Belveir et multi alii.

NOTE. Warin son of Simon first occurs in 1166 (see no. 398 note). This gift was confirmed by pope Alexander III, 31 March 1173.[3]
Roger de Cundy's charter is in MS. Dodsworth 7 fo. 329r.[4] The origin of the Mowbray interest in Eltisley is obscure.[5]

---

[1] See nos. 38, 40, 99, 238, 297.   [2] *E.Y.C.* ii no. 981.   [3] *P.U.E.* i no. 117.
[4] For the Cundy fee, see Fees [27].
[5] Cf. W. Farrer, *Feudal Cambridgeshire* (Cambridge, 1920) p. 173.

306 *Notification by Roger de Mowbray of his gift to St. Leonard's hospital, York, of the ninth sheaf of corn on all his English demesne lands; and precept to his reeves to sustain the gift.*   [*c.* 1166 × March 1173]

> Cartulary copies: B.M., Cotton MS. Nero D iii fo. 65*r* (old fo. 63*r*) (two versions, A and B). Charter roll copy: P.R.O., Charter Roll 22 Edw. I (C. 53/80) m. 9 (version C).
> Pd. (abstract), *C.Ch.R.* ii 441 (18), and (abbreviated), *Mon. Ang.* vi (2) 612 (XIV), from Charter Roll. Also pd. (abbreviated), *Mon. Ang.* vi (2) 611 (XI), from an *inspeximus* by William de Mowbray.

Notum sit omnibus sancte matris ecclesie filiis tam presentibus quam futuris quod ego Rogerus*ᵃ* de Molbray et heredes mei concessimus et in perpetuam elemosinam dedimus Deo et Sancto Leonardo et pauperibus hospitalis Sancti Petri nonam garbam bladi nostri de omni dominio nostro quod habemus in Anglia. Quare volumus et firmiter precipimus quatinus predictorum pauperum ministri a prepositis nostris prenominatam elemosinam sine aliqua contradictione ad sustentacionem dilectorum amicorum Christi suscipiant *ᵇ*et quiete*ᵇ* et honorifice possideant ut eterne felicitatis participes existere mereamur. Et si forte contigerit ut nos aliquibus *ᶜ*personis vel religioni vel viris secularibus*ᶜ* ad tenendum de nobis dominia nostra sive ad tempus sive imperpetuum concedamus elemosinam prefatam possessores dominiorum pauperibus hospitalis reddant.*ᵈ* Hiis testibus, Nigello et Roberto filiis meis, Roberto de Daivill, Rogero de Condio,*ᵉ* Gwaltero Buhin,*ᶠ* Hugone Malebisse, Radulfo de Belun, Rollando de Landel',*ᵍ* Gwarino filio Simonis, Hamone Beler, Roberto Beler,*ʰ* Roberto de Crevequer, Radulfo de Belveir.*ⁱ*

> NOTE. The composition of the witness-list suggests that this charter was issued at the same time as no. 305 above.

307 *Gift by Roger de Mowbray to St. Leonard's hospital, York, of a moiety of the church of Althorpe (Axholme, Lincs.).*   [*c.* 1170 × March 1173]

> Cartulary copy: B.M., Cotton MS. Nero D iii fo. 15*r* (old fo. 13*r*). Charter roll copy: P.R.O., Charter Roll 22 Edw. I (C. 53/80) m. 9.
> Pd. (abstract), *C.Ch.R.* ii 441 (17), and (abbreviated) *Mon. Ang.* vi (2) 612 (XIV), from Charter Roll.

Rogerus de Moubray universis filiis sancte matris ecclesie presentibus et futuris salutem. Notum sit vobis me et heredes meos concessisse et dedisse et presenti carta confirmasse Deo et pauperibus hospitalis Sancti Petri Ebor(aci) medietatem ecclesie de Aletorp' cum omnibus pertinenciis

---

ᵃ Robertus, A.   *ᵇ⁻ᵇ* Omitted in C.   *ᶜ⁻ᶜ* Omitted in B and C, which read: *hominibus*.   *ᵈ reddant*, B.   *ᵉ Cundeyo*, C.   *ᶠ Galtero Buhery*, C.   *ᵍ Hudles*, A.   *ʰ* This witness omitted in B.   *ⁱ Belveer*, C.

suis in puram et perpetuam elemosinam liberam et quietam ab omni
exactione et seculari servicio pro salute anime mee et omnium antecessorum meorum et heredum, ut simus participes omnium beneficiorum
que fient illa domo nunc et imperpetuum. Hiis testibus, Roberto capellano,
Roberto de Daivilla, Willelmo fratre suo, Ricardo de Avvers, Roberto
de Busci, Radulfo de Bevven,[a] Petro de Bilingheia, Gileberto de Rompan, Hugone Malebisse, Alano de Limeseia,[b] Willelmo camerario,
Hugone fratre suo, Roberto de Bello Campo.

> NOTE. The appearance of Alan de Limesey suggests a date after *c.* 1170 (see
> no. 66 note). The church of Althorpe was confirmed to the hospital by
> Alexander III, 31 March 1173.[1] The other moiety belonged to the Templars
> (no. 273).
> The cartulary copy has the heading: *Rogerus de Moubray de ecclesia de
> Alethorp' cum sigillo W. Ebor. archiepiscopi eidem apposito.* If the above dating
> is correct, 'W.' is not to be identified with William Fitz Herbert (1143–7 and
> 1153–4). The archiepiscopal seal was therefore perhaps appended at the time
> of an *inspeximus* by a later archbishop, such as Walter de Gray (1214–55).

308 *Gift by Roger de Mowbray to St. Leonard's hospital, York, of 32 acres
of meadow in (? South) Cave (Yorks., E.R.), and of Swain son of Dune
in Thirsk (N.R.), with his tenement.*   [*c.* 1160 × Sept. 1182]

> Cartulary copy: Bodl., MS. Rawlinson B 455 fo. 228v.

Universis filiis sancte matris ecclesie Rogerus de Molbrai salutem.
Notum sit vobis me et heredes meos dedisse et presenti carta confirmasse
Deo et pauperibus hospitalis Sancti Petri Ebor(aci) triginta duas acras
prati in Cava et Suanum filium Dune in Tresco et toftum suum et
croftum et duas bovatas terre plenarie in omnibus in liberam et puram
et perpetuam elemosinam que scilicet prius dederamus Warino vielatori
pro servicio suo. Cujus etiam petitione et concessu predictis Dei
pauperibus hec in puram et perpetuam elemosinam dedimus et predictus
Warinus hanc elemosinam tenebit in vita sua de prefatis pauperibus,
reddendo eis annuatim unam libram piperis. Hiis testibus, Roberto de
Molbrai, Hugone Malabissa, Adam Luvel, Rodberto de Bucei, Herberto
filio Ricardi, Nicholao de Bellun, Willelmo de Daivilla, Radulfo de
Bevver, Rodberto de Tresco, Rogero fratre archid(iaconi), Willelmo de
Tichehil, Hugone filio Lewini.

> NOTE. Nicholas de Bellun does not occur before *c.* 1160 (no. 343 note), and
> Herbert son of Richard's first certainly dated appearance is 1166 (no. 401).[2]
> William of Tickhill died by Sept. 1182 (no. 388 note).

---

[a] *Beauuer*, Charter Roll.   [b] *Lymeseya*, Charter Roll.

[1] *P.U.E.* i no. 117.   [2] See Fees [32].

309 *Confirmation by Nigel de Mowbray to St. Leonard's hospital, York, of the previous gift by Roger de Mowbray.* [*c.* 1160 × Sept. 1182]

Cartulary copy: Bodl., MS. Rawlinson B 455 fo. 228*v.*

Universis filiis sancte matris ecclesie Nigellus de Molbrai salutem. Notum sit vobis me et heredes meos dedisse et presenti carta confirmasse Deo et pauperibus hospitalis Sancti Petri Ebor(aci) triginta duas acras prati in Cava et Suanum filium Dune in Tresco et croftum suum et toftum et duas bovatas terre plenarie in omnibus in liberam et puram et perpetuam elemosinam que scilicet pater meus prius dederat Warino vielatori pro servicio suo. Cujus etiam petitione et concessu predictis Dei pauperibus hec in puram et perpetuam elemosinam dedimus. Hiis testibus, Roberto de Molbrai, Hugone Malabissa, Adam Luvel, Rodberto de Bucei, Herberto filio Ricardi, Nicholao de Bellun, Willelmo de Daivilla, Radulfo de Bevver, Rogero fratre archid(iaconi), Willelmo de Tichehil, Hugone filio Lewini.

NOTE. For the date, see note to no. 308.

310 *Confirmation by Nigel de Mowbray to St. Leonard's hospital, York, of all the gifts and alms given by his father.* [*c.* 1170 × Sept. 1182]

Charter roll copy: P.R.O., Charter Roll 22 Edw. I (C. 53/80) m. 9.
Pd. (abstract), *C.Ch.R.* ii 441–2 (19).

Notum sit omnibus sancte matris ecclesie filiis tam futuris quam presentibus quod ego Nigellus de Mulbray concessi et dedi et presenti carta confirmavi Deo et pauperibus hospit(alis) Sancti Petri Ebor(aci) omnes donationes et elemosinas in omnibus quas pater meus eisdem pauperibus in elemosinam dederat sicut carte ipsius testantur. Hoc feci pro salute anime mee et pro anima patris mei et matris mee et animabus omnium antecessorum meorum parentum et propinquorum ut simus participes omnium bonorum et orationum que fiunt sive facienda sunt in illa sancta domo nocte et die. Hiis testibus, Johanne abbate de Jeresvalle, Roberto capellano, Hugone Malebisse, Willelmo de Tikehil, Hamone Beler, Radulfo de Belver, Rogero filio Gaufridi, Bertranno Hagat, Roberto de Bucy, Ricardo de Cardunel, Hugone de Lungevilers, Adam de Reynesvilla, Warino filio Simonis, Rogero de Ardek'ne, Roberto de Belcamp, Roberto filio Alfudin.

NOTE. This confirmation was almost certainly subsequent to nos. 305–8. William of Tickhill died by Sept. 1182 (no. 388 note).

311 *Gift by Roger de Mowbray to St. Leonard's hospital, York, of Richard de Geroldethorp with his messuage [in Thirsk].*   [*c.* 1154×1186]

> Extract, from fo. 194 of a lost volume of the cartulary of St. Leonard's, York: Bodl., MS. Dodsworth 120 B fo. 78*r*.

Rogerus de Molbray amicis et hominibus suis Francis et Anglis salutem. Sciatis me dedisse hospitali Sancti Petri Ebor(aci) Ricardum de Geroldethorp cum mess(uagio) suo in tofto et crofto et duabus bovatis terre 20 acrarum cum omnibus pertinenciis. Testes, Nigellus filius domini, Rob(ertus) de Daivilla, et Hugo de Malabisse, Robertus de Molbray, Tho(mas) de Colevill, Rogerus de Ardene.

> NOTE. Thomas de Coleville first occurs after 1154 (see no. 356 note). Richard de Geroldethorp probably came from Thorpe Acre ('Torp' in 1086 and 'Thorp' in 1129) near Garendon in Leicestershire ('Geroldon' in 12th-century documents).[1]

312 *Gift by Roger de Mowbray to St. Leonard's hospital, York, of William de Leicestria and his tenement in Thirsk.*   [*c.* 1166×1186]

> Extract, from fo. 194 of a lost volume of the cartulary of St. Leonard's, York: Bodl., MS. Dodsworth 120 B fo. 78*r*.

Omnibus sancte matris etc. Rogerus de Molbray salutem. Sciatis me dedisse et [concessisse]*ᵃ* hospitali Sancti Petri Ebor(aci) Willelmum de Leicestria et totum tenementum suum in Tresc infra villam et extra. Teste, Nigello de Molbrai, Roberto de Molbrai, Hamone Beler, Roberto de Buci, Gaufrido Dela Hay, Adam Luvel, Roberto de Bellocampo, Roberto Beler.

> NOTE. Geoffrey de la Haia does not occur until after *c.* 1166 (no. 364 note).

313 *Notification by Roger de Mowbray to his men and friends, of his reception into his own protection of the possessions on his fee of St. Leonard's hospital, York.*   [*c.* 1170×1186]

> Cartulary copy: B.M., Cotton MS. Nero D iii fo. 68*r–v* (old fo. 66*r–v*).

Rogerus de Molbrai omnibus hominibus suis Francis et Anglis et amicis suis salutem. Sciatis me concessisse et hac presenti carta mea confirmasse et in manu mea ac defensione mea accepisse omnes possessiones hospitalis beati Leonardi in Ebor(aco) que de feudo meo sunt tam de donatione mea quam de donatione hominum meorum. Et volo et precipio ut omnes

---

ᵃ Omitted in MS.

[1] e.g. nos. 155–6, 158–9.

homines mei ita custodiant et manuteneant omnes possessiones illas etiam in absencia mea ne quis eas ab hospitali auferat vel minuat vel in aliquis perturbet. Insuper volo et precipio eas omnes ita firmiter observari sicut in carta donationis mee et in cartis donationis hominum meorum continetur. Et si aliquis hominum meorum eas in aliquis contra tenorem carte mee vel contra tenorem cartarum hominum meorum perturbaverit senescaldus meus faciat et compellat ita servari sicut me diligit et salutem anime mee. Hii sunt testes, Robertus de Daivilla, Thomas de Colevilla, Hugo Mala bestia, Radulfo de Bealuer, Robertus Buci, Robertus capellanus, Robertus de Molbrai, Robertus hostiarius, Martinus Mala herba.

NOTE. The appearance of the last two witnesses suggests a date after c. 1170.[1] Perhaps Roger de Mowbray was about to leave the country, in 1177 or 1186.

314 *Mandate by Roger de Cundy, steward of Roger de Mowbray, concerning the render to St. Leonard's hospital of the ninth sheaf from the English demesne lands.* [c. 1170 × 1186]

Transcript, probably from a York register, 'Liber D fo. 142': Bodl., MS. Dodsworth 9 fo. 19r. Cartulary copy: B.M., Cotton MS. Nero D iii fo. 68v. Pd., *Mon. Ang.* vi (2) 609, from Cotton MS.

Rogerus de Condeio dapifer Rogeri[a] de Molbrai omnibus ministris domini mei Rogeri[b] salutem. Vobis mando atque precipio quatenus habere faciatis fratribus hospitalis de Eboraco nonam garbam de dominico domini mei Rogeri[c] per totam Angliam, et sibi hominibusque suis[d] predictum bladum ante hostium grangie sue liberare faciatis. Valete.

NOTE. Roger de Cundy occurs as steward in 1174 or 1175 (nos. 110–11; cf. no. 381).[2] Perhaps this mandate was issued when Roger de Mowbray was out of the country, in 1177–8 or 1186–8.

315 *Mandate of Roger de Mowbray to Hamo Beler, Roger de Daiville, and Hugh son of Lewin of York and other tenants of his demesne lands, ordering them to cease withholding from St. Leonard's hospital, York, the thraves he had given.* [1182 × 1186]

Cartulary copy: B.M., Cotton MS. Nero D iii fo. 65r (old fo. 63r).

Rogerus de Moubr' Hamoni Beler et Rogero de Daivilla et Hugoni filio Lewini de Ebor(aco) et universis aliis hominibus suis tenentibus dominia

---

^a *Rogerus*, cart. ^b *Regis*, cart. ^c *R.*, cart. ^d Omitted in MS. Dodsw.

---

[1] Robert 'portarius' occurs *E.Y.C.* ii nos. 706, 1199, 1225; Martin Malherbe occurs *E.Y.C.* i nos. 55–6, 59, 84, 226, 546, 625, and in many other charters after c. 1170.
[2] For his fee, see Fees [27].

sua in Anglia salutem. Fratres hospitalis Sancti Petri Ebor(aci) michi
conquesti sunt quod vos elemosinam meam, scilicet nonam garbam
omnium dominiorum meorum in Anglia quam eis in puram et perpetuam elemosinam dedi et Nigellus filius et heres meus concessit et
confirmavit unde etiam ipsi cartas nostras habent detinetis. Sciatis igitur
vos nullatenus eis predictam elemosinam posse detinere. Quia nec ego
eis prefatam elemosinam possem detinere si vellem. Si enim detinerem
liceret eis de jure rigore ecclesiastice justicie in me agere donec sepe-
dictam elemosinam plenarie eis redderem. Sciatis autem me vobis dominia mea non liberius dedisse quam ego ea tenui et quod eis in puram
et perpetuam elemosinam dedi nullatenus vobis dare posse. Vobis ergo
generaliter mando atque precipio quatinus predictam elemosinam prefatis pauperibus Christi scilicet ix garbam totius terre quam tenetis de
dominiis meis in Anglia plenarie sine omni contradictione et impedimento
solvatis. Hiis testibus, fratre Roberto de Constantino, Radulfo de Bevver
dapifero, Filippo de Monte pincun, Radulfo filio Ricardi, Petro clerico,
Arnaldo dispensario, Willelmo de Camera.

NOTE. Hugh son of Lewin probably succeeded William of Tickhill in the
manor of Askham Richard, 1182.[1] All these witnesses, except the first, occur
in no. 276, which may belong to the year 1185–6.
    Hamo Beler held demesne land in Axholme and Hovingham, and Roger de
Daiville in South Cave.[2]

316 *Confirmation by Roger de Mowbray to St. Mary's, York (Ben.), of the
vill of Hutton le Hole (Yorks., N.R.) from the river Dove to the boundary
of Spaunton and on the moor to the boundary of Cleveland; and of all the
lands and tithes of the grant of Nigel d'Aubigny, his father.*

[1142 × c. 1150]

Pd., *E.Y.C.* ix no. 136, from York, D. & C. Muniments, MS. xvi A. 1 fo. 176v.

Hiis testibus, Rogero abbate de Beeland, Roberto de Alne(to), Sampsone
de Albinio, Radulfo de Bellu(n), et multis aliis.

NOTE. For Nigel d'Aubigny's gifts to St. Mary's, see nos. 2, 3, 12.

317 *Gift by Roger de Mowbray to St. Mary's, York, of the island of Sandtoft
(Axholme, Lincs.), with fisheries, land, and pasture, and certain renders of
food and other rights.* [1142 × c. 1150]

13th-cent. copy of an *inspeximus* by R. dean of York: Bodl., MS. Dodsworth
76 fo. 121r.
Pd., *Mon. Ang.* iii 617 (I) (edn. of 1682, i 405).

[1] See no. 388, and cf. *E.Y.C.* i 427–8.
[2] See above, p. xliv n. 9; and nos. 61, 342, 360.

Notum sit omnibus videntibus vel audientibus literas has quod ego Rogerus de Mubray cum consilio heredum meorum et amicorum meorum consensu, pro salute anime mee et animarum patris et matris mee et omnium parentum meorum, concessi et dedi et hac mea carta confirmavi ecclesie beate Marie Ebor(aci) et monachis ibidem Deo servientibus, in puram et perpetuam elemosinam, insulam que vocatur Santoft' cum omnibus pertinenciis suis, et cum piscariis que vocantur Sister et Carleflet', et cum Heselholm' et Munkeholm'[a] et Hailwaldholm' et Calvecroft', et totam terram et pasturam inter Calvecroft et Carleflet usque ad Heselholm' et usque ad aquam que vocatur Ydel, libere et quiete. Et concedo eis ad opus monachi Santoft' sex sceppas ordei de hominibus meis de Appewyt omni anno in die Omnium Sanctorum, et medietatem decimarum omnium ciborum meorum ubicunque fuero in Haxolm'. Et quindecim porcos habeant per totum annum sine pannagio in bosco meo que vocatur Ros, et pasturam decem vaccarum in eodem bosco, et quicquid inde capere voluerit de mortuo ad comburendum bosco et de viridi ad edificandum, sine vasto et venditione. Insuper concedo monacho de Santoft' ut habeat unum mastivum ad custodie[ndum domum][b] suam et croftum suum de extraneis animalibus, et quicquid poterit lucrari de communi palude et de rebus suis venditis ad [utilitatem][b] suam, sine impedimento hominum meorum. Si quis heredum meorum, instigante diabolo, hanc confirmationem violare [presumpserit][b], maledictionem Dei et mei et omnium parentum meorum habeat, quia sicut didicimus antecessores nostri hec omnia eis concess[erunt et plurima][b] alia eis contulerunt. Testibus hiis, Roberto de Alneto, Sampsone de Albino, Radulfo de Bellum, Roberto de Davilla, et m[ultis aliis.][b]

NOTE. The witnesses suggest that the charter belongs to the same occasion as no. 316. The island of Sandtoft, which had been given to St. Mary's by Geoffrey de La Guerche,[1] became a cell for one monk, sustained by the food and other rights conveyed in the present charters.

318 *Grant by Roger de Mowbray to St. Mary's, York, in satisfaction for injuries done to the church, of freedom from castle-works and tensarie; of their mill, pool, and fishery at Myton on Swale (Yorks., N.R.), and of a boat there; settlement of a dispute over land between Beningbrough and Overton and Shipton (N.R.); and restoration of their land of Ousefleet (W.R.).* [1142×c. 1154]

Cartulary copy: York, D. & C. Muniments, MS. xvi A. 1 fo. 138r.
Pd., *Mon. Ang.* iii 558 (XLI).

[a] *Mon. Ang.* has *Munbeholm'*.   [b] Edge of folio torn; lacunae supplied from *Mon. Ang.*

[1] *E.Y.C.* i 276.

Universis ecclesie filiis Rogerus de Moubray salutem. Quoniam tam per me quam per meos multa dampna multociens abbatie Ebor(aci) illata sunt, in recompensationem et satisfactionem eorum firmam et perpetuam pacem futuris temporibus a me et heredibus meis et omnibus qui ad me pertinent, predicte ecclesie concessi et presenti cartula confirmavi, videlicet ut ipsa ecclesia deinceps libera et quieta sit ab omni exactione mei et meorum tam de operibus castrorum quam de tensariis que violenter et injuste a castrensibus exigi solent. Concessi etiam prefate ecclesie ut habeant apud Mitonam villam suam molendinum et stagnum et piscariam suam sicut unquam melius preteritis temporibus habuerunt. Quoniam vero pontem ejusdem ville destruxi, ad proprium transitum suum et suorum et omnium salva pace et indemnitate castri mei transire volentium et ad deferenda sive referenda quecunque eis necessaria sunt, navim eis concessi donec eis pontem suum quem in tempore patris mei et meo habuerunt reparere licuerit. Contentionem quoque illam que diu habita fuit inter Benyngburgh et duas villas eorum, Overtonam scilicet et Schuptonam de terra interjacente in bosco et plano, per juramentum duodecim legitimorum virorum quos abbas predicte ecclesie supposuit, presente Augustino priore de Novo Burgo et hominibus Willelmi de Arches ad cujus feodum predicta villa de Benyngburgh pertinet, Widone scilicet de Wivelesthorp', Alberico de Merstona, Fulcone de Hammertona, qui ex precepto meo ad diem statutum interfuerunt, prorsus pacificando removi ita videlicet ut terram illam ab omni calumpnia deinceps quietam et liberam futuris temporibus possideant. Terram etiam de Ufflet in prato et in terra culta quam Normannus et Willelmus [filii]ᵃ Mazeline ob patrocinium et tuitionem meam michi dederant prefate ec[clesie]ᵃ libere et quiete reddidi. Hanc conventionem et pactionem inviolabiliter tenendam propria manu affidavi et Robertus de Dayvilla et Hugo Mala Bissa similiter affidaverunt.

NOTE. Augustine was prior of Newburgh from 1142 to some time between 1154 and 1157.[1] William de Arches died in c. 1154 (below, no. 359 note).

319 *Release by R(oger) de Mowbray to St. Mary's, York, of all forensic service due to him in Wroot (Lincs.).* [c. 1160×c. 1170]

> 13th-cent. copy of an *inspeximus* by R. dean of York: Bodl., MS. Dodsworth 76 fo. 121r.
> Pd., *Mon. Ang.* iii 618 (II) (edn. of 1682, i 405).

Sciant omnes tam presentes quam futuri quod ego R. de Mubray totum forense servicium et quicquid ego solebam habere in Wroth s[ive in una

ᵃ Illegible in MS.

---

[1] See *E.Y.C.* ix 248.

re]*ᵃ* sive in alia, liberum et quietum reddidi Deo et Sancte Marie et monachis Ebor(aci), pro amore Dei et pro salute mea et filiorum me[orum et pro animabus]*ᵃ* patris et matris mee omniumque parentum meorum. Volo itaque ut Wroth, cum omnibus rebus quas inde solebam habere, qui[eta et libera in]*ᵃ* pura elemosina in perpetuum eisdem monachis permaneat, eorumdem usibus modis omnibus pro futura. Testibus hiis, T[homa de Colevi]*ᵃ*lla, Roberto de Davilla, Radulfo de Belwer, Roberto fratre ejus, Johanne Cruequer', Willelmo filio Ingeler, Willelmo de Langetof[t, Roberto capellano.]*ᵃ*

NOTE. Five of these witnesses occur in *c.* 1160 × 1169 (no. 247) and in 1163 × 1169 (no. 249). Wroot had been granted to St. Mary's by Geoffrey de Stuteville, probably in the time of William Rufus.[1]

320 *Confirmation by Roger de Mowbray to St. Mary's, York, of 6 bovates in Hayton (Yorks., E.R.), given by Richard de Moreville.* [*c.* 1154×1183]

Transcript, from cartulary of St. Mary's, York, fo. 90r: Bodl., MS. Dodsworth 9 fo. 89r.

Rogerus de Molbrai confirmat ecclesie beate Marie Eboraci sex bovatas terre in Haitona preter dimidiam illam carrucatam terre quam prius concessit eisdem monachis et quam habent ex dono Ricardi filii et heredis Hereberti de Morevilla in eadem villa.

NOTE. Richard de Moreville succeeded to his father's 5 fees after *c.* 1154 and probably died by 1183 (no. 384 note). Land in Hayton was held of Moreville by the family of Rudston.[2]

321 *Confirmation by Roger de Mowbray to St. Peter's, York (secular cathedral), and William of Winchester, canon of York, of the church of Bubwith (Yorks., E.R.), founded on his fee, given by Warin of Bubwith.*

[*c.* 1138×1143]

Pd., *York Min. Fasti* i no. 2, from B.M., Cotton MS. Claud. B iii fo. 25r. Also pd. (abbreviated), *Mon. Ang.* vi (3) 1189 (LXVI) from York D. & C. Muniments, Registrum Magnum Album III fo. 18.

Hiis testibus, Herberto de Cuningburg', Waltero Buher(i), Bertram(o) Aget, Mathia de Rampayg', Ricardo de More Villa, Olivero de Buc(i), Rogero de C(un)dio.

NOTE. Bubwith was part of the Tison fee (Fees [3]). Warin of Bubwith's charter, and William Tison's confirmation are both attested by William de

---

ᵃ Edge of folio torn; *lacunae* supplied from *Mon. Ang.*

[1] *E.Y.C.* i 276.   [2] Cf. Fees [22]; *E.Y.C.* x no. 28.

Sainte-Barbe as dean of York, and therefore belong to the period before June 1143.[1]

For Nigel d'Aubigny's gifts to York, see above, nos. 2, 3.

322 *Gift by Roger de Mowbray, with the consent of Alice his wife and Nigel his heir, to St. Peter's, York, by way of restoration of the losses caused by him to the church and to obtain absolution for the same, of £10 worth of land in South Cave (Yorks, E.R.), i.e. £4 worth in 4 carucates of tilled land and £6 worth in meadow land.* At St. Peter's, York, 17 April 1153

Pd., *E.Y.C.* iii no. 1823, from York, D. & C. Muniments, Registrum Magnum Album III fo. 16v.

Presentibus et pro teste assistentibus, Radulfo episcopo,[2] Sampsone de Albenni et Rogero de Cundi clericis meis, Hugone de Malebys et Olivero de Buscy et Hamone Beler et Herberto pincerna, hominibus meis, et preter hos clericorum et proborum hominum civitatis copiosa multitudine.

323 *Gift by Alice de Gant to St. Peter's, York, for the absolution of Roger de Mowbray and for her admission to the fraternity of St. Peter's, of £10 worth of land in South Cave.* At St. Peter's, York, 9 June 1154

Pd., *E.Y.C.* iii no. 1824, from York, D. & C. Muniments, Registrum Magnum Album II fo. 36v. Also pd., *Mon. Ang.* vi (2) 611 (XII), from an original charter formerly in St. Mary's Tower, York (cf. transcript, Bodl., MS. Dodsworth 7 fo. 170r). Another cartulary copy: B.M., Cotton MS. Claud. B iii fo. 32r.

Hiis testibus, Willelmo de Widowilla, Rogero de Flamvilla, Bertram Haget, Hugone Malebissa, Radulfo de Beauver, Radulfo Rugemund, David lardiner, Waltero de Karletuna; presente Roberto filio Rogeri.

NOTE. The text as given in *Mon. Ang.*, and in the Dodsworth and Cotton MSS., confirms Farrer's conjecture that the dating clause in the Reg. Mag. Album version—'post obitum archiepiscopi Willelmi, eodem etiam non diu sepulto'—should be emended, *nondum* being read for *non diu*.

324 *Gift by Roger de Mowbray to the church of South Cave (a prebend of St. Peter's, York) of the tithe of the mills of that town.* [1154×1157]

Confirmation by Roger of Pont l'Évêque of this and of restorations by Bertram Haget of a *mansura* in Cave, and by Robert of the hospital (of St. Leonard's) in Broomfleet, pd., *E.Y.C.* iii no. 1825, from York, D. & C. Muniments, Registrum Magnum Album II fo. 38v. Another cartulary copy: B.M., Cotton MS. Claud. B iii fo. 34r.

[1] *York Min. Fasti* i nos. 1, 3. [2] Ralph Noel, bishop of Orkney.

Testes sunt prefate donationis decime molendinorum: Osebertus Arundel canonicus Beverlacensis, Rogerus de Cunde canonicus Eboracensis, Petrus de Carcasona, Radulfus de Sancto Gregorio clerici archiepiscopi, Willelmus medicus canonicus Lund',[1] Turstinus dapifer domini archiepiscopi, Robertus de Daivilla, Olivarus de Buscy, Radulfus Beler, Radulfus de Beslun, Walterus de Karletuna, homines Rogeri de Moubray.

> NOTE. In view of the appearance among the witnesses of Ralph Beler, Farrer's terminal date, 1160, can be put back to 1157.[2] The church of York had probably possessed South Cave church since the time of Robert Malet.[3]

325 *Gift by Roger de Mowbray to St. Peter's, York, of the churches of Masham (Yorks., N.R.), Kirkby Malzeard (W.R.), Haxey, Owston (Axholme, Lincs.), Langford (Notts.), and Smite (Warwicks.).* [Oct. 1154 × 1157]

> Cartulary copy: B.M., Cotton MS. Claud. B iii fo. 51v.
> Pd. (transl.), J. Fisher, *History of Masham* (1895) p. 531.

Rogerus de Molbrai omnibus sancte matris ecclesie filiis ad quos litere iste pervenerint salutem et dilectionem. Notum sit vobis omnibus me concessisse in prebendam quantum ad laicam personam pertinet et Rogerum archiepiscopum concessisse et confirmasse ecclesie beati Petri de Ebor(aco) ecclesiam de Masham et ecclesiam de Kirkebi Malsard et ecclesiam de Halsay et ecclesiam de Haustun' et ecclesiam de Landesford et ecclesiam de Hesmit cum omnibus pertinenciis earum in perpetuam elemosinam libere et quiete ab omni exactione et consuetudine. Teste, Rogero archiepiscopo et capitulo Ebor', et Radulfo Beler, et Olivero[a] de Buci, et Rogero de Flamanvilla, et Waltero de Charletona.

> NOTE. The appearance together as witnesses of Roger of Pont l'Évêque, archbishop of York, and Ralph Beler, gives the outside limits of date (cf. no. 324).
> The first five churches had already been given to Newburgh (nos. 196–9) and the sixth to Kenilworth (nos. 175–7). Much earlier, Geoffrey de La Guerche had given the church of Langford to Monks Kirby.[4] The dispute between York and Newburgh was referred to pope Alexander III.[5] Newburgh retained Haxey and Owston, with the other Axholme churches, and York kept Masham, Malzeard, and Langford, which were established as the prebend of Masham (no. 326). Kenilworth retained Smite (no. 178).

> [a] *Oliver*, MS.

---

[1] William medicus was a canon of St. Paul's, London.   [2] See *E.Y.C.* ix 212.
[3] See *York Min. Fasti* ii 18.   [4] *Mon. Ang.* vi (2) 996.
[5] *Corpus Iuris Canonici*, ed. E. Friedberg (Leipzig, 1879–81) ii, *Decretales* bk. iii tit. 38 can. 20

326 *Gift by Roger de Mowbray, with the consent of his sons, to St. Peter's, York, of the churches of Masham, Kirkby Malzeard, and Langford to form a prebend in the church of York.* [*c.* 1163×*c.* 1169]

Pd., *York Min. Fasti* i no. 34, from B.M., Cotton MS. Claud. B iii fo. 51*v.* Also pd. (transl.), J. Fisher, *History of Masham* (1895) p. 531.

Hiis testibus, Radulfo de Belveer, Roberto de Buci, Thoma de Colvila, Ricardo de Widevilla, Rogero de Ardane, Samsone Cornuwalla, Roberto capellano, Johanne archidiacono, mag. Mainard', Alano can(onicis) Ebor(acensibus).

NOTE. Five of the witnesses occur in 1163 × 1169 (no. 249). Samson d'Aubigny's son, Roger, became prebendary, and was confirmed in the prebend by Walter Buher, Mowbray's tenant in Masham.[1] The prebend was exempted from archidiaconal dues by archbishop Geoffrey.[2] In 1291 it was York's most valuable prebend, being assessed at £166. 13*s.* 4*d.*[3]

327 *Quitclaim by Roger de Mowbray to St. Peter's, York, of land in Bishopside (Yorks., W.R.) within specified bounds, made before the king in his court at Northampton.* At Northampton [Aug. 1174]

Pd., *York Min. Fasti* ii no. 53, from B.M., Cotton MS. Claud. B iii fos. 50*v*–51*r.*

Hiis testibus, Clemente abbate Sancte Marie Ebor(acensis), Roberto abbate de Fontibus, Rogero abbate de Bellalanda, Willelmo cantore Ebor(acensi), Johanne archidiacono de Notingham, Willelmo senescaldo, Hamone et Ad(a) canonicis Ebor(acensis), Gilberto de Sancto Claro, Johanne hostiario, Hugone de Redenesse, Hugone Malebissa, Nicholao canonico de Ripon(a).

NOTE. This charter was confirmed by Henry II at Woodstock.[4]

327A *Similar quitclaim by Roger de Mowbray to St. Peter's, York.* [At Northampton, Aug. 1174]

Cartulary copy: B.M., Cotton MS. Claud. B iii fo. 51*r.*

Text identical with 327, with the omission of the clause recording that the quitclaim was made before the king in his court at Northampton. Witnesses as in 327, with the omission of Nicholas canon of Ripon.

[1] *York Min. Fasti* i no. 35; cf. charter no. 174 above.
[2] *York Min. Fasti* i no. 36; cf. ibid. no. 37.
[3] *Taxatio Nicholai IV* (Record Comm., 1802) p. 297.
[4] *York Min. Fasti* ii 99, probably at the same time as *E.Y.C.* i no. 508.

328 *Similar quitclaim by Nigel de Mowbray to St. Peter's, York.*

[At Northampton, Aug. 1174]

Cartulary copy: B.M., Cotton MS. Claud. B iii fo. 51*r*.

Nigellus de Molbrai omnibus hominibus Francis et Anglis hanc cartam visuris vel audituris salutem. Sciatis quod . . . continues in identical terms and with same witnesses as 327A.

329 *Gift by Nigel de Mowbray to Roger archbishop of York of the service of Samson of Cornwall for the land held of him at Brinklow (Warwicks.).*

[1174 × Nov. 1181]

Pd., *York Min. Fasti* ii no. 55, from B.M., Cotton MS. Claud. B iii fo. 92*v*.

Hiis testibus, Roberto de Molbrei, Roberto de Butthi, Nicholao de Bellung, Johanne archidiacono, Radulfo capellano, magistro Vaccario, Gaufrido, Ada clericis archiepiscopi, Roberto marescald(o), Johanne hostiar(io), Aug(us)tino camerario, Willelmo de Insula.

> NOTE. An entry of 1226 in archbishop Gray's register records that Samson of Cornwall had sold to the archbishop 2¾ roods of land and 2 burgages in Brinklow.[1]

330 *Gift by Roger de Mowbray to Robert de Arden, clerk, of the wood of 'Bederichellea' (? Birch Leyes in Hampton in Arden, Warwicks.),[2] for which Robert gave Roger £10 Anjou, and was to render a sore sparrow-hawk annually.*

[1154 × c. 1170]

> Transcript, from an original charter formerly in the possession of Symon Mountfort of Bescote, Staffs., 1637: Bodl., MS. Dugdale 13 p. 211.

Rogerus de Molbr' omnibus hominibus et fidelibus suis Normannis et Anglis salutem. Sciatis quod ego concessi Roberto de Ardenna clerico et amico meo totum nemus de Bederichellea cum omnibus antiquis libertatibus et consuetudinibus ejusdem nemoris ad tenendum de me in capite et heredibus meis ita libere et quiete et integre sicut ego unquam illud liberius quietius et integrius tenui. Et ipse propter hanc concessionem meam dedit michi in introitu x libras Andeg', et singulis annis daturus est michi loco servicii nisum unum sorum. Talis quoque conventio facta est inter me et illum de nemore illo quod si ego recuperavero totam terram quam tenet de me Radulfus de Haia in manerio meo de Hantun vel eam totam terram quam habet de me Tustinus de Monte-

---

[1] *Register of Walter Gray*, ed. J. Raine (S.S. lvi) p. 223.

[2] *Place-Names Warwicks.* (English Place-Name Soc. xiii) p. 346, gives 1589 as the first appearance of Birch Leyes.

forti in eodem manerio seu pertinenciis ejus, ut teneam utramque vel alteram in dominico meo, ita quod nec donem eam nec invadiem nec vendam nec commodem nec alio modo alienem a dominico meo, et tunc voluero nemus illud habere et similiter retinere in dominico meo, reddam Roberto x libras And' et nemus potero habere in dominico meo ita quod illud nullo modo alienem a dominico meo. Et si postquam illud aliquo tempore tenuero voluero aliquo modo alienare a me ad Robertum denuo pro easdem x libras revertetur. Si Robertus etiam nemus clauserit reddam ei cum x libris juxta probationem suam quantum miserit in clausura. Et si numquam contigerit me tenere aliquam predictarum terrarum in dominico meo, remaneat Roberto predictum nemus imperpetuum ita vel possit illud cum eisdem conventionibus dare Rogero fratri suo, et post Rogerum si Robertus supervixerit, cui aliorum fratrum suorum vel cui propinquorum vel amicorum suorum voluerit. Ego autem debeo nemus illud warantizare Roberto et post eum Rogero fratri suo contra omnes homines, et pepigi quod illud omnino liberabo ei a canonicis quibus illud commendaveram ad graantum eorum, ita quod unquam oportebit Roberto contra eos inde placitare. Hoc autem totum factum est assensu et concessione Nigelli filii mei, qui similiter sicuti et ego recuperare potest predictum nemus hac conventione. T(estibus), Arnulfo Lex(oviensi) episcopo, Nigello filio meo, Roberto capellano, Roberto de Crevequeor, Roberto de Bucceio, Radulfo de Bealveer, Alexandro de Barent', Rogero de Ard', Simone et aliis pluribus.

NOTE. The appearance of Arnulf, bishop of Lisieux, suggests a date after 1154.[1] Thurstan de Montfort died c. 1170.[2]

Robert de Arden, who appears as clerk of Arden in no. 271, was son of Ralph de Hamton, who was perhaps a son of Turkill of Warwick.[3] Robert became archdeacon of Lisieux (no. 334). The present charter, and nos. 331–8, relate to the Arden subtenancy of the Montfort fee.

331 *Gift by Roger de Mowbray to Roger (de Arden), son of Ralph de Hamton, of the land of 'Langruge' (? in Hampton in Arden), for the tenth part of the service of one knight.* [1154×c. 1170]

Transcript, from an original charter formerly in the possession of Symon Mountfort, 1637: Bodl., MS. Dugdale 13 p. 213.

Rogerus de Molbr' omnibus etc. Sciatis me dedisse et concessisse Rogero filio Radulfi de Hamt' et heredibus suis ad tenendum de me et de

---

[1] Cf. *Letters of Arnulf of Lisieux*, ed. F. Barlow (Camden 3rd ser. lxi) pp. xxv–ix.
[2] *Complete Peerage* ix 120–1.
[3] See W. Dugdale, *Antiquities of Warwickshire*, 2nd edn., W. Thomas (1730) ii 970.

heredibus meis in feudo et hereditate totam terram de Langruge et boscum per divisam de Smalebroc usque ad Chadleswic et de Chadleswic per
viam que vadit ad Benetleie et per viam de Benetleie usque ad Merebroc
et de Merebroc usque ad Blie, et terram Ewini sutoris de Coppthorn et
ipsum Ewinum, et unam virgatam terre que fuit Chippingi in Hampt'
et terram que fuit Eilrici, et Birchile, et terram que fuit Amet, et Brom-
croft cum omnibus suis pertinenciis et adjacentiis in boscis et in planis
etc. per servicium decime partis unius militis. Preter hec concedo huic
Rogero et omnibus hominibus suis suum pasnagium quietum et quod ipse
et homines sui habeant omnia sua necessaria in meis boscis exceptis haiis
meis etc. Hujus mee donationis et concessionis sunt testes Nigellus filius
meus qui hanc donationem fecit et ex sua parte concessit et ita quod
Rogerus dedit ei unum annulum aureum in recognitionem, Willelmus
de Sules, Turstanus de Munfor, Hugo Maleb' etc.

NOTE. Thurstan de Montfort died c. 1170 (no. 330 note). As Roger was
younger than Robert de Arden, this charter presumably cannot have been
given before no. 330. The grant may be referred to in no. 193. In 1174 this
land was temporarily confiscated by the king for Roger de Arden's participation in the rebellion.[1]

332 *Confirmation by Roger de Mowbray of Ralph de la Haia's gift to Roger de
Arden of one virgate in Hampton in Arden, for which Roger de Arden was
to render to Ralph a sore sparrow-hawk annually, and for which he gave
a palfrey in recognition, the agreement being made in the presence of Roger
de Mowbray.*   [c. 1166 × 1177]

Note, from an original charter formerly in the possession of Symon Mountfort, 1637: Bodl., MS. Dugdale 13 p. 213.

Ista carta [i.e. of Ralph de la Haia] confirmata fuit per Rogerum de
Molbrai coram predictis testibus.

The witnesses to Ralph de la Haia's charter, in addition to Roger de
Mowbray himself, are: His testibus, Rogero de Condeio, Waltero
Buerei, Waltero de Scoteni, Radulfo de G'ingb', Gaufrido de Haia,
Henrico Foliot, Hamone Beler, Ricardo Cole, Rogero coco, Radulfo
Carbun, Johanne de Crocheslai, Gaufrido pincerna, Johanne de
Wappenbiri, Roberto de Belchamp, Balduino clerico qui scripsit hanc
cartam.

NOTE. The appearance of Geoffrey de la Haia suggests a date after c. 1166
(see no. 364 note). Walter Buher was dead by 1177 (no. 143 note).

[1] P.R. 20 Hen. II p. 143.

333 *Notification by Roger de Mowbray of Ralph de la Haia's sale to Robert de Arden of all the land and wood in Hampton in Arden which Roger had previously given to Ralph, to be held for half the service of one knight, for which Robert gave Roger a palfrey.* [1154 × 1179]

Transcript, from an original charter formerly in the possession of Symon Mountfort, 1637: Bodl., MS. Dugdale 13 p. 211.

Rogerus de Molbr' omnibus hominibus suis Francis et Anglis salutem. Sciatis quod Radulfus de la Haia voluntate et assensu meo vendidit Roberto de Ardena imperpetuum ad tenendum de me et heredibus meis in capite totam terram et nemus, quod ego dederam ei apud Hantun in Ardena in escambium pro terra quam clamabat tenere de me in Ever-wichesira, scilicet cortem dominicam et gardinum et advocationem ecclesie et totam terram arabilem de dominico et prata dominica de Hant' et molendinum cum terra ad illud pertinente et fabrum cum tota terra sua et omnes bovarios cum terris eorum et terram Kippingi qui faciebat summonitionem et terram messarii et terram et silvam de Birchelea et Hespeleia et silvam de la Leia et nemus operabilem apud Chedleswic et omnes haias que pertinent ad dominicum de Hantun, que omnia predicta dederam et cartam meam ei inde feceram. Post-modum vero voluntate et concessione mea sicut dictum est superius omnem terram predictam cum dignitatibus et libertatibus suis et advoca-tionem ecclesie vendidit Radulfus predicto Roberto Lex(oviensi) archi-diacono pro l marcas argenti et reddidit eam cum omnibus pertinenciis in manum meam liberam et absolutam et quietam clamavit omnino. Et ego ipso Radulfo petente et presente totam terram cum advocatione ecclesie et ceteris omnibus predictis dedi et concessi sepedicto archi-diacono Roberto imperpetuum et homagium ejus inde accepi ad tenen-dum de me et heredibus meis in capite per servicium dimidii militis et ad dandum cui fratrum vel amicorum suorum voluerit salvo predicto servicio michi et heredibus meis. Pepigit quoque idem Radulfus de Haia fide corporaliter prestita quod terram et nemus et advocationem ecclesie et cetera predicta que ei vendidit ei et cui ea ipse daret pro posse suo bona fide warantizaret. Robertus vero pro concessione mea dedit michi unum palefridum bonum. Et ego concessi ei quod si terram predictam et advocationem ecclesie et cetera sepedicta in vita sua nemini dederit justi heredes ejus eam hereditario jure teneant de me et here-dibus meis imperpetuum per predictum servicium. Sed si ea dederit ipse ea teneat et habeat integre et quiete cui ab eo data fuerint. Quare volo etc. quod predictus Robertus etc. teneant etc. terram predictam etc. bene et in pace etc. sicut Nigellus pater meus et ego post eum ea unquam melius etc. tenuimus in bosco et plano etc. T(estibus), Willelmo de Sola, Radulfo de Belvaco, Roberto de Buci, Willelmo de Solariis, Adam Luvel, Adam de Archeteio, Roberto de Baioc, Willelmo de Novilla, Petro de Ard', Huberto clerico, Rogero, Simone, Willelmo Bello Vasleto et pluribus aliis.

> NOTE. The sale by Ralph de la Haia must have been subsequent to no. 330. Robert de Arden was dead by 1179 (no. 179 note).

334 *Confirmation by Nigel de Mowbray to Robert de Arden, archdeacon of Lisieux, of Roger de Mowbray's gift to Robert in Hampton in Arden, for which Robert gave Nigel 100s.* [c. 1160 × 1179]

> Transcript, from an original charter formerly in the possession of Symon Mountfort, 1637: Bodl., MS. Dugdale 13 p. 212.

Nigellus de Moubrai omnibus hominibus suis Francis et Anglis salutem. Sciatis quod ego concessi et confirmavi Roberto Lex(oviensi) archidiacono quicquid pater meus ei concesserat et carta sua confirmaverat in Hantona de Ard', in advocatione ecclesie et terris et pratis et molendinis et aquis et bosco et plano et libertatibus et consuetudinibus et hominibus et virgultis et omnibus aliis rebus. Concessi etiam secundum concessionem patris mei quod idem Robertus possit terram predictam cum libertatibus et dignitatibus et consuetudinibus suis et pertinenciis dare vel vendere cui fratrum vel amicorum suorum voluerit salvo servicio meo. Ipse vero pro concessione mea dedit michi centum solidos et inde homagium ejus accepi. Quare volo etc. quod predictus Robertus etc. habeant et teneant predictam terram imperpetuum de me et heredibus meis libere etc. Testibus, domino et patre meo Rogero de Moubrai, Rainaldo de Gerponvilla, Willelmo de Veteriponte, Galerano vicecomite, Rogero de Perceio, Olivero de Boceio, Adam Lovel, Roberto de Boceio, Radulfo de Millai, Galtero, Andrea et aliis pluribus.

> NOTE. It is unlikely that Nigel de Mowbray issued charters before c. 1160, and Robert de Arden was dead by 1179 (no. 179 note).

335 *Concession by Roger de Mowbray to Peter de Arden of Chadwick (in Hampton in Arden), which Peter's father had bought from Roger and given to Peter, for the tenth part of the service of one knight.* [c. 1154 × 1183]

> Transcript, from an original charter formerly in the possession of Symon Mountfort, 1637: Bodl., MS. Dugdale 13 p. 212.

Rogerus de Molbr' omnibus etc. Sciatis quod ego concessi Petro de Ard' totam terram de Cheddleswic quam pater suus donavit ei pro servicio

suo, quam etiam ipse pater ejus emerat a me cum omnibus hominibus
et libertatibus et consuetudinibus in bosco et plano etc. ad tenendum de
me et heredibus meis imperpetuum pro decima parte servicii militis
unius. Concessi etiam Petro quod ipse terram illam possit dare cui
fratrum suorum voluerit ad tenendum de me et heredibus meis. Et si
ipse nulli fratrum suorum eam donaverit, eo decedente ad proximos et
justissimos ejus transeat heredes cum omnibus libertatibus etc. imperpetuum ad tenendum de me et heredibus meis in capite. Volo itaque
etc. quod ipse teneat etc. hoc modo terram illam etc. per predictum
servicium sicut aliquis militum meorum liberius et honorificentius
feodum suum tenet de me. Ego vero de terra illa homagium ejus accepi.
Testes sunt, Robertus capellanus, Oliverus de Buceio, Hugo Malabissa,
Robertus de Buceio, Ricardus de Morevilla, Hamo Belverius, Rogerus
de Ard' frater Petri et aliis.

NOTE. Roger de Arden occurs first after c. 1154 (nos. 191, 330). Richard de
Moreville was probably dead by 1183 (see note to no. 384).

336 *Gift by Roger de Mowbray to Roger de Arden of the advowson of Hampton
in Arden and of land and wood which Robert, archdeacon of Lisieux, had
bought from Ralph de la Haia, for half the service of one knight.*

[*c.* 1170 × 1184]

Transcript, from an original charter formerly in the possession of Symon
Mountfort, 1637: Bodl., MS. Dugdale 13 p. 213.

Rogerus de Molbrai omnibus etc. salutem. Sciatis me dedisse et concessisse et hac carta mea confirmasse Rogero de Ardena advocationem
ecclesie de Hamtona in Ardena et totam terram et tenementum et nemus
quod Robertus Lexov(iensis) archidiaconus frater ejus emerat de Radulfo de la Haia ad tenendum de me et heredibus meis in capite et de
me tenuit et possedit et ei in vita et libera potestate sua dedit et concessit
et carta sua confirmavit ad tenendum de me per servicium dimidii
militis, videlicet cortam dominicam et gardinium et donationem et
advocationem ecclesie predicte et totam terram arabilem de dominio
etc. Quare volo etc. quatinus Rogerus de Ardena predictam terram etc.
habeat et teneat ita bene etc. sicut carta Roberti Lex(oviensis) archi-
diaconi quam de me habuit testatur et sicut Nigellus pater meus et ego
post eum prefatam advocationem ecclesie et terram et nemus etc. unquam
melius etc. tenuimus in bosco et plano etc. Hiis testibus, Roberto de
Daivilla, Hugone Maleb', Radulfo de Bevver, Nicholao de Bellund,
Roberto de Buci, Warino filio Simonis, Philippo de Munpinchun,
Roberto capellano, Henrico de Steinegrif, Waltero filio Rag', Radulfo

filio Radulfi, Waltero de Hudicote, Johanne de Ludinton, Rogero de Camvilla, Alano de Limesei, Petro clerico, Radulfo clerico et aliis.

Drawing of seal no. 3 of Roger de Mowbray (above, p. lxxxiii).

NOTE. The witness-list is not unlike to those of nos. 343, 346, 349, 360, 364-5, of c. 1170 × 1184, possibly c. 1175 × 1176. Cf. note to no. 343. Arnulf, bishop of Lisieux, and Fulk the dean and the chapter of Lisieux issued a notification to Roger and Nigel de Mowbray before 1179, that Robert de Arden, archdeacon of Lisieux, had given his land of Hampton, with the advowson of the church, to his brothers Peter and Roger.[1]

337 *Confirmation by Nigel de Mowbray to Roger de Arden of the previous gift.*
[c. 1170 × 1190]

Transcript, from an original charter formerly in the possession of Symon Mountfort, 1637: Bodl., MS. Dugdale 13 p. 214.

Nigellus de Molbr' omnibus hominibus etc. Sciatis me dedisse etc. Rogero de Ardena donationem et advocationem ecclesie de Hamtona in Ardena et totam terram et tenementum quod Robertus Lexov(iensis) archidiaconus frater ejus emerat de Radulfo de la Haia ad tenendum etc. sicut in carta Rogeri patris sui videlicet in iisdem verbis et testibus.

Drawing of seal no. 2 of Nigel de Mowbray (above, pp. lxxxiii–iv).

NOTE. Of even date with no. 336, if the witnesses were the same.

338 *Gift by Nigel de Mowbray to Roger de Arden of Chadwick, which his father Ralph[2] and his brother Peter had held, in increment of his other fee in Hampton in Arden, whence he does half the service of one knight.*
[c. 1170 × 1184]

Transcript, from an original charter formerly in the possession of Symon Mountfort, 1637: Bodl., MS. Dugdale 13 p. 212.

Nigellus de Molbr' omnibus etc. Sciatis me dedisse etc. Rogero de Ardena totam terram de Chedleswic cum omnibus pertinenciis suis et divisis quam Radulfus pater suus tenuit et post eum Petrus frater suus illi et heredibus suis in feodo et hereditate libere etc. in bosco et plano etc. in incrementum alterius feudi sui quod tenet de me in Hamtona in Ardena unde facit michi servicium dimidii militis. Hiis testibus, Hugone Malebisse, Adam Luvel, Herberto filio Ricardi, Roberto de Buci, Nicholao de Bellund, Gaufrido de Haia, Radulfo de Bevver etc.

NOTE. Five of these witnesses appear in no. 343 and five in no. 349, of c. 1170 × 1184, possibly c. 1175 × 1176. Cf. note to no. 343. The charter may therefore belong to the same occasion as nos. 336-7.

[1] B.M., Cotton Ch. xi 35.　　[2] De Hamton, see no. 331.

339 *Gift by Roger de Mowbray to Roger de Arden of Richard* nepos *of Uviet,
Roger's man of the Isle of Axholme (Lincs.), for building and restoring his
land.*   [*c.* 1166 × 1186]

Pd., *Danelaw Charters* no. 472, from B.M., Cotton Ch. xxvii. 123.

His testibus . Radulfo de Beluer tunc dapifero . Roberto capellano .
Radulfo Carbun . Roberto de Bello Campo . Balduino clerico;;

Size: 12·9 × 7·7 cm.
Seal: missing; was appended on tongue; also tie-tongue.

NOTE. The last three witnesses occur in the charter for Roger de Arden of
c. 1166 × 1176 (no. 332). Possibly this gift was made soon after the rebellion
of 1174–5, in which Arden's property in Axholme may have been damaged.

340 *Gift by Nigel de Mowbray to Augustine of 2 bovates in Kirkby Malzeard
(Yorks., W.R.), for a rent of spurs or 4d. p.a.*   [1186 × 1190]

Cartulary copies (Fountains): B.M., Add. MS. 37770 fo. 67*v* (old p. 134);
Add. MS. 18276 fo. 109*v* (abstract).
Pd. (transl.), *Fount. Cart.* i 408 (i), from Add. MS. 37770.

Nigellus de Moubr' omnibus hominibus et amicis suis presentibus et
futuris salutem. Sciatis me dedisse et hac carta confirmasse Augustino
pro servicio et homagio suo duas bovatas terre in Malesard quas Acca
tenuit, illi et heredibus suis tenendas de me et heredibus meis jure hereditario, annuatim reddendo pro omnibus serviciis et consuetudinibus
quedam calcaria seu iiij denarios. Hiis t(estibus), Roberto de Moubr',
Rogero de Daivilla, Hamone Beler, Roberto de Castell', W. camerario,[1]
Roberto de Bozci, W. de Mainnill',[2] Radulfo clerico et aliis multis.

NOTE. In 1268 this land was given to Fountains, by a deed which reveals that
Augustine had been chamberlain of Nigel de Mowbray.[3]

341 *Gift by Roger de Mowbray to Hamo Beler of 7½ carucates in Eye Kettleby
and 3 carucates in Burton Lazars (Leics.), and a mill at Norby (par. Thirsk,
Yorks., N.R.), for the service of one knight.*   [1138 × Apr. 1153]

Confirmation by Henry II [1156 × 1158]: pd., *Recueil des Actes de Henri II*,
ed. L. V. Delisle and E. Berger (Paris, 1909–27) i no. LXXXVI, from
P.R.O., Patent Roll 3 Edw. IV pt. iii (C. 66/507) m. 23. Also pd., *C.P.R.
1461–67* p. 306.

NOTE. Hamo is described as one of the *homines* of Roger de Mowbray on
17 April 1153 (no. 322), so that he had presumably been enfeoffed by that
date. He held one new fee in 1166.[4]

---

[1] Presumably William the chamberlain.   [2] Perhaps Walter de Meinil.
[3] *Fount. Cart.* i 408 (2).   [4] No. 401; see Fees [43].

342 *Grant by Nigel de Mowbray to Hamo Beler of free pannage in Axholme* (*Lincs.*). [1186×1190]

Original charter: B.M., Add. Ch. 20607.

Nigellus de Molbrai omnibus hominibus suis presentibus et futuris salutem. Sciatis me dedisse et hac mea presenti carta confirmasse Hamundo Beler et suis heredibus padnagium de Insula porcorum suorum et hominum suorum quietum . tenendum de me et meis heredibus. Hiis testibus . Rogero de Sancto Martino . Nicholao de Betlung . Roberto de Castellun . Ricardo Bacun . Radulfo clerico.

No endorsement.

Size: 9·8 × 4·2 cm.; 1·3 cm. turn-up.

Seal: seal no. 2 of Nigel de Mowbray (above, pp. lxxxiii–iv), red wax varnished; legend broken off; appended on silk strings.

NOTE. Hamo Beler had land in Axholme by 1179–80, when he and other men were amerced for constructing an illegal fosse.[1] His meadow in Moss wood is mentioned in no. 276.

343 *Confirmation by Nigel de Mowbray to Nicholas de Bellun of Winksley and* ½ *carucate in Azerley* (*Yorks., W.R.*), *and other tenements, and 100s. worth of land in* (*South*) *Cave* (*E.R.*), *given by Roger de Mowbray, for half the service of one knight.* [*c.* 1170×1184]

Cartulary copies (Fountains): Manchester, John Rylands Libr., Lat. MS. 224 fo. 372r–v; B.M., Add. MS. 18276 fo. 246v (abstract).
Pd. (transl.), *Fount. Cart.* ii 746 (1), from Rylands MS.

Nigellus de Molbr' omnibus hominibus suis et amicis Francis et Anglis clericis et laicis tam presentibus quam futuris salutem. Sciatis me concessisse et hac carta mea confirmasse donationem quam pater meus fecit Nicholao de Bellund, scilicet Winkesle cum omnibus pertinenciis ejus, et dimidiam carrucatam terre in Azerle, scilicet in Flatscouh, et pannagium porcorum suorum et porcorum hominum suorum quietum in omni foresta mea de Malesard et de Masham, et servicium et tenementum Marcelli de Mildeby et heredum suorum, et pastualia et pascualia per totas forestas prefatas quieta ad animalia sua et hominum suorum, et aisiamenta forestarum predictarum sibi et hominibus suis ad edificandum et ardendum et ad alia necessaria sua; et centum solidatas terre in Cava, scilicet Gamel cum dimidia carrucata terre, Reinerum filium Hugonis cum dimidia carrucata terre, Gamel prepositum cum duabus bovetis, Petrum cum duabus bovetis, Robertum filium Toke cum duabus bovetis, Thoche filium Lete cum duabus bovetis terre, et eos et infantes

[1] *P.R. 26 Hen. II* p. 52.

eorum, et triginta acras in eadem villa de prato recenti et antiquo. Hec omnia concessi et confirmavi predicto Nicholao et heredibus suis ad tenendum in feudo et hereditate de me et heredibus meis per servicium dimidii militis. Quare volo et firmiter precipio quatinus omnia hec predicta teneat in bene pace libere et quiete et honorifice sicut unquam pater meus ea liberius vel quietius tenuit, cum omni communitate quam pater meus in illis habuit, tam versus homines quam versus vicinos suos, in boscho et plano in viis et semitis in pratis et pascuis et moris in aquis et stagnis^a et molendinis et in omnibus locis, cum soc et sac et thol et them et infangenþef, cum omnibus libertatibus et liberis consuetudinibus ad liberum feodum pertinentibus. Hiis test(ibus), Roberto de Mubr', Roberto capellano, Roberto de Daivilla, Hugone Malebisse, Radulfo de Bevv(er), Roberto fratre ejus, Roberto de Buci, Hamone Beler, Warin filio Simonis, Gaufrido de la Haie, Adam Luvel, Willelmo de Daivilla, Rogero fratre ejus, Petro de Bilingheia, Philippo de Munpinchun, Roberto de Beucamp, Folcone de Casteillun, Giliberto Bove, Giliberto de Arches, Gaufrido coco, Radulfo clerico, Petro clerico, Adam capellano.

NOTE. The appearance of Philip de Montpincon suggests a date after *c.* 1170 (see no. 376 note). Peter of Billinghay died by 1184 (see note to no. 349). Ten of the witnesses are found in no. 119, of Sept. 1175 × March 1176, which is perhaps the date of this charter, and also of nos. 346, 349, 360, 364–5, whose witness-lists so closely resemble that of the present charter.
    Ralph de Bellun gave land in Redley to Fountains before November 1156.[1] The Bellun tenancy therefore originated earlier than this charter would suggest. Perhaps the present charter converted a socage tenure into military fee.
    Nicholas de Bellun's interest in South Cave is mentioned in the Templars' Inquest of 1185.[2] His first occurrence in Mowbray charters is after *c.* 1160 (nos. 247, 249).

344 *Agreement between Nigel de Mowbray and Nicholas de Bellun concerning the issues of the wood [near Winksley].*   [1186 × 1190]

Cartulary copies: Manchester, John Rylands Libr., Lat. MS. 224 fo. 372*v*; B.M., Add. MS. 18276 fo. 246*v* (abstract).
Pd. (transl.), *Fount. Cart.* ii 746 (2), from Rylands MS.

Hec est conventio inter Nigellum de Mubray et Nicholaum de Bellun. Idem Nigellus de Mubray concessit Nicholao de Bellun totam medietatem de exitibus illius nemoris de quo lis fuit inter eos et de quo Nicholaus de Bellun posuit se in misericordia predicti Nigelli de Mubrai, scilicet illius quod est inter Beremore et magnam viam que vadit per medium lande de Hellei et sicut antiquus Taga[t]e^b descendit in

---

^{a} *stangnis*, MS. ^{b} Ink-smudge in MS.

[1] *Fount. Cart.* ii 705 (6); cf. above, nos. 105, 107.
[2] *Records of Templars* p. 125 (cal. above, no. 273).

Gunremiresic et sicut Gunremiresic descendit in Lavere et sicut magna via vadit in Cravenegile usque ad Stochebrige et sicut Cravengile descendit in Holebrun, predicto Nicholao et heredibus suis de predicto Nigello et heredibus suis. Hiis testibus, Roberto de Mubray, Rogero de Sancto Martino, Ricardo Bacun, Hereberto filio Ricardi, Radulfo clerico, Rogero de Condeio et aliis multis.

345 *Gift by Roger de Mowbray to Ralph de Belvoir and Robert his brother of wood and land in Mickley (Yorks., W.R.) by specified bounds, for scarlet hose p.a.; and grant of free pannage throughout Roger's forests.*

[Sept. 1175 × March 1176]

Pd., *Hatton's Book of Seals* no. 462, from facsimile in the custody of Northants Record Society.

His testibus, Nigello de Mubr', Roberto de Daivilla, Hugone Malebisse, Thoma de Colevilla, Hamone Beler, Adam Luvel.

NOTE. All the witnesses occur in no. 119, of Sept. 1175 × March 1176. Ralph occurs in charters from *c.* 1150 (no. 77) to after 1186 (no. 72), and was steward of Roger de Mowbray, occurring in office before 1169 and also in 1175–6 and after 1182 (above, p. lxiii n. 1). Robert his brother occurs from *c.* 1150 (no. 77) to after 1175 (no. 388). For other estates held by Ralph, see nos. 213, 293, and by Robert, see no. 190.

346 *Gift and restoration by Roger de Mowbray to Ralph de Belvoir of one carucate in 'Kerhae' (? Carr House in Azerley, Yorks., W.R.), in increment of his other fee in Mickley.*

[*c.* 1170 × 1184]

Transcript, from an original charter formerly in St. Mary's Tower, York: Bodl., MS. Dodsworth 7 fo. 94*v*.

Rogerus de Molbrai omnibus hominibus suis et amicis Francis et Anglis clericis et laicis presentibus et futuris salutem. Sciatis me dedisse et reddisse sicut suum jus et hac carta mea confirmasse Radulfo de Bevver carrucatam terre in Kerhae cum omnibus pertinenciis suis et divisis, quam Willelmus de Chamonfled tenuit, illi et heredibus suis ad tenendum in feudo et hereditate de me et heredibus meis libere et quiete et honorifice in incrementum alterius feudi sui in Miclehahe. His testibus, Roberto de Daivilla, Hugone Maleb', Toma de Colevilla, Hamone Beler, Nicholao de Bellund', Adam Luvel, Philippo de Munpinchun, Roberto Beler, Gaufrido de Lahaia, Warino filio Simonis, Henrico de Lubeham.

NOTE. Philip de Montpincon and Henry of Lubbenham do not appear before *c.* 1170.[1] The similarity between this witness-list and those of nos. 343, 349, 360, and 364–5 suggests that the gift was made at the same time, before 1184, and perhaps *c.* 1175 × 1176 (see note to no. 343).

[1] For Philip see no. 376 note, and for Henry see no. 274 note.

347 *Confirmation by Roger de Mowbray to Roger son of Haldan de Berlay of his tenure in Wothersome (Yorks., W.R.), given by Richard de Moreville, for the eighth part of the service of one knight.* [c. 1176]

Transcript, from an original charter: Leeds, Yorks. Archaeol. Soc. Libr., MS. 869 (Farrer MS.) E.Y.C. box 7.
Pd. (transl.), *Yorks. Deeds* iii no. 425, from the original then in the possession of William Brown of Sowerby; and *Archaeol. Jnl.* xxxvi (1879) 272, from the original then in the possession of D. Brown, Q.C.

Rogerus de Mubrai omnibus hanc cartam audituris et visuris salutem. Sciatis me concessisse et hac mea carta confirmasse Rogero filio Haldani de Berlai et heredibus ejusdem Rogeri confirmationem et donationem et relaxationem quam illi fecit Ricardus de Morevilla, scilicet de tenura quam tenet in Wudehusum, tam in boscho quam in plano et in molendinis et in pascuis et in pratis et in*a* omnibus libertatibus ejusdem ville, scilicet tres carrucatas terre in Wudehusum cum omnibus pertinentiis suis, perinde forinsecum tantum faciendo servicium quantum pertinet ad octavam partem feodi unius militis. His testibus, Roberto capellano Rogeri de Mubrai, Roberto de Mubrai, Ricardo de Morevilla, Radulfo de Beiaveir dapifero Rogeri de Mubrai, Hamundo Beler, Roberto Beiaschamp, Adam Luvel, Roberto le Norreis, Roberto de Trehamtun, Willelmo de Tikehil, Ranulfo*b* de Rigetun, Edwardo de Tikehil, Petro clerico Rogeri de Mubrai, Adam de Torneure et Roberto fratre ejus, Gerardo filio Lewini filii Colling et Thoma filio Gerardi, Roberto de Cundi.

Seal: left-hand half of seal no. 3 of Roger de Mowbray (above, p. lxxxiii), red wax.

NOTE. Ten of these witnesses appear at York in March 1176 (nos. 125–30). The text of Richard de Moreville's charter is not known to survive. In 1166 Richard de Moreville held 5 old fees.

348 *Gift by Roger de Mowbray to Bernard the miller of a* mansura *in Thirsk (Yorks., N.R.) with appurtenances and* ½ *acre, for a rent of spurs worth 4d. p.a.* [c. 1170 × 1186]

Original charter: Durham, D. & C. Archives, 3.1. Ebor. 4.

Rog(erus) de Moubrai omnibus hominibus suis et amicis Francis et Anglis clericis et laicis presentibus et futuris salutem. Sciatis me dedisse et hac carta mea confirmasse Bernardo molendinario mansuram quandam in Tresch cum tofto et omnibus pertinentiis suis illam scilicet quam Robertus filius Radulfi tenuit et dimidiam acram terre extra uillam quam idem Robertus tenuit . pro hommagio et seruicio suo . sibi et heredibus

a in repeated in MS.   *b Ranulfus*, MS.

¹ No. 401, Fees [22].

suis ad tenendum de me et heredibus meis in feudo et hereditate . libere
et quiete et honorifice . reddendo annuatim quedam calcaria . de iiij^{or}.
denariis . ad Natale Domini . pro omnibus seruiciis. His testibus .
Rob(erto) de Moubr' . Ham(one) Beler . Rob(erto) de Buci . Gam(ello)
decano . Rogero filio eius . Willelmo filio Ingel(rami) . Adam capellano . Rob(erto) filio Matildis . Helia . Ailmero . Ernaldo nepote
capellani . Philippo de Balio . et aliis multis.

Endorsements: *Carta Rogeri de Mulbreio data Bernardo molendinario* (13th
cent.); *.3^a. .1^e. Ebor' D.1.* (later medieval hand).

Size: 16 × 7·6 cm.; 2·6 cm. turn-up.

Seal: seal no. 3 of Roger de Mowbray (above, p. lxxxiii), white wax; appended
on tag.

Script: same hand as no. 366. See Fig. 2 (above, p. lxviii).

NOTE. The appearance of Adam the chaplain and Robert son of Maud
suggests a date after *c.* 1170 (cf. nos. 92, 140). Bernard the miller gave to
Durham a toft which Roger de Mowbray had given him in Thirsk,[1] possibly
that confirmed by Roger de Mowbray to Durham in no. 92, of *c.* 1170 × 1186.

349 *Gift by Roger de Mowbray to Peter of Billinghay of 100s. worth of land in
Hovingham (Yorks., N.R.), for the fourth part of the service of one knight.*
[*c.* 1170 × 1184]

Transcript, from an original charter formerly in St. Mary's Tower, York:
Bodl., MS. Dodsworth 91 fo. 36v.

Rogerus de Molb' omnibus hominibus et amicis suis clericis et laicis
tam presentibus quam futuris salutem. Sciatis me dedisse et hac presenti
carta confirmasse Petro de Bilingeia centum solidatas terre in Hovinge-
ham: duas bovatas quas Martinus tenuit, et duas bovatas quas Willelmus
Abelot tenuit, et illas duas bovatas quas Willelmus Carpent(arius) tenuit,
et duas bovatas quas Gilleb(ertus) Litle tenuit, et duas bovatas quas
Rogerus filius Albrici tenuit, et duas bovatas quas Samson Malassis
tenuit, et duas bovatas quas Radulfus filius Wulrici tenuit, et illas duas
bovatas quas Robertus filius Edwini tenuit, et duas bovatas quas Ulf
filius Reginaldi tenuit, et duas bovatas quas Elfuat filius Rogeri tenuit,
et eos et liberos suos; pratum vero in his locis assignatis juxta Holebec
tres acras juxta Tuft, et juxta Gaufridi de Stutevill quinque acras, juxta
Aust [.]^{a}lres tres acras et dimidiam, in Pening eus[.]^a octo acras et dimidiam. Hec omnia ei dedi et confirmavi et heredibus suis ad tenendum
de me et heredibus meis libere et quiete et honorifice pro servicio quarte
partis militis, cum omnibus communitatibus in bosco et plano in viis et

^{a} Illegible.

[1] D. & C. Archives, 3.1. Ebor. 3.

semitis in pratis et pascuis et moris in aquis et in omnibus locis et omnibus libertatibus et liberis consuetudinibus libero feodo pertinentibus
cum tol et them et soc et sac et infangentheof. Testibus his, Roberto
capellano, Radulfo de Belveeir, Herberto filio Ricardi, Rogero de
Daievill, Willelmo de Daievill fratre ejus, Adam Lovel, Roberto de
Boci, Warino filio Symonis, Nicholao de Bellum, Gilleberto Levot,
Fulcone de Castellun, Roberto de Casteillun, Osberto Britone, Philippo
de Munpincon, Roberto de Bello Campo, Henrico de Lubbeham,
Roberto Beler, Petro clerico et aliis multis.

Drawing of seal: 'A greate greene seale with a man on horsebacke the super-
scription defaced'; appended on tag.

NOTE. Peter of Billinghay (Lincs.), who held a fee of the archbishop of York,[1]
first occurs in Mowbray charters before 1173 (no. 307), but does not occur
in the *carta* of 1166. He died by 1184.[2] The witness-clause of this charter is
very similar to those of nos. 343, 346, 360, 364–5. Philip of Billinghay, Peter's
brother, who succeeded to his fee, sold 2 bovates in Hovingham, with other
parcels of land, to Newburgh for 50 marks.[3]

350 *Gift by Roger de Mowbray to Richard de Camville of the vill of Smite*
(Warwicks.).   [1143 × July 1150]

Cartulary copies (Combe): B.M., Cotton MSS. Vit. A i fo. 37r; Vit. D xviii
fo. 1r (fragment). Transcripts, from cartulary of Combe fo. 50r (Vit. D
xviii before Cotton fire): Bodl., MSS. Dugdale 12 p. 112, Dodsworth 110
fo. 4v.
Pd., *Mon. Ang.* v 584 (II), from Vit. A i.

Rogerus de Moubray comiti de Leicestr(ie) et matri sue et filio suo et
omnibus hominibus suis Francis et Anglis salutem. Sciatis quia dedi et
concessi Ricardo de Camvilla et heredibus suis villam de Smite et teneat
bene et in pace et honorifice in bosco et plano in pratis et pasturis et in
omnibus bonis consuetudinibus de me tenendum et heredibus meis.
T(estibus), comite de Arundel et comite Simone.

NOTE. The reference to Roger de Mowbray's son indicates that 1143 is the
earliest possible date. Richard de Camville gave this property for the foundation of Combe in July 1150 (see no. 77). The service of one knight was due
from Mowbray to the earl of Leicester for Smite (no. 78 note). Richard de
Camville was probably a cousin of Walter de Camville, who held 9 old fees
of Mowbray in 1166.[4]

---

[1] *R.B.* i 414.
[2] See *P.R. 30 Hen. II* p. 40; *Rotuli de Dominabus*, ed. J. H. Round (P.R.S. xxxv)
pp. xx, 3–4.
[3] Bodl., MS. Dodsworth 91 fo. 46v.   [4] No. 401, Fees [10].

351 *Notification by Roger de Mowbray to the sheriff and citizens of York of his gift to Alice Careu, when her husband Geoffrey de Rouen went on pilgrimage to St. James, of all Geoffrey's house and land [in York], for a rent of 12d. p.a.* [c. 1147 × 1157]

> Cartulary copy: B.M., Add. MS. 40009 (cart. of Fountains) fo. 113r (old p. 225).
> Pd., *Fount. Cart.* i 277 (38).

Rogerus de Molb' vic(ecomiti) et omnibus civibus Eborac(i) Francis et Anglis clericis et laicis salutem. Sciatis quod quando Galfridus de Rotomago viam Sancti Jacobi incepit ego dedi et concessi Adelicie Careu uxori sue et heredibus suis totam domum suam et terram in feudo et in hereditate, tenendam de me et de heredibus meis et eodem servicio quo ipse Gaufridus tenuit, scilicet xij denarios reddendo per annum. Quare deprecor omnes amicos meos quod ipsam pro amore meo adjuvent et manuteneant ad hanc domum et terram tenendam, quia non erit michi amicus qui ei inde contumeliam fecerit. Test(ibus), Nigello filio meo, Olivero de Buc', Bertrammo Hag', Rogero de Flamevilla, Rogero de Cundi, Radulfo Beler, Rogero de Cun' et Baldewino fratre suo.

> NOTE. Nigel de Mowbray did not attest charters before c. 1147. Ralph Beler was dead by 1157.[1] The *mansura terre* in York which Geoffrey de Rouen and his wife held of Mowbray is mentioned in a charter of Robert de Daiville, granting to them the next *mansura* on the Ouse in free burgage for 12d. p.a.[2] In her widowhood Alice Careu granted the houses to Fountains,[3] a gift which was confirmed by Henry II in August 1175.[4]

352 *Gift by Roger de Mowbray to W[?alter of Carlton] of [? Carlton Miniott, Yorks., N.R.].* [1138 × 1165]

> Fragment of an original charter attached by string to seal-tag of no. 353: York, D. & C. Muniments, Vicars Choral deeds, Vv. 21.

Rog(erus) de Molb' . omnibus bailliuis[..............................]
me dedisse . et concessisse W[......................................]
nem sicuti jus suum . insuper[......................................]
feudi in feudo [et] hereditate[.....................................]
Teste . Willelmo de [.....]ll[......................................]
Hugone . Malab[...]

No endorsement.

Size: 4·9 [+lost 6·4] × 4·8 cm.

Seal: missing; was appended on tongue from left (now 11·3 cm.), tie-tongue below.

> NOTE. Walter first occurs before 1145 (no. 95). His son Roger had succeeded before 1166 (no. 353). Another Walter of Carlton occurs however in 1174 or 1175 (nos. 110–12).

---

[1] See *E.Y.C.* ix 212.   [2] *Fount. Cart.* i 277 (37).   [3] Ibid. p. 278 (39).
[4] *E.Y.C.* i no. 78.

353 *Restoration by Roger de Mowbray to Roger of Carlton, son of Walter of Carlton, and Maud his mother, of Old Carlton (Miniott) and Islebeck and a house in Thirsk (Yorks., N.R.), for the third part of the service of one knight.* [1154 × 1166]

Original charter: York, D. & C. Muniments, Vicars Choral deeds, Vv. 21.

Rog(erus) de Molb' constabul(ario) suo de Tresc et dapifero suo et omnibus balliuis suis et omnibus hominibus et amicis suis Francis et Anglicis salutem. Notum sit uobis omnibus presentibus et futuris me concessisse et reddidisse Rogero de Carletun filio Walteri de Carletun et Mahald(e) matri sue Carletun cum omnibus pertinentiis et uetus Carletun . et Hiserbec cum omnibus pertinentiis ·' exceptis pratis . et domum suam et mansuram in Tresc . que fuit Gerod'*a* de Sancto Rich'er . illis et heredibus suis hereditario tenend(a) de me et de here-dibus meis per seruicium tercie partis unius militis libere et quiete et honorifice cum socco et sacca et tol et them et infanghenthef et cum omnibus liberis consuetudinibus. His testibus . Richardo priore de Neub(urgo) . Rob(erto) de Daiuilla . Rog(ero) de Cund' . Rob(erto) capell(ano) . Walt(ero) Bured . Tom(a) de Coleuilla . Hug(one) Maleb' . Rad(ulfo) de Beuuer . Ham(one) Beler . Rob(erto) Beler . Rog(ero) de Bell(und) . Willelmo cam(erario) . Hug(one) fratre eius . Rog(ero) coco . Rad(ulfo) Carbun . Rog(ero) de Hotun . Rob(erto) de Beuchamp . Rad(ulfo) can(onico) . Bald(wino) cler(ico).

No medieval endorsement.

Size: 15·7 × 15·3 cm.

Seal: seal no. 3 of Roger de Mowbray (above, p. lxxxiii), white wax varnished; appended on tag (to which no. 352 is attached by string).

Script: same hand as no. 354.

> NOTE. Richard did not become prior of Newburgh until after 1154.[1] Presum-ably the restoration was made before the Mowbray *carta* of 1166 was drawn up, in which Roger of Carlton appears holding ⅓ fee of the new enfeoffment.[2]

354 *Confirmation by Nigel de Mowbray to Roger son of Walter of Carlton and Maud his mother of Carlton Miniott etc., given by Roger de Mowbray, for the third part of the service of one knight.* [1154 × 1166]

Original charter: York, D. & C. Muniments, Vicars Choral deeds, Vv. 22.

Nigellus de Molbr' constabulario suo de Tresc et dapifero suo et omni-bus balliuis suis et omnibus hominibus et amicis suis Francis et Anglicis salutem. Notum sit uobis omnibus presentibus et futuris me concessisse

a *Sic.*

----

[1] See *E.Y.C.* ix 248.   [2] No. 401, Fees [44].

Rogero de Carlet' filio Walteri de Carl' . et Mahald(e) matri sue donationem quam Rog(erus) de Molbr' pater meus dedit illis uidelicet Carlet' cum omnibus pertinentiis et uetus Carlet' et Hiserbec cum omnibus pertinentiis exceptis pratis . et domum suam et mansuram in Tresc . que fuit Geroldi de Sancto Richero tenend(a) de me et heredibus meis per seruicium tercie partis unius militis. Ideo uolo et precipio quod ipsi et heredes sui teneant predictam tenuram in bene et in pace libere et quiete et honorifice cum socco et sacca et tol et them et infanghenthef et cum omnibus liberis consuetudinibus sicut in carta patris mei continetur. His testibus . Ricardo priore de Neub(urgo) . Rob(erto) de Daiuilla . Rog(ero) de Condi . Rob(erto) capell(ano) . Walt(ero) Bured . Toma Coleuill' . Hug(one) Maleb' . Rad(ulfo) de Beuuer . Ham(one) Beler . Rob(erto) Beler . Rog(ero) de Bellund . Willelmo cam(erario) . Hug(one) fratre eius . Rog(ero) c[oco]ᵃ Rad(ulfo) Carbun . Rog(ero) de Hotun . Rob(erto) de Beuchamp . Rad(ulfo) canonico . Bal[dw]ᵃino clerico.

No medieval endorsement.
Size: 16 × 15·5 cm.; 2·3 cm. turn-up.
Seal: missing; was appended on tag.
Script: same hand as no. 353.
NOTE. For the date, see note to no. 353.

355 *Gift by Roger de Mowbray to William of Clapham of land in Clapham (Yorks., W.R.), by specified bounds.* [1138 × 1154]

Pd. (text corrupt), T. D. Whitaker, *An History of Richmondshire* (1823) ii 348.

Test(ibus), Rob. de Wensbrough, Wulfurd Kipox, Rogero de Tendeo, Alfred de Mercrio, Augustino de Ustwice, Olivero de Horton, Nic. de Otterburn, Car. de Cansfield, Radulpho Bellax, Willelmo Dautry, Rolando de Lasse.

NOTE. Farrer noted the similarity between this witness-list and that of no. 383 (Leeds, Yorks. Archaeol. Soc. MS. 869). Comparison suggests that the first four names here are corrupt forms of 'Herberto de Queniborough, Waltero de Riparia, Rogero de Condeio, Alfredo camerario', and the last three, corruptions of 'Radulpho Beler, Willelmo Baldri, Rollando de Landeles'.

356 *Gift by Roger de Mowbray to Thomas de Coleville of Coxwold, Oulston, and Yearsley (Yorks., N.R.), for the service of one knight.*

[c. 1154 × 1157]

Pd., *C.P.R. 1354–58* p. 315, from P.R.O., Patent Roll 29 Edw. III pt. iii (C. 66/247) m. 9.

ᵃ Charter damaged; letters supplied from no. 353.

Hiis testibus, Willelmo de Colevill, Neel filio domini, Olivero*a* de Buceio, Waltero Buhere, Roberto de Buceio, Hamone Beler, Waleran vice-comite, Willelmo de Croschelaio, G. pincerna, Rogero de Flammvill, Roberto de Alemvill, Willelmo de Wivill, Waltero de Riveria, Waltero de Karlent', Roberto de Kervelia, Gisleberto de Sancto Laudo, Gaufrido Salvagio, Roberto capellano, Radulfo Beler et multis aliis.

NOTE. Thomas de Coleville first occurs 1154×1157 (nos. 202, 236 note, 302). Ralph Beler died by 1157.[1] The enfeoffment was confirmed by king Henry II at Tours, 1156×1158.[2] Thomas de Coleville held one new fee in 1166 (no. 401 and Fees [40]).

357 *Gift by Nigel de Mowbray to Thomas de Coleville of one carucate in Melton Mowbray (Leics.), for a rent of silver spurs.*   [*c.* 1166×1190]

Transcript, from an original charter formerly in St. Mary's Tower, York: Bodl., MS. Dodsworth 94 fo. 28*r*.

Nigellus de Molbrai omnibus hominibus et amicis suis tam presentibus quam futuris salutem. Sciatis me dedisse et hac karta mea confirmasse Thome de Colevilla unam carucatam terre in Melthetona, scilicet dimidiam carucatam de meo dominio et duas bovatas quas tenuit Wimundus Mus et alias duas in eadem villa, illi et heredibus tenenda de me et heredibus meis in feodo et hereditate libere et quiete [et] honorifice, annuatim reddendo pro omnibus serviciis et consuetudinibus quedam calcaria cum argento de Lincoln. Testibus hiis, Roberto de Daivilla, Hugone de Malebisse, Herberto filio Ricardi, Galfrido de Haja, Nicolao de Bell(un), Roberto de Bellocampo, Willelmo camerario, Radulfo clerico et multis aliis clericis et laicis.

'The seale faire on horsbake'.

NOTE. Geoffrey de la Haia does not occur before *c.* 1166 (see no. 364 note).

358 *Gift by Roger de Mowbray to Samson of Cornwall of 2 bovates in Grewel-thorpe (Yorks., W.R.).*   [1138×1186]

Record of gift: B.M., Add. MS. 18276 (cart. of Fountains) fo. 109*v*.

Rogerus de Moubray dedit Samsoni de Cornubio pro servicio duas bovatas terre in Thorp.

NOTE. Samson of Cornwall had been given 4 bovates in 'Hoveton' (N.R.) by Gundreda de Gournay (see above, no. 249). He also had land in Brinklow (no. 329).

---

a *Oliveri*, MS.

---

[1] See *E.Y.C.* ix 212.
[2] *Recueil des Actes de Henri II*, ed. L. V. Delisle and E. Berger (Paris, 1909–27) i no. LXXXV.

359 *Gift by Roger de Mowbray to Hugh de Cramaville in Sleningford, Grantley, and Skelden (Yorks., W.R.), for the fourth part of the service of one knight.*

[*c.* 1154]

> Cartulary copies: York, Borthwick Institute of Historical Research, Register of Melton fo. 593*v* (lacks all but first five witnesses); Manchester, John Rylands Libr., Lat. MS. 224 (cart. of Fountains) fo. 166*r–v*. Transcript, probably from Register of Melton: Bodl., MS. Dodsworth 121 fo. 85*v*.
> Pd., *Kirkby's Inquest*, ed. R. H. Skaife (S.S. xlix) p. 417 n., from Reg. Melton; (transl.) *Fount. Cart.* ii 646 (1), from Rylands MS.

Rogerus de Moubray dapiferis suis et omnibus hominibus suis et amicis Francis et Anglis clericis et laicis salutem. Sciatis me dedisse et concessisse et presentis carte testimonio confirmasse Hugoni de Cramanvilla et heredibus suis imperpetuum villam de Sleningford et Grantelay et Cnarreford et totum feodum quod Nigellus pater meus tenuit de archiepiscopo Ebor(acensi) et quod ego de eo teneo, in feodum et hereditatem de me et heredibus meis tenendum, cum omni eo quod ad illud feodum pertinet in bosco et plano, in pratis et pascuis et aquis et molendinis et stagnis et omnibus aliis aysiamentis tam ipsi quam hominibus suis,[a] cum socca et sacca et tol et them et infangenthef et omnibus aliis liberis consuetudinibus, pro servicio dimidii militis. Ita quidem quod nichil exigam ab eo aliquando nisi quando archiepiscopus Ebor(acensis) exiget a me servicium quarte partis unius militis, et tunc non exigam amplius nisi quantum ad servicium dimidii militis pertinebit, secundum quod pro quarta parte unius militis a me exigetur. Hiis testibus, Adelr' abbate Rievall(is), Johanne thesaurario Ebor', Osberto Arundell', Rogero de Cunde, Willelmo de Arches, Roberto de Davidvilla, Willelmo de Widvilla, Rogero de Flamvilla, Ricardo de Morvilla, Waltero de la Rivere, Olivero de Buci et Roberto fratre ejus, Radulfo Beler et Hamone fratre ejus, Willelmo filio Aldelini, Radulfo filio Nicholai, Willelmo filio Haconis, Radulfo Ruuecest', Willelmo de Cramanvilla, Hugone de Verli, Ricardo Hareng, Petro pincerna, Ricardo filio Andkil, Bernardo filio Gamelli de Rypona.

> NOTE. John of Canterbury did not become treasurer of York until *c.* 1154.[1] Nine of the witnesses occur in 1154 (no. 236). This charter shows that William de Arches did not die in *c.* 1150, as was thought by Farrer,[2] but it is his last occurrence, and it is unlikely that he survived much later than *c.* 1154.
> The land granted comprised the entire ¼ fee held by Mowbray of the archbishop of York, by whom this charter was confirmed between 1154 and 1162.[3] Crémanville (Calvados, arr. Lisieux, cant. Honfleur), from which Hugh de

[a] Rylands MS. adds *preter cervum et bissa[m] et porcum.*

---

[1] See C. T. Clay, in *Y.A.J.* xxxv (1943) 11–16.   [2] *E.Y.C.* i 420.
[3] *Fount. Cart.* ii 646 (2).

Cramaville may have come,[1] is not far from Pont l'Évêque, the presumed place of origin of Roger archbishop of York. Before 1181 Robert the dean and the chapter of York confirmed Roger de Mowbray's gift of the estate to Ralph de Cramaville, as it had been held by Ralph's brother Hugh.[2]

360 *Gift by Roger de Mowbray to Roger de Daiville of all the remaining demesne in South Cave (Yorks., E.R.), after the enfeoffment of Nicholas de Bellun and Robert le Norreis, for half the service of one knight.* [c. 1170 × 1184]

Patent roll copy: P.R.O., Patent Roll, 7 Edw. II pt. ii (C. 66/141) m. 18.
Pd. (abstract), *C.P.R. 1313–17* p. 96.

Rogerus de Molbr' omnibus hominibus suis et amicis Francis et Anglis clericis et laicis presentibus et futuris salutem. Sciatis me dedisse et hac carta mea confirmasse Rogero de Daivilla totum dominium de Cava quod habui in manu mea post feoffamentum Nicholai de Bellund et Roberti le Norreis, scilicet tres carucatas terre in dominio et in terris bubulcorum cum prato recenti et salsato quod pertinet ad dominicum et xxiiij toftos in Marchedcava et octo toftos et dimidium in villa de Cava et Gregorium prepositum cum ij bovetis terre, Radulfum fabrum cum una boveta, Lewin cum una boveta, Robertum fratrem Albini cum ij bovetis in Bagefled', Godewin et filium ejus cum ten(emento) suo, Everardum cum suo ten(emento), j ten(ementum) quod Sewardus tenuit de me, in passagio de Bagefled' x solidos et viij denarios. Unum furnum de Marchedcava cum hoc quod ei pertinet. Hec omnia concessi et dedi illi et heredibus suis ad tenendum in feudo et hereditate de me et heredibus meis per servicium dimidii militis. Et volo et precipio quatinus omnia hec predicta teneat in bene et pace libere et quiete et honorifice, sicut ego unquam ea liberius et quietius tenui, in pratis et pasturis, in viis et semitis, in aquis et marescis, in stagnis et molendinis, in foro et in omnibus locis, cum soc et sac et thol et them et infangenþef cum omnibus libertatibus et liberis consuetudinibus ad liberum feudum pertinentibus. Hiis testibus, Nigello de Molbr', Roberto de Daivilla, Hugone Maleb', Thoma de Colevilla, Radulfo de Belv(er), Roberto fratre ejus, Hamone Beler, Herberto filio Ricardi, Roberto de Beucamp, Roberto Bel(er), Henrico de Lubeham, Petro de Bilinge, Roberto de Bucy, Adam Luvel, Willelmo de Daivilla, Nicholao de Daivilla, Waltero de Daivilla, Roberto de Beueraus.

Marginal note: 'Pro Petro de Daivilla'.

NOTE. For the date, cf. nos. 343, 349. Roger de Daiville was brother of William de Daiville (no. 349) and therefore brother also of Robert de Daiville, the

---

[1] Cf. *Magni Rotuli Scaccarii Normanniae*, ed. T. Stapleton (1840–4) ii p. clviii.
[2] *Fount. Cart.* ii 674 (4). Ralph first occurs in York in Feb. 1173 (*E.Y.C.* i no. 123).

tenant in 1166 of four old and one new fees (cf. nos. 122, 307, etc.; see no. 401, and Fees [24], [38]).

The interests in South Cave of Roger de Daiville, Nicholas de Bellun, and Robert le Norreis are mentioned in the Templars' Inquest of 1185.[1]

361 *Restoration by Nigel de Mowbray to John son of Robert de Daiville of the land which Robert de Daiville, his father, had held of Nigel's father and himself.* [1186 × 1190]

Pd., *E.Y.C.* ix no. 137, from a transcript from an original charter formerly in the possession of William Brown of Sowerby: Leeds, Yorks. Archaeol. Soc. Libr., MS. 869 (Farrer MS.). Also pd. (transl.), *Yorks. Deeds* iii no. 424, from the original in the possession of Brown; and *Archaeol. Jnl.* xxxvi (1879) 272, from the original then in the possession of D. Brown, Q.C.

Hiis testibus, Rogero de Sancto Martino, Radulfo de Cramavil(la), Radulfo de Bealveer, Nicholao de Beelun, Adam Luvel, Roberto de Chast(ellione), Ricardo Bacun, Waltero de Daivila, Hugone de Munfort, Nicholao de Daivila, Eudone de Daivila, Rogero de Daivila, Willelmo de Daivila, Willelmo Malerbe, et multis aliis clericis et laicis.

Seal: seal no. 2 of Nigel de Mowbray (above, pp. lxxxiii–iv), yellow wax; cast in B.M., MSS. Dept. xlix. 12.

NOTE. The land restored was probably Kilburn.[2] John de Daiville already had an interest in Mowbray property in Axholme (Lincs.) in 1180, when his father was still alive.[3] The present charter mentions that Robert de Daiville had charters from both Roger and Nigel de Mowbray.

362 *Gift by Roger de Mowbray and Nigel his son to Adam Fossard, in the wood and land of 'Bagwith' (Yorks., N.R.).* [1166 × 1186]

Reference in a charter of Adam Fossard for Byland: B.M., Egerton Ch. 2145.

. . . quicquid juris ego et Hugo frater meus unquam habuimus ex donatione et concessione Rogerii de Molbrai et Nigelli filii ejus in bosco et in terra de Baggewith . . .

NOTE. Adam did not succeed his father Geoffrey in the fee held of Stuteville until after 1166.[4] Another charter of Adam Fossard shows that 'Bagwith' was near Bagby (N.R.), and was therefore not the same as Bagwith near Kirkby Malzeard (W.R.).[5]

363 *Gift by Roger de Mowbray to Bertram Haget, of the land of Dacre (Yorks., W.R.), in the service of his other land.* [1138 × 1145]

Cartulary copies (Fountains): B.M., Add. MS. 40009 fo. 9r (old p. 17); Bodl.,

[1] *Records of Templars* p. 125 (cal. above, no. 273). For Bellun see no. 343.
[2] See *E.Y.C.* ix no. 137 note. [3] *P.R. 26 Hen. II* p. 55.
[4] See *E.Y.C.* ix nos. 15, 16, and pp. 152 ff.
[5] B.M., Egerton ch. 2142; pd. (transl.), *Yorks. Deeds* ii no. 30.

MS. Rawlinson B 449 fo. 151*r* (lacks all but one witness); B.M., Add. MS. 18276 fo. 46*r* (abstract).
Pd. (transl.), *Fount. Cart.* i p 203 (1), from Add. MS. 40009.

Rogerus de Molb'*a* omnibus hominibus suis et amicis salutem. Sciatis me dedisse et concessisse Bertramo*b* Haget terram de Dacra cum omni re terre illi pertinente, in feudo et hereditate, et heredi suo libere in servicio alie terre ejus. Test(ibus), Ricardo Burdet, et Willelmo Bac', et Olivero de Buc', et pinc(erna), et Roberto Maltal', et G. de Condeio, et Rogero fratre ejus, et Willelmo de Ercheslai.

NOTE. The latest possible date is Jan. 1146, when Bertram Haget had already given Dacre to Fountains abbey (see no. 96). Bertram's son William had succeeded by 1165[1] and held two fees of Mowbray in 1166.[2]

364 *Gift by Roger de Mowbray to Geoffrey de la Haia of £6 worth of land in Grewelthorpe (Yorks., W.R.), for the fourth part of the service of one knight, in exchange for Brinklow (Warwicks.).* [*c.* 1170 × 1184]

Original charter: Ribston Hall deeds deposited at Leeds, Yorks. Archaeol. Soc. Libr., DD 59/xv.
Pd. (incompletely), *Y.A.J.* viii (1884) 267 (XV), from the original charter then at Ribston Hall.

Rog(erus) de Moubr' omnibus hominibus et amicis suis . clericis et laicis presentibus et futuris . salutem. Sciatis me dedisse et concessise*c* et hac presenti cartha mea confirmasse Gaufrido de la Haia pro seruitio et hominagio suo sex libratas terre in parrochia de Kyrkebi Malesart . scilicet in territorio de Thorp . duas uidelicet carrucatas terrę in eadem uilla quas isti decem homines tenebant pro .iiij*or*. libris . scilicet . Suanus Neubonde .i. bouatam Gamel de Birnebem .ij. bouatas . Hulf filius Duue .i. bouatam . Willelmus Eltefoster .ii. bouatas . Gamel Eltebroder .ij. bouatas . Thorbrant filius Accheman .i. bouatam . Fareman filius Ede .i. bouatam . Thorbrant filius Orm .ij. bouatas . Baudra' filius Kethel .ij. bouatas . Hernaldus filius Normanni .ij. bouatas . cum essartis suis que facte fuerant ante hanc donationem . et quas dedi ei incrementum desuper predictas bouatas . et .ij. carucatas terre cum carucis in dominio pro quadraginta solidis scilicet . in Naurethorp et in Tinchehoucroft . et octo acras terre desuper ad unam mansuram . ad domum suam faciendam. In his uero duabus carucatis terre sunt sexdecim bouate . et in qualibet bouata .xij*cim*. acrę cum pertica .xviij*to*. pedum et dimidio. Concessi etiam ei et hominibus suis

a *Molbray*, MS. Rawl.   *b* *Bertrammo*, MS. Rawl.   *c* *Sic.*

---

[1] *P.R. 11 Hen. II* p. 48.   [2] No. 401, Fees [4].

communem pasturam in foresta mea . et ligna sibi et hominibus suis ad ignem et ad edificia ibidem facienda sine wasto . et pasnagium quietum in predicta foresta mea de propriis porcis et hominum suorum. Hec autem omnia dedi et concessi et confirmaui sibi et heredibus suis . tenenda de me et heredibus meis in feudo et hereditate libere et quiete et honorifice . cum omnibus libertatibus et liberis consuetudinibus ad liberum feudum pertinentibus in boscho et plano in pratis et pascuis in uiis et semitis et in omnibus locis per seruitium quartę partis unius militis. Et sciant omnes quod hec omnia donaui in excambium de Brinkelauu . quam prius dedi ei . et quam michi quietam clamauit pro hoc excambio. Et ego et heredes mei debemus illi et heredibus suis warantizare predictum excambium ab omnibus calengiis contra omnes homines. Test(ibus) his . Rob(erto) de Moubr' . Rob(erto) d[e Daeuilla]ᵃ Hug(one) Maleb' . Rad(ulfo) de Beluario . Thom(a) de Coleuilla . Rad(ulfo) [filio Audl']ᵃ Hamund(o) Beler . Rob(erto) de Buci . Adam Loue' Rob(erto) Beler . Johanne [de Creu]ᵃequer . Rog(ero) de Daieuilla . Nichol(ao) de Beslun . Henric(o) d[e Lubeham]ᵃ Will(elmo) camerario . Pet(ro) de Hume.

Endorsements: *Richemundesir'* (late 12th or early 13th cent.); *Malesart Thorp* (later medieval hand).

Size: 22·8 × 16·1 cm.; 4·2 cm. turn-up.

Seal: fragment of seal no. 3 of Roger de Mowbray (above, p. lxxxiii), brown wax; appended on tag.

Script: same hand as no. 365.

> NOTE. Geoffrey de la Haia first occurs before 1177 (no. 332), but does not occur in the *carta* of 1166. The witness-list of the present charter suggests a date similar to that of nos. 343, 349, 360. Perhaps the charter is to be related to the Pipe Roll of 1179, where Geoffrey accounted 10 marks for having recognition against Roger de Mowbray.[1] The exchange of Brinklow is possibly to be connected with Nigel de Mowbray's grant to the archbishop of York, 1174 × 1181 (no. 329). Haia's tenure in Brinklow is illustrated by a charter for Combe (no. 81 note).

365 *Confirmation by Nigel de Mowbray to Geoffrey de la Haia of his father's gift in Grewelthorpe, in identical terms.* [c. 1170 × 1184]

> Original charter: Ribston Hall deeds deposited at Leeds, Yorks. Archaeol. Soc. Libr., DD 59/xvii.
> Pd. (incompletely), *Y.A.J.* viii (1884) 275 (XVII), from the original charter then at Ribston Hall.

Nig(ellus) de Moubr' omnibus hominibus et amicis suis clericis et laicis

---

ᵃ Charter damaged; text supplied from no. 365.

[1] *P.R. 25 Hen. II* p. 21.

presentibus et futuris . salutem. Sciatis me concessisse et hac carta mea confirmasse donationem quam pater meus Rog(erus) de Moubr' fecit Gaufrido de Lahaia . scilicet .vi. libratas terrę pro seruitio et homagio suo in Kyrkebi Malesart . scilicet in territorio de Thorp . duas uidelicet carucatas terre in eadem uilla . quas isti decem homines tenebant pro .iiij^or. libris scilicet Suanus Neubonde .i. bouatam . Gamel de Bernebem . duas bouatas . Hulf filius Duue .i. bouatam . Willelmus Eltefoster .ij. bouatas . Gamel Eltebroder .ij. bouatas . Thorbrant filius Accheman .i. bouatam . Faraman filius Edę .i. bouatam . Thorbrant filius Orm .ij. bouatas . Baudra' filius Kethel .ij. bouatas . Hernaldus filius Normanni .ij. bouatas cum essartis suis que facte fuerant ante hanc donationem et quas dedi ei incrementum desuper predictas bouatas . et duas carucatas terre cum carrucis in dominio . pro quadraginta solidis . scilicet in Naurethorp et in Tingehoucroft . et octo acras terre desuper ad unam mansuram ad domum suam faciendam. In his uero duabus carucatis terre sunt sexdecim bouate . et in qualibet bouata .xij. acre cum pertica .xviij. pedum et dimidio. Concessi etiam ei et hominibus suis communem pasturam et ligna sibi et hominibus suis ad ignem et ad edificia ibidem facienda sine wasto . et pasnagium quietum in predicta foresta mea de propriis portis^a et porcis hominum suorum. Hec autem omnia dedi et concessi et confirmaui sibi et heredibus suis tenenda de me et heredibus meis . in feudo . et hereditate libere et quiete et honorifice cum omnibus libertatibus et liberis consuetudinibus ad liberum feudum pertinentibus in boscho et plano in pratis et pascuis . in uiis et semitis et in omnibus locis per seruitium quarte parte militis. Et sciant omnes quod hec omnia ei donaui in excambium de Brinchelau quam prius dedi ei . et quam michi quietam clamauit pro hoc excambio. Et ego et heredes mei debemus illi et heredibus suis warantizare predictum excambium ab omnibus calengiis contra omnes homines. Test(ibus) his . Rob(erto) de Moubr' . Rob(erto) de Daeuilla . Hug(one) Maleb' . Rad(ulfo) de Beluario . Thom(a) de Coleuilla Rad(ulfo) filio Audl(ini) . Ham(one) Beler . Rob(erto) de Buci . Rob(erto) Beler . Johanne de Creuequer . Rog(ero) de Daeuilla . Nich(olao) de Beslun . Henric(o) de Lubeham . Will(elmo) camerario . Pet(ro) de Hume.

Endorsements: *Richemundesir'* (late 12th or early 13th cent.); *Thorp* (later medieval hand).

Size: 19·1 × 13·8 cm.; 1·7 cm. turn-up.

Seal: seal no. 1 of Nigel de Mowbray (above, p. lxxxiii), brown wax; appended on tag.

Script: same hand as that of no. 364.

   ^a *Sic*; *porcis* intended.

NOTE. For the date, see note to no. 364. Nigel de Mowbray's interest in la Haia's enfeoffment probably stemmed from his tenure of Brinklow from before 1181 (above, no. 329).

366 *Gift by Roger de Mowbray to Richard de Hedona of 60 acres in Nutwith (Yorks., N.R.), for his service.* [*c.* 1170 × *c.* 1181]

> Original charter: Vyner deeds deposited at Leeds Archives, V.R. 25. Cartulary copies (Fountains): B.M., Cotton MS. Tib. C xii fo. 28*r–v*; Bodl., MS. Rawlinson B 449 fo 23*r–v* (lacks last 7 witnesses); B.M., Egerton MS. 3053 fo. 5*r–v* (lacks all witnesses); Add. MS. 18276 fo. 5*r* (abstract).
> Pd., *Mon. Ang.* v 306 (LVI) (lacks last 7 witnesses), from MS. Rawlinson; (transl.) *Fount. Cart.* i 17 (13), from Cotton MS.

Rog(erus) de Moubrai omnibus hominibus suis et amicis Francis et Anglis clericis et laicis presentibus et futuris . salutem. Sciatis me dedisse et hac carta mea confirmasse Ricardo de Hedona sexaginta acras terre in Nutewid iuxta uiam que uadit de*a* Torp apud Masham uersus lecasteler usque ad diuisas Aldredi . et usque ductum de Musebec . illi et heredibus suis tenendas de me et heredibus meis in feudo et hereditate libere et quiete et honorifice per seruicium quantum pertinet sexaginta acris unde duodecim carrucate terre faciunt seruicium unius militis. His test(ibus) . Rob(erto) de Moubrai . Philippo de Munpinchun . Warino filio Simonis . Rog(ero) filio Gaufridi . Rob(erto) Beler . Rob(erto) de Beucamp . Will(elmo) pincerna . Willelmo le Gramari . Hug(one) de Leheleia . Rad(ulfo) de Chinun.

Endorsements: *Carta R. de Mubr' de lx. acris in Notewid | Aldeburch' | Nutewith'.* (late 12th or early 13th cent.); *xiii* (? 14th cent.); *Aldeburgh' carta .13.* (? 15th cent.).

Size: 12·3 × 11·1 cm.; 2·5 cm. turn-up.

Seal: seal no. 3 of Roger de Mowbray (above, p. lxxxiii), white wax varnished; appended on tag.

Script: same hand as no. 348. See Fig. 1 (above, p. lxviii).

> NOTE. Philip de Montpincon does not occur before *c.* 1170 (no. 376 note). This charter was issued before Richard de Hedona's gift to Fountains, probably made in *c.* 1181,[1] and confirmed by Roger de Mowbray, *c.* 1176 × 1183, probably *c.* 1181 (no. 142).

367 *Confirmation by Nigel de Mowbray to Richard de Hedona of 60 acres in Nutwith, given by his father Roger, for a pound of cumin p.a.* [*c.* 1170 × *c.* 1181]

> Original charter: Vyner deeds deposited at Leeds Archives, V.R. 27. Cartu-

---

a *ad*, MS. Rawl.

---

[1] Vyner deeds deposited at Leeds Archives, V.R. 26; cf. incomplete text *Mon. Ang.* v 307 (LVII).

lary copies: B.M., Cotton MS. Tib. C xii fo. 28v; Bodl., MS. Rawlinson B
449 fo. 23v (lacks last 3 witnesses); B.M., Egerton MS. 3053 fo. 5v (lacks
all witnesses); B.M., Add. MS. 18276 fo. 5r (abstract).
Pd. (transl.), *Fount. Cart.* i 17 (14), from Cotton MS.

Nigellus de Moubr' omnibus hominibus et amicis suis presentibus et
futuris salutem. Sciatis me concessisse et hac carta confirmasse Ric(ardo)
de Hedona et heredibus suis tenendas de me et heredibus meis in feodo
et hereditate .lx. accras terre in Nutuwit quas pater meus ei dederat.
Hanc terram prefatam concessi ei et confirmaui pro seruicio et hominagio suo secundum diuisas que in carta patris mei continentur . annuatim
reddendo unam libram cumini pro omnibus seruiciis. Hiis t(estibus) .
Herb(erto) filio Ricardi . Nicoll(ao) de Beelun . Galfr(ido) de Beellun .
Willelmo de Belmainnil . Galfr(ido) coco . Ric(ardo) de Richem' .
Rad(ulfo) clerico.

Endorsements: *Confirmatio Nigelli de Mubray.* (12th cent.); *Nutewyd.* (early
13th cent.); *xiii* (? 13th cent.); *Aldeburgh. carta 14.* (? 15th cent.).

Size: 14·4×7 cm.; 1·5 cm. turn-up.

Seal: fragment of seal no. 1 of Nigel de Mowbray (above, p. lxxxiii), brown wax;
appended on tag.

NOTE. For the date, see note to no. 366. This charter seems to convert the
tenancy granted in no. 366 from military fee to free socage.

368 *Gift by Roger de Mowbray to Richard de Hedona of all his land in Nutwith,*
for a rent of a pound of pepper p.a.   [*c.* 1176×*c.* 1181]

Cartulary copies: B.M., Cotton MS. Tib. C xii fos. 28v–29r (old fos. 25v–
26r); Bodl., MS. Rawlinson B 449 fo. 23v (lacks last 11 witnesses); B.M.,
Egerton MS. 3053 fo. 5r (lacks all witnesses); B.M., Add. MS. 18276 fo. 5r
(abstract).
Pd. (transl.), *Fount. Cart.* i 17 (15), from Cotton MS.

Rogerus de Mubr'[a] omnibus hominibus suis et amicis clericis et laicis
presentibus et futuris salutem. Sciatis me dedisse et concessisse et hac
carta mea confirmasse Ricardo de Hedune totam terram quam habui in
Nutewit,[b] preter quandam carrucatam quam Aldredus illic habet et
preter vj acras Liulfi et preter duas bovatas Hacke,[c] scilicet per has
divisas sicuti Musebec descendit in Musecodc[d] usque in Hior[e] et sic
amunt[f] Hior[e] usque ad divisas monachorum et sic per divisas inter me et
Johannem de Wautune[g] usque in Musescod,[d] illi et heredibus suis
tenendam de me et heredibus meis libere quiete et honorifice in bosco
et plano, in pratis et pascuis, in viis, in semitis et in omnibus locis, cum

[a] *Mubrai*, MS. Rawl.   [b] *Nutewith*, MS. Rawl.   [c] *Acke*, MS. Rawl.
[d] *Musecloh*, MS. Rawl.   [e] *Jor*, MS. Rawl.   [f] *Sic.*   [g] *Wattun*, MS. Rawl.

omnibus libertatibus libero feudo pertinentibus, reddendo annuatim pro omnibus serviciis et consuetudinibus unam libram piperis. Concedo etiam illi et heredibus suis communem pasturam per forestam meam*a* de Malesard*b* et pasnagium porcorum suorum quietum. Hanc donationem*c* quam illi dedi pro homagio suo et servicio illi warentizabo contra omnes homines. Hiis test(ibus), Roberto de Mubr',*d* Willelmo de Mubr',*d* Philippo de Muntpincun, Herberto filio Ricardi, Willelmo cam(erario), Roberto Beler, Rogero filio Gaufridi, Roberto de Belcamp, Roberto de Buci, Alano Fossard, Willelmo filio cam(erarii), Willelmo Gramaire, Radulfo de Scoteni, Roberto clerico et multis aliis.

NOTE. The reference to John de Wauton's bounds indicates that the charter was probably given after 1176.[1] The *terminus ad quem* is the same as for no. 366.

369 *Gift by Roger de Mowbray to William de Immingham, the reeve of 'Bee-loda', of land between the house of Wibald of Belwood and the vaccary, and 2 bovates and a toft in 'Litlehasel' (Axholme), for an annual rent of 4s., which Roger gave to the cell of Nostell at Hirst.* [1138×1154]

Transcript, from an original charter formerly in St. Mary's Tower, York: Bodl., MS. Dodsworth 8 fo. 198*v*. Cartulary copy: B.M., Cotton MS. Vesp. E xix (cart. of Nostell) fo. 131*r* (old p. 323) (lacks all witnesses).

Rogerus de Molb' omnibus ballivis et amicis et omnibus hominibus suis tam Francis quam Anglicis de wapatac de Insula*e* salutem. Sciatis me dedisse et concessisse Willelmo de Himigh' le rifle[2] de Beeloda, que est inter domum*f* Wibaldi de Belwoda et vacer,*g* et .ij. bovatas et .i. toft in Litlehasel, pro .iiij. solidis donandis per annum, pro servicio suo, et .iiij. solidos de his .ij. bovatis terre concessi domine Sancte Marie de Herst,*h* pro anima patris mei Nigelli, et pro animabus omnium fidelium, et pro michimet ipsis, quiet' per tantum, pro omnibus serviciis et querelis, in feudo*i* et hereditate, sibi et heredi suo. Et volo et*j* firmiter*k* precipio ut terram istam de me et de heredibus meis teneat in bene et in*j* pace, libere et quiete et honorifice. Teste, Hereberto de Morevilla, Rogero de Flam'villa, Bertram Haghet, Hugone de Maisnihermer, et W. fratre ejus, Olivero de Boceio, Aluredo cam(erario), et probis hominibus de Insula.

Dodsworth notes: 'On horsebacke sword & sheild*l* yellow wax +SIGILLVM: ROGERI'.

a *foresta mea*, MS. Rawl.   *b* *Malesart*, MS. Rawl.   *c* MS. Rawl. inserts *vero*.   *d* *Mubrai*, MS. Rawl.   *e* *et wapentac*, omitting *de Insula*, cart. *f* *dom'*, cart.   *g* *Wacer'*, cart.   *h* *Hirst'*, cart.   *i* *feodo*, cart.   *j* Omitted in Dodsw. version.   *k* Omitted in cart.   *l* *Sic*.

---

[1] Cf. *P.R. 23 Hen. II* p. 78.   [2] Reeve; cf. above, nos. 219, 221.

NOTE. Alfred the chamberlain had been succeeded by his son William before 1154 (nos. 235, 300). The appearance of Hugh and W(illiam) de Meisnil-hermer suggests a date in the 1140s (see note to no. 400). For charters in favour of Hirst, a cell of Nostell, see nos. 15, 215–21.

370 *Gift by Roger de Mowbray to William son of Gilbert of Lancaster, of Lonsdale, Kendale (Westmorland), and Horton in Ribblesdale (Yorks., W.R.), for the service of 4 knights.* [probably 1149]

> Transcript: Bagot deeds at Levens Hall, 'Register of deeds written about 1639' fo. 79r.
> Pd., *Lancs. Pipe Rolls and Early Charters*, ed. W. Farrer (Liverpool, 1902) p. 389; and W. Farrer, *Records relating to the Barony of Kendale*, ed. J. F. Curwen (Cumb. and Westm. Antiq. and Archaeol. Soc., Rec. ser. iv–vi) i 377–8, from transcript.

Rogerius de Mowbray omnibus hominibus suis Francis et Anglicis salutem. Sciatis me dedisse et concessisse Willelmo filio Gilberti de Lancastr(ia) in feodo et hereditate scilicet totam terram meam de Lonsdall et de Kendall et Hortuna de Riblesdala, cum omnibus suis pertinenciis tenere bene et in pace, quiete et libere et honorifice, in bosco, in plano, in aquis, in molendinis, in omnibus rebus cum soco et sacca et tolneto et infangentheefe, cum omnibus consuetudinibus, libertatibus et rectis, per servicium quatuor militum. Test(ibus), Richardo Burdet, Mathia de Rampenne, Roberto Boscer, Turgilo*a* filio Malger, Ricardo Farser, Galtero de Davilla, Gilberto Bacun et Clemente fratre suo, Botselmo Neillecien,*b* Rogero de Daltuna.

> NOTE. The appearance of the first three witnesses suggests a date before c. 1150.[1] This enfeoffment probably belongs to 1149, when Roger de Mowbray may have recovered these estates at the time of the alliance between king David of Scotland, Henry of Anjou, and Ranulf of Chester (above, p. xxvi).
> William son of Gilbert's mother was Goditha, probably the daughter of the thegn Eldred. William was therefore probably cousin of Orm, the father of Gospatric, ancestor of the Curwens of Workington.[2] In 1166 William held two new fees of Mowbray, representing the Yorkshire estates granted in the present charter.[3]

371 *Gift by Roger de Mowbray to Hugh Malebisse of Carlton (? Miniott), (Over) Silton, Kepwick, Scawton, Murton, Dale Town, Stainton, Arden, Hawnby, and 2 carucates in Broughton (? in Appleton le Street) (all Yorks., N.R.), and a mill in York, for the service of one knight.* [c. 1147 × c. 1157]

a Read *Turgisio.*   *b* ? Read *Gocelino Veillekin.*

---

[1] For Richard Burdet, cf. nos. 48, 98, 230, 363. For Matthew de Rampan, see note to no. 35. For Robert Boscer, see note to no. 36.

[2] See G. Washington, in *Trans. Cumb. and Westm. Antiq. and Archaeol. Soc.* N.S. lxii (1962) 95–100.

[3] No. 401, Fees [39]. Cf. Farrer, *Barony of Kendale* i p. xi, and *Lancashire Pipe Rolls* pp. 389–90.

Transcript, from an original charter formerly at Gilling Castle: Leeds, Yorks. Archaeol. Soc. Libr., MS. 282 (notes by Dodsworth) fo. 17r.
Pd. (abstract), *Kirkby's Inquest*, ed. R. H. Skaife (S.S. xlix) p. 97 n., citing *York Corporation Papers* ii 950.[1]

Rog' de Molbr' conest' et dapif' et baillivis et hominibus et amicis suis salutem. Sciatis me dedisse et concessisse Hugoni Maleb' Carlcho et Siltuna et Chiepewic et Scaltona et Mortuna et Dala et Steintona et Erdena et Helbi et .ij. carucatas terre in Broctuna, et quicquid illis terris pertinet, bene et in pace, quiete et libere et honorifice, in bosco, in plano, in stagnis, in molendinis, in pratis, in aquis, in piscariis, et in omnibus rebus eisdem terris pertinentibus, cum soco et saca et tolla et them et infanghentef, et molendinum de Eboraco, et tali conditione de molendinis, quod si dominus Rogerus eas rehabere voluerit dabit sibi in escambium et precium, in feudo et hereditate sibi et heredibus suis, tenendum de me et heredibus meis per servicium unius militis. Test-(ibus), Nigello de Molb', Roberto fratre ejus, R. de Davilla,[2] W. de Widvilla,[3] W. Buere,[4] Rogero de Flam', Bertram Haget, Radulfo Beler, Rogero de Condeio, Waltero de Rivera, Radulfo de Bel', Radulfo de Rug', Roberto de Bocei, Adam Luvel, W. Maleb',[5] Hamone Beler.

> NOTE. Nigel and Robert de Mowbray did not attest charters before *c.* 1147. Ralph Beler was probably dead by 1157,[6] and W(illiam) de Wyville does not occur after this date.[7] For charters with similar witness-clauses, all belonging to 1154 × 1157, see, e.g., nos. 236, 242-3, 323.
> Hugh Malebisse held one fee of the old enfeoffment in 1166 (no. 401, where he is called 'Hugo Malherbe').[8] Farrer suggested that Malebisse's ancestor may have been enfeoffed by Robert Malet before 1106.[9] The present charter was therefore a restoration and not a new enfeoffment. The beneficiary was probably the son of Hugh Malebisse the *dapifer*, who had been succeeded in office by William de Wyville by 1154 (cf. no. 237). Land in Bagby was granted by Mowbray in augmentation of the fee before *c.* 1181 (see no. 58).

372 *Memorandum that Roger de Mowbray and Henry de Montfort quitclaimed to Richard Malebisse land in (Little) Ayton (Yorks., N.R.), in the king's court.* 12 June 1179

> Extract, ? from original charters formerly at Gilling Castle: Leeds, Yorks. Archaeol. Soc. Libr., MS. 282 (notes by Dodsworth) fo. 27v.

Rogerus de Molbray et Henricus de Munford quietum clam(averunt) Ricardo Malebisse et heredibus suis capitale messuagium et totam

---

[1] It has been impossible to trace these papers. Skaife made copies which were used by W. T. Lancaster, but Lancaster's extracts (Yorks. Archaeol. Soc. Libr., MS. 405 pp. 29 ff.) do not contain the present charter.   [2] Probably Robert rather than Roger.
[3] Presumably William.   [4] Walter Buher.   [5] Presumably William Malebisse.
[6] See *E.Y.C.* ix 212.   [7] Cf. nos. 202, 242-3, 281 note.   [8] See Fees [23].
[9] *E.Y.C.* iii 457; charters relating to the Malet lands are pd. ibid. pp. 434-66.

medietatem totius terre de Etona in curia regis H(enrici) 2, die Martii proxima post festum Sancti Barnabi Apostoli anno xxv. H(enrici) 2, tenendum de dicto rege in capite et ad pertinendum ad feudum sui militis quod tenet de me de honore Eye.

NOTE. Richard Malebisse, who in 1176 had paid 100s. relief for his fee of the honour of Eye, owed 40 marks in 1180 for having judgement of the land of Ayton against Roger de Mowbray and Henry de Montfort.[1] The honour of Eye, like Malebisse's lands of Mowbray, had originally belonged to Robert Malet.[2]

373 *Gift by Roger de Mowbray to William de Martona of 2 bovates and 9 acres of marsh in Kelfield (Axholme, Lincs.) for a rent of 8s. p.a.*

[*c.* 1170 × 1184]

Pd., *Danelaw Charters* no. 393, from B.M., Add. Ch. 20847.

Testibus hiis . Nigello de Molbr' . Roberto . capellano . Roberto . de Nouilla . Roberto . de Boceo . Petro de Billingeia . Herberto filio Ricardi . Nicolao de Besl'o . Willelmo camerario . Rogero coco . Willelmo de Thalamo . Ricardo . Malherba .

Size: 18·2 × 12 cm.; 2 cm. turn-up.

Seal: fragment of seal no. 3 of Roger de Mowbray (above, p. lxxxiii), red wax; appended on tag.

Script: same hand as that of nos. 272 and 282. See Fig. 5 (above p. lxviii).

NOTE. Four of these witnesses appear in no. 349, in favour of a fifth witness, Peter of Billinghay. Possibly this charter belongs to the same period as nos. 343, 349, 360, 364–5. William de Martona gave this land to Welford (see no. 284). He is perhaps to be identified with William de Martona who appears in Lincolnshire in 1191 and 1193, on the second occasion as *camerarius*.[3]

374 *Restoration and confirmation by Roger de Mowbray to Walter de Meinil of Thirkleby of 2 carucates in Little Thirkleby (Yorks., N.R.) which his father had held and another carucate from Roger de Mowbray's demesne there, in marriage with Ascelina his wife, for the fifth part of the service of one knight.*

[1138 × 1148]

Original charter: archives of Viscount Downe, deposited at Northallerton, North Riding R.O.

Rogerius de Molbrai omnibus hominibus suis Francis et Anglis presentibus et futuris salutem. Sciatis me reddidisse et concessisse et presenti carta mea confirmasse Valtero de Meinil de Turkillebi duas carrucatas

---

[1] *P.R. 22 Hen. II* p. 77; *26 Hen. II* p. 74.   [2] See *E.Y.C.* iii 455–9, 463–6.
[3] *P.R. 3 Ric. I* p. 21; *5 Ric. I* p. 35.

terre in Parua Turkillebi quas pater eius tenuit. Et in eadem uilla dedi ei unam carrucatam terre de meo dominio cum Ascelina sponsa sua in liberum maritagium ; illi et heredibus suis tenendas de me et heredibus meis libere . quiete . et solute et honorifice . in bosco et plano . in pratis et pasturis . in uiis et . aquis . et semitis . et ceteris omnibus communitatibus . et libertatibus . et aisiamentis . perfaciendo seruicium quinte partis feudi unius militis . sicut contingit feudo militis . decem carrucatas terre. His test(ibus) . Sansone de Albeneio . Rogero de Flammauilla . Roberto de Daiuilla . Oliuero de Buzi . Willelmo de Ages . Roberto de Buzzi . Waltero de Daiuilla . Roberto Boscher . Herberto de Cunigburch . Helia de Sancto Martino . Landrico de Ages.

No endorsement.

Size: 14·3 × 13 cm.; 1·7 cm. turn-up.

Seal: missing; was appended on tag.

NOTE. The latest possible date, in view of the appearance of Elias de Sancto Martino, is probably 1148 (cf. no. 89 note); four other charters in which he occurs belong to 1138 × 1143.[1] Thirkleby was part of the Buscy fee, in which the Meinil family held a sub-tenure, but it is possible that this charter precedes the enfeoffment of Oliver de Buscy in one new fee, which his brother Robert held in 1166.[2] The parentage of Ascelina is unknown.

375 *Gift by Roger de Mowbray to Rainald de Mildeby of one carucate in Brimham (Yorks., W.R.), for the fifteenth part of the service of one knight.*
[1138 × 1157]

Cartulary copy: Bodl., MS. Rawlinson B 449 (cart. of Fountains) fo. 91r.

[R]ogerus de Mubray dapifero suo et omnibus hominibus suis salutem. Sciatis me concessisse et dedisse Reynaldo de Mildeby unam carucatam terre in Birnebem pro quinta decima parte servicii militis, donec reddidero ei suum plenum servicium sicut carta mea testatur quam habet. T(este), Radulfo Beler etc.

NOTE. The date is determined by the appearance of Ralph Beler, who died by 1157.[3] Rainald restored this land to Mowbray before 1176, and it was given to Fountains (no. 116).

376 *Gift by Roger de Mowbray to Philip de Montpincon of Swetton (Yorks., W.R.), by specified bounds.*
[c. 1170 × 1186]

Reference in a charter of Philip de Montpincon for Newburgh: Newburgh Priory deeds deposited at Northallerton, North Riding R.O.
Pd. (abstract), H.M.C., *Various Collections* ii (1903) 9.

---

[1] Nos. 32, 37–8, 195; cf. no. 294.   [2] No. 401, Fees [42].
[3] See *E.Y.C.* ix 212.

NOTE. Philip de Montpincon attests more than forty charters, of which the earliest that are dated belong to 1176 (nos. 125–7), and all seem to be after *c.* 1170. Philip made a gift on entering Newburgh, of a third of the vill of Swetton, consisting of 4 bovates held by tenants, a third of the mill, a third of one mark p.a. from Carlesmoor, a third of the demesne 'tam sartandam quam sartatam', a toft, a third of the wood for building, burning, and selling, and a third of pasture, pannage, and easements. The boundaries of the vill were 'sicut carta Rogeri de Mubrai testatur'.

377 *Gift by Roger de Mowbray to Noel of one carucate in Sleningford (Yorks., W.R.), rendering 20 lengths of cord[1] p.a.* [1138 × 1169]

> Cartulary copy: Manchester, John Rylands Libr., Lat. MS. 224 (cart. of Fountains) fos. 185v–186r.
> Pd. (transl.), *Fount. Cart.* ii 658 (56).

Rogerus de Molbray omnibus suis Francis et Anglicis salutem. Sciatis me dedisse et concessisse Noel unam carucatam terre in Slaingford, in bosco et plano, libere et quiete, cum saca et soca et tol et tem et infanganthef, reddendo annuatim xx taises de laz[1] michi et uxori mee. His t(estibus), Wat' Bueri, Roberto de Daivile, Radulfo de Bellun, Rogero de Flamanvile et aliis pluribus.

> NOTE. Roger de Flamville probably died by 1169.[2]
> Sleningford was part of the fee which Roger de Mowbray held of the archbishop and had subenfeoffed to Cramaville (no. 359). The cartulary of Fountains records a final concord whereby in 1204 Alan Noel remitted his right to Sleningford to Robert de Cramaville in return for £10 silver.[3]

378 *Gift by Roger de Mowbray to Ralph de Normanville of Empingham (Rutland), for his service; and later gift of the same to Gerold de Normanville.* [1142 × 1157]

> Confirmation by Henry II for Gerold de Normanville [1154 × 1157]: pd., *C.P.R. 1494–1509* p. 268, from P.R.O., Patent Roll 17 Hen. VII pt. ii (C. 66/590) m. 5.

> NOTE. Empingham formed the dowry of Alice de Gant (above, no. 182). The Normanville family was connected with the counts of Eu,[4] of whom Mowbray held a fee in Normandy.[5] Both Ralph and Gerold de Normanville occur in 1147.[6] Gerold may have been succeeded in some Lincolnshire estates by his son Ralph in 1169 or 1170.[7] The Normanville holding of Mowbray in Empingham consisted of two knights' fees in 1259.[8]

---

[1] See Glossary, below, p. 267. Lancaster's conjecture, 'wolves' heads', is clearly wrong.
[2] *E.Y.C.* i 415. Roger last occurs in 1167 (*P.R. 13 Hen. II* p. 1), but had been dead for 1½ years (3 terms) in Sept. 1170, so presumably died before Easter 1169 (*P.R. 16 Hen. II* p. 49).
[3] Manchester, John Rylands Libr., Lat. MS. 224 fo. 186r.
[4] G. R. Sitwell in *The Genealogist* N.S. xiii (1896–7) 11–15.
[5] Above, no. 19. Cf. also Daiville, above, p. xxxiv n. 1.
[6] *Mon. Ang.* v 522–3.   [7] *P.R. 15 Hen. II* p. 14, *16 Hen. II* p. 147.
[8] *Cal. Inq. P.M.* i 117.

379 *Gift by Roger de Mowbray to Rainald Puher of 2 bovates in (Middle)thorpe (Yorks., W.R.), held by Osbert [? Bustard], and the homage and service of Osbert, for a rent of one pound of pepper p.a.* [1138×c. 1154]

> Cartulary copy: cartulary of Whitby, in the possession of Miss M. L. A. Strickland, of Whitwell, York, fo. 72r.
> Pd., *Whitby Cart.* i no. 281.

Rogerus de Molbray omnibus ministris suis et hominibus Francis et Anglis salutem. Notum sit vobis me dedisse et concessisse Rainaldo Poher duas bovatas terre in Thorp juxta Eboracum quas Osbertus tenet et homagium et servicium ipsius Osberti et suorum heredum, liberas et quietas et solutas ab omni servicio et consuetudine, per servicium unius libre piperis annuatim. Illi et suo heredi concedo hanc terram predictam et homagium et servicium hujus Osberti et suorum heredum, ita quod Osbertus et omnes sui filii sint liberi et quieti a me et meis heredibus intendentes de homagio et servicio suo Rainaldo et suis heredibus. Et volo et jubeo quod Rainaldus et suus heres teneant libere et quiete in feudum et hereditatem in bosco in plano et in omnibus ad supradictam terram pertinentibus de me et meis heredibus. Testibus, Willelmo de Arch', Radulfo de Widvilla, Philippo Pumtel, Helya de Dol, Osberto filio W. filii Herm', Roberto filio Bald', Ricardo filio Widonis.

> NOTE. Ralph de Wyville was probably dead some time before *c.* 1154 (no. 400 note). Cf. charters for Whitby, nos. 290–1.

380 *Gift by Roger de Mowbray to Rainald Puher of a* mansura *in York and* ½ carucate *in (Middle)thorpe, held by Herbert* pincerna, *for an annual rent of scarlet hose.* [1138×c. 1154]

> Cartulary copy: cartulary of Whitby (Strickland) fo. 65r.
> Pd., *Whitby Cart.* i no. 258.

Rogerus*a* de Molbrai constabulariis suis et dapiferis et baronibus et omnibus hominibus et amicis suis Francisque Anglicis de Eborascira salutem. Sciatis me dedisse et concessisse Reginaldo Pouherio mansuram quam Herbertus pincerna in Eboraco tenebat, et dimidiam carucatam terre in Thorp quam predictus Herbertus tenebat, in feudo et hereditate et heredibus suis solutam*a* liberam et quietam cum omnibus rebus terre predicte pertinentibus et cum omnibus consuetudinibus liberis et per servicium unarum caligarum de scarlet annuatim reddend(arum). Teste, Willelmo de Archis, Herberto Quonigburc,*c* Willelmo Malebisse et aliis.

> NOTE. William de Arches probably died by *c.* 1154 (cf. note to no. 359). Herbert *pincerna* occurs only once, 17 April 1153 (no. 322).

> *a* Rogero, MS.   *b* solam, MS.   *c* ? read Queningburg.

381 *Gift by Roger de Mowbray to Ralph of Queniborough of his tenure in Queni-borough and Burton on the Wolds (Leics.), for the service of one knight, which before he had for the service of 2 knights.* [*c.* 1170 × 1186]

> Cartulary copy: B.M., Add. MS. 37771 (cart. of Selby) fo. 194*r* (old fo. 192*r*). Pd., *Selby Coucher* ii no. 1123.

Rogerus de Molb' omnibus baronibus et hominibus suis tam Francis quam Anglis salutem. Sciatis me dedisse et concessisse Radulfo de Quenig-burg' totam tenuram suam, scilicet Queningburg' et Burton'*ᵃ* heredibus suis a me et heredibus meis imperpetuum, pro servicio unius militis quam antea habebat pro servicio duorum militum, et hoc amore et petitione fratris Herberti de Quenigburg'. Et ego Johannes capellanus hoc breve scripsi quia interfui, et inde sunt testes, Rogerus de Cod'*ᵇ* senescallus etc.

> NOTE. John the chaplain does not appear before *c.* 1170 (see no. 166 note). In 1166 Ralph of Queniborough held 2 old fees.¹ The reason for the reduction of service was the grant to Selby of land in Queniborough.²

382 *Confirmation by Roger de Mowbray to Ralph of Queniborough of Queni-borough, for the service of one knight.* [*c.* 1170 × 1186]

> Cartulary copy: B.M., Add. MS. 37771 fo. 194*r* (old fo. 192*r*). Pd., *Selby Coucher* ii no. 1124.

Rogerus de Moubr' omnibus hominibus suis et amicis clericis et laycis presentibus et futuris salutem. Sciatis me concessisse et hac carta con-firmasse Radulfo de Queningburg' Queningburg' cum omnibus perti-nenciis illi et heredibus suis tenendum de me et heredibus meis libere quiete et honorifice per servicium faciendum*ᶜ* unius militis. Ego vero et heredes mei warantizabimus illi et heredibus suis hanc donationem per idem servicium contra omnes homines. Hiis testibus, Hub' de Daivil(la), Hugone Maleb(is)se etc.

> NOTE. Presumably this is subsequent to no. 381.

383 *Restoration by Roger de Mowbray to Ralph son of Aldelin of his father's land, i.e. all the land of Aldfield and 7 bovates in Studley (Roger) and 2 mansurae in Kirkby Malzeard (Yorks., W.R.), for the fourth part of the service of one knight.* [1138 × 1154]

> Cartulary copy: B.M., Cotton MS. Tib. C xii (cart. of Fountains) fo. 37*v*. Pd. (transl.), *Fount. Cart.* i 22 (1).

Rogerus de Molb' omnibus hominibus et amicis suis tam Francis quam Anglicis et Eboraci scira salutem. Sciatis me reddidisse et dedisse et

---

ᵃ Some words omitted.   *ᵇ* ? read *Condeio*.   *ᶜ* *faciendo*, MS.

¹ No. 401, Fees [15].   ² See *Selby Coucher* ii nos. 1125 ff.

concessisse Radulfo filio Aldelini terram patris sui, videlicet totam terram de Aldefeld' et vij bovatas terre in Stodleia quas tenuit Ricardus parvus clericus et duas masuras in Mapeshard, in feudo et in hereditate et heredibus suis. Quare volo et precipio quod iste Radulfus hanc terram predictam totam bene et in pace, quiete et libere et honorifice teneat, cum bosco, in plano, in pratis, in aquis, in stagnis, in molendinis, in vivariis, in virgultis, in viis, in semitis, in paschuis, et in omnibus rebus cum socho et sacha, ethol, ethem, et in fagentheof,[a] et cum omnibus consuetudinibus liberis, et per servicium quarte partis unius militis. Test(ibus), Herberto de Queniburc, Waltero de Ripar', Rogero de Condeio, Alfredo camerario, Willelmo de Colevilla, Radulfo Beler, Willelmo Baldri, Turgis filio Malgeri, Rollando de Landeles, Stephano Junni', Helto de Boisdela, Radulfo Malchael.

> NOTE. The appearance of Alfred the chamberlain suggests a date before 1154 (cf. note to no. 369). The charter was confirmed by Henry II, probably in January 1156.[1]
>
> Ralph son of Aldelin and Roger son of Geoffrey held ½ fee of Mowbray in 1166.[2] Ralph did not recover all the land which had belonged to his father: the present charter omits reference to Winterburn, which had been held by Aldelin of Aldfield by hereditary right in 1135, and which passed, probably after c. 1149, to the Graindorge fee (no. 150 note). Ralph's brother William was *dapifer* to Henry II.[3]

384 *Confirmation by Roger de Mowbray to William de Rudeville of Lindley (Leics.), given by Richard de Moreville.*   [c. 1150 × 1183]

> Transcript, from an original charter formerly in the possession of Cassibelan Burton, 1649: Bodl., MS. Dugdale 13 p. 516.
> Pd., Nichols, *Leics.* iv (2) 645, from 'Burton MS.'.

Rogerus de Molbrai omnibus hominibus suis Francis et Anglis tam presentibus quam futuris salutem. Sciatis me concessisse et presenti carta mea confirmasse illam donationem de terra de Lindleja que de feodo meo est quam Ricardus de Morevilla fecit Willelmo de Arodevilla consanguineo suo et dedit. Quare volo et firmiter precipio quod hec donatio de Lindleja firma sit et rata Willelmo de Aroudevilla et heredibus suis erga me et heredes meos, et quod predictus Willelmus et heredes sui teneant hanc prescriptam terram de Lindleja bene et in pace et honorifice et integre de Ricardo de Morevilla et de heredibus suis per tale servicium quale continetur in carta Ricardi de Morevilla. T(estibus), Roberto

---

[a] *Sic.*

[1] *Fount. Cart.* i 23 (2); cf. Eyton, *Itinerary* pp. 15-16.
[2] No. 401 and Fees [29].
[3] *E.Y.C.* iii 299-300; *Recueil des Actes de Henri II*, ed. L.V. Delisle and E. Berger (Paris, 1909-27), Introduction, p. 478.

comite Legr(ecestrie), Roberto de Molbraj, Radulfo de Belvario, Roberto de Butej, Samsone de Cornubia, Radulfo de Turrevilla, Philippo Sorel, Rogerio de Cranford, Bertolomeo de Sifflewast, Willelmo Sansonei.

NOTE. Richard de Moreville did not succeed to his father's fee until after *c.* 1154, when his father Herbert was still alive (no. 191). Richard last occurs in 1178,[1] and had probably died by 1183, perhaps by 1181.[2] Richard de Moreville and William de Rudeville appear together in no. 159, of *c.* 1160 × 1183.

Richard de Moreville's charter grants Lindley to William de Rudeville in exchange for Withybrook and records that Rudeville gave 10 marks for the exchange. If Rudeville had legitimate heirs, the land was to be held for the third part of two knights' service; if not, it was to return to Moreville and his heirs.[3]

William de Rudeville's origin was probably Éroudeville (Manche, arr. Valognes, cant. Montebourg),[4] not far from Morville (arr. Valognes, cant. Bricquebec).[5]

385 *Acquittance by Roger de Mowbray to Alan de Ryedale and his heirs of 10s. yearly rent from the land of Bowforth (Yorks., N.R.), to be held for a yearly payment of a pound of pepper for all services.*

At Nottingham [*c.* 24 March 1176]

Quitclaim by Alan de Ryedale and Maud his wife to Roger de Mowbray and Rievaulx of claims [in Welburn], made at Nottingham [*c.* 24 March 1176]: pd., *E.Y.C.* ix no. 160, from B.M., Cotton MS. Julius D i fo. 90*r* (old fo. 85/2). Also pd. (incompletely), *Riev. Cart.* no. 132.

NOTE. The date is given in a notification by Gregory, prior of Bridlington, before whom, with Master Vacarius, the suit was heard and settled between Alan de Ryedale and the monks of Rievaulx.[6]

386 *Gift by Roger de Mowbray to Robert de Stuteville of Kirkby Moorside (Yorks., N.R.) and appurtenances, for the service of (? 9 or) 10 knights, to settle Stuteville's claim on the barony.*

[1154 × 1166, perhaps before 1157]

Reference in narrative pd. as *E.Y.C.* ix no. 42, from *Houeden* iv 117–18.

NOTE. This enfeoffment is also referred to in the settlement between William de Mowbray and William de Stuteville, made in the king's court at Westminster on 2 April 1201.[7] For the date of the enfeoffment, see *E.Y.C.* ix 5 and ibid. no. 19 and note (cal. above as no. 239) and no. 62 and note. In the *carta* of 1166, Robert de Stuteville is recorded as holding eight old fees and one new fee.[8] For a list of the lands granted, see *E.Y.C.* ix 75, and for charters relating to the tenancy, see ibid. pp. 200–48.

1 *P.R. 24 Hen. II* p. 68.
2 *P.R. 29 Hen. II* p. 48; cf. *P.R. 27 Hen. II* p. 42. For his fee, see Fees [22].
3 Nichols, *Leics.* iv (2) 645.
4 Cf. *Recueil des Historiens des Gaules et de la France* xxiii 521*k*.
5 See *Ang.-Norm. Families* pp. 49, 70.   6 *E.Y.C.* ix no. 159.
7 *E.Y.C.* ix no. 43.   8 No. 401, Fees [2], [37].

387 *Gift by Nigel de Mowbray to Richard de Thorp of 'Alnetescroft' (? in Thorpe Arnold, Leics.) with 12 acres of land, for a rent of 18d. p.a.*

[*c.* 1166 × 1186]

Cartulary copy: B.M., Cotton MS. Nero C xii (cart. of Burton Lazars) fo. 5*r* (old p. 5).

Nigellus de Moubraio omnibus hominibus suis tam presentibus quam futuris salutem. Notum sit omnibus vobis me dedisse et concessisse Ricardo de Thorp' Alnetescroft cum xij acris terre et licenciam faciendi fossetum circa croftum scilicet in*ᵃ* suo illi et heredibus suis, tenendum de me et heredibus meis libere et quiete sine*ᵃ* omnibus aliis consuetudinibus et serviciis annuatim reddendo xviij denarios. His testibus, Hugone Maleb', Warino filio Simonis, Radulfo de Quenib', Roberto de Berci, Radulfo filio Turb', Reg(inaldo) preposito, Durando de Scaldeford', Gilberto de Caldwella, Thoma de Wikeham, Nicolao de Torp'.

NOTE. Warin son of Simon does not occur before 1166 (see no. 398 note). This estate was granted to Burton Lazars before 1186 (nos. 29–31).

388 *Gift by Roger de Mowbray to William of Tickhill of his manor of Askham Richard (Yorks., W.R.), with the advowson, in fee and heredity for a rent of one mark p.a., the gift being made when Roger promised to visit the Holy Land.*

[1175 × 1177]

Pd., *E.Y.C.* i no. 547, from B.M., Add. MS. 40008 fo. 178*v*. Also pd. (transl.), *Abstract of the Chart. of Bridlington*, ed. W. T. Lancaster (Leeds, 1912) p. 232.

Hiis testibus, Roberto [de] Dayvilla, Hugone Malebis(sa), Radulfo de Belver, Roberto fratre ejus, Thoma de Colvilla, Hamone Beler, Nicholao de Belun, Roberto capellano, Erniso Ultra Usam, Ger(vasio) gen(ero) Herb(erti) coc(i), Roberto Barri, Pagano fratre ejus, Roberto de Arden, Willelmo pincerna, Baldewino clerico, Edwardo et aliis.

NOTE. The gift was probably made after the settlement of the rebellion in 1175.[1] William of Tickhill died by Sept. 1182,[2] so that Mowbray's reference to his visit to the Holy Land must be to the expedition of 1177. Two charters of March 1176 were given in William of Tickhill's house in York (nos. 126–7). Askham Richard was part of the Arches fee (no. 389), and the church had already been given by William de Arches to the nunnery of Nun Monkton.[3]

ᵃ Presumably some words omitted.

---

[1] Cf. *P.R. 21 Hen. II* p. 182.
[2] *P.R. 28 Hen. II* p. 46, where Albreda his widow, Benedict son of Aldred and his wife, and Hugh son of Lewin and his wife proffered £100 for his debts and rights.
[3] *E.Y.C.* i no. 535.

389 *Gift by Nigel de Mowbray to William of Tickhill of Askham Richard, for a rent of one mark p.a., the land having been bought by Nigel and his father Roger from Juetta de Arches for 220 marks.* [1175 × 1179]

Transcript, from an original charter formerly at Gilling Castle: Leeds, Yorks. Archaeol. Soc. Libr., MS. 282 (notes by Dodsworth) fo. 23v.

Nigellus de Molbrai omnibus sancte matris ecclesie filiis etc. salutem. Notum sit vobis omnibus me dedisse et concessisse et hac carta mea confirmasse Willelmo de Ticheille et heredibus suis pro servicio et homagio suo Escham cum omnibus pertinenciis suis videlicet in bosco et plano etc., reddendo annuatim unam marcam argenti. Hanc terram prenominatam dedi predicto Willelmo et heredibus suis, sicuti illam que erat de feudo meo et quam Rogger de Molbrai pater meus et ego emimus de Jueta de Arches pro xi^{cim} xx^{ti} marcis argenti, sicut de recto herede Willelmi de Arches, qui habuit et tenuit hereditarie illam terram prenominatam etc. His testibus, Willelmo comite Albemarle, Roberto constabulario, Roberto de Daiville, Nicholao de Daiville, Rogero de Ardene, Henrico de Staingreve, Bertramo de Stivetune, Baldwino le despenser, Willelmo de Bonevilla etc.

Drawing of outline of circular seal: 'The seale red wax very faire on horsback'.

NOTE. The charter was probably given at the time of no. 388, and certainly before 1179, when William count of Aumale died.[1] In view of Roger de Mowbray's need to raise money for his projected crusade, it seems likely, as suggested by Farrer[2] and Professor Miller,[3] that he accepted a large sum from the merchant William of Tickhill in return for the grant of Askham Richard. The purchase from Juetta de Arches was therefore a means of raising a loan without diminishing the Mowbray demesne.

390 *Restoration by Roger de Mowbray to Arthur son of William de Torp of ½ carucate in Osgoodby (Yorks., N.R.), which his father had held of Roger's father, for a rent of 40d. p.a.* [c. 1147 × c. 1154]

Transcript, from an original charter formerly in St. Mary's Tower, York: Bodl., MS. Dodsworth 91 fo. 129r.

Rogerus de Molbray omnibus suis hominibus Francis et Anglis salutem. Sciatis me reddidisse Arturo filio Willelmi de Torp terram suam quam pater ejus tenuerat de Nigello patre meo, scilicet dimidiam carucatam terre in Angoteby cum omnibus que ad terram illam pertinent in bosco et plano. Et volo ut teneat terram illam libere et quiete pro quadraginta denariis per annum pro omni servicio. Teste Nigello filio meo qui et ipse hanc donationem concessit, et testibus, Willelmo de Widevilla, Willelmo de Arches, Waltero de Riveria, Radulpho de Bethlun, Waltero de Karletona.

[1] *Complete Peerage* i 353.   [2] *E.Y.C.* i 427.
[3] *V.C.H. Yorks. City of York* p. 45.

NOTE. In view of Nigel de Mowbray's active participation, the earliest possible date is *c.* 1147. All the witnesses, except William de Arches who died *c.* 1154 (no. 359 note), occur in 1154 × 1157 (no. 243). If William de Wyville's prominent position indicates that he was *dapifer, c.* 1154 would be the probable date.[1]

Osgoodby was part of the enfeoffment made to Oliver de Buscy.[2] The land which is the subject of the present charter seems to have been given to Byland.[3] Roger, abbot of Byland, granted to Geoffrey, son of Arthur de Torp, ½ carucate in Ampleforth, presumably in exchange.[4]

391 *Gift by Roger de Mowbray to Engelram de Torp of 3 bovates and a* mansura *before the castle gate in Thirsk (Yorks., N.R.).* [1138 × 1176]

Reference in charter of Engelram de Torp for Byland: Bodl., MS. Dodsworth 7 fo. 166r, transcript from an original charter in St. Mary's Tower, York.

. . . tres bovatas terre in Tresc cum toftis et croftis, cum pratis et pascuis et omnibus aisiamentis que ad illas bovatas pertinent . . . et unam mansuram ante portam castelli ubi domus mea sedet sicut continetur in carta domini Rogeri de Molbrai quam tradidi predictis monachis.

NOTE. The monks were to pay 2*s.* p.a. to Roger de Mowbray and his heirs at Christmas for the three bovates. Presumably Engelram's charter was given before the razing of Thirsk castle in 1176. Robert Beler confirmed Engelram's gift to Byland, and the donation is mentioned in no. 73 above.

392 *Concession by Roger de Mowbray to Uctred son of Dolfin of the land of Uctred's grandfather, Gospatric, of Ilton (par. Masham, Yorks., N.R.), to be held of Turgis (son of Malger) for the fourth part of the service of one knight.* [1138 × ? 1145]

13th-cent. copy: Ingilby of Ripley deeds, deposited at Leeds Archives, no. 12. 14th-cent. copy: Bodl., Yorks. Rolls 21 (cartulary of Hebden family) m. 3.

Rogerus de Moubray dapifero et omnibus hominibus suis Francis et Anglicis de Ebor(aci) Skyra salutem. Sciatis me concessisse Hucthred[a] filio Dolfini[b] terram avi sui Gospatric(i) de Ilketon(a)[c] cum omnibus pertinenciis ejusdem ville, in feodo et hereditate sibi et heredibus suis de Turgisso tenendam sibi et heredibus suis, pro servicio quarte partis feodi unius militis. Quare volo et firmiter precipio quod predictus Ucthred'[d] hanc terram teneat in pace, quod pro nullo calumpniatore in placito ponatur nisi in presencia mea, quia inde homo meus est et ego ei presidium. Hiis testibus etc.

[a] *Huthred*, Ingilby MS.   [b] *Dofini*, Ingilby MS.   [c] *Iyquetonia*, Bodl. MS.
[d] *Uthred'*, Ingilby MS.

---

[1] Cf. above, no. 237.   [2] See note to no. 374, and Fees [42].
[3] Bodl., MS. Dodsworth 63 fo. 62v.   [4] MS. Dodsworth 91 fo. 120r.

NOTE. Uctred of Ilton occurs before 1145 (no. 95).

In 1086 Ilton (2 carucates) was held of count Alan by Gospatric, son of the tenant of 1066, Archil. A fifteenth-century genealogy gives Gospatric a son Dolfin, to whom three sons, Torfin, Swein, and Uctred are assigned.[1] Torfin and Swein retained some of Gospatric's lands, and Swein was the ancestor of the families of Thoresby and Staveley.[2] The present charter shows Gospatric's third grandson, Uctred, in possession of part of the ancient family estate.

Uctred was the ancestor, through his son Simon, of the Hebden family, holding land in Conistone of the Skipton honour, and in Burnsall of Bulmer.[3] Another son, Ketel, witnesses no. 95. The land of Ilton was held of Turgis son of Malger, who himself held of Walter Buher, Mowbray's immediate sub-tenant in the Masham fee, held of the honour of Richmond.[4]

393 *Concession by Roger de Mowbray to Uctred of Ilton (son of Dolfin) of pannage for his pigs and those of his men of Ilton.* [1138 × 1186]

14th-cent. copy: Bodl., Yorks. Rolls 21 m. 3.

Rogerus de Moubray omnibus hominibus et amicis suis Francis et Anglicis clericis et laycis tam presentibus quam futuris salutem. Sciatis [me]*a* condona[sse]*a* Huthredo de Ilketona pannagium porcorum suorum et hominum suorum de Ilketona, sibi et heredibus suis de me et heredibus meis liberum et quietum in foresta mea. Hiis test(ibus) etc.

NOTE. The charter is subsequent to no. 392, but it is impossible to say how much later it may have been issued. Uctred son of Dolfin occurs last after 1179;[5] his son Simon first occurs as a landowner in 1192.[6]

394 *Gift by Roger de Mowbray to Uctred son of Dolfin of pasture for his cattle in Ilton, by specified bounds.* [1138 × 1186]

14th-cent. copy: Bodl., Yorks. Rolls 21 m. 3.

Rogerus de Mulbray omnibus hominibus presentibus et futuris salutem. Sciatis me dedisse concessisse Hucthred filio Dolfini pasturam peccudibus suis in*b* Ilketona in foresta mea juxta Ilketon', videlicet sicut Postebeck' descendit in brureiam et sicut Postebec [as]*a*cendit superius. Hanc pasturam predictam, videlicet illam que jacet inter Postesbec et Ilketon' per divisas prenominatas, concedo predicto Ucthredo sibi et heredibus suis, tenendam de me et heredibus meis in feodo et hereditate, quiete, libere et honorifice. Hiis testibus etc.

NOTE. For the date, see note to no. 393.

a Not clear in MS.   *b* ? read *de*.

---

[1] *Registrum Honoris de Richmond* (ed. R. Gale, 1722) app. pp. 56–7, table I.
[2] See *E.Y.C.* v 122–3; cf. *V.C.H. Yorks.* ii 184.   [3] See *E.Y.C.* vii 248 ff.
[4] Cf. no. 108; and *Fount. Cart.* ii 856–7.   [5] *E.Y.C.* vii no. 92 and p. 248.
[6] Ibid. no. 106 and p. 249.

395 *Gift by Roger de Mowbray to Uctred son of Dolfin of the manor of Hebden (Yorks., W.R.) by specified bounds, for a rent of 8s. p.a.* [1138 × 1186]

> 14th-cent. copy: Bodl., Yorks. Rolls 21 m. 4.
> Pd. (incompletely), T. D. Whitaker, *History and Antiquities of the Deanery of Craven*, 3rd edn., ed. A. W. Morant (Leeds, 1878), p. 500, retranslated into Latin from abstracts supplied by Mr. Swale of Settle.

Rogerus de Moubb' omnibus hominibus suis Francis et Anglicis presentibus et futuris salutem in Domino. Noveritis me dedisse concessisse Vhtredo filio Dolfyn et heredibus suis totum manerium de Hebbeden' cum omnibus suis pertinenciis, per divisas de Eskedensik usque Loutanstan et [Stanwath et Brokeshougill et inde usque ad Bradden]*ᵃ*-ford' in Gathopbeck juxta Holmkeld' et sicut divise extendunt inter Apletrewyk [et Hebbedene]*ᵃ* usque Sameleseng' et Gathophou et sicut Swargil extendit se in Grisdale et ad Stanrayse juxta Magare et ultra Tranber mire et Hissendene que extendit usque in Werf. Habendum et tenendum predictum manerium cum pertinenciis dicto Vhctredo et heredibus suis [? libere et quiete]*ᵇ* et pacifice cum omnibus libertatibus [? et consuetudinibus]*ᵇ* ad manerium meum de [. . . . .]*ᶜ* per dominum regem michi concessis. Reddendo inde [? de . . . . ? Galfrido de Stav . . . .]*ᵇ* heredibus suis viij solidos annuatim, medietatem ad Pentecosten et aliam med[ietatem ad festum Sancti]*ᵇ* Martini in hyema [. . . . .]*ᵇ* Et ego Rogerus et heredes mei dictum manerium cum omnibus suis [pertinenciis . . . . . Uh]*ᵇ*tred filio Dolfini et heredibus suis contra omnes homines warantizabimus et defendemus imperpetuum. His test(ibus) etc.

> NOTE. The boundaries and reference to liberties conceded by the king render this charter suspect. Perhaps it is an interpolated version of a genuine charter.

396 *Gift by Roger de Mowbray to Uctred son of Gamel of all his assarts in Brimham (Yorks., W.R.), for the service of ½ mark p.a. and aid.*

[c. 1147 × c. 1157]

> Cartulary copies (Fountains): B.M., Cotton MS. Tib. C xii fo. 229r; Add. MS. 18276 fo. 30v (abstract).
> Pd. (transl.), *Fount. Cart.* i 145 (10), from Cotton MS.

Rogerus de Molbraio omnibus hominibus suis Francis et Anglis salutem. Notum sit vobis omnibus tam presentibus quam futuris me dedisse et

---

ᵃ Illegible where parchment cracked and ink rubbed away; lacunae supplied from Whitaker's version.   *ᵇ* Illegible; not found in Whitaker's version.   *ᶜ* A hole cut out of the parchment. Whitaker's source also lacked the name of the manor, which he suggested might be Kirkby Malzeard.

concessisse et hac carta mea confirmasse Huctredo filio Gamelli omnes esarz que michi jurate fuerunt in Birnebem, et totam dominiam terram meam cultam ultra aquam, nominatim infra Wineslay, propter*a* unam carucatam terre, et communem pasturam et pasnagium suum de dominia domo sua quietum, annuatim reddendo dimidiam marcam argenti et auxilium quantum pertinet ad unam aliam carrucatam terre. Homines vero ejus pasnagium justum [habebunt]*b* cum vicinis suis et molendinum suum sibi concedo faciendum. Ideo precipio et volo ut iste Huctredus teneat istam tenuram predictam in bene et in pace et libere et quiete predictum servicium faciendo et in feudo et in hereditate tenendo ipse et heredes ejus de me et de heredibus meis. Testibus istis, Nigello de Molb', Rogero de Condeio, Ricardo clerico de Malessart, Hamone Beler, Rodberto de Buci, Huctredo filio Dolfini, Thoma de Walchingham, Samsone Cornewal', Baldwino clerico qui hanc eandem scripsit cartulam.

NOTE. Nigel de Mowbray did not attest charters before *c.* 1147. Richard clerk of Malzeard occurs last 1154 × *c.* 1157 (no. 109).[1] Three of the witnesses occur in *c.* 1147 × Nov. 1156 (no. 107). Uctred son of Gamel attests a charter of 1147 × 1153.[2]

397 *Restoration and confirmation by Roger de Mowbray to William de Vescy of the fee which his father, Eustace Fitz John, held—one fee held by Rolland Hachet, one fee in Brompton (Yorks., N.R.), 3 fees held by William and Peter Mauleverer, 6 fees held by William Tison, 2 fees in Gainsborough (Lincs.) and Thrussington (Leics.), and one fee in Stathern (Leics.), i.e. 14 fees, for the service of 11 knights.* [1157 × 1169]

Pd., *Cal. Close Rolls 1313–18* p. 286, from P.R.O., Close Roll 9 Edw. II (C. 54/133) m. 9.

Testibus istis, Roberto de Deyvilla, et Rogero de Flammengvilla, Hugone Malebissa, Bertrammo Haget, Waltero de Riparia, et Thoma de Colevilla.

NOTE. Eustace Fitz John died in July 1157.[3] Roger de Flamville had probably died by 1169 (no. 377 note). Sir Charles Clay dates this charter after 1166, on the ground that the Mowbray *carta*'s entry for Vescy, of 2 new fees (no. 401, Fees [36]), must have been made before this enfeoffment.[4] But the *carta* is not without other discrepancies (cf. no. 386 note), and it seems best to assign the present charter to the wide limits given above. There is no reason, however, why it should not have been given soon after the death of Eustace Fitz John in 1157.

The enfeoffment of Eustace presumably took place after his return from

---

a Sic; ? read *preter*.   *b* Illegible in MS.

[1] Cf. nos. 104, 106–7, 197.   [2] *E.Y.C.* i no. 535.
[3] See *Complete Peerage* xii (2) 272–4.   [4] *E.Y.C.* xii 22–3.

Scotland in 1143 or 1144, perhaps at about the time that he became constable of earl Ranulf of Chester.[1] To only one of the fourteen fees did he have a genuine claim: this was Brompton, which he had held as early as 1130.[2] In the other fees Eustace seems to have been interposed above established tenants. The Vescy interest in the Tison estates in the East Riding and in Gainsborough and Thrussington persisted into the thirteenth century.[3] The fee in Stathern was probably that which Elias d'Aubigny held in 1166; there is no evidence of Vescy interest there, although Tolebut, who was Vescy's tenant in Gainsborough, is found in Stathern in the later twelfth century.[4] The fees of Rolland Hachet (or Haget) and William and Peter Mauleverer cannot be identified. The Mauleverers held 3 fees of Brus in Garrowby (E.R.) and Allerton Mauleverer (W.R.),[5] but it is difficult to see what claim Mowbray had on these, and there is nothing to suggest a later Vescy interest. For another estate where Mowbray and Eustace Fitz John apparently had a dispute, see nos. 198, 297.

398 *Gift by Roger de Mowbray to Warin son of Simon of 2 mills outside Melton Mowbray and one bovate, a toft, and a meadow in Melton Mowbray (Leics.).* [*c.* 1166]

Reference in charter of Simon son of Richard son of Warin for Burton Lazars: B.M., Cotton MS. Nero C xii (cartulary of Burton Lazars) fo. 6r.

. . . duo molendina extra villam de Meltona que Rogerus de Mumbrai dedit Warino filio Simonis . . . pro servicio suo et unam bovatam terre et unum toftum in villa de Meltona quod pertinet ad illam bovatam terre et unum pratum cum omnibus pertinenciis suis que ad prefatam bovatam spectant . . .

NOTE. Warin son of Simon first occurs in the *carta* of 1166, holding ⅔ fee of the new enfeoffment.[6] It is unlikely that he was enfeoffed long before 1166.

399 *Gift by Roger de Mowbray to William son of Ucce of one carucate in Ampleforth, in exchange for his patrimony in Bagby (Yorks., N.R.), for a rent of ½ mark p.a.* [1142 × 1157]

Transcript, from an original charter formerly in St. Mary's Tower, York: Bodl., MS. Dodsworth 94 fo. 48v.

Rogerus de Molbr' omnibus suis hominibus Francis et Anglis salutem. Sciatis me dedisse et confirmasse Willelmo filio Ucce unam carrucatam terre in Ampleforda, cum omnibus que ad illam carrucatam pertinent

---

[1] *Symeonis Dunelmensis Opera Omnia*, ed. T. Arnold (R.S. lxxv) i 154; *Early Scottish Charters, prior to A.D. 1153*, ed. A. C. Lawrie (Glasgow, 1905) no. 177; G. Barraclough, 'Some charters of the earl of Chester', in *A Medieval Miscellany for D. M. Stenton*, ed. P. M. Barnes and C. F. Slade (P.R.S. N.S. xxxvi) pp. 25–9.

[2] *Regesta* ii nos. 1722, 1730.

[3] See Fees [9]; cf. also [11] and *E.Y.C.* ix no. 44.

[4] Bodl., MS. Dodsworth 144 fo. 93r; cf. Fees [20].   [5] *E.Y.C.* ii 13.

[6] No. 401, Fees [46].

in terra et aqua, in plano et bosco, pro escambio patrimonii sui in Baggebi, tenendam libere et quiete pro dimidia marca argenti reddenda annuatim, salvo etiam forensi servicio. Dedi autem terram hanc ipsi et heredibus ejus tenendam perpetuo. Hiis testibus, Augustino priore Neuburgi, Samsone de Albeneio, Rogero de Cundi, Waltero de Riparia, Waltero de Carletuna.

NOTE. Augustine, prior of Newburgh, held office from 1142 to some time between 1154 and 1157.[1] Despite this exchange, William son of Ucce seems to have retained an interest in Bagby, and granted land there to Byland (nos. 59 and note, 73). He also held $\frac{1}{5}$ fee of Brus.[2]

400 *Gift by Roger de Mowbray to Ralph de Wyville of Thorpe le Willows (par. Coxwold, Yorks., N.R.).* [c. 1147]

Transcript, from an original charter formerly in St. Mary's Tower, York: Bodl., MS. Dodsworth 7 fo. 105r.

Rogerus de Molb' dapifero et omnibus bajulis suis et ministris et hominibus et amicis Francis et Anglis salutem. Sciatis me dedisse et concessisse Radulfo de Widevilla Torp cum omnibus appentitiis suis in feudo et hereditate sibi et heredibus suis, tenendam de me et de heredibus meis in bosco et plano in aquis in pratis in molendinis et cum omnibus liberis consuetudinibus, eodem visu et pacto quo unquam melius vel liberius tenuit Willelmus de Meisnilhermer. Teste, Herberto de Morevilla, Willelmo de Arcis, Herberto de Queniburc, Bertramo Haget, Waltero de Rivera, Petro de Tresc, Radulfo de Bel[. .]*a* et multis aliis.

NOTE. Five witnesses appear in 1147 (nos. 43–4). Ralph de Wyville (?heir of Robert de Wyville) last occurs in ? c. 1147 (no. 200), and had been succeeded by his brother William (no. 195) before c. 1154, by which time William had given Thorpe to Byland (no. 50). In 1166 William's son Richard held 5 fees of Mowbray.[3]

The chronicler William of Newburgh was a relative of the Meisnilhermer family.[4] A William de Meisnilhermer had land in the forest of Gouffern,[5] and a man of the same name was commemorated at Durham.[6] The William de Meisnilhermer of the present charter, and his brother Hugh, appear in several Mowbray charters of the 1140s.[7] William had given land in Coxwold to Byland before 1147 (no. 44).

a Obliterated by ink-smudge, but presumably *Bellun* rather than *Belvoir*.

---

[1] See *E.Y.C.* ix 248.   [2] See *E.Y.C.* ii no. 692.   [3] No. 401, Fees [21].
[4] See H. E. Salter, in *E.H.R.* xxii (1907) 510–14.
[5] Caen, Archives of Calvados, H. 6510 (cartulary of Gouffern) fo. 14v.
[6] *Liber Vitae Dunelm.*, facsimile ed. A. H. Thompson (S.S. cxxxvi) fo. 52r.
[7] Nos. 38, 94, 98–9, 177, 369, perhaps also no. 33; cf. *E.Y.C.* iii no. 1495.

401 *Return of English knights' fees by the men of Roger de Mowbray.*   1166

13th-cent. copies: P.R.O., Liber Niger (Parvus) (E. 164/12) fo. 68*v*; Liber Rubeus (E. 164/2) fo. 118*r–v*.
Pd., *Liber Niger Scaccarii*, ed. T. Hearne (1771–4) i 309–11; *R.B.* i 418–21.

Carta de feodis Rogeri de Moubrai.[a]

Domino suo karissimo H(enrico) Dei gracia regi Angl(orum) homines Rogeri de Moubrai[b] salutem. Secundum preceptum vestrum mandamus vobis quot milites dominus noster Rogerus de Molbrai[a] habet de antiquo feodo et novo.

[1] Rogerus de Flammavill'[c] tenet feoda viij militum et dimidii.
[2] Robertus de Stutevill'[d] viij militum.
[3] Willelmus Tisun feoda xv militum.
[4] Willelmus Haget[e] ij militum.
[5] Walterus de Riparia j militis.
[6] Adam Luvel j militis.
[7] Walterus filius Asketin j militis.
[8] Rogerus de Sancto Martino duorum[f] militum.
[9] Willelmus de Gainesburg'[g] ij militum.
[10] Walterus de Camvill'[h] ix militum.
[11] Thomas de Wppenberi[i] v militum.
[12] Walterus de Wiseg'[j] j militis.
[13] Robertus de Griselee[k] j militis.
[14] Henricus de Arden'[l] j militis.
[15] Radulfus de Quenigburc'[m] ij militum.
[16] Hugo de Rampan j militis.
[17] Sanson Tachel j militis.
[18] Simon filius Simonis dimidii militis.
[19] Willelmus de Reimes j militis.
[20] Helias de Abbaneio[n] j militis.
[21] Ricardus de Wivill' v militum.
[22] Ricardus de Morevill' v militum.
[23] Hugo Malherbe j militis.
[24] Robertus de Dauuill'[o] iiij militum.
[25] Turstanus de Munfort[p] iij militum et tres partes militis.
[26] Willelmus de Moles j militis.
[27] Rogerus de Condeio dimidii militis.

---

[a] *Munbray*, Liber Rubeus.   [b] *Monbray*, L.R.   [c] *Flamvill'*, L.R.
[d] *Stotevill'*, L.R.   [e] *Haket*, L.R.   [f] *ij*, L.R.   [g] *Cainesburg'*, L.R.
[h] *Campvill'*, L.R.   [i] *Woppenberi*, L.R.   [j] *Wileng*, L.R.   [k] *Criselee*, L.R.
[l] *Harden'*, L.R.   [m] *Queningbun'*, L.R.   [n] *Elyas de Albaineio*, L.R.
[o] *Dayvill'*, L.R.   [p] *Muntfort*, L.R.

[28] Rogerus filius Parces*a* j militis.
[29] Rogerus filius Galfridi et Radulfus filius Aldelin dimidii militis.
[30] Rogerus Prince terciam partem militis.
[31] Robertus Dapifer dimidii militis.
[32] Hubertus filius Ricardi terciam partem militis.
[33] Ricardus de Crosseslai*b* terciam partem militis.
[34] Ricardus Grammaticus*c* quartam partem j militis.
[35] Willelmus de Bolemer j militis.

Tot habuit milites feodatos in tempore H(enrici) regis, scilicet quater viginti et octo, videlicet lx de antiquo feodo, et viginti octo istorum feodavit Nigellus de Albaneio*d* de dominio suo.
Et de novo feodo

[36] Willelmus de Vesci*e* duos*f* milites.
[37] Robertus de Stutevill'*g* j militem.
[38] Robertus de Dauuill'*h* j militem.
[39] Willelmus de Lanc' ij milites.
[40] Thomas de Colevill' j militem.
[41] Albricus Comes j feodum.*i*
[42] Robertus de Busci j feodum.*i*
[43] Hamon Beler*j* j feodum.*k*
[44] Rogerus de Charleton'*l* dimidium feodum.
[45] Willelmus Grain dorge*m* dimidium feodum.
[46] Warinus filius Simonis duas partes j feodi.*n*

Hii sunt de novo feodo Rogeri de Molbrai*o* post mortem Henrici regis, videlicet xi feoda militum et tres partes feodi unius militis.

NOTE. The figures in square brackets refer to the notes on the English knights' fees below, pp. 262–6.

402 *Inquisition of Norman knights' fees.*   1220
Pd., *Recueil des Historiens des Gaules et de la France* xxiii 619.

Isti tenent de honore de Monbrai, qui est in manu domini Regis.
Willelmus Malerbe tenet de domino de Monbrai, qui est in manu domini regis, unum feodum et quartam partem unius feodi apud Nouvi et apud Basoches.[1]

a *Perces*, L.R.   *b* *Trusselai*, L.R.   *c* *Gramaticus*, L.R.   *d* *Albeneio*, L.R.
e *Vescy*, L.R.   *f* *ij*, L.R.   *g* *Stotevill'*, L.R.   *h* *Daumvill'*, L.R.
i *militem*, L.R.   *j* *Hamo Berler*, L.R.   *k* L.R. adds *militis.*   *l* *Carleton'*,
L.R.   *m* *Grain de or*, L.R.   *n* *ij partes j militis*, L.R.   *o* *Monbray*, L.R.

[1] Neuvy-au-Houlme and Bazoches-en-Houlme (Orne, arr. Argentan, cant. Putanges). Probably also in Villers-Canivet (Calvados, arr. Caen, cant. Falaise) (Léchaudé d'Anisy, *Extrait* ii 307, and ibid. i 449) and Marcei (Orne, arr. Argentan, cant. Mortrée) (*Magni Rotuli Scaccarii Normanniae*, ed. T. Stapleton (1840–4) ii p. lxxxv).

Girardus Boel tenet unum feodum apud Sanctum Briccium.[1]

Isabellis de Cuelaio, apud Cueleium unum feodum.[2]

Willelmus Borrel tenet dimidium feodum.[3]

Galfridus Barle dimidium feodum.[4]

Willelmus Corbet tenet duas partes unius feodi.[5]

Willelmus de Vaus tenet quartam partem unius feodi.[6]

Johannes de Torigneio tenet quartam partem similiter.[7]

Ranulfus Farsi tenet dimidium feodum.[8]

Ricardus Bacon tenet unum feodum.[9]

Godefridus de la Mosce et ejus participes tenent unum feodum.[4]

Fulco de Huchon et Ranulfus de Cruis tene[n]t dimidium feodum.[4]

Robertus de Grantvilla tenet dimidium feodum.[10]

Dominus Engerranus de Hommet tenet in maritagium ex parte sororis Willelmi de Montbrai apud Escouceium duo feoda.[11]

NOTE. This inquisition may be compared with that of 1172, which reads as follows: 'Nigellus de Montbrai servicium v militum de honore de Montbrai et Castri Gonteri[12] et ad suum servicium xi milites et quartam partem et septimam militis.'[13]

[1] Saint-Brice-sous-Rânes (Orne, arr. Argentan, cant. Écouché); also in next parish Saint-Ouen-sur-Maire (Léchaudé d'Anisy, *Extrait* i 418).

[2] Rabodonges (Orne, arr. Argentan, cant. Putanges); cf. above, no. 17. Perhaps also in Pertheville-Ners (Calvados, arr. Caen, cant. Falaise) (Léchaudé d'Anisy, *Extrait* i 336, 421, 424).

[3] Perhaps in Quetiéville (Calvados, arr. Lisieux, cant. Mézidon) (Léchaudé d'Anisy, *Extrait* i 131, 132).

[4] Unknown.

[5] Perhaps Crocy (Calvados, arr. Caen, cant. Morteaux-Coulibœuf) (Léchaudé d'Anisy, *Extrait* i 409, 412, 425).

[6] ? Vaux-sur-Seulles (Calvados, arr. Caen, cant. Creully) (Léchaudé d'Anisy, *Extrait* ii 183).

[7] ? Torigny-sur-Vire (Manche, arr. Saint-Lô).

[8] Probably Pontfarcy (Calvados, arr. Vire, cant. Saint-Sever-Calvados) (*Magni Rotuli Scaccarii Normanniae*, ed. T. Stapleton (1840–4) ii pp. ccxli, 359).

[9] ? Landelles (Calvados, arr. Vire, cant. Saint-Sever-Calvados) (*Magni Rotuli Scaccarii Normanniae* ii p. ccxlii).

[10] ? Grainville-Langannerie (Calvados, arr. Caen, cant. Bretteville-sur-Laize) (cf. *Gallia Christiana* xi instr. col. 60).

[11] Écouché (Orne, arr. Argentan).

[12] Château-Gontier (Orne, arr. Argentan, cant. Écouché).

[13] *Recueil des Historiens des Gaules et de la France* xxiii 695

ADDENDUM

403 *Confirmation by Roger de Mowbray to St. Andrew's, Northampton (Clun.), of the mill of Welford (Northants).* [1138 × c. 1150]

Cartulary copies: B.M., Royal MS. 11 B ix fo. 66v; Cotton MS. Vesp. E xvii fo. 234v.

Rogerus*a* de Mulbr' omnibus baronibus suis tam Francis quam Anglis et ministris tam*b* futuris quam presentibus salutem. Notum sit vobis me concessisse dominis monachis Norht'*c* molendinum de Welleford in feudo et elemosina, libere et quiete absque omni calumpnia et consuetudine, pro anima Roberti de Witville,*d* scilicet molendinum tenendum de me et meis heredibus et de heredibus supradicti Roberti, libere et quiete sine omni consuetudine. Testibus,*e* Ricardo*f* de Camvilla, Mathia dap(ifero), Rogero de Flamengvilla, Willelmo Flameng', Roberto de*f* Warre*f* et Landrico, Gillberto de Rampenn', Hugone de Maisnill' Hermeri, Thoma capellano,*f* Osmundo*f* de Waspreo, Hugone Gobiun, Ranulfo clerico com(itis) Sim(onis).*g*

NOTE. The gift of the mill of Welford had been made by Robert de Wyville,[1] who was apparently dead by the time Roger de Mowbray issued the present confirmation. Robert de Wyville last occurs between 1130 and 1136, and had been succeeded in the Wyville fee by 1147.[2] The mill was confirmed to Northampton by pope Eugenius III, between 1145 and 1153,[3] and by king Henry II, in January 1155.[4]

The witness-list suggests that the present charter was given in the early years of Roger de Mowbray's lordship. Neither Gilbert de Rampan nor Hugh de Meisnilhermer appear after c. 1150.[5] Possibly the witness Landric is to be identified with Landric de Ages, who occurs in the 1140s.[6]

The charter records the only known occurrence of Matthew the *dapifer*. If he was the predecessor of Hugh Malebisse as steward of the Mowbray household, he must have held office before c. 1147.[7] The only other Matthew to appear in Mowbray charters of this period is Matthew de Rampan, brother of Gilbert de Rampan who attests this charter. Matthew de Rampan witnesses nine early charters of Roger de Mowbray but is never called *dapifer*.[8]

a Initial *R* lacking in Royal MS.   *b* Vesp. MS. inserts *presentibus*.
c Northampton', Vesp. MS.   *d* Wytvylle, Vesp. MS.   *e* T', Royal MS.
f Word lacking in Royal MS. (damaged by fire).   *g* comite Simone, Vesp. MS.

[1] B.M., Royal MS. 11 B ix fo. 66r–v; Cotton MS. Vesp. E xvii fo. 234v.
[2] See notes to nos. 22 and 400.
[3] P.U.E. I no. 55.
[4] Royal MS. 11 B ix fo. 15v; for the date cf. Eyton, *Itinerary* p. 3.
[5] For Gilbert cf. nos. 21, 94, 107, and 156; for Hugh see note to no. 400.
[6] See above, p. lxi n. 7.
[7] See p. lxii.
[8] See note to no. 35.

PEDIGREE I. THE ELEVENTH-CENTURY FAMILY OF AUBIGNY

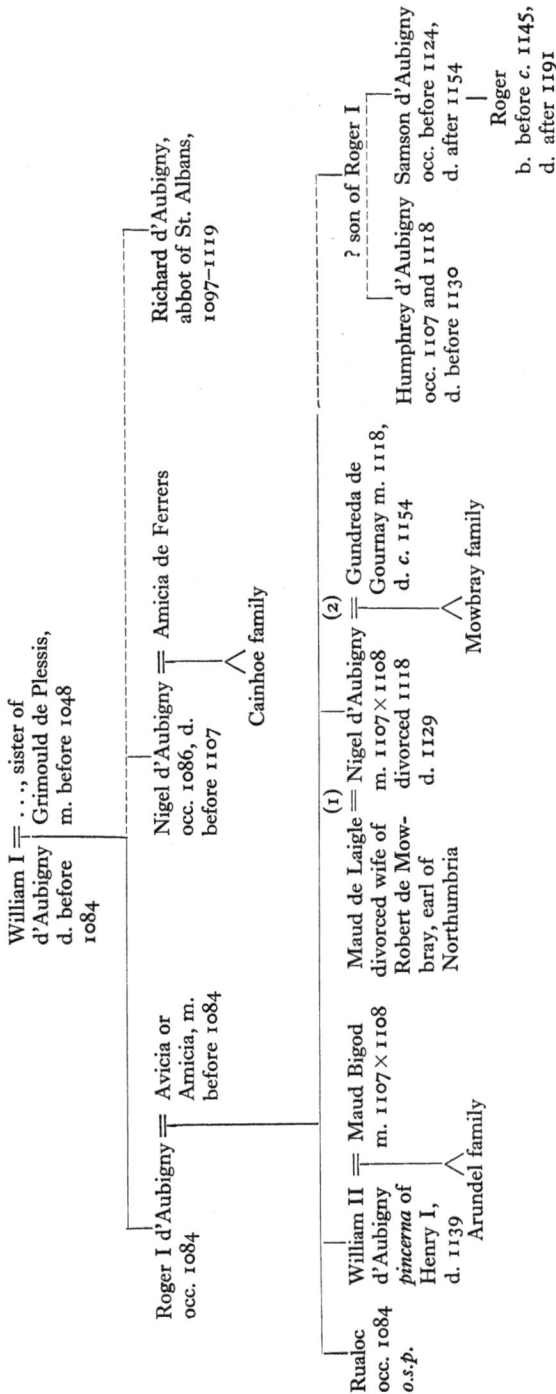

William I = ..., sister of
d'Aubigny Grimould de Plessis,
d. before m. before 1048
1084

Roger I d'Aubigny = Avicia or
occ. 1084 Amicia, m.
before 1084

Nigel d'Aubigny = Amicia de Ferrers
occ. 1086, d.
before 1107

Cainhoe family

Richard d'Aubigny,
abbot of St. Albans,
1097–1119

Rualoc
occ. 1084
o.s.p.

William II = Maud Bigod
d'Aubigny m. 1107 × 1108
pincerna of
Henry I,
d. 1139

Arundel family

(1)
Maud de Laigle = Nigel d'Aubigny = Gundreda de (2)
divorced wife of m. 1107 × 1108 Gournay m. 1118,
Robert de Mow- divorced 1118 d. c. 1154
bray, earl of d. 1129
Northumbria

Mowbray family

? son of Roger I

Humphrey d'Aubigny Samson d'Aubigny
occ. 1107 and 1118 occ. before 1124,
d. before 1130 d. after 1154

Roger
b. before c. 1145,
d. after 1191

PEDIGREE II. THE TWELFTH-CENTURY FAMILY OF MOWBRAY

Nigel d'Aubigny = Gundreda de Gournay
d. 1129   m. 1118, d. c. 1154

Walter de Gant d. 1139 = Maud, daughter of Stephen count of Britanny

Gilbert de Gant
d. 1156

(1)
Roger de Mowbray = Alice de Gant = Ilbert de Lacy
came of age 1138,   d. after 1176   d. 1141 × 1142
m. 1142 × 1143,
d. 1188

(2)

daughter = William de Daiville

Robert de Mowbray
d. after 1199

Nigel de Mowbray = Mabel, ? daughter
d. 1191   of William Patri,
m. before 1170,
d. c. 1203

daughter = Engerran du Hommet

William de Mowbray
born c. 1171, d. 1223

Philip

Robert

Roger

NOTES ON THE LOCATION OF THE ENGLISH KNIGHTS' FEES

THE following notes on the 46 military tenancies recorded in 1166 are arranged in the order in which the tenants occur in the *carta* (charter no. 401). In many cases the evidence for the location of the fees comes from the thirteenth century, and unless another name is given in the notes, the tenant family of 1166 was still in occupation.

The thirteenth-century evidence is found in lists cited as follows:

1212	*Book of Fees*, ed. H. C. Maxwell Lyte (1920–31) i 192–3 (Lincs.)
1224–30	Ibid. ii 1460–2 (entire honour)
1232–3	Ibid. p. 1467 (honour south of Trent)
1235–6	Ibid. i 496, 498 (Northants.); ibid. p. 519 (Leics.); ibid. p. 538 (Notts.)
1242–3	Ibid. ii 997 (Notts.); ibid. p. 1095 (Lincs.)
1284–5	*Feudal Aids* vi 1–105 (Yorks.)
1297–1300	*Cal. Inq. P.M.* iii 358–64 (entire honour)

[1] *Roger de Flamville 8¼ fees*

This represents *Arches 7 fees* (gained by Roger de Flamville in marriage with Juetta de Arches) and *Flamville 1¼ fees*.

Arches: The Domesday tenancy of Osbern de Arches in Yorks., W.R. See *E.Y.C.* i 408–36. The under-tenants were probably as follows:

Bertram of Steeton in Scagglethorpe and Steeton 1 fee
Eustace de Merc and Peter de Fauconberg in Appleton Roebuck, Scagglethorpe, and Steeton 1 fee
William Haget in Bilton 1 fee
Guy son of Aubrey of Marston in Marston 1 fee
Richard of Wilstrop in Wilstrop 1 fee
William of Rufforth in Marston and Rufforth ½ fee
Fulk son of John ¼ fee
Elias de Hou ¼ fee
Also Henry of Beningbrough in Beningbrough (N.R.) 1 fee, perhaps as a result of exchange by Arches with d'Aubigny for Robert Dapifer [31]

Flamville: Fryton, High Hutton (Yorks., N.R.), Marton (W.R.), Norton, Sutton, Welham (E.R.)—1 fee in 1224–30 (cf. charters nos. 183–4, 189).

[2] *Robert de Stuteville 8 fees*
[37] *Robert de Stuteville 1 fee (new)*
Actually 10 fees settled on Robert de Stuteville 1154 × 1166 (charter no. 386). For location and history, see *E.Y.C.* ix 75, 80–1.

[3] *William Tison 15 fees*
The Domesday tenancy of Gilbert Tison in Yorks., Lincs., and Notts. See *E.Y.C.* xii 19–23. 6 fees assigned to Fitz John (charter no. 397).

[4] *William Haget 2 fees*

Bainton (Yorks., E.R.), Caldwell (N.R.), Dacre, Easedike, Follifoot, Healaugh, Wighill (W.R.)—Sancta Maria ¾ fee in 1224–30 (cf. charters nos. 96, 117, 128, 363). Also Welby (Leics.)—above, nos. 157–8.

[5] *Walter de Riparia 1 fee*

Brafferton, Brandsby, Stearsby (Yorks., N.R.)—1 fee in 1224–30 (cf. charters nos. 204, 206–7, 209, 213). Also Cundall (N.R.)—1 carucate in 1284–5; and Harome—1 carucate in 1224–30.

[6] *Adam Luvel 1 fee*

Gilling, South Holme (Yorks., N.R.)—Etton 1 fee in 1224–30.

[7] *Walter son of Asketil 1 fee*

Grimston, Nawton, Welburn (Yorks., N.R.)—Burdun, Eyville, Mauley in 1284–5. Also Coney St., York—*Fount. Cart.* i 275 (27).

[8] *Roger de Sancto Martino 2 fees*

Blyborough, Somerby (nr. Corringham), Yawthorpe (Lincs.)—1 fee in 1212 (cf. charters nos. 89–91). Also Kinnard's Ferry and Melwood—*Danelaw Charters* no. 398.

[9] *William of Gainsborough 2 fees*

Thrussington (Leics.), Gainsborough (Lincs.)—Tolebut 2 fees of Vescy in 1212 (cf. charters nos. 231, 397).

[10] *Walter de Camville 9 fees*

Leesthorpe, Cold Newton, East Norton, Pickwell (Leics.), Crick (Northants), Bentley, Cesters Over, Newnham Paddox, Shustoke (Warwicks.)—8 fees in Leics. and Warwicks., 1 fee in Northants in 1232–3.

[11] *Thomas of Wappenbury 5 fees*

Thrussington, Sysonby (Leics.)—2½ fees in 1235–6; Newbold Revel, Wappenbury (Warwicks.)—2 fees in 1235–6. Cf. the assignment of Wappenbury's 4½ fees to Stuteville in 1201 (*E.Y.C.* ix no. 44).

[12] *Walter de 'Wiseg' or 'Wileng' 1 fee*

Probably 'Bisege' who held 1 fee in Bitteswell, Ullesthorpe, Walton (nr. Kimcote) (Leics.), and Baddesley Clinton (Warwicks.) in 1224–30 and 1235–6.

[13] *Robert de 'Griselee' or 'Criselee' 1 fee*

Possibly Langford (Notts.), held by Grey for ½ fee in 1235–6.

[14] *Henry of Arden 1 fee*

Hampton in Arden (Warwicks.)—½ fee in 1224–30; Humburton (Yorks., N.R.)—⅙ fee in 1284–5.

[15] *Ralph of Queniborough 2 fees*

Burton on the Wolds, Queniborough (Leics.)—Curcun 1 fee and Selby 1 fee in 1235–6 (cf. charters nos. 381–2; 159). Also Coxwold (Yorks., N.R.)—no. 24.

[16] *Hugh de Rampan 1 fee*

Kirby Bellars (Leics.)—Monks Kirby 1 fee in 1235–6 (cf. nos. 3 (p. 9), 26).

[17] *Samson Takel 1 fee*

Butterwick, Haxey, Scawby, Yawthorpe (Lincs.)—1 fee in 1212.

[18] *Simon son of Simon ½ fee*

Possibly Kyme family, but location unknown.

[19] *William de Rames 1 fee*

Stathern (Leics.)—½ fee in 1428 (*Feudal Aids* iii 119; cf. charter no. 167).

[20] *Elias d'Aubigny 1 fee*

Stathern (Leics.)—John de Stathern 1 fee in 1235–6.

[21] *Richard de Wyville 5 fees*

Cold Ashby, Elkington, Sulby, Welford (Northants.)—1½ fees in 1235–6 (cf. no. 403); Burnby, Sherburn, Sledmere (Yorks., E.R.), Coulton, Slingsby, Thornton Dale (N.R.)—3 fees in 1284–5 (cf. no. 22). Also Thorpe le Willows (N.R.) (nos. 50–1, 400).

[22] *Richard de Moreville 5 fees*

Lindley (Leics.)—Rudeville ½ fee in 1224–30 (cf. charter no. 384); Binley, Hopsford, Nuthurst, Withybrook (Warwicks.)—Hastings ½ fee, Neuham 1 fee, Waure 1 fee in 1224–30 (cf. nos. 82–3); Hayton (Yorks., E.R.)—Rudston ⅓ fee in 1224–30 (cf. no. 320); Bardsey, Collingham, Micklethwaite, Wothersome (W.R.)—Berlay (cf. above, nos. 181, 347), and Kirkstall in 1284–5.

[23] *Hugh Malebisse 1 fee* (entered in *carta* as 'Malherbe')

Arden, Broughton (? in Appleton le Street), Carlton (? Miniott), Dale Town, Hawnby, Kepwick, Murton, Scawton, Silton, Snilesworth, Stainton (Yorks., N.R.)—charter no. 371 (and cf. nos. 75, 244); ½ fee in 1224–30. Also Bagby (N.R.)—no. 58. See also *E.Y.C.* iii 456–9.

[24] *Robert de Daiville 4 fees*

[38] *Robert de Daiville 1 fee* (*new*)

Freeby, Kirby Bellars, Welby (Leics.)—2 fees in 1224–30 (cf. no. 3 p. 9); Egmanton, Tuxford, Weston (Notts.)—1 fee in 1235–6; Baxby, Butterwick, Kilburn, Nawton, Thornton Bridge, Thornton on the Hill (Yorks., N.R.), Adlingfleet (W.R.)—2½ fees in 1224–30 (cf. nos. 245, 361). Also in York— *Fount. Cart.* i 277 (37).

[25] *Thurstan de Montfort 3¾ fees*

Chadwick (Warwicks.)—⅛ fee in 1224–30 (½ fee in 1232–3) (cf. charter no. 338); Hampton in Arden (Warwicks.)—¼ fee in 1224–30 (cf. nos. 330–7). Also in York—no. 195.

[26] *William de Moles 1 fee*

Serlby, Torworth (Notts.)—½ fee in 1235–6 (¾ fee in 1241–2).

[27] *Roger de Cundy ½ fee*

Burton Lazars (Leics.), Axholme (Lincs.)— $\frac{1}{12}$ fee in 1224–30. Also Eltisley (Cambs.)—charters nos. 168–9, 305. Great and Little Wildon (Yorks., N.R.) —*E.Y.C.* ix no. 167; and Bagby (N.R.)—charters nos. 205, 212.

[28] *Roger 'filius Parces' or 'Perces' 1 fee*

Perhaps error for 'de Pereres', who held 1 fee in Sysonby and Welby (Leics.) in 1235–6.

[29] *Roger son of Geoffrey and Ralph son of Aldelin ½ fee*

Son of Geoffrey: Studley Roger (Yorks., W.R.)—¼ fee in 1224–30 (? cf. charter no. 147).
Son of Aldelin: Aldfield, Kirkby Malzeard, Studley Roger (W.R.)—¼ fee in 1224–30 (cf. nos. 99, 129–30, 383).

[30] *Roger Prince ⅓ fee*

Family and location unknown. Robert Prince occurs in Cumberland in 1177 (*P.R. 23 Hen. II* p. 121).

[31] *Robert Dapifer ½ fee*

Catterton and Toulston (Yorks., W.R.), held of Arches for 1 fee—see *E.Y.C.* i 415 and charter no. 289.

[32] *Herbert son of Richard ⅓ fee* (entered in *carta* as 'Hubert')

Herbert son of Richard who lost land in Kirby Hill (Yorks., N.R.) to William son of Aldelin in 1185 (*P.R. 31 Hen. II* p. 63).

[33] *Richard de 'Crosseslai' or 'Trusselai' ⅓ fee*

Family and location uncertain: perhaps either Croxley (Herts.), claimed by Richard de 'Crokeslea' against Mowbray in 1176 (*P.R. 22 Hen. II* p. 5) or in Axholme (Lincs.), held by heirs of Richard de 'Crokelega' in 1224–30.

[34] *Richard Grammaticus ¼ fee*

Bickerton (Yorks., W.R.)—¼ fee in 1224–30.

[35] *William de Bulmer 1 fee*

Hartlington (Yorks., W.R.), Kepwick, Over or Nether Silton (N.R.)—1 fee in 1224–30.

[36] *William de Vescy 2 fees (new)*

Enfeoffed in 14 fees for service of 11 knights—charter no. 397. Gainsborough (Lincs.)—2 fees in 1212; Brompton (wap. Pickering Lythe, Yorks., N.R.)—7 fees in 1224–30. See *E.Y.C.* xii 22–3 and note to charter no. 397 above. Cf. assignment to Stuteville of 4½ fees held by Vescy in 1201 (*E.Y.C.* ix no. 44).

[37] *Robert de Stuteville 1 fee (new)*

See above [2].

[38] *Robert de Daiville 1 fee (new)*

See above [24].

[39] *William son of Gilbert of Lancaster 2 fees (new)*

Kendale, Lonsdale (Westmorland), and Horton in Ribblesdale (Yorks., W.R.)
—4 fees *c.* 1150 (charter no. 370 and note).

[40] *Thomas de Coleville 1 fee (new)*

Coxwold, Oulston, Yearsley (Yorks., N.R.)—charter no. 356, and cf. no. 68;
1 fee in 1224–30. Also in Melton Mowbray (Leics.)—above, no. 357.

[41] *Aubrey de Vere 1 fee (new)*

Possibly Goadby Marwood (Leics.), held by Quatremans and Vere for ½ fee
in 1235–6.

[42] *Robert de Buscy 1 fee (new)*

Osgoodby, Over Silton, Thirkleby (Yorks., N.R.)—1 fee in 1224–30. Also
Grewelthorpe (W.R.)—2 carucates in 1224–30.

[43] *Hamo Beler 1 fee (new)*

Burton Lazars, Eye Kettleby (Leics.), and in Norby (par. Thirsk, Yorks.,
N.R.)—charter no. 341; 1 fee in 1235–6. Also in Axholme (Lincs.)—above,
no. 342; and Hovingham (N.R.)—above, no. 61.

[44] *Roger of Carlton ½ fee (new)*

Carlton Miniott, Islebeck (Yorks., N.R.)— ⅓ fee in 1224–30 (cf. charters nos.
63, 352–4); Sand Hutton (N.R.)—¼ fee in 1224–30. Also in Thirsk (N.R.)—
nos. 353–4.

[45] *William Graindorge ½ fee (new)*

Elslack, Flasby, Winterburn (Yorks., W.R.)—½ fee in 1224–30 (cf. charters
nos. 150–3).

[46] *Warin son of Simon ⅔ fee (new)*

Burton Lazars, Melton Mowbray (Leics.); Azerley, Kirkby Malzeard (Yorks.,
W.R.)—¼ fee in 1224–30 (cf. charters nos. 139, 398).

GLOSSARY

alnetum, alder grove
annona, grain, crop
bajulus, official, bailiff
barra, bar, rail, barrier
brureia (for *brueria*), heath
calcedum, causeway
canabus, canvas, hemp
chevescii, headlands
consistor, constable
folerez (French), fulling (of a mill)
frutectum, orchard, thicket
garba, garb, sheaf
gigator, minstrel
grodis (ablative) (? for *grovis*), mine-shafts
hostricer (as *hostrifer*), hawk-bearer
laz (French), cord, lace, rope
nisus, hawk, sparrow-hawk
ortus (*hortus*), garden
parmentarius, parmenter, robe-trimmer, furrier
plaga, stretch of country, quarter, region

platea, open space, plot
pretor, reeve, provost
roda, rood, cross
rogus (? for *rogus calcis*), ? lime-kiln
salcetum, osier bed
salsatum pratum, salt meadow
sceppa, *scheppa*, 'skep', basket, dry measure
sichet, syke, stream, ditch
sorus, 'sore', unmewed (of a hawk)
spina, thorn tree
spinetum, thorn thicket, spinney
sutor, cobbler
taise (French) (for *toise*), length of about 6 feet, fathom
telarius, weaver (? of linen)
tremeia, hopper of mill
vielator, fiddler
vinator, vinitor, 'viner', vine-dresser
virgultum, orchard

INDEX OF PERSONS AND PLACES

References are to pages. The following abbreviations are used in the index:

A   addressee of charter
B   beneficiary of charter
W   witness to a charter (number of occurrences on one page, if more than one, shown in square brackets)
abp. archbishop
bp. bishop

Personal and place-names are given in their modern form where possible. Variant forms are given only where identification of the modern name is not made on the relevant page. Patronymics are indexed under the name of the son.

INDEX OF SUBJECTS

eels, xlvii, li n., 18, 151–6
endorsements, lxx, and *passim*
enfeoffment, xxvi n., xxvii–viii, xxxiii–iv, xliv, lvii, lx
— charters of, lvii, 212–55 *passim*
— *see also* fee; homage
exchange of property, xxxvi–vii, lvii–viii, 7–9, 12–13, 15, 32, 36, 45, 47, 82–5, 96, 107, 118–19, 138, 142, 150, 162, 166, 172–8, 191–2, 215, 233–5, 240, 254–5

faith, pledge of, 67, 84–6, 90–1; *see also* affidation; oath
falconers, lxii; *see also* hawk-bearer
famulus, xlvii; *see also* Walter
farm (*firma*), 42–3, 104, 140, 151–6
fee, free (*liberum feudum*), 221, 225, 231, 234–5, 238
fee, grant in: fee and alms, 74–5, 259; fee and heredity, xxxvi, xxxix, 19, 102, 119, 194, 214, 218, 221–2, 224, 226, 229–31, 233–40, 244, 246, 248, 250–1, 253, 255
fee (*feodum, feudum*), held by Mowbray, 20, 230
— held of Mowbray, 8, 114, 158, 207, 217–18, 222
— Mowbray, 21, 34, 53–4, 62–3, 100, 117, 119, 141, 150, 159, 172–3, 198, 203, 208, 246, 249
— *see also* enfeoffment; knights' fees
fences, 103
— wood for making, xlix, 105–7, 184
feudal incidents, xxxviii–ix; *see also* aid; marriage; relief; wardship
fields, lii, 28–30, 51, 113, 123–4, 189–90; *see also* arable; culture
fish, 16
— right to, 125
fisheries, xlvii, li, 7–8, 154–6, 173, 183, 187, 205–7
flax, 18
foods, tithe of, xlvi, 205–6
— *see also* rents, food-
ford, 74, 95
forest, Mowbray, xlviii–l, 29, 32–5, 37–8, 40–2, 44–5, 47–8, 54, 56, 75–7, 79, 82–7, 90–1, 93–4, 102, 104–7, 148, 150, 183, 220, 222, 234–5, 238, 251
— royal, xxix and n., l; *see also* Galtres; Knaresborough
forester, of Mowbray honour, xlviii, l, 38, 41, 44, 48, 54, 82, 89–92, 95, 102, 106–7; A 37, 132–3; *see also* Drogo; Hovingham; John; Roger; Uctred
forge, xlix, 86, 94, 104; *see also* charcoal; smith
forged charters, lxxiv–v, 31–2, 37–8, 40–2,

44, 177–8; interpolated charters, 28–31, 33, 35, 53, 59–60
fosse (*fossa, fossatum*), as boundary, 43, 48, 78, 80, 95, 103, 147, 154, 177–8, 220
— land to make, 73–4, 95
— right to make, 47, 248
frankalmoin, xli–iii, and *passim*
fraternity, religious, 17, 209
free tenants, xxxix–xli, xlvi, 43, 126, 150, 177–8
fuel: wood for burning, xlix, 105–7, 145–6, 184, 206, 220, 234–5, 243

gallows, lviii n.
game, xlviii, 38, 41, 44, 48, 54, 84–6, 102, 164; *see also* birds of prey; boar; deer; hunt
garb, lxiv, 18, 193, 200, 204–5
garden (*gardinium, gardinum, ortus*), 18, 41, 63, 86, 215, 217
gifts in return for charters: *destrier*, xxxviii, 20; gold ring, xxxviii, 101, 214; money, 20, 63–7, 77, 79, 83, 85–6, 90–3, 95, 97, 99, 111–12, 212, 216; palfrey, xxxviii, 112, 214–15
grange, 71, 75–6, 79, 82, 86–7, 92, 94–5, 104, 164, 189 n., 204
grooms, lxii

haia (enclosure in a wood), 214–15
hawk-bearer, *see* Thomas; *see also* falconers
hay (*fenum*), xlvi, 41, 88, 94
hayward (*messarius*), 215
heirs (not *sui et heredibus suis*), 7–9, 11, 55–6, 60, 162, 177, 185, 195, 199, 206, 208–9, 215, 217, 247, 249; A 152, 156
herbergiamentum, 41
hereditary right, xxxvi, 215, 219, 227, 249; *see also* fee, grant in fee and heredity; heirs; patrimony
homage, lvii, 114, 157, 215–17
— and service, 109, 119, 219, 223, 233, 235, 237–8, 244, 249
honor, lvi, 5, 8, 100–1, 104, 122, 257–8
horses, liii; *destrier*, xxxviii, 20; foals, liii n., 36, 40; mares, liii n., 36, 40, 42; pack animals, liii n., 44; palfrey, xxxviii, 112, 214–15
hose, scarlet, as rent, xl, 50, 55, 222, 244
hosteler, *see* Hugh
house (*domus*, not religious), liv, lxiv, 8, 15, 32, 114, 130, 147, 150, 181, 188, 206, 226–8, 233, 235, 250; *see also* building; *mansio*; *mansura*; messuage
household, Mowbray, xlii, xliv, lvi, lvii, lix–lxx
— — chapelry of, 143
hue and cry, lix

RECORDS OF THE SOCIAL AND ECONOMIC HISTORY OF ENGLAND AND WALES

RECORDS OF SOCIAL AND ECONOMIC HISTORY
New Series

MAP III. The Honour of Mowbray in Yorkshire.

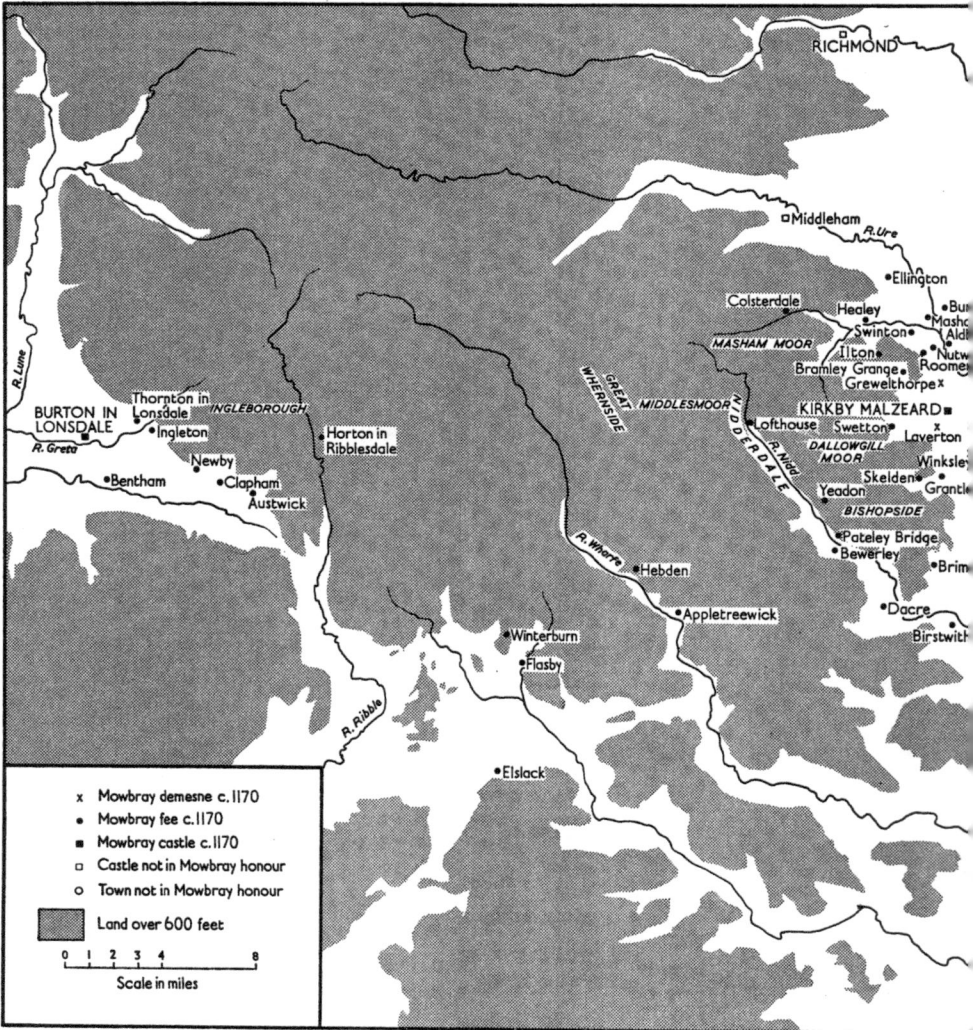

RICHMOND

Middleham
R. Ure

Ellington

Colsterdale
Healey
Bu
Swinton
Masha
MASHAM MOOR
Ald
Ilton
Nutw
Bramley Grange
Roome
Grewelthorpe ×

GREAT
WHERNSIDE
MIDDLESMOOR
KIRKBY MALZEARD ■
Lofthouse
Swetton
Laverton ×
MIDDERDALE
DALLOWGILL
MOOR
Winksle
Skelden
Yeadon
Grantle
BISHOPSIDE

Thornton in
Lonsdale
INGLEBOROUGH
BURTON IN
LONSDALE
Ingleton
R. Greta
Horton in
Ribblesdale
Newby
Bentham
Clapham
Austwick

R. Lune

Pateley Bridge
Bewerley
Brim

R. Wharfe
Hebden
Dacre

Appletreewick
Birstwith

Winterburn
Flasby

R. Ribble

Elslack

x Mowbray demesne c.1170
• Mowbray fee c.1170
■ Mowbray castle c.1170
□ Castle not in Mowbray honour
○ Town not in Mowbray honour

   Land over 600 feet

0 1 2 3 4   8
     Scale in miles

RTHALLERTON

FARNDALE MOOR

SNILESWORTH MOOR

Over Silton

Kepwick

Arden

Dale Town

Murton

Old Byland

Hawnby

Gillamoor

Fadmoor

Skiplam

Hutton le Hole

Welburn

Kirkby Moorside

Norby

THIRSK

Hood

Scawton

Nawton

Wombleton

Bowforth

R. Rye

R. Dove

Thornton Dale

Brompton

Hutton

on Miniott

Balk

Bagby

Osgoodby

Oldstead

Thorpefield

Thirkleby

Byland Abbey

Ampleforth

Harome

Little Barugh

Normanby

Kirby Misperton

R. Derwent

Sherburn

Islebeck Coxwold

Newburgh Priory

Gilling

HOVINGHAM

South Holme

Great Barugh

Butterwick

Cundall

Fawdington

Oulston

Thornton Hill

Brandsby

Yearsley

Scackleton

Grimston

Coulton

Fryton

Slingsby

Airyholme

Ryton

Broughton

MALTON

Thornton Bridge

Brafferton

Humburton

Stearsby

Dalby

Norton

Sutton

Welham

Kirby Hill

Myton on Swale

Sledmere

Kirkby

Whixley

Nun Monkton

Beningbrough

Green Hammerton

Kirk Hammerton

Wilstrop

Stockton on the Forest

R. Nidd

Cattal

Tockwith

Rufforth

Bickerton

Long Marston

YORK

Bainton

Bilton

Walton

Healaugh

Askham Richard

Middlethorpe

Thorpe Arch

Wighill

Catterton

Copmanthorpe

Burnby

Hayton

Collingham

Easedike

Steeton

Thorpe le Street

Goodmanham

Bardsey

Toulston

Appleton

Roebuck

Wothersome

R. Wharfe

Acaster Selby

Nun Appleton

Laytham

Houghton

Hessleskew

Sancton

North Duffield

Harlthorpe

Holme upon Spalding Moor

Bubwith

Foggathorpe

Gribthorpe

Gunby

Willitoft

Bursea

Lund

Spaldington

www.ingramcontent.com/pod-product-compliance
Lightning Source LLC
Chambersburg PA
CBHW070841100426
42813CB00003B/708